Lecture Notes in Computer Science 12957

More information about this subseries at http://www.springer.com/series/7407

Osvaldo Gervasi · Beniamino Murgante ·
Sanjay Misra · Chiara Garau ·
Ivan Blečić · David Taniar ·
Bernady O. Apduhan · Ana Maria A. C. Rocha ·
Eufemia Tarantino · Carmelo Maria Torre (Eds.)

Computational Science and Its Applications – ICCSA 2021

21st International Conference
Cagliari, Italy, September 13–16, 2021
Proceedings, Part IX

Springer

Editors
Osvaldo Gervasi (iD)
University of Perugia
Perugia, Italy

Sanjay Misra (iD)
Covenant University
Ota, Nigeria

Ivan Blečić (iD)
University of Cagliari
Cagliari, Italy

Bernady O. Apduhan
Kyushu Sangyo University
Fukuoka, Japan

Eufemia Tarantino (iD)
Polytechnic University of Bari
Bari, Italy

Beniamino Murgante (iD)
University of Basilicata
Potenza, Potenza, Italy

Chiara Garau (iD)
University of Cagliari
Cagliari, Italy

David Taniar (iD)
Monash University
Clayton, VIC, Australia

Ana Maria A. C. Rocha (iD)
University of Minho
Braga, Portugal

Carmelo Maria Torre (iD)
Polytechnic University of Bari
Bari, Italy

ISSN 0302-9743   ISSN 1611-3349   (electronic)
Lecture Notes in Computer Science
ISBN 978-3-030-87012-6   ISBN 978-3-030-87013-3   (eBook)
https://doi.org/10.1007/978-3-030-87013-3

LNCS Sublibrary: SL1 – Theoretical Computer Science and General Issues

This Springer imprint is published by the registered company Springer Nature Switzerland AG
The registered company address is: Gewerbestrasse 11, 6330 Cham, Switzerland

Preface

These 10 volumes (LNCS volumes 12949–12958) consist of the peer-reviewed papers from the 21st International Conference on Computational Science and Its Applications (ICCSA 2021) which took place during September 13–16, 2021. By virtue of the vaccination campaign conducted in various countries around the world, we decided to try a hybrid conference, with some of the delegates attending in person at the University of Cagliari and others attending in virtual mode, reproducing the infrastructure established last year.

This year's edition was a successful continuation of the ICCSA conference series, which was also held as a virtual event in 2020, and previously held in Saint Petersburg, Russia (2019), Melbourne, Australia (2018), Trieste, Italy (2017), Beijing, China (2016), Banff, Canada (2015), Guimaraes, Portugal (2014), Ho Chi Minh City, Vietnam (2013), Salvador, Brazil (2012), Santander, Spain (2011), Fukuoka, Japan (2010), Suwon, South Korea (2009), Perugia, Italy (2008), Kuala Lumpur, Malaysia (2007), Glasgow, UK (2006), Singapore (2005), Assisi, Italy (2004), Montreal, Canada (2003), and (as ICCS) Amsterdam, The Netherlands (2002) and San Francisco, USA (2001).

Computational science is the main pillar of most of the present research on understanding and solving complex problems. It plays a unique role in exploiting innovative ICT technologies and in the development of industrial and commercial applications. The ICCSA conference series provides a venue for researchers and industry practitioners to discuss new ideas, to share complex problems and their solutions, and to shape new trends in computational science.

Apart from the six main conference tracks, ICCSA 2021 also included 52 workshops in various areas of computational sciences, ranging from computational science technologies to specific areas of computational sciences, such as software engineering, security, machine learning and artificial intelligence, blockchain technologies, and applications in many fields. In total, we accepted 494 papers, giving an acceptance rate of 30%, of which 18 papers were short papers and 6 were published open access. We would like to express our appreciation for the workshop chairs and co-chairs for their hard work and dedication.

The success of the ICCSA conference series in general, and of ICCSA 2021 in particular, vitally depends on the support of many people: authors, presenters, participants, keynote speakers, workshop chairs, session chairs, organizing committee members, student volunteers, Program Committee members, advisory committee members, international liaison chairs, reviewers, and others in various roles. We take this opportunity to wholehartedly thank them all.

We also wish to thank Springer for publishing the proceedings, for sponsoring some of the best paper awards, and for their kind assistance and cooperation during the editing process.

We cordially invite you to visit the ICCSA website https://iccsa.org where you can find all the relevant information about this interesting and exciting event.

September 2021

Osvaldo Gervasi
Beniamino Murgante
Sanjay Misra

Welcome Message from the Organizers

COVID-19 has continued to alter our plans for organizing the ICCSA 2021 conference, so although vaccination plans are progressing worldwide, the spread of virus variants still forces us into a period of profound uncertainty. Only a very limited number of participants were able to enjoy the beauty of Sardinia and Cagliari in particular, rediscovering the immense pleasure of meeting again, albeit safely spaced out. The social events, in which we rediscovered the ancient values that abound on this wonderful island and in this city, gave us even more strength and hope for the future. For the management of the virtual part of the conference, we consolidated the methods, organization, and infrastructure of ICCSA 2020.

The technological infrastructure was based on open source software, with the addition of the streaming channels on YouTube. In particular, we used Jitsi (jitsi.org) for videoconferencing, Riot (riot.im) together with Matrix (matrix.org) for chat and ansynchronous communication, and Jibri (github.com/jitsi/jibri) for streaming live sessions to YouTube.

Seven Jitsi servers were set up, one for each parallel session. The participants of the sessions were helped and assisted by eight student volunteers (from the universities of Cagliari, Florence, Perugia, and Bari), who provided technical support and ensured smooth running of the conference proceedings.

The implementation of the software infrastructure and the technical coordination of the volunteers were carried out by Damiano Perri and Marco Simonetti.

Our warmest thanks go to all the student volunteers, to the technical coordinators, and to the development communities of Jitsi, Jibri, Riot, and Matrix, who made their terrific platforms available as open source software.

A big thank you goes to all of the 450 speakers, many of whom showed an enormous collaborative spirit, sometimes participating and presenting at almost prohibitive times of the day, given that the participants of this year's conference came from 58 countries scattered over many time zones of the globe.

Finally, we would like to thank Google for letting us stream all the live events via YouTube. In addition to lightening the load of our Jitsi servers, this allowed us to record the event and to be able to review the most exciting moments of the conference.

Ivan Blečić
Chiara Garau

Organization

ICCSA 2021 was organized by the University of Cagliari (Italy), the University of Perugia (Italy), the University of Basilicata (Italy), Monash University (Australia), Kyushu Sangyo University (Japan), and the University of Minho (Portugal).

Honorary General Chairs

Norio Shiratori	Chuo University, Japan
Kenneth C. J. Tan	Sardina Systems, UK
Corrado Zoppi	University of Cagliari, Italy

General Chairs

Osvaldo Gervasi	University of Perugia, Italy
Ivan Blečić	University of Cagliari, Italy
David Taniar	Monash University, Australia

Program Committee Chairs

Beniamino Murgante	University of Basilicata, Italy
Bernady O. Apduhan	Kyushu Sangyo University, Japan
Chiara Garau	University of Cagliari, Italy
Ana Maria A. C. Rocha	University of Minho, Portugal

International Advisory Committee

Jemal Abawajy	Deakin University, Australia
Dharma P. Agarwal	University of Cincinnati, USA
Rajkumar Buyya	University of Melbourne, Australia
Claudia Bauzer Medeiros	University of Campinas, Brazil
Manfred M. Fisher	Vienna University of Economics and Business, Austria
Marina L. Gavrilova	University of Calgary, Canada
Yee Leung	Chinese University of Hong Kong, China

International Liaison Chairs

Giuseppe Borruso	University of Trieste, Italy
Elise De Donker	Western Michigan University, USA
Maria Irene Falcão	University of Minho, Portugal
Robert C. H. Hsu	Chung Hua University, Taiwan
Tai-Hoon Kim	Beijing Jaotong University, China

Vladimir Korkhov   St. Petersburg University, Russia
Sanjay Misra   Covenant University, Nigeria
Takashi Naka   Kyushu Sangyo University, Japan
Rafael D. C. Santos   National Institute for Space Research, Brazil
Maribel Yasmina Santos   University of Minho, Portugal
Elena Stankova   St. Petersburg University, Russia

Workshop and Session Chairs

Beniamino Murgante   University of Basilicata, Italy
Sanjay Misra   Covenant University, Nigeria
Jorge Gustavo Rocha   University of Minho, Portugal

Awards Chair

Wenny Rahayu   La Trobe University, Australia

Publicity Committee Chairs

Elmer Dadios   De La Salle University, Philippines
Nataliia Kulabukhova   St. Petersburg University, Russia
Daisuke Takahashi   Tsukuba University, Japan
Shangwang Wang   Beijing University of Posts and Telecommunications,
                              China

Technology Chairs

Damiano Perri   University of Florence, Italy
Marco Simonetti   University of Florence, Italy

Local Arrangement Chairs

Ivan Blečić   University of Cagliari, Italy
Chiara Garau   University of Cagliari, Italy
Alfonso Annunziata   University of Cagliari, Italy
Ginevra Balletto   University of Cagliari, Italy
Giuseppe Borruso   University of Trieste, Italy
Alessandro Buccini   University of Cagliari, Italy
Michele Campagna   University of Cagliari, Italy
Mauro Coni   University of Cagliari, Italy
Anna Maria Colavitti   University of Cagliari, Italy
Giulia Desogus   University of Cagliari, Italy
Caterina Fenu   University of Cagliari, Italy
Sabrina Lai   University of Cagliari, Italy
Francesca Maltinti   University of Cagliari, Italy
Pasquale Mistretta   University of Cagliari, Italy

Augusto Montisci   University of Cagliari, Italy
Francesco Pinna   University of Cagliari, Italy
Davide Spano   University of Cagliari, Italy
Giuseppe A. Trunfio   University of Sassari, Italy
Corrado Zoppi   University of Cagliari, Italy

Program Committee

Vera Afreixo   University of Aveiro, Portugal
Filipe Alvelos   University of Minho, Portugal
Hartmut Asche   University of Potsdam, Germany
Ginevra Balletto   University of Cagliari, Italy
Michela Bertolotto   University College Dublin, Ireland
Sandro Bimonte   INRAE-TSCF, France
Rod Blais   University of Calgary, Canada
Ivan Blečić   University of Sassari, Italy
Giuseppe Borruso   University of Trieste, Italy
Ana Cristina Braga   University of Minho, Portugal
Massimo Cafaro   University of Salento, Italy
Yves Caniou   University of Lyon, France
José A. Cardoso e Cunha   Universidade Nova de Lisboa, Portugal
Rui Cardoso   University of Beira Interior, Portugal
Leocadio G. Casado   University of Almeria, Spain
Carlo Cattani   University of Salerno, Italy
Mete Celik   Erciyes University, Turkey
Maria Cerreta   University of Naples "Federico II", Italy
Hyunseung Choo   Sungkyunkwan University, South Korea
Chien-Sing Lee   Sunway University, Malaysia
Min Young Chung   Sungkyunkwan University, South Korea
Florbela Maria da Cruz   Polytechnic Institute of Viana do Castelo, Portugal
  Domingues Correia
Gilberto Corso Pereira   Federal University of Bahia, Brazil
Fernanda Costa   University of Minho, Portugal
Alessandro Costantini   INFN, Italy
Carla Dal Sasso Freitas   Universidade Federal do Rio Grande do Sul, Brazil
Pradesh Debba   The Council for Scientific and Industrial Research
                            (CSIR), South Africa
Hendrik Decker   Instituto Tecnolčgico de Informática, Spain
Robertas Damaševičius   Kausan University of Technology, Lithuania
Frank Devai   London South Bank University, UK
Rodolphe Devillers   Memorial University of Newfoundland, Canada
Joana Matos Dias   University of Coimbra, Portugal
Paolino Di Felice   University of L'Aquila, Italy
Prabu Dorairaj   NetApp, India/USA
Noelia Faginas Lago   University of Perugia, Italy
M. Irene Falcao   University of Minho, Portugal

Cherry Liu Fang	Ames Laboratory, USA
Florbela P. Fernandes	Polytechnic Institute of Bragança, Portugal
Jose-Jesus Fernandez	National Centre for Biotechnology, Spain
Paula Odete Fernandes	Polytechnic Institute of Bragança, Portugal
Adelaide de Fátima Baptista Valente Freitas	University of Aveiro, Portugal
Manuel Carlos Figueiredo	University of Minho, Portugal
Maria Celia Furtado Rocha	Universidade Federal da Bahia, Brazil
Chiara Garau	University of Cagliari, Italy
Paulino Jose Garcia Nieto	University of Oviedo, Spain
Jerome Gensel	LSR-IMAG, France
Maria Giaoutzi	National Technical University of Athens, Greece
Arminda Manuela Andrade Pereira Gonçalves	University of Minho, Portugal
Andrzej M. Goscinski	Deakin University, Australia
Eduardo Guerra	Free University of Bozen-Bolzano, Italy
Sevin Gümgüm	Izmir University of Economics, Turkey
Alex Hagen-Zanker	University of Cambridge, UK
Shanmugasundaram Hariharan	B.S. Abdur Rahman University, India
Eligius M. T. Hendrix	University of Malaga, Spain/Wageningen University, The Netherlands
Hisamoto Hiyoshi	Gunma University, Japan
Mustafa Inceoglu	EGE University, Turkey
Peter Jimack	University of Leeds, UK
Qun Jin	Waseda University, Japan
Yeliz Karaca	University of Massachusetts Medical School, USA
Farid Karimipour	Vienna University of Technology, Austria
Baris Kazar	Oracle Corp., USA
Maulana Adhinugraha Kiki	Telkom University, Indonesia
DongSeong Kim	University of Canterbury, New Zealand
Taihoon Kim	Hannam University, South Korea
Ivana Kolingerova	University of West Bohemia, Czech Republic
Nataliia Kulabukhova	St. Petersburg University, Russia
Vladimir Korkhov	St. Petersburg University, Russia
Rosa Lasaponara	National Research Council, Italy
Maurizio Lazzari	National Research Council, Italy
Cheng Siong Lee	Monash University, Australia
Sangyoun Lee	Yonsei University, South Korea
Jongchan Lee	Kunsan National University, South Korea
Chendong Li	University of Connecticut, USA
Gang Li	Deakin University, Australia
Fang Liu	Ames Laboratory, USA
Xin Liu	University of Calgary, Canada
Andrea Lombardi	University of Perugia, Italy
Savino Longo	University of Bari, Italy

Tinghuai Ma	Nanjing University of Information Science and Technology, China
Ernesto Marcheggiani	Katholieke Universiteit Leuven, Belgium
Antonino Marvuglia	Research Centre Henri Tudor, Luxembourg
Nicola Masini	National Research Council, Italy
Ilaria Matteucci	National Research Council, Italy
Eric Medvet	University of Trieste, Italy
Nirvana Meratnia	University of Twente, The Netherlands
Giuseppe Modica	University of Reggio Calabria, Italy
Josè Luis Montaña	University of Cantabria, Spain
Maria Filipa Mourão	Instituto Politécnico de Viana do Castelo, Portugal
Louiza de Macedo Mourelle	State University of Rio de Janeiro, Brazil
Nadia Nedjah	State University of Rio de Janeiro, Brazil
Laszlo Neumann	University of Girona, Spain
Kok-Leong Ong	Deakin University, Australia
Belen Palop	Universidad de Valladolid, Spain
Marcin Paprzycki	Polish Academy of Sciences, Poland
Eric Pardede	La Trobe University, Australia
Kwangjin Park	Wonkwang University, South Korea
Ana Isabel Pereira	Polytechnic Institute of Bragança, Portugal
Massimiliano Petri	University of Pisa, Italy
Telmo Pinto	University of Coimbra, Portugal
Maurizio Pollino	Italian National Agency for New Technologies, Energy and Sustainable Economic Development, Italy
Alenka Poplin	University of Hamburg, Germany
Vidyasagar Potdar	Curtin University of Technology, Australia
David C. Prosperi	Florida Atlantic University, USA
Wenny Rahayu	La Trobe University, Australia
Jerzy Respondek	Silesian University of Technology Poland
Humberto Rocha	INESC-Coimbra, Portugal
Jon Rokne	University of Calgary, Canada
Octavio Roncero	CSIC, Spain
Maytham Safar	Kuwait University, Kuwait
Francesco Santini	University of Perugia, Italy
Chiara Saracino	A.O. Ospedale Niguarda Ca' Granda, Italy.
Haiduke Sarafian	Pennsylvania State University, USA
Marco Paulo Seabra dos Reis	University of Coimbra, Portugal
Jie Shen	University of Michigan, USA
Qi Shi	Liverpool John Moores University, UK
Dale Shires	U.S. Army Research Laboratory, USA
Inês Soares	University of Coimbra, Portugal
Elena Stankova	St. Petersburg University, Russia
Takuo Suganuma	Tohoku University, Japan
Eufemia Tarantino	Polytechnic University of Bari, Italy
Sergio Tasso	University of Perugia, Italy

Ana Paula Teixeira	University of Trás-os-Montes and Alto Douro, Portugal
Senhorinha Teixeira	University of Minho, Portugal
M. Filomena Teodoro	Portuguese Naval Academy/University of Lisbon, Portugal
Parimala Thulasiraman	University of Manitoba, Canada
Carmelo Torre	Polytechnic University of Bari, Italy
Javier Martinez Torres	Centro Universitario de la Defensa Zaragoza, Spain
Giuseppe A. Trunfio	University of Sassari, Italy
Pablo Vanegas	University of Cuenca, Equador
Marco Vizzari	University of Perugia, Italy
Varun Vohra	Merck Inc., USA
Koichi Wada	University of Tsukuba, Japan
Krzysztof Walkowiak	Wroclaw University of Technology, Poland
Zequn Wang	Intelligent Automation Inc, USA
Robert Weibel	University of Zurich, Switzerland
Frank Westad	Norwegian University of Science and Technology, Norway
Roland Wismüller	Universität Siegen, Germany
Mudasser Wyne	National University, USA
Chung-Huang Yang	National Kaohsiung Normal University, Taiwan
Xin-She Yang	National Physical Laboratory, UK
Salim Zabir	National Institute of Technology, Tsuruoka, Japan
Haifeng Zhao	University of California, Davis, USA
Fabiana Zollo	University of Venice "Cà Foscari", Italy
Albert Y. Zomaya	University of Sydney, Australia

Workshop Organizers

Advanced Transport Tools and Methods (A2TM 2021)

Massimiliano Petri	University of Pisa, Italy
Antonio Pratelli	University of Pisa, Italy

Advances in Artificial Intelligence Learning Technologies: Blended Learning, STEM, Computational Thinking and Coding (AAILT 2021)

Alfredo Milani	University of Perugia, Italy
Giulio Biondi	University of Florence, Italy
Sergio Tasso	University of Perugia, Italy

Workshop on Advancements in Applied Machine Learning and Data Analytics (AAMDA 2021)

Alessandro Costantini	INFN, Italy
Davide Salomoni	INFN, Italy
Doina Cristina Duma	INFN, Italy
Daniele Cesini	INFN, Italy

Automatic Landform Classification: Spatial Methods and Applications (ALCSMA 2021)

Maria Danese   ISPC, National Research Council, Italy
Dario Gioia   ISPC, National Research Council, Italy

Application of Numerical Analysis to Imaging Science (ANAIS 2021)

Caterina Fenu   University of Cagliari, Italy
Alessandro Buccini   University of Cagliari, Italy

Advances in Information Systems and Technologies for Emergency Management, Risk Assessment and Mitigation Based on the Resilience Concepts (ASTER 2021)

Maurizio Pollino   ENEA, Italy
Marco Vona   University of Basilicata, Italy
Amedeo Flora   University of Basilicata, Italy
Chiara Iacovino   University of Basilicata, Italy
Beniamino Murgante   University of Basilicata, Italy

Advances in Web Based Learning (AWBL 2021)

Birol Ciloglugil   Ege University, Turkey
Mustafa Murat Inceoglu   Ege University, Turkey

Blockchain and Distributed Ledgers: Technologies and Applications (BDLTA 2021)

Vladimir Korkhov   St. Petersburg University, Russia
Elena Stankova   St. Petersburg University, Russia
Nataliia Kulabukhova   St. Petersburg University, Russia

Bio and Neuro Inspired Computing and Applications (BIONCA 2021)

Nadia Nedjah   State University of Rio de Janeiro, Brazil
Luiza De Macedo Mourelle   State University of Rio de Janeiro, Brazil

Computational and Applied Mathematics (CAM 2021)

Maria Irene Falcão   University of Minho, Portugal
Fernando Miranda   University of Minho, Portugal

Computational and Applied Statistics (CAS 2021)

Ana Cristina Braga   University of Minho, Portugal

Computerized Evaluation of Economic Activities: Urban Spaces (CEEA 2021)

Diego Altafini   Università di Pisa, Italy
Valerio Cutini   Università di Pisa, Italy

Computational Geometry and Applications (CGA 2021)

Marina Gavrilova	University of Calgary, Canada

Collaborative Intelligence in Multimodal Applications (CIMA 2021)

Robertas Damasevicius	Kaunas University of Technology, Lithuania
Rytis Maskeliunas	Kaunas University of Technology, Lithuania

Computational Optimization and Applications (COA 2021)

Ana Rocha	University of Minho, Portugal
Humberto Rocha	University of Coimbra, Portugal

Computational Astrochemistry (CompAstro 2021)

Marzio Rosi	University of Perugia, Italy
Cecilia Ceccarelli	University of Grenoble, France
Stefano Falcinelli	University of Perugia, Italy
Dimitrios Skouteris	Master-Up, Italy

Computational Science and HPC (CSHPC 2021)

Elise de Doncker	Western Michigan University, USA
Fukuko Yuasa	High Energy Accelerator Research Organization (KEK), Japan
Hideo Matsufuru	High Energy Accelerator Research Organization (KEK), Japan

Cities, Technologies and Planning (CTP 2021)

Malgorzata Hanzl	University of Łódź, Poland
Beniamino Murgante	University of Basilicata, Italy
Ljiljana Zivkovic	Ministry of Construction, Transport and Infrastructure/Institute of Architecture and Urban and Spatial Planning of Serbia, Serbia
Anastasia Stratigea	National Technical University of Athens, Greece
Giuseppe Borruso	University of Trieste, Italy
Ginevra Balletto	University of Cagliari, Italy

Advanced Modeling E-Mobility in Urban Spaces (DEMOS 2021)

Tiziana Campisi	Kore University of Enna, Italy
Socrates Basbas	Aristotle University of Thessaloniki, Greece
Ioannis Politis	Aristotle University of Thessaloniki, Greece
Florin Nemtanu	Polytechnic University of Bucharest, Romania
Giovanna Acampa	Kore University of Enna, Italy
Wolfgang Schulz	Zeppelin University, Germany

Digital Transformation and Smart City (DIGISMART 2021)

Mauro Mazzei	National Research Council, Italy

Econometric and Multidimensional Evaluation in Urban Environment (EMEUE 2021)

Carmelo Maria Torre	Polytechnic University of Bari, Italy
Maria Cerreta	University "Federico II" of Naples, Italy
Pierluigi Morano	Polytechnic University of Bari, Italy
Simona Panaro	University of Portsmouth, UK
Francesco Tajani	Sapienza University of Rome, Italy
Marco Locurcio	Polytechnic University of Bari, Italy

The 11th International Workshop on Future Computing System Technologies and Applications (FiSTA 2021)

Bernady Apduhan	Kyushu Sangyo University, Japan
Rafael Santos	Brazilian National Institute for Space Research, Brazil

Transformational Urban Mobility: Challenges and Opportunities During and Post COVID Era (FURTHER 2021)

Tiziana Campisi	Kore University of Enna, Italy
Socrates Basbas	Aristotle University of Thessaloniki, Greece
Dilum Dissanayake	Newcastle University, UK
Kh Md Nahiduzzaman	University of British Columbia, Canada
Nurten Akgün Tanbay	Bursa Technical University, Turkey
Khaled J. Assi	King Fahd University of Petroleum and Minerals, Saudi Arabia
Giovanni Tesoriere	Kore University of Enna, Italy
Motasem Darwish	Middle East University, Jordan

Geodesign in Decision Making: Meta Planning and Collaborative Design for Sustainable and Inclusive Development (GDM 2021)

Francesco Scorza	University of Basilicata, Italy
Michele Campagna	University of Cagliari, Italy
Ana Clara Mourao Moura	Federal University of Minas Gerais, Brazil

Geomatics in Forestry and Agriculture: New Advances and Perspectives (GeoForAgr 2021)

Maurizio Pollino	ENEA, Italy
Giuseppe Modica	University of Reggio Calabria, Italy
Marco Vizzari	University of Perugia, Italy

Geographical Analysis, Urban Modeling, Spatial Statistics (GEOG-AND-MOD 2021)

Beniamino Murgante	University of Basilicata, Italy
Giuseppe Borruso	University of Trieste, Italy
Hartmut Asche	University of Potsdam, Germany

Geomatics for Resource Monitoring and Management (GRMM 2021)

Eufemia Tarantino	Polytechnic University of Bari, Italy
Enrico Borgogno Mondino	University of Turin, Italy
Alessandra Capolupo	Polytechnic University of Bari, Italy
Mirko Saponaro	Polytechnic University of Bari, Italy

12th International Symposium on Software Quality (ISSQ 2021)

Sanjay Misra	Covenant University, Nigeria

10th International Workshop on Collective, Massive and Evolutionary Systems (IWCES 2021)

Alfredo Milani	University of Perugia, Italy
Rajdeep Niyogi	Indian Institute of Technology, Roorkee, India

Land Use Monitoring for Sustainability (LUMS 2021)

Carmelo Maria Torre	Polytechnic University of Bari, Italy
Maria Cerreta	University "Federico II" of Naples, Italy
Massimiliano Bencardino	University of Salerno, Italy
Alessandro Bonifazi	Polytechnic University of Bari, Italy
Pasquale Balena	Polytechnic University of Bari, Italy
Giuliano Poli	University "Federico II" of Naples, Italy

Machine Learning for Space and Earth Observation Data (MALSEOD 2021)

Rafael Santos	Instituto Nacional de Pesquisas Espaciais, Brazil
Karine Ferreira	Instituto Nacional de Pesquisas Espaciais, Brazil

Building Multi-dimensional Models for Assessing Complex Environmental Systems (MES 2021)

Marta Dell'Ovo	Polytechnic University of Milan, Italy
Vanessa Assumma	Polytechnic University of Turin, Italy
Caterina Caprioli	Polytechnic University of Turin, Italy
Giulia Datola	Polytechnic University of Turin, Italy
Federico dell'Anna	Polytechnic University of Turin, Italy

Ecosystem Services: Nature's Contribution to People in Practice. Assessment Frameworks, Models, Mapping, and Implications (NC2P 2021)

Francesco Scorza	University of Basilicata, Italy
Sabrina Lai	University of Cagliari, Italy
Ana Clara Mourao Moura	Federal University of Minas Gerais, Brazil
Corrado Zoppi	University of Cagliari, Italy
Dani Broitman	Technion, Israel Institute of Technology, Israel

Privacy in the Cloud/Edge/IoT World (PCEIoT 2021)

Michele Mastroianni	University of Campania Luigi Vanvitelli, Italy
Lelio Campanile	University of Campania Luigi Vanvitelli, Italy
Mauro Iacono	University of Campania Luigi Vanvitelli, Italy

Processes, Methods and Tools Towards RESilient Cities and Cultural Heritage Prone to SOD and ROD Disasters (RES 2021)

Elena Cantatore	Polytechnic University of Bari, Italy
Alberico Sonnessa	Polytechnic University of Bari, Italy
Dario Esposito	Polytechnic University of Bari, Italy

Risk, Resilience and Sustainability in the Efficient Management of Water Resources: Approaches, Tools, Methodologies and Multidisciplinary Integrated Applications (RRS 2021)

Maria Macchiaroli	University of Salerno, Italy
Chiara D'Alpaos	Università degli Studi di Padova, Italy
Mirka Mobilia	Università degli Studi di Salerno, Italy
Antonia Longobardi	Università degli Studi di Salerno, Italy
Grazia Fattoruso	ENEA Research Center, Italy
Vincenzo Pellecchia	Ente Idrico Campano, Italy

Scientific Computing Infrastructure (SCI 2021)

Elena Stankova	St. Petersburg University, Russia
Vladimir Korkhov	St. Petersburg University, Russia
Natalia Kulabukhova	St. Petersburg University, Russia

Smart Cities and User Data Management (SCIDAM 2021)

Chiara Garau	University of Cagliari, Italy
Luigi Mundula	University of Cagliari, Italy
Gianni Fenu	University of Cagliari, Italy
Paolo Nesi	University of Florence, Italy
Paola Zamperlin	University of Pisa, Italy

13th International Symposium on Software Engineering Processes and Applications (SEPA 2021)

Sanjay Misra   Covenant University, Nigeria

Ports of the Future - Smartness and Sustainability (SmartPorts 2021)

Patrizia Serra	University of Cagliari, Italy
Gianfranco Fancello	University of Cagliari, Italy
Ginevra Balletto	University of Cagliari, Italy
Luigi Mundula	University of Cagliari, Italy
Marco Mazzarino	University of Venice, Italy
Giuseppe Borruso	University of Trieste, Italy
Maria del Mar Munoz Leonisio	Universidad de Cádiz, Spain

Smart Tourism (SmartTourism 2021)

Giuseppe Borruso	University of Trieste, Italy
Silvia Battino	University of Sassari, Italy
Ginevra Balletto	University of Cagliari, Italy
Maria del Mar Munoz Leonisio	Universidad de Cádiz, Spain
Ainhoa Amaro Garcia	Universidad de Alcalà/Universidad de Las Palmas, Spain
Francesca Krasna	University of Trieste, Italy

Sustainability Performance Assessment: Models, Approaches and Applications toward Interdisciplinary and Integrated Solutions (SPA 2021)

Francesco Scorza	University of Basilicata, Italy
Sabrina Lai	University of Cagliari, Italy
Jolanta Dvarioniene	Kaunas University of Technology, Lithuania
Valentin Grecu	Lucian Blaga University, Romania
Corrado Zoppi	University of Cagliari, Italy
Iole Cerminara	University of Basilicata, Italy

Smart and Sustainable Island Communities (SSIC 2021)

Chiara Garau	University of Cagliari, Italy
Anastasia Stratigea	National Technical University of Athens, Greece
Paola Zamperlin	University of Pisa, Italy
Francesco Scorza	University of Basilicata, Italy

Science, Technologies and Policies to Innovate Spatial Planning (STP4P 2021)

Chiara Garau	University of Cagliari, Italy
Daniele La Rosa	University of Catania, Italy
Francesco Scorza	University of Basilicata, Italy

Anna Maria Colavitti   University of Cagliari, Italy
Beniamino Murgante   University of Basilicata, Italy
Paolo La Greca   University of Catania, Italy

Sustainable Urban Energy Systems (SURENSYS 2021)

Luigi Mundula   University of Cagliari, Italy
Emilio Ghiani   University of Cagliari, Italy

Space Syntax for Cities in Theory and Practice (Syntax_City 2021)

Claudia Yamu   University of Groningen, The Netherlands
Akkelies van Nes   Western Norway University of Applied Sciences,
                                Norway
Chiara Garau   University of Cagliari, Italy

Theoretical and Computational Chemistry and Its Applications (TCCMA 2021)

Noelia Faginas-Lago   University of Perugia, Italy

13th International Workshop on Tools and Techniques in Software Development Process (TTSDP 2021)

Sanjay Misra   Covenant University, Nigeria

Urban Form Studies (UForm 2021)

Malgorzata Hanzl   Łódź University of Technology, Poland
Beniamino Murgante   University of Basilicata, Italy
Eufemia Tarantino   Polytechnic University of Bari, Italy
Irena Itova   University of Westminster, UK

Urban Space Accessibility and Safety (USAS 2021)

Chiara Garau   University of Cagliari, Italy
Francesco Pinna   University of Cagliari, Italy
Claudia Yamu   University of Groningen, The Netherlands
Vincenza Torrisi   University of Catania, Italy
Matteo Ignaccolo   University of Catania, Italy
Michela Tiboni   University of Brescia, Italy
Silvia Rossetti   University of Parma, Italy

Virtual and Augmented Reality and Applications (VRA 2021)

Osvaldo Gervasi   University of Perugia, Italy
Damiano Perri   University of Perugia, Italy
Marco Simonetti   University of Perugia, Italy
Sergio Tasso   University of Perugia, Italy

Workshop on Advanced and Computational Methods for Earth Science Applications (WACM4ES 2021)

Luca Piroddi	University of Cagliari, Italy
Laura Foddis	University of Cagliari, Italy
Augusto Montisci	University of Cagliari, Italy
Sergio Vincenzo Calcina	University of Cagliari, Italy
Sebastiano D'Amico	University of Malta, Malta
Giovanni Martinelli	Istituto Nazionale di Geofisica e Vulcanologia, Italy/Chinese Academy of Sciences, China

Sponsoring Organizations

ICCSA 2021 would not have been possible without the tremendous support of many organizations and institutions, for which all organizers and participants of ICCSA 2021 express their sincere gratitude:

Springer International Publishing AG, Germany (https://www.springer.com)

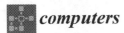

Computers Open Access Journal (https://www.mdpi.com/journal/computers)

IEEE Italy Section, Italy (https://italy.ieeer8.org/)

Centre-North Italy Chapter IEEE GRSS, Italy (https://cispio.diet.uniroma1.it/marzano/ieee-grs/index.html)

Italy Section of the Computer Society, Italy (https://site.ieee.org/italy-cs/)

University of Perugia, Italy (https://www.unipg.it)

University of Cagliari, Italy (https://unica.it/)

University of Basilicata, Italy
(http://www.unibas.it)

Monash University, Australia
(https://www.monash.edu/)

Kyushu Sangyo University, Japan
(https://www.kyusan-u.ac.jp/)

University of Minho, Portugal
(https://www.uminho.pt/)

Scientific Association Transport Infrastructures,
Italy
(https://www.stradeeautostrade.it/associazioni-e-
organizzazioni/asit-associazione-scientifica-
infrastrutture-trasporto/)

Regione Sardegna, Italy
(https://regione.sardegna.it/)

Comune di Cagliari, Italy
(https://www.comune.cagliari.it/)

Città Metropolitana di Cagliari

Cagliari Accessibility Lab (CAL)
(https://www.unica.it/unica/it/cagliari_
accessibility_lab.page/)

Referees

Nicodemo Abate	IMAA, National Research Council, Italy
Andre Ricardo Abed Grégio	Federal University of Paraná State, Brazil
Nasser Abu Zeid	Università di Ferrara, Italy
Lidia Aceto	Università del Piemonte Orientale, Italy
Nurten Akgün Tanbay	Bursa Technical University, Turkey
Filipe Alvelos	Universidade do Minho, Portugal
Paula Amaral	Universidade Nova de Lisboa, Portugal
Federico Amato	University of Lausanne, Switzerland
Marina Alexandra Pedro Andrade	ISCTE-IUL, Portugal
Debora Anelli	Sapienza University of Rome, Italy
Alfonso Annunziata	University of Cagliari, Italy
Fahim Anzum	University of Calgary, Canada
Tatsumi Aoyama	High Energy Accelerator Research Organization, Japan
Bernady Apduhan	Kyushu Sangyo University, Japan
Jonathan Apeh	Covenant University, Nigeria
Vasilike Argyropoulos	University of West Attica, Greece
Giuseppe Aronica	Università di Messina, Italy
Daniela Ascenzi	Università degli Studi di Trento, Italy
Vanessa Assumma	Politecnico di Torino, Italy
Muhammad Attique Khan	HITEC University Taxila, Pakistan
Vecdi Aytaç	Ege University, Turkey
Alina Elena Baia	University of Perugia, Italy
Ginevra Balletto	University of Cagliari, Italy
Marialaura Bancheri	ISAFOM, National Research Council, Italy
Benedetto Barabino	University of Brescia, Italy
Simona Barbaro	Università degli Studi di Palermo, Italy
Enrico Barbierato	Università Cattolica del Sacro Cuore di Milano, Italy
Jeniffer Barreto	Istituto Superior Técnico, Lisboa, Portugal
Michele Bartalini	TAGES, Italy
Socrates Basbas	Aristotle University of Thessaloniki, Greece
Silvia Battino	University of Sassari, Italy
Marcelo Becerra Rozas	Pontificia Universidad Católica de Valparaíso, Chile
Ranjan Kumar Behera	National Institute of Technology, Rourkela, India
Emanuele Bellini	University of Campania Luigi Vanvitelli, Italy
Massimo Bilancia	University of Bari Aldo Moro, Italy
Giulio Biondi	University of Firenze, Italy
Adriano Bisello	Eurac Research, Italy
Ignacio Blanquer	Universitat Politècnica de València, Spain
Semen Bochkov	Ulyanovsk State Technical University, Russia
Alexander Bogdanov	St. Petersburg University, Russia
Silvia Bonettini	University of Modena and Reggio Emilia, Italy
Enrico Borgogno Mondino	Università di Torino, Italy
Giuseppe Borruso	University of Trieste, Italy

Michele Bottazzi	University of Trento, Italy
Rahma Bouaziz	Taibah University, Saudi Arabia
Ouafik Boulariah	University of Salerno, Italy
Tulin Boyar	Yildiz Technical University, Turkey
Ana Cristina Braga	University of Minho, Portugal
Paolo Bragolusi	University of Padova, Italy
Luca Braidotti	University of Trieste, Italy
Alessandro Buccini	University of Cagliari, Italy
Jorge Buele	Universidad Tecnológica Indoamérica, Ecuador
Andrea Buffoni	TAGES, Italy
Sergio Vincenzo Calcina	University of Cagliari, Italy
Michele Campagna	University of Cagliari, Italy
Lelio Campanile	Università degli Studi della Campania Luigi Vanvitelli, Italy
Tiziana Campisi	Kore University of Enna, Italy
Antonino Canale	Kore University of Enna, Italy
Elena Cantatore	DICATECh, Polytechnic University of Bari, Italy
Pasquale Cantiello	Istituto Nazionale di Geofisica e Vulcanologia, Italy
Alessandra Capolupo	Polytechnic University of Bari, Italy
David Michele Cappelletti	University of Perugia, Italy
Caterina Caprioli	Politecnico di Torino, Italy
Sara Carcangiu	University of Cagliari, Italy
Pedro Carrasqueira	INESC Coimbra, Portugal
Arcangelo Castiglione	University of Salerno, Italy
Giulio Cavana	Politecnico di Torino, Italy
Davide Cerati	Politecnico di Milano, Italy
Maria Cerreta	University of Naples Federico II, Italy
Daniele Cesini	INFN-CNAF, Italy
Jabed Chowdhury	La Trobe University, Australia
Gennaro Ciccarelli	Iuav University of Venice, Italy
Birol Ciloglugil	Ege University, Turkey
Elena Cocuzza	Univesity of Catania, Italy
Anna Maria Colavitt	University of Cagliari, Italy
Cecilia Coletti	Università "G. d'Annunzio" di Chieti-Pescara, Italy
Alberto Collu	Independent Researcher, Italy
Anna Concas	University of Basilicata, Italy
Mauro Coni	University of Cagliari, Italy
Melchiorre Contino	Università di Palermo, Italy
Antonella Cornelio	Università degli Studi di Brescia, Italy
Aldina Correia	Politécnico do Porto, Portugal
Elisete Correia	Universidade de Trás-os-Montes e Alto Douro, Portugal
Florbela Correia	Polytechnic Institute of Viana do Castelo, Portugal
Stefano Corsi	Università degli Studi di Milano, Italy
Alberto Cortez	Polytechnic of University Coimbra, Portugal
Lino Costa	Universidade do Minho, Portugal

Alessandro Costantini	INFN, Italy
Marilena Cozzolino	Università del Molise, Italy
Giulia Crespi	Politecnico di Torino, Italy
Maurizio Crispino	Politecnico di Milano, Italy
Chiara D'Alpaos	University of Padova, Italy
Roberta D'Ambrosio	Università di Salerno, Italy
Sebastiano D'Amico	University of Malta, Malta
Hiroshi Daisaka	Hitotsubashi University, Japan
Gaia Daldanise	Italian National Research Council, Italy
Robertas Damasevicius	Silesian University of Technology, Poland
Maria Danese	ISPC, National Research Council, Italy
Bartoli Daniele	University of Perugia, Italy
Motasem Darwish	Middle East University, Jordan
Giulia Datola	Politecnico di Torino, Italy
Regina de Almeida	UTAD, Portugal
Elise de Doncker	Western Michigan University, USA
Mariella De Fino	Politecnico di Bari, Italy
Giandomenico De Luca	Mediterranean University of Reggio Calabria, Italy
Luiza de Macedo Mourelle	State University of Rio de Janeiro, Brazil
Gianluigi De Mare	University of Salerno, Italy
Itamir de Morais Barroca Filho	Federal University of Rio Grande do Norte, Brazil
Samuele De Petris	Università di Torino, Italy
Marcilio de Souto	LIFO, University of Orléans, France
Alexander Degtyarev	St. Petersburg University, Russia
Federico Dell'Anna	Politecnico di Torino, Italy
Marta Dell'Ovo	Politecnico di Milano, Italy
Fernanda Della Mura	University of Naples "Federico II", Italy
Ahu Dereli Dursun	Istanbul Commerce University, Turkey
Bashir Derradji	University of Sfax, Tunisia
Giulia Desogus	Università degli Studi di Cagliari, Italy
Marco Dettori	Università degli Studi di Sassari, Italy
Frank Devai	London South Bank University, UK
Felicia Di Liddo	Polytechnic University of Bari, Italy
Valerio Di Pinto	University of Naples "Federico II", Italy
Joana Dias	University of Coimbra, Portugal
Luis Dias	University of Minho, Portugal
Patricia Diaz de Alba	Gran Sasso Science Institute, Italy
Isabel Dimas	University of Coimbra, Portugal
Aleksandra Djordjevic	University of Belgrade, Serbia
Luigi Dolores	Università degli Studi di Salerno, Italy
Marco Donatelli	University of Insubria, Italy
Doina Cristina Duma	INFN-CNAF, Italy
Fabio Durastante	University of Pisa, Italy
Aziz Dursun	Virginia Tech University, USA
Juan Enrique-Romero	Université Grenoble Alpes, France

Annunziata Esposito Amideo	University College Dublin, Ireland
Dario Esposito	Polytechnic University of Bari, Italy
Claudio Estatico	University of Genova, Italy
Noelia Faginas-Lago	Università di Perugia, Italy
Maria Irene Falcão	University of Minho, Portugal
Stefano Falcinelli	University of Perugia, Italy
Alessandro Farina	University of Pisa, Italy
Grazia Fattoruso	ENEA, Italy
Caterina Fenu	University of Cagliari, Italy
Luisa Fermo	University of Cagliari, Italy
Florbela Fernandes	Instituto Politecnico de Braganca, Portugal
Rosário Fernandes	University of Minho, Portugal
Luis Fernandez-Sanz	University of Alcala, Spain
Alessia Ferrari	Università di Parma, Italy
Luís Ferrás	University of Minho, Portugal
Ângela Ferreira	Instituto Politécnico de Bragança, Portugal
Flora Ferreira	University of Minho, Portugal
Manuel Carlos Figueiredo	University of Minho, Portugal
Ugo Fiore	University of Naples "Parthenope", Italy
Amedeo Flora	University of Basilicata, Italy
Hector Florez	Universidad Distrital Francisco Jose de Caldas, Colombia
Maria Laura Foddis	University of Cagliari, Italy
Valentina Franzoni	Perugia University, Italy
Adelaide Freitas	University of Aveiro, Portugal
Samuel Frimpong	Durban University of Technology, South Africa
Ioannis Fyrogenis	Aristotle University of Thessaloniki, Greece
Marika Gaballo	Politecnico di Torino, Italy
Laura Gabrielli	Iuav University of Venice, Italy
Ivan Gankevich	St. Petersburg University, Russia
Chiara Garau	University of Cagliari, Italy
Ernesto Garcia Para	Universidad del País Vasco, Spain,
Fernando Garrido	Universidad Técnica del Norte, Ecuador
Marina Gavrilova	University of Calgary, Canada
Silvia Gazzola	University of Bath, UK
Georgios Georgiadis	Aristotle University of Thessaloniki, Greece
Osvaldo Gervasi	University of Perugia, Italy
Andrea Gioia	Polytechnic University of Bari, Italy
Dario Gioia	ISPC-CNT, Italy
Raffaele Giordano	IRSS, National Research Council, Italy
Giacomo Giorgi	University of Perugia, Italy
Eleonora Giovene di Girasole	IRISS, National Research Council, Italy
Salvatore Giuffrida	Università di Catania, Italy
Marco Gola	Politecnico di Milano, Italy

A. Manuela Gonçalves	University of Minho, Portugal
Yuriy Gorbachev	Coddan Technologies LLC, Russia
Angela Gorgoglione	Universidad de la República, Uruguay
Yusuke Gotoh	Okayama University, Japan
Anestis Gourgiotis	University of Thessaly, Greece
Valery Grishkin	St. Petersburg University, Russia
Alessandro Grottesi	CINECA, Italy
Eduardo Guerra	Free University of Bozen-Bolzano, Italy
Ayse Giz Gulnerman	Ankara HBV University, Turkey
Sevin Gümgüm	Izmir University of Economics, Turkey
Himanshu Gupta	BITS Pilani, Hyderabad, India
Sandra Haddad	Arab Academy for Science, Egypt
Malgorzata Hanzl	Lodz University of Technology, Poland
Shoji Hashimoto	KEK, Japan
Peter Hegedus	University of Szeged, Hungary
Eligius M. T. Hendrix	Universidad de Málaga, Spain
Edmond Ho	Northumbria University, UK
Guan Yue Hong	Western Michigan University, USA
Vito Iacobellis	Polytechnic University of Bari, Italy
Mauro Iacono	Università degli Studi della Campania, Italy
Chiara Iacovino	University of Basilicata, Italy
Antonino Iannuzzo	ETH Zurich, Switzerland
Ali Idri	University Mohammed V, Morocco
Oana-Ramona Ilovan	Babeş-Bolyai University, Romania
Mustafa Inceoglu	Ege University, Turkey
Tadashi Ishikawa	KEK, Japan
Federica Isola	University of Cagliari, Italy
Irena Itova	University of Westminster, UK
Edgar David de Izeppi	VTTI, USA
Marija Jankovic	CERTH, Greece
Adrian Jaramillo	Universidad Tecnológica Metropolitana, Chile
Monalisa Jena	Fakir Mohan University, India
Dorota Kamrowska-Załuska	Gdansk University of Technology, Poland
Issaku Kanamori	RIKEN Center for Computational Science, Japan
Korhan Karabulut	Yasar University, Turkey
Yeliz Karaca	University of Massachusetts Medical School, USA
Vicky Katsoni	University of West Attica, Greece
Dimitris Kavroudakis	University of the Aegean, Greece
Shuhei Kimura	Okayama University, Japan
Joanna Kolozej	Cracow University of Technology, Poland
Vladimir Korkhov	St. Petersburg University, Russia
Thales Körting	INPE, Brazil
Tomonori Kouya	Shizuoka Institute of Science and Technology, Japan
Sylwia Krzysztofik	Lodz University of Technology, Poland
Nataliia Kulabukhova	St. Petersburg University, Russia
Shrinivas B. Kulkarni	SDM College of Engineering and Technology, India

Pavan Kumar	University of Calgary, Canada
Anisha Kumari	National Institute of Technology, Rourkela, India
Ludovica La Rocca	University of Naples "Federico II", Italy
Daniele La Rosa	University of Catania, Italy
Sabrina Lai	University of Cagliari, Italy
Giuseppe Francesco Cesare Lama	University of Naples "Federico II", Italy
Mariusz Lamprecht	University of Lodz, Poland
Vincenzo Laporta	National Research Council, Italy
Chien-Sing Lee	Sunway University, Malaysia
José Isaac Lemus Romani	Pontifical Catholic University of Valparaíso, Chile
Federica Leone	University of Cagliari, Italy
Alexander H. Levis	George Mason University, USA
Carola Lingua	Polytechnic University of Turin, Italy
Marco Locurcio	Polytechnic University of Bari, Italy
Andrea Lombardi	University of Perugia, Italy
Savino Longo	University of Bari, Italy
Fernando Lopez Gayarre	University of Oviedo, Spain
Yan Lu	Western Michigan University, USA
Maria Macchiaroli	University of Salerno, Italy
Helmuth Malonek	University of Aveiro, Portugal
Francesca Maltinti	University of Cagliari, Italy
Luca Mancini	University of Perugia, Italy
Marcos Mandado	University of Vigo, Spain
Ernesto Marcheggiani	Università Politecnica delle Marche, Italy
Krassimir Markov	University of Telecommunications and Post, Bulgaria
Giovanni Martinelli	INGV, Italy
Alessandro Marucci	University of L'Aquila, Italy
Fiammetta Marulli	University of Campania Luigi Vanvitelli, Italy
Gabriella Maselli	University of Salerno, Italy
Rytis Maskeliunas	Kaunas University of Technology, Lithuania
Michele Mastroianni	University of Campania Luigi Vanvitelli, Italy
Cristian Mateos	Universidad Nacional del Centro de la Provincia de Buenos Aires, Argentina
Hideo Matsufuru	High Energy Accelerator Research Organization (KEK), Japan
D'Apuzzo Mauro	University of Cassino and Southern Lazio, Italy
Chiara Mazzarella	University Federico II, Italy
Marco Mazzarino	University of Venice, Italy
Giovanni Mei	University of Cagliari, Italy
Mário Melo	Federal Institute of Rio Grande do Norte, Brazil
Francesco Mercaldo	University of Molise, Italy
Alfredo Milani	University of Perugia, Italy
Alessandra Milesi	University of Cagliari, Italy
Antonio Minervino	ISPC, National Research Council, Italy
Fernando Miranda	Universidade do Minho, Portugal

B. Mishra	University of Szeged, Hungary
Sanjay Misra	Covenant University, Nigeria
Mirka Mobilia	University of Salerno, Italy
Giuseppe Modica	Università degli Studi di Reggio Calabria, Italy
Mohammadsadegh Mohagheghi	Vali-e-Asr University of Rafsanjan, Iran
Mohamad Molaei Qelichi	University of Tehran, Iran
Mario Molinara	University of Cassino and Southern Lazio, Italy
Augusto Montisci	Università degli Studi di Cagliari, Italy
Pierluigi Morano	Polytechnic University of Bari, Italy
Ricardo Moura	Universidade Nova de Lisboa, Portugal
Ana Clara Mourao Moura	Federal University of Minas Gerais, Brazil
Maria Mourao	Polytechnic Institute of Viana do Castelo, Portugal
Daichi Mukunoki	RIKEN Center for Computational Science, Japan
Beniamino Murgante	University of Basilicata, Italy
Naohito Nakasato	University of Aizu, Japan
Grazia Napoli	Università degli Studi di Palermo, Italy
Isabel Cristina Natário	Universidade Nova de Lisboa, Portugal
Nadia Nedjah	State University of Rio de Janeiro, Brazil
Antonio Nesticò	University of Salerno, Italy
Andreas Nikiforiadis	Aristotle University of Thessaloniki, Greece
Keigo Nitadori	RIKEN Center for Computational Science, Japan
Silvio Nocera	Iuav University of Venice, Italy
Giuseppina Oliva	University of Salerno, Italy
Arogundade Oluwasefunmi	Academy of Mathematics and System Science, China
Ken-ichi Oohara	University of Tokyo, Japan
Tommaso Orusa	University of Turin, Italy
M. Fernanda P. Costa	University of Minho, Portugal
Roberta Padulano	Centro Euro-Mediterraneo sui Cambiamenti Climatici, Italy
Maria Panagiotopoulou	National Technical University of Athens, Greece
Jay Pancham	Durban University of Technology, South Africa
Gianni Pantaleo	University of Florence, Italy
Dimos Pantazis	University of West Attica, Greece
Michela Paolucci	University of Florence, Italy
Eric Pardede	La Trobe University, Australia
Olivier Parisot	Luxembourg Institute of Science and Technology, Luxembourg
Vincenzo Pellecchia	Ente Idrico Campano, Italy
Anna Pelosi	University of Salerno, Italy
Edit Pengő	University of Szeged, Hungary
Marco Pepe	University of Salerno, Italy
Paola Perchinunno	University of Cagliari, Italy
Ana Pereira	Polytechnic Institute of Bragança, Portugal
Mariano Pernetti	University of Campania, Italy
Damiano Perri	University of Perugia, Italy

Federica Pes	University of Cagliari, Italy
Marco Petrelli	Roma Tre University, Italy
Massimiliano Petri	University of Pisa, Italy
Khiem Phan	Duy Tan University, Vietnam
Alberto Ferruccio Piccinni	Polytechnic of Bari, Italy
Angela Pilogallo	University of Basilicata, Italy
Francesco Pinna	University of Cagliari, Italy
Telmo Pinto	University of Coimbra, Portugal
Luca Piroddi	University of Cagliari, Italy
Darius Plonis	Vilnius Gediminas Technical University, Lithuania
Giuliano Poli	University of Naples "Federico II", Italy
Maria João Polidoro	Polytecnic Institute of Porto, Portugal
Ioannis Politis	Aristotle University of Thessaloniki, Greece
Maurizio Pollino	ENEA, Italy
Antonio Pratelli	University of Pisa, Italy
Salvatore Praticò	Mediterranean University of Reggio Calabria, Italy
Marco Prato	University of Modena and Reggio Emilia, Italy
Carlotta Quagliolo	Polytechnic University of Turin, Italy
Emanuela Quaquero	Univesity of Cagliari, Italy
Garrisi Raffaele	Polizia postale e delle Comunicazioni, Italy
Nicoletta Rassu	University of Cagliari, Italy
Hafiz Tayyab Rauf	University of Bradford, UK
Michela Ravanelli	Sapienza University of Rome, Italy
Roberta Ravanelli	Sapienza University of Rome, Italy
Alfredo Reder	Centro Euro-Mediterraneo sui Cambiamenti Climatici, Italy
Stefania Regalbuto	University of Naples "Federico II", Italy
Rommel Regis	Saint Joseph's University, USA
Lothar Reichel	Kent State University, USA
Marco Reis	University of Coimbra, Portugal
Maria Reitano	University of Naples "Federico II", Italy
Jerzy Respondek	Silesian University of Technology, Poland
Elisa Riccietti	École Normale Supérieure de Lyon, France
Albert Rimola	Universitat Autònoma de Barcelona, Spain
Angela Rizzo	University of Bari, Italy
Ana Maria A. C. Rocha	University of Minho, Portugal
Fabio Rocha	Institute of Technology and Research, Brazil
Humberto Rocha	University of Coimbra, Portugal
Maria Clara Rocha	Polytechnic Institute of Coimbra, Portugal
Miguel Rocha	University of Minho, Portugal
Giuseppe Rodriguez	University of Cagliari, Italy
Guillermo Rodriguez	UNICEN, Argentina
Elisabetta Ronchieri	INFN, Italy
Marzio Rosi	University of Perugia, Italy
Silvia Rossetti	University of Parma, Italy
Marco Rossitti	Polytechnic University of Milan, Italy

Francesco Rotondo	Marche Polytechnic University, Italy
Irene Rubino	Polytechnic University of Turin, Italy
Agustín Salas	Pontifical Catholic University of Valparaíso, Chile
Juan Pablo Sandoval Alcocer	Universidad Católica Boliviana "San Pablo", Bolivia
Luigi Santopietro	University of Basilicata, Italy
Rafael Santos	National Institute for Space Research, Brazil
Valentino Santucci	Università per Stranieri di Perugia, Italy
Mirko Saponaro	Polytechnic University of Bari, Italy
Filippo Sarvia	University of Turin, Italy
Marco Scaioni	Polytechnic University of Milan, Italy
Rafal Scherer	Częstochowa University of Technology, Poland
Francesco Scorza	University of Basilicata, Italy
Ester Scotto di Perta	University of Napoli "Federico II", Italy
Monica Sebillo	University of Salerno, Italy
Patrizia Serra	University of Cagliari, Italy
Ricardo Severino	University of Minho, Portugal
Jie Shen	University of Michigan, USA
Huahao Shou	Zhejiang University of Technology, China
Miltiadis Siavvas	Centre for Research and Technology Hellas, Greece
Brandon Sieu	University of Calgary, Canada
Ângela Silva	Instituto Politécnico de Viana do Castelo, Portugal
Carina Silva	Polytechic Institute of Lisbon, Portugal
Joao Carlos Silva	Polytechnic Institute of Cavado and Ave, Portugal
Fabio Silveira	Federal University of Sao Paulo, Brazil
Marco Simonetti	University of Florence, Italy
Ana Jacinta Soares	University of Minho, Portugal
Maria Joana Soares	University of Minho, Portugal
Michel Soares	Federal University of Sergipe, Brazil
George Somarakis	Foundation for Research and Technology Hellas, Greece
Maria Somma	University of Naples "Federico II", Italy
Alberico Sonnessa	Polytechnic University of Bari, Italy
Elena Stankova	St. Petersburg University, Russia
Flavio Stochino	University of Cagliari, Italy
Anastasia Stratigea	National Technical University of Athens, Greece
Yasuaki Sumida	Kyushu Sangyo University, Japan
Yue Sun	European X-Ray Free-Electron Laser Facility, Germany
Kirill Sviatov	Ulyanovsk State Technical University, Russia
Daisuke Takahashi	University of Tsukuba, Japan
Aladics Tamás	University of Szeged, Hungary
David Taniar	Monash University, Australia
Rodrigo Tapia McClung	Centro de Investigación en Ciencias de Información Geoespacial, Mexico
Eufemia Tarantino	Polytechnic University of Bari, Italy

Sergio Tasso	University of Perugia, Italy
Ana Paula Teixeira	Universidade de Trás-os-Montes e Alto Douro, Portugal
Senhorinha Teixeira	University of Minho, Portugal
Tengku Adil Tengku Izhar	Universiti Teknologi MARA, Malaysia
Maria Filomena Teodoro	University of Lisbon/Portuguese Naval Academy, Portugal
Giovanni Tesoriere	Kore University of Enna, Italy
Yiota Theodora	National Technical Univeristy of Athens, Greece
Graça Tomaz	Polytechnic Institute of Guarda, Portugal
Carmelo Maria Torre	Polytechnic University of Bari, Italy
Francesca Torrieri	University of Naples "Federico II", Italy
Vincenza Torrisi	University of Catania, Italy
Vincenzo Totaro	Polytechnic University of Bari, Italy
Pham Trung	Ho Chi Minh City University of Technology, Vietnam
Dimitrios Tsoukalas	Centre of Research and Technology Hellas (CERTH), Greece
Sanjida Tumpa	University of Calgary, Canada
Iñaki Tuñon	Universidad de Valencia, Spain
Takahiro Ueda	Seikei University, Japan
Piero Ugliengo	University of Turin, Italy
Abdi Usman	Haramaya University, Ethiopia
Ettore Valente	University of Naples "Federico II", Italy
Jordi Vallverdu	Universitat Autònoma de Barcelona, Spain
Cornelis Van Der Mee	University of Cagliari, Italy
José Varela-Aldás	Universidad Tecnológica Indoamérica, Ecuador
Fanny Vazart	University of Grenoble Alpes, France
Franco Vecchiocattivi	University of Perugia, Italy
Laura Verde	University of Campania Luigi Vanvitelli, Italy
Giulia Vergerio	Polytechnic University of Turin, Italy
Jos Vermaseren	Nikhef, The Netherlands
Giacomo Viccione	University of Salerno, Italy
Marco Vizzari	University of Perugia, Italy
Corrado Vizzarri	Polytechnic University of Bari, Italy
Alexander Vodyaho	St. Petersburg State Electrotechnical University "LETI", Russia
Nikolay N. Voit	Ulyanovsk State Technical University, Russia
Marco Vona	University of Basilicata, Italy
Agustinus Borgy Waluyo	Monash University, Australia
Fernando Wanderley	Catholic University of Pernambuco, Brazil
Chao Wang	University of Science and Technology of China, China
Marcin Wozniak	Silesian University of Technology, Poland
Tiang Xian	Nathong University, China
Rekha Yadav	KL University, India
Claudia Yamu	University of Groningen, The Netherlands
Fenghui Yao	Tennessee State University, USA

Fukuko Yuasa	KEK, Japan
Moayid Ali Zaidi	Ostfold University College Norway, Norway
Paola Zamperlin	University of Pisa, Italy
Peter Zeile	Karlsruhe Institute of Technology, Germany
Milliam Maxime Zekeng Ndadji	University of Dschang, Cameroon
Nataly Zhukova	ITMO University, Russia
Ljiljiana Zivkovic	Ministry of Construction, Transport and Infrastructure/Institute of Architecture and Urban and Spatial Planning of Serbia, Serbia

Contents – Part IX

**International Workshop on Sustainability Performance Assessment:
Models, Approaches and Applications Toward Interdisciplinary
and Integrated Solutions (SPA 2021)**

13th International Symposium on Software Engineering Processes and Applications (SEPA 2021)

Commercial Entry Control Using Robotic Mechanism and Mobile Application for COVID-19 Pandemic

José Varela-Aldás[1,3](✉) ⓘ, Jefferson Pilla[1], Víctor H. Andaluz[2] ⓘ,
and Guillermo Palacios-Navarro[3] ⓘ

[1] SISAu Research Group, Universidad Tecnológica Indoamérica, Ambato, Ecuador
josevarela@uti.edu.ec
[2] Universidad de las Fuerzas Armadas ESPE, Sangolquí, Ecuador
vhandaluz1@espe.edu.ec
[3] Department of Electronic Engineering and Communications, University of Zaragoza,
Teruel, Spain
guillermo.palacios@unizar.es

Abstract. The control of entry to commercial premises has always existed, but with the pandemic, this has been adapted to include biosecurity measures that guarantee the safety of customers. Technology makes it possible to automate these activities, among the most popular tools are mobile applications that allow easy implementation and good reception from users. This work presents the entrance control to a commercial premise using a robotic mechanism and a mobile application connected through a cloud database. The system is implemented using accessible and low-cost components, among the tools are 3D printing, the ESP32 board, servo motors, proximity sensors, temperature, and heart rate. The mobile application is developed in App Inventor and Firebase is used for the remote database. The system automates the provision of hand sanitizer at the entrance and records these vital signs of the customers, allowing to generate a report of the attendees. The results show the readings carried out by validating the implemented system and a measure of acceptance of this technology is applied with a score of 73%, evidencing the deficiencies of the proposal from the users' perspective.

Keywords: Robotic mechanism · Mobile application · Cloud database · COVID-19

1 Introduction

The pandemic caused by COVID-19 has caused great changes worldwide, countries have had to incorporate biosecurity measures to take care of citizens [1, 2]. Commerce has been directly affected, requiring adaptations in the facilities to continue commercial activities, among the measures are social distancing, use of a mask, application of hand sanitizer, and others [3, 4]. Another action to take is monitoring vital signs, body temperature is the first variable to be checked, although an increase in heart rate has also been recorded in

O. Gervasi et al. (Eds.): ICCSA 2021, LNCS 12957, pp. 3–14, 2021.
https://doi.org/10.1007/978-3-030-87013-3_1

some cases [5]. In optimizing these activities, technological options have been developed that help control biosafety measures [6, 7]. These systems are commonly implemented when entering the local, using sensors and actuators that automate the control processes [8].

Robotics has been a tool used in the fight against COVID-19, robots are installed in different fields to control biosafety measures, in some cases robots assist medical activities avoiding the exposure of doctors, disinfect buildings using different technologies cleaning, controlling the temperature of people in closed places, providing disinfectant gel and more [9, 10]. Robotics still has more solutions that have not yet been explored and in the future, there will be greater dependence on this technology, but the implementation costs are high, this has forced the use of more accessible technologies in solving the problems caused by the pandemic [11, 12].

Mobile devices such as smartphones and tablets are widely used to achieve fast and effective solutions, developing mobile applications that allow the incorporation of support measures to prevent the spread of the virus [13]. In some cases, mobile devices alert users in areas with a high number of infections to avoid these places, some applications allow entering information on the user's health status to make decisions regarding a possible contagion, ruling out symptoms not related to the disease [14, 15]. These solutions incorporate other technologies such as the internet of things, databases, cloud computing, and others [16].

Cloud databases have been useful when implementing mobile applications and web applications displaying information of interest in real-time, in the development of telemedicine solutions, and remote data monitoring [17]. These technologies are constantly growing, allowing the creation of portable applications that guarantee the availability of information from anywhere in the world [18]. The combination of robotics, mobile applications, and cloud databases promises multi-featured tools to improve user acceptance.

This work presents a support system in the commerce entry control in the context of COVID-19, for a robotic mechanism is built for the reading of vital data through sensors and the activation of a hand sanitizer, managing the system from a mobile application that uses a database in Firebase. The document is distributed as follows: i) An introduction to the subject; ii) Materials and methods, iii) Results; iv) Conclusions [19].

2   Materials and Methods

In the context of the COVID-19 pandemic, the business's adaptations have been very creative, using mechanical devices to dispense gel through digital skin thermometers to control the temperature of those attending the premises. Thus, it is important to develop new tools that help to combat contagion, the main objective of this work is to implement a system to control entry through low-cost technology, Fig. 1 shows the general scheme of this proposal. The scheme is presented based on referential images and boxes of continuous lines (__) that contain blocks of some function or action within the scheme, the dashed lines (--) group the three main elements of the control system. The requirements include measuring vital signs and providing disinfectant to the user, for this the construction of a robotic mechanism with an electronic circuit and integrated programming for operation, and a mobile application for the management of the system through the global network is designed. Once the proposal is implemented, tests of the system are carried out through measurements of the temperature and heart rate of the users. Finally, a measurement of acceptance of the proposal is applied to measure satisfaction with the characteristics of the system.

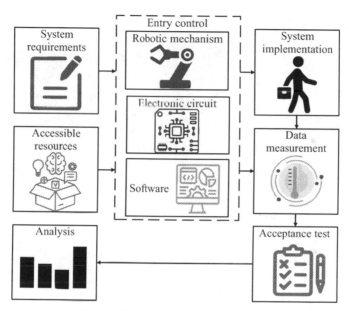

Fig. 1. General scheme of the proposal.

2.1 Components

Figure 2 presents the components to be used in the implementation of this proposal, these resources have been selected mainly for the accessibility and ease of use. In the hardware, a 3D printer is used to manufacture the mechanical components of the robotic mechanism, the required actuators are servomotors for the joints and a buzzer to generate alerts, the required sensors are proximity detectors and temperature and heart rate meters. To manage these elements, the ESP32 board is used, which is a System On Chip device that is characterized by WiFi connectivity, in this way the system is connected to the net. On the other hand, the application is developed in App Inventor and the remote database is implemented in Firebase, both tools belong to Google.

2.2 Hardware

In hardware development, two components are distinguished, the mechanical structure and the electronic circuit. Figure 3 presents images of the mechanism in 3D design computer-assisted. The mechanism starts from a dark gray lower base that contains the

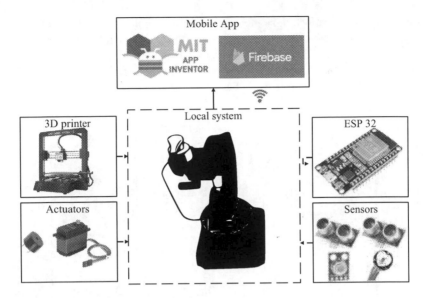

Fig. 2. Selected components to implement the system.

circuitry and one of the proximity sensors, and the yellow cylindrical base that contains the first servomotor that rotates the entire upper mechanism. Then there are have two links driven by servo motors that are placed serially to build a kinematic chain, similar to a robotic arm. At the end there is an extrusion mechanism to provide the hand sanitizer, this works by converting rotating movement to linear movement using a gear and rack, the mechanism includes a circular bracket to place the alcohol bottle.

The electronic circuit in this proposal is based on the 30-pin ESP 32 Dev Module board, Fig. 4 shows the design of the connections to the sensors and actuators. The proximity sensors (HC-SR04) use 4 pins configured as digital inputs and outputs, one of these sensors is located at the base of the robot to detect the presence of the user, and the other is located at the end to detect the hands and provide the disinfectant. The infrared temperature sensor (GY-906 MLX90614) uses pins D21 and D22 for synchronous serial communication (I2C). The heart rate sensor (XD-58C) uses pin D34 configured as an analog input. Regarding the actuators, the buzzer uses a digital output and the servo-motors are connected to a 16-channel motor driver (PCA9685) that is controlled using I2C communication. The first three servomotors (SF3218MG) reach a torque of up to 20 kg-cm and the fourth servomotor (MG995) maximum torque of 10 kg-cm. The entire system uses a 5 V 4 amperes electrical dependent supply.

The components of the mechanical structure of the robot are manufactured using the Anycubic Mega S 3D printer and PLA material, Fig. 5 shows the robotic mechanism built, observing a rectangular wooden base that fixes all the robot and the circuitry, evidencing the correct assembly of the entire mechanical system. Preliminary tests show the correct operation of all built-in sensors and actuators.

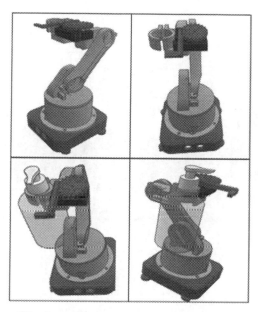

Fig. 3. 3D design of the robotic mechanism.

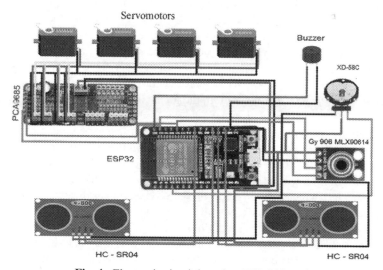

Fig. 4. Electronic circuit based on ESP 32 board.

2.3 Software

Regarding the software, it is necessary to develop the programming of the control board and the user interface of the mobile application. The ESP 32 is programmed using Arduino IDE with the required libraries for the compatibility of the board, the libraries for the WiFi communication (WiFi.h), the temperature sensor (Adafruit_MLX90614.h), and

Fig. 5. Photos of the robotic mechanism built.

the driver of the devices are also included. servomotors (Adafruit_PWMServoDriver.h). The robot is programmed to initiate actions when it detects a presence, activities with measuring body temperature, heart rate, give disinfectant, possible alerts, and communication with the mobile application through the cloud.

The mobile application allows viewing the vital parameters (temperature and heart rate) of the user, control the actions of the robot, and present alerts. Alerts consist of an audible and visual warning at the remote site and an audible warning at the local site, at the remote site the alert is played on the administrator's phone, and at the local site, the audible alert is played with the circuit buzzer electronic. Figure 6 shows some screens of the mobile application, the interface includes control of access to the application and registration of frequent users. In addition, the generation of reports is implemented that allows reviewing the history of customers who attended the commercial.

The entire mobile application is developed in App Inventor. Figure 7 shows some blocks of the implemented application, each color implies a different function that is assigned by default (e.g. red = text, green = set). The greatest complexity of the software is in the communication with the remote database, for this Firebase is used, this platform is located in the cloud, it supports easily synchronizes the data without managing connections or using complex synchronization logic and does not require a server. In addition, allowing to implement functions of communication in App Inventor. In the Arduino IDE program, the database is managed through the FirebaseESP32.h library that allows reading and writing registers. The database created in the Firebase web interface is presented in Fig. 8, showing the elements of the tables for the clients, the robot, and the administrator.

3 Results

The proposed system is evaluated in a hardware store for a week, registering the owner of the premises as administrator and entering the most frequent customers to the database, while infrequent customers have a number assigned as they enter local, without wasting

Fig. 6. Mobile app screens.

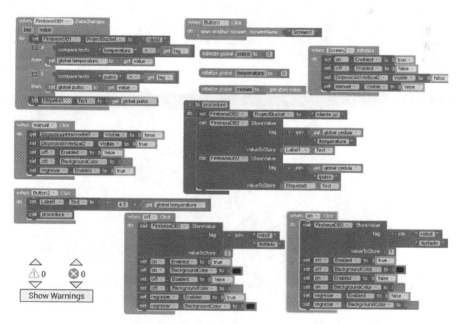

Fig. 7. Block diagram segment implemented in App inventor.

time. Figure 9 shows photos of the system in operation, observing a client receiving the
sanitizer in their hands and the mobile application showing the information obtained

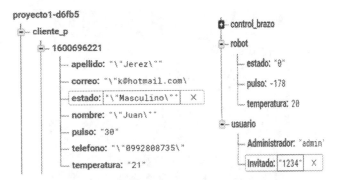

Fig. 8. Database implemented in Firebase.

from the local site. The dispenser works manually and automatically, so that the client receives the disinfectant upon entering and when the application administrator wishes.

3.1 Measurements

During the testing period, data from 41 people are taken, which are reported in the mobile application, the report shows the customer data, entered manually to the database, and the history of the measurements taken by the sensors, as shown in Fig. 10. The alert trigger is configured for temperatures above 37.5 °C, and in the evaluation period no alerts are generated, i.e., 100% of the participants had adequate temperature values.

Fig. 9. Photos of the system in operation.

Temperature and heart rate measurements are presented in Fig. 11. The unit of measurement for temperature is in degrees Celsius ([°C]), with an average temperature of 35.9 [°C] and a standard deviation of 0.8 [°C], these data are consistent with common

Fig. 10. Mobile app report.

human temperatures, since the sensor is calibrated using a commercial thermometer. Heart rate is presented in units of beats per minute ([bpm]), with a mean rate of 78 [bpm] and a standard deviation of 8 [bpm].

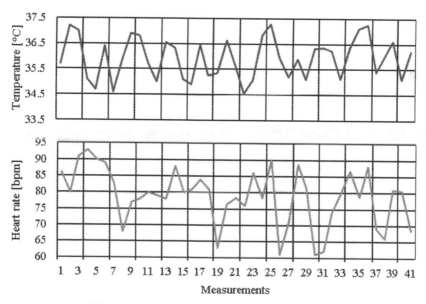

Fig. 11. Temperature and heart rate measurements.

3.2 Acceptance

As a complementary tool, an acceptance indicator is applied to clients and the manager of the commercial premises, using measure of technology acceptance model of [20], this is evaluated with each participant using the Likert scale, the scores are in the range from

"I disagree" (1) to "totally agree" (5). Table 1 presents Acceptance scores, the system has a final score of 73%, which is favorable for this proposal, but in productivity the customers believe that the system does not help in the commerce and does not facilitate entry control, while that measures of ease of use have good scores.

Table 1. Results of the acceptance measure

Measure	Score
Using the system would improve control entry performance	3.3
Using the system would enhance the effectiveness on the control entry	3.2
I would find the system useful in the control entry	3.9
Using the system in the control entry would increase the productivity	2.7
Using the system would enable me to accomplish control entry quickly	3.1
Using the system would make it easier to do the control entry	3.0
Learning to operate the system would be easy for me	4.2
I would find the system easy to use	4.2
I would find it easy to get the system to do what I want it to do	4
It would be easy for me to become skillful at using the system	4.4
Learning to operate the system would be easy for me	4.2
Total	40.2/55 (73%)

4   Conclusions

The COVID-19 pandemic changed the shape of trade around the world, and although there is currently a vaccine, it is not yet available to everyone, especially in developing countries. Thus, biosafety measures continue to be applied and it is necessary to continue developing technological tools to combat the spread of this or any other virus. The entry control in times of pandemic includes the measurement of body temperature and disinfecting the assistants. This work proposes an automated mechanism based on a space robot to measure physical health variables and provide disinfectant, managing the information through a mobile application. The system is implemented using accessible resources for easy reproduction. In addition, the system includes a cloud database to access the records from the application and from anywhere in the world.

The results of the system evaluate the operation of the proposal through the readings obtained and an acceptance indicator. The measurements made are within the correct range, showing normal temperatures and heart rates in all readings. The mobile application allows reviewing the history of customers who attended the commercial in a report generated from the remote database. The acceptance measure indicates a score of 73/100, expressing some dissatisfaction with the proposal, the participants rate the system as unproductive. In summary, some characteristics and conditions of this system are not accepted by users, requiring improvements to achieve a more effective product. The robot's appearance can be improved to achieve greater user acceptance. This information is useful in future work by authors or readers who propose an entry control system that considers the current health problem.

References

1. Trump, B.D., Linkov, I.: Risk and resilience in the time of the COVID-19 crisis. Environ. Syst. Decis. **40**(2), 171–173 (2020). https://doi.org/10.1007/s10669-020-09781-0
2. Bagchi, B., Chatterjee, S., Ghosh, R., Dandapat, D.: Presented at the Impact of COVID-19 on Global Economy (2020). https://doi.org/10.1007/978-981-15-7782-6_3
3. Ortega, R., Gonzalez, M., Nozari, A., Canelli, R.: Personal protective equipment and Covid-19. N. Engl. J. Med. **382**, e105 (2020). https://doi.org/10.1056/NEJMvcm2014809
4. Khan, M.M., Parab, S.R.: Simple economical solution for personal protection equipment (face mask/shield) for health care staff during COVID 19. Indian J. Otolaryngol. Head Neck Surg. 1–5 (2020). https://doi.org/10.1007/s12070-020-01863-4
5. Pavri, B.B., Kloo, J., Farzad, D., Riley, J.M.: Behavior of the PR interval with increasing heart rate in patients with COVID-19. Hear. Rhythm. **17**, 1434–1438 (2020). https://doi.org/10.1016/j.hrthm.2020.06.009
6. Ting, D.S.W., Carin, L., Dzau, V., Wong, T.Y.: Digital technology and COVID-19. Nat. Med. **26**, 459–461 (2020). https://doi.org/10.1038/s41591-020-0824-5
7. Madurai Elavarasan, R., Pugazhendhi, R.: Restructured society and environment: A review on potential technological strategies to control the COVID-19 pandemic. Sci. Total Environ. **725**, 138858 (2020). https://doi.org/10.1016/j.scitotenv.2020.138858
8. Tong, A., et al.: Research priorities for COVID-19 sensor technology. Nat. Biotechnol. **39**, 144–147 (2021). https://doi.org/10.1038/s41587-021-00816-8
9. Murphy, R.R., Gandudi, V.B.M., Adams, J.: Applications of Robots for COVID-19 Respons (2020)
10. Guettari, M., Gharbi, I., Hamza, S.: UVC disinfection robot. Environ. Sci. Pollut. Res. **28**(30), 40394–40399 (2020). https://doi.org/10.1007/s11356-020-11184-2
11. Varela-Aldás, J., Moreira, A., Criollo, P., Ruales, B.: Body temperature control using a robotic arm. In: Botto Tobar, M., Cruz, H., Díaz Cadena, A. (eds.) CIT 2020. LNEE, vol. 762, pp. 280–293. Springer, Cham (2021). https://doi.org/10.1007/978-3-030-72208-1_21
12. Varela-Aldás, J., Pilla, J., Llugsha, E., Cholota, O.: Application of hand disinfectant gel using a SCARA. In: Rocha, Á., Ferrás, C., López-López, P.C., Guarda, T. (eds.) ICITS 2021. AIS'C, vol. 1331, pp. 13–23. Springer, Cham (2021). https://doi.org/10.1007/978-3-030-68418-1_2
13. Kondylakis, H., et al.: COVID-19 mobile apps: a systematic review of the literature. J. Med. Internet Res. **22**, e23170 (2020). https://doi.org/10.2196/23170
14. Drew, D.A., et al.: others: rapid implementation of mobile technology for real-time epidemiology of COVID-19. Science (80) (2020). https://doi.org/10.1126/science.abc0473
15. Altmann, S., et al.: Acceptability of app-based contact tracing for COVID-19: cross-country survey study. JMIR mHealth uHealth **8**, e19857 (2020). https://doi.org/10.2196/19857
16. Ndiaye, M., Oyewobi, S.S., Abu-Mahfouz, A.M., Hancke, G.P., Kurien, A.M., Djouani, K.: IoT in the wake of COVID-19: a survey on contributions, challenges and evollution. IEEE Access **8**, 186821–186839 (2020). https://doi.org/10.1109/ACCESS.2020.3030090
17. Warren, M.S., Skillman, S.W.: Mobility Changes in Response to COVID-19 (2020)
18. Mallik, R., Hazarika, A.P., Ghosh Dastidar, S., Sing, D., Bandyopadhyay, R.: Development of an android application for viewing Covid-19 containment zones and monitoring violators who are trespassing into it using firebase and geofencing. Trans. Indian Nat. Acad. Eng. **5**(2), 163–179 (2020). https://doi.org/10.1007/s41403-020-00137-3

19. Misra, S.: A Step by Step Guide for Choosing Project Topics and Writing Research Papers in ICT Related Disciplines. In: Information and Communication Technology and Applications: Third International Conference, ICTA 2020, Minna, Nigeria, November 24–27, 2020, Revised Selected Papers 3. pp. 727–744 (2021). https://doi.org/10.1007/978-3-030-69143-1_55
20. Lin, C.-C.: Exploring the relationship between technology acceptance model and usability test. Inf. Technol. Manage. **14**(3), 243–255 (2013). https://doi.org/10.1007/s10799-013-0162-0

Software Process Metrics in Agile Software Development: A Systematic Mapping Study

Syeda Sumbul Hossain[(✉)], Pollab Ahmed, and Yeasir Arafat

Daffodil International University, Dhaka, Bangladesh
{syeda.swe,pollab35-1732,yeasir35-1501}@diu.edu.bd

Abstract. Software process metrics are being used for improving agile processes in software companies. This helps a lot in managing customer satisfaction and the growth of the company. Different studies have stated different process metrics and practitioners are using various metrics in terms of software process improvement. However, it is difficult to find out the best-suited metrics for every company as per the project nature. A systematic mapping study is used to identify potential process improvement metrics and finding the best metrics in agile development. We have found only 13 papers on process metrics. Finally, we have classified them into three categories assuming their impacting factors. This study provides an overview of agile software development process metrics that will help the practitioners to adopt efficient process metrics in Global Software Development (GSD).

Keywords: Software process improvement · Global Software Development (GSD) · Agile · Distributed software development · Process metrics · Systematic mapping study

1 Introduction

Maintaining software development life cycle models (SDLC) throughout the software development is crucial for the success of the software and also for the business. With this point of view, various SDLC models were introduced and practiced and the agile development model had got the most popular for its incremental development attitude. Agile works in an iteration or in a small module where every iteration takes 2–4 weeks. And every iteration implements some functions. Jinzenji [8] explained iterative software development in a very understanding manner. The main benefit of agile is that it can incorporate any valid functionalities at any time of the development process. Improving the agile software development process requires a lot of work for the development team as it requires maintaining multiple things at a time. Everything in agile is managed in phases and metrics come in help for this matter. Concas [3] implemented agile project phases with software metrics which provides a brief overview on how we

© Springer Nature Switzerland AG 2021
O. Gervasi et al. (Eds.): ICCSA 2021, LNCS 12957, pp. 15–26, 2021.
https://doi.org/10.1007/978-3-030-87013-3_2

can implement and ease our agile project development by applying metrics in different phases. Traditional software development models used a lot of metrics in their development phase which has a great impact in managing, organizing, and improving the development process. Many companies implemented those metrics in agile but found that they are not fully capable of utilizing agile development. So, they tried to create new metrics according to their business and development needs and also fused some metrics with agile. Padmini [14] made a comparison of traditional software metrics and agile software metrics. A lot of literature reviews, case studies on companies, and empirical studies have been done for finding the metrics which will provide the highest amount of benefit in agile software development. A survey was done by Sanjay Misra and Martha Omorodion [12] where different software metrics are classified as Product Metrics, Process Metrics, Objective Metrics, Subjective Metrics, Resource Metrics, Project Metrics, Direct Metrics, and Indirect Metrics.

Process metrics are further classified into different metrics and a lot of those are already being used by different software companies according to their usages and needs. A lot of research had been done on this topic and many metrics also found out. It will be worth the findings if we can summarize the most common metrics that might be effective mostly in software process improvement. From that, we are motivated to identify the most common metrics that are stated in the literature through a systematic mapping study.

The further sections of this study are assembled as follows. Related works are presented in Sect. 2. In Sect. 3, the overall research methodology is described which is followed by results and analysis in Sect. 4. And finally, the conclusion is furnished in Sect. 5.

2   Related Work

Measuring the agile software development process is not that much different than traditional software development. But it still has some differences. For a software company practicing agile, measuring its projects under development and the quality of the products they create and serve is very much essential. It helps to understand the project's progression rate and manage it for further improvement [4]. Metrics are used for this aspect so that better visibility and insight can be found. It also helps for analyzing how well it is doing in development and did [16]. In general terms, it is a defining factor for agile process management. By my systematic mapping study, we have found very little study on agile process metrics. And it is also seen that many of the studies done in recent years which refer to agile are gaining popularity and it needs a lot of concentration from the researchers. Gustafsson [5] made a category of five metrics as Lean, Business value, Cost, Quality, and Predictability. Predictability and Business value refers to different surveys on business for finding a future insight of the business and predicting its shortcomings. Cost refers to the measurement of cost per function. Finally, Quality and Lean are for ensuring product quality assurance and working progress. Downey and Sutherland [4] found some remarkable metrics which are very much beneficial for making decisions on managerial aspects. There are nine of them and they are, Focus Factor, Percentage of Found Work, Percentage of Adopted work, Velocity, Work Capacity, Targeted Value Increase, Win/Loss Record, Accuracy of Forecast, and Success at Scale. Oza and Korkala [13] divided agile software development into three categories, productivity level, economic level, and code level. Though they further divided this into seven, their primary motive is to find out good metrics for improving team performance in the agile process. Ram [18] had done a multiple case study on process metrics that provides effective operationalization is agile. Though agile works in big projects, many small projects are applying agile process metrics for better results [2]. According to ISO/IEC 9126:1991, software quality metric is a metric of quantity and the value of a feature of any software product can be measured by it. Metrics play a vital role in software development as it ensures the validity of certain factors of the product under development and already developed. So, finding out proper metrics for agile process improvement is a must for the growth of software development companies.

3   Research Methodology

For finding potential information about certain research areas, reviewing previous research papers is a must and well-established path. Kai Petersen et al. [15] performed a thorough analysis and discussion on systematic review and systematic mapping study where he suggested that systematic mapping study is better in finding potential information than a systematic review. We are also motivated to perform a systematic mapping study from one of our prior works [6].

3.1   Systematic Mapping Study

According to Kitchenham [15], getting an overview of a specific research area, a systematic mapping study is a perfect method. It keeps my focus on the research area and helps to find relevant papers. We have followed the overall mapping study process from [6,15]. Figure 1 represents the overall research methodology of this study.

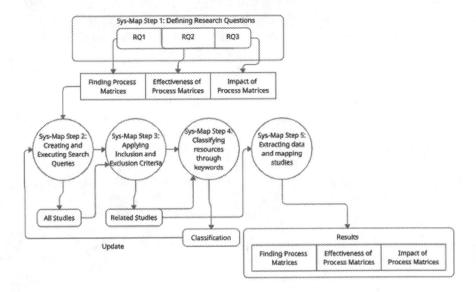

Fig. 1. Design of systematic mapping

Systematic Mapping Step 1: Defining Research Questions. Budgen and other researchers [1] agreed that the research question is the key point of every systematic mapping study. We have also specified research questions for conducting a systematic mapping study. We were driven by the following research questions:

– *Which software process improvement metrics are reported in the current state-of-the-art that has succeeded in terms of business, development, and customer satisfaction in global agile software development?*

Table 1 is presenting the breakdown of our Research Question.

Table 1. Systematic mapping research questions

Serial No.	Systematic Mapping Research Questions	Objective
RQ1	What are the process metrics that are used by software companies stated in the current state of the art?	To find out the process metrics used by software companies.
RQ2	Which process metrics have higher effectiveness in software process improvement?	To find out the matrices that provide more effect than others in process improvement.
RQ3	What is the impact of applying metrics in software process improvement?	To find the impact of process matrices in software companies

Systematic Mapping Step 2: Creating and Executing Search Queries.
In this stage, we have designed our search strategy to define the searching process, digital databases, searching timeline. Then we have created our search string based on the research question and research scope. Digital sources and databases are used for applying search queries. For systematic search, the following procedures are performed. Software process improvement, quality metrics, and agile represent a multi-dimensional area of context. By observing, it is found that every study consists of keywords for referencing their terms and values. Snowballing approach [7] is proved to be the best approach for gathering and analyzing all the potential keywords. Search queries are specified by the following steps:

- All the potential keywords are identified by observing research titles, abstracts, and index terms of a paper.
- Including research area and mediation into the search queries find most relevant research papers.
- For finding similar keywords, thesaurus or reference book is used.
- Incorporating Boolean operators like AND and OR into search queries.

Table 2 shows the summary of the search strategy.

Table 2. Summary of search strategy

Data Items	Values
Databases	IEEE Xplore, Springer, Science Direct, ACM, Google Scholar
Scope Area	Software process improvement, quality matric, agile
Mediation	Keywords
Outcomes	Identify the gap, following the research questions and the amount of contribution done in this research area.
Reference Management	Mendeley
Year	2000 - 2020
Study Target	Journal and Conference Papers

Systematic Mapping Step 3: Applying Inclusion and Exclusion Criteria for Finding Relevant Resources. Inclusion and exclusion criteria are applied for finding relevant research papers and omitting papers that do not go with this research goal. According to Kitchenham, B. [9], introductory sentences and abstract hold were the main focus for excluding research papers. The below steps are followed for finding relevant papers:

- Papers must be written in English, there is no duplication, and peer-reviewed.

– The purpose of the primary study must be on keywords followed by abstract and title to be studied for further classification of the papers. If the motive of the paper is unclear, the introduction and conclusion can be studied for clarification.
– Only the relevant papers that are available in full text and clear were included.

Figure 2 represents the Inclusion & Exclusion Process of this mapping study.

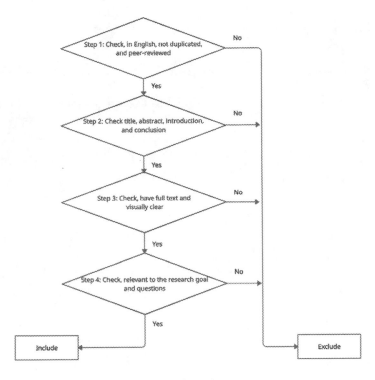

Fig. 2. Inclusion & exclusion process

Systematic Mapping Step 4: Classifying Resources Through Keywords. Resources are classified according to the objective or goal of the research area. Kitchenham elaborated that [9], keyword finding can be done with only two steps. At the first stage, we have gone through the title and abstract to find potential keywords and ideas about the contribution of any research. If the title and abstract could not provide enough details about the research, we have moved to the further stages by going through the introduction and conclusion to classify research papers accordingly.

Systematic Mapping Step 5: Extracting Data and Mapping Studies.
All the related studies are mapped and reported visually by graphs and figures. They are listed by different perspectives like challenging issues, mitigation approaches, advantageous points, disadvantageous points, years, etc. Duplicate data are omitted from lists. Finally, they are summarized for a clearer overall view of the whole systematic mapping study.

4   Results and Analysis

4.1   Systematic Mapping Results

Initially, we have found 38 papers that were published between 2010 to 2021. After applying inclusion and exclusion criteria along with the snowballing process, we have selected 20 papers. After investigating all the 20 papers we have conclusively determined 13 papers that are most relevant to our research. Figure 3 represents the Systematic Mapping Results.

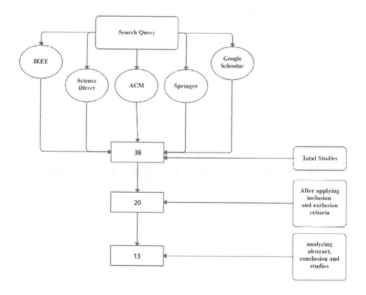

Fig. 3. Systematic mapping results

4.2   Process Metrics

From the study of systematic mapping, we have found a total of 19 software process metrics that have a direct impact on the agile software development process and used by software companies in the current state of the art. This answers our research question RQ1. Though some of them have higher and some of them have lower impact rates, their presence makes the agile development process successful. Table 3 summarizes all process metrics that are stated in different literature.

Table 3. Summary of process metrics

Metric Name	Metric Description	Study References
Data Quality Cost	Time, budget and resource to collect real data	[14, 18, 19, 22]
Functional Quality Cost	Time, budget and resource to ensure functional quality	[5, 14, 18, 22]
Client Communication	Effective communication with client in every phase	[5, 14, 17]
Forecast Accuracy	Clear outcome and risk measure	[4, 14, 19]
Estimation Accuracy	Accurate time, budget and resource estimation	[14, 18]
Performance on Delivery	Reporting to client at delivery	[5, 11, 14, 17, 18, 22]
Coverage of Unit Test	Code or function coverage at early development phase	[11, 13, 14]
Development Speed	Core development time	[4, 5, 14, 17, 18]
Focus Factor	Purpose of developing and testing a software	[4, 14]
Team Assessment	The skills and capabilities of the team members	[4, 17]
Work Adaptation Rate	The ratio of the requirements can be adapted by the team for the development purposes	[4, 5, 14]
Cycle Completion Rate	Ratio of complete a sprint successfully	[11, 14, 17, 20, 22]
Severe Defect Rate	Critical defects which have high risk	[10, 14]
Slipping Defect Rate	The ratio of the number of defects found in the development and the execution phase	[5, 14]
Defect Correction Time	Defect fixing turn around time	[10, 11]
Clarity in Requirements	Understand-ability of the requirements to the development team	[14]
Defect Correction Efficiency	Ratio of defect correction and rejection	[10, 14]
Team Communication	The communication between the team members	[21]
System Test	System test for ensuring client requirements	[5, 11, 21]

Table 3 is summarized in a column chart with an overview of the appearance of all the process metrics had been stated in different studies (Fig. 4).

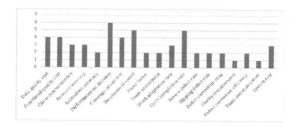

Fig. 4. Study frequency in terms of process metrics

4.3   Systematic Mapping Analysis

Padmini and Bandara [14] made a detailed overview of process metrics where
the percentage of the most used metrics in software companies were included.
We have categorized the metrics of the above table into three effective metrics
according to the company usages and research studies, they can be referred to
as high, mid, and low-level impact metrics. We can elaborate on the effectiveness of process metrics from two different perspectives. The first one goes to
the companies which are practicing agile methodologies and the other goes to
the research communities which are studying agile software development process
improvements. Every company tends to follow the steps which lead them to earn
more money. High-level effective metrics are highly regarded by every company
and they are kind of a standard that a company should follow for improving the
development process. Especially, Functional quality cost, Development speed,
and Cycle completion rate are a must to maintain. By applying these metrics,
companies can easily calculate the functional requirements and its quality maintenance cost. Every sprint cycle completion time can be observed which helps to
measure team performance and find a lack of manpower or training sessions of
the team members. Development speed also helps in monitoring the team's performance. Moreover, it helps to show off the company's capabilities in developing
certain categories of software with other companies.

High-Level Impact Metrics. The high-level effective metrics Fig. 5 are Data quality cost, Functional quality cost, Performance on delivery, Coverage of unit tests,
Development speed, and Cycle completion rate. Development speed and Cycle
completion rate greatly depend on team assessment.

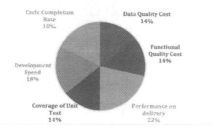

Fig. 5. High level impact metrics

Mid-Level Impact Metrics. The mid-level effective metrics Fig. 6 are Client communication, Forecast accuracy, System test, Work adaptation rate, Estimation accuracy, Team assessment, Severe defect rate, Focus factor, Slipping defect rate, Defect correction time, and Defect correction efficiency.

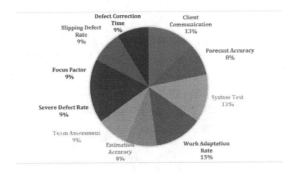

Fig. 6. Mid level impact metrics

Low-Level Impact Metrics. Finally, the low-level effective metrics Fig. 7 are Clarity in requirements and Team communications. So, the -level effective metrics answer our second research question.

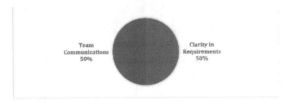

Fig. 7. Low level impact metrics

5   Conclusions

Agile software development metrics are divided into different categories. In this work, we focus on process metrics and make a comparative analysis through a systematic mapping study. This analysis shows that some metrics have a high effective ratio and some have not. Some metrics are constantly practiced by companies and researchers and some are less practiced. By following this systematic mapping study, a researcher can easily find out the more studied area and less studied areas of agile process metrics. On the other hand, applying these metrics according to their effectiveness in agile practicing companies will benefit them highly. This systematic mapping study tells the most studied areas and the lowest studied areas of agile process metrics. It also shows in which area the researcher should give their focus for improvement. Based on the findings from this study, we will conduct a case study research on how practitioners focus on improving process quality by imposing different process quality metrics.

Acknowledgements. We thank Mr. Razzak M Abdur, Ph.D., who is working as Software Quality Coordinator at Ocuco Limited, Dublin, Ireland for his continuous support towards our research journey.

References

1. Budgen, D., Turner, M., Brereton, P., Kitchenham, B.A.: Using mapping studies in software engineering. Ppig. **8**, 195–204 (2008)
2. Choraś, M., et al.: Measuring and improving agile processes in a small-size software development company. IEEE Access **8**, 78452–78466 (2020)
3. Concas, G., Marchesi, M., Destefanis, G., Tonelli, R.: An empirical study of software metrics for assessing the phases of an agile project. Int. J. Softw. Eng. Knowl. Eng. **22**(04), 525–548 (2012)
4. Downey, S., Sutherland, J.: Scrum metrics for hyperproductive teams: how they fly like fighter aircraft. In: 2013 46th Hawaii International Conference on System Sciences, pp. 4870–4878. IEEE (2013)
5. Gustafsson, J.: Model of agile software measurement: a case study (2011)
6. Hossain, S.S., Arafat, Y., Amin, T., Bhuiyan, T.: Requirements re-usability in global software development: a systematic mapping study. In: Gervasi, O., et al. (eds.) ICCSA 2020. LNCS, vol. 12252, pp. 960–974. Springer, Cham (2020). https://doi.org/10.1007/978-3-030-58811-3_68
7. Jan, N., Ibrar, M.: Systematic mapping of value-based software engineering: a systematic review of value-based requirements engineering (2010)
8. Jinzenji, K., Hoshino, T., Williams, L., Takahashi, K.: Metric-based quality evaluations for iterative software development approaches like agile. In: 2012 IEEE 23rd International Symposium on Software Reliability Engineering Workshops, pp. 54–63. IEEE (2012)
9. Kitchenham, B.: Procedures for performing systematic reviews. Keele UK Keele Univ. **33**(2004), 1–26 (2004)
10. Korhonen, K.: Supporting agile transformation with defect management in large distributed software development organisation (2012)
11. Mannila, J.: Key performance indicators in agile software development (2013)
12. Misra, S., Omorodion, M.: Survey on agile metrics and their inter-relationship with other traditional development metrics. ACM SIGSOFT Softw. Eng. Notes **36**(6), 1–3 (2011)
13. Oza, N., Korkala, M.: Lessons learned in implementing agile software development metrics. In: UKAIS, p. 38 (2012)
14. Padmini, K.J., Bandara, H.D., Perera, I.: Use of software metrics in agile software development process. In: 2015 Moratuwa Engineering Research Conference (MERCon), pp. 312–317. IEEE (2015)
15. Petersen, K., Feldt, R., Mujtaba, S., Mattsson, M.: Systematic mapping studies in software engineering. In: 12th International Conference on Evaluation and Assessment in Software Engineering (EASE) 12, pp. 1–10 (2008)
16. Pfleeger, S.L.: Software metrics: progress after 25 years? IEEE Softw. **25**(6), 32–34 (2008)

17. Pinto, N., Acuña, C., Cuenca Pletsch, L.R.: Quality evaluation in agile process: a first approach. In: XXII Congreso Argentino de Ciencias de la Computación (CACIC 2016) (2016)
18. Ram, P., Rodriguez, P., Oivo, M.: Software process measurement and related challenges in agile software development: a multiple case study. In: Kuhrmann, M., et al. (eds.) PROFES 2018. LNCS, vol. 11271, pp. 272–287. Springer, Cham (2018). https://doi.org/10.1007/978-3-030-03673-7_20
19. Rathore, S.S., Kumar, S.: A study on software fault prediction techniques. Artif. Intell. Rev. **51**(2), 255–327 (2017). https://doi.org/10.1007/s10462-017-9563-5
20. Sandu, I.A., Salceanu, A.: Metrics improvement for phase containment effectiveness in automotive software development process. In: 2017 10th International Symposium on Advanced Topics in Electrical Engineering (ATEE), pp. 661–666. IEEE (2017)
21. Sandu, I.A., Salceanu, A.: System testing in agile sw development of the electronic components based on software from the automotive industry. In: 2019 11th International Symposium on Advanced Topics in Electrical Engineering (ATEE), pp. 1–4. IEEE (2019)
22. Sneed, H.M., Prentner, W.: Analyzing data on software evolution processes. In: 2016 Joint Conference of the International Workshop on Software Measurement and the International Conference on Software Process and Product Measurement (IWSM-MENSURA), pp. 1–10. IEEE (2016)

Failures Forecast in Monitoring Datacenter Infrastructure Through Machine Learning Techniques: A Systematic Review

Walter Lopes Neto⬤ and Itamir de Morais Barroca Filho⁽⊠⁾⬤

Metropole Digital Institute, Federal University
of Rio Grande do Norte Natal, Lagoa Nova, Brazil
walter.lopes@ifrn.edu.br, itamir.filho@imd.ufrn.br
http://www.imd.ufrn.br, http://www.ufrn.br

Abstract. With the trend of accelerating digital transformation processes, datacenters (DC) are gaining prominence as increasingly critical components for business success. Modern DC are complex systems. To maintain the operation with high efficiency and high availability, it is necessary to carry out detailed monitoring, which easily results in hundreds or thousands of items being monitored. Also, the large number of possible configurations is a challenge for monitoring and correcting failures on time. However, recent advances in the field of Artificial Intelligence (AI), especially in the area of Machine Learning (ML), have been generating unprecedented opportunities to improve the efficiency of the analysis of historical monitoring data, facilitating the recognition of patterns and enabling scenarios for early detection of failures. In this sense, significant research has been published discussing the applications of ML techniques in the context of DC monitoring. Based on this context, in this paper, we aim to present a systematic literature review (SLR) that helps to understand the current state and future trends of the application of ML techniques in DC monitoring, specifically those aimed at early fault detection. This SLR also aims to identify gaps for further investigations. As main results, we identified 51 papers reporting unique studies published in conferences and journals between 2009 and 2020. Most of the works (60%) were applied in supervised algorithms, in which the most used algorithm was the Random Forest (19,60%). The main types of data used were S.M.A.R.T attributes (14 papers) and log data (10 papers).

Keywords: Machine learning · Monitoring · Data center · Systematic literature review

1 Introduction

With the trend towards accelerating digital transformation processes, datacenters (DC) have gained prominence as increasingly critical components for business success. If, on the one hand, the dependence on the high availability of DCs

© Springer Nature Switzerland AG 2021
O. Gervasi et al. (Eds.): ICCSA 2021, LNCS 12957, pp. 27–42, 2021.
https://doi.org/10.1007/978-3-030-87013-3_3

has become increasingly greater, on the other hand, the complexity of these systems has also increased.

Datacenters are buildings specifically designed to host multiple servers and communication devices with common environmental requirements and physical security needs [8]. Modern DCs are complex systems composed of multiple electrical and electronic, mechanical, digital, and control subsystems. To maintain efficient and highly available operation, monitoring each subsystem sometimes results in hundreds of thousands of items being monitored. In addition, a large number of possible configurations and the interdependence of these various subsystems and their configurations, make effective and dynamic monitoring of failures difficult. This makes it difficult especially with regard to early corrective actions in the face of those that generate unavailability and consequently impact the business. Thus, developing automatic ways of detecting anomalous event sources based on either their historical behavioral analysis or run-time status is not a trivial task [43].

However, recent advances in the field of Artificial Intelligence (AI), especially in the area of Machine Learning (ML), have generated unprecedented opportunities to improve the efficiency of the analysis of historical monitoring data, facilitating the recognition of patterns and enabling scenarios of early failure detection. Based on this context, the objective of this paper is to describe a systematic literature review (SLR) that aim to understand the current state and future trends of the application of ML techniques in the monitoring of DC, which aim at the early detection of failures, in addition to identifying gaps for future investigations.

Kitchenham, Dybå, and Jørgensen proposed the use of software engineering SLR to support Evidence-based Software Engineering (EBSE) [29]. According to Kitchenham, the most common reasons for undertaking SLRs are to summarise the existing evidence concerning treatment or technology, to identify gaps in current research (proposing areas for further investigation), and to provide appropriate background to position new research activities. Additionally, according to Kitchenham, the main rationale for undertaking SLRs instead of a literature review in a traditional manner is because the first one result in a relevant scientific value. Despite a SLR requires considerably more effort than a traditional review, it has the advantage of providing information about the effects of certain events on a wide range of settings and empirical methods [28].

This trend is reflected in Gartner's forecast that AI-derived business values may reach the 3.9 trillion USD mark in 2022 [1]. Machine learning has become one of the trends for improving the impact on business operations in several segments. It has been providing real impacts such as increased efficiency and accelerated innovation.

Nevertheless, the objects of study, solutions, and implementations are diverse and there is no consensus or guideline for strategies aimed at the broad monitoring of the various DC subsystems with a focus on failure early detection. Most of the studies present strategies/solutions aimed specifically for a particular application, for instance, storage disks such as Solid State Drives (SSDs) [5, 34] and Hard Disk Drive (HDDs) [19, 23, 54], to name a few.

As main results, we identified that 10 of the 51 works applied the Random Forest (RF) algorithm in a supervised way. We also identified that all works focused on history data-based methods. To achieve this goal, we seek to answer the research questions identified in Sect. 2 through an SLR.

The main contributions of this work are the review of the state of the art of machine learning applications in the early detection of failures in monitoring data center infrastructures.

This work is organized as follows: In Sect. 2, we present the method of this review, identifying the research questions, the research strategy, the inclusion and exclusion criteria and procedures, the quality assessment, and the data collection. In Sect. 3 we present the results of this method, focusing on the results of the research, on the overview of the studies, and on the results of the quality assessment. In Sect. 4 we present the results and discussions. Finally, in Sect. 5 we present the conclusions and future work for this research.

2 Method

This study was conducted as a systematic literature review (SLR). The main objective of this review was to understand the state of the art and future trends in the use of machine learning techniques in the context of monitoring data center infrastructure. As a way of achieving this objective with scientific rigor, the review was structured in a three-phase process, as described by Kitchenham [28], named: Planning, Conduction and Communication.

Kitchenham [28] argued that the most common reasons for conducting an SLR are: 1) Aiming to summarise the existing evidence concerning technology or treatment, investigating the advantages and the limitations of a particular technology. 2) Aiming to identify gaps in current research and recognizing the challenges in present studies, in this way, grounding complementary research. 3) Aiming to provide an appropriate framework to ground new research activities.

These stages were carried out to identify the current state and main trends related to the theme of machine learning applications in the context of monitoring data center infrastructure. The review was carried out through the mapping of algorithms applied, architectural models, source data, and application challenges. The review process will be described in detail next.

2.1 Research Questions

As a way of identifying primary studies, this study considered the following research questions:

RQ1. What are the main characteristics of the machine learning algorithms and models that are being applied to the monitoring of data center infrastructure?

RQ2. What types of data are being used in the proposed models? (For example, sensor data, images, event logs)

RQ3. What are the main challenges in applying machine learning to data center infrastructure monitoring?

RQ4. What are the most common types of failures identified in data center infrastructure monitoring?

Regarding RQ1, about the characteristics of ML algorithms and models, we intend to analyze the main algorithms and methods applied to historical monitoring data.

2.2 Research Strategy for Primary Studies

Primary studies were selected through the Scopus repository (Elsevier)[1]. Examples of indexed sources are: ACM Digital Library at http://dl.acm.org, IEEE Xplore at http://ieeexplore.ieee.org, Science Direct at http://www.sciencedirect.com and Springer Link at http://link.springer.com.

In order to identify the largest number of works related to research questions, the defined search string was: (datacenter OR datacenters OR "data center" OR "data centers") AND "machine learning" AND (monitoring OR faut* OR fail* OR detection OR predic*).

2.3 Inclusion and Exclusion Criteria and Procedures

As proposed by Kitchenham [26] the inclusion and exclusion criteria are the basis for the selection of primary studies and must be defined in advance, to avoid bias. The review included peer-reviewed papers, which included topics related to the application of machine learning techniques applied to datacenter monitoring for early failure detection. 1) Studies on the following topics were excluded: Studies that have not clearly defined the research questions, research process and data extraction process. 2) Duplicate studies. In cases of duplicity for the same study, the most complete work was considered. 3) Studies in languages other than English.

2.4 Study Quality Assessment

All studies included were assessed using the assessment questions (QA), adapted from Dyba [18] and described as following: QA1. Does this report empirical research? Or is the report restricted to just "lessons learned" based on an expert opinion? QA2. Does the study clearly present the objectives and rationale of the research in the report? (Including why the survey was carried out) QA3. Is the description of the research context reported adequate? QA4. Does the study report clearly the results found? All studies were evaluated to answer the 5 evaluation questions according to the following scale of scores adapted from

---

[1] http://www.scopus.com/.

Dyba [18]: 1 - Fully meets the criteria; 0.5 - Partially meets the criteria; 0 - does not meet the criteria. Thus, the total sum of points for each study can vary between 0 (Very bad) to 7 (Very good).

2.5 Data Collect

During this phase, the data extracted from primary studies of the review were: title, keywords, authors, country of authors, year of publication, type (newspaper, conference, workshop), objective, field of application, challenges and opportunities, context (educational/industry), methodology, algorithms, types of data used, protocols, contributions, tools/infrastructure, future work and additional comments.

3 Results

This section presents the results of the literature review. The stages of conducting the review and a summary of the works that contributed to answer the research questions are also presented. At the end, the results of the quality assessment of the studies are discussed.

3.1 Search Results

The review process started with the application of the search string defined in Sect. 2 in the Scopus repository (Stage 1), which returned 446 studies. Stage 2 was carried out by analyzing the title, abstract, and keywords of each of the articles, which resulted in 53 articles. Of the 53 articles resulting from stage 2, we performed a careful reading (Stage 3) and identified that 51 papers were useful to help answer the research questions. The data extraction spreadsheet is available at https://cutt.ly/wz87CG3. The Fig. 1 presents the study selection and analysis process.

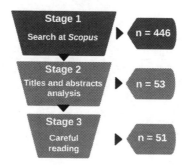

Fig. 1. Stages of the study selection and analysis process.

Table 1. 51 studies object of stage 3 - careful reading.

Id	Author	Year	Venue	Reference
T1	Zhang, J. et al.	2020	Journal	[56]
T2	Liu, C. et al.	2020	Journal	[37]
T3	Ren, H. et al.	2020	Conference	[44]
T4	Jiang, T. et al.	2020	Journal	[24]
T5	Ricci, P.P. et al.	2020	Conference	[45]
T6	Decker, L. et al.	2020	Conference	[16]
T7	Liu, X. et al.	2020	Conference	[39]
T8	Zhao, J. et al.	2020	Conference	[59]
T9	Glavan, A.F. et al.	2020	Conference	[21]
T10	Lin, F. et al.	2020	Conference	[36]
T11	Das, A. et al.	2020	Conference	[14]
T12	Shimizu, D.Y. et al.	2020	Conference	[47]
T13	Balakir, A. et al.	2020	Conference	[7]
T14	Lanciano, G. et al.	2020	Conference	[31]
T15	Kheradmandi, M. et al.	2020	Conference	[27]
T16	Zeydan, E., Arslan, S.S	2020	Conference	[54]
T17	Gao, J. et al.	2020	Journal	[20]
T18	Marahatta, A. et al.	2020	Journal	[40]
T19	Cucinotta, T. et al.	2020	Conference	[13]
T20	Alter, J. et al.	2019	Conference	[5]
T21	Zhang, J. et al.	2019	Conference	[55]
T22	Satpathi, S. et al.	2019	Journal	[46]
T23	Berezovskaya, Y. et al.	2019	Conference	[9]
T24	Huang, S. et al.	2019	Conference	[23]
T25	Borghesi, A. et al.	2019	Conference	[11]
T26	Liang, S. et al.	2019	Conference	[34]
T27	Poghosyan, A. et al.	2019	Conference	[43]
T28	Harutyunyan, A.N. et al.	2019	Journal	[22]
T29	Mozo, A. et al.	2019	Journal	[41]
T30	Diotalevi, T. et al.	2019	Conference	[17]
T31	Su, C.-J., Huang, S.-F	2018	Journal	[49]
T32	Anantharaman, P., Qiao, M., Jadav, D	2018	Conference	[6]
T33	Xiao, J. et al. et al.	2018	Conference	[51]
T34	Lin, F. et al.	2018	Conference	[35]
T35	Ahmed, J. et al.	2018	Conference	[4]
T36	Zhang, S. et al.	2018	Journal	[57]
T37	Nagashree, N. et al.	2018	Journal	[42]
T38	Adamu, H. et al.	2017	Conference	[3]
T39	Davis, N.A. et al.	2017	Conference	[15]
T40	Buda, T.S., Assem, H., Xu, L	2017	Conference	[12]
T41	Zhang, S. et al.	2017	Conference	[58]
T42	Liu, C. et al.	2017	Journal	[38]
T43	Lee, Y.-L. et al.	2017	Conference	[32]
T44	Sîrbu, A., Babaoglu, O	2016	Journal	[48]
T45	Ganguly, S. et al.	2016	Conference	[19]
T46	Yang, W. et al.	2015	Conference	[53]
T47	Bogojeska, J. et al.	2014	Conference	[10]
T48	Li, J. et al.	2014	Conference	[33]
T49	Kumar, R. et al.	2014	Conference	[30]
T50	Teixeira, P.H.D.S. et al.	2010	Conference	[50]
T51	Xu, W. et al.	2009	Conference	[52]

3.2 Overview of Studies

Considering the venue of the selected studies (journal or conference), 78.8 % were related to conferences and 21.2 % were related to journal articles. Regarding the year of publication, 37 % were published in 2020, 20.4 % in 2019, 2018, and 2017 each with 13 % with the remaining 16.6 % distributed between the years 2016 and 2009.

It is possible to notice a tendency to increase the volume of publications for selected studies on this field over the years, demonstrating a tendency to increase interest in the field of research.

3.3 Quality Assessment Results

The studies were evaluated according to the criteria defined in Sect. 2.4. The table with the detailed score of the studies is presented at https://cutt.ly/akspG0v. The studies will be referenced in this work by the ID that can be consulted in Table 1. The results demonstrate that 2 studies scored 3.5 (T6 and T8) and 49 studies reached the maximum score (5).

4 Discussions

In this section, we will discuss the answers to the research questions, as well as present the limitations and conclusions of the review.

4.1 What are the Main Characteristics of the Machine Learning Algorithms and Models that are Being Applied to the Monitoring of Datacenter Infrastructure?

In general, the analyzed researches presented a wide variety of Machine Learning (ML) strategies and algorithms applied to the monitoring of datacenter infrastructure components. In these studies, the RF algorithm was used more often (in 10 papers). The methods related to fault detection can be classified into three groups: quantitative model-based methods, qualitative model-based methods, and history data-based methods [9]. We also identified that all papers focused on history data-based methods. The ML algorithms presented in the papers were classified into three main categories: supervised, unsupervised and semi-supervised. Two studies [16] and [11] used semi-supervised algorithms. The graph presented in Fig. 2 shows the distribution of researches with a focus on each of the categories mentioned.

The supervised methods were widely applied in strategies for solving classification problems and regression problems. The main supervised algorithms were: Random Forests (RF): The algorithm has been applied to several strategies for early failure detection presenting advantages such as: having presented the best prediction accuracy, having few parameters for fine adjustments (which facilitates the training process) [5,24,39], as well as being able to handle a large

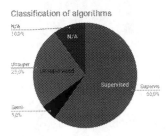

Fig. 2. Distribution of supervised and unsupervised algorithms in studies.

number of input variables without discarding these variables (facilitating the processing of multi-dimensional data) [49]. The presented disadvantage was also that of having few parameters for fine adjustments [24]. Random Forest was applied to predict disk failures in [24] and [49]. It was applied with an online approach to disk failure detection in [6] and applied to identify the remaining lifetime for Hard Disk Drives (HDDs) in [54]. There were also more extensive applications in log data in [48], in switch log data in [57] and with a focus on anticipating server failures in [39] and [32]. Other algorithms that were applied in a supervised manner were: TrAdaBoost + IMDA [56], ExtraTreeClassifier (ETC) [44], Multilayer Perceptron Networks (MPLs) [21] and [15], Ridge [9], XGBboost [12], Linear Logistic Regression [53], Gradient Boosting Machine (GBM) [10] and Parallel SVM [30], where SVM (Support Vector Machine) refers to an algorithm that can be used for classification [2]. Studies [19] (non-parametric method using decision tree) and [36] (NLP (Natural Language Processing) + GBDT (Gradient Boosted Decision Trees)) use techniques related to Decision Trees, which are essentially classifiers tree-based techniques that forecast the values using a certain number of input attributes [25]. Machine Learning algorithms with an unsupervised approach were also presented, mainly in two groups of clustering and classification problems. Regarding algorithms applied to unsupervised strategies, the main applications were based on Self-Organizing Maps(SOM) to detect anomalies based on the degradation behavior of resource consumption in the datacenter [13] and [4].

The Fig. 3 shows the main algorithms and applied techniques in the papers.

4.2 What Types of Data are Being Used in the Proposed Models? (For Example: Sensor Data, Images and Event Logs)

The researches included in this SLR are heterogeneous in terms of applications of the types of data used to train the models of failure prediction. The main types of data used as the focus of the studies were Self-Monitoring, Analysis and Reporting Technology (S.M.A.R.T) attributes (14 papers), and log data (10 papers). The S.M.A.R.T attributes refer to data collected based on the sensors of the Hard Disk Drives (HDD), such as temperature and error rates by sector.

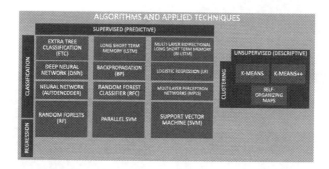

Fig. 3. Main algorithms and applied techniques.

This type of data has been widely used by HD manufacturers to determine when disk failures are likely to occur [6].

The main data sources identified in the works can be grouped into the following categories: Logs, S.M.A.R.T attributes, Performance data from CPU, Memory, I/O, Network utilization, Sensor data from hardware, and Incident tickets.

Some studies seek to identify failures in advance through logs, such as T7 that proposes a smart server crash prediction method for triggering early warning and migration in Cloud Service datacenter, [57] that seeks to determine during runtime whether a switch failure will happen soon and [48] that present a data-science study of a large amount of cluster data with the goal of building and evaluating predictive models for node failures. T6 proposes a real-time approach to monitor and classify log records based on sliding time windows and provides the basis for extracting information from log content. [14] tackles online anomaly prediction in computing systems by exploiting context-free grammar-based rapid event analysis. In [43] the authors seek to identify changes of an event source an off-line change point detection algorithm and diagnosing sick resources. [22] address several problems in intelligent log management of distributed cloud computing application and [17] implementation of a system that collects, parses, and displays the log information from specific data sources. The category S.M.A.R.T attributes refer to studies that focused on predicting failures based on historical data on health attributes of HDDs or SSDs registered by S.M.A.R.T. Performance data refers to studies that used historical performance data and its possible degradation as a mechanism for predicting failures. Hardware sensor data grouped papers that analyzed especially data collected from sensors with environmental data such as temperature and humidity. Finally, the incident tickets category refers to jobs that used metadata in incident tickets to extract the historical fault behavior and thereby make the prediction

The Fig. 4 shows the graph relating the frequency of occurrence of data types.

During the research, it was possible to notice that, in general, the studies included in this review did not demonstrate in detail the description of the tools

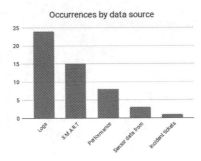

Fig. 4. Occurrences by data source.

used in the data collection stage used as a source for training machine learning models.

4.3 What are the Main Challenges in Applying Machine Learning to Datacenter Infrastructure Monitoring?

The main challenges identified in this research can be classified into the following groups:

Challenges related to Machine Learning models: ML models fail to describe the gradual change precisely [53]. Another important challenge described is called Model Aging Problem presented by [6] demonstrates that over time the data may change and the model may need to be retrained. One stable way to calibrate the model is presented in [19]. Despite the crucial role that Syslog processing plays in switch failure diagnosis, detection, or prediction, existing Syslog processing techniques have low accuracies [58].

Challenges related to complexity: An approach based on direct statistical analysis faces the challenge of the complexity of the data [5]. A large amount of information in the system log files makes it difficult to find the right pattern(s) [30]. Complexity of failure root causes [39], Complex problems can have various sources on the information Technology (IT) stack [21]. Another challenge identified was Heterogeneous minority disks [56].

Challenges related to missing data: Transient failures such as processor and memory overheating are not persistent [35], The impracticality of collecting specific service level events from inside the datacenter infrastructure [41], Lack of standard to S.M.A.R.T. data [56], and the temporary blackout of monitoring data. Also, no labels to indicate which disk was replaced [19].

The Fig. 5 summarize the main challenges identified in the works.

4.4 What are the Most Common Types of Failures Identified in Datacenter Infrastructure Monitoring?

The failures monitored in the datacenters identified in the SLR were classified in the following areas: Specific Hardware Failure, General Failure (hardware,

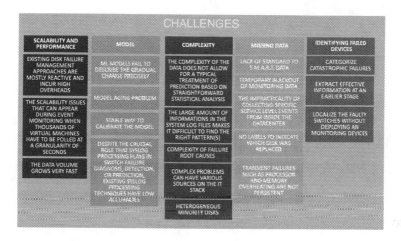

Fig. 5. Main challenges.

firmware, software, and application), Network Failure, Scheduling Failure, Software Failure, and Service Failure.

The type of failure Hardware Failure refers to studies that focused on using historical data of hardware failures as a source for predictions. General Failure refers to jobs that more broadly analyzed data such as log data, which could refer to any type of failure. The other groups were also used to group researches that focused on detecting failures based on the history of network failures, software failures, task/process scheduling (scheduling failure), and services at a higher level of abstraction (service failure).

The Fig. 6 shows the graph relating the frequency of occurrence of each type of failure in the works.

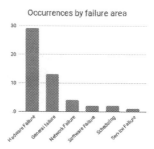

Fig. 6. Occurrences by failure area.

The most common types of failures identified during the survey were classified: General Failure (hardware, firmware, software, and application), Specific Hardware Failure, Storage disk component failure (SSDs and HDDs to name a few), Task or process execution, Network Failure, Machine or Node failure,

Service level events, Hardware Failure on Switch, Optical link failure, Software (Network Functions Virtualization - NFV and Resource Consumption) and Hardware Sensor.

4.5   Limitations of this Review

The main related limitations of this review include bias during the study selection and data extraction steps. As a way to remove the bias from these processes, we strictly followed the protocol described in Sect. 2. Another limitation of this research was the inclusion of studies in English only since publications made only in other languages may have been omitted. As a final limitation of this review, we can mention the time of conducting the review, in which some new publications may have been made and not included.

5   Conclusions and Future Work

This systematic review has discussed 51 papers reporting unique studies published in conferences and journals between 2009 and 2020. Most of the researches (60%) was applied in supervised algorithms, in which the most used algorithm was the RF (19,60%). The main types of data used were S.M.A.R.T attributes (14 papers) and log data (10 papers). The main types of failures were hardware failures. The heterogeneity of the studies concerning data sources and strategies made the data synthesis process challenging. These studies have identified an increase in interest in sustainable failure prediction strategies based on machine learning techniques. There is no consensus on the strategies to be adopted to anticipate monitoring failures in a more general way, in which the research, in general, focuses on some subsystem of the datacenter specifically. Also, it was possible to notice the lack of detailed description of the tools used for data collection in the researched papers. Based on the research we were able to identify that currently there is a growing trend towards the use of machine learning strategies applied to the monitoring of data center infrastructure through different strategies. As future work, we will use the insights identified in this review as the basis for the development of a predictive monitoring platform for the data center that will deal in particular with issues such as anticipating failure through machine learning techniques.

References

1. Gartner says global artificial intelligence business value to reach $1.2 trillion in 2018. https://www.gartner.com/en/newsroom/press-releases/2018-04-25-gartner-says-global-artificial-intelligence-business-value-to-reach-1-point-2-trillion-in-2018
2. Abolade, R.O., Famakinde, S.O., Popoola, S.I., Oseni, O.F., Atayero, A.A., Misra, S.: Support vector machine for path loss predictions in urban environment. In: Gervasi, O., et al. (eds.) ICCSA 2020. LNCS, vol. 12255, pp. 995–1006. Springer, Cham (2020). https://doi.org/10.1007/978-3-030-58820-5_71

3. Adamu, H., Mohammed, B., Maina, A.B., Cullen, A., Ugail, H., Awan, I.: An approach to failure prediction in a cloud based environment. In: 2017 IEEE 5th International Conference on Future Internet of Things and Cloud (FiCloud), pp. 191–197. IEEE (2017)

4. Ahmed, J., et al.: Automated diagnostic of virtualized service performance degradation. In: 2018 IEEE/IFIP Network Operations and Management Symposium, NOMS 2018, pp. 1–9. IEEE (2018)

5. Alter, J., Xue, J., Dimnaku, A., Smirni, E.: SSD failures in the field: symptoms, causes, and prediction models. In: Proceedings of the International Conference for High Performance Computing, Networking, Storage and Analysis, pp. 1–14 (2019)

6. Anantharaman, P., Qiao, M., Jadav, D.: Large scale predictive analytics for hard disk remaining useful life estimation. In: 2018 IEEE International Congress on Big Data (BigData Congress), pp. 251–254. IEEE (2018)

7. Balakir, A., Yang, A., Rosenbaum, E.: An interpretable predictive model for early detection of hardware failure. In: 2020 IEEE International Reliability Physics Symposium (IRPS), pp. 1–5. IEEE (2020)

8. Barroso, L.A., Clidaras, J., Hölzle, U.: The datacenter as a computer: an introduction to the design of warehouse-scale machines. Synth. Lect. Comput. Architect. 8(3), 1–154 (2013)

9. Berezovskaya, Y., Yang, C.W., Mousavi, A., Zhang, X., Vyatkin, V.: A hybrid fault detection and diagnosis method in server rooms' cooling systems. In: 2019 IEEE 17th International Conference on Industrial Informatics (INDIN), vol. 1, pp. 1405–1410. IEEE (2019)

10. Bogojeska, J., Giurgiu, I., Lanyi, D., Stark, G., Wiesmann, D.: Impact of HW and OS type and currency on server availability derived from problem ticket analysis. In: 2014 IEEE Network Operations and Management Symposium (NOMS), pp. 1–9. IEEE (2014)

11. Borghesi, A., Libri, A., Benini, L., Bartolini, A.: Online anomaly detection in HPC systems. In: 2019 IEEE International Conference on Artificial Intelligence Circuits and Systems (AICAS), pp. 229–233. IEEE (2019)

12. Buda, T.S., Assem, H., Xu, L.: ADE: an ensemble approach for early anomaly detection. In: 2017 IFIP/IEEE Symposium on Integrated Network and Service Management (IM), pp. 442–448. IEEE (2017)

13. Cucinotta, T., et al.: Behavioral analysis for virtualized network functions: a SOM-based approach. In: CLOSER, pp. 150–160 (2020)

14. Das, A., Mueller, F., Rountree, B.: Aarohi: making real-time node failure prediction feasible. In: 2020 IEEE International Parallel and Distributed Processing Symposium (IPDPS), pp. 1092–1101. IEEE (2020)

15. Davis, N.A., Rezgui, A., Soliman, H., Manzanares, S., Coates, M.: Failuresim: a system for predicting hardware failures in cloud data centers using neural networks. In: 2017 IEEE 10th International Conference on Cloud Computing (CLOUD), pp. 544–551. IEEE (2017)

16. Decker, L., Leite, D., Giommi, L., Bonacorsi, D.: Real-time anomaly detection in data centers for log-based predictive maintenance using an evolving fuzzy-rule-based approach. In: 2020 IEEE International Conference on Fuzzy Systems (FUZZ-IEEE), pp. 1–8. IEEE (2020)

17. Diotalevi, T., et al.: Collection and harmonization of system logs and prototypal analytics services with the elastic (elk) suite at the infncnaf computing centre. In: International Symposium on Grids & Clouds (ISGC), Proceedings of Science, Taipei, pp. 1–15 (2019)

18. Dybå, T., Dingsøyr, T.: Empirical studies of agile software development: a systematic review. Inf. Softw. Technol. **50**(9–10), 833–859 (2008)
19. Ganguly, S., Consul, A., Khan, A., Bussone, B., Richards, J., Miguel, A.: A practical approach to hard disk failure prediction in cloud platforms: Big data model for failure management in datacenters. In: 2016 IEEE Second International Conference on Big Data Computing Service and Applications (BigDataService), pp. 105–116. IEEE (2016)
20. Gao, J., Wang, H., Shen, H.: Task failure prediction in cloud data centers using deep learning. IEEE Trans. Serv. Comput. (2020)
21. Glavan, A.F., Marian, C.V.: Cognitive edge computing through artificial intelligence. In: 2020 13th International Conference on Communications (COMM), pp. 285–290. IEEE (2020)
22. Harutyunyan, A.N., Poghosyan, A.V., Grigoryan, N.M., Hovhannisyan, N.A., Kushmerick, N.: On machine learning approaches for automated log management. J. UCS **25**(8), 925–945 (2019)
23. Huang, S., Liang, S., Fu, S., Shi, W., Tiwari, D., Chen, H.B.: Characterizing disk health degradation and proactively protecting against disk failures for reliable storage systems. In: 2019 IEEE International Conference on Autonomic Computing (ICAC), pp. 157–166. IEEE (2019)
24. Jiang, T., Huang, P., Zhou, K.: Cost-efficiency disk failure prediction via threshold-moving. Concurr. Comput. Pract. Exp. **32**(14), e5669 (2020)
25. Jonathan, O., Misra, S., Osamor, V.: Comparative analysis of machine learning techniques for network traffic classification. In: IOP Conference Series: Earth and Environmental Science, vol. 655, p. 012025. IOP Publishing (2021)
26. Keele, S., et al.: Guidelines for performing systematic literature reviews in software engineering. Technical report. Citeseer (2007)
27. Kheradmandi, M., Down, D.G.: Data driven fault tolerant thermal management of data centers. In: 2020 International Conference on Computing, Networking and Communications (ICNC), pp. 736–740. IEEE (2020)
28. Kitchenham, B.: Procedures for performing systematic reviews. Keele, UK, Keele University **33**(2004), 1–26 (2004)
29. Kitchenham, B., Brereton, P.: A systematic review of systematic review process research in software engineering. Inf. Softw. Technol. **55**(12), 2049–2075 (2013)
30. Kumar, R., Vijayakumar, S., Ahamed, S.A.: A pragmatic approach to predict hardware failures in storage systems using MPP database and big data technologies. In: 2014 IEEE International Advance Computing Conference (IACC), pp. 779–788. IEEE (2014)
31. Lanciano, G., et al.: SOM-based behavioral analysis for virtualized network functions. In: Proceedings of the 35th Annual ACM Symposium on Applied Computing, pp. 1204–1206 (2020)
32. Lee, Y.-L., Juan, D.-C., Tseng, X.-A., Chen, Y.-T., Chang, S.-C.: DC-prophet: predicting catastrophic machine failures in DataCenters. In: Altun, Y., et al. (eds.) ECML PKDD 2017. LNCS (LNAI), vol. 10536, pp. 64–76. Springer, Cham (2017). https://doi.org/10.1007/978-3-319-71273-4_6
33. Li, J., et al.: Hard drive failure prediction using classification and regression trees. In: 2014 44th Annual IEEE/IFIP International Conference on Dependable Systems and Networks, pp. 383–394. IEEE (2014)
34. Liang, S., et al.: Reliability characterization of solid state drives in a scalable production datacenter. In: 2018 IEEE International Conference on Big Data (Big Data), pp. 3341–3349. IEEE (2018)

35. Lin, F., Beadon, M., Dixit, H.D., Vunnam, G., Desai, A., Sankar, S.: Hardware remediation at scale. In: 2018 48th Annual IEEE/IFIP International Conference on Dependable Systems and Networks Workshops (DSN-W), pp. 14–17. IEEE (2018)
36. Lin, F., et al.: Predicting remediations for hardware failures in large-scale datacenters. In: 2020 50th Annual IEEE-IFIP International Conference on Dependable Systems and Networks-Supplemental Volume (DSN-S), pp. 13–16. IEEE (2020)
37. Liu, C., Dai, L., Lai, Y., Lai, G., Mao, W.: Failure prediction of tasks in the cloud at an earlier stage: a solution based on domain information mining. Computing 1–23 (2020)
38. Liu, C., Han, J., Shang, Y., Liu, C., Cheng, B., Chen, J.: Predicting of job failure in compute cloud based on online extreme learning machine: a comparative study. IEEE Access **5**, 9359 9368 (2017)
39. Liu, X., et al.: Smart server crash prediction in cloud service data center. In: 2020 19th IEEE Intersociety Conference on Thermal and Thermomechanical Phenomena in Electronic Systems (ITherm), pp. 1350–1355. IEEE (2020)
40. Marahatta, A., Xin, Q., Chi, C., Zhang, F., Liu, Z.: PEFS: AI-driven prediction based energy-aware fault-tolerant scheduling scheme for cloud data center. IEEE Trans. Sustain. Comput. (2020)
41. Mozo, A., Segall, I., Margolin, U., Gomez-Canaval, S.: Scalable prediction of service-level events in datacenter infrastructure using deep neural networks. IEEE Access **7**, 179779–179798 (2019)
42. Nagashree, N., Tejasvi, R., Swathi, K.: An early risk detection and management system for the cloud with log parser. Comput. Ind. **97**, 24–33 (2018)
43. Poghosyan, A., Grigoryan, N., Kushmerick, N., Beybutyan, H., Harutyunyan, A.: Identifying changed or sick resources from logs. In: 2018 IEEE 3rd International Workshops on Foundations and Applications of Self* Systems (FAS* W), pp. 86–91. IEEE (2018)
44. Ren, H., Nie, L., Gao, H., Zhao, L., Diao, J.: NetCruiser: localize network failures by learning from latency data. In: 2020 IEEE International Conference on Smart Internet of Things (SmartIoT), pp. 23–30. IEEE (2020)
45. Ricci, P., Donatelli, M., Onofri, M., Scarponi, L., Velardo, A.: An innovative monitoring and maintenance model for the INFN CNAF Tier-1 data center infrastructure. In: Journal of Physics: Conference Series, vol. 1525, p. 012039. IOP Publishing (2020)
46. Satpathi, S., Deb, S., Srikant, R., Yan, H.: Learning latent events from network message logs: a decomposition based approach. arXiv preprint arXiv:1804.03346 (2018)
47. Shimizu, D.Y., Mayer, K.S., Soares, J.A., Arantes, D.S.: A deep neural network model for link failure identification in multi-path ROADM based networks. In: 2020 Photonics North (PN), p. 1. IEEE (2020)
48. Sîrbu, A., Babaoglu, O.: Towards operator-less data centers through data-driven, predictive, proactive autonomics. Clust. Comput. **19**(2), 865–878 (2016)
49. Su, C.J., Huang, S.F.: Real-time big data analytics for hard disk drive predictive maintenance. Comput. Electr. Eng. **71**, 93–101 (2018)
50. Teixeira, P.H.D.S., Clemente, R.G., Kaiser, R.A., Vieira Jr., D.A.: HOLMES: an event-driven solution to monitor data centers through continuous queries and machine learning. In: Proceedings of the Fourth ACM International Conference on Distributed Event-Based Systems, pp. 216–221 (2010)

51. Xiao, J., Xiong, Z., Wu, S., Yi, Y., Jin, H., Hu, K.: Disk failure prediction in data centers via online learning. In: Proceedings of the 47th International Conference on Parallel Processing, pp. 1–10 (2018)
52. Xu, W., Huang, L., Fox, A., Patterson, D., Jordan, M.I.: Detecting large-scale system problems by mining console logs. In: Proceedings of the ACM SIGOPS 22nd Symposium on Operating Systems Principles, pp. 117–132 (2009)
53. Yang, W., Hu, D., Liu, Y., Wang, S., Jiang, T.: Hard drive failure prediction using big data. In: 2015 IEEE 34th Symposium on Reliable Distributed Systems Workshop (SRDSW), pp. 13–18. IEEE (2015)
54. Zeydan, E., Arslan, S.S.: Cloud 2 HDD: large-scale HDD data analysis on cloud for cloud datacenters. In: 2020 23rd Conference on Innovation in Clouds, Internet and Networks and Workshops (ICIN), pp. 243–249. IEEE (2020)
55. Zhang, J., et al.: Transfer learning based failure prediction for minority disks in large data centers of heterogeneous disk systems. In: Proceedings of the 48th International Conference on Parallel Processing, pp. 1–10 (2019)
56. Zhang, J., et al.: Minority disk failure prediction based on transfer learning in large data centers of heterogeneous disk systems. IEEE Trans. Parallel Distrib. Syst. **31**(9), 2155–2169 (2020)
57. Zhang, S., et al.: Prefix: switch failure prediction in datacenter networks. Proc. ACM Meas. Anal. Comput. Syst. **2**(1), 1–29 (2018)
58. Zhang, S., et al.: Syslog processing for switch failure diagnosis and prediction in datacenter networks. In: 2017 IEEE/ACM 25th International Symposium on Quality of Service (IWQoS), pp. 1–10. IEEE (2017)
59. Zhao, J., et al.: Disk failure early warning based on the characteristics of customized smart. In: 2020 19th IEEE Intersociety Conference on Thermal and Thermomechanical Phenomena in Electronic Systems (ITherm), pp. 1282–1288. IEEE (2020)

Empirical Analysis on Effectiveness of NLP Methods for Predicting Code Smell

Himanshu Gupta[✉], Abhiram Anand Gulanikar[✉], Lov Kumar[✉], and Lalita Bhanu Murthy Neti[✉]

BITS Pilani, Hyderabad Campus, Hyderabad, India
{f20150339h,f20150105h}@alumni.bits-pilani.ac.in,
{lovkumar,bhanu}@hyderabad.bits-pilani.ac.in

Abstract. A code smell is a surface indicator of an inherent problem in the system, most often due to deviation from standard coding practices on the developer's part during the development phase. Studies observe that code smells made the code more susceptible to call for modifications and corrections than code that did not contain code smells. Restructuring the code at the early stage of development saves the exponentially increasing amount of effort it would require to address the issues stemming from the presence of these code smells. Instead of using traditional features to detect code smells, we use user comments (given on the packages' repositories) to manually construct features to predict code smells. We use three Extreme learning machine kernels over 629 packages to identify eight code smells by leveraging feature engineering aspects and using sampling techniques. Our findings indicate that the radial basis functional kernel performs best out of the three kernel methods with a mean accuracy of 98.52.

Keywords: Extreme learning machine · Natural language processing · Radial basis kernel

1 Introduction

The existence of code smells in source code points towards poor design and violations in standard coding practices [1]. The code smells may not necessarily be identified as defects in the software in the current phase, but these code classes have a high likelihood of developing bugs in the future. Since these code smells do not cause defects, the only way to identify them is based on inspection, i.e., manually combing through thousands of lines of code to find code smells. This method is highly disorganized and costly and becomes more inefficient along with scaling of code package size. In our work, we are automating this process of identifying code smells. We are using the input source code packages to build our set of source

H. Gupta and A. A. Gulanikar—The research associated to this paper was completed during author's undergraduate study at BITS Pilani, Hyderabad Campus.

O. Gervasi et al. (Eds.): ICCSA 2021, LNCS 12957, pp. 43–53, 2021.
https://doi.org/10.1007/978-3-030-87013-3_4

code metrics to develop a model to locate and predict code smells in the application packages. These models will reduce the cost and efficiency of maintaining software while enforcing standard coding practices and improving its quality.

In this paper, we used three kernels: Linear kernel, radial basis function kernel, and polynomial kernel to develop models to predict the following eight code smells, namely, Swiss Army Knife (SAK), Long Method (LM), Member Ignoring Method (MIM), No Low Memory Resolver (NLMR), Blob Class (BLOB), Internal Getter/Setter (IGS), Leaking Inner Class (LIC) and Complex Class (CC). These source code metrics are from the application's source code packages and are used to engineer relevant features and select relevant metrics. We used the Wilcoxon Rank Sum Test to achieve the second of these objectives. In this work, we have analyzed the performance with various kernel functions using accuracy, area under the curve (AUC), and F-measure to predict code smells. We have attempted to answer three research questions in this paper:

- **RQ1: Discuss the ability of different NLP Methods to generate features that help detect code smells.** In traditional code smell detection techniques, code smell metrics are present, which help detect code smells. We have manually constructed 100 features derived from reviews of peer developers' software about the software's source code in this problem. We have a Continuous Bag of words and the Skip-gram method to construct features for detection. We will use accuracy, Area under the curve, and F1 Score to compare each technique's performance.
- **RQ2: Explore the potential of Data Sampling Techniques to discover code smells** Instead of using just the original data, we have used three sampling techniques to generate datasets. SMOTE [2] (Synthetic Minority Over-sampling), borderline SMOTE [3], and SVM SMOTE (Support Vector Machine SMOTE) [4], along with original data, gives us four sets of data. We compare the performance of these datasets using Area under curve and statistical significance tests.
- **RQ3: Study the capacity of various ELM Kernels to predict code smells.** We have used three Extreme Learning Machine kernels to detect code smells from the various features and datasets. Linear Kernel (LINK), Radial Basis Function kernel (RBF), and Polynomial kernel have been used for classification. Their performance has been compared using statistical significance tests and Area Under the Curve Analysis.

Organization: The paper is prepared as follows: The 2nd section summarizes the associated work. The 3rd section offers an in-depth review of all the components used in the experiment. The 4th section describes the study's framework pipeline and how the components described in Sect. 3 interact with each other. The 5th section provides the experimental outcome and the 6th section answers the questions raised in the introduction. In the 7th section we conclude our research.

2   Related Work

Evgeniy et al. used contextual analysis of document data to generate features making use of word sense clarification. Long Ma et al. used Word2Vec to output word

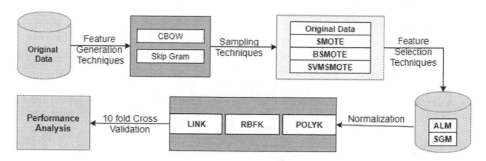

Fig. 1. Flowchart of the research framework

vectors to represent large pieces of texts or entire documents. He used CBOW and skip-grams as component models of Word2Vec to create word vectors and then evaluate word similarity [5]. Hui Han et al. introduced over-sampling techniques of Borderline-SMOTE as a variant of SMOTE where only minority examples near borderline are over-sampled [3]. Josey Mathew et al. proposed a kernel-based SMOTE (SVM SMOTE) algorithm which directly generates the minority data points. His proposed SMOTE technique performs better than other SMOTE techniques in 51 benchmark datasets [4]. Guang-Bin Huang et al. proposed Extreme Learning Machine (ELM), which randomly chooses hidden nodes and determines the Single-hidden Layer Feed forward Neural Networks (SLFN) weights [6]. Francisco Fernández-Navarro et al. proposed a modified version of ELM, which uses Gaussian distribution to parameterize the distribution called the radial basis function. She used ELM is used to optimize the parameters of the model [7].

3 Research Methodology

A detailed description of the Dataset, Data Sampling Techniques, Feature Generation Techniques, Feature Selection Techniques, and Classification Algorithms is given below.

3.1 Experimental Data Set

In this research, our main database comprised of 629 freely available software packages. Our dataset consisted of a list of packages, and the code smells present

Table 1. Statistics on code smell distribution by type

Code smell names	Repository without any code smell	Repository with code smell	Percent of classes without code smell	Percent of classes with code smell
Complex Class (CC)	230	399	63.4%	36.5%
Leaking Internal Class (LIC)	160	469	74.5%	25.4%
Blob Class	460	169	26.8%	73.1%
No Low Memory Resolver (NLMR)	190	439	69.7%	30.2%
Internal Getter Setter (IGS)	264	365	58.02%	41.9%
Member Ignoring Method (MIM)	265	364	57.8%	42.1%
Swiss Army Knife (SAK)	155	474	75.3%	24.6%
Long method (LM)	225	404	64.2%	35.7%

in them. The characteristics and patterns exhibited by all of the code smells are presented in Table 1. Table 1 shows that the code smells are present in a range from 25.4% to 73.1%. We also observed that the lowest presence of any code smell we found was 25.4% for the BLOB Class code smell, while the highest presence observed at 75.04% was for Swiss Army Knife (SAK) code smell.

3.2   Data Sampling Techniques

We use three data sampling techniques to generate additional datasets to mitigate the bias in the dataset:

- **SMOTE** [2] randomly chooses samples from K nearest neighbors from minority class. The synthetic data would be made between the randomly selected sample and the k nearest neighbor.
- **Borderline SMOTE** [3] works on a similar principle but creates data only along the classes' boundary line, not to introduce external bias.
- **SVM-SMOTE** [4,8] uses Support Vector Machine instead of K nearest neighbor to generate samples between a chosen sample and the decision boundary.

3.3   Feature Generation Techniques

We use two architectures from the word2vec [5] techniques, namely the Continuous Bag of Words (CBOW) and Skip-gram. Continuous Bag of Words method [9] uses the surrounding words to speculate the present word. Since it derives from the bag of words model, words present in the window (surrounding the current word) are not differentiated based on the current word's distance. The skip-gram model [10] makes use of the current word to predict the context. Here words nearer are more heavily weighted than words farther away from the present word. Comparing the two models, the CBOW model is faster than skip-grams, but skip-grams perform better when uncommon words are involved.

3.4   Feature Selection Techniques

We have generated 100 feature metrics, but they might not be relevant to the code smells we have considered. We use the Wilcoxon signed-rank test to get the statistical relation between the smelly and clean applications. We have set 0.05 as the outset for the p-value, and we reject the hypothesis if the value is lower. We employ cross-correlation analysis to select uncorrelated features. Our selected variables share a high correlation to the output variables and have a low correlation between themselves.

3.5   Classification Algorithms

This paper uses three ELM kernel functions [6,11] to train models to predict code smells, namely the Linear Kernel function, Radial basis kernel function, and

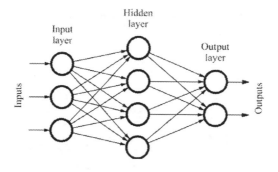

Fig. 2. Architecture diagram of extreme machine learning kernel

polynomial kernel function [12]. As shown in Fig. 2, Extreme Learning Machines (ELM) can be simply defined as feed-forward neural networks, and they can be used for clustering, classification, regressing, among other things. These three kernel methods work best for different data types based on whether it is linearly separable and the problem is linear or nonlinear. Kernel functions are mathematical functions used to transform training data into higher dimensions. The linear kernel is generally chosen when dealing with linearly separable data; it is also most commonly used when many features are in a dataset. The Radial basis function kernel is a non-linear kernel used for training SVMS when solving nonlinear problems. The polynomial kernel function is also used to train nonlinear models. It is faster and requires fewer resources to train the linear or polynomial kernel functions than radial basis functions. Still, they are less accurate in comparison to the RBF kernel. We also use ten-fold cross-validation to overcome overfitting and selection-bias issues and obtain insights on our model's performance on an independent dataset. We use the area under the curve (AUC) and F-measure, among other tests, to compare their performance.

4 Research Framework

We make use of the code data from 629 open-source software packages on GitHub. To eliminate the class imbalance problem in the data, we use SMOTE, Borderline SMOTE, and SVM SMOTE [2–4]to get four datasets: the Original Dataset (ORD) SMOTE Dataset, Borderline SMOTE Dataset, and SVM SMOTE Dataset. We use three kernel functions, the linear kernel function, the radial basis kernel function, and the polynomial kernel function. To compare the accuracy over all the four datasets, we have created and used the area under the curve (AUC) and F-measure, among other tests, to compare their performance. Figure 1 provides a clear representation of the same.

5 Experimental Results

Tables 2A and 2B give accuracy and AUC values for all the ELM methods, using feature engineering methods and all feature selection techniques. Table 3

Table 2. Area Under Curve and Accuracy figures for ELM models trained on the original dataset

(a) Accuracy values

Original Data

	ALM						SGM					
	CBOW			SKG			CBOW			SKG		
	LINK	RBFK	POLYK	LINK	RBFK	POLYK	LINK	RBFK	POLYK	LINK	RBFK	POLYK
BLOB	62.80	100.00	100.00	73.77	100.00	100.00	62.64	100.00	72.02	63.91	68.04	76.63
LM	75.36	100.00	100.00	75.68	99.84	100.00	75.36	100.00	100.00	75.36	100.00	100.00
SAK	75.20	100.00	100.00	74.72	100.00	100.00	75.83	75.83	100.00	73.77	100.00	94.28
CC	71.70	100.00	100.00	71.54	100.00	100.00	70.27	100.00	100.00	70.75	100.00	93.80
IGS	67.73	99.68	100.00	68.04	63.43	100.00	61.84	100.00	65.66	57.71	74.56	100.00
MIM	58.98	100.00	100.00	59.46	82.35	100.00	59.62	100.00	94.59	59.62	88.71	100.00
NLMR	81.08	100.00	100.00	81.56	100.00	100.00	75.04	100.00	99.84	75.04	94.75	93.16
LIC	70.11	100.00	100.00	65.18	85.06	100.00	64.86	100.00	97.46	66.45	78.54	100.00

(b) AUC Values

Original Data

	ALM						SGM					
	CBOW			SKG			CBOW			SKG		
	LINK	RBFK	POLYK	LINK	RBFK	POLYK	LINK	RBFK	POLYK	LINK	RBFK	POLYK
BLOB	0.64	1.00	1.00	0.78	1.00	1.00	0.60	1.00	0.78	0.62	0.86	0.84
LM	0.72	1.00	1.00	0.75	1.00	1.00	0.72	1.00	1.00	0.67	1.00	1.00
SAK	0.71	1.00	1.00	0.68	1.00	1.00	0.69	0.72	1.00	0.65	1.00	0.99
CC	0.75	1.00	1.00	0.70	1.00	1.00	0.65	1.00	1.00	0.69	1.00	0.98
IGS	0.74	1.00	1.00	0.74	0.74	1.00	0.65	1.00	0.73	0.61	0.84	1.00
MIM	0.63	1.00	1.00	0.61	0.91	1.00	0.62	1.00	0.99	0.61	0.96	1.00
NLMR	0.84	1.00	1.00	0.85	1.00	1.00	0.71	1.00	1.00	0.67	0.99	0.98
LIC	0.76	1.00	1.00	0.67	0.98	1.00	0.67	1.00	1.00	0.68	0.94	1.00

and Table 4 summarize the various statistical measures of different metrics used in our research. It is pretty evident from Tables 2A and 2B that Radial Basis Function and polynomial perform much better for most samples than Linear kernel. Table 3B Fig. 3 shows that models trained using all metrics perform better than those using significant metrics. The high values of the performance indicators encourage the use of the code smell prediction model. The following observations can be made from the Results obtained:

- The performance of all models varies greatly with the minimum accuracy being 56.41% and the maximum accuracy being 100% AUC follows similar trend to accuracy but f-measure varies the most from minimum value being 0.02 and maximum being 1.
- It is observed that radial basis kernel and polynomial kernel perform much better than linear kernel across all three statistical measures that is AUC, accuracy and f-measure and they also indicate the high efficiency of the models which are developed.
- It is observed that Linear kernel performs the best with Class NLMR (77.5%) and the worst with MIM class (61.95%).

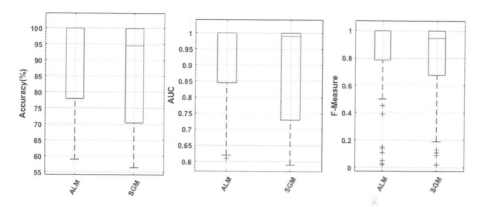

Fig. 3. Box plot comparison between All Metrics

Table 3. Statistical measure

(a) Feature Generation Techniques

	Min	Max	Mean	Median	25th	75th
Accuracy						
CBOW	57.98	100.00	88.63	100.00	74.61	100.00
SKM	56.41	100.00	87.82	99.85	73.98	100.00
AUC						
CBOW	0.59	1.00	0.90	1.00	0.78	1.00
SKM	0.59	1.00	0.90	1.00	0.80	1.00
F Measure						
CBOW	0.02	1.00	0.86	1.00	0.74	1.00
SKM	0.05	1.00	0.84	1.00	0.72	1.00

(b) Features Selection Metrics

	Min	Max	Mean	Median	25th	75th
Accuracy						
ALM	58.98	100.00	90.72	100.00	77.94	100.00
SGM	56.41	100.00	85.73	94.55	70.46	100.00
AUC						
ALM	0.61	1.00	0.93	1.00	0.84	1.00
SGM	0.59	1.00	0.88	0.99	0.73	1.00
F Measure						
ALM	0.02	1.00	0.88	1.00	0.78	1.00
SGM	0.02	1.00	0.83	0.95	0.68	1.00

6 Comparison

RQ1: Discuss the ability of different NLP Methods to generate features that help detect code smells. Table 3A and Fig. 4 shows that CBOW performs slightly better than skip-grams across accuracy and F-measure metric. It is a known fact that CBOW is many times faster to train compared to skip-grams. CBOW performs marginally better when common words are considered, while skip-gram performs better on rare words or phrases [8]. Our model performs better on CBOW, indicating that user comments from which the feature vectors are generated have a higher occurrence of common words over rare words. Table 6B shows us the result of the Ranksum test of vectors generated using these two methods, and we can conclude that the vectors generated are highly uncorrelated.

RQ2: Explore the potential of Data Sampling Techniques to discover code smells. Table 4B and Fig. 5 shows that the data sampling techniques perform better than the original data in AUC, accuracy, and F-measure. Although all three SMOTE techniques, BorderlineSMOTE and SVM-SMOTE, perform nearly the same, SVM-SMOTE performs the best. SVM-SMOTE performs better than others because they use KNN. SVM can employ kernels to lead to a better hyperplane in higher dimensions. KNN uses euclidean distance, on the other hand, which may not work well in the same case. Also, KNN computes the nearest neighbors' distance, leading to more unsatisfactory performance when working on a large dataset.

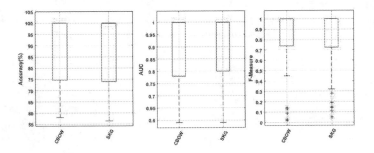

Fig. 4. Accuracy, AUC and F-measure box-plot of different feature generation techniques

Table 4. Statistics about different datasets and machine learning models

(a) Performance on various ELM Kernels

Accuracy

	Min	Max	Mean	Median	25th	75th
LINK	56.41	82.59	69.84	70.57	64.39	75.11
RBFK	63.43	100.00	98.52	100.00	100.00	100.00
POLYK	64.92	100.00	96.32	100.00	95.57	100.00

AUC

	Min	Max	Mean	Median	25th	75th
LINK	0.59	0.90	0.74	0.74	0.66	0.80
RBFK	0.72	1.00	0.99	1.00	1.00	1.00
POLYK	0.71	1.00	0.98	1.00	0.99	1.00

F Measure

	Min	Max	Mean	Median	25th	75th
LINK	0.02	0.86	0.62	0.69	0.59	0.75
RBFK	0.32	1.00	0.98	1.00	1.00	1.00
POLYK	0.45	1.00	0.96	1.00	0.96	1.00

(b) Performance on different Datasets

Accuracy

	Min	Max	Mean	Median	25th	75th
ORD	57.71	100.00	86.66	96.10	73.77	100.00
SMOTE	57.02	100.00	88.78	100.00	74.46	100.00
BSMOTE	56.41	100.00	88.50	100.00	73.14	100.00
SVMSMOTE	58.69	100.00	88.96	99.95	74.61	100.00

AUC

	Min	Max	Mean	Median	25th	75th
ORD	0.60	1.00	0.88	0.99	0.72	1.00
SMOTE	0.61	1.00	0.91	1.00	0.81	1.00
BSMOTE	0.59	1.00	0.91	1.00	0.80	1.00
SVMSMOTE	0.61	1.00	0.92	1.00	0.82	1.00

F Measure

	Min	Max	Mean	Median	25th	75th
ORD	0.02	1.00	0.74	0.96	0.50	1.00
SMOTE	0.58	1.00	0.89	1.00	0.75	1.00
BSMOTE	0.57	1.00	0.89	1.00	0.74	1.00
SVMSMOTE	0.59	1.00	0.89	1.00	0.75	1.00

Table 5A gives us the result of the Ranksum test of the datasets generated using these methods. We observe that all the datasets generated from smoothing techniques vary a lot from the original dataset, and we can conclude that the datasets are highly uncorrelated. We also observe that SMOTE,

Borderline-SMOTE, and SVM-SMOTE are very similar to each other, and hence the performance of the models trained over them also show similar trends.

RQ3: Study the capacity of various ELM Kernels to predict code smells. Table 4A and Fig. 6 shows the three kernel methods' performance in terms of accuracy, AUC, and F-measure. Since our data does not have a linear distribution, we observe that the linear kernel method's performance is relatively lackluster. Polynomial and RBF both perform significantly better than the linear kernel due to a fixed small number of features. It is observed that the RBF kernel shows the best performance of the three. Table 5B shows the result of the Ranksum tests on models generated using the different ELM kernels. We can observe that the prediction models developed using the various methods are significantly different from each other, and the models are highly unrelated.

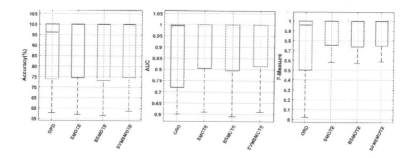

Fig. 5. Comparison between different data sampling techniques.

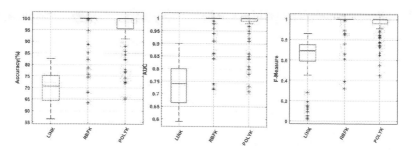

Fig. 6. Box-plot comparison between different ELM Kernel methods

Table 5. Ranksum Test

(a) Different sampling methods

	ORD	SMOTE	BSMOTE	SVMSMOTE
ORD	1.00	0.12	0.19	0.12
SMOTE	0.12	1.00	0.76	0.89
BSMOTE	0.19	0.76	1.00	0.83
SVMSMOTE	0.12	0.89	0.83	1.00

(b) Model similarity

	LINK	RBFK	POLYK
LINK	1.00	0.00	0.00
RBFK	0.00	1.00	0.00
POLYK	0.00	0.00	1.00

H. Gupta et al.

Table 6. Ranksum Test

(a) Feature Combination

	ALM	SGM
ALM	1.00	0.00
SGM	0.00	1.00

(b) Feature Generation Methods

	CBOW	SKM
CBOW	1.00	0.43
SKM	0.43	1.00

7 Conclusion

This paper provides the empirical evaluation of code smell prediction utilizing various ELM methods, feature generation methods using NLP techniques, feature selection, and data sampling techniques. The models are evaluated using ten-fold cross-validation, and their prediction abilities are compared using accuracy, AUC, and F-measure. We draw the following conclusions from our research study:

- CBOW performs better than skip-grams in feature generation.
- SVM-SMOTE performs best among the data sampling techniques.
- Models based on all metrics perform better than models based on significant metrics created using the Wilcoxon signed-rank test.
- RBF kernel performs best among the EML methods in predicting code smells.

References

1. Van Emden, E., Moonen, L.: Java quality assurance by detecting code smells. In: 2002 Proceedings of the Ninth Working Conference on Reverse Engineering, pp. 97–106. IEEE (2002)
2. Chawla, N.V., Bowyer, K.W., Hall, L.O., Kegelmeyer, W.P.: Smote: synthetic minority over-sampling technique. J. Artif. Intell. Res. **16**, 321–357 (2002)
3. Han, H., Wang, W.-Y., Mao, B.-H.: Borderline-SMOTE: a new over-sampling method in imbalanced data sets learning. In: Huang, D.-S., Zhang, X.-P., Huang, G.-B. (eds.) ICIC 2005. LNCS, vol. 3644, pp. 878–887. Springer, Heidelberg (2005). https://doi.org/10.1007/11538059_91
4. Mathew, J., Luo, M., Pang, C.K., Chan, H.L.: Kernel-based smote for SVM classification of imbalanced datasets. In: IECON 2015–41st Annual Conference of the IEEE Industrial Electronics Society, pp. 001127–001132. IEEE (2015)
5. Ma, L., Zhang, Y.: Using Word2Vec to process big text data. In: 2015 IEEE International Conference on Big Data (Big Data), pp. 2895–2897. IEEE (2015)
6. Huang, G.-B., Zhu, Q.-Y., Siew, C.-K.: Extreme learning machine: theory and applications. Neurocomputing **70**(1–3), 489–501 (2006)
7. Fernández-Navarro, F., Hervás-Martínez, C., Sanchez-Monedero, J., Gutiérrez, P.A.: MELM-GRBF: a modified version of the extreme learning machine for generalized radial basis function neural networks. Neurocomputing **74**(16), 2502–2510 (2011)
8. Wang, Q., Luo, Z., Huang, J., Feng, Y., Liu, Z.: A novel ensemble method for imbalanced data learning: bagging of extrapolation-SMOTE SVM. Comput. Intell. Neurosci. **2017** (2017)

9. Wang, Q., Xu, J., Chen, H., He, B.: Two improved continuous bag-of-word models. In: 2017 International Joint Conference on Neural Networks (IJCNN), pp. 2851–2856. IEEE (2017)
10. Guthrie, D., Allison, B., Liu, W., Guthrie, L., Wilks, Y.: A closer look at skip-gram modelling. In: LREC, vol. 6, pp. 1222–1225. Citeseer (2006)
11. Micchelli, C.A., Pontil, M., Bartlett, P.: Learning the kernel function via regularization. J. Mach. Learn. Res. **6**(7) (2005)
12. Prajapati, G.L., Patle, A.: On performing classification using SVM with radial basis and polynomial kernel functions. In: 2010 3rd International Conference on Emerging Trends in Engineering and Technology, pp. 512–515. IEEE (2010)

Machine Learning Applied for Spectra Classification

Yue Sun[1,2(✉)] ⓘ, Sandor Brockhauser[1,2] ⓘ, and Péter Hegedűs[1,3] ⓘ

[1] University of Szeged, Szeged, Hungary
{yue.sun,sandor.brockhauser}@xfel.eu, hpeter@inf.u-szeged.hu
[2] European XFEL GmbH, Schenefeld, Germany
[3] MTA-SZTE Research Group on Artificial Intelligence, ELKH, Szeged, Hungary

Abstract. Spectroscopy experiment techniques are widely used and produce a huge amount of data especially in facilities with very high repetition rates. In High Energy Density (HED) experiments with high-density materials, changes in pressure will cause changes in the spectral peak. Immediate feedback on the actual status (e.g. time-resolved status of the sample) would be essential to quickly judge how to proceed with the experiment. The two major spectral changes we aim to capture are either the change of intensity distribution (e.g., drop or appearance) of peaks at certain locations, or the shift of those on the spectrum.

In this work, we apply recent popular machine learning/deep learning models to HED experimental spectra data classification. The models we presented range from supervised deep neural networks (state-of-the-art LSTM-based model and Transformer-based model) to unsupervised spectral clustering algorithm. These are the common architectures for time series processing. The PCA method is used as data preprocessing for dimensionality reduction. Three different ML algorithms are evaluated and compared for the classification task. The results show that all three methods can achieve 100% classification confidence. Among them, the spectra clustering method consumes the least calculation time (0.069 s), and the transformer-based method uses the most training time (0.204 s).

Keywords: Spectral data · Classification · PCA · LSTM · Transformer · Clustering

1 Introduction

High Energy Density (HED) scientific instrument focuses on the investigation of matter at high density, temperature, pressure, electric, and/or magnetic field [1]. In HED experiments with high-density materials, changes in pressure will cause changes in the spectral peaks (vanishing, shifting, or splitting). To evaluate the experiment status, the measured spectra need to be classified so that each class is assigned to a different state of the system under investigation. The two major spectral changes that we aim to capture in this study are.

© Springer Nature Switzerland AG 2021
O. Gervasi et al. (Eds.): ICCSA 2021, LNCS 12957, pp. 54–68, 2021.
https://doi.org/10.1007/978-3-030-87013-3_5

- the change of intensity distribution (e.g. drop or appearance) of peaks at certain locations, or
- the shift of those in the spectrum.

With recent developments in machine learning, data-driven machine learning/deep learning (ML/DL) methods have turned out to be very good at discovering intricate structures in high-dimensional data [2]. The ML/DL-based methods have applied broadly to a set of algorithms and techniques that train systems from raw data rather than a priori models [3], thus useful for research facilities that produce large, multidimensional datasets.

In this study, we aim to derive a statistical model for the application of HED spectra data classification. In this way, the actual status of the experiment can be fed back instantly according to the classification result, and the follow-up experiment can be better guided. We presented a simple and strong baseline range from supervised DL networks to unsupervised spectral clustering architecture for time series spectra data classification. Three commonly used ML/DL-based models are explored and evaluated on the same HED benchmark datasets, namely, the supervised LSTM-based, Transformer-based DL models and the unsupervised Spectral clustering ML algorithm. The PCA method is used here as data preprocessing for dimensionality reduction and speed up training or calculation. The experiment results show that all three methods can find a clear classification boundary and achieve 100% classification confidence. Among them, the spectra clustering method consumes the least calculation time (0.069 s). Although the data set is not clearly labeled, we use representative spectral curves as the training data set, which makes supervised DL models possible. Related work.

1.1 Deep Learning Approaches

Deep neural networks have received an increasing amount of attention in time series analysis in recent years [4, 14]. A large variety of deep learning modeling approaches for time series analysis have been exploited for a wide range of tasks, such as forecasting, regression, and classification [5, 9, 14 15, 36]. The most common established deep learning models in this area are convolutional neural network (CNN) [13, 42, 43], recurrent neural networks (RNN) [5, 7, 8], and attention-based neural networks [10, 11, 14–16, 34]. Since CNN-based models can only learn local neighborhood features, recently, RNN-based models and attention-based models which can learn long-range dependencies are increasingly popular for learning from time series data [5].

Recurrent Approach. Two variants of the recurrent neural networks (RNN) models, Long Short Term Memory [6], GRU (Gated Recurrent Unit) [40], in particular, can effectively capture long term temporal dependencies, thus can work efficiently on various complex time series processing, prediction, recognition, and classification tasks [5, 7, 8, 38]. for example, in [8], Lipton et al. use clinical episodes as examples to first illustrate that LSTM has multi-label classification capabilities in multivariate time series. In the meantime, RNN-based architectures have also been used in combination with the CNN-based module to automatically extract the features and capture their long-term dependencies at the same time. The hybrid neural architectures have shown promising results for the automated analysis of time series [5, 9, 33, 38]. Lai et al. [5] proposed a Long- and Short-term Time-series network (LSTNet) framework for multivariate time series forecasting. The method combines the strengths of CNN and RNN, can effectively extract short-term and long-term dependencies in data at the same time. In addition, they considered attention mechanism to alleviate nonseasonal time series prediction issue. Wu et al. [9] applied a convolutional recurrent neural network (CRNN) for hyperspectral data classification and achieved state-of-the-art performance. In 2017, Karim et al. [33] proposed two deep learning models for end-to-end univariate time series classification, namely LSTM RNN and ALSTM-FCN. The proposed model is an enhancement of a Fully Convolutional Network (FCN) with LSTM sub-module or attention LSTM sub-module. In 2019, the authors [35] introduced squeeze-and-excitation block to augment the FCN block, which can capture the contexture information and channel-wise dependencies, so that the model can be used for multivariate time series classification [35]. Interdonato et al. [37] proposed and end-to-end DuPLO DL architecture for the analysis of Satellite Image Time Series data. It involves branches of CNN and GRU, which can better represent remote sensing data and achieve better quantitative and qualitative classification performance.

Attention-Based Approach. Very recently, inspired by the Transformer scaling successes in NLP [10], researches have also successfully developed their Transformer-based or attention-based models for time series analysis task, such as video understanding [11], forecasting of multivariate time series data [14, 15], satellite image time series classification [12], and hyperspectral image (HSI) classification [16]. Unlike sequence-aligned models, Transformer or other attention-based models can process data sequences in more parallel and the applied attention mechanism can learn global dependencies in the sequence [4]. Ma et al. [39] first proposed a novel approach called Cross-Dimensional Self-Attention (CDSA) for the multivariate, geo-tagged time series data imputation task. The CDSA model can jointly capture the self-attention across multiple dimensions (time, location, measurement), yet in an order-independent way [39]. Garnot et al. [12] proposed a spatio-temporal classifier for automatic classification of satellite image time series, in which a Pixel-Set Encoder is used to extract spatial features, and a self-attention-based temporal encoder is used to extract temporal features. This architecture has made significant improvements in accuracy, time, and memory consumption. Rußwurm et al. [34] explored and compared several commonly used state-of-the-art deep learning mechanisms on preprocessed and raw satellite data, such as convolution, recurrence, and self-attention—for crop type identification. They pointed out that preprocessing can improve the classification performance of all models they applied, while the choice of model was less crucial [34]. Although in most cases, the attention-based architecture used for time series analysis is used as a supervised learning method, in 2020, Zerveas et al. [15] first proposes a transformer-based framework for unsupervised representation learning of multivariate time series. Even with very limited training samples, this model can still exceed the current state-of-the-art performance in the classification and regression tasks of multivariate time series, and can potentially be used for other downstream tasks, such as forecasting and missing value imputation [15].

1.2 Clustering Approach

In the field of unsupervised learning, many machine learning methods for data classification have also been developed, such as k-nearest neighbor (KNN) [17], partial least-squares discrimination analysis (PLS-DA) [18, 19], support vector machine (SVM) [20], Extreme Learning Machine (ELM) [21], kernel extreme learning machine (KELM) [22]. As an unsupervised learning algorithm, clustering is one of the common nonparametric ML techniques and is widely used for exploratory data analysis [23]. Among them, spectral clustering is a clustering method that does not make assumptions about the global structure of the data [24]. It can solve very general problems like intertwined spirals and can be implemented efficiently even for large data sets [23]. For example, Jebara et al. [41] combined non-parametric spectral clustering with parametric hidden Markov models for time series data analysis, and achieved great clustering accuracy.

In this work, we apply three commonly used machine learning/deep learning architectures to time series spectral data classification. Our proposed baseline models are based on the same PCA preprocessing process. The LSTM-based, Transformer-based and Spectral clustering network range from supervised DL neural networks to unsupervised ML algorithm are explored and evaluated on the same benchmark datasets.

2 Method

2.1 Dataset Description

The spectral data used in this work was collected during the HED experiment, and it was obtained by azimuthal integration of raw X-ray diffraction images. The data set consists of 349 samples with each of 4023 features and is publicly available at https://zenodo.org/record/4424866. To show more clearly how the diffraction changes while the pressure on the sample is changing, we show one for every 10 diffractograms, as shown in Fig. 1. It can be clearly seen from this figure that the amplitude of spectral peaks changes (increases, decreases, vanishes) at certain locations, and the peaks also shift at 2θ-angle position, or split, or start to broaden. These changes correspond to the modification of the crystal lattice (e.g. indicating phase changes). Among them, 28 original spectra samples (the 16 marked in red belong to class label 0 and the 12 marked in blue belong to class label 1) are used as the training dataset in supervised methods. We also added 2800 simulated ones for training (by adding sufficiently small random noise, 100 simulated spectral curves can be added to each original diffractogram).

During the experiment, we should be able to track these changes and determine the actual state of the system in near real-time. Scientifically, the most relevant question is whether the phase transition in the sample has occurred. Since there is no ground truth information, in order to determine this, for supervised learning approaches, we got representative spectra measured (and simulated) at both the initial and final stages for training, which is marked in red or blue in Fig. 1. Based on this input, we should provide a judgment with minimum ambiguity at each point during the experiment.

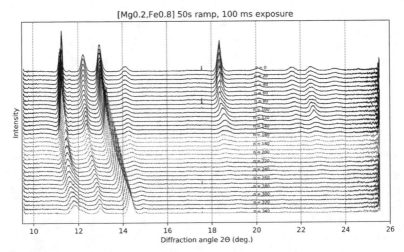

Fig. 1. Spectral data (one for every 10 diffractograms) collected during the experiment after baseline subtraction. Please note that the 28 spectra marked in red or blue are used as the basis for the LSTM or Transformer-based ML training set. Among them, the 16 marked in red belong to class label 0 and the 12 marked in blue belong to class label 1.

2.2 PCA for Dataset Preprocessing

In spectroscopy experiments, it is very common that the number of input variables (features) is greater than the number of training samples, which will more easily lead to the problem of overfitting. Our data has the same characteristic. In order to facilitate the ML/DL training process, the PCA algorithm is applied to data dimensionality reduction while speeding up the training process. PCA uses an orthogonal transformation to convert data (of possibly correlated variables) into a set of new uncorrelated variables called principal components that successively maximize variance [26]. It is proved to be a simple and effective dimensionality reduction method for spectra data [22, 25].

Data Centering. Before applying the PCA algorithm, the dataset features should be centered by removing the mean. Centering is performed independently on each feature by computing the relevant statistics on the samples [44], as shown in Fig. 2.

PCA Preprocessing. In the PCA method, the number of principal components (PCs) required to describe the data can be determined by looking at the cumulative explained variance ratio as a function of the number of PCs [45]. The cumulative explained variance of PCA is shown in Fig. 3a), the first 2 PCs explain more than 60% of the variance. Some of the new projected orthogonal variables' (PCs) values distribution can be seen from Fig. 3b). It can be clearly seen that the first PC explains the most variance in the data with each subsequent component explaining less.

When converted back to the original space, you can see the information retained or lost by the PCA algorithm more vividly, the comparison between the inverse transformation of PCA with different explained variance and the original spectra data is shown in Fig. 4. We can get that the first few PCs can describe the basic distribution of the data,

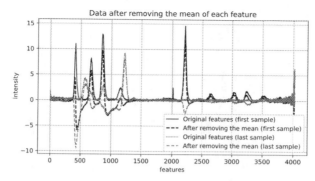

Fig. 2. Centering the dataset (take the first and last samples are used as an example).

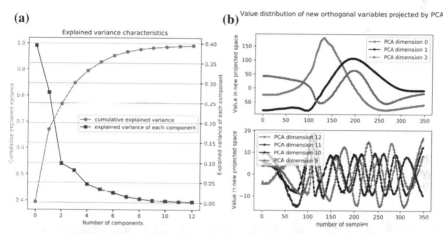

Fig. 3. a) Cumulative explained variance. b) Value distribution of new orthogonal variables projected by PCA.

with other PCs providing more details. In order to retain as many features as possible, we choose 13 components which can explain 99% of the variance. Then our new projected data consist of 349 samples with each of 13 features.

Contributions of Variables to PCs. In PCA, the correlation between components and variables is called loadings, it is the element of the eigenvectors and estimates the information they share [26].

The loadings (marked with blue line) and contributions (marked with red line) of variables/features in accounting for the variability to the first PC are shown in Fig. 5 (top row). The sum of loadings and the contributions of each original variable/feature to selected PCs are shown in Fig. 5 (bottom row). It shows that the more obvious the features/variables, the greater the contribution to the selected PCs.

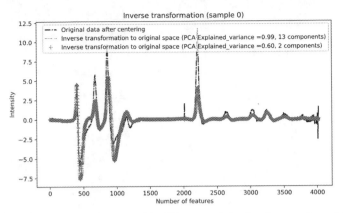

Fig. 4. Inverse transformation with different explained variances of sample 0.

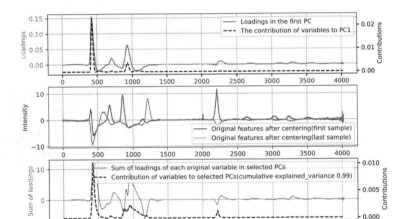

Fig. 5. Sum of loadings over variable and the contributions of each original variable/feature to the first PC and selected PCs.

2.3 LSTM-Based Model

As a variance of RNN in particular, Long short-term memory (LSTM), originally applied in NLP tasks, also yielded promising results for time series classification [5, 34, 36]. The cell unit and three gates (input gate, output gate and forget gate) in the LSTM unit allow this architecture to remember values over arbitrary time intervals and regulate the flow of information [27]. The point-wise operations used to update cell state and hidden state in the LSTM architecture can assign different weights to different features/variables in our time series spectra data, thereby improving the role of obvious features in the classification task and weakening the impact of unobvious features on classification.

Here, we do not consider the connections between different spectral observations at different time steps, but only consider the relationship between different features, that is, the sequence length is set to 1.The spectra data classification model based on LSTM structure is shown in Fig. 6, where the selected PCs after PCA preprocessing are fed into the LSTM unit. Here we use a single layer of LSTM cell, followed by a dense layer (64 input neurons and 1 output neuron) with Sigmoid as the activation function for the classification task. 64 neurons are used in the hidden state. The hidden states are initialized with zero-valued vectors. The PCA preprocessing process can also be regarded as an input embedding.

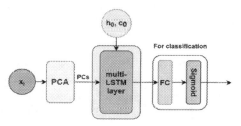

Fig. 6. Multi-LSTM layers solution for spectra data classification. PCA method is used as data preprocessing for dimensionality reduction that can also serve as an input embedding.

2.4 Transformer-Based Model

Transformer model relies on the so-called self-attention mechanism and is found to be superior in quality while being more parallelizable [10]. There are many successful applications of Transformers in time series processing tasks such as the spectra data classification [15, 16].

We adopted the encoder architecture of the self-attention Transformer network, as illustrated in Fig. 7. below. The same PCA preprocessing process is used to reduce dimensionality and save the amount of calculation. Since our spectra time series data lives in a continuous space of spectral intensity values [34], we use the dense layer or the convolutional layer for input embedding instead of a word embedding step. In addition, as with the LSTM-based method, in each batch, we only process one spectral data vector, without considering the sequential correlation of the time series, so we discarded the step of positional encoding. In this work we employed 8 attention layers, or heads, running in parallel. And the input embedding layer produces outputs of dimension 16.

In the decoder part, similarly to the input embedding, the dense layer with Sigmoid as the activation function is used to predict the class label of each spectral curve. Here, the dense layer has an input dimensionality of 16, output dimensionality of 1.

2.5 Spectral Clustering Method

Spectral Clustering uses information from the eigenvalues (spectrum) of special matrices (i.e., Affinity Matrix, Degree Matrix, and Laplacian Matrix) derived from the graph or

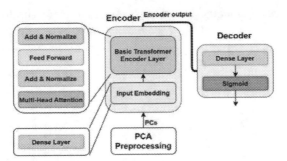

Fig. 7. Single transformer layer solution for spectra data classification. In the decoder part, the dense layer with Sigmoid as the activation function is used for the classification task.

the data set [28] and makes no assumptions about the form of the clusters. The method shows great clustering performance for data with non-convex boundaries. It is usually used when the dataset has a non-flat geometry and needs to be divided into a small number of clusters with even cluster size [30], which is well suitable for our case.

In this method, PCA preprocessing with the same parameters is used for dimensionality reduction, immediately followed by the standard spectral clustering algorithm. The clustering metrics used in the spectral clustering algorithm is graph distance, a graph of nearest neighbors [29], which is constructed to perform a low-dimension embedding of the affinity matrix between samples. And the K-Means label assignment strategy is applied in the approach, which is a popular choice [23].

2.6 Implementation

Implementation Details. All the models are implemented on the Jupyter notebook plat-form using Pytorch and Scikit-learn libraries and use the same PCA preprocessing method with the same parameters.

The Transformer-based model and LSTM-based model are performed as supervised learning. 28 original spectra samples with 2800 simulated ones as mentioned above (by adding some random noise, 100 simulated spectral curves are generated based on each original spectrum), a total of 2828. The small random noise in simulated spectral data is generated using the Mersenne Twister [31] as the core generator. The 28 original spectra samples used as the basis for training is shown in Fig. 1. All training data including the simulated ones obtained after PCA preprocessing is shown in Fig. 8. The two models are trained by backpropagation using gradient descent, with the adaptive learning-rate method Adam [32] as the optimizer (learning rate is set to $2e^{-3}$, and weight decay is $2e^{-5}$). We use the cross-entropy loss function for our classification task. The statistical models are obtained by minimizing the loss function on the training data set. In the Transformer-based model, 15 epochs are used for iteration, and in the LSTM-based model, 45 epochs are used. The two models are trained on one machine with Tesla P100-PCIE-16GB GPU.

Jupyter Notebook for Reproducibility. In this work, we use Jupyter notebooks for data analysis. The analysis scripts as Jupyter notebooks are publicly available at https://github.com/sunyue-xfel/Machine-Learning-applied-for-spectra-classification.

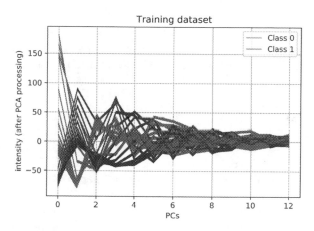

Fig. 8. Training dataset (including original spectra data and simulated ones) used in Transformer-based model and LSTM-based model.

3   Results and Discussions

3.1   Performance Metrics

In this study, we aim to find the phase transition point, which also means classifying the spectra into 2 phases or classes during the experiment. As there is no ground-truth phase transition information, we are interested in whether there is a clear boundary or an ambiguity zone during the experiment when the classification jumps inconsistently between the phases. Hence, our performance metric shall how small this ambiguous zone is. To explain what an ambiguity zone is, an illustrative example is shown in Fig. 9. Suppose we have 24 samples, corresponding to class 0 or class 1, and their classification results are shown in Fig. 9, the zone marked with red for the class label jump is an ambiguity zone. From the physics point of view, a proper interpretation would require the phases and the ambiguity zone to be linked to specific pressure ranges. Unfortunately, the available data is not complete and does not contain such information.

00000000 00101001 11111111

Fig. 9. An illustrative example of ambiguity zone.

Let N_f represent the number of spectral curves in ambiguous region, N_t represent the number of test spectral curves, then the classification confidence can be defined as

$$P_{conf} = 1 - \frac{N_f}{N_t} \qquad (1)$$

The clear boundary between these two types of spectra yields 100% confidence. If phase transition or boundary between two classes is not detected, then all the spectral curves are in the ambiguous region, and the classification confidence is 0.

3.2 Results Comparison and Discussion

Classification confidence and training time consumption of these three methods are shown in Fig. 10. All methods can achieve 100% classification confidence with the same PCA preprocessing process. Among them, the spectra clustering algorithm uses the least calculation time (0.069 s), and the transformer-based method consumes the most training time (0.204 s). Regarding reproducibility, all these methods have been run at least 20 times, and we get the same classification confidence and with almost the same training time, which means that they have high stability and reproducibility. Regarding complexity, for supervised learning algorithms, the parameters that need to be trained using the LSTM-based method are 20289, while the transformer-based method requires 5633. And the training losses for these two methods are 0.11917 and 0.113147, respectively.

For the spectral clustering method, we also test the classification confidence with different explained variance value which ranges from 55% to 99.99% (the corresponding number of PCs range from 2 to 301), the result shows that this method achieves consistent high-precision classification results (100% classification confidence), at the same time, the classification boundary is very stable and fluctuates only in a small range, as can be seen from Fig. 11. From another aspect, it also shows that the PCA algorithm can obtain the main feature information of the original data.

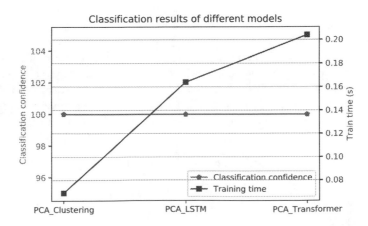

Fig. 10. Classification confidence and training time of the three models.

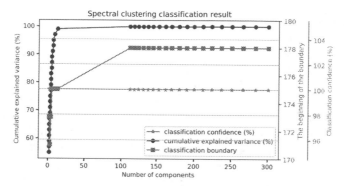

Fig. 11. Classification confidence with different explained variance value and PCs.

4 Threats to Validity

Although we obtained nice results on ML-based spectral classification, there are still some threats to validity. It can be clearly seen that in our original spectral data set, the number of training samples is limited, and the number of features is much larger than the number of samples, which will cause over-fitting problems. In this case, the PCA method is used for dimensionality reduction, and more simulated spectral curves are added to the LSTM-based and transformer-based supervisory architecture for training. However, the effect of simulation data is limited after all, and it may not reflect the real experimental data well.

In addition, since there is no ground truth information for the phase transition, the process of selecting/creating the training set is still limited. When the data is not correctly labeled and lacks some key explanatory information, we can only choose some representative spectra as training data, thus reducing the efficiency and validity of the supervised learning algorithms.

Moreover, in our current work, only one data set is used. To improve reliability and validity, multiple data sets should be used for performance evaluation and comparison.

5 Conclusion and Future Work

In this work, we provide a simple and strong baseline range from supervised deep neural networks to unsupervised spectral clustering architecture for time series spectra data classification. Here, the PCA method is used as data preprocessing to reduce the dimensionality and speed up the subsequent training or clustering process. The state-of-the-art supervised LSTM-based and transformer-based models are applied for spectra data classification. In these two methods, the context between different time series (sequential correlation of time series) is not considered, but only the connection between different features. Despite this, both methods achieve 100% classification confidence, a clear boundary can be found. Regarding the training time, the Transformer-based method (0.204 s) consumes more time than the LSTM-based method (0.164 s). The unsupervised spectral clustering method is also shown to be very suitable for the HED spectra data analysis with non-flat geometries. It achieves 100% classification confidence and consumes the least amount of time (0.069 s). In addition, we provide the data analysis scripts as Jupyter notebooks for reproducibility.

In the future, for the LSTM-based and transformer-based models, we will consider using the connection between different spectral samples to better utilize the advantages of these two algorithms in time series processing. Currently, the parameters and hyperparameters of these algorithms in our work are manually selected. In subsequent research, we consider conducting parameter analysis work, for example, using some optimization algorithms to fine-tune these parameters. We will also consider applying other different deep neural network architectures, such as convolutional neural network (CNN) and its combination with LSTM or attention mechanism, to improve the model architecture of spectral classification tasks. And in future work, an end-to-end classification model without preprocessing will be introduced. Similarly, other different unsupervised clustering algorithms can be explored and compared to provide a strong baseline. At the same time, in order to better evaluate and verify the algorithm, multiple data sets from multiple experiments could be tested.

Acknowledgement. The authors would like to thank Christian Plueckthun and Zuzana Konopkova at European XFEL for providing the HED experimental spectral data.

This work was supported by China Scholarship Council (CSC). Furthermore, Péter Hegedűs was supported by the Bolyai János Scholarship of the Hungarian Academy of Sciences.

References

1. Nakatsutsumi, M., et al.: Scientific Instrument High Energy Density Physics (HED) (2014)
2. LeCun, Y., Bengio, Y., Hinton, G.: Deep learning. Nature **521**, 436–444 (2015)
3. Edelen, A., et al.: Opportunities in machine learning for particle accelerators. arXiv:1811.03172 (2018)
4. Wu, N., Green, B., Ben, X., O'Banion, S.: Deep transformer models for time series forecasting: The influenza prevalence case. arXiv:2001.08317 (2020)
5. Lai, G., Chang, W.C., Yang, Y., Liu, H.: Modeling long-and short-term temporal patterns with deep neural networks. In: The 41st International ACM SIGIR Conference on Research & Development in Information Retrieval, pp. 95–104 (2018)
6. Hochreiter, S., Schmidhuber, J.: Long short-term memory. Neural Comput. **9**(8), 1735–1780 (1997)
7. Hammerla, N.Y., Halloran, S., Plötz, T.: Deep, convolutional, and recurrent models for human activity recognition using wearables. arXiv:1604.08880 (2016)
8. Lipton, Z.C., Kale, D.C., Elkan, C., Wetzel, R.: Learning to diagnose with LSTM recurrent neural networks. arXiv:1511.03677 (2015)
9. Wu, H., Prasad, S.: Convolutional recurrent neural networks for hyperspectral data classification. Remote Sens. **9**(3), 298 (2017)
10. Vaswani, A., et al: Attention is all you need. arXiv:1706.03762 (2017)
11. Bertasius, G., Wang, H., Torresani, L.: Is Space-Time Attention All You Need for Video Understanding?. arXiv:2102.05095 (2021)
12. Garnot, V.S.F., Landrieu, L., Giordano, S., Chehata, N.: Satellite image time series classification with pixel-set encoders and temporal self-attention. In: Proceedings of the IEEE/CVF Conference on Computer Vision and Pattern Recognition, pp. 12325–12334 (2020)

13. Wang, Z., Yan, W., Oates, T.: Time series classification from scratch with deep neural networks: a strong baseline. In:2017 International joint conference on neural networks (IJCNN), pp. 1578–1585. IEEE (2017)
14. Shih, S.-Y., Sun, F.-K., Lee, H.: Temporal pattern attention for multivariate time series forecasting. Mach. Learn. **108**(8–9), 1421–1441 (2019). https://doi.org/10.1007/s10994-019-058 15-0
15. Zerveas, G., Jayaraman, S., Patel, D., Bhamidipaty, A., Eickhoff, C.: A Transformer-based Framework for Multivariate Time Series Representation Learning. arXiv:2010.02803 (2020)
16. He, X., Chen, Y., Lin, Z.: Spatial-spectral transformer for hyperspectral image classification. Remote Sens. **13**(3), 498 (2021)
17. Zhang, S., Li, X., Zong, M., Zhu, X., Cheng, D.: Learning k for knn classification. ACM Trans. Intell. Syst. Technol. **8**(3), 1–19 (2017)
18. Vitale, R., Bevilacqua, M., Bucci, R., Magri, A.D., Magri, A.L., Marini, F.: A rapid and non-invasive method for authenticating the by NIR spectroscopy and chemometrics. Chemometr. Intell. Lab. Syst. **121**, 90–99 (2013)
19. Chen, H., Lin, Z., Tan, C.: Nondestructive discrimination of pharmaceutical preparations using near-infrared spectroscopy and partial least-squares discriminant analysis. Anal. Lett. **51**, 564–574 (2018)
20. Zou, A.M., Shi, J., Ding, J., Wu, F.X.: Charge state determination of peptide tandem mass spectra using support vector machine (SVM). IEEE Trans. Inf Technol. Biomed. **14**(3), 552–558 (2010)
21. da Costa, N.L., Llobodanin, L.A.G., de Lima, M.D., Castro, I.A., Barbosa, R.: Geographical recognition of Syrah wines by combining feature selection with Extreme Learning Machine. Measurement **120**, 92–99 (2018)
22. Zheng, W., Shu, H., Tang, H., Zhang, H.: Spectra data classification with kernel extreme learning machine. Chemomet. Intell. Laboratory Syst. **192**, 103815 (2019)
23. Von Luxburg, U.: A tutorial on spectral clustering. Stat. Comput. **17**(4), 395–416 (2007)
24. Jia, H., Ding, S., Xu, X., Nie, R.: The latest research progress on spectral clustering. Neural Comput. Appl. **24**(7–8), 1477–1486 (2013). https://doi.org/10.1007/s00521-013-1439-2
25. Tan, N., Sun, Y.D., Wang, X.S., Huang, A.M., Xie, B.F.: Research on near infrared spectrum with principal component analysis and support vector machine for timber identification. Spectrosc. Spectr. Anal. **37**, 3370–3374 (2017)
26. Jolliffe, I.T., Cadima, J.: Principal component analysis: a review and recent developments. Philos. Trans. Royal Soc. A: Math. Phys. Eng. Sci. **374**(2065), 20150202 (2016)
27. Van Houdt, G., Mosquera, C., Nápoles, G.: A review on the long short-term memory model. Artif. Intell. Rev. **53**(8), 5929–5955 (2020). https://doi.org/10.1007/s10462-020-09838-1
28. Mall, R., Langone, R., Suykens, J.A.: Kernel spectral clustering for big data networks. Entropy **15**(5), 1567–1586 (2013)
29. White, S., Smyth, P.: A spectral clustering approach to finding communities in graphs. In: Proceedings of the 2005 SIAM International Conference on Data Mining, Newport Beach, CA, USA, 21–23 April 2005; pp. 274–285 (2005)
30. Catak, F.O., Aydin, I., Elezaj, O., Yildirim-Yayilgan, S.: Practical implementation of privacy preserving clustering methods using a partially homomorphic encryption algorithm. Electronics **9**(2), 229 (2020)
31. Matsumoto, M., Nishimura, T.: Mersenne twister: a 623-dimensionally equidistributed uniform pseudo-random number generator. ACM Trans. Model. Comput. Simul. **8**(1), 3–30 (1998)
32. Kingma, D.P., Ba, J.: Adam: A method for stochastic optimization. arXiv:1412.6980.(2014)
33. Karim, F., Majumdar, S., Darabi, H., Chen, S.: LSTM fully convolutional networks for time series classification. IEEE Access **6**, 1662–1669 (2017)

34. Rußwurm, M., Körner, M.: Self-attention for raw optical satellite time series classification. ISPRS J. Photogramm. Remote. Sens. **169**, 421–435 (2020)
35. Karim, F., Majumdar, S., Darabi, H., Harford, S.: Multivariate LSTM-FCNs for time series classification. Neural Netw. **116**, 237–245 (2019)
36. Belagoune, S., Bali, N., Bakdi, A., Baadji, B., Atif, K.: Deep learning through LSTM classification and regression for transmission line fault detection, diagnosis and location in large-scale multi-machine power systems. Measurement **177**, 109330 (2021)
37. Interdonato, R., Ienco, D., Gaetano, R., Ose, K.: DuPLO: A DUal view point deep learning architecture for time series classification. ISPRS J. Photogramm. Remote. Sens. **149**, 91–104 (2019)
38. Behera, R.K., Jena, M., Rath, S.K., Misra, S.: Co-LSTM: Convolutional LSTM model for sentiment analysis in social big data. Inf. Process. Manage. **58**(1), 102435 (2021)
39. Ma, J., Shou, Z., Zareian, A., Mansour, H., Vetro, A., Chang, S.F.: CDSA: cross-dimensional self-attention for multivariate, geo-tagged time series imputation. arXiv:1905.09904 (2019)
40. Cho, K., et al.: Learning phrase representations using RNN encoder-decoder for statistical machine translation. arXiv:1406.1078 (2014)
41. Jebara, T., Song, Y., Thadani, K.: Spectral clustering and embedding with hidden markov models. In: Kok, J.N., Koronacki, J., Lopez, R., de Mantaras, S., Matwin, D.M., Skowron, A. (eds.) Machine Learning: ECML 2007, pp. 164–175. Springer Berlin Heidelberg, Berlin, Heidelberg (2007). https://doi.org/10.1007/978-3-540-74958-5_18
42. Abayomi-Alli, A., Abayomi-Alli, O., Vipperman, J., Odusami, M., Misra, S.: Multi-class classification of impulse and non-impulse sounds using deep convolutional neural network (DCNN). In: Misra, S., (eds.) ICCSA 2019. LNCS, vol. 11623, pp. 359–371. Springer, Cham (2019). https://doi.org/10.1007/978-3-030-24308-1_30
43. Ismail Fawaz, H., Forestier, G., Weber, J., Idoumghar, L., Muller, P.-A.: Deep learning for time series classification: a review. Data Min. Knowl. Disc. **33**(4), 917–963 (2019). https://doi.org/10.1007/s10618-019-00619-1
44. Lazzeri, F.: Machine Learning for Time Series Forecasting with Python®. Wiley (2020). https://doi.org/10.1002/9781119682394
45. VanderPlas, J.: Python data science handbook: Essential tools for working with data. "O'Reilly Media, Inc." (2016)

Design of Smart Cities Dimensions Using the SmartCitySysML Profile

Layse Santos Souza(iD) and Michel S. Soares(✉)(iD)

Department of Computing Federal University of Sergipe, São Cristóvão, Brazil
michel@dcomp.ufs.br

Abstract. Dimensions of smart cities are identified and described from essential factors and characteristics to improve efficiency, sustainability, and quality of life for the citizens living in these cities. It is possible to note in the literature that the domains areas are not yet consolidated for structuring the dimensions of a smart city. In this article, the main idea is to describe the extension of a SysML profile to model dimensions of smart cities as native elements of system design. The profile extension, named SmartCitySysML, has been extended from SysML Internal Block Definition diagrams. The conception of this extension arose from the need to think about different dimensions to separate interests and to improve the focus on problem-solving. As a result, the SmartCitySysML profile facilitates the use of common elements of smart cities and provides a visual representation to evaluate the quality of diagrams from a practical point of view, as it provides using common terminology well-known by the stakeholders that are responsible for managing a variety of aspects of a smart city.

Keywords: SysML · Smart Cities · Dimensions

1 Introduction

Modern life in cities is highly dependent on infrastructures such as roads, energy, water, and waste supply. These infrastructures are in high demand by citizens and organizations, and their design and maintenance are crucial to our daily activities. Cities infrastructures' receive data and retrieve information, and consequently present high complexity and demand, which leads to the need to apply Information and Communication Technologies and Processes for their design, control, and management.

The term smart city generally refers to the search and identification of smart solutions that allow modern cities to improve the quality of services provided to citizens through creativity, innovation, and decision-making in a fast and efficient way [11]. A smart city has a good prospective performance in the economy, improves governance and mobility, and provides better daily life for citizens [15]. According to Nilssen [23], smart cities are considered as representations of holistic ideas and sustainable development, considering the focus on technology,

O. Gervasi et al. (Eds.): ICCSA 2021, LNCS 12957, pp. 69–83, 2021.
https://doi.org/10.1007/978-3-030-87013-3_6

human resources, and collaborative governance, or the combination of the three as a defining resource.

Adapting and evolving a city to new processes and applications is a strategy adopted to mitigate the problems generated by urban population growth and rapid urbanization, e.g., air pollution, resource scarcity, waste management, inadequate infrastructure due to deterioration, health concerns, and traffic congestion [7].

Currently, many modeling languages are used for modeling software systems that are responsible for the control of city infrastructures'. SysML [24], for example, is a UML profile applied to systems that include hardware, software, information, processes, people, and procedures. SysML has gained attention in recent years [29–31, 33, 35] as it also models elements of systems that are not software.

This article proposes to identify several areas, separate interests, represent elements focused on the dimensions of a smart city, and improve the focus on problem-solving by adapting an existing SmartCitySysML profile, improved in this article.

Dimensions proposed in the SmartCitySysML profile have been identified and described from essential factors for a smart city to improve efficiency, sustainability, and quality of life for the citizens of these cities. For the dimensions of the SmartCitySysML profile, the SysML Internal Block diagram is extended to describe the internal structure of a block in terms of properties and connectors between properties. A block can include elements, properties, values, parts, and references to other blocks. In the SmartCitySysML profile, the SysML Internal Block diagram is used to describe the main dimensions of a smart city.

2   Background

This section presents a brief overview of the concepts of Smart Cities and SysML.

2.1   Smart Cities

A smart city is a safe, efficient, and environmentally friendly urban center with infrastructure designed, built, and maintained through technology [36]. A smart city can be explained in terms of complex services and products designed to provide solutions to efficiently improve the management of modern cities. These solutions gather information from citizens about their activities, preferences, and habits [34, 41]. Smart cities depend upon creative and knowledge resources to maximize their innovation potential.

Smart cities are portrayed as the association of several connected networks, that is, an integrated and multidimensional system that provides continuous data on the movements of people and materials in terms of the flow of decisions on the physical and social form of the city to face urban challenges [3, 13]. Smart cities act as distributed systems to facilitate the analysis and interpretation of large-scale, real-time data, the creation of new urban services, and the deployment and optimization of infrastructures [25, 27].

Urban challenges stimulated the search for better quality services, therefore, they encouraged cities to find a way to integrate technology in all aspects of the urban environment to offer better quality of life to citizens [4]. According to Albino et al. [1], there are four commonest characteristics of emerging smart cities. First, the network infrastructure of a city that permits political and social efficiency and cultural development. Second, a stress on urban development led by companies and inventive activities for promoting urban growth. Third, social inclusion of varied urban residents and social capital in urban development. Finally, the natural environment may be a strategic component for the longer term.

Cities, however, become smart when they make use of Information and Communication Technologies (ICT) to integrate and synthesize these data for some purpose, for example, ways to improve efficiency, equity, sustainability, and quality of life in cities [3]. A smart city is intended as an urban environment that, supported by pervasive ICT systems, can offer advanced and innovative services to citizens to improve the overall quality of their daily life [10, 26].

2.2 Brief Introduction to SysML

SysML [24] has been developed by the Object Management Group (OMG) and International Council on Systems Engineering (INCOSE) to develop a unified language for general-purpose modeling for systems engineering applications. SysML is a UML profile applied to systems that include hardware, software, information, processes, people, and procedures. The SysML diagrams are [24]:

- Activity, Sequence, State Machine, and Use Cases diagrams to model behavior;
- Requirements diagram to model requirements;
- Block Definition, Internal Block, Parametric, and Package diagrams to model structure.

Sequence, State Machine, Use Cases, and Package diagrams have not been changed from UML 2.0, except that their focus is broader, regarding software as well as systems elements. Block Definition, Activity, and Internal Blocks diagrams have been modified from UML, and the Requirements and Parametric diagrams are new [24].

SysML reuses parts of UML and additionally offers new language elements, such as value types, type of quantity, and the opportunity to describe the functionality of systems. Therefore, it allows one to model a wide variety of systems from different perspectives [44]. Current version of SysML, named SysML 1.6, was released in December 2019 [24].

It is worth mentioning that SysML also allows modeling in multiple architectural views, through diagrams that can model the structure, behavior, and requirements of a system. In this way, SysML is characterized through diagrams, models, structural and behavioral elements, effective in specifying requirements, allocations, and restrictions on system properties to support a systems engineering project [5, 14].

SysML limitations have been identified regarding formal modeling and mathematical analysis of models, thus limiting the ability to analyze and verify the specifications of systems [40, 44].

3   Related Work

This section presents work related to the dimensions of a smart city for the elaboration of the extension of a SysML profile.

Giffinger et al. [15] declare that a smart city has six dimensions for urban development with awareness and participation of citizens of a city. These six dimensions, defined by Giffinger et al., are the smart economy, smart people, smart environment, smart governance, smart mobility, and smart living. Cohen [8], Moustaka et al. [19] and Staffans and Horelli [39] also declared the same dimensions, but with different factors and/or characteristics for smart cities.

Nam and Prado [22] present technology, people, and institutions as the main dimensions of an intelligent city. The technology dimension is composed of a digital city, intelligent city, ubiquitous city, wired city, hybrid city, and information city. The people dimension is composed of a creative city, a learning city, a human city, and a knowledge city. Finally, the institution's dimension is composed of a smart community.

Chourabi et al. [7] proposed a framework for smart city dimensions using a set of factors that affect the design, implementation, and usability of smart cities from smart initiatives, shared services, and challenges. These factors are management and organization, technology, governance, policy context, people and communities, economy, built infrastructure, and natural environment.

Reichwein et al. [28] present a high-level system architecture model defined in SysML and a dynamic system model defined in Modelica. The system components, as well as their interfaces, can be represented through the definition of SysML Block Definition and Internal Block diagrams.

Roche [32] represents an intelligent city, digital city, open city, and live city as the main dimensions of an intelligent city. The intelligent city dimension is composed of social infrastructure. The digital city dimensions are composed of an informational infrastructure. The open city dimension is composed of open governance. Finally, the live city dimension is composed of a continuously adaptive urban living fabric.

Barbieri et al. [2] proposed a SysML modeling architecture and design pattern to build models that enhance traceability of information, facilitating the analysis of change influences in later life cycle phases of the system and reuse for future projects.

Jucevičius et al. [17] introduced a model for the dimensions of smart cities based on the characteristics of smart agile, smart digital, smart learning, smart sustainable, smart knowledge-driven, smart network, and smart innovation.

Fagioli [12] states that a smart city must follow standards of quality of life and productivity from social assets, environment, economy, governance, mobility, and housing. The author adds that the main problems of a sensible city are energy, pollution, and infrastructure.

Nilssen [23] elaborated a typology composed of four dimensions of smart cities (technological, organizational, collaborative, and experimental) focused on technological innovations, for example, new practices, products, and services focused on organizational and collaborative innovations.

4 SmartCitySysML Profile Dimensions

This section is an extension of the profile, named SmartCitySysML [38], proposed by the authors themselves and based on the dimensions of people, governance, environment, economy, and mobility. The development of a profile for smart cities arose from the challenges resulting from urban growth and the need to develop smart, transparent, and sustainable urban strategies, as well as the structuring and illustration of the characteristics and peculiarities of a city to make decisions quickly and efficiently.

A profile makes it easier to compose decisions based on better-described facts, encourages stakeholder involvement, promotes the exchange of experiences by analyzing the strengths and weaknesses of a city, engages in the needs of each dimension of a city, and uses smarter technologies and approaches to provide better services and quality of life for citizens.

Dimensions of a smart city are considered as part of the development to be pursued, to allow the equity of present and future generations equity in living conditions and have relevant factors that reflect the important aspects of each intelligent characteristic. These dimensions approximate the needs of the applications and the elements in the field of modeling applications in smart cities, both in design and software architecture, improve the monitoring of the city, as they gather information (incidents or emergencies) from all sources with easy and quick access, act dynamically on the needs of citizens, comprise useful services and information for better decision-making, and offer different types of innovation and initiatives [20, 21, 23].

The Dimensions of people, economy, mobility, governance, environment, and living are illustrated in Fig. 1 and identified in Cohen [8], Giffinger and Gudrun [15], Moustaka et al. [19], and Staffans and Horelli [39].

4.1 People

People, as depicted in Fig. 2, refers to social and human capital, social learning and education, the level of qualification of women and men from different backgrounds, motivation to learn and participate in the co-creation of public life, affinity to lifelong learning, social ethnic plurality, open-mindedness and individuals' participation in public life. Some values are equity, creativity, flexibility, cosmopolitanism, and tolerance [8, 15, 19, 39].

For the people dimension, people's needs have to be identified, modeled, understood, and designed as solutions to provide education and training that

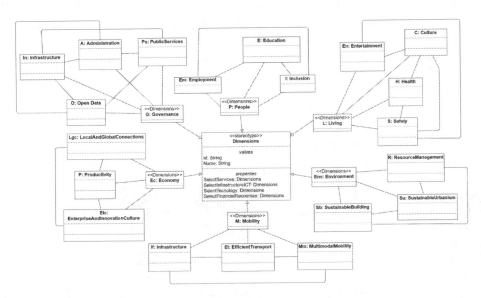

Fig. 1. SysML internal block diagram for the dimensions of interest in a Smart City.

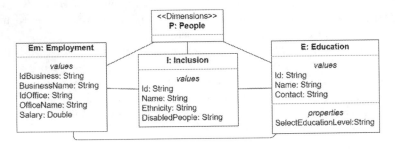

Fig. 2. SysML internal block diagram for the people dimension of a Smart City.

promote innovation and creativity [6]. Kumar and Dahiya [18] complement by stating that smart people are fundamental in a smart city. Smart people are open-minded, have a multicultural perspective, maintain a healthy lifestyle, and are actively involved in the sustainable and harmonious development of their cities. Therefore, without the active participation and involvement of smart people, a smart city will not be able to function.

4.2   Economy

Economy, as depicted in Fig. 3, refers to a number of characteristics, including innovative spirit, entrepreneurship, productivity, economic image, trademarks, flexibility of labor market, internationalization, local and global interconnect-edness, effective production of goods and services for new business models, enhanced by connectivity through Information and Communication Technologies (ICTs) [8, 15, 19, 39].

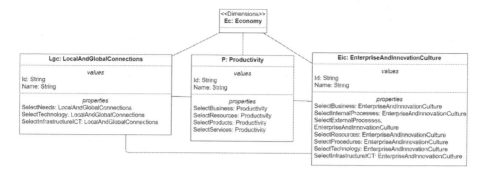

Fig. 3. SysML internal block diagram for the economy dimension of a Smart City.

The economy dimension requires a smart city to present many attributes such as entrepreneurial leadership, valuing creativity, preparing for the challenges and opportunities of economic globalization, as well as driving innovation, making strategic investments, standing out in productivity and flexibility, and insisting on balanced and sustainable economic development and growth [18].

4.3 Mobility

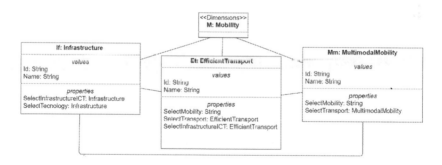

Fig. 4. SysML internal block diagram for the mobility dimension of a Smart City.

Mobility, as illustrated in Fig. 4, refers to sustainable innovative, safe transport systems, mixed modal access, logistics, and communication systems, availability of ICT infrastructure, local and international accessibility. Real-time information improves the management of public and personal mobility, increasing the use of appropriate mobility options and chains, for example, cars, trams, trains, subways, buses and bicycles [8, 15, 19, 39].

The mobility dimension aims to facilitate the flexibility of people within a city, and consequently generates benefits including reduced traffic, reduced travel time and costs, reduced pollution and noise pollution, and greater safety during travel. Furthermore, mobility can change constantly, have immediate communication with users of mobile applications and ensure an intelligent and smooth travel process [42].

4.4   Governance

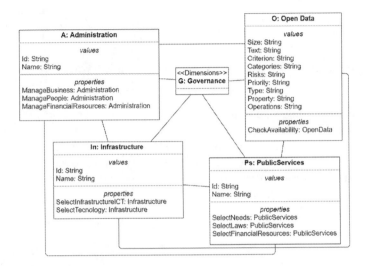

Fig. 5. SysML internal block diagram for the governance dimension of a Smart City.

Governance, as depicted in Fig. 5, refers to public strategies and policies, including urban planning, which enables the co-production of public services, that is, participation in decision-making, public and social services, transparent governance, and political strategies and perspectives. Governance needs to be a transparent process and open data that allows a variety of participation at different levels for decision-making. It is characterized by the orchestration and balance of processes, partnerships, networks, and formal, semi-formal, and informal spheres [8, 15, 19, 39].

The governance dimension plays an important role in a smart city. Its goal is to better serve citizens and communities by linking data, institutions, procedures, and physical infrastructure based on ICT. Also, a smart government allows citizens to be involved in city planning and public decisions. Therefore, the smart government can improve efficiency at the same time as increasing the transparency of information [9].

4.5   Environment

Environment, as depicted in Fig. 6, refers to the care with natural resources and planetary culture, that is, it includes sustainable resource management, pollution

Fig. 6. SysML internal block diagram for the environment dimension of a Smart City.

reduction, and environmental protection with green construction, green urban planning, green production, green buildings, and consumption of green energy [8,15,19,39].

The environment dimension uses the technological resources to detect, act, communicate and enable the infrastructure and technologies to provide services, acquire and exploit knowledge about the environment, so that its citizens live and protect nature, as well as can adapt their preferences and needs [18,37].

4.6   Living

Living, as depicted in Fig. 7, refers to the quality of life and safe environments. It comprises infrastructure to support everyday life, which involves decent housing options, work opportunities, good health conditions, access to nature, touristic attractiveness, individual safety, housing quality, educational and cultural facilities incorporated into social cohesion, enhanced by co-governance [8,15,19,39].

The living dimension is considered a key element for the development and management of a smart city. The services provided by this dimension are based on ICT for the dissemination of information and the involvement of citizens in cultural activities and tourism [16,43].

5   Discussion

A smart city is an urban center that integrates a variety of solutions to mitigate problems generated by the growth of urbanization, improve the efficiency and performance of infrastructures, enable the quality of life of citizens living in these cities, and achieve sustainable urban development with focus on technology, human resources and collaboration of citizens for active governance.

The dimensions of a smart city have relevant factors that reflect the important aspects of each intelligent characteristic, for example, smart people have human and social capital, the smart environment has natural resources, the smart economy has competitiveness, smart mobility has transport and ICT,

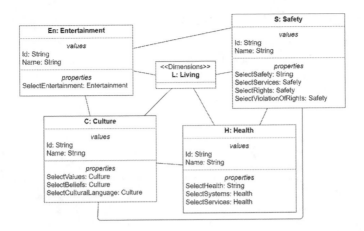

Fig. 7. SysML internal block diagram for the living dimension of a Smart City.

smart living has the quality of life, and smart governance has citizen participation.

In the literature, many modeling languages are used for modeling smart city software systems. In this article, SysML is used to model elements of systems that are not software, that is, elements of the dimensions of smart cities at a higher level of granularity in a complex system.

The SmartCitySysML Dimensions profile extension facilitates the use of common elements of smart city dimensions and provides a visual representation to assess the quality of the diagrams from a practical point of view. The conception of this extension arose from the need to think in different dimensions to separate interests and improve the focus on problem-solving.

This profile is extended from the SysML Internal Block Definition diagram and considers the dimensions thinking about modeling systems with SysML for smart cities. During the design process, some challenges related to formalism and consistency arose, mainly due to the lack of software tools that can fully implement all SysML resources.

Dimensions of the SmartCitySysML Dimensions profile, which includes people, governance, economy, mobility, environment, and living, were based on the dimensions presented by Cohen [8], Giffinger and Gudrun [15], Moustaka et al. [19] and Staffans and Horelli [39].

Table 1 illustrates the different dimensions described by various authors of a smart city. The authors of the dimensions are on the horizontal, and the dimensions are on the vertical. SmartCitySysML stands for the dimensions described by the authors of this article, GG stands for Giffinger and Gudrun [15], NP stands for Nam and Prado [22], R stands for Roche [32], N stands for Nilssen [23], and J stands for Jucevičius et al. [17].

In Table 1, it is possible to note that the areas related to dimensions of a smart city are not yet consolidated. For example, in SmartCitySysML, Giffinger and Gudrun [15], and Nam and Prado [22] the people dimension is presented.

Table 1. Dimensions for Smart City.

	SmartCitySysML	GG	NP	R	N	J
People	•	•	•			
Governance	•	•			•	
Economy	•	•				
Mobility	•	•				
Environment	•	•				
Living	•	•				
Technology			•	•	•	•
Institutions			•			
Intelligent				•		
Open				•		
Live				•		
Collaborative					•	
Experimental					•	
Agile						•
Learning						•
Knowledge-driven						•
Network						•
Innovation						•

In SmartCitySysML, Giffinger and Gudrun [15], and Nilssen [23] the governance dimension is presented, in the works of authors, Nam and Prado [22] and Nilssen [23] and Jucevičius et al. [17] the technology dimension is presented, and the other dimensions are presented only once.

It is worth noting that although the dimensions proposed by Giffinger and Gudrun [15] and the dimensions proposed in the SmartCitySysML profile are the same, they have different characteristics. The characteristics and factors of each dimension of the SmartCitySysML profile are described in Sect. 4, while the characteristics and factors proposed by Giffinger and Gudrun [15] are:

- Economy dimension: an innovative spirit, entrepreneurship, economic image and trademarks, productivity, the flexibility of labor market, international embeddedness, and ability to transform;
- People dimension: level of qualification, affinity to lifelong learning, social and ethnic plurality, flexibility, creativity, cosmopolitanism/open-mindedness, and participation in public life;
- Governance dimension: participation in decision-making, public and social services, transparent governance and political strategies and perspectives;
- Mobility dimension: local accessibility, national and international accessibility, availability of ICT-infrastructure and sustainable, innovative, and safe transport systems;

- Environment dimension: lack of pollution of natural conditions, pollution, environmental protection, and sustainable resource management;
- Living dimension: cultural facilities, health conditions, individual safety, housing quality, education facilities, touristic and social cohesion.

The proposal of this article is different from the articles illustrated in Table 1 for including the factors and characteristics of the dimensions of smart cities as native SysML components, adapting the language to represent the elements related to smart cities, using terminology well-known for stakeholders.

Another difference from the articles published by Barbieri et al. [2] and Reichwein et al. [28] is the creation of a SysML profile for smart cities, with the extension of the dimensions, to help in modeling the needs of applications in a smart city both in software design and architecture activities.

6   Conclusion

Modeling software systems for smart cities is a complex activity, as there is not a single standard to be used, since there are many modeling languages proposed in past years, and a diversity of problems and domains. Therefore, a variety of legacy software systems were developed using many different software modeling languages, which are mostly not tailored to express stakeholders' terminology.

The focus of this article is to adapt and extend a SysML profile for smart cities introduced in the article proposed by the authors themselves, named SmartCitySysML, to model systems for smart cities through several important dimensions for smart cities applications.

The proposed extension of the profile, SmartCitySysML Dimensions, arose from the need to think in different dimensions to identify various areas, separate interests, improve the focus of solving problems generated by the growth of urbanization, represent and facilitate the use of common elements of smart city dimensions and provide a visual representation to evaluate quality of the diagrams from a practical point of view.

The dimensions proposed in SmartCitySysML Dimensions were identified and described from characteristics and essential factors for a smart city to improve efficiency, sustainability, and quality of life of citizens of these cities. The SysML Internal Block diagram is used to model the profile dimensions.

It is worth mentioning that this work of developing a profile for smart cities is still in progress. Future work will focus on software modeling and simulation of various case studies of smart cities related to infrastructure systems, for example, traffic signal control, water and sewage treatment, energy, and health information systems.

Acknowledgments. This study was financed by Fundação de Apoio à Pesquisa e à Inovação Tecnológica do estado de Sergipe (FAPITEC/SE) and the Coordenação de Aperfeiçoamento de Pessoal de Nível Superior - Brasil (CAPES) - Finance Code 001.

References

1. Albino, V., Berardi, U., Dangelico, R.M.: Smart Cities: definitions, dimensions, performance, and initiatives. J. Urban Technol. **22**(1), 3–21 (2015)
2. Barbieri, G., Kernschmidt, K., Fantuzzi, C., Vogel-Heuser, B.: A SysML based design pattern for the high-level development of mechatronic systems to enhance re-usability. IFAC Proc. Vol. **47**(3), 3431–3437 (2014)
3. Bibri, S.E., Krogstie, J.: Smart sustainable cities of the future: an extensive inter-disciplinary literature review. Sustain. Urban Areas **31**, 183–212 (2017)
4. Bifulco, F., Tregua, M., Amitrano, C.C., D'Auria, A.: ICT and sustainability in Smart Cities management. Int. J. Public Sector Manag. **29**(2), 132–147 (2016)
5. Biggs, G., Sakamoto, T., Kotoku, T.: A profile and tool for modelling safety information with design information in SysML. Softw. Syst. Model. **15**(1), 147–178 (2016)
6. Calderón, M., López, G., Marín, G.: Smart Cities in Latin America. In: Ochoa, S.F., Singh, P., Bravo, J. (eds.) UCAmI 2017. LNCS, vol. 10586, pp. 15–26. Springer, Cham (2017). https://doi.org/10.1007/978-3-319-67585-5_2
7. Chourabi, H., et al.: Understanding Smart Cities: an integrative framework. In: Hawaii International Conference on System Sciences, pp. 2289–2297 (2012)
8. Cohen, B.: Key Components for Smart Cities. UBM's Future Cities (2012)
9. Cui, L., Xie, G., Qu, Y., Gao, L., Yang, Y.: Security and privacy in Smart Cities: challenges and opportunities. IEEE Access **6**, 46134–46145 (2018)
10. Desogus, G., Mistretta, P., Garau, C.: Smart Islands: a systematic review on urban policies and smart governance. In: Misra, S., et al. (eds.) ICCSA 2019. LNCS, vol. 11624, pp. 137–151. Springer, Cham (2019). https://doi.org/10.1007/978-3-030-24311-1_10
11. Duarte, A., Oliveira, C., Bernardino, J.: Smart Cities - an architectural approach. In: International Conference on Enterprise Information Systems - ICEIS 2015, vol. 2, pp. 563–573 (2015)
12. Fagioli, M.C.: Human smarties: the human communities of the future. In: International Conference on Computational Science and Its Applications - ICCSA 2015, pp. 57–61 (2015)
13. Fernandez-Anez, V., Fernández-Güell, J.M., Giffinger, R.: Smart City implementation and discourses: an integrated conceptual model. The case of Vienna. Cities **78**, 4–16 (2018)
14. Friedenthal, S., Moore, A., Steiner, R.: A Practical Guide to SysML: The Systems Modeling Language, 3rd edn. Morgan Kaufmann Publishers Inc., San Francisco (2014)
15. Giffinger, R., Gudrun, H.: Smart Cities ranking: an effective instrument for the positioning of the cities? Architect. City Environ. **4**(12), 7–26 (2010)
16. Girardi, P., Temporelli, A.: Smartainability: a methodology for assessing the sustainability of the Smart City. Energy Procedia **111**, 810–816 (2017)
17. Jucevičius, R., Patašienė, I., Patašius, M.: Digital dimension of Smart City: critical analysis. Procedia Soc. Behav. Sci. **156**(26), 146–150 (2014)
18. Vinod Kumar, T.M.: Smart environment for Smart Cities. In: Vinod Kumar, T.M. (ed.) Smart Environment for Smart Cities. ACHS, pp. 1–53. Springer, Singapore (2020). https://doi.org/10.1007/978-981-13-6822-6_1
19. Moustaka, V., Theodosiou, Z., Vakali, A., Kounoudes, A.: Smart Cities at risk! Privacy and security borderlines from social networking in cities. In: Companion Proceedings of the the Web Conference 2018, pp. 905–910 (2018)

20. Murgante, B., Borruso, G.: Smart City or Smurfs City. In: Murgante, B., et al. (eds.) ICCSA 2014. LNCS, vol. 8580, pp. 738–749. Springer, Cham (2014). https://doi.org/10.1007/978-3-319-09129-7_53

21. Muvuna, J., Boutaleb, T., Baker, K.J., Mickovski, S.B.: A methodology to model integrated Smart City system from the information perspective. Smart Cities 2(4), 496–511 (2019)

22. Nam, T., Pardo, T.A.: Conceptualizing Smart City with dimensions of technology, people, and institutions. In: International Digital Government Research Conference: Digital Government Innovation in Challenging Times, pp. 282–291 (2011)

23. Nilssen, M.: To the Smart City and beyond? Developing a typology of smart urban innovation. Technol. Forecast. Soc. Chang. 142, 98–104 (2018)

24. OMG: Systems Modeling Language (OMG SysML) Version 1.6 (2019)

25. de Paz, J.F., Bajo, J., Rodríguez, S., Villarrubia, G., Corchado, J.M.: Intelligent system for lighting control in Smart Cities. Inf. Sci. 372, 241–255 (2016)

26. Piro, G., Cianci, I., Grieco, L.A., Boggia, G., Camarda, P.: Information centric services in Smart Cities. J. Syst. Softw. 88, 169–188 (2014)

27. Puiu, D., et al.: CityPulse: large scale data analytics framework for Smart Cities. IEEE Access 4, 1086–1108 (2016)

28. Reichwein, A., et al.: Maintaining consistency between system architecture and dynamic system models with SysML4Modelica. In: International Workshop on Multi-Paradigm Modeling, pp. 43–48 (2012)

29. Ribeiro, F.G.C., Misra, S., Soares, M.S.: Application of an extended SysML requirements diagram to model real-time control systems. In: Murgante, B., et al. (eds.) ICCSA 2013. LNCS, vol. 7973, pp. 70–81. Springer, Heidelberg (2013). https://doi.org/10.1007/978-3-642-39646-5_6

30. Ribeiro, Q.A.D.S., Ribeiro, F.G.C., Soares, M.S.: A technique to architect real-time embedded systems with SysML and UML through multiple views. In: Hammoudi, S., Smialek, M., Camp, O., Filipe, J. (eds.) ICEIS 2017 - Proceedings of the 19th International Conference on Enterprise Information Systems, Porto, Portugal, 26–29 April, vol. 2, pp. 287–294. SciTePress (2017)

31. Ribeiro, Q.A., Ribeiro, F.G.C., Soares, M.S.: A technique to architect real-time embedded systems with SysML and UML through multiple views. In: International Conference on Enterprise Information Systems - ICEIS 2017, vol. 2, pp. 287–294 (2017)

32. Roche, S.: Geographic information science I: why does a Smart City need to be spatially enabled? Prog. Hum. Geogr. 38(5), 703–711 (2014)

33. Rosenberger, P., Gerhard, D., Rosenberger, P.: Context-aware system analysis: introduction of a process model for industrial applications. In: International Conference on Enterprise Information Systems - ICEIS 2018, pp. 368–375 (2018)

34. Sánchez Alcón, J.A., López, L., Martínez, J.F., Rubio Cifuentes, G.: Trust and privacy solutions based on holistic service requirements. Sensors 16(1), 16 (2016)

35. Savoska, S., Ristevski, B., Bogdanoska, A.: A Functional Model of Information System for IT Education Company, pp. 365–372 (2019)

36. Shahidehpour, M., Li, Z., Ganji, M.: Smart Cities for a sustainable urbanization: illuminating the need for establishing smart urban infrastructures. IEEE Electrification Mag. 6(2), 16–33 (2018)

37. Silva, B.N., Khan, M., Han, K.: Towards sustainable Smart Cities: a review of trends, architectures, components, and open challenges in Smart Cities. Sustain. Urban Areas 38, 697–713 (2018)

38. Souza, L.S., Misra, S., Soares, M.S.: SmartCitySysML: a SysML profile for Smart Cities applications. In: Gervasi, O., et al. (eds.) ICCSA 2020. LNCS, vol. 12254, pp. 383–397. Springer, Cham (2020). https://doi.org/10.1007/978-3-030-58817-5_29
39. Staffans, A., Horelli, L.: Expanded urban planning as a vehicle for understanding and shaping smart, liveable cities. J. Commun. Inform. 10(3) (2014)
40. Steimer, C., Fischer, J., Aurich, J.C.: Model-based design process for the early phases of manufacturing system planning using SysML. Procedia CIRP 60, 163–168 (2017)
41. Štepánek, P., Ge, M.: Validation and extension of the Smart City ontology. In: International Conference on Enterprise Information Systems - ICEIS 2018, vol. 2, pp. 406–413 (2018)
42. Šurdonja, S., Giuffrè, T., Deluka-Tibljaš, A.: Smart mobility solutions-necessary precondition for a well-functioning Smart City. Transp. Res. Procedia 45, 604–611 (2020)
43. Vázquez, J.L., Lanero, A., Gutiérrez, P., Sahelices, C.: The contribution of Smart Cities to quality of life from the view of citizens. In: Leitão, J., Alves, H., Krueger, N., Park, J. (eds.) Entrepreneurial, Innovative and Sustainable Ecosystems. AQLR, pp. 55–66. Springer, Cham (2018). https://doi.org/10.1007/978-3-319-71014-3_3
44. Wolny, S., Mazak, A., Carpella, C., Geist, V., Wimmer, M.: Thirteen years of SysML: a systematic mapping study. Softw. Syst. Model. 19(1), 111–169 (2020)

A Scalable Blockchain Implementation Model for Nation-Wide Electronic Voting System

Apeh Jonathan Apeh[1](✉), Charles K. Ayo[2], and Ayodele Adebiyi[1]

[1] Covenant University, Ota, Ogun State, Nigeria
[2] Trinity University, Yaba, Lagos State, Nigeria

Abstract. Blockchain technology adoption rate is fast growing as seen in cryptocurrency and distributed finance (DiFi) domains. It is also getting lots of attention in many other application areas including electronic voting(e-voting) systems. The electronic voting system is an interesting application use case for blockchain because it helps to solve critical problems within that space- the integrity of voting data, the secrecy of the ballot, and single point of failure. This is because of the characteristics that blockchain technology embodies. One of the challenges, however, is with the scalability of the blockchain network, how the blockchain technology can power the scalability of systems built on it. The aim of this paper, therefore, is to present a Blockchain Implementation Model that tackles scalability concerns for E-Voting System. This model can be adaptable in any national election, specifically, Nigeria's national elections. The resulting model would present a scalable electronic voting framework by leveraging the security and integrity infrastructures that blockchain technology brings to bear.

Keywords: Implementation model · Election · Ballot · Electronic voting system · Suffrage · Integrity infrastructure · Digital signature · Public key

1 Introduction

Security is considered the biggest concern with any electronic voting system [1]. This could be either the security of the ballot or even the election result. For an e-voting system to be trusted, people want to see that their ballot is not tempered with, nobody has control to manipulate the outcome of an election.

Blockchain technology has security infrastructures that make the electronic voting system an interesting application use case. These infrastructures include immutability, auditability, decentralization, and smart contract [2]. Leveraging on these properties of the blockchain helps to solve popular problems associated with most e-voting systems (i.e. compromise of the secrecy of the ballot and that of the election results). Despite the promises of blockchain technology, a major challenge has to do with its scalability [1, 3].

Scalability simply means the ability of a computing system to increase or decrease computing resources depending on the workload need of the system. There are two types of scalability in a computing system. These are vertical and horizontal scalability.

© Springer Nature Switzerland AG 2021
O. Gervasi et al. (Eds.): ICCSA 2021, LNCS 12957, pp. 84–100, 2021.
https://doi.org/10.1007/978-3-030-87013-3_7

In vertical scalability, the system scales up or down, depending on the workload. For a scale-up, the system resources like the Random Access Memory (RAM), the processor can increase in size to be able to support the demand of the workload. In a scaled-down scenario, the compute resources will have to reduce in size. In horizontal scalability, however, the system scales out or in. In this situation, there is either an increase or a decrease in the number of system instances available to manage the workload.

In a blockchain network, scalability is simply the measure of the ability of the network to add new nodes. It is also a reflection of its throughput i.e. transactions per second (TPS) [1]. It is one of the performance challenges associated with blockchain. There are different approaches to improving the blockchain scalability available in the literature. Some of these approaches published in the literature are mentioned in Sect. 2.4.

The rest of this paper is organized as follows: Sect. 2 provides a review of the Electronic Voting System, and Blockchain Technology. In Sect. 3, the design of the proposed system is presented; Sect. 4 represents the methodology adopted; Sect. 5 contains the results and discussions.

2 Literature Review

2.1 Electronic Voting System

An electronic voting system is any computing system or electronic device that is used in the conduct of elections. Major components of a typical electronic voting system include haptic touchscreens, thermal printers, smartcard reader, external LCD, Uninterruptible Power Supply (UPS), and a standard computer [4, 5].

This description is typical of most electronic voting systems including the Direct Recording Electronic (DRE) machine used in the United States of America (USA), Netherlands, Brazil, Mexico, Australia, India [6]. These democracies have varying e-voting systems [7, 8] base on their peculiar situations.

For an e-voting system to be considered secured or credible, it must exhibit the following characteristics [9]: fairness, eligibility, privacy, verifiability [10], and coercion-resistance.

2.2 Blockchain Technology

Blockchain technology otherwise known as a Distributed Ledger Technology [2], is a fully distributed, peer-to-peer software network that rides on cryptography and distributed computing as underlying technologies. It makes use of cryptography to host applications and store data in a secured manner and to easily transfer digital instruments(value) that could represent real-world money [11–13].

It uses community validation (i.e. consensus) to keep committed transactions synchronized (this could be cast votes) and ledger replicated across multiple nodes or miners in a way that it is decentralized, transparent, immutable, auditable, persistent, and secured [2, 3, 14, 15]. Figure 1 shows how blockchain technology works [16].

Major steps in how the technology works include: i.Transaction Request ii.Transaction broadcast iii.validation iv.A verified transaction is combined with other

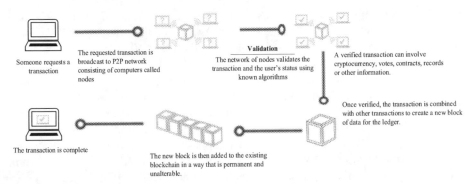

Fig. 1. How blockchain works [16]

Table 1. Blockchain structure

TXN ID	Timestamp	Transaction(txn) details (hash, size, status)	Last txn (current txn hash details, previous txn hash)
1	1585735315(Wed 1st April, 2020; 10:01:55 UTC)	0xfd36ebd112d79348246f 4e08f6a312d80060be7d044 ca7030417a0f6b3b02be6; 234MB, COMFIRMED	0xfd36ebd112d793482 46f4e08f6a312d80060be 7d044ca7030417a0f6b3b 02be6 + genesis hash
2	1586127600 (Sunday, 05-Apr-20 23:00:00 UTC)	0xd980b87683ea92c86edeb 5c2109ac681ebbd8f2f71d 4408b53123c09f782f01a; 230MB, COMFIRMED	0xfd36ebd112d79348246 f4e08f6a312d80060be7d044ca 7030417a0f6b3b02be6 + genesis hash + 0xd980b87683ea92c86edeb 5c2109ac681ebbd8f2f71d4408 b53123c09f782f01a
3	1590042600 (Thursday, 21-May-20 06:30:00 UTC)	0x485155c53688fc0061f7 a91ac211540b73aae020d0ee 9f7e84e7e45c756e6b6f; 301MB; COMFIRM	0xfd36ebd112d79348246 f4e08f6a312d80060be7d044ca 7030417a0f6b3b02be6 + genesis hash + 0xd980b87683ea92c86edeb 5c2109ac681ebbd8f2f71d4408 b53123c09f782f01a + 0x485155c53688fc0061f7a 91ac211540b73aae020d0ee 9f7e84e7e45c756e6b6f

transactions to create a new block of data for the ledger. **v.**The new block is then added to the existing blockchain in a way that is permanent and immutable.

Given that Table 1 typically represents a blockchain, when a new record is inserted into it, the last computed hash is broadcasted to every interested party. Every party doesn't need to keep a copy of the entire transaction history as only a few parties are sufficient. Given that everyone knows the last hash, anyone can verify that the data hasn't been altered since it would be impossible without obtaining a different and thus invalid hash. The only way to tamper with the data while preserving the hash would be to find a collision in the data, and that's computationally impossible. It would require so much computing power that it's practically uneconomical.

Blockchain Deployment Types

There are different types of blockchains. The most common classifications are public, private, and consortium blockchains. Table 2 shows the main properties of these blockchain types.

Table 2. Blockchain types [3]

Properties	Public	Private	Consortium
Ownership	For the people by the people and of the people	Own by individuals or organizations	Own by a group of individuals or organizations
Read/write/audit permission	All	Restricted	Restricted
Consensus Process	Permission-less	Permissioned	Permissioned
Consensus determination	All miners	A selected set of peers	A selected set of peers
Examples	Bitcoin, Ethereum, Litecoin	Multichain	Energy Web

Blockchain has applications in some interesting areas such as Finance, Supply Chain Management, Digital Content Management, Public Services, Telecoms, Electronic Voting. Top four blockchain implementations: Bitcoin, Litecoin, Dogecoin, Ethereum.

Security Features of Blockchain

Blockchain technology is characterized by certain security features [2] that define its applicability in varying domains. These include:

i   Decentralized, peer-to-peer network (i.e. no central controlling authority). This promotes fairness in an e-voting system as it does not allows any peer to have a controlling influence on any outcome.

ii Distributed Ledger- all peers on the blockchain network have a copy of the ledger. They validate transactions using a defined consensus algorithm. This feature promotes fairness in the e-voting system as no single peer/authority can decide acceptable votes. Fairness is about impartiality, equal treatment, and integrity.

iii Immutable history of transaction: each new block contains the hash of the previous one. It is impossible to change existing or committed transactions on a blockchain network without being detected. This feature promotes verifiability in an e-voting system.

iv Transparency: transaction on a blockchain network is only visible to authorized participants. This feature allows for the privacy of a voter in an e-voting system. It also helps enforce coercion-resistance.

v   Smart Contracts: these are business logic deployed on the blockchain, they are shared and validated by participants or peers on the network. This can enforce eligibility of an e-voting system by ensuring failure-proof authentication into the e-voting system.

2.3 Blockchain and E-voting System

E-voting systems generally automate the electoral processes: e-registration, e-verification, e-voting, e-counting, e-transmission, and e-reporting. The ability of e-voting systems to implement these electoral processes shows their potential in enhancing the efficient and effective conduct of elections except for their vulnerabilities [6].

Hao and Ryan [6] posit that most fielded e-voting systems are found to have some vulnerabilities. Most common susceptibilities have to do with the compromise of the voting outcome of election and secrecy of the ballot. Abayomi-Zannu et al. [17] and Awotunde et al. [18] suggest blockchain technology has security infrastructures that the e-voting system can leverage to eliminate the inherent vulnerabilities points. For instance, the blockchain network is a decentralized, peer-to-peer network. This means, in a blockchain network, there is no central controlling authority for validating transactions. Instead, it utilizes the consensus between the peers to validate a transaction. Applying this in an e-voting system would mean that vote cast is a transaction. Also, rather than using the regular server-client deployment model which is prone to single-point-of-failure, a decentralized and consensus-driven approach is used to validate cast votes. Blockchain also ensures that a distributed ledger or record of cast votes exists on all authorized peers on the decentralized network. To ensure that a cast vote cannot be changed, blockchain ensures that transaction history (i.e. history of cast votes) is immutable and it is transparent enough that all authorized participants can view it.

2.4 Scalability Problem in Blockchain

Scalability has been identified as a performance and capacity concern in blockchain technology [1] hence a lot of efforts are on improving it. There have been different solutions proposed to improve it without compromising the security and decentralization of the blockchain. These include solutions that deal with adjusting some system parameters (e.g. the block size of the blockchain network, throughput, or TPS), sharding and consensus strategy of the blockchain (i.e. modifying the consensus mechanism).

i   Block size approach

The block size of a blockchain network indicates the number of transactions a network can validate and add to the ledger per time. The higher the size of the block, the more transactions can be processed per time. Also, the block size of a blockchain network has storage implications on the nodes on the network hence, compressed blocks have less storage overhead. This increases linearly the bootstrap time of existing nodes with growth in the blockchain history and delays the process for adding new nodes as well. The proposed solution to handle this capacity and performance concern is targeted in compressing the block size of the blockchain system [1]. Some of these projects are Segregated Witnesses (SegWit), Bitcoin-cash, block compression, and storage scheme optimization [19, 20].

ii Sharding

This is a traditional technology for the optimization of large commercial database systems. The whole idea is to divide and conquer. It is used in this category of database systems to divide database data into different fragments and get them shared across several servers. This allows for improved search performance and storage management. It is applied in the blockchain space by dividing the whole blockchain network into smaller networks called shards. The nodes are a part of each smaller network fragment.

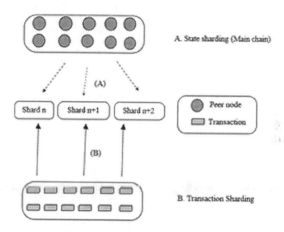

Fig. 2. Sharding architecture [1]

Sharding technology has been used in lots of blockchain projects including Elastico, OminiLedger, RapidoChain, and Monoxide [20–23]. An example of sharding architecture is shown in Fig. 2. The architecture shows that the blockchain network is divided into 3 shards using 3 procedures:

- firstly, each peer in the network (i.e. main net) is assigned to different shards. To reduce the storage overhead of each node, State sharding enables nodes in each shard to only store the state of their shard.
- Transaction sharding distributes transactions across the available shards and allows their parallel processing. Apart from transactions being executed within a single shard, cross-shard transactions are very common in a large system. Consequently, the system must be equipped with some protocols that would handle cross-shard transactions carefully and efficiently.

iii Consensus strategy

Consensus means agreement. So simply, consensus algorithms are those algorithms in a distributed or decentralized network that help them to unanimously take a decision when it is necessary without the need of a third party trusted authority [24]. Its major functions on the blockchain network include ensuring and maintaining decentralized governance, quorum structure, authentication, integrity, non-repudiation, byzantine fault tolerance, and performance [3].

They are critical to the way of working of the blockchain network as a result, the last category of proposed solutions to the scalability concern on the blockchain is the modification of the consensus mechanism. Popular consensus algorithms like Proof of Work(PoW), Proof of Stake and Distributed Denial of Service, Practical Byzantine Fault Tolerance, Hybrid Consensus, and others have gone through varying modifications and improvements geared towards optimizing their TPS and scalability [1].

The original PoW mechanism, for instance, has been improved through the Bitcoin-NG and GHOST projects. Bitcoin-NG improves on the original PoW by dividing time into epochs [1], a leader responsible for transaction serialization is assigned to each epoch. To support this improvement strategy, Bitcoin-NG introduced two types of blocks, namely: key block and microblock. The key block is generated by the miners through the PoW mechanism. It does not contain transaction data and is only used for the election of the leader. The leader is allowed to generate the microblock which contains the packaged transaction data. Consequently, transactions can be processed continually until the next leader that significantly reduces transaction confirmation time and improves the scalability is elected.

GHOST also builds upon PoW but in its case, it re-organizes Bitcoin's data structure to eliminate double-spending [25] attacks, a security concern caused by network delay which has to do with spending the same asset more than once. Another project which improves on PoW is SPECTRE [26]. It utilizes the structure called direct acyclic graph (DAG) to improve the transaction throughput and reduce the confirmation time of Bitcoin.

3 Design

This research proposed a scalable blockchain-based e-voting system (BEV) implementation. As indicated in the network view of our architecture in Fig. 5, our proposed system does not only achieve the end-to-end implementation of the electoral process but more importantly, showcases how scalability can be improved via the combination of lightweight peers and cache database. The e-voting system developed was built on the Ethereum Virtual Machine (EVM) which is the Ethereum blockchain network deployment environment.

The implementation model shown in Fig. 3 is made up of 4 layers interacting together. These include the presentation, business logic, data, and the Ethereum Virtual Machine tiers. The presentation layer which provides the user interface to the blockchain-based (DAPP) e-voting system, is the component via which voters can securely cast their votes. It has the Web3.js API which is a collection of JavaScript libraries that are used

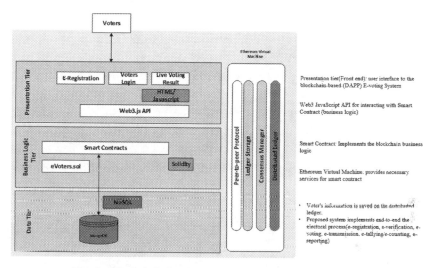

Fig. 3. Blockchain Implementation Framework for e-voting

for interacting with local or remote Ethereum nodes [27] through the smart contract. The business logic tier otherwise known as the application layer hosts the smart contract which implements the blockchain business logic. The data tier implements the state caching on the model's PU modules. The EVM provides critical services like peer-to-peer protocol, consensus manager for the management of the blockchain network.

Unlike the BEV model design [28] presented in Fig. 4, in which voter's registration and verification were done on a centralized system and only the cast votes are placed on the blockchain, the proposed design supports the end-to-end management of the entire electoral process (i.e. e-registration, e-verification, e voting, e transmission, e-counting, and e-reporting) on the blockchain. The proposed design recognizes how critical e-registration and voters' register are to the integrity of a voting result, hence, it implements the voter's database on the immutable, auditable blockchain ledger alongside the other steps in the electoral process. Figure 5 represents the architecture of the proposed design. It shows voters can interface with the proposed model through the voting device for registration and vote cast. Both the voter's details and their votes are signed, encrypted, and submitted on the blockchain network.

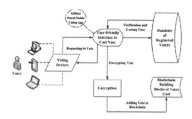

Fig. 4. Existing blockchain-based electronic voting system [28]

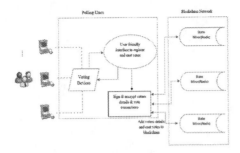

Fig. 5. Proposed blockchain-based e-voting model architecture

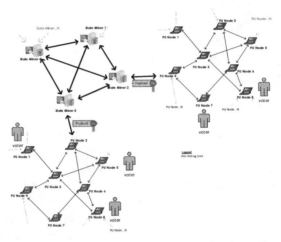

Fig. 6. Network view of the blockchain-enabled model for electronic voting system

The network view of the proposed model as shown in Fig. 6, is made up of two logical blockchains- Federal and State blockchains. This is to better handle latency issues related to querying the blockchain.

The Federal blockchain constitutes 36 state miners (representing the 36 states in Nigeria) and the Federal Capital Territory (FCT). While the State blockchain is made up of all the Polling Units (PU) in each state and the State Miner(node). Miners are nodes on the network with the capability to validate transactions.

The state miners are full nodes while the PU nodes are lightweight. Each full node has a complete copy of the distributed ledger (information about all registered voters and cast votes in the country), can validate new vote blocks, and verify transactions (i.e. cast votes).

For latency's purpose, PU nodes (i.e. lightweight nodes), don't store a full copy of the blockchain- they have a copy of the block header (i.e. metadata) to stay updated with the main blockchain and to verify transactions. Using the web3.js API, a copy of the blockchain with only eligible voters in every state is made available at the respective state PUs.

Communications between state miners and the PUs are digitally signed. The PU sends a payload that is signed with its public key. Hence during voting, voters get verified, then they cast vote. The cast votes are sent as a payload which is digitally signed with each PU public key. If for any reason, the PU loses connectivity to the blockchain, voting would be done offline, but verification gets done online later once connectivity is restored. A wrong actor engaging in double voting would be able to vote offline but when the PU connects, such votes would be invalidated because they had voted.

4 Methodology

The methodology includes the processes and methods followed to implement the proposed design above. The Nigerian Independent National Electoral Commission (INEC) was used as a case study for the blockchain-based model. Nigeria currently conducts her electronic verification(e-verification) using the Smart Card Reader (SCR) [29] and uses the INEC result viewing portal for collation of results as demonstrated in the 2020 Edo state gubernatorial election [30]. Electoral processes like e-voting, e-counting, and e-reporting are still not allowed under the Nigerian Electoral Law [31].

4.1 Setting up the Model

Ethereum network was used to set up the model. This is because, beyond the fact that Ethereum is open source and it provides blockchain developer the ability to build private blockchain networks on top of the ethereum environment when compared with other blockchain networks(Bitcoin, Litecoin, and Dogecoin), it outperforms them with respect to block-release time, transaction size, transaction rate, consensus model and consensus algorithm [32]. The following steps were taken to set up the proposed scalable blockchain-based electronic voting system for national election: Setting up the First Node on the Private Blockchain, Deploying the Smart Contract, Creating the Network, Deploying the Polling Units(PU) Module.

Setting up the First Node on the Private Blockchain
To set up our private blockchain (Dapp) called eVoters, we started with the first node among the three full nodes in our proposed model's proof of concept (PoC). The nodes which are called state miners are setup on the cloud:
eth-node1.codecounty.com, eth-node2.codecounty.com, eth-node3.codecounty.com. Each has Ubuntu Operating System (OS) installed on it. On top of the OS is installed the Ethereum "Geth" application. A secure shell protocol (SSH) is used to connect to each node from a Git bash tool:
$ ssh-i custom-eth.pem ubuntu@eth-node1.codecounty.com.
The "custom-eth.pem" file is the identity file with the public key of the eth-node1.codecounty.com node for a secured connection between the source machine and the blockchain node. Geth is installed to set up a custom/private ethereum node using the command: # sudo add-apt-repository -y ppa:ethereum/ethereum.
Below set of commands is used to update the repositories and install Ethereum alongside its command line (CLI) environment "Geth":

sudo apt-get update.
sudo apt-get -y install Ethereum.

Genesis Block

The genesis block holds the first/initial state of the entire network. In it, the network "blueprint" or "DNA" is determined. The genesis block is created using a genesis file. It is a JSON file with the required parameters to initialize the blockchain. Below is the genesis file used for eVoters:

```
{   "config": { "chainId": 19xx, "homesteadBlock": 0, "eip155Block": 0, "eip158Block": 0 },
    "difficulty": "10000", "gasLimit": "2100000",
    "alloc": {
        "e662...aa87": {"balance":"100000000000000000"},
        "e662...aac6": {"balance":"100000000000000000"},
    } }
```

The chain is a unique identifier for the network and is used in the signing and validation of transactions. The difficulty is used to specify the hash iteration, this directly affects the rate at which new blocks are mined. Note that 10,000 is low difficulty number, "gasLimit" specifies the maximum number amount of gas (fees) allowed for a transaction, while "alloc" pre-funds specified accounts with "Ether".

Once the genesis file has been created the blockchain and genesis block is initialized using the command below: geth --datadir "./db" init genesis.json.

With the above command, a new chain is created and committed in the database. To run the newly created blockchain node use the following command:

```
geth --datadir "./db" --networkid 19xx
```

With this, the first blockchain node is deployed successfully.

Deploying the Smart Contract

An Ethereum based decentralized application isn't complete without the smart contract. A smart contract is a self-executing contract. It is built to enforce an agreement between multiple parties, in this case, an election.

To build and deploy a smart contract, remix and ethfiddle were used as recommended tool. EthFiddle is a browser-based solidity Integrated Development Environment (IDE) which allows users to write and test their solidity codes without deploying to a blockchain while "remix" (which is also a browser-based IDE) generates the bytes codes used to deploy the smart contract and Application Binary Interface (ABI) data which used to interact with the smart contract over the RPC protocol.

Upon generating the byte code of the contract on "Remix" a transaction is created and broadcasted to the network and in response, a transaction hash is generated, this hash acts as a transaction reference and can be used to get the transaction details.

The contract byte data is first read from a file and is used to create a transaction object. The transaction is then signed using a private key and sent to the blockchain network.

Upon propagation, a view into the transaction using the transaction hash generated above would reveal the new contract's address. This address is copied to the "app-config.json" file of the NodeJS application.

Creating the Network

To create a network, first, a new node has to be created, then a second node to communicate and synchronize with the first node. There are different ways to go about this. A simpler alternative is reusing the exact same genesis file and chain ID. Once the node has been created, run geth --datadir "./db" --networkid 1946 console to initialize the node and access its console.

Deploying the Polling Units (PU) Module

So far, we have set up and deployed the state miners on the blockchain network. This is important as the PU module will need the state miner blockchain network for connectivity, voter's verification, validation of cast votes and adding them to the blockchain.

As represented in Sect. 3, the PU is the module of our proposed model that is deployed at various polling units across the country. For our model to run optimally without feeling the full effect of network instability and latency, the PU module is set up with MongoDB to cache voting transactions on the voting device used at every PU. It also has a file called "app-config.json" which the PU module uses to communicate and sync with the federal blockchain network. The file contains critical configuration information like the provider's (parent node) RPC information (URL and port number), the private key, and address of the PU, alongside the application's configurations and smart contract address.

As a proof of concept, the PU module was installed on ten laptops operated by Service Integrators (SIs). These SIs are tech-savvy, well-educated and at different locations. Their laptops have the same specifications except one as indicated in Table 3. From records obtained from these SIs, it takes a maximum of three minutes to get it installed and to set up the PUs for voter verification and voting.

To set up the PU device, the SIs downloaded the PU module from the OneDrive repository, extract and navigate it to the folder where the packaged PU is stored, double click on the "run.bat" file. This installs and connects the PU device to the state miner that it has been configured to connect within the config.json file.

Once the setup is completed, the eVoter web module interface is loaded on port 5000 as shown in Fig. 7 below.

Fig. 7. eVoter web interface

The config.json does not just specify the address of the state miner that each PU should connect to, it also specifies other critical parameters including the private key and address of the state miner the PU is connecting to, contract details; the MongoDB configuration details; the provider parameter defines the state miner which the PU is securely communicating with. This variable also determines the state in which the PU is. MongoDB is a NoSQL (Structured Query Language) Database Management System.

Performance Impact of Proposed Model Design

The proposed design is meant to improve the scalability performance matrix of the blockchain-based e-voting system. The method for implementing this matrix is presented below.

Scalability Matrix

For the purposes of secured communication and scalability, the model design adopts the use of the Rivest, Shamir, Adleman (RSA) encryption scheme. All PUs are set up on-demand to communicate with the state miners on the blockchain network by utilizing the RSA scheme. This means that communication between state miners and the PUs is digitally signed. The PU sends a payload that is signed with its private key. During voting, voters get verified, before voting. The cast votes are sent as a payload which is digitally signed with each PU's private key. If for any reason, the PU loses connectivity to the blockchain network, voting could still be done offline, but verification and validation get done online later when connectivity is restored.

From the scalability standpoint of the proposed model performance, we considered how long it takes to deploy a new PU and the cost of the computing device including the cost of Uninterrupted Power Supply(UPS) and MODEM/subscription for internet connectivity as critical factors. As represented in Sect. 4.1.5, to set up PUs, pre-packaged PU modules are transferred, extracted, and then installed on the computer systems designated as PU nodes. The result from the scalability evaluation done with the ten volunteering SIs from a multinational telecommunications company, each setting up a PU is captured in Table 3.

Overall, the Keccak algorithm, MongoDB, and Web3.js are used to enhance the overall performance of our model by reducing response time between the PU nodes and the state miners on the blockchain network. Also, the more nodes that are added to the blockchain network, the more secure the network becomes since it relies on consensus to verify transactions and validate blocks.

5   Results and Discussions

Base on the aim of this research work which is to advance a scalable blockchain-enabled electronic voting model, we present below performance results from the experimentations conducted with respect to the scalability of our model.

5.1   Scalability

To evaluate the system scalability, we considered the time and cost of setting up the PUs. To set up PUs, we packaged the PU application module, port and install the packaged file created on the computer system designated as PU node. To conduct the scalability evaluation, we engaged ten system integrators (SI) from a multinational telecommunications company that volunteered to participate in setting up a system each as PUs, making ten PUs in effect. Table 3 represents how long it took each of them to set up each PU.

Table 3. Evaluation of systems integrators' setup time

SI ID	Device type	Device RAM size	Processor spec	Estimated cost price (NGN)	PU name	Download time (min)	Setup time (min)
SI1	HP Laptop	16GB	CORE i5	300,000	LA-Ajah	3:00	2:37
SI2	HP Laptop	16GB	CORE i5	300,000	LA-Surulere	4.00	2:50
SI3	HP Laptop	16GB	CORE i5	300,000	LA-Alimosho	2:11	3:42
SI4	HP Laptop	16GB	CORE i5	300,000	R-Ikwerre	3:10	2:31
SI5	HP Laptop	16GB	CORE i5	300,000	R-Bonny	2:20	1:67
SI6	HP Laptop	16GB	CORE i5	300,000	R-Okrika	1:00	2:90
SI7	HP Laptop	16GB	CORE i5	300,000	K-Municipal	3:00	2.50
SI8	HP Laptop	16GB	CORE i5	300,000	K-Gwale	2:00	2.45
SI9	HP Laptop	4.0GB	Pentium	130,000	K-Dala	4:00	3:00
SI10	HP Laptop	16GB	CORE i5	300,000	A-Abaji	2:01	2:17
Average							2.64

From the recorded experiences of the ten SIs who volunteered as electoral technical officers-in-charge of the PUs, it takes an average of 2.64 min to get a PU ready once the module is on hand. Once the PU is set up, voter's accreditation and voting can start immediately provided it is time to start voting as scheduled by the election management body (i.e. the INEC). From experiences in elections in Nigeria, the INEC faces varying difficulties in starting polls at the stipulated time. Apart from logistics challenges like transportation of the INEC staff and sensitive materials to the PUs, at the PUs, it takes a lot of time and effort to get them ready to commence voting. This often leads to frustration and sometimes, the disenfranchisement of the electorate.

As seen in the result obtained in Table 3, we presented how the proposed system can be set up on an average of 2.64 min. This is a far cry from what is obtainable in the existing system manned by the INEC where it takes an average of 10 min to set up or reconfigure the Smart Card Reader (SCR).

The significance of the proposed model setup time is not just in the ability to set up new PUs but also in the ease of deploying replacements for malfunctioning PU modules. This ability to easily scale out is very critical in ensuring that voters are not disenfranchised on account of delays in getting the PUs ready for suffrage.

5.2   Assumptions

i.   All peers on the network have internet connectivity
ii.   Miners do NOT have equal system specification- some miners could have higher compute capacity than those in polling units
iii. Miners and lightweight nodes are added to the private blockchain network on demand
iv.   All miners have a copy of the blockchain
v.   All payloads are digitally signed.

5.3   Conclusion

In this paper, we focus on how to improve the scalability of a blockchain-based e-voting system. We conducted a review of four major blockchain networks (Bitcoin, Litcoin, Dogecoin and Ethereum). The review showed the Ethereum network has better block-release time, transaction size, transaction rate, and consensus algorithm. As a Proof of Concept, a private blockchain-based e-voting system was set up using cloud infrastructure and lightweight nodes called PUs across. The rate of spinning up the ten PUs was recorded. The average PU spin-up time (scalability) was compared with INEC's existing system PU setup time. Our model's was found to be much better.

References

1. Zhou, Q., Huang, H., Zheng, Z., Bian, J.: Solutions to scalability of blockchain: a survey. IEEE Access **8**, 16440–16455 (2020)
2. Sarah, G.: Blockchain- What is the Business Value?. A paper presented at the Oracle Modern Business Talks, Webinar (2018)
3. Zheng, Z., Xie, S., Dai, H., Chen, X., Wang, H.: An overview of blockchain technology: architecture, consensus, and future trends. In: IEEE 6th International Congress on Big Data, pp. 557–564 (2017)
4. Vaibhav, et al.: literature survey- online voting: voting system using blockchain. Int. Res. J. Eng. Technol. **6**(6), 534–536 (2019)
5. Komminist, W., Adolfo. V., Andrea, M.: Experiments and data analysis of electronic voting system. IEEE, pp105–112 (2009)
6. Hao., F., Ryan, P.Y.A.: Practical attacks on real-world e-voting. In: Hao, F., Ryan, P.Y.A., (eds.) Real-World Electronic Voting: Design, Analysis and Deployment, pp. 45–196. Auerbach Publications, US (2016)
7. Ayo, C.K., Adebiyi, A.A., Sofoluwe, A.B.: E-voting implementation in nigeria: the success factors. Int. J. Comput. Sci. Appl. **15**(2), 91–105 (2008)

8. Sheriff, F.F., Ayo, C.K., Oni, A.A., Gberevbie, D.E.: Challenges and prospects of e-elections in Nigeria. In: Proceeding of 14th European Conference on E-Government, Brasov Romania, 13–14 June 2014
9. Mohammad, H.S., Essam, M.: A secure e-Government's e-Voting system. Sci. Inf. Conf. **44**(12), 1365–1373 (2015)
10. Gharadaghy, R., Volkamer, M.: Verifiability in electronic voting explanations for non security experts. 4th International Conference on Electronic Voting 2010 EVOTE 2010 **4**(4), 1–13 (2010)
11. Dannen, C.: Introducing Ethereum and Solidity: Foundations of Cryptocurrency and Blockchain Programming for Beginners. Apress, Brooklyn, New York, USA (2017)
12. Deloittecom. Deloittecom. Retrieved from 20 Nov 2017. https://www2.deloitte.com/content/dam/Deloitte/ie/Documents/Technology/IE_C_BlockchainandCyberPOV_0417.pdf
13. Philip, B.: European Union Parliamentary Research Services; How blockchain technology could change our lives. European Union, Brussels (2017)
14. Ansif, A., Mohsin, R.: Electronic voting with biometric verification offline and hybrid EVMS solution. The Sixth International Conference on Innovative Computing Technology (INTECH 2016), pp. 332–337 (2016)
15. Cortie, V., Constantin, C.D., Francois, D., Benedikt, S., Pierre, Y.S., Bogdan, W.: Machine-checked proofs of privacy for electronic voting protocols. In: 2017 IEEE Symposium on Security and Privacy, pp. 993–1008 (2017)
16. Blockgeekscom. What is blockchain technology?. Retrieved from 17 July 2020. https://blockgeeks.com/guides/what-is-blockchain-technology/ (2020)
17. Abayomi-Zannu T.P., Odun-Ayo I., Tatama B.F., Misra S.: Implementing a mobile voting system utilizing blockchain technology and two-factor authentication in Nigeria. In: Singh, P., Pawłowski, W., Tanwar, S., Kumar, N., Rodrigues, J., Obaidat, M. (eds.) Proceedings of First International Conference on Computing, Communications, and Cyber-Security (IC4S 2019). Lecture Notes in Networks and Systems, vol. 121. Springer, Singapore (2020). https://doi.org/10.1007/978-981-15-3369-3_63
18. Awotunde, J.B., Ogundokun, R.O., Misra, S., Adeniyi, E.A., Sharma, M.M.: Blockchain-based framework for secure transaction in mobile banking platform. In: Abraham, A., Hanne, T., Castillo, O., Gandhi, N., Rios, T.N., Hong, T.-P. (eds.) Hybrid Intelligent Systems: 20th International Conference on Hybrid Intelligent Systems (HIS 2020), December 14-16, 2020, pp. 525–534. Springer International Publishing, Cham (2021). https://doi.org/10.1007/978-3-030-73050-5_53
19. Lombrozo, E., Lau, J., Wuille, P.: Segregated witness (consensus layer) (2015). https://github.com/bitcoin/bips/blob/master/bip-0141.mediawiki
20. Luu, L., Narayanan, V., Zheng, C., Baweja, K., Gilbert, S., Saxena, L.P.: A secure sharding protocol for open blockchains. In: Proceedings of the 2016 ACM SIGSAC Conference on Computer and Communications Security, pp. 17–30. ACM (2016)
21. Kokoris-Kogias, E., et al.: IEEE symposium on security and privacy (SP). IEEE **2018**, 583–598 (2018)
22. Zamani, M., Movahedi, M., Raykova, M.: Rapidchain: scaling blockchain via full sharding. In: Proceedings of the 2018 ACM SIGSAC Conference on Computer and Communications Security, pp. 931–948. ACM (2018)
23. Wang, J., Wang, H.: Monoxide: Scale out blockchains with asynchronous consensus zones. In: 16th USENIX Symposium on Networked Systems Design and Implementation (NSDI 19), pp. 95–112 (2019)
24. Li, X., Jiang, P., Chen, T., Luo, X., Wen, Q.: A survey on the security of blockchain systems. Future Generation Computer System (2017)

25. Sompolinsky, Y., Zohar, A.: Secure high-rate transaction processing in bitcoin. In: Böhme, R., Okamoto, T. (eds.) Financial Cryptography and Data Security, pp. 507–527. Springer Berlin Heidelberg, Berlin, Heidelberg (2015). https://doi.org/10.1007/978-3-662-47854-7_32s
26. Sompolinsky, Y., Lewenberg, Y., Zohar, A.: Spectre: a fast and scalable cryptocurrency protocol. IACR Cryptol. ePrint Arch. **2016**, 1159 (2016)
27. Web3js.readthedocs.io. 2021. web3.js - Ethereum JavaScript API — web3.js 1.0.0 documentation. https://web3js.readthedocs.io/en/v1.3.4/. Accessed on 15 June 2021
28. Dogo, et al.: Blockchain 30: Towards a secure ballotcoin democracy through a digitized public ledger in developing countries. In: 2nd International Conference on Information and Communication Technology and Its Applications (ICTA 2018), pp. 477–484 (2018)
29. INEC (2015). www.inecnigeria.org. www.inecnigeria.org/wp./FactSheet-on-PVC-and-Card-Readers.docx
30. Independent National Electoral Commission. INEC - Result viewing portal. Retrieved from 4 Oct 2020. https://inecelectionresults.com/
31. Independent national electoral commission. Regulations and Guidelines For The Conduct of Elections. Retrieved from 6 Oct 2020. https://www.inecnigeria.org/elections/regulations-and-guidelines-for-the-conduct-of-elections/
32. Hintzman, Z.: Comparing Blockchain Implementations. NCTA Technical Papers. Nctatechnicalpapers.com. https://www.nctatechnicalpapers.com/Paper/2017/2017-comparing-blockchain-implementations. Accessed on 16 June 2021

A Hybrid Metaheuristic Algorithm for Features Dimensionality Reduction in Network Intrusion Detection System

Bukola Fatimah Balogun[1], Kazeem Alagbe Gbolagade[1], Micheal Olaolu Arowolo[2], and Yakub Kayode Saheed[3(✉)]

[1] Department of Computer Science, Kwara State University, Malete, Nigeria
[2] Department of Computer Science, Landmark University, Omu-Aran, Nigeria
[3] School of Information Technology and Computing, American University of Nigeria, Yola, Nigeria
yakubu.saheed@aun.edu.ng

Abstract. The advent of the Internet computer, and thus the amounts of connected computers in the last few decades, has opened vast quantities of intelligence to attackers and intruders. Firewalls are designed to identify, and block potentially harmful incoming traffic based on a predefined rule set. But, as attack tactics evolve, it becomes more difficult to differentiate anomalous traffic from regular traffic. Numerous detection strategies using machine-learning approaches have been suggested. However, there are issues with the high dimensional data of network traffic, the performance accuracy, and the high rate of false-positive and false-negative. In this paper, we propose a hybrid metaheuristic features dimensionality reduction method for Intrusion Detection Systems (IDSs). We used metaheuristic Bat algorithm for feature selection. The Bat algorithm selects sixteen (16) attributes. Subsequently, RNS was used to obtain the residues of the sixteen features selected. Then, the PCA was used to get the residues by extracting it. The experimental analysis was performed on NSLKDD dataset. The propose Bat-RNS + PCA + RF achieved 98.95% accuracy, sensitivity of 99.40% and F-score of 97.70%. The findings were also benchmarked with existing studies and our results were superior.

Keywords: Bat algorithm · Residue number system · Principal component analysis · Random forest · Intrusion detection system · Dimensionality reduction

1 Introduction

Network technology has been a critical component in advancing the industrial revolution 4.0, serving as a platform for the development of industrial technology automation and as a means of sharing knowledge [1]. However, the advancement in communication and information technology is also harmed by several threats to network security. Numerous threats posed by black attackers or ransomware can result in widespread attacks on information technology and computer system [2–5]. Due to the widespread use of the

© Springer Nature Switzerland AG 2021
O. Gervasi et al. (Eds.): ICCSA 2021, LNCS 12957, pp. 101–114, 2021.
https://doi.org/10.1007/978-3-030-87013-3_8

internet computer and increased usage, and access to online content, cyber-crime is also growing in frequency [6, 7]. Intrusion detection is the first line of defense against a security breach [8–10]. As a result, studies focus heavily on security technologies like IDSs, intrusion prevention systems (IPS), firewalls, and unified threat modeling. Intrusion detection detects computer threats by the review of different network records [11, 12].

Intrusion detection models are divided into two types: those that detect misuse and those that detect anomalies. Misuse detection may identify intrusions based on a recognized pattern, referred to as a signature [13, 14]. By detecting deviations from the usual network traffic pattern, anomaly detection may recognize malicious activities [15–17]. As a result, anomaly detection will detect novel anomalies. The issue with current developmental strategies is their high-rate of false-positives and low-rate of false- negatives. Therefore, how to reduce the high rate of false-positives and low-rate of false-negatives have been an important issue in cybersecurity field.

Numerous machine learning based approaches such as genetic algorithm [18–20], SVM [21, 22], RF [22, 23], DT [24], PSO [25], KNN [26, 27], ANN [28, 29], and NB [30, 31] have been proposed to address these issues in the past. None of the techniques, however, can detect all intrusion attempts and resulting in a higher detection accuracy and a lower false alarm rate. As a result, it is essential to incorporate feature selection and classifier techniques in order to improve the efficiency of IDSs.

Feature selection phase is a critical step in solving classification tasks because it leads to the elimination of redundant and irrelevant features, and does not just decreases learning-time nonetheless, also advances classification performance [32, 33]. The methods for selecting features can be categorized as filter, wrapper, or hybrid. Filter methods pick a function subgroup as the pre- processing phase based on a predefined standard and without regard for the classifier's efficiency. Thus, filter techniques are typically less computationally intensive than costly wrapper methods that test feature selection methods using the classification results. Though wrapper methods typically outperform filter techniques in terms of classifier accuracy, the obtained results are often unusable when the classifier is modified. Thus, the methods that combined the filter method and wrapper method is known as hybrid methods. The method considered in this paper can be regarded as wrapper methods.

Efficient and cost-effective IDS are typically built using data mining algorithms as a result of the fact that they can spot intrusions and performing simplifications with ease [34]. Though, such systems are inherently complicated to incorporate and deploy. The inherent complexities of the systems can be divided into dissimilar collections of problem on the basis of accuracy, capability, and adaptability criteria [35, 36]. Yet, IDS developed because of data mining methods, particularly those that are focused on anomaly detection, have a superior rate of false-positive instances than earlier techniques for identification focused on hand-crafted signatures.

One of the most significant obstacles to assessing the efficiency of network intrusion detection systems is the absence of a robust network-protocol based data collection [37]. Majority of the anomaly IDS studies in the literatures were experimented on KDDCup'99 dataset [38]. We utilized the NSLKDD [39] dataset which is a standard dataset for IDS in this research. PCA is used in this work to produce a new collection of uncorrelated characteristics, removing noise and avoiding the use of small variance attributes (that is, variables that are single-valued). Additionally, these newest attributes are chosen for their discriminative potential. Following that, the Random forest algorithm is being used to represent and categorize the feature vectors. Numerous models for intrusion detection have been produced using technique for selection and classification of features. The proposed metaheuristic Bat-RNS model differs from conventional IDS methods in that the Bat algorithm is optimized using residue number system.

This paper is structed as follows. Section 2 is the related work. We highlight the methodology employed in Sect. 3 and in Sect. 4, we present the results and discussion. The conclusion is presented in Sect. 5.

2 Related Work

Numerous investigations have been carried out on IDSs with ML technique. Their primary objective is to address the feature selection issue which is known to be costly in time and efforts, increase the output accuracy, sensitivity, F-score and recommend the standard dataset.

Recently, Ref. [40] proposed a feature selection approach for improving the IDS performance. The authors proposed Information Gain and Ranker technique as the feature selection method and they performed classification with KNN, NB and SVM. The evaluation was done on NSLKDD dataset. The results obtained gave more than 95% accuracy for the three classifiers with low false positive and false alarm rate.

Ref. [41] proposed a model utilizing the LDA and GA as the feature selection algorithms. The LDA is implemented to find the best features set while the GA is presented to obtain the novel features from the fitness score. The experimental analysis was done on KDD Cup'99 IDS dataset.

Ref. [42] presented a wrapper feature-selection approach for network IDS. They used ANN and SVM for the classification method using the NSLKDD dataset. The findings exposed that the ANN with wrapper feature selection outperformed the SVM with wrapper feature selection. The results obtained was efficient as compared to reported works.

Ref. [43] proposed a method on IDS by using a ranking based method with chi-square for feature selection. The classification was done with SVM. The work was evaluated on both KDD Cup99 and the NSL-KDD datasets. The method gave better results on NSL-KDD in comparison to KDDCup'99. Authors in [21] presented feature selection weight and Genetic algorithm for optimizing parameter of SVM. The results obtained showed a reduced rate of false positive and false negative.

Ref. [44] presented a method that used PCA to select subsets of the features based on the PCA eigenvalues. They presented a genetic algorithm based principal components in order to select attributes with higher eigen values to pick the SVM subset attributes for the classification.

Ref. [45] presented three methods for feature selection issues in IDS. They used information reinforcement, gain ratios and correlation based. The authors also suggest a new feature selection method using attribute vitality reduction approach to find less significant features. The findings of their results showed that with features selection they obtained superior performance.

Ref. [46] proposed two feature selection approaches which are correlation coefficient measure and information gain method. The proposed method gave high performance accuracy in detecting attacks on the IDS.

Ref. [47] utilized correlation feature selection and particle swarm optimization as feature selection method to eliminate redundant features. This was done to increase the performance of the classifier accuracy. The experiment was done on KDDCup '99 dataset and findings obtained reached an accuracy up to 99%.

The authors [48] utilize K-means method of clustering for feature engineering. In this method, the evaluation value of the correlation is first determined in which a cluster is molded founded on the clustering algorithm K-means.

3 Materials and Method

We presented the proposed methodology in this section. In the first line of our methodology, we used metaheuristic Bat algorithm for feature selection that belong to the family of wrapper techniques. The Bat algorithm selects sixteen (16) attributes. Subsequently, the fusion of RNS was performed on the sixteen features selected from the Bat algorithm to obtain the residues of the sixteen features selected. Then, the PCA was used to get the residues by extracting it. PCA is used in this work to produce a new collection of uncorrelated characteristics, removing noise and avoiding the use of small variance (that is, attributes that are single-valued). Additionally, these newest attributes are chosen for their discriminative potential. Following that, the Random forest algorithm was implemented to model and categorize the feature vector.

3.1 Bat Algorithm

The Bat Algorithm was created in response to bats' echolocation activity. Bats typically produce a brief tone pulse and detect a fractional echo in a second, that is employed to assess their distance after an entity [49]. Additionally, they possess the ability to discriminate between obstacles and target, which enables them to search in completely dim environments [50]. Each bat represents a solution in the BAT algorithm, which is algorithm for population-based evolution. It was created using the echolocation activity of virtual bats as a guide. This ability allows them to detect their prey's location. For echolocation, frequency modulated pulses are used [51]. Because as bat gets closer to its prey, the volume of their reverberation decreases and the rate of the sound pulse increases.

3.2 Principal Component Analysis

PCA is a commonly used algorithm for mining the most important information from a dataset in a variety of applications [52, 53]. Indeed, it has been successfully applied to applications involving facial recognition. PCA is used in this case to generate an entirely new collection of unrelated attributes drawn from a collection of related attributes [54, 55]. Therefore, PCA produces a collection of orthogonal functions that are used to shown data as a weighted sum of those basis vectors [56].

3.3 Residue Number System

For many decades, the residue number system (RNS) has been a significant area of investigation in computer arithmetic, owing to its carry-free design, which enables the development of architectures for high-performance computing with superior delay requirements [57]. RNS have several benefits over binary number systems in general. This is due to their intrinsic characteristics, which include the absence of carry, parallelism, modularity, and fault tolerance [58].

3.4 Random Forest Algorithm

Random Forests are algorithms for supervised learning [59]. RF is a type of ML technique that combines many decision trees to construct an algorithm for generating an accurate and robust prediction equation for results. These multiple trees are created arbitrarily and trained for a particular action that becomes the model's final outcome [60]. RF is usually utilized in distributed denial of service attack prediction [61] and anomaly prediction.

3.5 Description of NSLKDD Dataset

The experimental work was carried out using the NSLKDD dataset, which is a typical dataset for intrusion detection. NSLKDD was created by Tavallaee et al. to address the inherent issues with the KDDCupp '99 data collection, as mentioned in [62]. However, some of the issues addressed by McHugh in [63] persist in this latest version of the dataset, and it may not be a complete illustration of actual real networks. This dataset is still used in most modern NIDS research, so we assume it is still a useful benchmark for researchers to compare various methods. The NSL-KDD database has a similar structure to the KDD Cup '99 dataset (that is it has normal traffic or twenty-two (22) attack patterns, and 41 attributes). For our evaluations, we will use the entire NSL-KDD dataset, the structure of which has been also shown in Table 1.

4 Results and Discussions

We used metaheuristic Bat algorithm with the fusion of RNS for feature selection in which sixteen (16) attributes were selected out of forty (40) attributes with one class label. PCA is then used for feature extraction. Thus, RF model was used for the classification in terms accuracy, false alarm, sensitivity, F-score, precision, and specificity. The feature selection time and the classifier training time was also noted in our experimental analysis. About 25% of the NSLKDD dataset was used for testing the model and 75% was used for training.

4.1 Performance Evaluation Metrics

i. True Positive rate (TP)/Sensitivity: Data about an attack that has been correctly identified as such.

ii. False Positive rate (FP): Data that is normal that has been mislabeled as an attack data.

Table 1. Attributes of the NSLKDD dataset

Attribute no	Attribute name	Attribute no	Attribute name	Attribute no	Attribute name
A1	Duration	A15	Su attempted	A29	Same server rate
A2	Type of protocol	A16	Number root	A30	Diff server rate
A3	Service	A17	Number file creation	A31	Srv diff host rate
A4	Flag	A18	Number shells	A32	Dst host count
A5	Source bits	A19	Number access files	A33	Dst host server count
A6	Destination bits	A20	Number outbound commands	A34	Dst host same server rate
A7	Land	A21	Is host log in	A35	Dst host diff server rate
A8	Error fragment	A22	Is guest log in	A36	Dst host same source port rate
A9	Critical	A23	Count	A37	Dst host server diff host rate
A10	Hot	A24	Server count	A38	Dst host serror rate
A11	Number Unsuccessful logins	A25	Server error rate	A39	Dst host server error rate
A12	Logged in	A26	Srverror rate	A40	Dst host rerror rate
A13	Num compromise	A27	R error rate	A41	Dst host srvr error rate
A14	Source shell	A28	Srverror rate	A42	Class Label

iii. True Negative rate (TN)/Specificity: Data that is normal that has been correctly categorized.

iv. False Negative rate (FN): Data that is attack that has been labeled incorrectly as normal data.

The following performance measures were adopted in this paper to evaluate the performance of the model.

$$\text{Accuracy} = \frac{TP + TN}{TP + TN + FP + FN} \tag{1}$$

The proportion of the total number of valid classifications is measured by the accuracy. The most critical measures in an intrusion detection system is accuracy [40, 64]. The accuracy, sensitivity, specificity, precision and F-score of our proposed model were used to evaluate its efficiency.

$$\text{Sensitivity} = \frac{TP}{TP + FN} \tag{2}$$

The sensitivity is a calculation that divides the number of valid classifications by the number of missing entries.

$$\text{Specificity} = \frac{TN}{FP + TN} \tag{3}$$

Specificity is proportional to the number of records admitted correctly, and it refers to the number of normal records known as normal.

$$\text{Precision} = \frac{TP}{TP + FP} \tag{4}$$

Precision is computed by separating the number of correctly classified instances by the amounts of incorrect categories.

$$\text{False Alarm} = \frac{FP}{FP + TN} \tag{5}$$

The false alarm rate calculates the percentage of benign incidents reported incorrectly as malicious.

$$\text{F - Score} = 2 \cdot \frac{Precision.Sensitivity}{Precision + Recall} \tag{6}$$

The F-score is a derived effectiveness metric that computes the harmonic mean of recall and precision.

4.2 Experimental Results of Bat-RNS + PCA + RF

The time taken by the metaheuristic Bat algorithm with the fusion of RNS for feature selection is depicted in Table 2 with the RF training time. The time taken to selects the sixteen features was 56.43 s with the RF training time of 22.05 s.

The performance measures of the proposed method Bat-RNS+PCA+RF is given in Table 3. The proposed method gave an accuracy of 98.95%, 99.4% sensitivity, 95.26% specificity, 96.0% precision and F-score of 97.7%

The feature selection time versus the training time is revealed in Fig. 1. The time taken by the proposed model to select the significant attributes is about 56.43 s. Whereas, the

Table 2. Feature selection time and training time

Feature selection time (s)	Training time (s)
56.43	22.05

Table 3. Performance measures of metaheuristic Bat-RNS + PCA + RF

Model/Metrics	Accuracy	Sensitivity	Specificity	Precision	F-score
Bat-RNS + PCA + RF	98.95	99.40	95.26	96.00	97.70

Fig. 1. Time taken for feature selection and training the proposed model

training time is 22.05 s. This is as a result of the facts that the metaheuristic Bat algorithm has eliminated the redundant features which made it possible for the RF classification algorithm to have few times for training the model.

The performance measures of the proposed model are depicted in Fig. 2. The proposed model gave higher sensitivity as compared to the accuracy, specificity, precision and F-score. Whereas, the accuracy gave higher value than the specificity, precision and f-score. The specificity gave the lowest performance as compared to other measures.

4.3   Comparison with the Recent Studies in IDS

The performance measures of the proposed model were bench marked with the existing model as presented in Table 4. As evident in Table 4, the proposed Bat-RNS+PCA+RF gave outstanding accuracy, sensitivity and F-score. However, the existing studies also gave better results in terms of accuracy. Though, we cannot

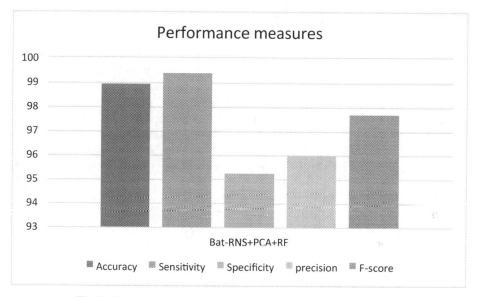

Fig. 2. Performance measures of the proposed Bat-RNS+PCA+RF

claim that the proposed Bat-RNS+PCA+RF outperforms the existing studies in all IDS performance measures, since all other metrics were unknown for the previous studies. In terms of validation dataset, the NSLKDD dataset was established to be the standard dataset. Our proposed method was evaluated on NSLKDD. However, some previous studies as shown in Table 4 still relied on KDDCup'99 which has some inherent issues as noted in [62].

Table 4. Performance of Bat-RNS + PCA + RF with the recent works in IDS

Authors	Accuracy	Sensitivity	F-score	Datasets
Saheed et al. [40]	94.00	x	X	NSLKDD
Kasliwal et al. [41]	83.25	x	85.2	KDDCup'99
Taher et al. [42]	94.02	x	X	NSLKDD
Thaseen et al. [43]	98.00	X	X	NSLKDD
Mukherjee et al. [45]	98.80	X	X	NSLKDD
Tsang et al. [65]	98.70	X	X	KDDCup'99
Raman et al. [66]	97.14	96.27	X	KDDCup'99
Proposed method	**98.95**	**99.40**	**97.70**	**NSLKDD**

5 Conclusion and Future Work

The traffic in network dataset is very huge with large number of distributions of connections of protocol. IDS with constraint of time find it difficult to process the whole network dataset. Hence, feature dimensionality is important for IDSs. Also, the feature selection phase is known to be critical both in efforts and time. Therefore, finding an effective and efficient feature dimensionality reduction is an issue in IDS. We proposed a metaheuristic Bat-RNS for feature dimensionality in this paper to selects the significant attributes in the network dataset. We adopt PCA for the feature extraction and performed our classification with RF algorithm. The experimental analysis was performed on the NSLKDD dataset. The results findings revealed an accuracy of 98.95%, sensitivity of 99.40% and F-score of 97.70%. Our results were also bench mark with existing studies and our findings showed better performance. The future work would be to introduce a deep learning method for IDS with the fusion of RNS.

References

1. Aziz, M.N., Ahmad, T.: Cluster analysis-based approach features selection on machine learning for detecting intrusion. Int. J. Intell. Eng. Syst. **12**(4), 233–243 (2019). https://doi.org/10.22266/ijies2019.0831.22
2. Gunduz, M.Z., Das, R.: Cyber-security on smart grid: threats and potential solutions. Comput. Netw. **169**, 107094 (2020). https://doi.org/10.1016/j.comnet.2019.107094
3. Alenezi, M.N., Alabdulrazzaq, H., Alshaher, A.A., Alkharang, M.M.: Evolution of malware threats and techniques: a review. Int. J. Commun. Networks Inf. Secur. **12**(3), 326–337 (2020)
4. Yaacoub, J.P.A., Salman, O., Noura, H.N., Kaaniche, N., Chehab, A., Malli, M.: Cyber-physical systems security: limitations, issues and future trends. Microprocess. Microsyst. **77**, 103201 (2020). https://doi.org/10.1016/j.micpro.2020.103201
5. Ogonji, M.M., Okeyo, G., Wafula, J.M.: A survey on privacy and security of Internet of Things. Comput. Sci. Rev. **38**, 100312 (2020). https://doi.org/10.1016/j.cosrev.2020.100312
6. Alaei, P., Noorbehbahani, F.: Incremental anomaly-based intrusion detection system using limited labeled data. In: 2017 3rd International Conference on Web Research ICWR 2017, pp. 178–184 (2017). https://doi.org/10.1109/ICWR.2017.7959324
7. Song, H., Lynch, M.J., Cochran, J.K.: a macro-social exploratory analysis of the rate of interstate cyber-victimization. Am. J. Crim. Justice **41**(3), 583–601 (2015). https://doi.org/10.1007/s12103-015-9308-4
8. Khan, K., Mehmood, A., Khan, S., Khan, M.A., Iqbal, Z., Mashwani, W.K.: A survey on intrusion detection and prevention in wireless ad-hoc networks. J. Syst. Arch. **105**, 101701 (2020). https://doi.org/10.1016/j.sysarc.2019.101701
9. Rubio, J.E., Alcaraz, C., Roman, R., Lopez, J.: Current cyber-defense trends in industrial control systems. Comput. Secur., 101561 (2019). https://doi.org/10.1016/j.cose.2019.06.015
10. Patil, S.S., Sonavane, S.P.: Data Science and Big Data: An Environment of Computational Intelligence, vol. 24, pp. 49–81 (2017). https://doi.org/10.1007/978-3-319-53474-9
11. Naganhalli, N.S., Terdal, S.: Network intrusion detection using supervised machine learning technique. Int. J. Sci. Technol. Res. **8**(9), 345–350 (2019)
12. Bhattacharya, S., et al.: A novel PCA-firefly based XGBoost classification model for intrusion detection in networks using GPU. Electron. **9**(2), 219 (2020). https://doi.org/10.3390/electronics9020219

13. Kaur, S., Singh, M.: Hybrid intrusion detection and signature generation using Deep Recurrent Neural Networks. Neural Comput. Appl. **32**(12), 7859–7877 (2019). https://doi.org/10.1007/s00521-019-04187-9

14. Gupta, A.R., Agrawal, J.: The multi-demeanor fusion based robust intrusion detection system for anomaly and misuse detection in computer networks. J. Ambient. Intell. Humaniz. Comput. **12**(1), 303–319 (2020). https://doi.org/10.1007/s12652-020-01974-4

15. Shijoe Jose, D., Malathi, B.R., Jayaseeli, D.: A survey on anomaly based host intrusion detection system. J. Phys.: Conf. Ser. **1000**, 012049 (2018). https://doi.org/10.1088/1742-6596/1000/1/012049

16. Anand, K., Kumar, J., Anand, K.: Anomaly detection in online social network: a survey. In: Proceedings of the International Conference on Inventive Communication and Computational Technologies, ICICCT 2017, pp. 456–459 (2017). https://doi.org/10.1109/ICICCT.2017.7975239

17. Zhou, L., Guo, H.: Anomaly detection methods for IIoT networks. In: Proceedings of the 2018 IEEE International Conference on Service Operations and Logistics, and Informatics, SOLI 2018, pp. 214–219 (2018). https://doi.org/10.1109/SOLI.2018.8476769

18. Gauthama Raman, M.R., Somu, N., Kirthivasan, K., Ramiro Liscano, V.S., Sriram, S.: An efficient intrusion detection system based on hypergraph - Genetic algorithm for parameter optimization and feature selection in support vector machine. Knowl.-Based Syst. **134**, 1–12 (2017). https://doi.org/10.1016/j.knosys.2017.07.005

19. Saheed, Y., Babatunde, A.: Genetic Algorithm Technique in Program Path Coverage For Improving Software Testing, vol. 7, no. 5, pp. 151–158 (2014)

20. Resende, P.A.A., Drummond, A.C.: Adaptive anomaly-based intrusion detection system using genetic algorithm and profiling. Secur. Priv. **1**(4), e36 (2018). https://doi.org/10.1002/spy2.36

21. Tao, P., Sun, Z., Sun, Z.: An improved intrusion detection algorithm based on GA and SVM. IEEE Access **6**, 13624–13631 (2018). https://doi.org/10.1109/ACCESS.2018.2810198

22. Ahmad, I., Basheri, M., Iqbal, M.J., Rahim, A.: Performance comparison of support vector machine, random forest, and extreme learning machine for intrusion detection. IEEE Access **6**, 33789–33795 (2018). https://doi.org/10.1109/ACCESS.2018.2841987

23. Aung, Y.Y., Min, M.M.: An analysis of random forest algorithm based network intrusion detection system. In: Proceedings - 18th IEEE/ACIS International Conference on Software Engineering, Artificial Intelligence, Networking and Parallel/Distributed Computing. SNPD 2017, pp. 127–132 (2017). https://doi.org/10.1109/SNPD.2017.8022711

24. Ahmim, A., Maglaras, L., Ferrag, M.A., Derdour, M., Janicke, H.: A novel hierarchical intrusion detection system based on decision tree and rules-based models. In: Proceedings - 15th Annual International Conference on Distributed Computing in Sensor Systems. DCOSS 2019, pp. 228–233 (2019). https://doi.org/10.1109/DCOSS.2019.00059

25. Syarif, A.R., Gata, W.: Intrusion detection system using hybrid binary PSO and K-nearest neighborhood algorithm," Proceedings of 11th International Conference on Information and Communication Technology and Systems. ICTS 2017, vol. 2018-January, pp. 181–18 (2018). https://doi.org/10.1109/ICTS.2017.8265667

26. Frp, V.J., et al.: *Hqhwlf 3Urjudpplqj Dqg . 1Hduhvw 1Hljkerxu &Odvvlilhu %Dvhg,Qwuxvlrq 'Hwhfwlrq 0Rgho, pp. 42–46 (2017)

27. Reazul, M., Rahman, A., Samad, T.: A network intrusion detection framework based on bayesian network using wrapper approach. Int. J. Comput. Appl. **166**(4), 13–17 (2017). https://doi.org/10.5120/ijca2017913992

28. Dias, L.P., Cerqueira, J.J.F., Assis, K.D.R., Almeida, R.C.: Using artificial neural network in intrusion detection systems to computer networks. In: 2017 9th Computer Science and Electronic Engineering Conference CEEC 2017 - Proceeding, pp. 145–150 (2017). https://doi.org/10.1109/CEEC.2017.8101615

29. Sumaiya Thaseen, I., Saira Banu, J., Lavanya, K., Rukunuddin Ghalib, M., Abhishek, K.: An integrated intrusion detection system using correlation-based attribute selection and artificial neural network. Trans. Emerg. Telecommun. Technol. **32**(2), 1–15 (2021). https://doi.org/10.1002/ett.4014

30. Gu, J., Lu, S.: An effective intrusion detection approach using SVM with naïve Bayes feature embedding. Comput. Secur. **103**, 10215 (2021). https://doi.org/10.1016/j.cose.2020.102158

31. Talita, A.S., Nataza, O.S., Rustam, Z.: Naïve bayes classifier and particle swarm optimization feature selection method for classifying intrusion detection system dataset. J. Phys.: Conf. Ser. **1752**, 012021 (2021). https://doi.org/10.1088/1742-6596/1752/1/012021

32. Zargari, S., Voorhis, D.: Feature selection in the corrected KDD-dataset. In: Proceedings - 3rd International Conference on Emerging Intelligent Data and Web. EIDWT 2012, pp. 174–180 (2012). https://doi.org/10.1109/EIDWT.2012.10

33. Saheed, Y.O.Y.K., Hambali, M.A., Arowolo, M.O.: Application of GA feature selection on Naive Bayes, Random Forest and SVM for Credit Card Fraud Detection. In: 2020 International Conference on Decision Aid Sciences and Application (DASA), pp. 1091–1097 (2020)

34. Aljawarneh, S., Aldwairi, M., Yassein, M.B.: Anomaly-based intrusion detection system through feature selection analysis and building hybrid efficient model. J. Comput. Sci. **25**, 152–160 (2018). https://doi.org/10.1016/j.jocs.2017.03.006

35. De la Hoz, E., De La Hoz, E., Ortiz, A., Ortega, J., Prieto, B.: PCA filtering and probabilistic SOM for network intrusion detection. Neurocomputing **164**, 71–81 (2015). https://doi.org/10.1016/j.neucom.2014.09.083

36. Ravale, U., Marathe, N., Padiya, P.: Feature selection based hybrid anomaly intrusion detection system using K Means and RBF kernel function. Procedia Comput. Sci. **45**, 428–435 (2015). https://doi.org/10.1016/j.procs.2015.03.174

37. Moustafa, N., Slay, J.: UNSW-NB15: a comprehensive data set for network intrusion detection systems (UNSW- NB15 network data set). In: 2015 Military Communications and Information Systems Conference MilCIS 2015 - Proceedings 2015. https://doi.org/10.1109/MilCIS.2015.7348942

38. Zargari, S.: Feature Selection in UNSW-NB15 and KDDCUP'99 datasets

39. Dhanabal, L., Shantharajah, S.P.: A study on NSL-KDD dataset for intrusion detection system based on classification algorithms. Int. J. Adv. Res. Comput. Commun. Eng. **4**(6), 446–452 (2015). 17148/IJARCCE.2015.4696

40. Saheed, Y.K., Hamza-usman, F.E.: Feature Selection with IG-R for Improving Performance of Intrusion Detection System, vol. 12, no. 3, pp. 338–344 (2020)

41. Kasliwal, B., Bhatia, S., Saini, S., Thaseen, I.S., Kumar, C.A.: A hybrid anomaly detection model using G-LDA. In: Souvenir 2014 IEEE International Advance Computing Conference. IACC 2014, pp. 288–293 (2014). https://doi.org/10.1109/IAdCC.2014.6779336

42. Taher, K.A., Mohammed Yasin Jisan, B., Rahman, M.M.: Network intrusion detection using supervised machine learning technique with feature selection. In: 1st International Conference on Robotics, Electrical and Signal Processing Techniques. ICREST, pp. 643– 646 (2019). https://doi.org/10.1109/ICREST.2019.8644161

43. Sumaiya Thaseen, I., Aswani Kumar, C.: Intrusion detection model using fusion of chi-square feature selection and multi class SVM. J. King Saud Univ. - Comput. Inf. Sci. **29**(4), 462–472 (2017). https://doi.org/10.1016/j.jksuci.2015.12.004

44. Guo, C., Zhou, Y., Ping, Y., Zhang, Z., Liu, G., Yang, Y.: A distance sum-based hybrid method for intrusion detection. Appl. Intell. **40**(1), 178–188 (2013). https://doi.org/10.1007/s10489-013-0452-6

45. Mukherjee, S., Sharma, N.: Intrusion detection using naive bayes classifier with feature reduction. Procedia Technol. **4**, 119–128 (2012). https://doi.org/10.1016/j.protcy.2012.05.017

46. Amiri, F., Rezaei Yousefi, M., Lucas, C., Shakery, A., Yazdani, N.: Mutual information-based feature selection for intrusion detection systems. J. Netw. Comput. Appl. **34**(4), 1184–1199 (2011). https://doi.org/10.1016/j.jnca.2011.01.002

47. Ahmad, T., Aziz, M.N.: Data preprocessing and feature selection for machine learning intrusion detection systems. ICIC Express Lett. **13**(2), 93–101 (2019). https://doi.org/10.24507/icicel.13.02.93

48. Fouedjio, F.: A hierarchical clustering method for multivariate geostatistical data. Spat. Stat. **18**, 333–351 (2016). https://doi.org/10.1016/j.spasta.2016.07.003

49. Natesan, P., Rajalaxmi, R.R., Gowrison, G., Balasubramanie, P.: Hadoop based parallel binary bat algorithm for network intrusion detection. Int. J. Parallel Program. **45**(5), 1194–1213 (2017). https://doi.org/10.1007/s10766-016-0456-z

50. Yang, X.S.: A new metaheuristic Bat-inspired Algorithm. Stud. Comput. Intell. **284**, 65–74 (2010). https://doi.org/10.1007/978-3-642-12538-6_6

51. Sreeram, I., Vuppala, V.P.K.: HTTP flood attack detection in application layer using machine learning metrics and bio inspired bat algorithm. Appl. Comput. Inf. **15**(1), 59–66 (2019). https://doi.org/10.1016/j.aci.2017.10.003

52. Uddin, M.P., Al Mamun, M., Hossain, M.A.: Effective feature extraction through segmentation-based folded-PCA for hyperspectral image classification. Int. J. Remote Sens. **40**(18), 7190–7220 (2019). https://doi.org/10.1080/01431161.2019.1601284

53. Bouwmans, T., Javed, S., Zhang, H., Lin, Z., Otazo, R.: On the applications of robust PCA in image and video processing. Proc. IEEE **106**(8), 1427–1457 (2018). https://doi.org/10.1109/JPROC.2018.2853589

54. Nobre, J., Neves, R.F.: Combining principal component analysis, discrete wavelet transform and XGBoost to trade in the financial markets. Expert Syst. Appl. **125**, 181–194 (2019). https://doi.org/10.1016/j.eswa.2019.01.083

55. Rajab, K.D.: New hybrid features selection method: a case study on websites phishing. Secur. Commun. Netw. **2017**, 1–10 (2017). https://doi.org/10.1155/2017/9838169

56. Bouhlel, J., et al.: Comparison of common components analysis with principal components analysis and independent components analysis: application to SPME-GC-MS volatolomic signatures. Talanta **178**, 854–863 (2018). https://doi.org/10.1016/j.talanta.2017.10.025

57. Navi, K., Molahosseini, A.S., Esmaeildoust, M.: How to teach residue number system to computer scientists and engineers,. IEEE Trans. Educ. **54**(1), 156–163 (2011). https://doi.org/10.1109/TE.2010.2048329

58. Gbolagade, K.A., Chaves, R., Sousa, L., Cotofana, S.D.: An improved RNS reverse converter for the {22n+1−1,2 n,2n−1} moduli set. ISCAS 2010 - 2010 International Symposium on Circuits and Systems, Nano-Bio Circuit Fabrics and Systems, pp. 2103–2106 (2010). https://doi.org/10.1109/ISCAS.2010.5537062

59. Al-Garadi, M.A., Mohamed, A., Al-Ali, A.K., Du, X., Ali, I., Guizani, M.: A survey of machine and deep learning methods for Internet of Things (IoT) security. IEEE Commun. Surv. Tutorials **22**(3), 1646–1685 (2020). https://doi.org/10.1109/COMST.2020.2988293

60. Tahsien, S.M., Karimipour, H., Spachos, P.: Machine learning based solutions for security of Internet of Things (IoT): a survey. J. Netw. Comput. Appl. **161**(February), 102630 (2020). https://doi.org/10.1016/j.jnca.2020.102630

61. Doshi, R., Apthorpe, N., Feamster, N.: Machine learning DDoS detection for consumer internet of things devices. In: IEEE Symposium on Security and Privacy Work. SPW 2018, no. Ml, pp. 29–35 (2018). https://doi.org/10.1109/SPW.2018.00013

62. Tavallaee, M., Bagheri, E., Lu, W., Ghorbani, A.A.: A detailed analysis of the KDD CUP 99 data set in Computational Intelligence for Security and Defense Applications. Comput. Intell. Secur. Def. Appl. no. Cisda, pp. 1– 6 (2009)

63. Mchugh, J.: Testing intrusion detection systems: a critique of the 1998 and 1999 DARPA intrusion detection system evaluations as performed by lincoln laboratory. ACM Trans. Inf. Syst. Secur. **3**(4), 262–294 (2000). https://doi.org/10.1145/382912.382923

64. Yin, C., Zhu, Y., Fei, J., He, X.: A deep learning approach for intrusion detection using recurrent neural networks. IEEE Access **5**, 21954–21961 (2017). https://doi.org/10.1109/ACCESS.2017.2762418

65. Tsang, C.H., Kwong, S., Wang, H.: Genetic-fuzzy rule mining approach and evaluation of feature selection techniques for anomaly intrusion detection. Pattern Recognit. **40**(9), 2373–2391 (2007). https://doi.org/10.1016/j.patcog.2006.12.009

66. Raman, M.R.G., Somu, N., Kirthivasan, K., Sriram, V.S.S.: A hypergraph and arithmetic residue-based probabilistic neural network for classification in intrusion detection systems. Neural Netw. **92**, 89–97 (2017). https://doi.org/10.1016/j.neunet.2017.01.012

Combining SysML with Petri Nets for the Design of an Urban Traffic Signal Control

Layse Santos Souza🄳 and Michel S. Soares$^{(\boxtimes)}$🄳

Department of Computing, Federal University of Sergipe, São Cristóvão, Brazil
`michel@dcomp.ufs.br`

Abstract. Urban roads are a crucial infrastructure highly demanded by citizens and organizations interested in their deployment, performance, and safety. Urban traffic signal control is an important and challenging real-world problem that aims to monitor and improve traffic congestion. Therefore, the deployment of traffic signals for vehicles or pedestrians at an intersection is a complex activity, as it is necessary to establish rules to control the flow of vehicles and pedestrians. Also, traffic flow at intersections changes constantly, depending, for instance, on weather conditions and day of the week, as well as road works and accidents that further influence complexity and performance. Thus, this work first uses the SysML Block Definition diagram to model the elements (sensor, controller, and actuator) of the architecture of an urban traffic signal control system. Next, Petri Nets models are proposed for the internal design of each of these elements. Finally, these Petri Nets models are combined into a complete model by merging common places. As a result, this article describes model integration, i.e., SysML Block Definition diagram and Petri Nets for modeling the architectural elements of an urban traffic signal control system.

Keywords: Urban traffic signal control · SysML Block Definition diagram · Petri Nets · System architecture

1 Introduction

Modern cities are highly dependent on infrastructures such as road, rail, and air traffic, energy distribution, water supply, and waste management. These infrastructures are highly demanded by citizens and organizations, their design and maintenance are crucial for daily activities, and they present high complexity and demand for their design, control, and management.

Urban traffic is considered a problem and a challenge for citizens and organizations in a city that aim to monitor and improve quality of life in a city [22]. Therefore, one of the most important infrastructure of a city is its urban road network, as traffic signals are the most basic elements for data acquisition, e.g., vehicle and pedestrian counts, congestion control, accident reports, speed

© Springer Nature Switzerland AG 2021
O. Gervasi et al. (Eds.): ICCSA 2021, LNCS 12957, pp. 115–126, 2021.
https://doi.org/10.1007/978-3-030-87013-3_9

management, and traffic control. The deployment of traffic signals both for vehicles and pedestrians is a complex activity as decisions have to be established to control the right-of-way for both vehicles and pedestrians [3,17].

At an intersection between two or more roads, there are conflicting movements that cannot be performed simultaneously. The control of an intersection is performed from the synchronization of traffic signals that minimizes fuel consumption, pollutant emissions and allows a better traffic flow by combining the green signal times (green wave), i.e., provides the passage of the maximum number of vehicles, reduces stops and delays for drivers at intersections [1,9,11].

Modeling for the control of infrastructure in cities is important to deliver better services and quality of life to the urban population, i.e., socioeconomic development. Currently, a large number of modeling languages are used to model the systems responsible for these infrastructures. For example, UML is used to design these systems with a focus on the software elements of the system, and SysML is used to model elements of systems that are not software [20]. Petri Nets are a formal graphical language that provides support for analysis of problems associated with systems, applicable to a wide variety of systems providing information about the structure and behavior of systems, e.g., resource sharing, concurrency, dynamic behavior, synchronous and asynchronous communication [10,15,27].

A Timed Petri Nets model for a traffic signal control policy system composed of two sensors for emergency vehicles preemption is proposed in [7], presenting the behavior of traffic signals in terms of conditions and events that cause phase preemption, i.e., it identifies and preempts urgent scenarios by conditions and events that control the alternating phases of the traffic signal (red, yellow, and green). After developing this model, the authors performed traffic analysis regarding the properties of liveliness and reversibility using the accessibility graph analysis method. In another related work, the authors of paper [20] used the SysML Requirements, Sequence, and Block Definition diagrams of the SmartCitySysML profile, an extension of SysML to include smart city elements as native SysML components, to model a road traffic control system, i.e., controller, actuator, and sensors for a specific region. The dynamic behavior of a group of traffic signals controlling a network of intersections is a complex discrete event system which can be modeled using Petri Nets [19]. Petri Nets have been considered as well to analyze good properties of models of road traffic signals, both for single intersections and for networks of roads. For instance, formal proofs of models can prove that unsafe states, such as two greens phases in a shared road intersection are not reached [18].

The proposal in this article is to address the architecture design problem of urban traffic signal control systems by using the SysML Block Definition diagram to model the architectural elements (sensor, controller, and actuator) of an urban traffic signal control, and Petri Nets to model the internal behavior of each of these elements, i.e., sub-models of Petri Nets, and then combine these sub-models into a single model to design the behavior of these elements in an urban traffic signal control.

2   Background

2.1   SysML

SysML [12] has been developed by the Object Management Group (OMG) and International Council on Systems Engineering (INCOSE) to develop a unified language for general-purpose modeling for systems engineering applications. SysML is a UML profile applied to systems that include hardware, software, information, processes, people, and procedures.

SysML reuses parts of UML and additionally offers new language elements, such as value types, type of quantity, and the opportunity to describe the functionality of systems. Therefore, it allows one to model a wide variety of systems from different perspectives [24].

It is worth mentioning that SysML also allows modeling in multiple architectural views, through diagrams that can model the structure, behavior, and requirements of a system. In this way, SysML is characterized through diagrams, models, structural and behavioral elements, effective in specifying requirements, allocations, and restrictions on system properties to support a systems engineering project [4,6].

Current version of SysML, named SysML 1.6, was released in December 2019. A full description of all SysML diagrams can be find in [12]. In this paper, the focus is on SysML Block Definition and SysML Internal Block diagrams, which are briefly introduced as follows, as the purpose is to model structural elements which will compose the system architecture.

SysML Blocks, as proposed by OMG, are based on UML Classes extended by UML Composite Structures. Blocks are modular units that are useful to create structural descriptions of a system. A block may include both structural and behavioral features, including properties and operations, to represent behavior and state of a system [12]. The SysML blocks are, respectively:

- **Block Definition Diagram:** defines resources and relationships between blocks, which includes associations, dependencies and generalizations. The Block Definition diagram characterizes blocks in terms of operations, properties, and relationships as a system hierarchy.
- **Internal Block Diagram:** captures the internal structure of a block in terms of properties and connectors between properties.

2.2   Petri Nets

Petri Nets are a graphical formal method applicable to a large variety of systems that provides important information about the structure and behavior of the modeled systems, i.e., simultaneity, concurrency, dynamic behavior, synchronous and asynchronous communication, and resource sharing need to be modeled [10,14–16].

A Petri Net is formally defined [10], as a tuple:

$$P = (P, T, F, W, M_0), \text{ where}$$

$$P = \{p_1, p_2, ..., p_3\} \quad \text{is a finite set of places;}$$

$$T = \{t_1, t_2, ..., t_3\} \quad \text{is a finite set of transitions;}$$

$$F \subseteq (PxT) \cup (TxP) \quad \text{is a set of arcs;}$$

$$W : F \to \{1, 2, 3, ...\} \quad \text{is a function of weights;}$$

$$M_0 : P \to \{1, 2, 3, ...\} \quad \text{is the initial marking,} \quad P \cap T = \varnothing \quad \text{e} \quad P \cup T \neq \varnothing;$$

According to Peterson [14], the graphic structure of a Petri Net is a bipartite directed graph composed of four elements, explained briefly below and shown in Fig. 1.

- *Places* can represent, for example, conditions, status, states, or operations;
- *Transitions* can represent, for example, start or stop events, which occurs to change the status of places;
- *Arcs* connect places and transitions;
- *Tokens* can represent the number of elements or the current availability of resources.

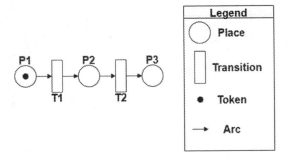

Fig. 1. Elements of Petri Nets.

An example of execution is shown in Fig. 2. Initially, places P1 and P2 with one token are enabling transition T1. After firing of transition T1, tokens in P1 and P2 are removed, and one token is deposited in place P3.

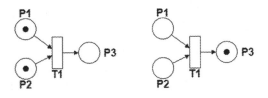

Fig. 2. Execution of a Petri Net.

3   Basic Architectural Elements of an Urban Traffic Signal Control

The design of city infrastructures is crucial for daily activities and is highly complex and demanding due to the need to apply processes and technologies for the control and management of architecture and system design. The main objective of this section is to model each architectural element of an urban traffic signal control system as a SysML Block Definition diagram and then as Petri Nets models.

Figure 3 shows a SysML Block Definition diagram that includes elements of the architecture of an urban traffic signal control. The controller, sensor, and actuator elements are specified using components of Petri Nets. The sensor sends data about the state of traffic to the controller. The controller sends signals to the actuator (traffic signals), and the actuator regulates traffic.

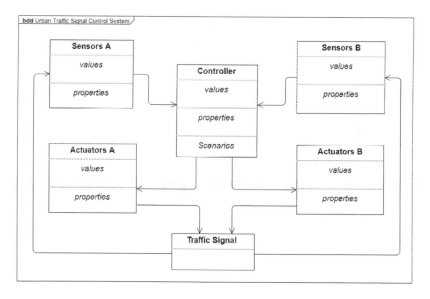

Fig. 3. SysML Block Definition diagram for the architecture of an urban traffic signal control.

Modeling of the controller, sensor, and actuator elements of an urban traffic control is modeled as a Petri Net with modular composition method, i.e., modular Petri Nets, as shown in Fig. 4, 5, 6, respectively.

Figure 4 shows the model of the actuator (traffic signal). This model consists of three phases (green, yellow, and red) together with the requests from the signal to the controller and the responses from the controller to the signal, i.e., places *Red, Green, Green_End, Yellow,* and *Yellow_End* represent the signal and places *Green_Start, Answers_Green, Yellow_Start, Answers_Yellow,* and

Red_Start represent the solicitations and responses between actuator and controller. For example, place *Green_Start* receives from the controller the response of the request to start the green phase of the corresponding road section, and place *Red_Start* receives from the controller the response of the request to start the red phase of the corresponding road section.

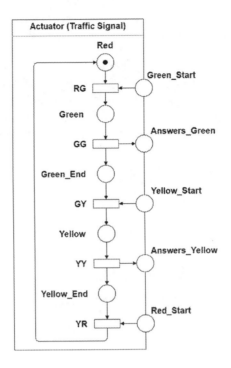

Fig. 4. SysML block definition diagram for the actuator components.

Figure 5 shows the controller model for controlling the traffic signal of an intersection. This model is composed of places *I, Green_Go, Yellow_Go, Green_Start, Answers_Green, Yellow_Start, Answers_Yellow, and Red_Start* and transitions *IGG, GGYG, and YGI*. For example, the controller *I* sends the green signal (token) command to the *Green_Go* actuator when the transition *IGG* is enabled and deposits a token in place *Green_Start*.

Figure 6 shows the sensor model. This model is composed of places *Detect_Vehicle and Answers_Detected_Vehicle*, place *Detect_Vehicle* sends information (token) to the controller warning that a vehicle has been detected and place *Answers_Detected_Vehicle* sends information (token) from the controller to the sensor as a form of response.

In these modular Petri Nets, each element (sensor, controller, and actuator) is modeled as a sub-model of the urban traffic control for easy understanding of future modifications. After these modular Petri Nets models have been developed, the sensor, controller, and actuator sub-models are integrated, forming a

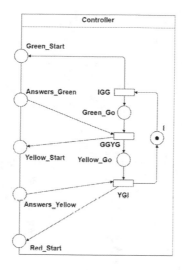

Fig. 5. SysML block definition diagram for the controller components.

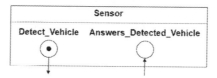

Fig. 6. SysML block definition diagram for the sensor components.

complete model of the urban traffic signal control system as shown in Fig. 9 in the next section.

4   Case Study: Urban Traffic Signal Control

The main objective of this section is to detail the architectural elements of an application for design an urban traffic signal control system. Traffic signal control is considered a competitive traffic management strategy to improve mobility and address environmental issues in urban areas, as they regulate traffic flows to achieve a more efficient traffic management strategy, i.e., one of the main tools to control congestion on roads [8], therefore, they are an important and challenging problem in the real world, which aims to monitor and improve traffic congestion [2, 21, 23, 25].

Traffic signals are control devices applied to urban traffic that aim to optimize the flow of vehicles, allowing safe, efficient, and appropriate crossings, i.e., it is the most basic instrument for collecting traffic data in a city, because they allow to control and manage the flow of vehicles and pedestrians [17, 26].

The deployment of traffic signals for vehicles or pedestrians at an intersection is a complex activity, as it is necessary to make decisions, e.g., to establish rules to

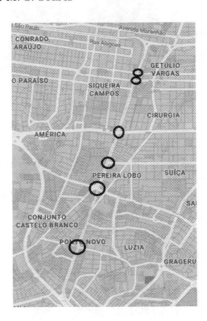

Fig. 7. Region of the urban network with visualization of traffic signals.

control the right of way, both for vehicles and pedestrians. Thus, it is necessary to determine new rules of priority between approaches to the intersection to permit crossing or prohibiting movement at the intersection, which could lead to accidents [5,13].

Current traffic signal control systems in use still rely heavily on simplified methods used in the control rules to decide whether to maintain or change the current phase [23]. An intersection between two or more roads is a complex infrastructure, thus the movements cannot be performed simultaneously, as they conflict with each other. As the traffic flow at the intersection changes constantly, depending on weather conditions, day of the week, and period of the day, in addition to works and accidents that further influence complexity and performance, it is necessary to make decisions, that is, to establish rules to control the right path for vehicles and pedestrians [3].

Figure 7 shows a region that presents high traffic flow in a city in northeastern Brazil. This region is composed of six traffic signals, illustrated by the black circles. In this article, the two chosen intersections are controlled by traffic signals, limiting left turns on either road.

Figure 8 shows the traffic signals chosen from this region to model this case study. The intersections in this region can be improved by providing green waves for the main roads (A and B), that is, providing maximum time to the green phase in a sequence of junctions, so that vehicles can cross as much as possible with few stops.

Figure 9 shows, at an abstract modeling level, the combination of SysML Block Definition diagrams for the urban traffic control elements (actuator in

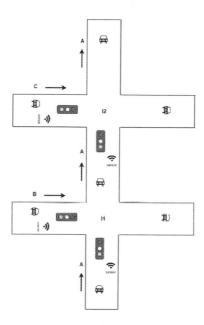

Fig. 8. Specific region of the urban network with visualization of traffic signals.

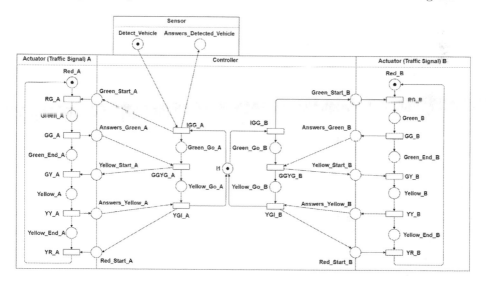

Fig. 9. SysML block definition diagrams of combined Petri Net elements for urban traffic signal control.

Fig. 4, controller in Fig. 5 and sensor in Fig. 6) for the region chosen in this case study, i.e., I1 composed of two traffic signals (A and B), a sensor and a controller for these signals. At this intersection, the A junction of the road has priority over the B one, thus the sensor is in the A junction of the road. A similar design is

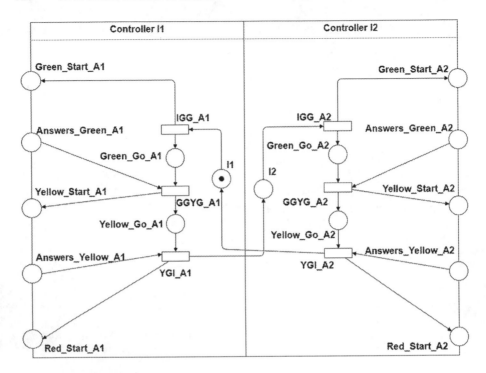

Fig. 10. Petri Nets for an urban traffic signal control (I1 and I2).

used for the sensor, controller, and actuator related to the other intersections of the region illustrated in Fig. 7. It is worth noting that Fig. 9 is depicted from the SysML Block Definition diagram in Fig. 3 and describes that it is possible to design the internal behavior of a SysML Block Definition diagram as a Petri Net model.

Figure 10 shows the behavior of the SysML Block Definition diagram of the controllers for intersections I1 and I2 shown in Fig. 8, that is, when the controller for intersection I1 sends the green signal to intersection I1, the controller for intersection I1 also sends the green signal to the controller for intersection I2. A similar design is used for the other controllers for the other intersections in the region shown in Fig. 7.

5   Conclusion

Modeling systems that control the infrastructure of a modern city is a complex activity, thus there is no single standard to be used, as there are many modeling languages proposed in the past decades for systems engineering activities. This paper proposed the modeling of architectural elements of an urban traffic control system using the SysML Block Definition diagram and Petri Nets to model the behavior of these elements.

The purpose of this paper is to describe the integration of models described using the SysML Block Definition diagram and Petri Nets to model the architectural elements of urban traffic signal control elements, i.e., controller, sensor, and actuator. Thus, the case study details the modeling of urban traffic signal control through the specification of the architectural elements of traffic signal control aiming at a better understanding of the problem. As a working example of a network of roads, a region of northeastern Brazil was defined, then the SysML Block Definition diagram was used to describe the characteristics of each element as a block. Then, Petri Nets models are proposed to represent the behavior of these elements of urban traffic signal control.

Future work will focus on modeling and software simulation of other case studies related to a city's infrastructure, as well as evaluating the Petri Net model developed for the case study (urban traffic signal control) by checking its performance and good behavioral properties to identify possible flaws and correct the functions of an urban traffic control system.

Acknowledgments. This study was financed by Fundação de Apoio à Pesquisa e à Inovação Tecnológica do estado de Sergipe (FAPITEC/SE) and the Coordenação de Aperfeiçoamento de Pessoal de Nível Superior - Brasil (CAPES) - Finance Code 001.

References

1. Adacher, L., Tiriolo, M.: A distributed approach for traffic signal synchronization problem. In: 2016 Third International Conference on Mathematics and Computers in Sciences and in Industry (MCSI), pp. 191–196 (2016)
2. An, Y., Zhu, C., Chen, P., Li, Y.: Modeling and analysis of transit signal priority control systems based on colored petri nets. In: IEEE International Conference on Systems, Man, and Cybernetics (SMC), pp. 2701–2706. IEEE (2017)
3. Asaithambi, G., Kuttan, M.O., Chandra, S.: Pedestrian road crossing behavior under mixed traffic conditions: a comparative study of an intersection before and after implementing control measures. Transp. Dev. Econ. **2**(2), 1–12 (2016). https://doi.org/10.1007/s40890-016-0018-5
4. Biggs, G., Sakamoto, T., Kotoku, T.: A profile and tool for modelling safety information with design information in SysML. Softw. Syst. Model. **15**(1), 147–178 (2016)
5. Castro, G.B., Hirakawa, A.R., Martini, J.S.: Adaptive traffic signal control based on bio-neural network. Procedia Comput. Sci. **109**, 1182–1187 (2017)
6. Friedenthal, S., Moore, A., Steiner, R.: A Practical Guide to SysML: The Systems Modeling Language. Morgan Kaufmann Publishers Inc., Burlington (2014)
7. Huang, Y.S., Shiue, J.Y., Luo, J.: A traffic signal control policy for emergency vehicles preemption using timed petri nets. IFAC-PapersOnLine **48**(3), 2183–2188 (2015)
8. Le, T., Kovács, P., Walton, N., Vu, H.L., Andrew, L.L., Hoogendoorn, S.S.: Decentralized signal control for urban road networks. Transp. Res. Part C Emerging Technol. **58**, 431–450 (2015)
9. Ma, C., He, R.: Green wave traffic control system optimization based on adaptive genetic-artificial fish swarm algorithm. Neural Comput. Appl. **31**(7), 2073–2083 (2019)

10. Murata, T.: Petri Nets: properties, analysis and applications. Proc. IEEE **77**(4), 541–580 (1989)
11. Ning, Z., Zhang, F., Remias, S.: Understanding the security of traffic signal infrastructure. In: Perdisci, R., Maurice, C., Giacinto, G., Almgren, M. (eds.) DIMVA 2019. LNCS, vol. 11543, pp. 154–174. Springer, Cham (2019). https://doi.org/10.1007/978-3-030-22038-9_8
12. OMG: Systems Modeling Language (OMG SysML) Version 1.6 (2019)
13. Oviedo-Trespalacios, O., Haque, M.M., King, M., Washington, S.: Effects of road infrastructure and traffic complexity in speed adaptation behaviour of distracted drivers. Accid. Anal. Prev. **101**, 67–77 (2017)
14. Peterson, J.L.: Petri Nets. ACM Comput. Surv. **9**(3), 223–252 (1977)
15. Petri, C.A.: Kommunikation mit Automaten. Ph.D. thesis, Universität Hamburg (1962)
16. Reisig, W.: Petri Nets: An Introduction. Springer, New York (1985). https://doi.org/10.1007/978-3-642-69968-9
17. Silvestre, E.A., Soares, M.S.: Modeling road traffic signals control using UML and the MARTE profile. In: Murgante, B., et al. (eds.) ICCSA 2012. LNCS, vol. 7336, pp. 1–15. Springer, Heidelberg (2012). https://doi.org/10.1007/978-3-642-31128-4_1
18. Soares, M.S., Vrancken, J.L.M.: Road traffic signals modeling and analysis with petri nets and linear logic. In: Proceedings of the IEEE International Conference on Networking, Sensing and Control, ICNSC 2007, London, UK, 15–17 April 2007, pp. 169–174. IEEE (2007)
19. Soares, M.S., Vrancken, J.L.M.: Responsive traffic signals designed with petri nets. In: Proceedings of the IEEE International Conference on Systems, Man and Cybernetics, Singapore, 12–15 October 2008, pp. 1942–1947. IEEE (2008)
20. Souza, L.S., Misra, S., Soares, M.S.: SmartCitySysML: a SysML profile for smart cities applications. In: Gervasi, O., et al. (eds.) ICCSA 2020. LNCS, vol. 12254, pp. 383–397. Springer, Cham (2020). https://doi.org/10.1007/978-3-030-58817-5_29
21. Vilarinho, C., Tavares, J.P., Rossetti, R.J.F.: Design of a multiagent system for real-time traffic control. IEEE Intell. Syst. **31**(4), 68–80 (2016)
22. Vrancken, J.L.M., van Schuppen, J.H., Soares, M.S., Ottenhof, F.: A hierarchical model and implementation architecture for road traffic control. In: Proceedings of the IEEE International Conference on Systems, Man and Cybernetics, San Antonio, TX, USA, 11–14 October 2009, pp. 3540–3544. IEEE (2009)
23. Wei, H., Zheng, G., Gayah, V., Li, Z.: A survey on traffic signal control methods. arXiv preprint arXiv:1904.08117 (2019)
24. Wolny, S., Mazak, A., Carpella, C., Geist, V., Wimmer, M.: Thirteen years of SysML: a systematic mapping study. Softw. Syst. Model. **19**(1), 111–169 (2020)
25. Yau, K.L.A., Qadir, J., Khoo, H.L., Ling, M.H., Komisarczuk, P.: A survey on reinforcement learning models and algorithms for traffic signal control. ACM Comput. Surv. **50**(3), 1–38 (2017)
26. Yuan, Y.: Application of intelligent technology in urban traffic congestion. In: 2020 International Conference on Computer Engineering and Application - ICCEA 2020, pp. 721–725 (2020)
27. Zhao, J., Duan, Z.: Verification of use case with petri nets in requirement analysis. In: Gervasi, O., Taniar, D., Murgante, B., Laganà, A., Mun, Y., Gavrilova, M.L. (eds.) ICCSA 2009. LNCS, vol. 5593, pp. 29–42. Springer, Heidelberg (2009). https://doi.org/10.1007/978-3-642-02457-3_3

A Bayesian Network Model for the Prognosis of the Novel Coronavirus (COVID-19)

Salisu Aliyu[1]([✉]) [iD], Aminu Salihu Zakari[2], Ibrahim Adeyanju[3], and Naseer Sanni Ajoge[4]

[1] Department of Computer Science, Ahmadu Bello University, Zaria, Nigeria
aliyusalisu@abu.edu.ng
[2] Department of Computer Science, Kaduna Polytechnic, Kaduna, Nigeria
[3] Department of Computer Engineering, Federal University Oye Ekiti, Oye Ekiti, Nigeria
[4] Open Distance and Flexible E-Learning Centre, Kaduna Polytechnic, Kaduna, Nigeria

Abstract. The World Health Organization (WHO) classified the new coronavirus disease 2019 (COVID-19) as a Public Health Emergency of International Concern on January 31, 2020. It is now clear that the dreadful virus has put a significant burden on the world's healthcare systems. Currently, the main techniques for diagnosing COVID-19 are viral nucleic acid testing and chest computed tomography (CT). Though proven to be effective, these methods are time consuming hence, the need for the use of non-clinical approaches for early detection, diagnosis and prognosis of the coronavirus. Using epidemiological dataset of COVID-19 patients, this study presents the use of Bayesian network model to predict contraction of the coronavirus disease. Following the application of several structural learning techniques, a causal Bayesian network based on the nodes: breathing problem, fever, dry cough, sore throat, running nose, asthma, chronic lung disease, headache, heart disease, diabetes, hypertension, fatigue, gastrointestinal, abroad travel, contact with COVID Patient, attended Large Gathering, visited public exposed places, family working in public exposed places and COVID-19 status, was estimated. The developed BN model correctly predicted the probability of contracting COVID-19 with an accuracy of 98%. The model also affirms that, individuals with contact history with a COVID-19 patient are the most susceptible to contracting the coronavirus disease.

Keywords: Coronavirus · COVID-19 · Pandemic · Bayesian networks · Model

1 Introduction

On January 31, 2020, the World Health Organization (WHO) proclaimed the new coronavirus disease 2019 (COVID-19) a Public Health Emergency of International Concern [1]. A disease that is said to have started in Wuhan, China, has now spread to other parts of the world. According to the situation reports by the World Health Organization as at

© Springer Nature Switzerland AG 2021
O. Gervasi et al. (Eds.): ICCSA 2021, LNCS 12957, pp. 127–140, 2021.
https://doi.org/10.1007/978-3-030-87013-3_10

10:21am CEST on September 14, 2020, there have been about 28,871,176 confirmed cases of COVID-19, including 921,801 deaths globally [2].

COVID-19, an infectious disease caused by a new coronavirus strain known as severe acute respiratory syndrome coronavirus 2 (SARS-CoV2), has as its primary source of infection patients who have already been infected with the disease, with or without clinical symptoms [3]. It is believed that the virus spread through respiratory droplets (e.g. cough, sneezes etc.). In the first week, symptoms like as fever, tiredness, cough, nasal congestion, runny nose, diarrhea, and headache may appear, with further symptoms such as dyspnea, cyanosis, malaise, bad appetite, and respiratory failure appearing as the disease develops [3].

There is currently no recognized medication or vaccine that has been clinically proven to treat COVID-19, and it is clear that the virus has wreaked havoc on healthcare systems throughout the world. Currently, the main techniques for diagnosing covid-19 are viral nucleic acid testing and chest computed tomography (CT) [4]. Though proven to be effective, these methods are time consuming hence, the need for the use of non-clinical techniques such as mathematical modelling, data mining, machine learning and expert system among other artificial intelligence techniques for efficient detection, diagnosis and prognosis of the coronavirus disease.

Bayesian Networks (BNs) are effective artificial intelligence tools for modeling problems in order to obtain a better understanding and perspective on uncertainties and complexities to assist decision makers. The use of BNs in modeling health care and disease-related problems has recently received remarkable interest from the scholarly community [5]. BNs have been used in a variety of applications in healthcare, including analyzing infection and death rates, modeling and forecasting patient outcomes, risk assessment, contact tracking, and epidemic curve prediction [6–8].

Despite the growing interest of the use of BNs in modeling infectious diseases and other health care related issues, the distribution of infectious diseases modeling in Bayesian Networks literature is only 4% [5].

At this point, the need for rapid diagnosis cannot be over-emphasized. Based on available patient data, a Bayesian Network model was created to estimate the likelihood of infection with the novel coronavirus disease. The model will help health workers to make effective use of the available scarce resources together with limited information, an advantage of modelling with BNs. The model was developed with the epidemiological information obtained from the World Health Organization. We also gave a thorough examination of the prediction of contracting the coronavirus diease and the connections between the disease's causative symptoms.

The key contributions of the work are summarized below:

- Identification of possible factors that are primary causes or poses a potential risk of contracting the coronavirus disease.
- Development of a Bayesian Network (BN), a probabilistic graphical approach for calculating the risk of specific variables/attributes in predicting the contraction of the dreadful coronavirus disease.
- Conduct a series of advanced studies, such as predictive inference reasoning and sensitivity analysis, to gain a better understanding of the effect of the generated model's outcomes.

The remaining sections of the paper are organized as follows: Sect. 2 explains the purpose of this work, Sect. 3 outlines the proposed model's general approach, including data collection and preparation, followed by an explanatory note on the Bayesian Network. The experimental results are explained in detail in Sect. 4. Finally, Sect. 5 concludes the paper.

2 Motivation

The following is the description of the motivation for doing this research:

- To avoid and reduce the effects of the coronavirus disease's spread, the primary causes of contracting the coronavirus disease must be thoroughly understood. With the huge amount of data collected with regards to coronavirus disease, the causes of one being infected with the disease can be mined out of these available dataset. Hence, the need for this study.
- There has been relatively few research into the prediction of the coronavirus disease. A number of prediction algorithms have been proposed towards enhancing healthcare decision making. Hence, the need to consider one for the coronavirus disease to aid decision makers. We therefore, propose utilizing the BN structure to predict coronavirus infection in this work.
- Bayesian networks have been used to assess risk and dependability, discover fault sources, minimize the likelihood of failures, examine how management activities influence sustainability, predict uncertainty and metrics in manufacturing, categorize data, and manage projects, among other applications. In Bayesian networks, conditionals are used to estimate risk based on a series of prior events that affects the outcomes. Without performing any further computations, one may deduce the causal linkages from the structure of a Bayesian model. These benefits associated with the use of BNs informed our decision of its usage in this study.

3 Related Works

Machine Learning algorithms are currently applied in a number of research [9]. In software development, Behera, Rath [10] examined the efficiency of machine learning models in predicting software dependability and reliability. Butt, Misra [11] identifies the major causes for the failure of the agile software development approach during the COVID-19 outbreak. In sentiment analysis, Behera, Jena [12] used the Convolutional LSTM learning model on big social media dataset. For stock prediction, Behera, Das [13] used machine learning algorithms on real-time streaming dataset. In healthcare, Guhathakurata, Kundu [14] used the Support Vector Machine (SVM) classifier to accurately classified patients' conditions into moderate, severe, or no infection based on coronavirus symptoms. Tezza, Lorenzoni [15] also used SVM to predict in-hospital mortality of COVID-19 patients in Italy. A number of machine learning algorithms some of which include: Decision Tree, K-Nearest Neighbour (KNN), Naïve Bayes, Random Forest and SVM were used in Rehman, Shafique [16] to effectively diagnose COVID-19 infection. Also, in the work of Muhammad, Algehyne [17], several machine learning algorithms were used for predicting the coronavirus disease. Using publicly accessible clinical and laboratory data, Alballa and Al-Turaiki [18] were able to review the potential of machine learning algorithms in diagnosing COVID-19 and estimating both the mortality risk and its severity. Wang, Zhai [19] utilized a Bayesian network model to investigate the impact of COVID-19 on Chinese visitors' mobility decision–making processes. Government information, traffic information, family structure, and social interaction networks are among the key factors impacting Chinese passengers' mobility, according to their results. Ojugo and Otakore [20] also used a Bayesian network to construct a model that was trained on a target system and can help anticipate the optimal parameters for classification of the novel coronavirus. In this paper, we propose the use of BN model to predict the potential risk of being infected with the coronavirus. To further validate our work, we evaluated the proposed model side by side with other machine learning techniques, including Nave Bayes, decision trees, and support vector machines.

4   Methodology

4.1   Data Collection and Description

Epidemiological dataset of COVID-19 patients based on information collected from the World Health Organization (WHO) and made available on Kaggle Website [21] was used. The dataset has 5434 instances with 21 Boolean typed attributes which include breathing problem, fever, dry cough, sore throat, running nose, asthma, chronic lung disease, headache, heart disease, diabetes, hypertension, fatigue, gastrointestinal, abroad travel, contact with COVID Patient, attended Large Gathering, visited public exposed places, family working in public exposed places, wearing masks, sanitization from market and COVID-19 status. Table 1 contains a list of the variables in the dataset used in this study as well as their definitions.

Table 1. Variables and their definitions

Nodes	Definitions
Contact with COVID Patient	Associating with an infected patient that is not cured
Chronic Lung Disease	A disorder that affects the lungs and other respiratory system
Diabetes	The body's capacity to metabolize blood glucose is impaired in this condition
Abroad travel	History of traveling

(continued)

Table 1. (*continued*)

Nodes	Definitions
Heart Disease	Range of conditions that affects the heart
Fatigue	A feeling of tiredness or lack of energy
Visited Public Exposed Places	Visit to public places
Hyper Tension	A condition in which the force of blood against the artery walls is too high
Asthma	A condition in which a person's airways become inflamed, narrow, swollen and produces extra mucus making it difficult to breath
Sore throat	Pain and irritation of the throat
Breathing Problem	Trouble or difficulty breathing
Fever	Increase in body temperature above normal
Dry Cough	Cough that does not bring up any mucus
Running Nose	Persistent watery discharge from the nose
Headache	Pain or discomfort in the head
Gastrointestinal	Diseases or disorder of digestive tract
Attended Large Gathering	Present in a crowded environment
Family working in Public Exposed Places	Associating with people that are publicly exposed

4.2 Data Preparation

The dataset was prepped and sanitized such that only relevant attributes were chosen. Irrelevant attributes like wearing masks and sanitization from market were removed because they are constant values. Constant values are generally not required in learning BN structures. For example, if an attribute y takes the same value in each of the records, then it cannot be a predictor for any other at-tribute. Fig. 1 depicts the frequency of each dataset attribute.

4.3 Bayesian Networks

A Bayesian Network (BN) is a directed acyclic network in which each node is tagged with quantitative probability information [10]. It is an efficient encoding of a domain's probabilistic model. BN are essentially used to indicate the dependencies between variables/attributes. Each node in a BN corresponds to a random variable, which might be discrete or continuous. A pair of nodes is connected by a set of directed links or arrows. If an arrow connects node X to node Y, X is said to be Y's parent. Each node Y_i has a conditional probability distribution $P(Y_i|Parents(Y_i))$ that measures the influence of the parents on the node.

The network's topology defines the conditional independence relationships that exist in a given domain (see Fig. 2).

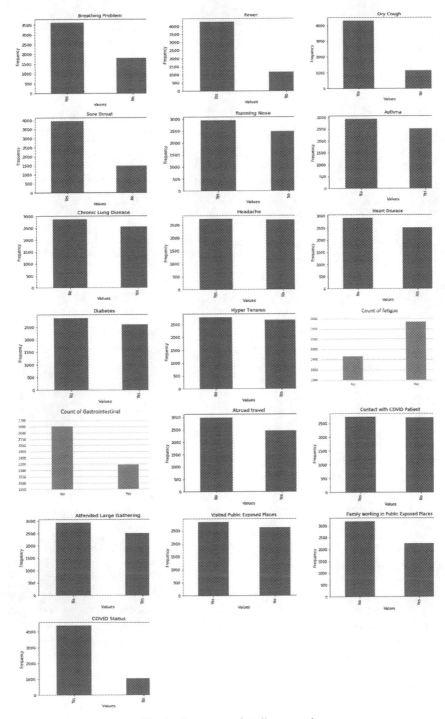

Fig. 1. Frequency of attributes used

Fig. 2. Topology of a Bayesian Network

From Fig. 2, node X has a direct influence on node Y. We often view the result of an unknown source as evidence, and we want to figure out what the cause is? In that case, Bayes' rule is expressed as:

$$P(cause|effect) = \frac{P(cause|effect)P(cause)}{P(effect)} \tag{1}$$

In Eq. 1, the conditional probability P(effect|cause) quantifies the causative link, whereas P(cause|effect) specifies the diagnostic direction. We often have conditional probabilities on causal links in tasks like medical diagnosis (that is, the doctor knows P (symptoms|disease) and wants to derive a diagnosis, P(disease|symptoms).

The domain expert is generally the one who determines what direct impact exists in a domain. We only need to describe a conditional probability distribution for each variable given its parents after the topology of the Bayesian network has been established.

There are basically two ways of building a BN structure/model:

i   Manually- where an expert determines the direction of arrows/edges between nodes and their associated Conditional Probability Tables (CPT).
ii Structural Learning- where the direction and location of arrows/edges are determined by means of some learning algorithms.

In this study, the structural learning approach was used. There are several structural learning algorithms, among which include the Peter-Clark (PC) algorithm [22], Bayesian Search (BS) algorithm [23], Greedy Thick Thinning (GTT) algorithm [24] etc. The logscore in equation 2 by [24] was chosen as the model selection criteria since it assesses the performances of the candidate BN models developed by the structural learning techniques.

The logscore is calculated as follows:

$$logscore(X_1, \ldots, X_N) = \frac{\sum_{i=1}^{N} \log_2 P(X_i|model)}{nN} \tag{2}$$

where X_i represent the nodes, N represents the total number of levels, and n represents the number of variables in the model. The BN model with the highest logscore is selected.

Sensitivity analysis was also done to see how changes in the levels of other nodes influence a node in a network.

5   Experimental Findings

In this section, we discuss the development of the Bayesian model for predictive inference reasoning. The GeNie [15] software was used in the model development process. The

Bayesian Search (BS) Algorithm [12], the Greedy Thick Thinning (GTT) algorithm [13] and the Peter-Clark (PC) algorithm [11] were employed to build different BN structures. In other to select the best algorithm to use for the current problem, the logscore for each algorithm is computed. The algorithm with the maximum logscore value is in turn selected. The logscore of each of the BN structure learning methods are shown in Table 2.

Table 2. Algorithms for Structural Learning and their associated Logscore Values

Algorithms	Logscore
Greedy Thick Thinning	−46210.7
Bayesian Search	−46601.8
Peter-Clark	−53828.5

Table 2 shows that the GTT method has the greatest logscore, indicating superior estimate performance. As a result, the BN estimated by the GTT method was chosen. The BN structural model is generated is as shown in Fig. 3. Upon completion of parameter modelling and quantification in the process of parameter learning from the dataset used, Fig. 4 shows the estimated BN with probabilities associated with each node in.

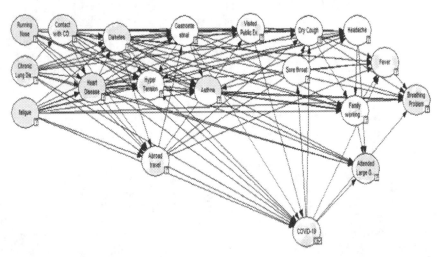

Fig. 3. GTT Algorithm-based Bayesian network structural model

The estimated BN in Fig. 4 can be used to predict the possibility of one being infected with the deadly coronavirus base on evidences observed. It can as well be used to analyze the factors causing one to be infected with the coronavirus and the relationships between those factors.

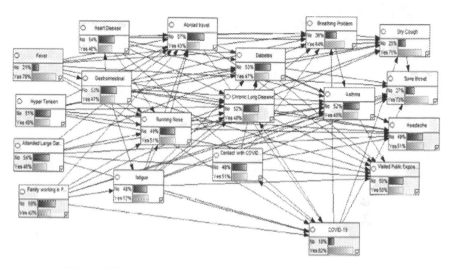

Fig. 4. GTT Algorithm-based Bayesian network model estimation

5.1 Validation of the Model

The developed model's prediction ability was verified using a measure of prediction accuracy and the Receiver Operating Characteristic (ROC) curve. Furthermore, a sensitivity analysis was carried out to determine which nodes are most likely to influence the likelihood of a patient contracting the deadly coronavirus disease.

Accuracy, as stated in Eq. 3, is the proportion of instances in the dataset correctly classified for the model. This is mathematically expressed as:

$$Accuracy = \frac{TP + TN}{TP + TN + FN + FP} \tag{3}$$

where *TP* denotes True Positive, TN denotes true negative, FP denotes false positive and FN denotes false negative.

The developed BN model correctly predicted the probability of contracting COVID-19 with an accuracy of 98%.

The ROC curve is a graph that compares the true positive rate (sensitivity) against the false positive rate (1- specificity). The area under the ROC curve is referred to as the Area Under the Curve (AUC). AUC values vary from 0 to 1. An AUC value of 1 indicates that the prediction is error-free, and as the AUC score drops, the model's prediction performance diminishes. Figure 5 depicts the ROC curve for the BN model prediction of contracting the coronavirus disease with an AUC of 0.997815.

Finally, a sensitivity analysis was performed to test the created BN model and assess the influence of additional variables/attributes (nodes) on the target node's result (COVID-19 status). In this study, the aim was to identify which node have the greatest impact on the probability of been infected by the deadly coronavirus.

Table 3 demonstrates how changes in the levels of other nodes impact the node "COVID-19". With a sensitivity value of 0.142, the most critical factor for predicting the contraction of the coronavirus disease is coming into contact with a COVID-19

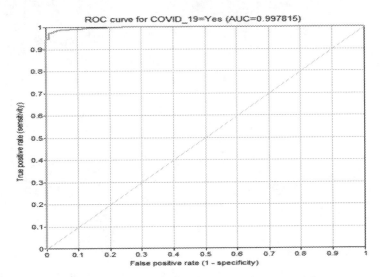

Fig. 5. ROC curve for the Bayesian network model.

patient, as shown in Table 3. This result is in accordance with the findings of [1, 3], the generally acknowledged views from centres of disease control across the globe and more importantly the World Health Organization.

This study hence concluded that patients with chronic lung diseases are the second category of people that are more susceptible to contracting the coronavirus disease. The third factor is diabetic patients followed by people with history of travelling abroad.

5.2 Other Machine Learning Algorithms

In addition to Bayesian Network, this study looked at the Nave Bayes Algorithm, J48 Algorithm, and Support Vector Machines, which are three common supervised machine learning techniques. We look at each machine learning process as thoroughly as possible in order to compute the best outcomes.

The Nave Bayes (NB) Algorithm is a popular machine learning approach based on the Bayes Rule. This approach is based on the independence of variables. The classes that would be calculated using the NB system must be unrelated to one another. One of the supervised learning algorithms is this one. Despite its simplicity, it yields excellent results in medical applications.

One of the most popular decision tree algorithms is J48. It also has the advantage of being able to make predictions using a smaller tree compares to other decision trees. As a result, the J48 algorithm is able to achieve more efficient results than its competitors.

Support Vector Machine (SVMs) are computational algorithms that use statistical learning theory to generate a coherent estimator from available data. It seeks to categorize the information into two groups. For this cause, the n-dimensional hyperplane is formed.

The WEKA software was used to develop programs for other machine learning algorithms used for comparison as shown in Table 4.

Table 3. Sensitivity analysis results using "COVID-19" as the target node.

Nodes	Sensitivity
Contact with COVID Patient	0.142
Chronic Lung Disease	0.046
Diabetes	0.022
Abroad travel	0.021
Heart Disease	0.018
Fatigue	0.018
Visited Public Exposed Places	0.012
Hyper Tension	0.000
Asthma	0.000
Sore throat	0.000
Breathing Problem	0.000
Fever	0.000
Dry Cough	0.000
Running Nose	0.000
Headache	0.000
Gastrointestinal	0.000
Attended Large Gathering	0.000
Family working in Public Exposed Places	0.000

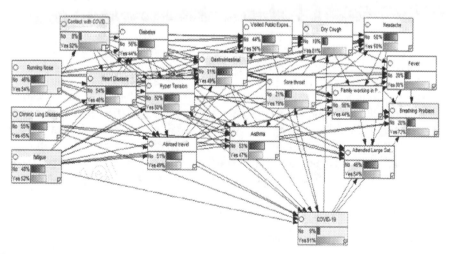

Fig. 6. The state of the Bayesian network in a situation where contact with a COVID-19 patient is estimated to be 92%.

Table 4. Comparison of machine learning algorithm

Algorithm	Accuracy	AUC
Naïve Bayes	96.5%	0.99
J48	98.2%	0.99
SVM	96.8%	0.91
Bayesian Network	**98.4%**	**0.99**

The Naïve Bayes, J48 Decision Tree, Support Vector Machine learning algorithms all correctly predicted the contraction of the coronavirus with an accuracy of 96.5%, 98.2% and 96.8% respectively.

The estimated BN depicting the level of probabilities of each node can be used to determine the patients that are more susceptible to contracting the coronavirus disease. For instance, given the evidence that there is 92% belief that a patient came in contact with another COVID-19 patient, the BN in Fig. 6 shows that there are 91% chances that the patient will likely contract the coronavirus disease. So, based on evidences provided by a patient, the BN model continues to adjust the probability of contracting the virus.

6   Conclusion

In the present study, a BN model was developed for estimating the probability of contracting the deadly coronavirus using epidemiological dataset. The BN quantifies the impact of several factors (attributes) on the probability of contracting the virus. With a 98% accuracy rate, the developed BN model successfully predicted the likelihood of contracting the coronavirus. Our model also affirms that contact with infected patient remains the sole cause for contracting the coronavirus disease. This is evident from the sensitivity analysis conducted which shows that contact with an infected patient has the highest sensitivity value of 0.142. The developed model can be used proactively to contain and manage the spread of the coronavirus in a cost effective manner. Furthermore, the BN model may be used to conduct scenario analysis in order to aid in the creation of a risk management strategy. In addition, the model may be modified to incorporate other features that are presently not captured, allowing for more effective tracking of vulnerable individuals and, as a result, more attention to be directed toward them. Finally, the proposed approach, as opposed to the existing random testing techniques, would aid in the early diagnosis of COVID-19 cases, decreasing the burden on healthcare institutions.

Funding:.   No funding sources.

Compliance with Ethical Standards.

Conflict of Interest:.   The authors declare that they have no conflict of interest

Ethical Approval:.   This article does not contain any studies with human participants or animals performed by any of the authors.

References

1. Zhou, M., Zhang, X., Qu, J.: Coronavirus disease 2019 (COVID-19): a clinical update. Front. Med. **14**(2), 126–135 (2020). https://doi.org/10.1007/s11684-020-0767-8
2. World Health Organization, Coronavirus disease (COVID-19) situation reports (2020). https://www.who.int/emergencies/diseases/novel-coronavirus-2019/situation-reports/.
3. Chen, Z.-M., et al.: Diagnosis and treatment recommendations for pediatric respiratory infection caused by the 2019 novel coronavirus. World J. Ped. 1–7 (2020). https://doi.org/10.1007/s12519-020-00345-5
4. Wynants, L., et al.: Prediction models for diagnosis and prognosis of covid-19 infection: systematic review and critical appraisal. BMJ **369** (2020). https://doi.org/10.1136/bmj.m1328
5. McLachlan, S., et al.: Bayesian networks in healthcare: distribution by medical condition. Artif. Intell. Med. **107**, 101912 (2020). https://doi.org/10.1016/j.artmed.2020.101912
6. Fenton, N.E., et al.: COVID-19 infection and death rates: the need to incorporate causal explanations for the data and avoid bias in testing. J. Risk Res. **23**, 1–4 (2020)
7. Fenton, N., et al.: A privacy-preserving Bayesian network model for personalised COVID19 risk assessment and contact tracing. medRxiv (2020)
8. Ucar, F., Korkmaz, D.: COVIDiagnosis-Net: deep bayes-squeezenet based diagnostic of the coronavirus disease 2019 (COVID-19) from X-ray images. Med. Hypoth. 109761 (2020). https://doi.org/10.1016/j.mehy.2020.109761
9. Jena, M., Dehuri, S.: DecisionTree for classification and regression: a state-of-the art review. Informatica **44**(4) (2020). https://doi.org/10.31449/inf.v44i4.3023
10. Behera, R.K., Rath, S.K., Misra, S., Leon, M., Adewumi, A.: Machine learning approach for reliability assessment of open source software. In: Misra, S., et al. (eds.) ICCSA 2019. LNCS, vol. 11622, pp. 472–482. Springer, Cham (2019). https://doi.org/10.1007/978-3-030-24305-0_35
11. Butt, S.A., Misra, S., Anjum, M.W., Hassan, S.A.: Agile project development issues during COVID-19. In: Przybyłek, A., Miler, J., Poth, A., Riel, A. (eds.) LASD 2021. LNBIP, vol. 408, pp. 59–70. Springer, Cham (2021). https://doi.org/10.1007/978-3-030-67084-9_4
12. Dehuri, R.K., et al.: Co-LSTM: Convolutional LSTM model for sentiment analysis in social big data. Inf. Process. Manage. **58**(1), 102435 (2021)
13. Behera, R.K., et al.: Comparative study of real time machine learning models for stock prediction through streaming data. J. Univ. Comput. Sci. **26**(9), 1128–1147 (2020)
14. Guhathakurata, S., et al.: A novel approach to predict COVID-19 using support vector machine. In: Data Science for COVID-19, pp. 351–364. Elsevier (2021)
15. Tezza, F., et al.: Predicting in-hospital mortality of patients with COVID-19 using machine learning techniques. J. Person. Med. **11**(5), 343 (2021)
16. Rehman, M.U., et al.: Future forecasting of COVID-19: a supervised learning approach. Sensors **21**(10), 3322 (2021)
17. Muhammad, L., et al.: Supervised machine learning models for prediction of COVID-19 infection using epidemiology dataset. SN Comput. Sci. **2**(1), 1–13 (2021)
18. Alballa, N., Al-Turaiki, I.: Machine learning approaches in COVID-19 diagnosis, mortality, and severity risk prediction: a review. Inf. Med. Unlocked **24**, 100564 (2021). https://doi.org/10.1016/j.imu.2021.100564
19. Wang, J., Zhai, X., Luo, Q.: How COVID-19 impacts chinese travelers' mobility decision-making processes: a bayesian network model. In: Wörndl, W., Koo, C., Stienmetz, J.L. (eds.) Information and Communication Technologies in Tourism 2021, pp. 557–563. Springer, Cham (2021). https://doi.org/10.1007/978-3-030-65785-7_53
20. Ojugo, A., Otakore, O.D.: Forging an optimized bayesian network model with selected parameters for detection of the coronavirus in Delta State of Nigeria. J. Appl. Sci. Eng. Technol. Educ. **3**(1), 37–45 (2021)

21. Symptoms and COVID Presence (2020). https://www.kaggle.com/hemanthhari/symptoms-and-covid-presence.
22. Spirtes, P., Glymour, C.: An algorithm for fast recovery of sparse causal graphs. Soc. Sci. Comput. Rev. **9**(1), 62–72 (1991)
23. Cooper, G.F., Herskovits, E.: A Bayesian method for the induction of probabilistic networks from data. Mach. Learn. **9**(4), 309–347 (1992)
24. Cheng, J., Bell, D.A., Liu, W.: An algorithm for Bayesian belief network construction from data. in proceedings of AI & STAT'97. Citeseer (1997)

Extending A+ with Object-Oriented Elements

A Case Study for A+.NET

Péter Gál[1(✉)] (ID), Csaba Bátori[1,2], and Ákos Kiss[1] (ID)

[1] Department of Software Engineering, University of Szeged,
Dugonics ter 13, Szeged 6720, Hungary
{galpeter,akiss}@inf.u-szeged.hu
[2] BlackRock, Vaci ut 47, Budapest 1134, Hungary
csaba.batori@blackrock.com

Abstract. This work presents a language extension to A+ that allows developers to conveniently handle external objects in A+ code. It discusses a set of object-oriented concepts and investigates their implications for the A+ language. For these new language elements, new symbols are added, and each of them represents basic operations (member access, member modification, type casting, and indexing) on objects. For each new operation the underlying mechanism is presented, and simple examples are provided showing their usage. Using these new operations, various .NET classes can be accessed and used from A+ programs without writing any additional code.

The presented language extension in this paper is runtime agnostic and it could enable the interoperation of A+ not only with the .NET framework but with other object oriented runtimes, too. Additionally this extension adds the basic mechanisms for implementing full object-oriented support for the A+ language in the future.

Keywords: A+ · Object-oriented programming · Language extension · DLR

1 Introduction

A+ is an array programming language [11] based on the APL language. The language was created more than 20 years ago to give an aid in real-life financial computations. Still, even in the present age, critical A+ programs are still used in computationally-intensive business environments. The original interpreter-based execution environment of A+ is implemented in C/C++ and is officially supported on Unix-like operating systems only. However, the development activity of this implementation is very low and the maintainability of the code is questionable, as discussed in the paper [6].

Csaba Bátori was with the Department of Software Engineering at the time of the language extension work.

© Springer Nature Switzerland AG 2021
O. Gervasi et al. (Eds.): ICCSA 2021, LNCS 12957, pp. 141–153, 2021.
https://doi.org/10.1007/978-3-030-87013-3_11

Thus in a previous work, the A+.NET project [5] was introduced, which is a cleanroom implementation of the original A+ environment for the .NET environment[1]. The goal of the .NET-based implementation was to allow the interoperability between A+ and .NET programs. This allows A+ scripts to call .NET methods, allows .NET applications to embed A+.NET as a domain-specific language, and A+ scripts could be executed just like any other application on Windows systems. In addition this provides a way for existing A+ applications to extend their lifetime, provide .NET developers existing financial routines in form of A+ code, and allow access for .NET libraries accessible for A+ developers.

However, using .NET classes and methods from A+.NET is not straight-forward. For each .NET method or class, specially formatted wrapper methods are required that need to be written by the developer. Fortunately, this extra burden can be removed by introducing language extensions that can handle external objects in the A+ language. In this paper a set of required operations for a language which is not object-oriented is presented to cooperate with the object-oriented concepts.

The rest of the paper is organized as follows. In order to make the paper self-contained, in Sect. 2 a short introduction into the A+ language is presented, focusing on distinguishing features. (This does not provide too in depth information, thus for further details the reader should refer to the A+ Language Reference [11] document.) In Sect. 3, we describe the current state of A+ and .NET interoperability. In Sect. 4, the proposed extensions are presented, and in Sect. 5, the implemented extensions for the A+.NET runtime are detailed. In Sect. 6, we overview the related work on extending legacy languages with object-oriented concepts, and finally, in Sect. 7, we conclude the paper and give directions for future work.

2   The A+ Programming Language

A+ derives from one of the first array programming languages, APL [2]. Due to this legacy, A+ have unusual aspects compared to other more recent programming languages. One of the most important one is that, although being a language of mathematical origin, all functions have equal precedence and every expression is evaluated from right to left.

There are more than 60 built-in functions, which are usually treated as operators in other languages. Among these functions there are simple arithmetic functions and also some other complex ones, like inner product or matrix inverse calculations. All built-in and user defined functions are treated as first class-citizens, which means that the programmer can assign functions to variables and is also able to pass functions as arguments to other functions. In addition almost all built-in functions have special non-ASCII symbols associated. This syntax makes the code compact and also allows mathematical-like notations in an A+ code. However, this could pose a challenge for the untrained eye when trying to read and understand the source code.

---

[1] Project hosted at: https://github.com/elecro/aplusdotnet.

```
1  (×/s) , +/s ← 1 + ι 10
```
Listing 1.1. Calculating the product and sum of the first 10 natural numbers in A+.

The language defines a very narrow set of types, it has integers, floats, characters, symbols – denoted by a starting backtick character –, functions, and a type named box – which is a special type wrapping another type. In A+ even the a single number or character is treated as an array.

Arrays can be placed in an array if they have the same type. This means that it is disallowed to put a character array inside an integer array. The programmer would need to convert the character array into an integer array first to be able to put it into the target array. Currently, the runtime environment only allows the creation of arrays with a maximum of 9 dimensions, as specified by the language reference [11].

In A+, there is a namespace-like concept called context. Each variable and function is in such a context and each context has a name. If one would like to access the `demo` variable from the context named `tst`, one would write `tst.demo` in A+. It is also possible to have a context named `tst.ctx` and then, one can use the `tst.ctx.var` identifier to access or modify the `var` in that context. This `<context name>.<var>` format is called the qualified name – note that there is one dot before the `<var>` part. The format `<var>` is called the unqualified name, when there is no dot character in the name. During the execution of an A+ code, the runtime always knows what context it is in and automatically extends all unqualified names. It is also possible to change context at runtime. There is a default root context that has no name. Thus, if one uses the `var` variable then it will return the value of the `.var` variable if the current context is the root context or it will return the `tst.var` value if the runtime is in the `tst` context.

The specialties mentioned above can be illustrated in Listing 1.1, which shows a way to calculate the product and sum of the first 10 natural numbers. Breaking down the example in smaller parts can help in understand how it works. The `ι 10` expression generates an 10-element array containing values from 0 to 9. The expression `1 +` will increment each element in this array by one. After this, the value is assigned to the variable `s`. By using the `+/` operator the sum of the vector is calculated. Similarly, the `*/` will calculate the product of the same vector. Lastly, using the concatenation function – which is denoted by a comma – the two values are merged into a single two-element array containing the `3628800 55` values. The parentheses around the product is important, as without it the variable `s` and the sum would be concatenated forming a two-element array and the product would be calculated on this new two-element vector because of the right-to-left evaluation order.

As the code above shows, quite complex computations can be easily expressed in a very compact form in A+. The Language Reference gives further examples, mostly from financial applications, e.g., how to compute the present value at various interest rates in a single line [11, page 62].

```
1  var scope = engine.CreateScope();
2  scope.SetVariable("tst.value", AFloat.Create(3.2);
```
Listing 1.2. Registering the constant 3.2 into an A+.NET scope

3   State of the Art of A+ and .NET Interoperability

A+.NET allows the developers to inject extra variables and functions into the scope of the runtime.

Each value that the developer wants to register into the runtime must be wrapped into an AType. There are four types of values that can be registered: numbers – integer and double –, characters, and symbols. The A+.NET types for these are AInt, AFloat, AChar, and ASymbol respectively. Naming the double type as float might seem strange at first sight, however, floats represent double precision floating point number in A+ terminology. Thus, AFloat adheres to the original naming conventions. Listing 1.2 depicts how someone can add the constant 3.2 into the A+.NET runtime under the name tst.value. The first line exemplifies the creation of a new scope in the runtime, which stores, all methods and variables and can be used when executing A+ code from .NET.

Each added method must adhere to some rules: First, the method must be a static method. Second, the return type must be AType, which is the base interface type for all types in the runtime. Third, the first argument must be an Aplus type, which contains the runtime environment information and can be accessed by the method. And fourth, any other arguments must be of AType type and – most importantly – they must be in reverse order. (The reverse order is required because the A+ language evaluates function arguments from right to left while the C# does not. Thus the A+.NET runtime performs a trick and requires all methods to have a reverse order of arguments. So for an A+ function that accepts two parameters, the second argument of the A+ function becomes the first non-environment argument of the registered C# method and the first argument in A+ will be the last parameter in C#. In Listing 1.3, a conforming method is shown, which meets all the requirements for the A+.NET.

There are two ways of adding a compatible method into the A+.NET runtime. The first one is to create scope – which contains the variables – for the A+.NET engine/runtime and then add the required method as a variable into the scope. The function must be wrapped into an AFunc which contains information about the callable method for the runtime. This approach is shown in Listing 1.4, where method Foo from Listing 1.3 is registered into the scope as tst.foo.

The second option is to create a class with the compatible methods and annotate all functions as AplusContextFunction and the class as AplusContext. The annotation AplusContext specifies the context name under which the methods should be registered. The function annotation specifies the name by which the method should be accessible from A+. Such annotated classes can be loaded via the $load system command specifying the name used in the annotation of the

```
1   static AType Foo(Aplus env, AType arg2, AType arg1) {
2     // ...
3   }
```

Listing 1.3. An A+.NET compatible C# method

```
1   var scope = engine.CreateScope();
2   scope.SetVariable("tst.foo",
3     AFunc.Create("foo", Foo, 2, "Test method"));
```

Listing 1.4. Registering a C# method into an A+.NET scope

class. Listing 1.5 depicts a class with all the annotations. For this specific case, the $load tst instruction in A+ will load the method into the context named tst with the name of foo.

After we have loaded the required function(s) into the A+.NET runtime – in any of the two ways described above –, it is possible to invoke them just like any other A+ functions, as shown in Listing 1.6.

As visible from the explanations and examples above, adding a method to A+.NET runtime requires writing a lot of code. Writing these wrapper methods or classes for each required .NET class is tedious and error prone, not to mention that there could be a lot of copy-paste code in the end.

Instead of writing these wrappers or providing tools to generate them, a better way would be to have a mechanism that allows run-time access for the required classes, methods, properties, and variables. For this, we have reviewed the object-oriented concepts and investigated requirements for the A+ language to handle external objects conveniently. These concepts will be described in the next section.

```
1   [AplusContext("tst")]
2   class Demo {
3     [AplusContextFunction("foo")]
4     static AType Method(Aplus env, AType arg2, AType arg1) {
5       // ...
6     }
7   }
```

Listing 1.5. A+.NET conformant C# method with annotations, registered as tst.foo in the A+ environment

```
1  tst.foo{1;2}
```
Listing 1.6. Invocation of a registered C# method from A+.NET

4   Language Extension

Due to the fact that the A+ language is not an object-oriented language by design, the investigation of the required operations to handle objects in a language was the first step.

During the investigation the base requirements to handle objects in a language were identified. First, the introduction of a way to represent objects in the runtime was required. This essentially means that a new type should be added to the language.

Second, there are four basic operations that should be supported by a language to handle the most basic tasks on objects. These are the following:

– Accessing members (methods, variables, and properties): this operation provides the means to read variables and properties, and to access methods.
– Modifying variables and properties: the operation makes it possible to assign new values to properties and values.
– Type casting: an important operation to resolve ambiguities.
– Using indexer properties: in .NET indexing objects is done via a special property and there are compound types where there is no other way of accessing elements e.g. in ArrayList. This is mainly required for the .NET binding.

Note that the method invocation is not among the operations. This is because most languages already support it in some way. So the existing method invocation syntax can be improved to handle the invocation of methods on instances and classes.

Also note that with the operations above the language will still not support native classes. That is, it is not possible to write classes in the same language for which the operations are implemented. Fortunately, the described operations take the language closer to the real object-oriented languages. So it becomes possible to build further object-oriented functionalities on top of these new operations. Also note that the concept of these operations is not tied to one specific language, in our case to A+. Thus, these could be added to other non-object-oriented languages as well.

5   Implemented Language Extension

As described in the previous section, four operations are a must for the A+.NET runtime to handle (external) objects. In the case of A+.NET, the implementation of the required operations can take advantage of the reflection capabilities of the .NET framework and also the code generation possibilities of the Dynamic Language Runtime (DLR) framework. The use of reflection provides ways to search for classes and methods, and the code generation capabilities of DLR enable the building of wrapper method(s) at runtime, thus eliminating the need for writing wrapper methods by hand. With these two techniques combined, it is possible to provide general functions for A+.NET which can perform the required lookups and code generations, thus avoiding unnecessary repetitive manual coding. Additionally, the implementation must take into account, that in A+ the order of evaluation is right to left and any changes to this rule could break existing code.

As mentioned in the previous section, a new type must be added into the runtime. In A+.NET, this new type is internally named **AObject** and its instances can store any .NET object. The subsequent sections will define each previously mentioned operation in more detail.

5.1   Accessing Methods, Variables, and Properties

In A+, functions are first class citizens, thus it must be ensured that each .NET method can also be used accordingly and not just for simple method invocation. Fortunately, this lenience is a win in our case as this will allow us to handle the methods, variables, and properties in a similar way, thus simplifying the implementation. The following algorithm describes the inner workings of the accessor operation. This operation has two input arguments, the name of the property, variable, or method to be looked up and the instance or class on which the lookup should be performed, and can be formulated as **SelectMemeber(x, y)**. Note that, both the member and class names must be passed as an A+ symbol type. This approach was chosen not to interfere with the context concept of the A+ language.

1. Collect all methods, variables, and properties of the instance or class specified by the second parameter (that is **y**).
2. For each method, variable, and property check if it has the same name as specified by the first parameter (that is **x**).
3. If no match is found, return an error, reporting that there is no member accessible with the given name.
4. If a variable or property was found, return it as an A+ type. In the case of a primitive type, such as string, number, or enum value, they be converted into their compatible A+.NET counterpart which are: array of **AChar**, **AInt**, **AFloat**, and **ASymbol** respectively. In any other case, the value must be returned as an **AObject**.
5. If the lookup found a method, construct a lambda function using the DLR capabilities, which accepts a variable number of arguments, performs the type matching algorithm – which is described in Sect. 5.5 – and invokes the method returned by type matching. The constructed lambda method is then returned as an A+ function type, represented by the **AFunc** type in A+.NET.

```
1  constructor ← ⊖ 'Bar
2  instance ← constructor{}
3  value ← 'variable ⊖ instance
4  ('method ⊖ instance){}
```
Listing 1.7. Example A+.NET accessor usage

Constructor access can be thought of as a special case of method access. The main difference, in this case, is that the function name parameter is always that of the class.

When the `SelectMember` returns a lambda function – either a constructor or another method – the A+ function containing it can be called a traditional function in the runtime. Thus, method invocation does not require additional implementation or functionality in the engine. The generated lambda function contains all required information on how to perform the .NET method invocation.

To integrate seamlessly into the syntax of the A+, the existing but hitherto unused ⊖ symbol was chosen for the `SelectMember` operation. The format $x \ominus y$ is treated as `SelectMember(x, y)`. Listing 1.7 shows an example use case for the `SelectMember` operation. In line 1, the constructor lookup for the .NET class named `Bar` is demonstrated, which is invoked in line 2. This invocation looks like any other A+ function invocation. Line 3 shows how variables can be accessed with the new operation. Finally, on line 4, the method access and invocation is demonstrated. As this line shows, the call to the ⊖ function is enclosed in parentheses to ensure the evaluation order dictated by A+, also this way the language grammar does not require radical changes to give the ⊖ function a higher precedence.

The described `SelectMember` operation provides a basic building block for handling the modification of variables and properties which is described in the next section.

5.2   Variable and Property Modification

The modification of variables and properties are similar to the access case, with the addition of a third parameter for the accessor algorithm. This third parameter will serve as the new value for the target variable or property. Additionally, searching for methods is not allowed when performing the member name lookup.

The following algorithm describes how to modify a variable or property on a given instance or class. It has three input parameters. The first is the name of the variable or property to modify. The second is the class or instance on which the variable/property lookup should be performed. And the third argument is the new value for the variable/property. The operation is named `SetMember(x, y, z)`

1. Get all variables and properties of the object or instance specified by the second parameter (that is y).

```
1  ('variable ⊖ instance) ← 42
```

Listing 1.8. Example A+.NET instance variable modification

2. For each variable and property check if it has a name which is specified by the first argument (that is x).
3. If no match is found, return an error, reporting that there is no such member to modify.
4. As the lookup found a variable or a property, try to cast the new value – specified by the third argument z – to the type of the variable/property.
5. If the cast is not possible, return with an error, stating that it is not possible to update the variable with the supplied new value.
6. If the cast was correctly performed, assign the cast value to the selected variable/property.
7. Return with the new value as specified by the third argument. Note that this is the original value of z, not the cast one.

For the `SetMember` operation the same ⊖ symbol was used, but to invoke the algorithm it must be used in the $(x \ominus y) \leftarrow z$ format. This can be detected during the parsing of the code, as the accessor function is on the left side of the assignment function. Note that the parentheses are required because of the strict right-to-left evaluation order of the A+ code and the fact that the assignment function has the same precedence as any other function in the language. Listing 1.8 exhibits a use case for the operation.

5.3   Indexers

In .NET, there are numerous objects that provide access to their individual elements. This is usually performed with the help of indexers. To have better integration with .NET types in the A+.NET runtime, it is important to provide an intuitive way to access such elements.

Fortunately, there is also the notation of indexing elements in A+ and, therefore, there is no need for introducing new syntactic elements. We can leverage the existing indexing mechanism and only improve its internal mechanisms to add the .NET indexer binding.

As the indexers in .NET are special properties that can be queried by reflection, the `SelectMember` algorithm can be used to get the value of an item at a given index from an object or instance. Thus, in the indexer case, the `SelectMember` algorithm will search for the indexer properties. In the case of element assignment at a given index, the `SetMember` algorithm will perform the same search as in the element access case.

An example of indexer usage is shown in Listing 1.9. After creating an instance of `ArrayList` in line 1, the code performs an element addition to the list in line 2. (The equivalent code in C# would be: `list.Add(1);`.) Then the usage of the indexers is shown: first, the access of a single element by its index on line 3, continued by the value modification of a given index in line 4.

```
1   list ← (⊖ 'ArrayList){}
2   ('Add ⊖ list){1}
3   list[0]
4   list[0] ← 2
```
Listing 1.9. Example indexer usage for .NET types

```
1   ('booleanVariable ⊖ instance) ← 'Boolean ◇ 1
```
Listing 1.10. Example A+.NET type casting for .NET types

5.4   Type Casting

Type casting is an important operation in the .NET world, as it allows developers to resolve ambiguities. A new ◇ symbol is introduced into the language, providing the means to perform the .NET type casting functionality in the runtime from the A+ code. This function can also be used for resolving method call ambiguities, which is detailed in Sect. 5.5.

Listing 1.10 depicts an example of the type casting function, represented by the ◇ symbol. In the example, the number 1 is initially represented as an A+ number type, but using the new type cast function, it will be changed to a Boolean type which is from the .NET world. The A+.NET symbol 'Boolean is used to specify the target type for the cast function. After the cast is performed, the value can be assigned to a boolean variable or property on a given instance if needed.

If the type cast operation cannot be accomplished, an error is reported to the A+.NET runtime. For example, if the developer wants to cast an integer to a string the error is returned, stating that an invalid cast was attempted.

5.5   Type Matching

As mentioned before in the SelectMember operations, .NET methods are looked up by their names. However, just a method name is not always enough to correctly match a method. It is possible that there is more than one method with the same name and the difference is only in the number of arguments or in their types. Thus, to correctly select a method, the types and number of parameters are also required.

The type matching algorithm should be performed after the potential methods based on their names have already been found. First, any method is ignored if it does not have the same number of arguments as the number of arguments supplied for the method invocation. In case there are no methods left to select from, an error is reported during runtime, that the number of parameters are incorrect. Second, as the number of arguments is now correct, a type distance vector calculation is performed. The basic building block of the calculation is the type distance notation.

```
1  class Place {}
2  class Bar : Place {}
3  class Vehicle {}
4  class Car : Vehicle {}
5
6  void Foo(Place arg1, Car arg2) {}
7  void Foo(Bar arg1, Vehicle arg2) {}
```

Listing 1.11. Example for C# method ambiguity

The type distance calculation of non-primitive types (i.e. classes) is based on the inheritance hierarchy of .NET types. If two types are in an inheritance relation, then the type distance of those types is the length of the shortest path between them in the inheritance graph, with the result of 0 if the two types are the same. If the two types are unrelated inheritance-wise, their type distance is specified as infinite. For example: if there is a class named Bar which is a subclass of class Place then the type distance between Bar and Place is one.

For primitive types, inheritance hierarchy is not applicable. However, the C# reference documentation [4, § 11.2] specifies conversion tables, which help to define a pseudo-hierarchy between them, which can be used the same way as the real inheritance for non-primitive types. This pseudo-hierarchy is as follows: Boolean → SByte → Byte → Int16 → UInt16 → Int32 → UInt32 → Int64 → UInt64 → Single → Double → Decimal → AType → Object, the Char type connects into the UInt16 type, the string values are starting with String → Enum and connecting into the AType. Thus, for example if there is an input argument with the type Byte and the method requires an Int32, the distance between the two types is 3. The A+ types are using this pseudo-hierarchy to allow interoperability with the .NET methods. A+ symbols are using the chain starting from the String type, integers either from Int32 or Double, and characters use the Char type as a starting point.

Based on this type of distance information, it is now possible to define the type distance vector. The type distance vector is a vector of N elements where N is the number of input parameters for the current method invocation and for each element the type distance is calculated between the input parameter and the parameter of the potential method. After the distance calculations, the best method is chosen. A method is considered better than the other if each element of its type distance vector is smaller or equal than the corresponding element in the other method's vector, but at least one element is strictly smaller than its corresponding element. This selection method is based on the better function member selection described in the C# language specification [4, § 12.6.4.3]. Note, however, that there may be incomparable elements in this relation. Only if there is a single method that is better than all other alternatives does the runtime select that method for invocation. Otherwise, the runtime reports an error because of the ambiguity. Such ambiguities can be resolved with the newly introduced type casting operation.

Listing 1.11 depicts a C# method ambiguity. For this use case the (`Foo ⊖ `class){(⊖ `Bar){}, (⊖ `Car){}} invocation would not be successful. The calculated type vector distance for the invocation and the first Foo method would be – based on the type hierarchy – the vector [1, 0], and for the second Foo method it would be [0, 1]. Thus, based on the better method selection rules, it is not possible to select one method and the ambiguity error is reported. However – as stated before – it is possible to resolve the ambiguity if e.g. the second parameter for the method invocation is cast to Vehicle. Then the type distance vector for the second case would result, in a [0, 0] vector and a perfect match would be found.

6   Related Work

Extending an already existing language with object-oriented capabilities is not a new thing in the world of programming languages. Even for APL – from which A+ derives – there are object-oriented extensions [1]. Before the creation of the A+ language, there were already experiments to incorporate object-oriented notations into the APL language [7]. Both of these implementations provide object-oriented notations, allowing the developers to create classes from APL code and not just operations for objects. However, in one case, the authors introduced the member access operation to be read from left-to-right thus making the right-to-left reading mode a bit awkward when such operations are performed. In the other case, the authors introduced a special system function (□NEW) to construct new instances from a given class. Additionally, possibility to interact with other objects – that are outside of the APL language – were not mentioned.

Moreover, the APL language is still in active use and there are different companies providing support for its implementations, the most notable one is provided by Dyalog Ltd. [3]. This version also provides object-oriented notations to make the developers' life easier. In addition, it is also gives a syntax to write classes, not just the option to instantiate them, and access its members. The variant took the approach to introduce a new system function to instantiate classes and use the dot syntax to select members on classes/instances [8].

Other array-based programing languages used in mathematics already have object-oriented support, for example the widely used Maple [9] and Matlab [10, 12] software packages.

7   Summary and Future Work

In this work, a set of requirements for a language with no object-oriented programming concepts were presented, to handle external objects. This can be achieved by adding a new type into the language and implementing four basic operations. The case study shows that with the new type and operations it is indeed possible to conveniently handle objects in A+.NET while also eliminating the need to write or generate wrapper methods to expose objects into the runtime. The introduction of only two new language elements into A+ was required for this extension and the refinement of the indexing, and assignment operations. Additionally, a type distance vector-based approach was presented for matching formal .NET and actual A+ method parameters.

However, there is still work to do as there are constructs in .NET which are not accessible in the current A+.NET extension. In the current approach there is no support for generics, parameter passing by reference, output parameters, and no support for invoking overloaded operators from A+. In addition, adding class support would be beneficial to further improve the language. The extension of the language with these new constructs may facilitate the more widespread use of A+.NET. Furthermore, after having a full object-oriented extension for the A+ language, a comparison with the APL object-oriented extension can be performed.

Acknowledgements. This research was supported by grant NKFIH-1279-2/2020 of the Ministry for Innovation and Technology, Hungary.

References

1. Brown, R.G.: Object oriented APL: an introduction and overview. In: Proceedings of the International Conference on APL-Berlin-2000 Conference, APL 2000, pp. 47–54. ACM, New York (2000). https://doi.org/10.1145/570475.570482
2. Clayton, L., Eklof, M.D., McDonnell, E.: ISO/IEC 13751:2000(E): Programming Language APL. Extended, International Standards Organization, June 2000
3. Dyalog Ltd.: Dyalog APL. http://www.dyalog.com/. Accessed 15 June 2021
4. ECMA International: ECMA-334 - C# Language Specification, 5th edn., December 2017. https://www.ecma-international.org/wp-content/uploads/ECMA-334_5th_edition_december_2017.pdf. Accessed 15 June 2021
5. Gál, P., Kiss, Á · Implementation of an A+ interpreter for .NET. In: Proceedings of the 7th International Conference on Software Paradigm Trends (ICSOFT 2012), Rome, Italy, pp. 297–302. SciTePress, 24–27 July 2012. https://doi.org/10.5220/0004129202970302
6. Gál, P., Kiss, Á.: A comparison of maintainability metrics of two A+ interpreters. In: Proceedings of the 8th International Joint Conference on Software Technologies - ICSOFT-EA, (ICSOFT 2013), pp. 292–297. INSTICC, SciTePress (2013). https://doi.org/10.5220/0004597702920297
7. Girardot, J.J., Sako, S.: An object oriented extension to APL. In: Proceedings of the International Conference on APL: APL in Transition, APL 1987, pp. 128–137. ACM, New York (1987). https://doi.org/10.1145/28315.28330
8. Kromberg, M.J.: Arrays of objects. In: Proceedings of the 2007 Symposium on Dynamic Languages, DLS 2007, pp. 20–28. Association for Computing Machinery, New York (2007). https://doi.org/10.1145/1297081.1297087
9. Bernardin, L., Chin, P., DeMarco, P., et al.: Maple Programming Guide. Maplesoft (2011)
10. MathWorks: Matlab Object-Oriented Programming (2021). https://www.mathworks.com/help/pdf_doc/matlab/matlab_oop.pdf. Accessed 15 June 2021
11. Morgan Stanley: A+ Language Reference (1995–2008). http://www.aplusdev.org/Documentation/. Accessed 15 June 2021
12. Register, A.H.: A Guide to MATLAB Object-Oriented Programming. Scitech Pub Inc. (2007). https://doi.org/10.5555/1202571

Rotation Forest-Based Logistic Model Tree for Website Phishing Detection

Abdullateef O. Balogun[1,2], Noah O. Akande[3(✉)], Fatimah E. Usman-Hamza[1],
Victor E. Adeyemo[4], Modinat A. Mabayoje[1], and Ahmed O. Ameen[1]

[1] Department of Computer Science, University of Ilorin, Ilorin PMB 1515, Nigeria
{balogun.ao1,usman-hamzah.fe,mabayoje.ma,
aminamed}@unilorin.edu.ng
[2] Department of Computer and Information Sciences, Universiti Teknologi PETRONAS,
Bandar Seri Iskandar 32610, Perak, Malaysia
abdullateef_16005851@utp.edu.my
[3] Department of Computer Science, Landmark University, Omu-Aran, Kwara State, Nigeria
akande.noah@lmu.edu.ng
[4] School of Built Environment, Engineering, and Computing, Leeds Beckett University,
Headingley Campus, Leeds LS6 3QS, UK
v.adeyemo5225@student.leedsbeckett.ac.uk

Abstract. The emergence of web and internet technology has led to its use in a broad array of services ranging from financial to educational services. This has led to a spike in the number of cybersecurity problems over the years, the most notable of which is the phishing attack, in which malicious websites imitate legitimate websites to capture gullible users' details needed for unauthorized access. However, current mitigation strategies, such as anti-phishing applications and Machine Learning (ML) methods, have been effective for detecting phishing activities. Hackers, on the other hand, are developing new ways to circumvent these countermeasures. Nevertheless, given the dynamism of phishing attempts, there is a continual demand for innovative and efficient solutions for website phishing detection. This study proposes a Rotation Forest-based Logistic Model Trees (RF-LMT) for website phishing detection. LMT is a technique that combines logistic regression and tree inference into a single model tree. Three datasets of different instance distributions, both balanced and imbalanced, are used to investigate the proposed RF-LMT. From the results, it was observed that LMT performed better than the selected baseline classifiers. This finding revealed that LMT can perform comparably to baseline classifiers. However, in comparison to LMT and experimented baseline classifiers, the proposed RF-LMT method showed superior performance in website phishing detection. Specifically, RF-LMT had a high detection accuracy (98.24%), AUC (0.998), f-measure (0.982) values with a low false-positive rate (0.018). Furthermore, RF-LMT outperformed existing ML-based phishing attack models. As a result, the proposed RF-LMT method is recommended for dealing with complex phishing attacks.

Keywords: Cybersecurity · Logistic Model Tree · Machine learning · Phishing attack · Rotation forest

O. Gervasi et al. (Eds.): ICCSA 2021, LNCS 12957, pp. 154–169, 2021.
https://doi.org/10.1007/978-3-030-87013-3_12

1 Introduction

The increased availability and application of Information Technology (IT) have increased the number of internet-based applications available in cyberspace. These operations range from vital services such as financial services to essential activities such as health and education applications [1, 2]. Financial purchases, online gaming platforms, and social media apps, according to data, are among the most popular and commonly used internet-based solutions with a large user base. The vast number of users who use these internet-based solutions demonstrate their recent successes.

According to research, financial transactions, online gaming sites, and social media applications are among the most common and widely used web-based solutions with a broad user base. The large number of people who use these web-based applications demonstrate their popularity in recent years. The aim is to increase the accessibility and availability of commonly used internet-based solutions. Nonetheless, since there are no generic cyberspace control mechanisms, the unrestricted mobility and affordability of these internet-based solutions in cyberspace open the door to cyber-attacks [3–5]. Cyber-attacks generate critical vulnerabilities and risks for both internet-based solutions and end-users, as well as important information and financial losses. Phishing attacks on websites are a typical example of these cyber-attacks. Cybercriminals are now setting up bogus websites to steal personal information from unsuspecting users and use it for illegal purposes [2, 6].

The website phishing attack is a significant cybersecurity issue that has overburdened cyberspace and has harmed internet users and internet-based solutions [7, 8]. According to [2], website phishing is a common deception in which an unauthorized website imitates a legitimate website for the sole intention of collecting data from unsuspecting users. As a result, phishing attacks pose a severe risk to web-based solutions [9–11]. In 2018, the Anti-Phishing Working Group (APWG) identified 51,401 phishing websites in cyberspace. According to RSA, international organizations lose almost $9 billion in 2016 due to phishing attacks [12, 13]. These incidents have shown that phishing attacks from unauthorized websites quickly gain ground, resulting in significant financial losses and burdens [9, 11, 14].

Numerous cybersecurity specialists and analysts have proposed and created various anti-phishing methods for identifying phishing websites [15–17]. One of these solutions is the use of a blacklist technique to avoid website phishing attacks. Web browsers' blacklisting mechanism matches the submitted universal resource locator (URLs) with previously-stored phishing website URLs to determine its authenticity. A significant disadvantage of blacklist anti-phishing methods is their failure to detect new phishing URLs due to their reliance on compiling blacklisted phishing URLs [3, 18]. Furthermore, cyber-attackers are deploying sophisticated techniques that enable them to circumvent the blacklisting process easily. Due to the dynamism of cyber-attacks, Machine Learning (ML)-based technologies are used to assess the credibility of websites to handle the complex existence of website phishing attacks on features derived from websites [12, 15, 19].

On the other hand, the efficacy of the ML-based phishing detection method depends on the success of the selected ML technique when detecting phishing websites. Several ML methods have been used to detect phishing websites, with low detection accuracy and high false-positive rates [6, 20–22]. This might be attributed to difficulties with data quality, like imbalanced datasets, that degrade the effectiveness of ML models [23, 24]. As a result of the dynamism of phishing websites, more sophisticated ML methods are needed.

Consequently, a rotation forest-based logistic model tree (RF-LMT) for identifying phishing websites is proposed. LMT is a model tree that integrates logistic regression and tree induction approaches. The cornerstone of LMT is the incorporation of a logistic regression model at the leaf nodes of the tree by systematically optimizing higher leaf nodes.

Summarily, the following are the specific contributions of this study:

1) RF-LMT algorithm is used to distinguish between legitimate and phishing websites.
2) An experimental evaluation and analysis of RF-LMT for website phishing detection in comparison to existing phishing approaches.

Furthermore, this research aims to address the following research questions:

1) How efficient is the LMT algorithm in detecting legitimate and phishing websites?
2) How efficient is the proposed RF-LMT algorithm in detecting legitimate and phishing websites?
3) How efficient is the proposed RF-LMT compared to existing phishing methods?

The rest of this paper is structured as follows. Section 2 examines existing related research. Section 3 portrays the analysis methodology, an overview of the experimental process, and the algorithms deployed. Section 4 discusses the research experiment and the analysis of the experimental findings. Finally, Sect. 5 concludes and suggests potential future works.

2   Related Works

This section investigates and discusses emerging phishing detection methods developed using different anti-phishing and ML techniques.

Mohammad, Thabtah and McCluskey [1] used a self-structuring neural network to identify phishing websites. Their model is based on an adaptive learning rate that varies before introducing new neurons and network structures. The suggested model's accuracy values were 94.07%, 92.48%, and 91.12% for the training, testing, and validation sets, respectively. Also, the bat meta-heuristics search algorithm was used by Vrbančič, Fister Jr and Podgorelec [2] to boost DNN. The proposed method had a maximum accuracy of 96.9%. These studies demonstrate that neural network models are almost as good as standard classifiers at detecting phishing websites.

Alqahtani [6] identified phishing websites using a novel association law induction strategy. The proposed solution employs an association law procedure to determine the authenticity of a page. Their experimental results showed the effectiveness of the proposed approach, as it outperforms baseline classifiers including DT, RIPPER, and some associative learning classification models with a precision of 95.20% and an F-measure value of 0.9511. Similarly, Abdelhamid, Ayesh and Thabtah [7] used a Multi-label Classifier-based Associative Classification (MCAC) technique to identify phishing. The MCAC technique was used for the detection mission to remove sixteen (16) unique features from a website URL using rules discovery, classifier creation, and class assignment. From their experimental results, MCAC outperformed the base classifiers RIPPER, DT, Component, CBA, and MCAR. Dedakia and Mistry [8] proposed a Content-Based Associative Classification (CBAC) approach for detecting phishing. The proposed method extends the Multi-Label Class Associative Classification (MCAC) algorithm by considering content-based properties. Based on the experimental results, the proposed solution (CBAC) had an accuracy value of 94.29%. Hadi, Aburub and Alhawari [10] created and tested a fast associative classification algorithm (FACA) for phishing website recognition against other known associative classification (AC) methods (CBA, CMAR, MCAR, and ECAR). Their experimental results show that FACA outperforms other AC methods in terms of accuracy and F-measure values. The effectiveness of these associative-based approaches shows their applicability for phishing detection. However, their low accuracy value is a disadvantage, and high detection accuracy phishing detection models are needed.

Rahman, Rafiq, Toma, Hossain and Biplob [11] investigated the effectiveness of various ML methods and ensemble methods in detecting website phishing (KNN, DT, SVM, RF, Extreme Randomized Tree (ERT), and Gradient Boosting Tree (GBT)). Similarly, Chandra and Jana [9] explored the usage of meta-classifiers to improve the detection of phishing websites. Their analyses showed that ensemble methods outperformed single classifiers. Alsariera, Elijah and Balogun [12] developed ensemble variants of Forest Penalizing by Attributes (ForestPA) to detect phishing websites. Forest employs weight assignment and an increment technique to grow healthy trees. According to their results, the proposed meta-learner ForestPA variants are very good at detecting phishing websites, with a minimum accuracy of 96.26%. Chiew, Tan, Wong, Yong and Tiong [13] proposed a Hybrid Ensemble FS (HEFS) approach based on a novel cumulative distribution function gradient (CDF-g) method to choose optimal functions. The RF estimation of HEFS was 94.6% accurate. Aydin and Baykal [14] used subset-based functionality extracted from a website URL to detect phishing. The extracted features were analyzed using alpha-numeric character, keyword, security, domain identity, and rank-based methods. The extracted features were then subjected to NB and Sequential Minimal Optimization (SMO). Precision was 83.96% for NB and 95.39% for SMO, respectively.

Ubing, Jasmi, Abdullah, Jhanjhi and Supramaniam [17] proposed a phishing approach focused on feature selection (FS) and Ensemble Learning Mechanism (ELM). The Random Forest Regressor (RFG) was used as the FS method, and the ELM was determined by majority voting. Their experimental findings revealed that the proposed methods outperform and perform comparably to existing baseline and ensemble methods.

As a result of the foregoing analyses, there is a need for more reliable and efficient solutions, as the majority of present approaches are relatively ineffective. Therefore, an RF-LMT method is proposed in this study for detecting phishing websites.

3 Methodology

This section describes the experimental methodology used in this study—specifically, Logistic Model Tree (LMT) and the proposed RF-LMT website phishing detection technique. The phishing datasets used for training and testing, detection performance metrics, and experimental procedure are discussed in this section.

3.1 Logistic Model Tree (LMT) Algorithm

The LMT algorithm is a hybrid of linear logistic regression and the decision tree algorithm. It can generate a model with high predictive precision while still generating an interpretable model. In this research, LMT is used to identify phishing websites, which is a difficult task in cybersecurity. LMT is a hierarchical architecture comprised of a single root, branches, leaves, and nodes. It constructs a standard C4.5 DT with an LR at the node level path down to the leaves. When making a splitting decision, it considers the information gain ratio [25, 26]. These distinguishing characteristics of LMT account for its inclusion as a base learner in this study. Table 1 shows the LMT parameter settings used in this analysis.

Table 1. Classification algorithm

Classification algorithm	Parameter setting
Logistic Model Tree (LMT)	splitOnResiduals = false; useAIC = false; batchSize = 100; fastRegression = True; weightTrimBeta = 0; numBoostingIterations = −1

3.2 Rotation Forest-Based Logistic Model Tree (RF-LMT) Method

Rotation Forest-based Logistic Model Tree (RF-LMT) is a meta-learner that produces classifier models using feature extraction. RF-LMT creates training data for a baseline learner (in this case, LMT) by randomly splitting the feature set into N subsets, and principal component analysis (PCA) is deployed on each of the generated subsets. To maintain the variability in the data, all principal components are kept. Hence, N axis rotations occur to create new features for the baseline learner LMT. The essence of the rotation is to allow concurrent independent accuracy and diversity within the ensemble. Diversity is attained via feature extraction for each baseline learner.

RF-LMT algorithm is presented in Algorithm 1 (See Fig. 1) with the assumption that X is the training dataset, Y is the class label, and F is the feature sets.

3.3 Website Phishing Datasets

Three phishing datasets were used in this study's experimentation phase. These datasets are commonly accessible and are often used in existing studies [1, 11–13, 15]. There

---

Algorithm 1. RF-LMT Algorithm

Input:

Training set $X = \{x_i, y_i\}, i = 1 \ldots m, y_i \in Y, Y = \{c_1, c_2, \ldots, c_k\}, c_k$ is the class label;

Base-Line Learner: *LMT*

$T = 100$ //Iteration count

1. Choose a value for K which is a factor of n, let F randomly divided into K parts of the distinct subsets while each subset must contain $N = n/k$ number of features.

2. Select the corresponding columns of attributes in the subset $T_{i,j}$ from the training dataset X, then form a new matrix $X_{i,j}$. Extract a bootstrap subset of objects ¾ of X to make a new training dataset $X'_{i,j}$.

3. Use Matrix $X'_{i,j}$ as feature transform to produce the co-efficient in the matrix $P_{i,j}$, which j^{th} column coefficient is the characteristic component j^{th}.

4. Construct a sparse rotation matrix S_i using the obtained coefficient obtained in the matrix $P_{i,j}$.

5. Classifier T_i of $d_{i,j}(XS_i^f)$ to determine x belonging to the class y_i, Then, calculate class confidence: $\alpha_j(x) = \frac{1}{L}\sum_{i=1}^{L} d_{i,j}(XS_i^f)$.

Output Assign the category with the largest $\alpha_j(x)$ value to x.

Fig. 1. Pseudocode for proposed RF-LMT method

are 11,055 instances in the first dataset (Dataset A; 4,898 phishing and 6,157 legitimate instances). Dataset A contains 30 distinct attributes that define the dataset [1]. The second dataset (Dataset B) contains 10,000 instances, 5,000 of which are legitimate and 5,000 of which are phishing. Dataset B comprises 48 discrete, continuous, and categorical functions. [11, 13]. The third dataset (Dataset C) comprises 1,353 instances with a total of ten attributes (702 phishing, 548 real, and 103 suspicious). Dataset C is distinguished from Datasets A and B, having three class labels. For more information on the phishing datasets, see [1, 11–13, 15].

3.4   Experimental Procedure

This section presents the experimental procedure as seen in Fig. 2 that was used in this study. The procedure is intended to empirically evaluate and validate the efficacy of the proposed methods for detecting phishing websites. Three phishing datasets from the UCI repositories are used for training and testing the proposed methods. The proposed website phishing detection model is developed and evaluated using K-fold ($k = 10$) Cross-Validation (CV) method. The 10-fold CV selection is based on its ability to create phishing models while minimizing the impact of the class imbalance problem [27, 28]. Since the K-fold CV technique allows each instance to be used iteratively for both training and testing [28–31], the proposed model (RF-LMT) and selected baseline classifiers (Multilayer Perceptron (MLP), K Nearest Neighbour (KNN), Decision Tree (DT), Bayesian Network (BN)) were deployed on phishing datasets based on 10-fold CV. The selected baseline classifiers were chosen based on their usage and performance from existing studies [32–35]. The phishing detection efficiency of the proposed phishing model (RF-LMT) was then evaluated and compared to other experimented and existing phishing detection approaches. All experiments were performed using the WEKA machine learning tool in the same environment [36].

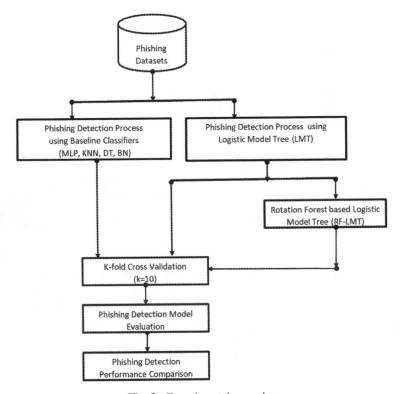

Fig. 2. Experimental procedure

3.5 Performance Evaluation Metrics

Accuracy, F-measure, Area under the Curve (AUC), False-Positive Rate (FPR), True Positive Rate (TPR), and Mathew's Correlation Coefficient (MCC) performance evaluation metrics are used to assess the detection performance of the experimented phishing models. The preference for these metrics stems from the widespread and regular use of these metrics for website phishing detection in existing studies [11, 12, 17–19, 37, 38].

i. Accuracy is the average degree at which the actual labels of all instances are predicted correctly. It is computed as outlined in Eq. (1):

$$Accuracy = \frac{TP + TN}{TP + FP + TN + FN} \tag{1}$$

ii. F-measure shows the weighted average of the Recall (R) and Precision (P). It stresses a classifier's ability to maximize both precision and recall at the same time. Equation 2 represents the computation of the F-measure.

$$F - \text{measure} = \frac{2 \times P}{2 \times TP + FP + FN} \qquad (2)$$

iii. The AUC plots the FP rate on the X-axis and the TP rate on the Y-axis. AUC is not vulnerable to plurality bias and does not overlook the minority samples during its assessment.

iv. The False Positive Rate (FPR) is the proportion of legitimate instances mistakenly reported as phishing attacks.

$$FPR = \frac{FP}{FP + TN} \times 100 \qquad (3)$$

v. True Positive Rate (TPR) is the rate at which actual phishing website instances are correctly classified as that phishing website.

$$TPR = \frac{TP}{TP + FN} \times 100 \qquad (4)$$

vi. The Mathews Correlation Coefficient (MCC) is a statistical rate that provides a high score if the prediction produces good outcomes in all four classes of the confusion matrix (true positives, false negatives, true negatives, and false positives), in proportion to the scale of the positive and negative elements in the dataset. MCC can be computed as shown in Eq. 5.

$$MCC = \frac{TP \times TN - FP \times FN}{\sqrt{(TP + FP) \times (TP + FN) \times (TN + FP) \times (TN + FN)}} \qquad (5)$$

4 Results and Discussion

This section discusses the experimental findings obtained when the experimental framework was implemented, trained, and tested with three phishing datasets.

4.1 LMT and Baseline Classifiers

As documented in Table 2, the performance of LMT was compared with selected experimented baseline classifiers on Dataset A. Six performance evaluation metrics were used for the performance comparison (See Sect. 3.5). Based on accuracy values, LMT yielded the highest accuracy value of 96.92% when compared with KNN (96.84%), DT (95.87%), MLP (94.76%), and BN (92.98%). Similar performance can be observed in terms of f-measure and AUC values. In particular, LMT recorded a f-measure and AUC values of 0.969 and 0.99 respectively which outperformed KNN (0.968, 0.967),

DT(0.959, 0.984), MLP(0.948, 0.983) and BN(0.93, 0.981). Also, LMT on Dataset A had the highest TP-Rate (0.969) and lowest FP-Rate (0.033) values compared with the baseline classifiers. Although it can be observed that the performance of LMT on Dataset A is comparable to baseline classifiers such as KNN, however, the hyper-parameterization of KNN is a drawback [39].

Table 2. Experimental results of LMT and baseline classifiers on Dataset A

	LMT	MLP	KNN	DT	BN
Accuracy (%)	96.92	94.76	96.84	95.87	92.98
F-Measure	0.969	0.948	0.968	0.959	0.93
AUC	0.990	0.983	0.967	0.984	0.981
TP-Rate	0.969	0.948	0.968	0.959	0.930
FP-Rate	0.033	0.053	0.034	0.045	0.075
MCC	0.938	0.894	0.936	0.916	0.858

Table 3. Experimental results of LMT and baseline classifiers on Dataset B

	LMT	MLP	KNN	DT	BN
Accuracy (%)	97.91	95.92	95.53	97.31	95.79
F-Measure	0.979	0.959	0.955	0.973	0.958
AUC	0.993	0.983	0.955	0.976	0.992
TP-Rate	0.979	0.959	0.955	0.973	0.958
FP-Rate	0.021	0.041	0.045	0.027	0.042
MCC	0.958	0.918	0.911	0.946	0.916

Table 4. Experimental results of LMT and baseline classifiers on Dataset C

	LMT	MLP	KNN	DT	BN
Accuracy (%)	89.36	84.77	86.32	87.58	84.33
F-Measure	0.894	0.840	0.863	0.891	0.828
AUC	0.972	0.927	0.880	0.916	0.948
TP-Rate	0.894	0.848	0.863	0.890	0.843
FP-Rate	0.079	0.108	0.104	0.082	0.118
MCC	0.813	0.742	0.761	0.803	0.727

Correspondingly, on Dataset B, the performance of LMT was superior to the baseline classifiers. As presented in Table 3, LMT achieved the highest accuracy value (97.91%),

F-Measure value (0.979), AUC value (0.993), TP-Rate value (0.979), MCC value (0.958), and the lowest FP-Rate value (0.021) when compared with the performance of the baseline classifiers. Furthermore, similar findings were observed on the performance of LMT on Dataset C, as presented in Table 4. LMT, in most cases, was significantly superior to most of the experimented baseline classifiers. These observations indicate that LMT provided equivalent results (performance) for phishing detection across all three datasets, regardless of dataset size. In other words, LMT showed competitive performance against baseline classifiers in website phishing detection. However, the performance of LMT can be amplified by augmenting it with an appropriate meta-leaner (Rotation Forest) as proposed in this study.

4.2 Rotation Forest-Based Logistic Model Tree (RF-LMT)

In this section, the performance of the proposed RF-LMT with the LMT classifier is presented and compared. Recall from the previous section (See Sect. 4.1), the superiority of the performance of LMT over selected baseline classifiers in website phishing detection has been emphasized. In this context, however, the objective is to see how well the proposed RF-LMT method will perform compared to the LMT classifier. The results of LMT and RF-LMT are presented in Table 5.

Observations from these results indicate that the proposed RF-LMT had promising results and, based on most performance metrics, outperformed the LMT classifier on Dataset A. For instance, RF-LMT recorded an accuracy value of 97.33% as against 96.92% produced by LMT. Also, a similar pattern of improvement can be observed on the evaluation metric, as shown in Table 5. Specifically, RF-LMT had a superior f-measure value (0.973), AUC value (0.997), TP-Rate value (0.973), and MCC value as compared with LMT.

Table 5. Experimental results of RF-LMT and LMT on Dataset A

	LMT	RF-LMT
Accuracy (%)	96.92	97.33
F-Measure	0.969	0.973
AUC	0.990	0.997
TP	0.969	0.973
FP	0.033	0.029
MCC	0.938	0.946

Furthermore, RF-LMT outperformed the LMT classifier on Dataset B and Dataset C based on performance evaluation metrics as used in this study. On Dataset B, RF-LMT achieved an accuracy of 98.24%, F-Measure of 0.982, AUC of 0.998, TP-Rate of 0.982, FP-Rate of 0.018, and MCC of 0.965, respectively, as shown in Table 6. This is better when compared with LMT results which had lower performance. Also,

Table 6. Experimental results of RF-LMT and LMT on Dataset B

	LMT	RF-LMT
Accuracy (%)	97.91	98.24
F-Measure	0.979	0.982
AUC	0.993	0.998
TP	0.979	0.982
FP	0.021	0.018
MCC	0.958	0.965

Table 7. Experimental results of RF-LMT and LMT on Dataset C

	LMT	RF-LMT
Accuracy (%)	89.36	90.61
F-Measure	0.894	0.906
AUC	0.972	0.977
TP	0.894	0.906
FP	0.079	0.068
MCC	0.813	0.835

on Dataset C, a similar pattern of results was observed (See Table 7) as the proposed RF-LMT outperformed the LMT classifier.

Consequently, the superior detection capabilities of RF-LMT on the experimented datasets imply that it has a lower likelihood of misclassifying phishing attacks than LMT. Additionally, the high AUC and MCC values of RF-LMT demonstrate its resistance and resilience to inherent data quality problems such as class imbalance and high dimensionality on the analyzed datasets than LMT. Although LMT performed comparably well and competitive with baseline classifiers such as KNN, MLP, BN, and DT. However, the proposed RF-LMT is better than LMT as the meta-learner (Rotation Forest) improved the performance of LMT. These results are consistent with observations on the application of ensemble techniques in other perspectives [27, 40, 41].

4.3 Rotation Forest-Based Logistic Model Tree (RF-LMT) with Existing Methods

In this section, the performance of the proposed RF-LMT is further compared with existing state-of-the-art methods for website phishing detection. Table 8 shows the performance comparison of RF-LMT with existing methods on Dataset A. Specifically, the experimental results from Al-Ahmadi and Lasloum [42], Alsariera, Elijah and Balogun [12], Ali and Malebary [21], and Vrbančič, Fister Jr and Podgorelec [2] are comparable to that of RF-LMT. However, RF-LMT still outperformed these models in accuracy and other metric values based on Dataset A.

Table 8. Performance evaluation of RF-LMT and existing models on Dataset A

Phishing models	Accuracy (%)	F-Measure	AUC	TP-Rate	FP-Rate	MCC
Aydin and Baykal [14]	95.39	0.938	0.936	–	0.046	–
Dedakia and Mistry [8]	94.29	–	–	–	–	–
Ubing, Jasmi, Abdullah, Jhanjhi and Supramaniam [17]	95.40	0.947	–	–	0.041	–
Hadi, Aburub and Alhawari [10]	92.40	–	–	–	–	–
Chiew, Tan, Wong, Yong and Tiong [13]	93.22	–	–	–	–	–
Rahman, Rafiq, Toma, Hossain and Biplob [11] (KNN)	94.00	–	–	–	0.049	–
Rahman, Rafiq, Toma, Hossain and Biplob [11] (SVM)	95.00	–	–	–	0.039	–
Chandra and Jana [9]	92.72	–	–	–	–	–
Folorunso, Ayo, Abdullah and Ogunyinka [19] (Stacking)	95.97	–	–	–	–	–
Folorunso, Ayo, Abdullah and Ogunyinka [19] (Hybrid NBTree)	94.10	–	–	–	–	–
Al-Ahmadi and Lasloum [42]	96.65	0.965	–	–	–	–
Alsariera, Elijah and Balogun [12]	96.26	–	–	–	0.040	–
Ali and Malebary [21]	96.43	–	–	–	–	–
Ferreira, Martiniano, Napolitano, Romero, Gatto, Farias and Sassi [43]	87.61	–	–	–	–	–
Vrbančič, Fister Jr and Podgorelec [2]	96.50	–	–	–	–	–
*Proposed RF-LMT	**97.33**	**0.973**	**0.997**	**0.973**	**0.029**	**0.946**

Likewise, Table 9 compared the performance of the proposed method with existing methods based on Dataset B. In particular, the performance of RF-LMT was superior to methods proposed by Chiew, Tan, Wong, Yong and Tiong [13] and Rahman, Rafiq, Toma, Hossain and Biplob [11]. Also, based on Dataset C, as shown in Table 10, RF-LMT outperformed existing methods as proposed by Rahman, Rafiq, Toma, Hossain

Table 9. Performance evaluation of RF-LMT and existing models on Dataset B

Phishing Models	Accuracy (%)	F-Measure	AUC	TP-Rate	FP-Rate	MCC
Chiew, Tan, Wong, Yong and Tiong [13]	94.60	–	–	–	–	–
Rahman, Rafiq, Toma, Hossain and Biplob [11] (KNN)	87.00	–	–	–	0.078	–
Rahman, Rafiq, Toma, Hossain and Biplob [11] (SVM)	91.00	–	–	–	0.067	–
Proposed RF-LMT	98.24	0.982	0.998	0.982	0.018	0.965

and Biplob [11]. These findings further show the superiority of the proposed RF-LMT as it in most cases outperformed existing website phishing methods based on multiple phishing datasets.

Table 10. Performance evaluation of RF-LMT and existing models on Dataset C

Phishing Models	Accuracy (%)	F-Measure	AUC	TP-Rate	FP-Rate	MCC
Rahman, Rafiq, Toma, Hossain and Biplob [11] (KNN)	88.00	–	–	–	0.099	–
Rahman, Rafiq, Toma, Hossain and Biplob [11] (SVM)	87.00	–	–	–	0.087	–
Proposed RF-LMT	90.61	0.906	0.977	0.906	0.068	0.835

Conclusively, the Research Questions (RQs) posed in the introduction were examined at the end of the experimentation. The following conclusions were reached:

RQ1: *How efficient is the LMT in detecting legitimate and phishing websites?*

LMT algorithm implementations indeed produced significant improvement as compared with baseline methods such as MLP, KNN, DT, and BN with better accuracy and other performance evaluation metrics. This performance is replicated across the three datasets that were considered in this study.

RQ2: *How efficient is the proposed RT-LMT algorithm in detecting legitimate and phishing websites?*

As compared to LMT for phishing website detection, the proposed RT-LMT leveraged the promising success of LMT and demonstrated a substantial increase in accuracy as well as a decrease in error rate. This progress was repeated and observed across the experimented three datasets.

RQ3: *How efficient is the proposed RF-LMT compared to existing phishing methods?*

The performance of the proposed RF-LMT is superior in terms of accuracy, F-Measure, AUC, TP-Rate, FP-Rate, and MCC values as used in this study compared with existing state-of-the-art methods using the three datasets for phishing website detection.

5   Conclusion and Future Works

Phishing attacks are one of the severe cyberattacks that have a global negative effect on internet users. A website phishing attack can be harmful to internet users and internet-based solutions in general. A website phishing attack helps an adversary access victims' personal information, which can then be used to conduct fraudulent transactions or capture users' identities. However, due to attackers' advanced and dynamic strategies, identifying phishing websites has proven difficult. Hence, this study proposed RF-LMT that leveraged the performance of the LMT classifier to detect phishing websites. RF-LMT recorded superior detection performance that outperformed **baseline** models such as MLP, KNN, DT, BN, and existing state-of-the-art methods for phishing website detection.

The authors plan to test the proposed RF-LMT on additional real-time phishing website datasets in the future to determine its generalization potential in detecting phishing websites. Also, more sophisticated models for developing scalable models will be investigated.

References

1. Mohammad, R.M., Thabtah, F., McCluskey, L.: Predicting phishing websites based on self-structuring neural network. Neural Comput. Appl. **25**(2), 443–458 (2013). https://doi.org/10.1007/s00521-013-1490-z
2. Vrbančič, G., Fister Jr, I., Podgorelec, V.: Swarm intelligence approaches for parameter setting of deep learning neural network: case study on phishing websites classification. In: Proceedings of the 8th International Conference on Web Intelligence, Mining and Semantics, pp. 1–8 (2018)
3. Ali, W., Ahmed, A.A.: Hybrid intelligent phishing website prediction using deep neural networks with genetic algorithm-based feature selection and weighting. IET Inf. Secur. **13**, 659–669 (2019)
4. Verma, R., Das, A.: What's in a url: Fast feature extraction and malicious url detection. In: Proceedings of the 3rd ACM on International Workshop on Security and Privacy Analytics, pp. 55–63 (2017)
5. Azeez, N., Misra, S., Margaret, I.A., Fernandez-Sanz, L.: Adopting automated whitelist approach for detecting phishing attacks. Comput. Secur. **108**, 102328 (2021)
6. Alqahtani, M.: Phishing Websites Classification using Association Classification (PWCAC). In: 2019 International Conference On Computer and Information Sciences (ICCIS), pp. 1–6. IEEE (2019)
7. Abdelhamid, N., Ayesh, A., Thabtah, F.: Phishing detection based associative classification data mining. Expert Syst. Appl. **41**, 5948–5959 (2014)
8. Dedakia, M., Mistry, K.: Phishing detection using content based associative classification data mining. J. Eng. Comput. Appl. Sci. **4**, 209–214 (2015)
9. Chandra, Y., Jana, A.: Improvement in phishing websites detection using meta classifiers. In: 2019 6th International Conference on Computing for Sustainable Global Development (INDIACom), pp. 637–641. IEEE (2019)
10. Hadi, W.e., Aburub, F., Alhawari, S.: A new fast associative classification algorithm for detecting phishing websites. Appl. Soft Comput. **48**, 729–734 (2016)

11. Rahman, S.S.M.M., Rafiq, F.B., Toma, T.R., Hossain, S.S., Biplob, K.B.B.: Performance assessment of multiple machine learning classifiers for detecting the phishing URLs. In: Raju, KSrujan, Senkerik, R., Lanka, S.P., Rajagopal, V. (eds.) Data Engineering and Communication Technology. AISC, vol. 1079, pp. 285–296. Springer, Singapore (2020). https://doi.org/10.1007/978-981-15-1097-7_25
12. Alsariera, Y.A., Elijah, A.V., Balogun, A.O.: Phishing website detection: forest by penalizing attributes algorithm and its enhanced variations. Arab. J. Sci. Eng. **45**(12), 10459–10470 (2020). https://doi.org/10.1007/s13369-020-04802-1
13. Chiew, K.L., Tan, C.L., Wong, K., Yong, K.S., Tiong, W.K.: A new hybrid ensemble feature selection framework for machine learning-based phishing detection system. Inf. Sci. **484**, 153–166 (2019)
14. Aydin, M., Baykal, N.: Feature extraction and classification phishing websites based on URL. In: 2015 IEEE Conference on Communications and Network Security (CNS), pp. 769–770. IEEE (2015)
15. Adeyemo, V.E., Balogun, A.O., Mojeed, H.A., Akande, N.O., Adewole, K.S.: Ensemble-based logistic model trees for website phishing detection. In: Anbar, M., Abdullah, N., Manickam, S. (eds.) ACeS 2020. CCIS, vol. 1347, pp. 627–641. Springer, Singapore (2021). https://doi.org/10.1007/978-981-33-6835-4_41
16. Pham, B.T., Nguyen, V.-T., Ngo, V.-L., Trinh, P.T., Ngo, H.T.T., Bui, D.T.: A novel hybrid model of rotation forest based functional trees for landslide susceptibility mapping: a case study at Kon Tum Province, Vietnam. In: Bui, D.T., Do, A.N., Bui, H.-B., Hoang, N.-D. (eds.) GTER 2017, pp. 186–201. Springer, Cham (2018). https://doi.org/10.1007/978-3-319-68240-2_12
17. Ubing, A.A., Jasmi, S.K.B., Abdullah, A., Jhanjhi, N., Supramaniam, M.: Phishing website detection: an improved accuracy through feature selection and ensemble learning. Int. J. Adv. Comput. Sci. Appl. **10**, 252–257 (2019)
18. Abdulrahaman, M.D., Alhassan, J.K., Adebayo, O.S., Ojeniyi, J.A., Olalere, M.: (2019): Phishing attack detection based on random forest with wrapper feature selection method. Int. J. Inf. Process. Commun. **7**, 209–224 (2019)
19. Folorunso, S.O., Ayo, F.E., Abdullah, K.-K.A., Ogunyinka, P.I.: Hybrid vs ensemble classification models for phishing websites. Iraqi J. Sci. 3387–3396 (2020). https://doi.org/10.24996/ijs.2020.61.12.27
20. Alsariera, Y.A., Adeyemo, V.E., Balogun, A.O., Alazzawi, A.K.: Ai meta-learners and extra-trees algorithm for the detection of phishing websites. IEEE Access **8**, 142532–142542 (2020)
21. Ali, W., Malebary, S.: Particle swarm optimization-based feature weighting for improving intelligent phishing website detection. IEEE Access **8**, 116766–116780 (2020)
22. Osho, O., Oluyomi, A., Misra, S., Ahuja, R., Damasevicius, R., Maskeliunas, R.: Comparative evaluation of techniques for detection of phishing URLs. In: Florez, H., Leon, M., Diaz-, J.M., Belli, S. (eds.) Applied Informatics: Second International Conference, ICAI 2019, Madrid, Spain, November 7–9, 2019, Proceedings, pp. 385–394. Springer International Publishing, Cham (2019). https://doi.org/10.1007/978-3-030-32475-9_28
23. Balogun, A.O., Basri, S., Abdulkadir, S.J., Adeyemo, V.E., Imam, A.A., Bajeh, A.O.: Software defect prediction: analysis of class imbalance and performance stability. J. Eng. Sci. Technol. **14**, 3294–3308 (2019)
24. Yu, Q., Jiang, S., Zhang, Y.: The performance stability of defect prediction models with class imbalance: an empirical study. IEICE Trans. Info. Sys. **100**, 265–272 (2017)
25. Lee, S., Jun, C.-H.: Fast incremental learning of logistic model tree using least angle regression. Expert Syst. Appl. **97**, 137–145 (2018)
26. Sumner, M., Frank, E., Hall, M.: Speeding up logistic model tree induction. In: Jorge, A.M., Torgo, L., Brazdil, P., Camacho, R., Gama, J. (eds.) PKDD 2005. LNCS (LNAI), vol. 3721, pp. 675–683. Springer, Heidelberg (2005). https://doi.org/10.1007/11564126_72

27. Balogun, A.O., et al.: SMOTE-based homogeneous ensemble methods for software defect prediction. In: Gervasi, O., et al. (eds.) ICCSA 2020. LNCS, vol. 12254, pp. 615–631. Springer, Cham (2020). https://doi.org/10.1007/978-3-030-58817-5_45

28. Yadav, S., Shukla, S.: Analysis of k-fold cross-validation over hold-out validation on colossal datasets for quality classification. In: 2016 IEEE 6th International Conference on Advanced Computing (IACC), pp. 78–83. IEEE (2016)

29. Arlot, S., Lerasle, M.: Choice of V for V-fold cross-validation in least-squares density estimation. J. Mach. Learn. Res. **17**, 7256–7305 (2016)

30. Balogun, A.O., et al.: Search-based wrapper feature selection methods in software defect prediction: an empirical analysis. In: Silhavy, R. (ed.) CSOC 2020. AISC, vol. 1224, pp. 492–503. Springer, Cham (2020). https://doi.org/10.1007/978-3-030-51965-0_43

31. Basri, S., Almomani, M.A., Imam, A.A., Thangiah, M., Gilal, A.R., Balogun, A.O.: The organisational factors of software process improvement in small software industry: comparative study. In: Saeed, F., Mohammed, F., Gazem, N. (eds.) IRICT 2019. AISC, vol. 1073, pp. 1132–1143. Springer, Cham (2020). https://doi.org/10.1007/978-3-030-33582-3_106

32. Ahmad, S.N.W., Ismail, M.A., Sutoyo, E., Kasim, S., Mohamad, M.S.: Comparative performance of machine learning methods for classification on phishing attack detection. Int. J. **9**, 349–354 (2020)

33. Jain, A.K., Gupta, B.: Comparative analysis of features based machine learning approaches for phishing detection. In: 2016 3rd International Conference on Computing for Sustainable Global Development (INDIACom), pp. 2125–2130. IEEE (2016)

34. Karabatak, M., Mustafa, T.: Performance comparison of classifiers on reduced phishing website dataset. In: 2018 6th International Symposium on Digital Forensic and Security (ISDFS), pp. 1–5. IEEE (2018)

35. Balogun, A.O., et al.: Empirical analysis of rank aggregation-based multi-filter feature selection methods in software defect prediction. Electronics **10**, 179 (2021)

36. Hall, M., Frank, E., Holmes, G., Pfahringer, B., Reutemann, P., Witten, I.H.: The WEKA data mining software: an update. ACM Sig. Exp. **11**, 10–18 (2009)

37. Adewole, K.S., Akintola, A.G., Salihu, S.A., Faruk, N., Jimoh, R.G.: Hybrid rule-based model for phishing URLs detection. In: Miraz, M.H., Excell, P.S., Ware, A., Soomro, S., Ali, M. (eds.) Emerging Technologies in Computing: Second International Conference, iCETiC 2019, London, UK, August 19–20, 2019, Proceedings, pp. 119–135. Springer International Publishing, Cham (2019). https://doi.org/10.1007/978-3-030-23943-5_9

38. AlEroud, A., Karabatis, G.: Bypassing Detection of URL-based phishing attacks using generative adversarial deep neural networks. In: Proceedings of the Sixth International Workshop on Security and Privacy Analytics, pp. 53–60 (2020)

39. Mabayoje, M.A., Balogun, A.O., Jibril, H.A., Atoyebi, J.O., Mojeed, H.A., Adeyemo, V.E.: Parameter tuning in KNN for software defect prediction: an empirical analysis. Jurnal Teknologi dan Sistem Komputer **7**, 121–126 (2019)

40. Adeyemo, V.E., Azween, A., JhanJhi, N., Mahadevan, S., Balogun, A.O.: Ensemble and deep-learning methods for two-class and multi-attack anomaly intrusion detection: an empirical study. Int. J. Adv. Comput. Sci. Appl. **10**, 520–528 (2019)

41. Balogun, A.O., Balogun, A.M., Sadiku, P.O., Amusa, L.: An ensemble approach based on decision tree and Bayesian network for intrusion detection. Ann. Comput. Sci. Ser. **15**, 82–91 (2017)

42. Al-Ahmadi, S., Lasloum, T.: PDMLP: phishing detection using multilayer perceptron. Int. J. Netw. Secur. Appl. **12**, 59–72 (2020)

43. Ferreira, R.P., et al.: Artificial neural network for websites classification with phishing characteristics. Soc. Netw. **7**, 97 (2018)

Mapping the Diversity of Agricultural Systems in the Cuellaje Sector, Cotacachi, Ecuador Using ATL08 for the ICESat-2 Mission and Machine Learning Techniques

Garrido Fernando[✉]

Faculty of Engineering in Applied Sciences, Department of Software Engineering and Artificial Intelligence, Technical University of the North, Avenue 17 de Julio 5-21, Ibarra, Ecuador
jfgarridos@utn.edu.ec

Abstract. The mapping of cropland helps to make decisions due to the intensification of its use, where the conditions of the crops change due to climatic variability and other socio-economic factors. In this way, the implementation of modern sustainable agriculture is essential to prevent soil degradation as measures to guarantee food security, propose sustainable rural development and protect the provision of different ecosystem services associated with the soil. NASA's Ice, Cloud, and Land Elevation Satellite-2 (ICESat-2) launched September 15, 2018, offers new possibilities for the mapping of global terrain and vegetation. An additional science objective is to measure vegetation canopy height as a basis for estimating large-scale biomass and biomass change. The Advanced Topographic Laser Altimeter System (ATLAS) instrument on-board ICESat-2 utilizes a photon-counting LIDAR and ancillary systems (GPS and star cameras) to measure the time a photon takes to travel from ATLAS to Earth and back again and to determine the photon's geodetic latitude and longitude. ICESat-2 ATL08 (Along-Track-Level) data product is developed for vegetation mapping with algorithms for along-track elevation profile of terrain and canopy heights retrieval of the from ATLAS point clouds. Thus, this study presents a brief look at the ATL08 product highlight the broad capability of the satellite for vegetation applications working with data of study area Seis de Julio de Cuellaje (SDJC), province of Imbabura, Ecuador. The study used Normalized Difference Vegetation Index (NDVI) by the year 2020 time-series at 30 m resolution by employing a Machine Learning (ML) approach. The results of this research indicate that the ATL08 data from the ICESat-2 product provide estimates of canopy height, show the potential for crop biomass estimation, and a machine learning land cover classification approach with a precision of 95.57% with Digital Elevation Model (DEM) data.

Keywords: ICESat-2 · ATLAS · Altimetry · Canopy height · LIDAR · Sentinel-2 · NDVI · Machine learning · Cropland

O. Gervasi et al. (Eds.): ICCSA 2021, LNCS 12957, pp. 170–181, 2021.
https://doi.org/10.1007/978-3-030-87013-3_13

1   Introduction

In the sector of Seis de Julio de Cuellaje (SDJC), the production and commercialization dynamics during the years 2015–2020 has revolved around the production and commercialization of three emerging crops: granadilla, naranjilla, and tree tomato, however, it is evident that one of the main problems faced by producers is due to the lack of technical knowledge about the weather conditions and the use of the soil to improve the production of these fruit trees. An important challenge to consider in the next decade is the appropriate use of the agricultural potential of Ecuador, this involves building an agricultural productive zone with updated cartographic information on the suitability of the soil, use of microclimates depending on the altitude of the land to establish the most economically important crop, support the efforts of the different producers to promote their integration, find better participation schemes to strengthen their development, achieve greater benefits in this important activity in the agricultural sector and, above all, determine the profitability that they have received. generated as a community.

Therefore, there is a need for regular mapping using satellite images with adequate spatial/temporal precision and resolution, generated regarding the crop's phenological stage and regional meteorological data. Users can track plant growth regularly by comparing maps from different dates. Governmental programs such as NASA's ICESat-2 [1] are taking significant efforts to make such data freely available with the intention to fuel innovation and entrepreneurship [2]. With access to such data, applications in the domains of agriculture, disaster recovery, climate change, urban development, or environmental monitoring can be realized [3]. The ICESat-2 mission has the goal of monitoring changes in the cryosphere, it is equipped with a high precision laser that provides routine measurements of the vegetation canopy height and also performs very high-resolution surface measurements around the world, to a wide range of terrestrial applications [4]. The ICESat-2 spacecraft provides power, propulsion, navigation, thermal control, data storage, handling, ground communication, and orbit control for ATLAS, the mission's height-measuring instrument. ICESat-2 in numbers: use ellipsoid WGS84, orbit repeats every 91 days, it is at an altitude of about 500 km, has an inclination of $92°$, covers up to $88°$ N & S at a speed of 7 km/s, the precision of flight time of a single photon is 800 ps, has 6 beams organized in 3 pairs, each beam of 90 m across the track, 3.2 km separating the pairs, diameter of the illuminated spot less than 17.5 m, the aperture diameter of the telescope of 0.8 m, 532-nm laser wavelength, 10-kHz pulse repetition rate, 1.5 ns transmitted pulse width, has 4 Solar panels average of 1320 W, onboard data recorder stores 580 gigabits/day, X-band downlink sends 220 Mbits a second [5]. ATLAS can take measurements every 0.7 m along the satellite's ground path. The ICESat-2 produces geophysical products over various surface types: inland water (ATL13), oceans (ATL12), atmosphere (ATL09), land/vegetation (ATL08), sea ice (ATL07), and land ice (ATL06) [6]. More information regarding the ICESat-2 mission can be found at https://icesat-2.gsfc.nasa.gov/.

In recent times, Machine Learning (ML) algorithms like Random Forest (RF), Support Vector Machines (SVM), and Artificial Neural Networks (ANN) have been used by researchers to classify satellite data and its derivatives into crop types. Feng [7] successfully used spectral bands, texture parameters, vegetation indices, and phenological parameters derived from Sentinel-2 time-series data as inputs to RF and SVM classification algorithms. They examined the use of short-wave infrared (SWIR) and water vapor bands of Sentinel-2 data for differentiating between crops [8]. Convolution Neural Network (CNN) bagged unprecedented accuracy in a variety of fields—object-based satellite image classification is one such application that proliferated in recent times. While high-resolution satellite image, required for object-based classification is not available for free, researchers often rely on freely available mid-resolution data (e.g. Landsat—each pixel represents a 30 m * 30 m land parcel). The mechanism of CNN elucidates that it considers the neighboring pixels and relies on the pattern and texture of it, and not just one pixel at a time [14]. In the land cover classification of mid-resolution satellite data (e.g. Landsat), the objective is to classify each pixel, based on its digital number (DN) values across different bands. In this post, we investigate the usability of the CNN model on mid-resolution data, where object-identification is neither possible nor the goal.

The objective of this research is to review the data dictionary for product ATL08 using an ICESat-2 transect over a vegetated region of SDJC, providing a quantitative evaluation of the recoveries of canopy and terrain height compared to observations of selected ecosystems to highlight the satellite's broad capacity for vegetation applications.

2 Methods and Materials

2.1 Overview of the Research Region

The study area is located in Imbabura province, Cotacachi region, parish "Seis de Julio de Cuellaje" in Ecuador (see Fig. 1.a.b) that lies between $0°23'15''$ N and $0°24'26''$ N latitudes and $78°32'35''$ W and $78°30'31''$ W longitudes. The parish SDJC is one of the 8 rural parishes of the Cotacachi canton, located in the southwestern part of the Intag area. It is 70 km 200 m from the city of Cotacachi, 71 km 200 m from Otavalo, 95 km 200 m from Ibarra, and 183 km 200 m from Quito, capital of Ecuador [10]. SDJC has a climate that ranges from temperate to very rainy sub temperate, depending on the altitude levels that range from 1750 m.a.m.s.l. to 2600 m.a.m.s.l. It has a climate that varies between 18 °C and 23 °C with average annual precipitation rainfall ranging from 1000 mm to 3000 mm (see Fig. 1.c). The soils are fine-silty [11], mixed, and mesic (see Fig. 1.d). The environmental conditions are favorable for agriculture, and cropland is the dominant land use class in the study site.

The main crops that are developed in the parish of SDJC are the tree tomato and the passion fruit in the first place, and the second place the cultivation of beans and naranjilla. The giant variety tree tomato is the main product of the parish, followed by the passion fruit, which has had an important rise in recent times. The bean variety one thousand one with a planted area of approximately 134 hectares, an important average production, and the naranjilla, white carrot with 6 hectares; the aforementioned crops are sown in monocultures or associated crops [12]. Approximately 27% of the population of the parish is dedicated to agriculture.

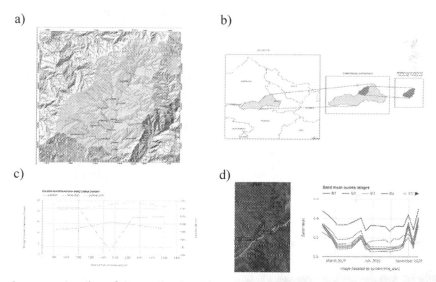

Fig. 1. a) Map location of the study area SDJC; b) map relative to the national, cantonal, and parish level of area of interest; c) elevation and temperatures along Cuellaje transect; d) band mean across images Landsat 8. Source: own study.

The naranjilla (solanum quitoense) is a fruit native to the subtropical understory of the Andes of Ecuador and grows mainly in places with good humidity, cool and shady regions around 800 and 1400 m.a.s.l. The cultivation of this fruit is highly important both nationally and internationally, due to the nutritional properties of both smell and color that make it a perfect fruit for agribusiness, as it allows the production of ice cream, preserves, jams, refreshing drinks, among other products [13].

2.2 Data

We collected Operational Land Imager (OLI) images present on the Landsat 8 satellite with less than 50% cloud cover from the United States Geological Survey (USGS) [29] between 01/01/2020 and 12/31/2020.

The large number of data points that ICESat-2 collects, coupled with the small size of the laser footprint of approximately 17 m [9], will mean that you will have information about changes in elevation measurements for a particular area. This, in turn, will allow a better understanding of the current situation and better predict how much the canopy level will increase and the impacts on vegetation [14]. The ATL08 algorithm was developed specifically for the extraction of ground heights including canopy height, canopy cover percentage, surface slope, roughness, and apparent reflectance from the ATL03 photon cloud data [15], for each beam presented along-track, which typically contain more than 100 signal photons. All ICESat-2 ATL08 data products were acquired from https://nsidc. org/data/atl08 [16]. This data set (ATL08) download contains an along-track (see Fig. 2).

2.3   ICESat-2 Data Processing

Laser pulses from ATLAS illuminate three left/right pairs of spots on the surface that as ICESat-2 orbits Earth trace out six ground tracks that are typically about 14 m wide. Each ground track is numbered according to the laser spot number that generates it, with ground track 1L (GT1L) on the far left and ground track 3R (GT3R) on the far right. The ATL08 data product is organized by ground track, with ground tracks 1L and 1R forming pair one, ground tracks 2L and 2R forming pair two, and ground tracks 3L and 3R forming pair three. Pair tracks are approximately 3 km apart in the across-track direction [17].

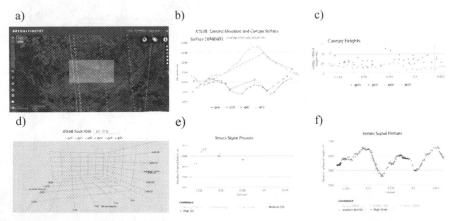

Fig. 2. a) ICESat-2 ATL08 transects (GT1R and GT2R) showing tracks over the extent of SDJC within the study site; b) ATL08: ground elevation and canopy surface; c) canopy heights; d) ATL08 track 1056 graph 3D; e) return signal photons: track ID: 1056 - beam: gt2r - showing 100% data sample rate; f) return signal photons: track ID: 1056 - beam: gt2l - showing 100% data sample rate. Source: own study.

The objective is to highlight the potential of ICESat-2 for the mapping of vegetation in three ecosystems: Montane evergreen forest, piemontan forest, xerophilous montane scrub present in the site of Cotacachi and provide a quantitative assessment of the accuracy of terrain and canopy height retrievals for the area of interest of SDJC. For this, the ATL08 software has been designed to accept multiple approaches to capture both the upper and lower surface signal photons. The algorithm utilizes iterative photon filtering in the along-track direction, which best preserves signal photons returned from the canopy and topography while rejecting noise photons [19]. To access the ATL08 product data dictionary and be able to establish an iterative photon filtering method along the track to preserve the topography and capture noble photons, while rejecting noise photons, thus having enough photons from both the canopy as off the ground [20], we use the icepyx [30] Python software library, which works with the ICESat-2 dataset, using OpenAltimetry for data discovery and NSIDC's Application Programming Interface (API). Photons that are reflected from the top of the canopy in vegetated areas are not always flagged as a signal. As such, before surface finding commences in ATL08, the input from ATL03 is passed through an additional signal finding method referred to as DRAGANN (Differential, Regressive, and Gaussian Adaptive Nearest Neighbor), which was developed specifically to identify and remove noise photons from histogrammed photon point clouds [17].

To generate a reference map for the study site encompassing the nearby ICESat-2 transect, Above Ground Biomass (AGB) [21] estimates from SDJC were aggregated to 30 m pixels, matching Landsat pixels. AGB was the dependent variable in a random forest (RF) regression model developed with input variables from NDVI from Landsat imagery. NDVI and enhanced vegetation index (EVI) was calculated for each image and combined with 2020 SDJC canopy cover and SDJC land cover as independent variables in the RF [22] model. The RF model was built and applied to generate the reference AGB map for the study site, using the Python over Euro Data Cube [23] (Cloud API to most important Earth Observation datasets) and Google Platform: Cloud, Colab, Earth Engine, and Drive [24]. This is a supervised, regression machine learning problem. During training, we give the RF both the features and targets and it must learn how to map the data to a prediction. Moreover, this is a regression task because the target value is continuous (as opposed to discrete classes in classification).

3   Results

The methodology adopted aims at predicting the crop yield of SDJC by providing the required dataset from that area. It involves the following steps:

1) Collection of the dataset ICESat-2 ATL08 and Landsat 8: In this step, we first create an ICESat-2 DAAC Data Access with the desired search parameters and download data from the NSIDC [28], we must first authenticate ourselves using a valid Earthdata login. This will create a valid token to interface with the DAAC as well as start an active logged-in session to enable data download. The token is attached to the data object and stored, but the session must be passed to the download function. Then we can order the granules (see Fig. 3).

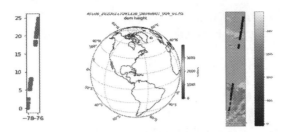

Fig. 3. ICESat-2 measurement plot on the surface showing the 2 laser beam pairs. Each beam pair contains a strong and weak beam. The relative positions of the beams on the surface provides the capability to determine regional and local surface slope. Source: own study developed python code. Source: own study developed python code.

2) Pre-Processing of data 2: Performing the pre-processing on the satellite image for extraction of data features for further analysis. Convert data into geopandas data frame, which allows for doing basing geospatial operations.

3) Deciding crop patterns with help of data filter points based on DEM extent: Use point cloud alignment techniques to align DEMs to points, we can use the transformation matrix to inform on the horizontal and vertical offset between ICESat-2 tracks and DEMs (see Figs. 4 and 5).

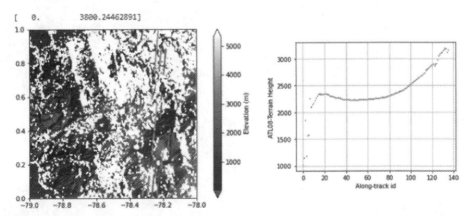

Fig. 4. ATL08 canopy top elevations plotted of the SDJC study site. Vertical offset between ICESat-2 tracks and DEMs. The area is a mix of urban, and forested landscapes on gently rolling terrain. Source: own study developed python code.

4) Applying the machine learning for accurate results: This is the step where we used TensorFlow, Keras, and machine learning algorithm given by Random Forest model so we can get high accurate identification. We will be using a flavor of the Iterative Closest Point alignment algorithm, implemented in NASA Ames Stereo Pipeline (ASP) [25] (see Fig. 6).

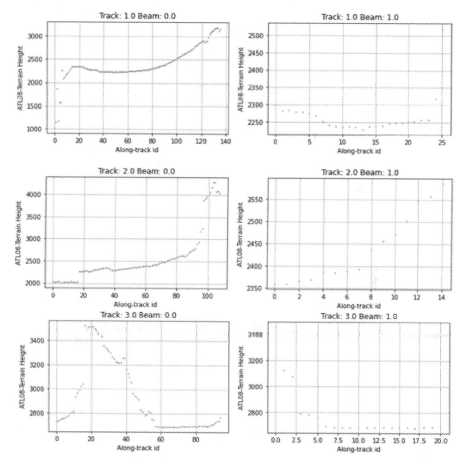

Fig. 5. ATL08 canopy heights were plotted against relative height metrics in SDJC. Source: own study developed python code.

a)

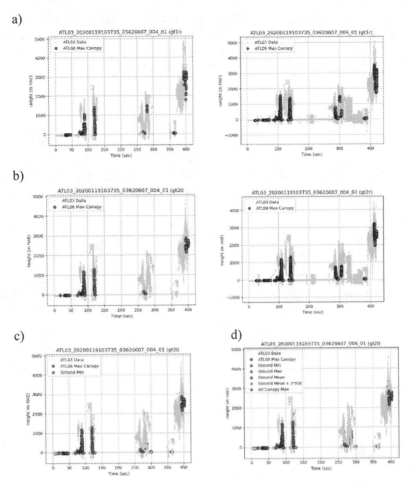

b)

c)   d)

Fig. 6. a) Filtered and classified data from GT1L and GT1R max Canopy ATL08; b) Filtered and classified data from GT2L and GT2R max Canopy ATL08; c) filtered and classified data from GT2L max canopy ATL08, ground min; d) filtered and classified data from GT2L max canopy ATL08, ground min; ground max, ground mean, ground mean + 3Std, all canopy max. Granule ID ATL08_20200119103735_03620607_004_01.h5. Source: own study developed python code.

4   Conclusions

This study has shown that the combination of ICESat2 ATL08 and DEM data can support the measurement of the composition of a cropped landscape to complement the use of satellite remote sensing to achieve some of the food productivity improvement goals. Therefore, crop mapping requires the development of new algorithms for the recovery of the land surface and the height of the canopy. Given the fact that commercial satellites with the high spatial resolution are becoming more affordable for remote sensing users, this study has the potential to support ongoing operational land and vegetation product programs which can benefit from these strategies/scheme for estimate yields, and the increased availability of new, large geospatial datasets on soils, management, and the weather should also benefit future efforts in this area.

Although the cost or availability of satellite data with sufficient spatial resolution to discriminate agricultural fields was an obstacle in the past, this barrier is rapidly diminishing. Improved algorithms to pre-process remote sensing data and estimate yields, and the increased availability of new, large geospatial datasets on soils, management, and the weather should also benefit future efforts in this area.

This research proposes a land cover classification approach using RF with remote sensing data and DEM. Given the sheer volume of altimetry data from ICESat-2, the is huge potential in extracting insights from the data with machine learning that were not possible before. Keep in mind that machine learning is a big field and here we focus on only a few specific approaches and a few computational tools. Additionally, DEM is very helpful for land cover classification. The final overall accuracy of the proposed approach is 95.57%. However, there are still some shortcomings. Compared with ground truth, the outline of ground objects in the final result is still not accurate enough, which should be solved in future research. According to the Chunked Dataset (canopy_h_metrics) found in ATL08_20200119103735_03620607_004_01.h5, which describes the height metric based on the cumulative distribution of canopy heights over the interpolated soil surface, and the Chunked Dataset (h_te_best_fit) that best fits the location of the midpoint of each 100m segments, a slope correction and weighting is applied to each ground photon based on the distance at the height of the slope at the center of the segment, in both fragments, the relationship between the photons of the canopy and the total number of signal photons, in each outgoing laser shot on the ecosystems of the area of interest produces the apparent density of the branches and leaves of the canopy; thus biases the canopy cover estimate high.

The advantage of using ICESat-2 with the ATLAS ATL08 micro-pulse, multi-beam instrument, is known global terrain elevation, global canopy heights, and global canopy coverage at resolutions ranging from 30 m to 100 m, along with data hyperspectral and multispectral it is possible to quantify the above-ground biomass of the vegetation of the ecosystems of the SDJC area, thus being able to improve agricultural production.

Crediting photographs and images:Imagery from the NASA ICESat-2 instrument, courtesy of NASA NSIDC DAAC.

References

1. Neuenschwander, A.L., et al.: ATLAS/ICESat-2 L3A Land and Vegetation Height, Version 4. Boulder, Colorado USA. NASA National Snow and Ice Data Center Distributed Active Archive Center (2021). https://doi.org/10.5067/ATLAS/ATL08.004. Accessed Nov 2020
2. Helber, P., Bischke, A., Dengel1, A., Borth, D.: EuroSAT: A Novel Dataset and Deep Learning Benchmark for Land Use and Land Cover Classification: German Research Center for Artificial Intelligence (DFKI), Germany (2019). arXiv:1709.00029v2
3. Bischke, B., Bhardwaj, P., Gautam, A., Helber, P., Borth, D., Dengel, A.: Detection of flooding events in social multimedia and satellite imagery using deep neural networks. In: MediaEval (2017)
4. Neuenschwander, A.L.: ICESat-2 and ATL08 (Land/Vegetation) Data: University of Texas at Austin. NASA's Applied Remote Sensing Training Program. 16 March 2021

5. Ice, Cloud, and Land Elevation Satellite-2, or ICESat-2, to access ICESat-2 data, visit the National Snow & Ice Data Center (NSIDC). https://icesat-2.gsfc.nasa.gov/how-it-works. Accessed 15 Feb 2021
6. Neuenschwander, A.L., Pitts, K.: The ATL08 land and vegetation product for the ICESat-2 Mission. Appl. Res. Lab. Remote Sens. Environ. **221**, 247–259 (2019). University of Texas at Austin, Elsevier. https://doi.org/10.1016/j.rse.2018.11.005
7. Feng, S., Zhao, J., Liu, T., Zhang, H., Zhang, Z., Guo, X.: Crop type identification and mapping using machine learning algorithms and sentinel-2 time series data. IEEE J. Sel. Top Appl. Earth Observ. Remote Sens. **12**(9), 3295–3306 (2019)
8. Krishna, M., et al.: Crop type identification and spatial mapping using Sentinel-2 satellite data with a focus on field-level information. Geocarto Int. (2020). https://doi.org/10.1080/10106049.2020.1805029
9. Neuenschwander, A.L., Magruder, L.A.: Canopy and terrain height retrievals with ICESat-2: a first look. Remote Sens. **11**, 1721 (2019)
10. Villacis, E.: Productive and marketing dynamics of: granadilla (passiflora ligularis), naranjilla (solanum quitoense) and tree tomato (solanum betaceum) in the parish of Cuellaje-Cotacachi, July 6, 2013–2017 period. Undergraduate work project to obtain the title of engineer in agribusiness appraisals and surveys, Faculty of Engineering in Agricultural and Environmental Sciences (FICAYA), Technical University of the North, August 2020
11. Zhua, L., Radeloffa, V., Ives, A.: Improving the mapping of crop types in the Midwestern U.S. by fusing Landsat and MODIS satellite data. Int. J. Appl. Earth Observ. Geoinf. **58**, 1–11 (2017). https://doi.org/10.1016/j.jag.2017.01.012
12. Gobierno Autómomo Descentralizado (GAD) Parroquial de Cuellaje. http://www.cuellaje.gob.ec. Accessed 2 Feb 2021
13. Castro, W., Herrera, L.: La naranjilla (Solanum quitoense Lam.) en Ecuador. Universidad Central "Marta Abreu" de las Villas, Cuba. Universidad Estatal Amazónica, Ecuador. Editorial Samuel Feijóo (2019). ISBN 978-959-250-337-2
14. Xing, Y., Huang, J., Gruen, A., Qin, L.: Assessing the Performance of ICESat-2/ATLAS Multi-Channel Photon Data for Estimating Ground Topography in Forested Terrain. Centre for Forest Operations and Environment, Northeast Forestry University, China; Institute of Theoretical Physics, Federal Institute of Technology (ETH), Switzerland. Remote Sensing, June 2020. https://doi.org/10.3390/rs12132084
15. Wang, Ch., et al.: Ground Elevation Accuracy Verification of ICESat-2 Data: A Case Study in Alaska, USA. Optical Society of America Under the Terms of the OSA Open Access Publishing Agreement, vol. 27, no. 26/23 December 2019/Optics Express 38168
16. Neuenschwander, A.L., et al.: ATLAS/ICESat-2 L3A Land and Vegetation Height, Version 4 [June to August 2020, 0°15'N, 78°32'W; 0°28'N, 78°21'W]. Boulder, Colorado USA. NASA National Snow and Ice Data Center Distributed Active Archive Center (2021). https://doi.org/10.5067/ATLAS/ATL08.004. Accessed 10 Feb 2021
17. Neuenschwander, A.L., et al.: Ice, Cloud, and Land Elevation Satellite 2 (ICESat-2) Algorithm Theoretical Basis Document (ATBD) for Land - Vegetation Along-Track Products (ATL08). Contributions by Land/Vegetation SDT Team Members and ICESat-2 Project Science Office, Winter (2021)
18. Khalsa, S.J.S., et al.: OpenAltimetry - rapid analysis and visualization of Spaceborne altimeter data. Earth Sci. Inf. (2020). https://doi.org/10.1007/s12145-020-00520-2
19. Chen, Y., Zhu, Z., Le, Y., Qiu, Z., Chen, G., Wang, L.: Refraction correction and coordinate displacement compensation in nearshore bathymetry using ICESat-2 lidar data and remote-sensing images. Optical Society of America under the terms of the OSA Open Access Publishing Agreement, vol. 29, no. 2/18 January 2021/Optics Express 2411
20. Luthcke, S., et al.: ICESat-2 pointing calibration and geolocation performance. Earth Space Sci. **8**, e2020EA001494 (2021). https://doi.org/10.1029/2020EA001494

21. Narine, L., Popescu, S., Malambo, L.: Using ICESat-2 to estimate and map forest aboveground biomass: a first example. Remote Sens. **12**(11), 1824 (2020). https://doi.org/10.3390/rs1211 1824

22. Koehrsen, W.: Random forest in Python. Towards data science. https://towardsdatascience.com/random-forest-in-python-24d0893d51c0

23. Euro Data Cube. https://eurodatacube.com/dashboard. Accessed 20 May 2021

24. Google Platform: Google Colab from https://drive.google.com/drive/folders/1kUy5yuWu TSOA70T825NFbeLV6BGTJAto?usp=sharing/ Google Cloud from https://console.cloud.google.com/storage/browser/crop_monitoring/ Google Drive from https://drive.google.com/drive/my-drive/ Google Earth Engine from https://code.earthengine.google.com/. Accessed 5 May 2021

25. Beyer, R., Alexandrov, O., McMichael, S.: Ames Stereo Pipeline DocumentationRelease 2.7.0. NASA Ames Stereo Pipeline (ASP), July 2020.

26. PhoREAL v3.24. Geospatial Analysis Toolbox for ICESat 2 Data. User Manual. Applied Research Laboratories, The University of Texas at Austin. https://github.com/icesat-2UT/PhoREAL

27. Liu, B., Du, S., Zhang, X.: Land cover classification using convolutional neural networkwith remote sensing data and digital surface model (2020). https://doi.org/10.5194/isprs-annals-V-3-2020-39-2020

28. National Snow and Ice Data Center (NSIDC): Boulder, Colorado USA. NASA National Snow and Ice Data Center Distributed Active Archive Center. https://nsidc.org/data/ATL08/versions/4. Accessed 10 May 2021

29. U.S. Geological Survey: Landsat ProductsLandsat Tools and Services EarthNow: Near Real-Time Imagery as Landsat Orbits the Earth (2020). https://earthexplorer.usgs.gov/. Accessed 15 Feb 2021

30. Scheick, J., et al.: icepyx: Python tools for obtaining and working with ICESat-2 data (2019). https://github.com/icesat2py/icepyx

Formal Method to Analyze Design Workflows in Software Development

N. N. Voit$^{(\boxtimes)}$ ⓘ and S. I. Bochkov$^{(\boxtimes)}$ ⓘ

Ulyanovsk State Technical University, Ulyanovsk, Russia
n.voit@ulstu.ru

Abstract. In this paper we present a new formal method for the design workflows and software algorithms analysis in the form of algorithm graph-schemes based on the graphic languages, using the EPC language example. This method is based on the RVTI temporal automaton grammar, it also provides detection of temporal and semantic errors in algorithm graph schemes. It differs from the existing ones in the linear analysis time and accounting the concept of "time". The application of this method to the design workflows and software algorithms analysis will reveal complex errors in computer programs at the design stage, provide an economic effect of the software development in most organizations.

Keywords: EPC · Grammar · Design workflows · Business process

1 Introduction

This work is a development of the topic of processing workflows in software development [1–5]. The software development success problem has been studied in the business process management theory and also in theoretical informatics and the CAD theory for more than 30 years. Such attention to the problem is caused by a high degree of software development terms beyond the planned time, financial and functional costs. In the mentioned above theories, the reasons have been identified and recommendations have been developed to improve the success of computer software development, however, according to The Standish Group [6], engaged in research in the field of software development success, nowadays only 40% of developments are successfully finished.

Thus, there is no formal method for analyzing the design workflows and algorithms presented based on the graphic languages, which has linear computational complexity and takes into account the concept of "clock", therefore, a new formal method that solves the above problems in the development of computer programs, providing an increase in the success of their development.

The paper consists of the following parts. Related works review on the research topic is given in Sect. 2, a new formal design workflows and algorithms analysis method is described in Sect. 3. Results of the computational experiment are presented in Sect. 4 and afterward conclusion on the gained results is given.

© Springer Nature Switzerland AG 2021
O. Gervasi et al. (Eds.): ICCSA 2021, LNCS 12957, pp. 182–194, 2021.
https://doi.org/10.1007/978-3-030-87013-3_14

2 Related Works

The software development success problem is of great interest to scientists, programmers, designers [7–50]. The following articles contain a description of formal methods for processing design workflows and algorithms at the conceptual level of software development.

Van der Aalst [7] analyzes BPM literature to identify trends, focusing on modeling and DesM and EnM use cases. However, there is no mention of improving the processes themselves in terms of compliance and performance. He also with a ter Hofstede, Kiepuszewski and Barros [8] prepared a foundational document on design workflow patterns, which defines the use of twenty patterns for identifying designs. The work was subsequently used in the study of design workflows based on graphical languages such as UML [9–11], BPEL4WS [12], BML [13] and BPMN [14–16].

Kindler et al. [17] and [18] describe "The Vicious Circle" paradox, which is a semantic error in the design workflows.

Rittgen [19], proposes an OR-join implementation taking into account the difference in the number of incoming links and the number of outgoing links to the OR-join.

Levmann et al. [20] introduced the concept of "dead path elimination" to the OR-join evaluation in FlowMark.

Kiepuszewski et al. [21] provided a comprehensive discussion of issues related to structured design workflows. In [22] they investigate several fundamental issues related to the design workflows outlook, including management ones, in workflow systems, including consideration of issues such as semantic correctness and the possibility of transforming semantically equivalent models of design workflows.

Wynn et al. [23] propose a general OR-join evaluation strategy. There is a set of articles about OR-join, for example [24–26].

Van der Aalst [27] discusses the use of Petri nets to describe the design workflows, including control ones, and to verify their performance. He also provides an overview [28] of how design workflows can be verified.

3 Formal Method to Analyze Design Workflows and Algorithms

The formal method is based on the temporal RVTI automaton grammar, which is well described in [1–5]. Therefore, in this paper, we describe the methodology for constructing an RVTI analyzer and present a graph diagram of design workflows and software analysis algorithm. This technique contains two phases: synthesis and analysis.

The RVTI analyzer synthesis consists of the following stages [51]:

1. Determination of the terminal alphabet of the controlled graphic language.
2. Description of labels location.
3. Revealing of the semantic differences for links having a common graphic form.
4. Construction of the quasitherms alphabet.
5. Construction of the matrix of admissible matchings for the quasi-terminal alphabet;
6. Determination of the relations over the internal memory, providing effective control of the graphic objects connectivity.

7. Construction of RVTI grammars graph using an admissible matchings matrix, i.e., a system of relations, the vertices of which are assigned the names of rule complexes, and the arcs are quasi-terms and operations on the internal memory.

It should be noted that in addition to the graphical form, the RVTI grammar can be presented in tabular and analytical ones.

The analysis phase is carried out in two stages:

1. Minimization of the RVTI grammar.
2. Elimination of non-determinism and uncertainty.

Figure 1 shows the structure of a linearly bounded automaton [52, 53] of the developed RVTI analyzer. Arrowheads allow writing and reading stacks, and rhomboids - only reading tape cells: $L_1, L_2, L_3, \ldots, L_n$.

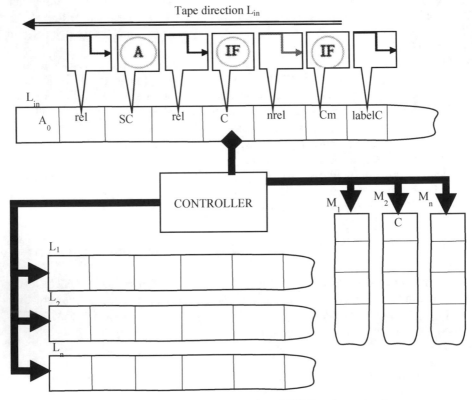

Fig. 1. Linearly bounded automaton-based RVTI analyzer structure

Design workflows and algorithms analysis method based on the graphic languages by the RVTI-analyzer is represented with the activity diagram in Fig. 2.

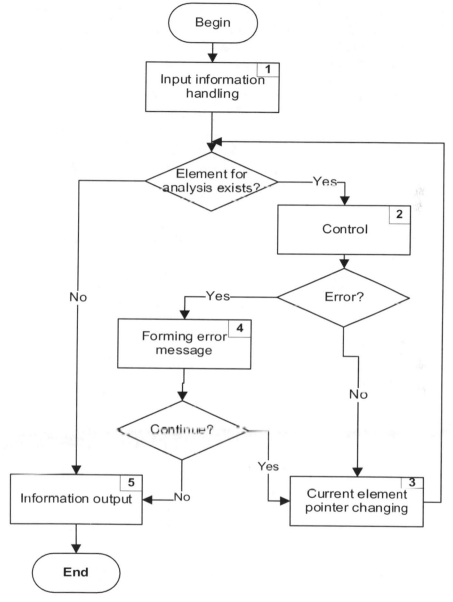

Fig. 2. Design workflows and algorithms analysis formal method

Blocks and fork items are described below.

- *Input information handling* processes the input design workflows and algorithms based on the graphic languages;
- *Element for analysis exists?* finds whether there are any unanalyzed design workflows and algorithms graphic elements;

- *Control* controls design workflows and algorithms;
- *Error?* finds whether the error is detected during the analysis;
- *Current element pointer changing* increases the counter of graphical elements;
- *Forming error message* outputs error notification;
- *Continue?* asks a designer whether to continue the analysis;
- *Information output* block displays the analysis result on the screen;
- *End* finishes the execution of the method.

The formal method has proof of linear time complexity analysis which is introduced in [4].

The list of errors detected with the authors' formal method is the following.

3. BPMN language:

   a. *Synonyms group with different parameters* – the diagram contains elements with synonymous names.
   b. *Antonyms group with same parameters* – the diagram contains elements with antonymic names.
   c. *Lack of conversion link* – elements have opposite names and there is no link between them.
   d. *No nested link to a diagram* – the diagram element is not associated with a suitable (with the same name) start element of another diagram.

4. EPC/UML language:

   a. *No start symbol* – no event found without incoming connections.
   b. *Too many outgoing links* – the event/function has more than one outgoing link.
   c. *Too many inbound links* – the event/function has more than one incoming link.
   d. *No end* – the last element is not an event/function.
   e. *Deadlock* – undecidable loop in the diagram.
   f. *Unanalyzed element* – there is an unreachable element in the diagram without incoming links.
   g. *The next figure was expected* – after the current element the next one must exist, but it does not.

5. IDEF3 language:

   a. *More than 1 initial characters* – units of behavior (UOB) with no incoming links count is greater than 1.
   b. *No start character* – no UOB without incoming links found.
   c. *Too many outcoming connections* – the UOB has more than one outcoming connection.
   d. *Too many incoming links* – the UOB has more than one incoming link.
   e. *No end* – the last element is not a UOB.
   f. *Deadlock* – an undecidable loop in a diagram.

   g. *Unanalyzed element* – there is an unreachable element in the diagram without incoming links.

   h. *The next figure was expected* – after the current element the next one must exist, but it does not.

6. IDEF5 language:

   a. *No end* – the last element is not a class.

   b. *Unanalyzed element* – there is an unreachable element in the diagram without incoming links.

   c. *The next figure was expected* – after the current element the next one must exist, but it is does not.

   d. *No start symbol* – class without incoming links is not found.

   e. *Unknown symbol* – the diagram contains elements that do not belong to IDEF5.

   f. *Many outputs* – there are elements with more than 1 outcoming link.

   g. *No outputs* – there is an element without outputs.

   h. *Incorrect link type* – there are links from another type of IDEF5 diagrams.

   i. *Incorrect vertex type* – there are vertices from another type of IDEF5 diagrams.

4 Computational Experiment

For certain time and quantitative characteristics of the design workflows and algorithms analysis, an experiment was carried out to analyze the metrics in the EPC language basis, or with EPC diagrams. For this, various diagrams are generated and the analysis time is measured.

Target metrics include analysis time and analysis steps count. The step is meant as the number of passes along the vertex or edge of the diagram.

When generating the diagram, the following parameters are determined: the vertices count and the probability of using the EPC linear template. The diagram is constructed as a serial connection of linear and branched EPC templates. The line template of the EPC diagram is a sequential chain of events and functions (Fig. 3). The branched pattern additionally includes OR elements (Fig. 4).

The following values are used in the diagrams generation process:

- vertices count is from 100 to 100000 with a step 100;
- EPC linear diagram template usage probability is form 0 to 1 with a step of 0.2.

Additionally, the diagram has such output characteristic as the fork ratio which is counted as the ratio of edges count from condition vertices to the total edges count. The fork ratio characterizes the diagram linearity.

In summary, 1200 diagrams were built during the experiment. Based on the data obtained, various dependency graphs were built:

- the analysis time on the vertices count with forks ratio 0.02 (Fig. 5);
- the analysis steps count on vertices count (Fig. 6);

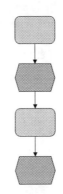

Fig. 3. Linear EPC diagram template

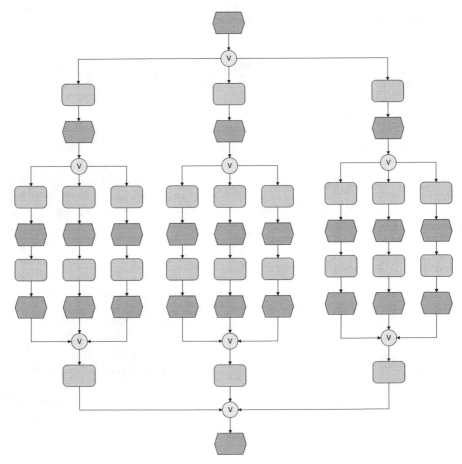

Fig. 4. Branched EPC diagram template

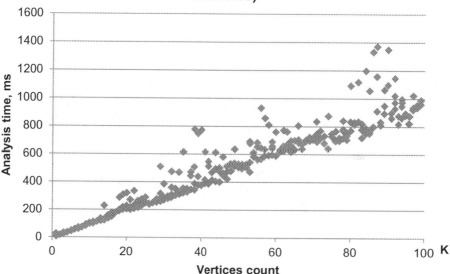

Fig. 5. Dependency graph of analysis time on the vertices count with fork ratio 0.02

- the analysis time on the elements count (Fig. 7);
- the analysis steps count on the elements count (Fig. 8).

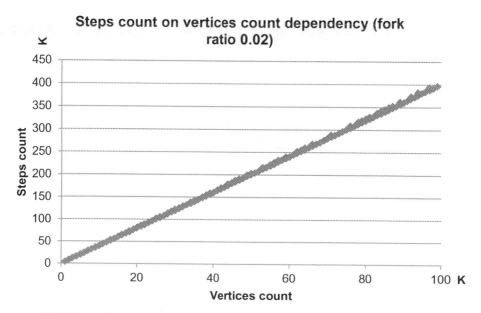

Fig. 6. Dependency graph of steps count on the vertices count with fork ratio 0.02

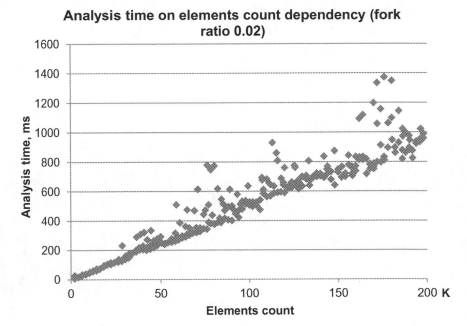

Fig. 7. Dependency graph of analysis time on the elements count with fork ratio 0.02

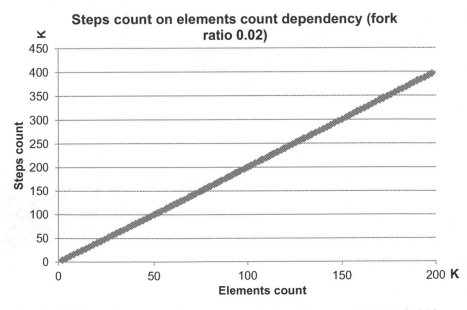

Fig. 8. Dependency graph of steps count on the elements count with fork ratio 0.02

Thus, the plotted graphs confirm the linear nature of the analysis time of the formal method.

5 Conclusion

The formal method of design workflows analysis in software development is described with the means of logic algebra and based on the temporal automaton RVTI grammar. The method differs from the existing ones in linear computational complexity in the analysis and taking into account the concept of "time". It allows the analysis of design workflows and algorithms based on various graphic languages, to identify syntactic (topological), semantic and temporal errors in design workflows and algorithms.

This novel method contributes to solving the successful software development problem. In practical terms, it allows to increase the number of detected errors at the software design stage and achieve an economic effect from its application in software development organizations.

In future works, the authors are going to draw attention to the expansion of the detected semantic errors class in the design workflows and software algorithms.

Acknowledgment. The reported research was funded by Russian Foundation for Basic Research and the government of the region of the Russian Federation, Grant no: 18-47-730032.

References

1. Afanasyev, A., Voit, N., Ukhanova, M., Ionova, I.: Development of the approach to check the correctness of workflows. Data Sci. Knowl. Eng. Sens. Decis. Support [Internet]. World Sci. https://doi.org/10.1142/9789813273238_0173. Accessed 30 July 2018
2. Afanasyev, A., Voit, N., Timofeeva, O., Epifanov, V.: Analysis and control of hybrid diagrammatical workflows. In: Abraham, A., Kovalev, S., Tarassov, V., Snasel, V., Vasileva, M., Sukhanov, A. (eds.) IITI 2017. AISC, vol. 679, pp. 124–133. Springer, Cham (2018). https://doi.org/10.1007/978-3-319-68321-8_13
3. Afanasyev, A., Voit, N., Ukhanova, M., Ionova, I.: Analysis of design-technology workflows in the conditions of large enterprise. In: Abraham, A., Kovalev, S., Tarassov, V., Snasel, V., Vasileva, M., Sukhanov, A. (eds.) IITI 2017. AISC, vol. 679, pp. 134–140. Springer, Cham (2018). https://doi.org/10.1007/978-3-319-68321-8_14
4. Voit, N., Bochkov, S., Kirillov, S.: Temporal automaton RVTI-grammar for the diagrammatic design workflow models analysis. In: 2020 IEEE 14th International Conference on Application of Information and Communication Technologies (AICT) [Internet]. IEEE, 7 October 2020. https://doi.org/10.1109/aict50176.2020.9368810
5. Afanasyev, A.N., Voit, N.N., Kirillov, S.Y.: Temporal automata RVTI-grammar for processing diagrams in visual languages as BPMN, eEPC and Askon-Volga. In: Proceedings of the 2019 5th International Conference on Computer and Technology Applications [Internet]. ACM, 16 Apr 2019. https://doi.org/10.1145/3323933.3324067
6. The Standish Group. https://www.standishgroup.com/
7. van der Aalst, W.M.P.: Business process management: a comprehensive survey. ISRN Software Engineering, pp. 1–37 (2013)
8. van der Aalst, W.M.P., ter Hofstede, A.H.M., Kiepuszewski, B., Barros, A.P.: Workflow patterns. Distrib. Parallel Databases **14**(3), 5–51 (2003)
9. Dumas, M., ter Hofstede, A.H.M.: UML activity diagrams as a workflow specification language. In: Gogolla, M., Kobryn, C. (eds.) UML 2001. LNCS, vol. 2185, pp. 76–90. Springer, Heidelberg (2001). https://doi.org/10.1007/3-540-45441-1_7

10. Russell, N., van der Aalst, W.M.P., ter Hofstede, A.H.M., Wohed, P.: On the suitability of UML 2.0 activity diagrams for business process modelling. In: Stumptner, M., Hartmann, S., Kiyoki, Y. (eds.) Proceedings of the Third Asia-Pacific Conference on Conceptual Modelling (APCCM2006). CRPIT, vol. 53, pp. 95–104. ACS, Hobart (2006)

11. Wohed, P., van der Aalst, W.M.P., Dumas, M., ter Hofstede, A.H.M., Russell, N.: Pattern-based analysis of the control-flow perspective of UML activity diagrams. In: Delcambre, L., Kop, C., Mayr, H.C., Mylopoulos, J., Pastor, O. (eds.) ER 2005. LNCS, vol. 3716, pp. 63–78. Springer, Heidelberg (2005). https://doi.org/10.1007/11568322_5

12. Wohed, P., van der Aalst, W.M.P., Dumas, M., ter Hofstede, A.H.M.: Analysis of web services composition languages: the case of BPEL4WS. In: Song, I.-Y., Liddle, S.W., Ling, T.-W., Scheuermann, P. (eds.) ER 2003. LNCS, vol. 2813, pp. 200–215. Springer, Heidelberg (2003). https://doi.org/10.1007/978-3-540-39648-2_18

13. Wohed, P., Perjons, E., Dumas, M., ter Hofstede, A.H.M.: Pattern based analysis of EAI languages—the case of the business modeling language. In: Camp, O., Piattini, M. (eds.) Proceedings of the 5th International Conference on Enterprise Information Systems (ICEIS 2003), vol. 3, pp. 174–184. Escola Superior de Tecnologia do Instituto Politécnico de Setúbal, Angers (2003)

14. OMG/BPMI: Business Process Model and Notation (BPMN) Version 2.0.2 (2014). http://www.omg.org/spec/BPMN/2.0.2/

15. White, S.: Process modeling notations and workflow patterns. In: Fischer, L. (ed.) Workflow Handbook 2004, pp. 265–294. Future Strategies Inc., Lighthouse Point (2004)

16. Wohed, P., van der Aalst, W.M.P., Dumas, M., ter Hofstede, A.H.M., Russell, N.: On the suitability of BPMN for business process modelling. In: Dustdar, S., Fiadeiro, J.L., Sheth, A.P. (eds.) BPM 2006. LNCS, vol. 4102, pp. 161–176. Springer, Heidelberg (2006). https://doi.org/10.1007/11841760_12

17. van der Aalst, W.M.P., Desel, J., Kindler, E.: On the semantics of EPCs: a vicious circle. In: Rump, M., Nüttgens, F.J. (eds.) Proceedings of the EPK 2002: Business Process Management Using EPCs, pp. 71–80. Gesellschaft fur Informatik, Trier (2002)

18. Kindler, E.: On the semantics of EPCs: resolving the vicious circle. Data Knowl. Eng. 56(1), 23–40 (2006)

19. Rittgen, P.: From process model to electronic business process. In: Avison, D., Christiaanse, E., Ciborra, C.U., Kautz, K., Pries-Heje, J., Valor, J. (eds.) Proceedings of the European Conference on Information Systems (ECIS 1999), Copenhagen, Denmark, pp. 616–625 (1999). http://www.adm.hb.se/~pri/ecis99.pdf

20. Leymann, F., Roller, D.: Production Workflow: Concepts and Techniques. Prentice Hall, Upper Saddle River (2000)

21. Kiepuszewski, B., ter Hofstede, A.H.M., Bussler, C.J.: On structured workflow modelling. In: Wangler, B., Bergman, L. (eds.) CAiSE 2000. LNCS, vol. 1789, pp. 431–445. Springer, Heidelberg (2000). https://doi.org/10.1007/3-540-45140-4_29

22. Kiepuszewski, B., ter Hofstede, A.H.M., van der Aalst, W.M.P.: Fundamentals of control flow in workflows. Acta Informatica 39(3), 143–209 (2003)

23. Wynn, M.T., Edmond, D., van der Aalst, W.M.P., ter Hofstede, A.H.M.: Achieving a general, formal and decidable approach to the OR-join in workflow using reset nets. In: Ciardo, G., Darondeau, P. (eds.) ICATPN 2005. LNCS, vol. 3536, pp. 423–443. Springer, Heidelberg (2005). https://doi.org/10.1007/11494744_24

24. Mendling, J., van der Aalst, W.: Formalization and verification of EPCs with or-joins based on state and context. In: Krogstie, J., Opdahl, A., Sindre, G. (eds.) CAiSE 2007. LNCS, vol. 4495, pp. 439–453. Springer, Heidelberg (2007). https://doi.org/10.1007/978-3-540-72988-4_31

25. Dumas, M., Grosskopf, A., Hettel, T., Wynn, M.: Semantics of standard process models with OR-joins. In: Meersman, R., Tari, Z. (eds.) OTM 2007. LNCS, vol. 4803, pp. 41–58. Springer, Heidelberg (2007). https://doi.org/10.1007/978-3-540-76848-7_5
26. Völzer, H.: A new semantics for the inclusive converging gateway in safe processes. In: Hull, R., Mendling, J., Tai, S. (eds.) BPM 2010. LNCS, vol. 6336, pp. 294–309. Springer, Heidelberg (2010). https://doi.org/10.1007/978-3-642-15618-2_21
27. van der Aalst, W.M.P.: The application of Petri nets to workflow management. J. Circ. Syst. Comput. **8**(1), 21–66 (1998)
28. van der Aalst, W.M.P., van Hee, K.M., ter Hofstede, A.H.M., Verbeek, H.M.W., Voorhoeve, M., Wynn, M.T.: Soundness of workflow nets: classification, decidability, and analysis. Formal Aspects Comput. **23**(3), 333–363 (2011)
29. Simsion, G., Witt, G.: Data Modeling Essentials, 3rd edn. Elsevier, San Francisco (2005)
30. Hay, D.C.: Data Model Patterns: Conventions of Thought. Dorset House, Wiley, New York (2001)
31. Gray, J., Reuter, A.: Transaction Processing: Concepts and Techniques. Morgan Kaufmann Publishers, San Francisco (1992)
32. Börger, E.: Approaches to modeling business processes. A critical analysis of BPMN, workflow patterns and YAWL. Softw. Syst. Model. **11**(3), 305–318 (2012)
33. Clarke, E.M., Grumberg, O., Peled, D.A.: Model Checking. The MIT Press, Cambridge (1999)
34. Eriksson, H.E., Penker, M.: Business Modeling with UML. OMG Press, New York (2000)
35. Gottschalk, F., van der Aalst, W.M.P., Jansen-Vullers, M.H., La Rosa, M.: Configurable workflow models. Int. J. Coop. Inf. Syst. **17**(2), 177–221 (2008)
36. Hagen, C., Alonso, G.: Exception handling in workflow management systems. IEEE Trans. Softw. Eng. **26**(10), 943–958 (2000)
37. ter Hofstede, A.H.M., van der Aalst, W.M.P., Adams, M., Russell, N. (eds.): Modern Business Process Automation: YAWL and Its Support Environment. Springer, Heidelberg (2009). https://doi.org/10.1007/978-3-642-03121-2
38. Holt, A.W.: Coordination technology and Petri nets. In: Rozenberg, G. (ed.) APN 1985. LNCS, vol. 222, pp. 278–296. Springer, Heidelberg (1986). https://doi.org/10.1007/BFb0016217
39. Huang, Y.N., Shan, M.C.: Policies in a resource manager of workflow systems: modeling, enforcement and management. Technical report HPL-98-156, Hewlett-Packard Company (1999). http://www.hpl.hp.com/techreports/98/HPL-98-156.pdf
40. Jablonski, S., Bussler, C.: Workflow Management: Modeling Concepts, Architecture and Implementation. Thomson Computer Press, London (1996)
41. Kiepuszewski, B.: Expressiveness and suitability of languages for control flow modelling in workflows. Ph.D. thesis, Queensland University of Technology, Brisbane, Australia (2003)
42. Marshall, C.: Enterprise Modeling with UML. Addison Wesley, Reading (1999)
43. zur Muehlen, M.: Workflow-Based Process Controlling: Foundation, Design and Application of Workflow Driven Process Information Systems. Logos, Berlin (2004)
44. OMG: OMG Unified Modeling Language (OMG UML), Version 2.5 (2015). http://www.omg.org/spec/UML/2.5
45. Russell, N., van der Aalst, W., ter Hofstede, A.: Workflow exception patterns. In: Dubois, E., Pohl, K. (eds.) CAiSE 2006. LNCS, vol. 4001, pp. 288–302. Springer, Heidelberg (2006). https://doi.org/10.1007/11767138_20
46. Sadiq, S., Orlowska, M., Sadiq, W., Foulger, C.: Data flow and validation in workflow modelling. In: Schewe, K.D., Williams, H.E. (eds.) Proceedings of the 5th Australasian Database Conference (ADC 2004). CRPIT, vol. 27, pp. 207–214. ACS, Dunedin (2004)
47. Verbeek, H.M.W., Basten, T., van der Aalst, W.M.P.: Diagnosing workflow processes using Woflan. Comput. J. **44**(4), 246–279 (2001)

48. Glushkov, V.M., Zeitlin, G.E., Yuschenko, E.L.: Algebra. Programming Languages, 2rd edn, 320 p. Naukova dumka, Kiev, USSR (1978)
49. Tonbul, G., et al.: Error density metrics for business process model. In: 2009 24th International Symposium on Computer and Information Sciences, pp. 513–517. IEEE (2009)
50. Misra, S., et al.: A proposed pragmatic software development process model. In: Intelligent Systems: Concepts, Methodologies, Tools, and Applications, pp. 448–462 (2018)
51. Afanasyev, A.N., Voit, N.N.: Structural-semantic workflows analysis and designers training in design automation. UlSTU, Ulyanovsk (2018). http://venec.ulstu.ru/lib/disk/2017/467.pdf
52. Myhill, J.: Linear Bounded Automata (WADD Technical Note). Wright Patterson AFB, Wright Air Development Division, Ohio (1960)
53. Kuroda, S.-Y.: Classes of languages and linear-bounded automata. Inf. Contr. **7**(2), 207–223 (1964)

Genetic Testing and Personalized Nutrition System for Men's Health Care

Jitao Yang(✉)

School of Information Science, Beijing Language and Culture University,
Beijing 100083, China
yangjitao@blcu.edu.cn

Abstract. Recent research data and evidence from multiple societies demonstrated that men's health problems have become increasingly worse than women around the world. A World Health Organization (WHO) report published recently described a significant gender gap in life expectancy that, in some regions the average life expectancy for men is 5.1 years less than for women. The primary causes of male premature mortality are cardiovascular disease, cancer, diabetes, and chronic respiratory diseases. The main risk factors for the aforementioned diseases, are caused by some bad lifestyle habits such as smoking, wine consumption, sedentary, counterbalanced diet, seldom exercise, irregular sleep and etc. Genetic factors are also known to play an important role in people's health, and much work has been done to identify the genes related specifically to men's health, such as the genes related to homocysteine level, alcohol metabolism ability, nicotine dependence, prostate specific antigen level, and so on. In this paper, we first describe the genetic risk factors that affect men's health, then we demonstrate the implementation of a personalized nutrition service specially designed for men based on men's genetic factors and lifestyles. The personalized nutrition service provides genetic testing, lifestyle assessment, personalized nutrition solution, and personalized nutritional supplements production, so that to improve men's health effectively.

Keywords: Men's health · Personalized nutrition · Genetic testing · Personalized solution

1 Introduction

In recent years, statistics found that men's health problems have become growing prominent in many countries. A recent World Health Organization (WHO) report [1] shows that, in some areas of the world the average life expectancy is 5.1 years less for men than for women [2]. The main causes of male death are cardiovascular disease, cancer, diabetes, and chronic respiratory diseases, which are caused by genetic factors and bad lifestyle habits. The bad lifestyle habits such as smoking, wine drinking, sedentary, counterbalanced diet, seldom exercise, and irregular sleep, are more prevalent among men than women. Therefore,

© Springer Nature Switzerland AG 2021
O. Gervasi et al. (Eds.): ICCSA 2021, LNCS 12957, pp. 195–204, 2021.
https://doi.org/10.1007/978-3-030-87013-3_15

it's necessary to design and implement a tailored personalized nutrition service for men's health.

2   Related Work

There are some data analysis [3,4] and models [5] in men's health, which analyzes and summarizes the factors affecting men's health, however most of the solutions for improving men's health are generic, and there are a lack of attempts to design and implement personalized solutions (especially based on genetic factors) to improve men's health specifically. Therefore, in this paper, we consider improving men's health from both genetic and lifestyle aspects, analyze multiple dimensional data and calculate personalized nutrition solution, as well as produce personalized nutrition product for each person to improve men's health effectively.

3   Genetic Factors and Men's Health

Many genes have associations with men's health considering men's unhealthy lifestyles, for example (just to name a few) the homocysteine level, alcohol metabolism, nicotine dependence, and prostate specific antigen (PSA) level are all affected by genes.

3.1   Homocysteine Level

Folic acid deficiency and elevated homocysteine (Hcy) levels are considered risk factors for many diseases, such as hypertension, stroke, and male infertility. Methylenetetrahydrofolate reductase (MTHFR) is a key enzyme in folate metabolism. The mutant genotype is closely related to decreased enzyme activity, as a result, the availability of folic acid is severely reduced, and the level of Hcy is significantly increased, which brings serious risks of diseases [6].

The results of meta-analysis suggest that blood Hcy is significantly related to the risk of stroke and coronary heart disease [8]. The level of folic acid will also affects the process of sperm production and probably reduces male fertility [9]. Individuals having TT genotype of MTHFR C677T will probably have significantly higher blood pressure risk than those having CC genotype [7].

3.2   Alcohol Metabolism

Alcohol consumption, a lifestyle much more popular in men than in women, is a relevant risk factor for atherosclerotic diseases, such as hypertension, dyslipidemia, and obesity. Different people's ability in alcohol consumption are partially decided by genetic factors. Aldehyde dehydrogenase is an important enzyme in alcohol metabolism, the Aldehyde dehydrogenase 2 (ALDH2) gene's mutation will greatly reduce the activity of the aldehyde dehydrogenase enzyme, which will result in a large accumulation of acetaldehyde [10].

The mutation of ALDH2*2 has an important impact on human health [11], the polymorphism of ALDH2 rs671 has been found to be an established genetic risk for coronary heart diseases and hypertension in Asian population [12].

3.3 Nicotine Dependence

Cigarette smoking is a leading contributor to men's disease and death, causing approximately five million premature deaths each year around the world. Cigarette smoking is a primary cause of lung cancer, and one of the major risk factors causing peripheral arterial disease. Genetic factors have been found to contribute to the development of nicotine dependence [13,15], some evidences for genetic influence on smoking behavior have also been identified [14].

3.4 Prostate Specific Antigen Levels

In some countries, prostate cancer is the most frequent cancer in men, prostate specific antigen (PSA) levels in the general population is also affected by inherited factors [16].

The mutation of rs17632542 in KLK3 was found to affect PSA levels [17], and this variant has a stronger effect on PSA levels than the variant of rs2735839 previously reported [18].

4 Personalized Nutrition Service for Men's Health

A personalized nutrition service for men's health includes four parts:

- genetic testing,
- lifestyle assessment,
- personalized nutrition solution, and
- personalized nutritional supplements product.

4.1 Genetic Testing

As shown in Fig. 1, a Men's Health Genetic Testing Report has four modules:

- Men's Health (in Fig. 1 left), which includes the testing items of: Male Pattern Baldness, Prostate-specific Antigen Level Elevation, Benign Prostatic Hyperplasia, Serum Testosterone Concentrations in Men, Norepinephrine and Epinephrine Concentrations at Rest and After Exercise, SSRI/SNRI-induced Sexual Dysfunction, Orepinephrine and Epinephrine Concentrations at Rest and After Exercise;
- Liver Protection, which includes the testing items of: Alcohol Dependence, Alcohol Consumption, Alcoholic Fatty Liver, Alcohol-related Cirrhosis, Inflammatory Bowel Disease, Duodenal Ulcer;

Fig. 1. The screen shots of the user interface (first level) of the Men's Health Genetic Testing Report.

- Influence of Smoking (in Fig. 1 right), which includes the testing items of: Lung Cancer, Nicotine Dependence, Etiology of Tobacco, Chronic Obstructive Pulmonary Disease; and
- Nutrient Absorption, which tests the nutritional requirement items of: DHA, Folate, Vitamin D, Zinc, Vitamin A, Vitamin E, Vitamin B1, Vitamin B2, Vitamin B6, Vitamin C, Magnesium, Selenium, Lycopene, Vitamin B12.

The men's health genetic testing report was implemented in Java web application using spring boot [19] and mybatis [20] framework, and the users can access the report both in personal computer and mobile phones. By clicking the name of each genetic testing item, a detail testing result report will be opened as described in Fig. 2.

Using the genetic testing item of Nicotine Dependence as an example, Fig. 2 demonstrates the screen shots of the user interface of a testing item. Each testing item report includes six parts:

- testing item name and its testing result (*e.g.*, Nicotine Dependence in Fig. 2 left, risk level: medium), which gives the testing result and the population gene frequency, explains the testing result, as well as provides some health advice based on the testing result;
- testing item introduction, which explains the testing contents of the item and emphasizes the importance of the testing item;
- testing item analysis (*e.g.*, Harms of Smoking), explains the relationship between the testing item and the health of a person, and analyzes why it is necessary to test the item;

Fig. 2. The screen shots of the user interface (second level) of the Men's Health Genetic Testing Report.

- the tested gene loci and genotype (*e.g.*, *CHRNA3* in Fig. 2 middle), lists the tested genes and loci and the corresponding genotypes;
- gene analysis (in Fig. 2 right) for the tested genes, explains the association between the genes and the testing item, for example explaining the association between the genes *CHRNA, CTNNA3* and nicotine dependence; and
- scientific references, list the scientific research papers and clinical evidences for the testing item.

4.2   Lifestyle Assessment

Not only the genetic factors affect men's health, the lifestyle also plays a very important role for men's health, such as smoking, wine drinking, sedentary, irregular sleep, obesity and etc. Therefore, we implemented a food frequency questionnaire (FFQ) [21–23] to assess a person's lifestyle.

4.3   Personalized Nutrition Solution

Based on the genetic testing results and food frequency questionnaire, the personalized nutrition service platform will calculate a personalized nutrition solution for each customer, the screen shots of the personalized nutrition report are described in Fig. 3. The personalized nutrition report includes three parts:

- daily personalized nutrition solution (in Fig. 3 left), which lists the recommended nutrition supplements, click each icon of the tablets, more detail information about the tablet will be shown describing the product information such as ingredients, subsidiary material, directions and dosage, and etc.;

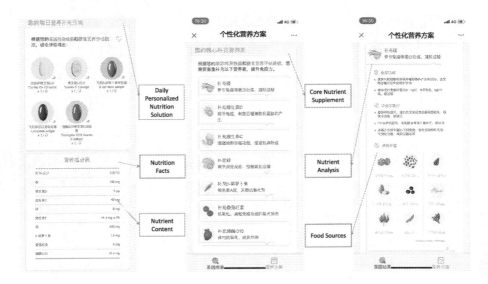

Fig. 3. The screen shots of the user interface of the personalized nutrition solution.

- nutrition facts, which list all the nutrient content (such as Vitamin C, 60 mg) in the daily personalized nutrition solution;
- core nutrition supplement (in Fig. 3 middle), explains why the suggested nutritional supplements are beneficial for the user, click each item, nutrient analysis will be displayed in a dropdownlist (in Fig. 3 right) to explain why the nutrient is recommended, including the functions of the nutrient, evaluation and suggestions, and food sources.

4.4 Personalized Nutritional Supplements Production

According to the personalized nutrition solution, the user can place an order to the nutrition factory to produce a monthly personalized nutrition box product including 30 daily nutrition packs. Each customer's name and the information of the tablets (inside the nutrition pack) will be printed on the pack, which means each customer will have a unique nutrition box.

The personalized nutrition box production requires nutrition factory to have the flexible manufacturing capability, which is a challenge for the traditional standardized production factory.

Figure 4 demonstrates the personalized nutrition box production process from order to delivery, in which multiple departments are involved in, such as Sales, Planning, Purchase, Workshop, Warehouse, Quality control, and Finance. Comparing to the standardized production pipeline that produces tens of thousands of exactly the same products at a time, the personalized production pipeline is much more complicated that each customer has a unique product composition with small production amount (such as 30 packs for one month per person, 90 packs for three months per person). Therefore, all the production process should

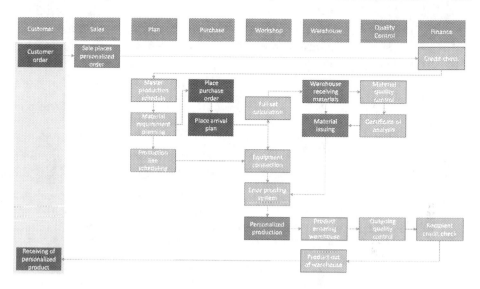

Fig. 4. The supply chain (from order to delivery) for personalized nutrition product production.

be digitalized so that to promote production efficiency as well as reduce or avoid production errors.

5   Conclusions

Men's health problem is partially caused by bad lifestyle habits, such as smoking, wine drinking, sedentary, counterbalanced diet, seldom exercise, and irregular sleep. Men's health is also closely related to genetic factors, for instance, the MTIIFR genetic polymorphism can assess an individual's ability for folic acid metabolism, the ALDH2 gene can be tested to evaluate a person's ability for alcohol metabolism, the CHRNA4 gene can be used to assess a person's nicotine dependence tendency.

Combining both the genetic testing data and lifestyle data, in this paper, we design and implement a tailored personalized nutrition service for men's health. The service requires the user to have a genetic testing, as well as finish online lifestyle assessment questionnaires, then the system will analyze both the genetic data and the lifestyle data together, using the genetic interpretation database (such as the Online Catalog of Human Genes and Genetic Disorders (OMIM) [24, 25], the AutDB [26]) and the scientific evidences [27–35] to calculate a genetic report and a personalized nutrition solution report, respectively. Based on the personalized nutrition solution, the nutrition factory will produce a monthly personalized nutrition box product for the customer. A personalized lifestyle solution will also be given to the customer. The personalized nutrition service for men has been delivered online, and has been used by tens of thousands of customers.

Concerning future work, we will combine more dynamic data such as sports data [36], physical examination data and sleep data to our data model to further perfect our service for men's health.

Acknowledgment. This research project is supported by Science Foundation of Beijing Language and Culture University (supported by "the Fundamental Research Funds for the Central Universities") (Approval number: 21YJ040002).

References

1. Rodrigues, R., Ilinca, S., Kai, L., et al.: The health and well-being of men in the WHO European Region: better health through a gender approach (2018). https://www.euro.who.int/en/publications/abstracts/the-health-and-well-being-of-men-in-the-who-european-region-better-health-through-a-gender-approach-2018. Accessed 29 Apr 2021
2. GBD 2017 Mortality Collaborators: Global, regional, and national age-sex-specific mortality and life expectancy, 1950–2017: a systematic analysis for the Global Burden of Disease Study 2017. Lancet **392**, 1684–1735 (2018)
3. Rajaratnam, J.K., et al.: Worldwide mortality in men and women aged 15–59 years from 1970 to 2010: a systematic analysis. Lancet **375**, 1704–1720 (2010)
4. Wang, H., et al.: Age-specific and sex-specific mortality in 187 countries, 1970–2010: a systematic analysis for the Global Burden of Disease Study 2010. Lancet **380**, 2071–2094 (2012)
5. Ashraf, K., Ng, C.J., Goh, K.L.: Theories, models and frameworks in men's health studies: a scoping review. J. Men's Health **17**(2), 15–24 (2021)
6. Ueland, P.M., Hustad, S., Schneede, J., et al.: Biological and clinical implications of the MTHFR C677T polymorphism. Trends Pharmacol. Sci. **22**(4), 195–201 (2001)
7. Saraswathy, K.N., Garg, P.R., Salam, K., et al.: MTHFR C677T polymorphism and its homocysteine-driven effect on blood pressure. Int. J. Stroke **9**(4), E20 (2014). Official Journal of the International Stroke Society
8. Holmes, M.V., Newcombe, P., Hubacek, J.A., et al.: Effect modification by population dietary folate on the association between MTHFR genotype, homocysteine, and stroke risk: a meta-analysis of genetic studies and randomised trials. Lancet **378**(9791), 584–594 (2011)
9. Gong, M., Dong, W., He, T., et al.: MTHFR 677C>T polymorphism increases the male infertility risk: a meta-analysis involving 26 studies. PLOS ONE **10**(3), e0121147 (2015)
10. Takeuchi, F., Isono, M., Nabika, T., et al.: Confirmation of ALDH2 as a Major locus of drinking behavior and of its variants regulating multiple metabolic phenotypes in a Japanese population. Circ. J. **75**(4), 911–918 (2011). Official Journal of the Japanese Circulation Society
11. Wang, L., Wu, Z.: ALDH2 and cancer therapy. Adv. Exp. Med. Biol. **1193**, 221–228 (2019)
12. Xia, C.L., Chu, P., Liu, Y.X., et al.: ALDH2 rs671 polymorphism and the risk of heart failure with preserved ejection fraction (HFpEF) in patients with cardiovascular diseases. J. Hum. Hypertens **34**(1), 16–23 (2020)
13. Carmelli, D., Swan, G.E., Robinette, D., et al.: Genetic influence on smoking-a study of male twins. N. Engl. J. Med. **327**(12), 829–833 (1992)

14. Thorgeirsson, T.E., Geller, F., Sulem, P., et al.: A variant associated with nicotine dependence, lung cancer and peripheral arterial disease. Nature **452**(7187), 638–642 (2008)
15. Bierut, L.J., Madden, P.A., Breslau, N., et al.: Novel genes identified in a high-density genome wide association study for nicotine dependence. Hum. Mol. Genet. **16**(1), 24–35 (2007)
16. Barry, M.J.: Screening for prostate cancer-the controversy that refuses to die. N. Engl. J. Med. **360**(13), 1351–1354 (2009)
17. Gudmundsson, J., Besenbacher, S., Sulem, P., et al.: Genetic correction of PSA values using sequence variants associated with PSA levels. Sci. Transl. Med. **2**(62), 62ra92 (2010)
18. Eeles, R.A., Kote-Jarai, Z., Giles, G.G., et al.: Multiple newly identified loci associated with prostate cancer susceptibility. Nat. Genet. **40**(3), 316–321 (2008)
19. Spring Boot. https://spring.io/projects/spring-boot/. Accessed 29 Apr 2021
20. MyBatis. https://mybatis.org/mybatis-3/index.html. Accessed 29 Apr 2021
21. Johns, R., Kusuma, J., Lie, A., Shiao, S.P.K.: Validation of macro- and micro-nutrients including methyl donors in social ethnic diets using food frequency questionnaire and nutrition data system for research (USDA computerized program). SDRP J. Food Sci. Technol. **3**(4), 417–430 (2018)
22. Affret, A., El Fatouhi, D., Dow, C., Correia, E., Boutron-Ruault, M.C., Fagherazzi, G.: Relative validity and reproducibility of a new 44-item diet and food frequency questionnaire among adults: online assessment. J. Med. Internet. Res. **20**(7), e227 (2018)
23. Thompson, F.E., Subar, A.F.: Chapter 1 - Dietary assessment methodology. In: Nutrition in the Prevention and Treatment of Disease, 4th edn. Academic Press (2017). ISBN 9780128029282
24. Hamosh, A., Scott, A.F., Amberger, J.S., Bocchini, C.A., McKusick, V.A.: Online Mendelian Inheritance in Man (OMIM), a knowledgebase of human genes and genetic disorders. Nucleic Acids Res. **33**(Database issue), D514–D517 (2005)
25. OMIM - Online Mendelian Inheritance in Man, an Online Catalog of Human Genes and Genetic Disorders. https://www.omim.org/. Accessed 20 May 2021
26. Pereanu, W., et al.: AutDB: a platform to decode the genetic architecture of autism. Nucleic Acids Res. **46**(D1), D1049–D1054 (2018)
27. Corella, D., Ordovas, J.M.: Nutrigenomics in cardiovascular medicine. Circ. Cardiovasc. Genet. **2**, 637–651 (2009)
28. Frazier-Wood, A.C.: Dietary patterns, genes, and health: challenges and obstacles to be overcome. Curr. Nutr. Rep. **4**, 82–87 (2015)
29. Vallee Marcotte, B.V., et al.: Novel genetic loci associated with the plasma triglyceride response to an omega-3 fatty acid supplementation. J. Nutrigenet. Nutrigenomics **9**, 1–11 (2016)
30. Ouellette, C., Rudkowska, I., Lemieux, S., Lamarche, B., Couture, P., Vohl, M.C.: Gene-diet interactions with polymorphisms of the MGLL gene on plasma low-density lipoprotein cholesterol and size following an omega-3 polyunsaturated fatty acid supplementation: a clinical trial. Lipids Health Dis. **13**, 86 (2014)
31. Rudkowska, I., et al.: Interaction between common genetic variants and total fat intake on low-density lipoprotein peak particle diameter: a genome-wide association study. J. Nutrigenet. Nutrigenomics **8**, 44–53 (2015)
32. Tremblay, B.L., Cormier, H., Rudkowska, I., Lemieux, S., Couture, P., Vohl, M.C.: Association between polymorphisms in phospholipase A2 genes and the plasma triglyceride response to an N-3 PUFA supplementation: a clinical trial. Lipids Health Dis. **14**, 12 (2015)

33. Palatini, P., et al.: CYP1A2 genotype modifies the association between coffee intake and the risk of hypertension. J. Hypertens. **27**, 1594–1601 (2009)
34. De Toro-Martin, J., Arsenault, B.J., Despres, J.P., Vohl, M.C.: Precision nutrition: a review of personalized nutritional approaches for the prevention and management of metabolic syndrome. Nutrients **9**(8), pii:E913 (2017)
35. Grimaldi, K.A., van Ommen, B., Ordovas, J.M., et al.: Proposed guidelines to evaluate scientific validity and evidence for genotype-based dietary advice. Genes Nutr. **12**, 35 (2017)
36. Patel, M.S., Asch, D.A., Volpp, K.G.: Wearable devices as facilitators, not drivers, of health behavior change. JAMA **313**, 459–460 (2015)

Reinforcement Learning Based Whale Optimizer

Marcelo Becerra-Rozas[1]([✉]) [ID], José Lemus-Romani[4] [ID], Broderick Crawford[1] [ID], Ricardo Soto[1] [ID], Felipe Cisternas-Caneo[1] [ID], Andrés Trujillo Embry[1] [ID], Máximo Arnao Molina[1] [ID], Diego Tapia[1] [ID], Mauricio Castillo[1] [ID], Sanjay Misra[2] [ID], and José-Miguel Rubio[3] [ID]

[1] Pontificia Universidad Católica de Valparaíso, Valparaíso, Chile
{marcelo.becerra.r,felipe.cisternas.c,andres.trujillo.e,
maximo.arnao.m,diego.tapia.r,mauricio.castillo.d}@mail.pucv.cl,
{broderick.crawford,ricardo.soto}@pucv.cl
[2] Covenant University, Ota, Nigeria
sanjay.misra@covenantuniversity.edu.ng
[3] Universidad Bernardo O'Higgins, Santiago, Chile
josemiguel.rubio@ubo.cl
[4] School of Civil Construction, Pontificia Universidad Católica de Chile,
Santiago, Chile
jose.lemus@uc.cl

Abstract. This work proposes a Reinforcement Learning based optimizer integrating SARSA and Whale Optimization Algorithm. SARSA determines the binarization operator required during the metaheuristic process. The hybrid instance is applied to solve benchmarks of the Set Covering Problem and it is compared with a Q-learning version, showing good results in terms of fitness, specifically, SARSA beats its Q-Learning version in 44 out of 45 instances evaluated. It is worth mentioning that the only instance where it does not win is a tie. Finally, thanks to graphs presented in our results analysis we can observe that not only does it obtain good results, it also obtains a correct exploration and exploitation balance as presented in the referenced literature.

Keywords: Metaheuristic · SARSA · Q-Learning · Swarm intelligence · Whale optimization algorithm · Combinatorial optimization

1 Introduction

The process of selecting the optimal solution from a collection of candidate solutions that satisfy all of the constraints of an optimization issue is referred to as optimization.

Beyond this, we find combinatorial optimization, where solutions are represented in variables that are in discrete domains. That is, the solutions can be subsets, permutations, graphs or integers, and have no polynomial solution. To

O. Gervasi et al. (Eds.): ICCSA 2021, LNCS 12957, pp. 205–219, 2021.
https://doi.org/10.1007/978-3-030-87013-3_16

obtain good quality solutions in reasonable times at the expense of the guarantee of finding the optimum, approximate methods are used given the complexity of solving combinatorial optimization problems.

A metaheuristic algorithm is a framework with numerous high-level purposes that can be used to construct heuristics or heuristic optimization algorithms using a variety of different tactics [11]. Various academics have employed metaheuristics to address a wide range of combinatorial optimization problems over the years. These algorithms have a distinguishing quality in that they can be employed and adapted to a variety of optimization problems in the same domain as the metaheuristic or even in distinct domains from the domain in which the metaheuristic operates.

Reinforcement learning is a class of methods that aim to try to find an optimal policy for complicated systems or agents [13,23,25]. Being efficient methods, they have been implemented in various areas or applications: model-free control, optimal control [26], ambidextrous metaheuristics [2,3,6,17,18]. Reinforcement learning can be divided according to the way it evaluates the policy: off-policy and on-policy. The most common reinforcement learning techniques include Q-Learning, SARSA, Temporal Difference(λ) [13].

In this paper, we present a general framework incorporating SARSA to determine a specific action: the selection of binarization schemes when solving binary domain problems with continuous swarm-based metaheuristic algorithms. SARSA is used to determine the selection of binarization schemes in binary domain problems. After evaluating 45 instances of the Set Covering Problem, it can be determined that the proposed implementation with SARSA outperforms the one presented in [2], where the binarization selector is Q-Learning by a statistically significant margin.

Some sections of the paper are modeled after the work of [9], and it is organized as follows: Sect. 2 presents related work, discussing swarm-based algorithms and how reinforcement learning has supported metaheuristics. Section 3 presents the Q-Learning and SARSA techniques with their respective reward function. Section 4 mentions the classical Whale optimization algorithm and then presents the proposal of a new Whale algorithm with the implementation of SARSA. Finally, the obtained results are evaluated and analyzed and a conclusion is drawn in Sects. 5 and 6 respectively.

2 Related Work

2.1 Swarm-Based Algorithms

Inspired often from nature and the collective behavior of biological systems, the swarm intelligence algorithms, corresponds to a group of algorithms that are based on the study of self-organized and distributed systems. Those systems usually consist of a population of agents with a limited individual capacity to perceiving and modifying their local environment. Such ability makes communication between individuals possible, detecting changes in the environment generated by the behavior of their peers. Local interactions between agents usually lead to the emergence of global behavior, which allows to the agents solve complex problems. Local interactions between agents often result in the formation of global behavior, which allows the agents to handle complicated problems successfully. Grey Wolf Optimization (GWO), Harris Hawk Optimization (HHO), Moth-Flame Optimization (MFO), Social Spider Optimization (SSO), Cuckoo Search (CS). [15] has further information about the Swarm Intelligence Algorithm and how it works.

Metaheuristics have a variety of elements that vary according to the metaphor they reflect. Metaheuristics are comprised mostly of the following elements: population, local search, instance, operators, parameters, evaluation, initialization, and decision variables [11]. Numerous experiments are required to calibrate the values of these parameters, which takes a significant amount of time and creates an imbalance between the exploitation and exploration of metaheuristics. As a result, the metaheuristics require incorporated dynamic features that can be changed as iterations go. SARSA and Q-Learning are utilized in this article to execute a dynamic selection of operators.

2.2   Reinforcement Learning into Metaheuristics

While metaheuristics have been proved to be quite beneficial in addressing difficult optimization problems [6, 20–22], it takes a long time and there is no guarantee that the approach will converge to an optimal solution; in fact, the method is frequently prone to falling into a local optimum. To address this issue, machine learning techniques were applied to shorten search durations and/or produce higher-quality results [16]. In [11], Song et al. offer a classification in which Machine Learning (ML) approaches assist metaheuristics.

The following are some of the reasons why hybridization is advantageous, which we consider noteworthy:

- It causes the metaheuristic to be adaptive, which allows the algorithm to apply to different problems.
- It does not require complete information about the problem since reinforcement learning models learn by collecting experience [14].
- By using independent learning agents [12], it allows in some cases, the computational cost to be lower. Since it uses a single update formula at each step.
- If general features are used, the information learned by the reinforcement learning can be used in other parts of the same problem [19].
- The behavior of various reinforcement learning methods end in optimal state-action pairs [13], which can be exploited. As an example of this, one can see how the policy choices the next action evolves at each step.

3   Reinforcement Learning Methods

Since in reinforcement learning the agent's goal is the maximization of the value function, at time t the agent chooses the action that maximizes the expected value of the total rewards it can obtain in the future from the state the agent is in. The expected reward R_t is generally defined as a function of the current and discounted future rewards. In general, we define the future reward from the time step t in Eq. (1).

$$R_t = \sum_{j=0}^{n} \gamma^j \cdot r_{t+j+1} \qquad (1)$$

Where $\gamma \in [0,1]$ is the discount factor, r_t is the reward when an action is taken at time t and n is often regarded as the time when the process terminates. Therefore, the agent's goal is to learn a policy capable of maximizing long-run rewards by interacting with the environment based on one's own experience. To do this, at each step t, starting from the state s_t, the agent has to compute as follows the value of the action-value function: $Q^\pi(s,a)$ for each possible action a_t on the basis of the policy π. The policy π can be defined as in Eq. (2):

$$Q^\pi(s,a) = \mathbb{P}_\pi\{R_t \mid s_t = s, a_t = a\} \qquad (2)$$

where $\mathbb{P}_\pi\{R_t \mid s_t = s, a_t = a\}$. Now the agent aims at obtaining the optimal state-action function Q*(s, a) which is usually relevant to the Bellman equation. Then two methods called Q-learning and SARSA will be compared to get the optimal state-action value function.

3.1   Q-Learning

Q-Learning is one of the most traditional reinforcement learning algorithms in existence [2], Q-learning is an off-policy method, in other words, the agent learns and selects action a independently of interaction with the environment. The impact of executing action a on the environment is obtained by reward or punishment (r) and this allows to decide which is the next state s_{t+1}. Therefore, the main objective is to maximize the function $Q(s,a)$ during the learning process to obtain the best action for a particular state. The way to mathematically represent the updating equation is Eq. (3):

$$Q(s_t, a_t) \longleftarrow (1 - \alpha) \cdot Q(s_t, a_t) + \alpha \cdot [r + \gamma \cdot maxQ(s_{t+1}, a_{t+1})] \qquad (3)$$

where α represents the learning rate, γ is the discount factor, r is the immediate reward or penalty received and $maxQ(s_{t+1}, a_{t+1})$ tells us that a_{t+1} is the best action for state s_{t+1}.

3.2   SARSA

Instead, SARSA is an on-policy method [13], the agent learns the value of the state-action pair based on the performed action, in other words, when the value of the current state-action is updated, the next action a_{t+1} will be taken. While in Q-Learning, the action a_{t+1} is completely greedy. Based on this, the state-action value update equation is defined as in Eq. (4):

$$Q(s_t, a_t) \longleftarrow Q(s_t, a_t) + \alpha \cdot [r + \gamma \cdot Q(s_{t+1}, a_{t+1}) - Q(s_t, a_t)] \qquad (4)$$

The procedure of forming the Q-table is the same for both algorithms. The only difference between them is the update rule that is being followed in every step, Eqs. (3) and (4). The different update rule enables SARSA to learn faster than the Q-learning algorithm. However, this makes SARSA a more conservative algorithm and the probability of finding the optimal policy is higher for Q-learning.

3.3   Reward Function

The big question when using reinforcement learning methods is: how to reward or punish the actions performed by the agent. The balance between reward and punishment achieves an equal variety of the selection of actions so that the best action found is more reliable.

Different learnheuristics have been found in the literature in which meta-heuristics incorporate reinforcement learning techniques as a machine learning technique. The classical reward function used by these learnheuristics is adapted to the behavior of the metaheuristic.

For example, we will use a simplified version of the version proposed by Yue Xu and Dechang Pi [24] for optimal topology selection in particle swarm optimization. The simplified performance-oriented version of the metaheuristic considers reward value +1 when fitness is improved or 0 otherwise. As a result, the reward or penalty visible in Eq. (5) and is born where only the reward is given. The type of reward mentioned above is shown in Table 1.

Table 1. Types of rewards

Reference	Reward Function
[24]	$r_n = \begin{cases} +1, & \textit{if the current action improves fitness} \\ 0, & \textit{otherwise.} \end{cases}$ \qquad (5)

4   Whale Optimization Algorithm

Whale Optimization Algorithm (WOA) is inspired by the hunting behavior of humpback whales, specifically, how they make use of a strategy known as "bubble netting". This strategy consists of locating the prey, and employing a spiral turn like a "9", enclosing the prey. This algorithm was invented by Mirjalili and Lewis in 2015 [8].

The WOA metaheuristic starts with a set of random solutions. At each iteration, the search agents update their positions concerning a randomly chosen search agent or the best solution obtained so far. There is a parameter "a" that is reduced from 2 to 0 to provide changes between exploration and exploitation. When the equation vector (6) has value: $|\vec{A}| \geq 1$ a new random search agent is chosen, while when $|\vec{A}| \leq 1$ the best solution is selected, all this in order to be able to update the position of the search agents.

On the other hand, the value of the parameter "p" allows the algorithm to switch between a spiral or circular motion. To assimilate this, three movements are crucial when working with the metaheuristic:

1. **Searching for prey:** The whales search for prey randomly based on the position of each prey. When the algorithm determines that $|\vec{A}| \geq 1$, then we can say that it is exploring and allows WOA to perform a global search. We represent this first move with the following mathematical model:

$$\vec{X}_i^{t+1} = \overrightarrow{X_{rand}^t} - \vec{A} \cdot \vec{D}$$
$$\vec{D} = |\vec{C} \cdot \overrightarrow{X_{rand}^t} - \vec{X}_i^t| \tag{6}$$

Where t denotes the current iteration, $\vec{A}$ and $\vec{C}$ are coefficient vectors, $\overrightarrow{X_{rand}}$ is a random position vector (i.e., a random whale) chosen from the current population. The vectors $\vec{A}$ and $\vec{C}$ can be computed according to Eq. (7):

$$\vec{A} = 2\vec{a} \cdot \vec{r} - \vec{a}$$
$$\vec{C} = 2 \cdot \vec{r} \tag{7}$$

Where, $\vec{a}$ decreases linearly from 2 to 0 over iterations (both in the exploration and exploitation phases) and $\vec{r}$ corresponds to a random vector of values between $[0, 1]$.

2. **Encircling the prey:** Once the whales have found and recognized their prey, they begin to encircle them. Since the position of the optimal design in the search space is not known in the first instance, the metaheuristic assumes that the current best solution is the target prey or is close to the optimum. Therefore, once the best search agent is defined, the other agents will attempt to update their positions toward the best search agent. Mathematically it is modeled as in Eq. (8):

$$\vec{X}_i^{t+1} = \overrightarrow{X_i^{*t}} - \vec{A} \cdot \vec{D}$$
$$\vec{D} = |\vec{C} \cdot \overrightarrow{X_i^{*t}} - \vec{X}_i^t| \tag{8}$$

Where $\vec{X^*}$ is the position vector of the best solution obtained so far and $\vec{X}$ is the position vector. The vector $\vec{A}$ and $\vec{C}$ are calculated as in Eq. (7). It is worth mentioning that $\vec{X}$ must be updated at each iteration if a better solution exists.

3. **Bubble net attack:** For this attack, the "shrinking net mechanism" is presented, this behavior is achieved by decreasing the value of a in the Eq. (7). Thus, as the whale spirals, it shrinks the bubble net until it finally catches the prey. This motion is modeled with the Eq. (9):

$$\overrightarrow{X}_i^{t+1} = \overrightarrow{D'} \cdot e^{bl} \cdot \cos(2\pi l) + \overrightarrow{X^*}_i^{t}$$
$$\overrightarrow{D'} = |\overrightarrow{X^*}_i^{t} - \overrightarrow{X}_i^{t}| \tag{9}$$

Where, $\overrightarrow{D'}$ is the distance of the i-th whale from the prey (the best solution obtained so far, b is a constant to define the shape of the logarithmic spiral. l is a random number between $[-1, 1]$.

It is worth mentioning that humpback whales swim around the prey within a shrinking circle and along a spiral trajectory simultaneously. In order to model this simultaneous behavior, there is a 50% probability of choosing between the encircling prey mechanism (2) or the spiral model (3) to update the position of the whales during optimization. The mathematical model is as follows:

$$\overrightarrow{X}_i^{t+1} = \begin{cases} \overrightarrow{X^*}_i^{t} - \overrightarrow{A} \cdot \overrightarrow{D} & \text{If } p < 0.5 \\ \overrightarrow{D'} \cdot e^{bl} \cdot \cos(2\pi l) + \overrightarrow{X^*}_i^{t} & \text{If } p \geq 0.5 \end{cases} \tag{10}$$

Figure 1 shows the behavior of the metaheuristic to improve the understanding of the above.

4.1 Ambidextrous Metaheuristics

Recent studies [2,17,18] built a general framework of ambidextrous metaheuristics [3,6] that incorporates Q-Learning as a reinforcement learning module for operator selection. Specifically, they select binarization schemes derived from combinations between transfer functions and discretization functions of the Two-Step Technique.

In this paper we present modifications of the classical whale [8], where both, SARSA and Q-Learning will be incorporated for later comparison. The **actions** to be taken by the agents are the **binarization schemes**, the **states** are the **phases of the metaheuristic**, i.e. exploration or exploitation, the **episodes** where an action is selected and applied in a particular state will be the **iterations** and the **agents** will be the **individuals** of the whale algorithm.

4.2 Balancing Exploration and Exploitation

During the search process, metaheuristics make decisions to discern whether to explore the search space or exploit promising regions. The decision criteria are specific to each metaheuristic and generating a good tuning allows obtaining a better balance. Ambidextrous algorithms were designed to balance exploration and exploitation from the point of view of decision-making. Before making a decision that affects the balancing, it is necessary to know in which phase the metaheuristic is.

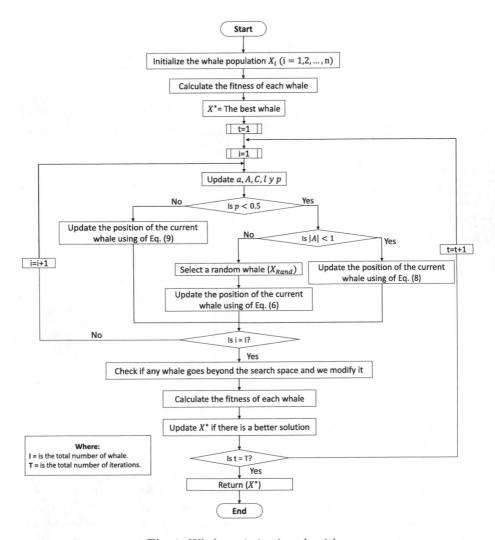

Fig. 1. Whale optimization algorithm

One of the techniques to measure the phase of a population metaheuristic is the diversity metrics. These metrics quantify diversity by the distances between individuals where distances increase during exploratory phases and decrease during exploitative phases. In the literature, there are different diversity metrics such as Dimensional Diversity-Hussain [4]. Dimensional-Hussain Diversity is defined as:

$$Div = \frac{1}{l \cdot n} \sum_{d=1}^{l} \sum_{i=1}^{n} |\bar{x}^d - x_i^d|, \tag{11}$$

Where X is the population under analysis, $\bar{x}^d$ is the mean of the d-th dimension, n is the number of individuals in the population X and l is the number of decision variables of the optimization problem.

Morales-Castañeda et al. in [10] propose equations that use the diversity obtained from a population to calculate an estimate of the exploration (XPL%) and exploitation (XPT%) phases using percentages. The equations mentioned are as follows:

$$XPL\% = \frac{Div}{Div_{max}} \cdot 100, \tag{12}$$

and

$$XPT\% = \frac{|Div - Div_{max}|}{Div_{max}} \cdot 100. \tag{13}$$

Where Div_t corresponds to the current diversity in the t-th iteration and Div_{max} corresponds to the maximum diversity obtained in the entire search process.

These exploration and exploitation percentages can be used to roughly determine the stage of the metaheuristic as follows:

$$Phase = \begin{cases} Exploration \ if \ XPL\% \geq XPT\% \\ Exploitation \ if \ XPL\% < XPT\% \end{cases} \tag{14}$$

This metaheuristic phase estimation is used for state determination in the Q-Learning and SARSA algorithms. Thus, their state transition is determined by the diversity of individuals during the search process. The proposal of this work is shown in Fig. 2.

4.3 A New Algorithm: Binary SARSA Whale Optimization Algorithm

Under the proposed implementation, a new algorithm based on Whale Optimization Algorithm is created, together with the incorporation of the reinforcement learning algorithm SARSA, which acts as the agent in charge of selecting the best binarization scheme to be used in each iteration according to what is learned during the iterative process of the metaheuristic.

The hybridization between the metaheuristic and the reinforcement learning algorithm SARSA is explained in the Fig. 2. Where the red boxes indicate the participation of the SARSA algorithm.

5   Experimental Results

Experiments solving the Set Covering Problem with Beasley's OR-Library instances totaled 45 instances. These instances were executed with a total of 40 population and 1000 iterations, having a total of 40,000 calls to the objective function, as used in [5]. The implementation was developed in Python 3.8.5 and processed using the free Google Colaboraty service [1]. The parameter settings for the SARSA and Q-Learning algorithm have been as follows: $\gamma = 0.4$ and $\alpha = 0.1$.

The results obtained are presented in the Table 2, which in its first column presents the name of each solved instance, in the second column, the optimal value of each instance. While the next 6 columns present the best results (Best), average results (Avg), and RPD according to Eq. 15 for each of the instances and both versions: BSWOA and Binary Q-WOA (BQWOA). The version of WOA hybridized with Q-Learning has been implemented according to the work of Cisternas et al. [2]. Finally, the last two rows of the table present the average values of all instances and the p-value obtained by the Wilcoxon-Mann-Whitney test [7]. The test allows us to determine whether the results obtained are significantly different to determine which of the two hybridized versions performs better on this subset of instances.

$$\text{RPD} = \frac{100 \cdot (Best - Opt)}{Opt}. \tag{15}$$

On the other hand, the exploration and exploitation graphs are presented as presented in Sect. 4.2, obtaining Fig. 3 and 4. Where we can observe that behaviors similar to those presented by Morales-Castañeda et al. [10] is presented as a correct balance of exploration and exploitation, starting with a diversification of the solutions in the search space to subsequently intensify the search.

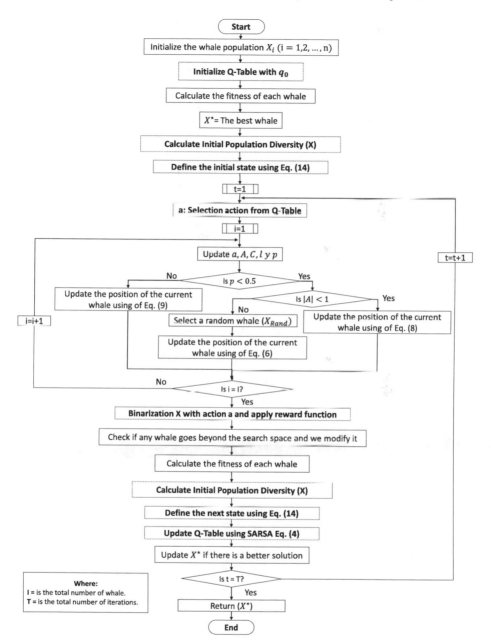

Fig. 2. Binary S-Whale optimization algorithm (Color figure online)

Table 2. Results obtained by BSWOA and BQWOA solving SCP

Inst.	Opt.	BSWOA			BQWOA		
		Best	Avg	RPD	Best	Avg	RPD
4.1	429	**430**	434.6	0.23	435	439.48	1.4
4.2	512	**523**	535.6	2.15	538	546.44	5.08
4.3	516	**525**	532.7	1.74	537	543.78	4.07
4.4	494	**497**	508.0	0.61	519	526.33	5.06
4.5	512	**523**	528.4	2.15	537	541.89	4.88
4.6	560	**567**	570.3	1.25	573	580.33	2.32
4.7	430	**435**	439.5	1.16	440	445.29	2.33
4.8	492	**496**	499.6	0.81	505	507.83	2.64
4.9	641	**671**	677.6	4.68	686	690.8	7.02
4.10	514	**521**	524.1	1.36	530	532.4	3.11
5.1	253	**258**	262.7	1.98	262	267.71	3.56
5.2	302	**319**	325.3	5.63	326	332.17	7.95
5.3	226	**230**	230.8	1.77	232	233.5	2.65
5.4	242	**247**	249.4	2.07	250	252.5	3.31
5.5	211	**212**	214.5	0.47	216	218.83	2.37
5.6	213	**218**	221.3	2.35	227	229.0	6.57
5.7	293	**302**	304.6	3.07	311	313.2	6.14
5.8	288	**291**	293.9	1.04	298	299.33	3.47
5.9	279	**282**	284.3	1.08	284	287.4	1.79
5.10	265	**267**	273.1	0.75	277	278.33	4.53
6.1	138	**141**	144.1	2.17	144	146.68	4.35
6.2	146	**147**	152.3	0.68	154	155.83	5.48
6.3	145	**147**	148.4	1.38	149	150.4	2.76
6.4	131	**131**	133.1	0.0	132	134.17	0.76
6.5	161	**163**	172.2	1.24	180	181.5	11.8
A.1	253	**260**	263.2	2.77	263	266.84	3.95
A.2	252	**261**	264.0	3.57	266	269.83	5.56
A.3	232	**240**	243.4	3.45	244	245.6	5.17
A.4	234	**238**	242.5	1.71	251	251.8	7.26
A.5	236	**241**	244.2	2.12	242	247.33	2.54
B.1	69	**69**	70.5	0.0	70	71.68	1.45
B.2	76	**76**	77.2	0.0	78	79.5	2.63
B.3	80	**81**	81.7	1.25	82	82.17	2.5
B.4	79	**79**	81.3	0.0	83	83.83	5.06
B.5	72	**72**	72.9	0.0	73	74.33	1.39
C.1	227	**234**	238.4	3.08	243	247.81	7.05
C.2	219	**229**	232.3	4.57	234	238.83	6.85
C.3	243	**249**	254.2	2.47	258	260.83	6.17
C.4	219	**227**	229.0	3.65	232	233.83	5.94
C.5	215	**221**	225.4	2.79	229	231.33	6.51
D.1	60	**61**	62.3	1.67	63	64.97	5.0
D.2	66	**67**	67.4	1.52	68	69.0	3.03
D.3	72	**73**	74.8	1.39	76	77.33	5.56
D.4	62	**62**	62.2	0.0	**62**	63.4	0.0
D.5	61	**61**	62.6	0.0	63	64.33	3.28
		258.76	262.44	1.73	264.93	267.99	4.27
p-value							0.00

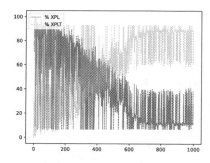
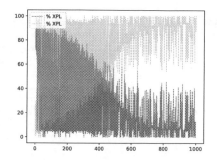

Fig. 3. Exploration and exploitation graphic - SARSA

Fig. 4. Exploration and exploitation graphic - Q-Learning

6 Conclusion

The implementation of reinforcement learning techniques to metaheuristics has presented a great contribution both to the improvement of fitness obtained and to obtain a better exploration-exploitation balance. In this work, SARSA has been implemented as a binarization scheme selector in the metaheuristic Whale Optimization Algorithm, solving 45 OR-Library instances of the Set Covering Problem. Where when compared with its closest version BQWOA, it has been shown that BSWOA obtains better quality results in 44 out of 45 instances and that these results are significantly better under the Wilcoxon-Mann-Whitney Test.

The proposal achieved the optimum in 7 instances (Instances 6.4, B.1, B.2, B.4, B.5, D.4, and D.5) versus 1 optimum of the version incorporating Q Learning (Instance D.4). As for the average RPD, the proposal achieves a value of 1.73 among all the instances executed, indicating a good performance by obtaining results that are not so far from the optimal ones.

The results obtained are promising since by implementing a binarization scheme selector, tuning times are reduced by not having to evaluate the combinations of the different binarization schemes present in the literature, providing the implementation of these techniques.

On the other hand, when observing in detail the exploration and exploitation graphs, it is observed that both have similar convergences, but in the case of BSWOA, the values tend to have variations of smaller magnitude and with the lower occurrence, which could be an indicator of its better performance in solving this problem, possibly having movements of smaller magnitude within the search space, but this statement must be validated by an analysis of the solution vectors during the iterative process.

As future work, along with the implementation of SARSA in other meta-heuristic techniques, there is a need to be able to parameterize the results obtained in the exploration and exploitation graphs, although it gives us valuable information of the search process, a metric for comparison is still needed, along with the option of incorporating this same metric to the learning process of the reinforcement learning agent.

Acknowledgements. Broderick Crawford is supported by Grant CONICYT/ FONDECYT/REGULAR/1210810. Ricardo Soto is supported by Grant CON-ICYT/FONDECYT/REGULAR/1190129. José Lemus-Romani is supported by National Agency for Research and Development (ANID)/Scholarship Program/ DOCTORADO NACIONAL/2019-21191692. Marcelo Becerra-Rozas is supported by National Agency for Research and Development (ANID)/Scholarship Program/ DOCTORADO NACIONAL/2021-21210740.

References

1. Bisong, E.: Google colaboratory. In: Bisong, E. (ed.) Building Machine Learning and Deep Learning Models on Google Cloud Platform, pp. 59–64. Springer, Heidelberg (2019). https://doi.org/10.1007/978-1-4842-4470-8_7
2. Cisternas-Caneo, F., et al.: A data-driven dynamic discretization framework to solve combinatorial problems using continuous metaheuristics. In: Abraham, A., Sasaki, H., Rios, R., Gandhi, N., Singh, U., Ma, K. (eds.) IBICA 2020. AISC, vol. 1372, pp. 76–85. Springer, Cham (2021). https://doi.org/10.1007/978-3-030-73603-3_7
3. Crawford, B., León de la Barra, C.: Los algoritmos ambidiestros (2020). https://www.mercuriovalpo.cl/impresa/2020/07/13/full/cuerpo-principal/15/. Accedeed 12 Feb 2021
4. Hussain, K., Zhu, W., Salleh, M.N.M.: Long-term memory Harris' hawk optimization for high dimensional and optimal power flow problems. IEEE Access **7**, 147596–147616 (2019)
5. Lanza-Gutierrez, J.M., Crawford, B., Soto, R., Berrios, N., Gomez-Pulido, J.A., Paredes, F.: Analyzing the effects of binarization techniques when solving the set covering problem through swarm optimization. Expert Syst. Appl. **70**, 67–82 (2017)
6. Lemus-Romani, J., et al.: Ambidextrous socio-cultural algorithms. In: Gervasi, O., et al. (eds.) ICCSA 2020. LNCS, vol. 12254, pp. 923–938. Springer, Cham (2020). https://doi.org/10.1007/978-3-030-58817-5_65
7. Mann, H.B., Whitney, D.R.: On a test of whether one of two random variables is stochastically larger than the other. Ann. Math. Stat. 50–60 (1947)
8. Mirjalili, S., Lewis, A.: The whale optimization algorithm. Adv. Eng. Softw. **95**, 51–67 (2016)
9. Misra, S.: A step by step guide for choosing project topics and writing research papers in ICT related disciplines. In: ICTA 2020. CCIS, vol. 1350, pp. 727–744. Springer, Cham (2021). https://doi.org/10.1007/978-3-030-69143-1_55
10. Morales-Castañeda, B., Zaldivar, D., Cuevas, E., Fausto, F., Rodríguez, A.: A better balance in metaheuristic algorithms: does it exist? Swarm Evol. Comput. 100671 (2020)
11. Song, H., Triguero, I., Özcan, E.: A review on the self and dual interactions between machine learning and optimisation. Progress Artif. Intell. **8**(2), 143–165 (2019). https://doi.org/10.1007/s13748-019-00185-z
12. Sutton, R.S.: Learning to predict by the methods of temporal differences. Mach. Learn. **3**(1), 9–44 (1988)
13. Sutton, R.S., Barto, A.G.: Reinforcement Learning: An Introduction. MIT Press, Cambridge (2018)
14. Sutton, R.: Generalization in reinforcement learning: successful examples using sparse coarse coding. In: Advances in Neural Information Processing Systems, vol. 8 (1996)

15. Talbi, E.G.: Metaheuristics: From Design to Implementation, vol. 74. Wiley, Hoboken (2009)
16. Talbi, E.G.: Machine learning into metaheuristics: a survey and taxonomy of data-driven metaheuristics (2020)
17. Tapia, D., et al.: A Q-learning hyperheuristic binarization framework to balance exploration and exploitation. In: Florez, H., Misra, S. (eds.) ICAI 2020. CCIS, vol. 1277, pp. 14–28. Springer, Cham (2020). https://doi.org/10.1007/978-3-030-61702-8_2
18. Tapia, D., et al.: Embedding q-learning in the selection of metaheuristic operators: the enhanced binary grey wolf optimizar case. In: Proceeding of 2021 IEEE International Conference on Automation/XXIV Congress of the Chilean Association of Automatic Control (ICA-ACCA), IEEE ICA/ACCA 2021, Article in Press (2021)
19. Taylor, M.E., Stone, P., Liu, Y.: Transfer learning via inter-task mappings for temporal difference learning. J. Mach. Learn. Res. **8**(9) (2007)
20. Valdivia, S., et al.: Bridges reinforcement through conversion of tied-arch using crow search algorithm. In: Misra, S., et al. (eds.) ICCSA 2019. LNCS, vol. 11623, pp. 525–535. Springer, Cham (2019). https://doi.org/10.1007/978-3-030-24308-1_42
21. Vásquez, C., et al.: Galactic swarm optimization applied to reinforcement of bridges by conversion in cable-stayed arch. In: Misra, S., et al. (eds.) ICCSA 2019. LNCS, vol. 11623, pp. 108–119. Springer, Cham (2019). https://doi.org/10.1007/978-3-030-24308-1_10
22. Vásquez, C., et al.: Solving the 0/1 Knapsack problem using a galactic swarm optimization with data-driven binarization approaches. In: Gervasi, O., et al. (eds.) ICCSA 2020. LNCS, vol. 12254, pp. 511–526. Springer, Cham (2020). https://doi.org/10.1007/978-3-030-58817-5_38
23. Wang, F.Y., Zhang, H., Liu, D.: Adaptive dynamic programming: an introduction. IEEE Comput. Intell. Mag. **4**(2), 39–47 (2009)
24. Xu, Y., Pi, D.: A reinforcement learning-based communication topology in particle swarm optimization. Neural Comput. Appl. **32**(14), 10007–10032 (2019). https://doi.org/10.1007/s00521-019-04527-9
25. Zhao, D., Zhu, Y.: MEC-a near-optimal online reinforcement learning algorithm for continuous deterministic systems. IEEE Trans. Neural Netw. Learn. Syst. **26**(2), 346–356 (2014)
26. Zhu, Y., Zhao, D., Li, X.: Using reinforcement learning techniques to solve continuous-time non-linear optimal tracking problem without system dynamics. IET Control Theory Appl. **10**(12), 1339–1347 (2016)

Changing Pattern of Human Movements
in Istanbul During Covid-19

Ayse Giz Gulnerman[✉] 📵

Ankara Haci Bayram Veli University, 06450 Ankara, Turkey
ayse.gulnerman@hbv.edu.tr

Abstract. Human trajectories provide spatial information on how citizens interact with the city. This information can explain the daily routine, economic and cultural cycle of citizens. In the last year, the pattern of human trajectories is expected to change over cities due to Covid-19. This paper investigates the change in human trajectories based on the social media data (SMD) before and after the Covid-19. This study aims to find out the differences between the years 2018, 2020, and 2021. Firstly, all accounts for each year are classified based on movement behaviors. Secondly, spatial distributions of the tweets in terms of classified accounts are visualized after the hierarchical clustering applied to each dataset. Lastly, the average step lengths (ASL) are calculated for each account and classified in terms of step length levels as no movement, neighborhood, district, inter-districts, inter periphery, and center, outbound. The number of tweets and distinct accounts decreased by 90% and 84% from 2018 to 2021. The decrease in the number of single tweeting accounts is 84%, it is 60% in stationary accounts, and 94% in moving ac-counts. The size of the spatial clusters also decreased for all types of accounts maps, however, some of the previously visited spatial points are disappeared while new ones appeared on maps of single tweeting and moving accounts. The ASL of moving accounts also confirms the human movement decrease. According to that, the max, mean, and median ASL decreased 22%, 13%, and 35%. Results point out outcomes vary in terms of accounts' movement behaviors. This study is expected to contribute the measuring the pandemic impacts on human movement with SMD.

Keywords: Human movement · Spatial trajectories · Social media analysis · Covid-19

1 Introduction

1.1 Human Trajectories and Mobility

A human is a moving object that interacts with the city [1–3] for diverse purposes and under diverse circumstances. Mobile technologies and apps have enabled the retrieval of this interaction as human trajectories. A trajectory is simply defined as an array of timestamped locations (a pair of latitude and longitude) with/-out attributes [4]. Trajectory data vary in terms of spatial and/or temporal frequency based on data collection settings

© Springer Nature Switzerland AG 2021
O. Gervasi et al. (Eds.): ICCSA 2021, LNCS 12957, pp. 220–230, 2021.
https://doi.org/10.1007/978-3-030-87013-3_17

(either pre-defined or controllable). Social media is one of the sources for crowdsourced trajectory data where each location pair is generated by geotagged social media posts [5]. In other words, social media is an unsystematic trajectory source since it has no pre-defined frequency settings and the data generation is entirely dependent on the users' instant preferences or un-consciously defined default settings.

Trajectory data with diverse data mining techniques provide diverse information. Zheng [6] defines the trajectory data mining flow in three bases; preprocessing (noise filtering, stay point detection, segmentation), indexing and retrieval, and processing (pattern mining, classification, anomaly detection). Buchin [7] categorizes the purpose of trajectory data analysis in terms of the number of trajectories (single, two, multiple). According to that, recurring pattern detection might be one purpose of single trajectory mining, while common or typical trajectory analysis could be performed with multiple trajectories.

Jurdak et al. [8] mention that there are diverse tracking systems (such as; mobile phones, GPS, and RFID) on human movement. However, these tracking systems have concerns such as; ethical breaching issues, data access problems, and low resolutions in data [5, 8]. Demšar [9] points out one of the big problems in movement science is modifiable areal unit problems (MAUP) that is different scales and shapes applied to movement data might return different insights. Dodge [5] also mentions responsible Computational Movement Analysis (CMA) is important to lead the vital studies that emerged and enhanced with the Covid-19 in this area.

Geospatial data analytics with trajectory analysis became a more important topic than ever before with the Covid-19 since the pandemic distort the usual human trajectories at any granularity (global and regional) [5, 10]. Jurdak et al. [8] demonstrated the social media (Twitter) is a reliable source for analyzing human movement patterns. So far, social media-based trajectory data is used to analyze human mobility patterns [11], to reveal trajectory patterns characteristic of traveling attendees of large-scale events [12], urban mobility patterns based on urban dynamics, and functional places [13, 14].

Social media is a wide data source that is used for the research on diverse topics such as; community detection [15], prediction of customers sentiments [16], and regulation of the use of social media to prevent disinformation during political campaigns [17]. In this study, social media data is assessed as a spatial trajectory source for monitoring human movement.

1.2 Aim of the Study

This study aims to demonstrate the change in human movement between the years (2018, 2020, 2021) based on social media (Twitter) data and search the impacts of Covid-19 on human movement within Istanbul city. In addition to the main aim, there are sub-objectives determined in order to reveal the possible indicators for monitoring the human movement change. The first sub-objective is finding out how the change in the number of tweets impacts the spatial distribution of tweets. The second objective is assessing the change in tweet distribution according to users' tweeting behavior. The third objective is revealing the change in step lengths of moving users under different circumstances. All these sub-objectives are aimed to define possible indicators to contribute algorithms built for human activity monitoring analytics based on social media data.

2   Data and Evaluation

This study investigates social media data (Twitter) for the years 2018, 2020, and 2021 collected via Twitter API. This API returns free data which is randomly selected 1% of all generated data in the meantime. Time interval is determined for each year in terms of the Covid-19 case declaration day (11th of March 2020) in Turkey. 15 days as one week before and after the 11th March accepted as the time interval and retrieved data for each year summarized in Table 1.

Table 1.   Social media data details in terms of year 2018, 2020, and 2021.

* (number of)	2018	2020	2021
* tweets	459,237	71,138	48,952
* distinct accounts	25,836	7278	4192
* single tweeting accounts	9612	3233	1552
* stationary accounts	4434	2039	1763
* moving accounts	11,790	2006	877

Accounts are categorized in terms of movement behaviors i.e., single tweeting, stationary, and moving. Accounts having single tweets have no values for movement step length comparison however contribute to change in the spatial density and place semantic interpretation. Accounts having multiple tweets classified as stationary or moving accounts depending on the calculated bounding box (BBOX) area for each. In this determination, 100 m^2 is accepted as GPS locating error for mobile devices in all directions. According to that, accounts having less than 0.04 km^2 BBOX area of their tweets are determined as stationary, others are determined as moving accounts.

It is clearly seen that the total amount of data in 2018 is quite high in every field when it is compared to the data in 2020 and 2021 in Table 1. Although the % of moving users decreased dramatically as well as the total amount, the % of stationary users increased more than double from 2018 to 2021 (Fig. 1). The single tweeting % represents the most

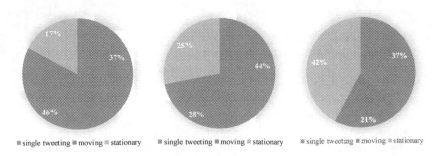

Fig. 1.   Users' moving behavior charts for the year (a) 2018 (b) 2020 (c) 2021.

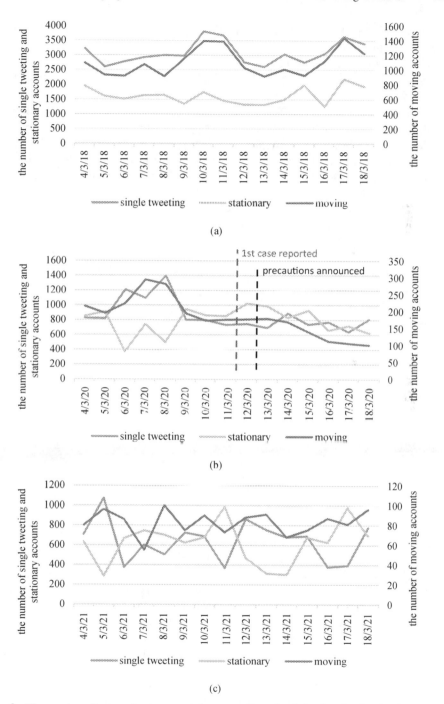

Fig. 2. The number of categorized accounts in terms of moving behaviors by day for the year (a) 2018 (b) 2020 (c) 2021.

stable part of this slicing comparison which might provide a valuable benchmark for further investigations.

Overall numbers of categorized accounts provide the information that the % of moving accounts and stationary accounts shifted between 2018 and 2021. In order to add a temporal fine-grained perspective, Fig. 2 shows the number of categorized accounts by day for the years 2018, 2020, and 2021. Trends for all category user counts are very similar in 2018 while in 2020, two of them (single tweeting and moving accounts) are similar in 2020. Also, none of the categories are showing a correlation in 2021. In 2018, single tweeting and moving users' counts are reaching a peak on the weekends. In 2020, single tweeting and moving users are reaching a peak in the weekends (7th-8th March) however after the Covid-19 declaration on 11th of March, the number of users for all kinds show decreasing trends even in the following weekends (14th–15th of March). In 2020, the number of moving accounts might be expected to decrease more with the 1st case declaration day however the partial precautions decision has been taken and announced on the late 12th of March for the later weeks. In 2021, all lines are fluctuating and the peaks seen in the former years' weekends are not seen this year.

Spatial footprints of the accounts for each categorization are visualized in Fig. 3 by year. A hierarchical clustering algorithm is used as an aggregation method to cluster spatial points (tweets). The evaluation process follows;

- geodesic distance calculation between spatial points with "distm" function from "geosphere" package [18]
- building hierarchical structure with "hclust" function from "stats" package [19]
- clustering points setting 5 km as distance threshold with the "cutree" function from "stats" package [19]
- calculating spatial center of each cluster with the "gCentroid" function from "rgeos" package [20]
- plotting each cluster centroid with "tm_bubbles" function from "tmap" package [21] defining size as point count facets by years

steps and applied to each set of tweets from single tweeting, stationary, and moving accounts. Since stationary accounts have tweets from the very same locations, an additional process is applied by grouping the tweets from each account beforehand.

Figure 3 shows the tweet density and distribution maps for each year in terms of movement behaviors of accounts. The overall decrease in the number of tweets between 2018, 2020, and 2021 is also spatially observed. Tweet clusters of single tweeting accounts, concentrated in the central part of the Istanbul city in 2018, dispersed to the outer parts and getting smaller in 2020, and get concentrated in the center again with a much smaller size in 2021 (Fig. 3 (a)). Tweet clusters of stationary accounts between years represent the most stable cluster distribution. These clusters emerged at very similar locations with the size reduction in years (Fig. 3 (b)). Tweet clusters of moving accounts also concentrated in the central for all years with the size reduction. Be-side the reducing size of the clusters, some of them disappeared in years in the outer parts and around the central parts of Istanbul (Fig. 3. (c)).

Human movement variation between years is analyzed referring to the moving accounts. Each step length and bearing angle is calculated between timely ordered tweets

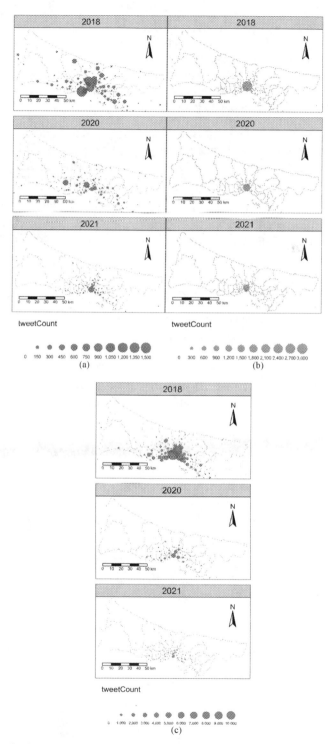

Fig. 3. Tweet distribution by year in terms of movement behavior of users (a) single tweeting users (b) stationary users (c) moving users.

for each user with the "moveHMM" R package [22]. A summary table for the movement data is given in Table 2. Mean step length and mean average step lengths are both decreased between years. In addition to that, median values are decreased more than mean values which means the number of tweets tends to right skewing in the step length distribution. Also, standard deviation increased in years and even higher than the mean value which represents the data widely distributed.

Table 2. Moving accounts movement details in terms of year 2018, 2020, and 2021.

(* km unit)	2018	2020	2021
Max. step length	123.98	132.24	165.12
Mean step length	9.36	9.06	8.91
Median step length	5.80	5.00	4.56
Std. dev. step length	11.00	11.78	11.94
Max average step lengths of an account	116.5	131.70	91.19
Mean average step lengths of accounts	10.83	9.81	9.41
Median average step lengths of accounts	8.24	6.08	5.35
Std. dev. of average step lengths of accounts	9.83	11.78	12.37

Furthermore, moving accounts steps are classified as to their step lengths and six levels are defined as no movement, neighborhood, district, inter-districts, inter periphery, and center, outbound. Break values are determined for the defined levels as 0.1 km, 1 km, 5 km, 10 km, 30 km, and above respectively considering the area of districts and distances to the central area. Figure 4 shows the number of steps with regards to moving length levels and years. No movement level steps are omitted in this representation. The number of steps in each level is ahead by far for the year 2018. However, the number of steps for each level decreased from 2018 to 2021, the decrease ratio between 2018 and 2020 is approximately three times higher than the de-crease ratio between 2020 and 2021.

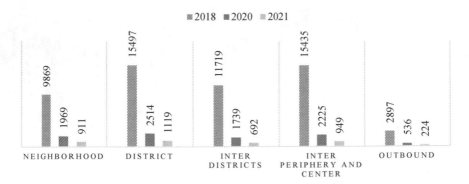

Fig. 4. The number of steps by each year in terms of step length levels.

Figure 5 represents the distribution of steps with regards to their length levels for the years 2018 (a), 2020 (b), and 2021 (c). While the neighborhood ratio is 18% in 2018, it is 22% in 2020 and 23% in 2021. Inter districts and inter periphery and center levels have a higher ratio in 2018 than in 2020 and in 2021. However, these ratio differences are not significant as in the number of differences seen in Fig. 4.

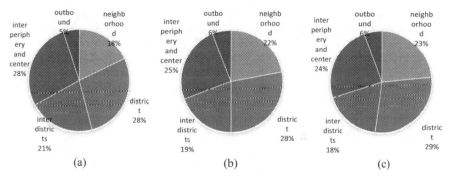

(a)   (b)   (c)

Fig. 5. The distribution of moving accounts step length levels for the year (a) 2018 (b) 2020 (c) 2021.

3 Results and Discussion

In the case study, three sets of data belong to years 2018, 2020, and 2021 are investigated and compared with regards to human movement behaviors. The first outcome of this investigation is the significant decrease in the number of tweets and the number of distinct accounts. This decrease is greater in the number of moving accounts while the least decrease seen proportionally in the number of stationary accounts. Therefore, omitting stationary users from the datasets in the pandemic estimation studies might not disrupt the results but benefit to reducing time cost. The change in number of accounts by day show while the all types of account movement behaviors show a similar trend after the pandemic declaration the number of single tweeting and moving accounts tend to decrease. However, the week after the Covid-19 declaration in 2020, the number of stationary accounts steadily tend to increase. Also, this second inference is supporting the stationary accounts can be omitted since it has no inferred change before and after Covid-19 declaration.

The spatial distribution of the stationary accounts is unchanged in years, however, the spatial cluster size changed proportionally between years. Since the number of tweets decreased, the size of the spatial clusters became small for all movement types. However, the single tweeting accounts map shows new locations become popular in the outer part of the Istanbul central area in 2020 and 2021. The map showing the clustered tweets of moving accounts shows that there is a significant decrease in cluster size and also many points are disappeared in 2020 and 2021. This reveals the certain change in moving accounts and the decreasing magnitude of its impact within the overall dataset. According to that, sets of tweets should be assessed separately based on accounts movement behaviors in order to see the real effects of the Covid-19.

Movement details of moving accounts show the shortening step lengths which means accounts travel to nearer locations than in 2018. Increasing standard deviations also reveals the growing disparities between accounts moving behaviors. Though the number of moving level decreases is higher between 2018 and 2020 than the decrease between 2020 and 2021, the decrease still continues. This might refer to adaptation to the pandemic normal but also refer to continuing migration from the city. As it is known mostly younger generations tend to share their locations and trajectories through social media. Millions of students are living in Istanbul and many of them immigrated back to their family houses in the other cities. So, the decrease in the number of moving accounts in each step length level is not surprising at all.

4 Conclusion

Geoinformatics has a leading role to manage the pandemics since Snow's Cholera Map [23]. Two centuries ago, data retrieval was a big problem, especially for wide areas. While several kinds of spatial data sources are available nowadays, the data need is still a big issue due to some reasons. Social media is a valuable continuous way of retrieving data, though it has data access limitations, representation and spatial bias, and uncertainty problems [24]. Therefore, social media is an open area to discover new geospatial data inferring techniques to diverse domains [25].

In this study, human movement change within Istanbul before and after Covid-19 is monitored with social media data. Tweets from classified accounts based on movement behaviors are investigated to reveal the change between years. According to that, the number of tweets and accounts decreased 90% and 84% between years. In a further look, this decrease in the number of accounts varies in terms of movement behaviors of accounts. While the number of single tweeting accounts decreased 84%, the decrease is 60% in stationary accounts and 94% in moving accounts. According to this, the most decrease was seen in the number of moving accounts.

The change in the spatial distribution of tweets is separately assessed with maps in terms of classified accounts. Generally, the size of the spatial clusters decreased in all maps of classified accounts. This unchanged spatial distribution is pointed out which might be omitted for further investigations to remove illusive weights on the spatial distribution. However, some of the spatial clusters are disappeared and new clusters emerged on maps of single tweeting and moving accounts. In addition to this spatial distribution, moving accounts add a new dimension to the results with the step length changes. According to that, human movement decrease is confirmed with the decrease in the max, mean, and median average step lengths of moving accounts which are 22%, 13%, and 35% respectively.

This study is limited with the data interval determined considering the first case of the Covid-19 declaration in Turkey. Only 15 days of each year is assessed and the outer regions of the Istanbul BBOX area discarded. The users that have only one tweet inside the BBOX of Istanbul and have other tweets outside are assessed within the single tweeting accounts. This study is planned to enhance the semantic segmentation of stay points of the single tweeting and moving users. In that way, the changing pattern of human movements is detailed with another dimension. In further studies, anomaly patterns of human behaviors are aimed to estimate the significant impacts of pandemics.

References

1. Ahas, R., et al.: Everyday space–time geographies: using mobile phone-based sensor data to monitor urban activity in Harbin, Paris, and Tallinn. Int. J. Geogr. Inf. Sci. **29**(11), 2017–2039 (2015)
2. Huang, Q., Wong, D.W.: Activity patterns, socioeconomic status and urban spatial structure: what can social media data tell us? Int. J. Geogr. Inf. Sci. **30**(9), 1873–1898 (2016)
3. Noulas, A., Scellato, S., Lambiotte, R., Pontil, M., Mascolo, C.: A tale of many cities: universal patterns in human urban mobility. PloS ONE **7**(5), e37027 (2012)
4. Buchin, K., Löffler, M., Popov, A., Roeloffzen, M.: Fréchet distance between uncertain trajectories: computing expected value and upper bound. In: 36th European Workshop on Computational Geometry (EuroCG 2020). Würzburg, Germany (2020)
5. Dodge, S., Gao, S., Tomko, M., Weibel, R.: Progress in computational movement analysis–towards movement data science (2020)
6. Zheng, Y.: Trajectory data mining: an overview. ACM Trans. Intell. Syst. Technol. (TIST) **6**(3), 1–41 (2015)
7. Buchin, K.: Trajectory Similarity. Winter School on Computational Geometry AUT, 11th Winter School on Computational Geometry. https://www.youtube.com/watch?v=GqOIzU EZgsA&list=LL&index=17. Accessed 03 May 2021
8. Jurdak, R., Zhao, K., Liu, J., AbouJaoude, M., Cameron, M., Newth, D.: Understanding human mobility from Twitter. PloS ONE **10**(7), e0131469 (2015)
9. Demšar, U., Long, J.A., Siła-Nowicka, K.: Integrated science of movement. J. Spat. Inf. Sci. **2020**(21), 25–31 (2020)
10. Minghini, M., Coetzee, S., Grinberger, A.Y., Yeboah, G., Juhász, L., Mooney, P.: Open-StreetMap research in the COVID-19 era. Editors **1** (2020)
11. Ma, D., Osaragi, T., Oki, T., Jiang, B.: Exploring the heterogeneity of human urban movements using geo-tagged tweets. Int. J. Geogr. Inf. Sci. **34**(12), 2475–2496 (2020)
12. Xin, Y., MacEachren, A.M.: Characterizing traveling fans: a workflow for event-oriented travel pattern analysis using Twitter data. Int. J. Geogr. Inf. Sci. **34**(12), 2497–2516 (2020)
13. Gabrielli, L., Rinzivillo, S., Ronzano, F., Villatoro, D.: From tweets to semantic trajectories: mining anomalous urban mobility patterns. In: Nin, J., Villatoro, D. (eds.) CitiSens 2013. LNCS, vol. 8313, pp. 26–35. Springer, Cham (2013). https://doi.org/10.1007/978-3-319-041 78-0_3
14. McKenzie, G., Janowicz, K., Gao, S., Gong, L.: How where is when? On the regional variability and resolution of geosocial temporal signatures for points of interest. Comput. Environ. Urban Syst. **54**, 336–346 (2015)
15. Kumari, A., Behera, R.K., Shukla, A.S., Sahoo, S.P., Misra, S., Rath, S.K.: Quantifying influential communities in granular social networks using fuzzy theory. In: Gervasi, O., et al. (eds.) ICCSA 2020. LNCS, vol. 12252, pp. 906–917. Springer, Cham (2020). https://doi.org/ 10.1007/978-3-030-58811-3_64
16. Behera, R.K., Jena, M., Rath, S.K., Misra, S.: Co-LSTM: convolutional LSTM model for sentiment analysis in social big data. Inf. Process. Manag. **58**(1), (2021)
17. Slös Wogu, I.A.P., Njie, S.N.N., Katende, J.O., Ukagba, G.U., Edogiawerie, M.O., Misra, S.: The social media, politics of disinformation in established hegemonies, and the role of technological innovations in 21st century elections: the road map to us 2020 presidential elections. Int. J. Electron. Gov. Res. (IJEGR) **16**(3), 65–84 (2020)
18. Hijmans, R.J.: Introduction to the "geosphere" package (Version 1.5-10) (2019)
19. R Core Team: R: A language and environment for statistical computing. R Foundation for Statistical Computing, Vienna, Austria (2020)

20. Bivand, V.R., Rundel, C.: rgeos: Interface to Geometry Engine - Open Source ('GEOS'). R package version (2020)
21. Tennekes, M.: tmap: Thematic maps in R. J. Stat. Softw. **84**(6), 1–39 (2018)
22. Michelot, T., Langrock, R., Patterson, T.A.: moveHMM: an R package for the statistical modelling of animal movement data using hidden Markov models. Methods Ecol. Evol. **7**(11), 1308–1315 (2016)
23. Snow, J.: On the Mode of Communication of Cholera. John Churchill (1855)
24. Gulnerman, A.G., Karaman, H., Pekaslan, D., Bilgi, S.: Citizens' spatial footprint on Twitter—anomaly, trend and bias investigation in Istanbul. ISPRS Int. J. Geo Inf. **9**(4), 222 (2020)
25. Gulnerman, A.G., Karaman, H.: Spatial reliability assessment of social media mining techniques with regard to disaster domain-based filtering. ISPRS Int. J. Geo Inf. **9**(4), 245 (2020)

Towards an Extensible Architecture for an Empirical Software Engineering Computational Platform

Fábio Fagundes Silveira[1]([⊠]) [iD], Rodrigo Avancini[1] [iD],
David de Souza França[1] [iD], Eduardo Martins Guerra[2] [iD],
and Tiago Silva da Silva[1] [iD]

[1] Federal University of São Paulo – UNIFESP, São José dos Campos, Brazil
fsilveira@unifesp.br
[2] Free University of Bolzen-Bolzano – UNIBZ, Bozen-Bolzano, Italy

Abstract. One of the main objectives of Empirical Software Engineering is the improvement of methods, techniques, and tools for Software Engineering (SE) through the conduction and execution of experiments. Although research in empirical software engineering is well established in the literature, it is possible to verify that there are few supporting environments for conducting experiments, despite the increasing demand for this kind of study within the SE community. Moreover, existing approaches lack a number of important features, such as extensible mechanisms for the required phases of an experimentation in different domains of SE, integration with existing software development environments, ways to define metrics to be collected, automatic organization mechanisms to analyze collected data using a specific statistical analyze method, and remote execution of experiments. This paper describes the *SCCOPLA – an extensible architecture for empirical software engineering computational platform.* Our approach aims to address the aforementioned functionalities missing in available environments to conduct empirical SE studies. Preliminary results show its feasibility by applying an architecture-based tool to some of our previous software testing empirical studies.

Keywords: Empirical software engineering · Controlled experiments · Experimental support environment

1 Introduction

Improving methods, techniques, and tools for Software Engineering (SE) through the conduction and execution of experiments are some of the main objectives of Empirical Software Engineering. Although research in empirical software engineering is well established in the literature, it is remarkable that there are few supporting environments for conducting experiments, despite the increasing

O. Gervasi et al. (Eds.): ICCSA 2021, LNCS 12957, pp. 231–246, 2021.
https://doi.org/10.1007/978-3-030-87013-3_18

demand for this kind of study within the SE community [8,10,30]. Additionally, existing approaches lack a number of important features. For instance, they do not offer extensible mechanisms for all required phases of experimentation in the different domains of SE, integration with existing software development environments, ways of how to define metrics to be collected, automatic organization mechanisms to analyze collected data using a specific statistical analyzes method, and remote execution of experiments. Notably, the capability to carry out remote experiments has become much more crucial after the onset of the COVID-19 pandemic and subsequent lockdowns.

It is essential to highlight that experiments have specific characteristics regarding their domains. These differences affect how computational environments that support empirical studies need to be extensible, allowing the highest possible flexibility to be tailored to different domains.

In this paper, we describe the *SCCOPLA* – an *extensible architecture for empirical software engineering computational platform*. Our approach aims to address the aforementioned functionalities missing in available environments to conduct empirical SE studies. Although our proposed architecture is an ongoing research and development project, preliminary results show its feasibility by applying an architecture-based tool to some of our previous software testing empirical studies.

The remaining of this paper is structured as follows: Sect. 2 reports the background notions related to empirical software engineering. Section 3 describes the extensible architecture for conducting SE experiments proposed in this work. Section 4 describes the tool developed to implement *SCCOPLA* and its main components. Also, discusses the present status, current results of our research and points out the next steps of the project. Finally, Sect. 5 summarizes our conclusion.

2   Empirical Software Engineering

A typical process of a controlled empirical study comprises the following phases: definition, planning, operation, analysis, interpretation, and packaging [29]. The seminal paper highlighting the importance of empirical studies in software engineering was published in the '80s by Basili et al. [3]. After that, several studies have been conducted in this area and reported in the literature.

Lately, the use of proof of concepts might not be enough in the assessment of proposed ideas in software engineering. This way, over the past years, the SE community has systematically increased its need for applying rigorous and systematic empirical studies, aiming to assess new scientific evidence about methods, techniques, and software technology proposals [21]. Reducing the risks involved in technology transfer to the industry is one of the clear benefits of such an approach. This way, hundreds of experiments have been conducted in the SE area [24].

Several researches on ESE applications show up important works in these areas. However, studies point out the lacking of automated and integrated tools or computational environments for supporting the experiment process phases [7,8,21,30], despite the growing demand for empirical studies in SE. Arisholm et al. [1] e Karahasanoviæ et al. [14] have proposed the SESE (*Simula Experiment Support Environment*), a web tool to support the participants' management, measures the time spent for each task, enable to download of additional information, and monitor participants activities. Nevertheless, it does not offer support to data acquiring and analyses.

The *Value-Based Empirical Research Planning Framework* (VBER) [4] was developed to help the study planning and evaluation, linking some deliverables to stakeholders propositions, aiming to compare the benefits and risks of empirical study variants. The *Mechanical Turk* [26] comprises a crowdsourcing tool to support empirical studies in SE, offering resources to access and manage a large number of participants, assisting in subjects recruitment to assess a technique or an ES tool. Torii et al. [27] have proposed the Ginger2, an experimental environment based on the CAESE (*Computer-Aided Empirical Software Engineering*) framework. According to the authors, even though the CAESE supports the whole experiment process, Ginger2 is still restricted to the analyses and execution phases. Mendonça et al. [19] have developed the FIRE (*Framework for Improving the Replication of Experiments*), focusing on sharing the knowledge generated by the study in a common body (intra and inter groups). However, they do not suggest how to organize lab packages.

The *Experiment Manager Framework* (EMF), proposed by Hochstein et al. [11] is a set of integrated tools to support experiments for the high-performance computing domain. The experiment framework supports many of the activities involved in a controlled experiment. Anyway, it does have some drawbacks. For example, it is not easy to adapt it to a particular domain language engineering since automated data capturing is customized for high-performance source code only. Another limitation is the lack of support for expanding statistical analyses beyond the ones built in the platform. Costa Araújo et al. [6] have presented the *Application of Reproducible Research on Evaluation of Software Testing Technique* (ARRESTT). Their main goal is to provide and encourage reproducible experimental artifacts, enabling the experimenter to develop, distribute and rerun studies within the software testing domain, such as test case selection and test suite minimization techniques. Although ARREST has several features that help the experiments with some replication issues, their uses have to know java to manipulate framework elements adequately. Neto and Scatalon [20] have shown up the ExpTool, a platform to carry out and packing experimental data in SE. On its current version, data are stored in XML files based on an ontology proposed for empirical studies in the literature [12].

It is possible to find out approaches specifically based on DSLs (*Domain Specific Languages*). For example, Freire et al. [8] have presented the ExpDSL, a tool, and a DSL to support experiments in SE. Basically, the approach encompasses the definition (scope) and the design experiment phases. Häser et al. [10] has developed an integrated end-to-end environment to perform experiments in DSL engineering, focusing on goal definition and experiment planning. As stated by the authors, the language offers to the experimenter to represent all the relevant data, while the tool automates the generation of interesting plots and testing the hypothesis.

Literature also reports approaches based on ontologies. The eSEE (*Experimentation Environment to Support Large-Scale Experimentation*), proposed by Travassos et al. [28] is an environment to manage several kinds of empirical studies in SE, including knowledge acquired when defining, planning, executing, and packaging studies. The eSSE is based on web services that facilitate instantiating environments to enable certain experimental study activities. It works in three different abstract levels: meta, configured, and execution, presenting an initial set of tools to populate its infrastructure. Garcia et al. [9] have developed an ontology to specify controlled experiments called *experOntology*. The main idea is to formalize the experiment plan through a body of knowledge previously recorded. It can model the design of an experiment, assigning, manually, different treatments to the participants. However, it is presented no empirical study to evaluate the ontology. The TESE (*Tool for Experimental Software Engineering*) [25] comprises a tool that, according to the authors, the main difference is the provision of aid its users about the main concepts involving empirical software engineering. TESE is implemented as a standalone application, which makes it difficult to manage geographically distributed experiments.

3   The *SCCOPLA* (An extenSible arChitecture for empiriCal sOftware Engineering comPutational pLAtform)

This section describes the architecture proposed in this work, particularly its components, their foundations, and how these components are integrated and extended.

During the design of our approach, aiming to fulfill the lacking of the flexibility of the existent approaches, the following main requirements were identified (reduced due to space limitations): *R1*) the system should support the whole workflow of a local or distributed controlled experiment, including online monitoring of participants; *R2*) the system should provide extensibility according to the experiment's study needs; *R3*) the system should provide flexible storage mechanisms; *R4*) ... provide extensible mechanisms to define and automatically collect metrics, preferable non-invasive ones; *R5*) ... provide extensible support to provide statistical analysis design; *R6*) ... provide mechanisms to allow conducting studies, including repeated measures with cross-over experimental design; and *R7*) ... provide extensible capabilities to integrate existing external tools. In particular, this requirement allows the users to either extend the environment to adapt it to different software engineering experiment domains through plugins or integrate it with existing technology solutions.

Considering the aforementioned main requirements of an ESE computational platform, *SCCOPLA* was designed based on microkernel architectural pattern [22]. Besides that, the proposed architecture highly adheres to the rules of the

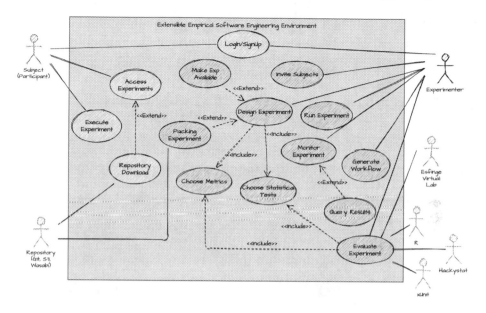

Fig. 1. Use cases diagram of the proposed platform.

Clean Architecture [18] and to the SOLID principles. Functional requirements and boundaries of the *SCCOPLA* can be seen in the use case diagram (Fig. 1).

Primarily, the *SCCOPLA* was sketched to be extended through the addition of plugins. Among the main advantages of this type of architecture, it is worth highlighting the extensibility via well-defined interfaces. Through this mecha-nism, it is often possible to build plugins without even knowing the source code of the application, being enough to implement the functions (or methods) of the interfaces that the host application is in charge of recognizing and using the plugin when needed.

Figure 2 presents a high-level view of the *SCCOPLA*: the core system and the independent plugin modules integrated into the reference implementation. We have defined custom interfaces (contracts) for each service to be developed adapters to connect to the desired services. This way, the independence of plug-ins is reached, providing extensibility, flexibility, and isolation to our application core features. This same view (Fig. 2) also presents some concepts of the applica-tion and their respective technologies and services available to assist in carrying out scientific experiments. At the right and left ends, one can see users of the application, experimenters, and participants. In the core system, some necessary plugins are displayed, such as: tools for statistical analysis, IDEs for experiments that require execution/development of source code, survey form services, cloud data storage services, and data analysis and manipulation tools.

Aiming to establish the boundaries of the architecture, as suggested by Mar-tin [18], the system was decomposed into components and distributed in layers as depicted in Fig. 3.

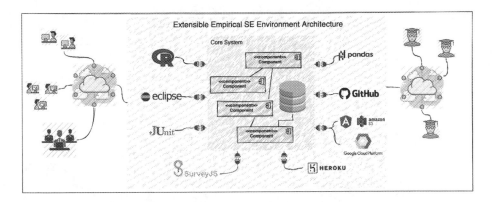

Fig. 2. The *SCCOPLA* architecture model.

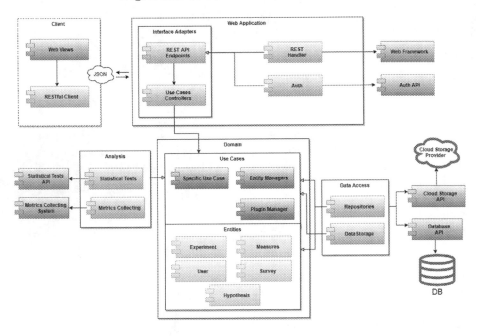

Fig. 3. Components diagram for the proposed platform.

In the Domain layer, entities refer to the business rules of the scientific experiment domain. They encapsulate the most general and high-level application rules. An entity can be an object with methods or a set of data structures and functions. In addition, entities are the most isolated objects and least prone to change. In the Use Cases layer, each use case represents an application-specific business rule. The use cases encapsulate and implement all the application's business logic, orchestrating the data flow using the entities to achieve the user's goals in the application. Here, there are two kinds of use cases: Entity Manager, responsible for some entity CRUD operations, and Specific Use Case, executed when it is necessary to interact with a more extensive set of entities and other tool resources.

According to the clean architecture guidelines, the Dependency Rule says that when a use case needs to use a resource provided by an API or framework, it uses an interface within its component instead of a concrete object that implements the resource. This rule is used to specify that the dependencies must always point from the lower-level components to the higher-level ones, considering the entities the highest level components.

Although the Clean Architecture ensures that components in the outer layers can act as plugins for business logic, which makes the architecture implicitly pluggable, the use case Plugin Manager has been defined to provide information about plugins used in the tool. Thus, an object that implements an external resource must also inherit from the Plugin interface provided by the Plugin Manager component.

The Web Application layer (or Back-end) provides a RESTful API that conforms to the constraints of REST (Representational State Transfer) architectural style. Thus, this layer is responsible for handling requests and responses for the Client, interacting with the use cases through the controllers. By convention, we define a corresponding endpoint for each entity, which, in turn, has a corresponding controller.

The Back-end also has a mechanism for authentication and authorization of access to endpoints represented by the Auth component. Hence, it prevents the endpoints from being accessed improperly. This mechanism also prevents the use cases from handling all user validation work, which improves the allocation of resources and the overall application's performance.

Regarding the Client layer (or Front end), we adopted a User-Centered Design approach in which we considered the user's needs as a basis to create and validate user interface possibilities. Thus, in order to meet the end users' goals in accordance with the proposed architecture, the Front-end was developed as a rich client standalone application, totally decoupled from the Back-end, using it only to consume web services provided by the REST API, as discussed in more detail later in this paper.

As shown in Fig. 4, the Clean Architecture is structured like an onion. The inner layers are comprised of more abstract parts, while the outer layers are implementation-specific with the glue code that communicates to the next circle inwards.

Noteworthy that internal elements do not depend on the external ones as it moves to the lower layers. Thus, the level of abstraction increases and the architecture level becomes higher. The most external elements are the concrete elements of the low-level ones (e.g., database and web framework). Figure 5 shows objects involved in the experiment registration.

Decomposing the software into layers and using the dependency rule makes it possible to build an intrinsically testable system with all the benefits it implies. When any of the external parts of the system become obsolete (e.g., database

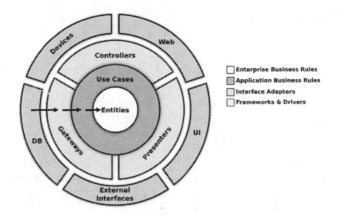

Fig. 4. The clean architecture [18].

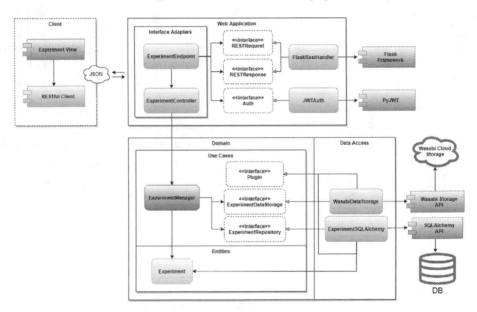

Fig. 5. Source code dependencies always point inwards.

or the web framework), it is possible to replace those obsolete elements with a minimum of maintainability effort.

Throughout the *SCCOPLA* development phases, we aimed to apply concepts from UX (User Experience), DX (Developer Experience), and End-User Development. We adopted a User-Centered Design approach in which we: carried out investigations by interviewing researchers and practitioners to understand their needs; carried out ideation rounds to bring up different ideas, and; prototyped different options to identify challenges and uncover subtleties. In order to improve the user experience, user testing sessions and questionnaires will be applied when the experiments are carried out.

3.1 Functionalities and Extension Points

One of the main requirements of the infrastructure is the ability to both support experiments with geographically distributed subjects and aggregate inter-institutional research groups. Hence, is mandatory to control and manage all the phases of an experimental study. Aiming to overcome this situation, the architecture implements a monitoring dashboard that presents to the experimenter data about the current status of a study and the status of each enrolled subject, as depicted by Fig. 7. It is essential to notice the UX aspects involved in the front-end GUI design: the accessibility concern. For example, the use of icons instead of only colors to make the GUI color-blind-friendly.

Yet, considering the geographical issues, to enable remote data access both to experimenters as well subjects, we decided to use distributed cloud infrastructure, as Google Cloud Firestore and Amazon S3. Actually, we are using noSQL databases to store the experiments data, since some kinds of experiments deal with non-structured data.

One of the main features of the proposed architecture regards its extensibility. So far, we have designed the following extension points: i) data storage; ii) collecting data forms (e.g., questionnaires); iii) software metrics collecting systems and; iv)statistical tests.

Concerning metrics collecting systems, according to Bykov et al. [5], for now, PRO Metrics (PROM) [23], and Hackystat [13] are the most widely known metric collection systems, developed initially to project monitoring rather than to run experiments. The former comprises a distributed architecture that collects various types of software data: software metrics and personal software process (PSP), an invasive method since PSP requires the participant's involvement. The latter enables automatic collecting software metrics from what authors called "sensors" attached to development tools via SOA. This way, data are sent to the servers to be analyzed. Some metrics include size and defect data. However, this collecting system is only for Java, and it is no longer under active development.

It is necessary to collect both software metrics and participant's behavior data in a most non-invasive way in an experiment monitoring approach. Moreover, since we are developing the system as a web application, it is important not to depend on installing a third-party application on the participant/experiment's computer to collect such metrics. This feature should integrate in a transparent way to the users. Currently, we are investigating how to use the approach proposed by Bykov et al. [5] to attach software sensors in our approach (both on the client and server-side) as observers to the experiment data uploaded to the storage solution plugged into our platform.

Regarding statistical tests extension, we are using an virtual laboratory called *Esfinge Virtual Lab*[1] (EVL). EVL allows users to upload java components to

---

[1] http://ssrn.inf.unibz.it/virtuallab/.

execute analysis on its plataform, accessing several datasets. This way, statistical tests are implement in java and deployed to the EVL, making them available as web services.

4   *K-Alpha*: A Tool for Managing SE Experiments

In order to provide a proof of concept for the *SCCOPLA*, we developed a tool called *K-Alpha*. This tool consists of a back-end Python Flask-based RESTful web services and a front-end React single-page web application. Figure 6 depicts the deployment diagram for the proposed system.

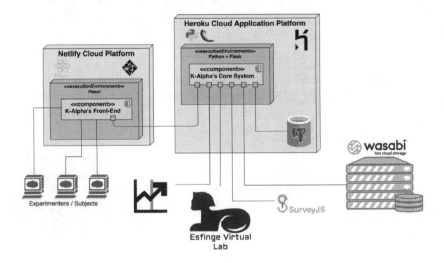

Fig. 6. Deployment diagram for the proposed system.

4.1   The Front-End Application

Among the myriad of possibilities, a single-page web application was chosen to consume the data provided by the endpoints. First of all, the front-end's application has been developed based on three main processes and using the tools provided by the API to do that: the edition of experiments, the application of experiments, and the experiments management. Noteworthy, these three main processes were identified from interviews with SE researchers during a User Research stage.

The edition of experiments includes the creation and edition of experiments to be applied to participants. The experimenter can control issues such as a number of hypotheses, analysis tools used, generation of questionnaires, and adding additional files to guide participants in its executions. Those stages help to create a complete experiment and describe the subject of it to clarify the participants.

The second process is the application experiments, where a set of participants is selected to become the experiment's target. Those participants can access through the web application custom areas to answer questionnaires, count the spent time reading, writing, or whatever the experiment requires, upload and download files needed to perform tasks.

Last but not least, we implemented a dashboard, accessible only to experimenters, where all pieces of information from experiments are compiled to become a valuable tool in managing experiment information. For example, how many and which participants are participating in the experiment, in which state is each of them. The views of the experiment's creation, participant area, and dashboard are shown in Fig. 7.

Fig. 7. Creation of a new experiment, addition of hypothesis in the experiment, *K-Alpha* participant's view of the experiment, and *K-Alpha*'s dashboard.

In order to reach the requirements described in Sect. 3, was decided to divide the *K-Alpha* into six components: Rest client: responsible for sending and receiving the messages to the back-end using RESTful services; Authentication: an orthogonal service that intercepts controllers' requests to guarantee the access rules for each profile; Controllers: they hold the business rules of each application screen and control the flow among them; Views: responsible for data presentation and interaction with users (experimenters and participants); Services: work as middlewares between controllers and rest clients. They are responsible for processing the data before sending it to the back-end or views, and; Entities: data models used by the application. Figure 8 shows the diagram with all components mentioned above that compose the front-end application architecture.

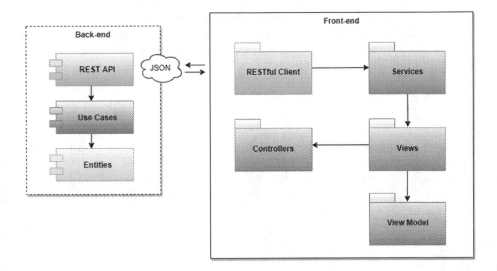

Fig. 8. *K-Alpha* front-end architecture.

4.2   Present Status and Next Steps

As part of the assessment of the approach, we have started reproducing previous experimental studies conducted by our research group [15–17] to observe whether reproductions of experiments are feasible through the proposed computational infrastructure. Preliminary results show that the tool helps guide both the experimenter and the participant to apply the experiment.

Regarding the experimenter, it was much easier to fill the experiment planning, filling out the context, hypotheses, variables, metrics, and experimental design (for now, only cross-over and control group experimental design (or prepost test) algorithm is implemented. Such facilities are especially significant for those who are learning to use or apply empirical studies.

As our previous experiments are related to software testing, we have implemented an adapter to plug in the *JUnit* framework to the *K-Alpha*, acting as the oracle that implements assertions. This way, it was possible to assess (almost in an automatic way) the source code uploaded by participants to the platform storage system in use (Wasabi). This reduced substantially the effort accomplished by the researcher to manually run participant's test cases.

Regarding the analysis phase, to test the integration of our platform with the EVL, we have deployed Java components to the EVL servers to run the same previously statistic tests: Shapiro-Wilk, Wilcoxon/Mann-Whitney, and paired Student t-test. Then, we have loaded the storage system with the same participant's results to verify if the statistic results differ or not from the expected ones described in our previous work.

Concerning participants, preliminary results indicate a good user experience when guiding the subject through the tasks assigned by the experimenter needed to conduct the experiment to extract the relevant data. Some of the most frequent questions made by subjects when applying local experiments in our laboratories, regarding, for example, the order of running activities, have practically disappeared. Besides that, automating the data upload to the central storage repository deals with common questions about submitting their data.

Even though some tests with Hackystat have been made (to Java only), we plan to integrate our architecture with the new non-invasive automatic software collecting metrics platform proposed in [5]. The main idea is to keep as much as possible the process of collecting metrics transparent and without requiring the personal involvement of users.

Currently, our efforts are also concentrated in how to implement the experiment packaging phase. Such phase is responsible for storing material, procedures, and data to allow subsequent replication of studies. We plan to implement a "reuse" experiment feature, setting up a new instance of a previous experiment. This way, it will be possible to compare results across different samples of the same study setup. Moreover, enabling users to choose statistic tests without the need for programming skills is on our radar. Here, the key to achieving this feature relies on introducing User-End Development concepts in our platform.

Finally, we are preparing a pilot study to empirically assessing a recent tool developed by our research group to evaluate API usage in the context of software ecosystems [2]. By conducting this study, we aim to assess the extensibility of the *SCCOPLA* for different SE empirical studies domains since evaluating a tool's usefulness differs from assessing testing techniques. The former, for example, need to have tasks set up to ask questions based on the tool's visualization, while the latter involves activities like test cases generation.

5   Conclusion

Nowadays, the development of computational environments to allow geographically distributed SE experiments has become even more critical. Beyond the fact that these platforms could improve the recruitment and participation of subjects in experiments, allowing large-scale studies [1], the COVID-19 pandemic and their physical barriers have enhanced their needs.

Notwithstanding the increased demand for this type of research, the existing few environments lack critical features such as defining metrics to be collected, automatic organization mechanisms to analyze collected data using a specific statistical analysis method, and remote experiment execution.

In this context, we have proposed an extensible architecture for an empirical software engineering computational platform. The *SCCOPLA* aims to address these missing functionalities by using plugins mechanisms. Among the main advantages of this type of architecture, it is worth highlighting the extensibility via well-defined interfaces. These mechanisms enable users to either extend the environment to adapt it to different software engineering experiment domains or integrate it with existing technology solutions.

Preliminary results on applying the proposed approach revealed benefits both to subjects and experimenters, such as guiding subjects through the tasks assigned by the experimenter and decreasing the effort accomplished by researchers to manually run participants' test cases when reproducing an empirical software testing study.

Future work includes finishing the *K-Alpha* implementation and plugins integration and concludes the replication of our previous experiments using the proposed computational infrastructure. Besides, a new empirical study to assess another recent tool developed by our research group will be conducted using this approach.

Acknowledgment. The authors would like to thank FAPESP (grant 2018/22064-4) for financial support.

References

1. Arisholm, E., Sjøberg, D.I.K., Carelius, G.J., Lindsjørn, Y.: A web-based support environment for software engineering experiments. Nord. J. Comput. **9**(3), 231–247 (2002). http://dl.acm.org/citation.cfm?id=766526.766530
2. Avancini, R., Silveira, F.F., Guerra, E.M., Andrade, P.R.: Software visualization tool for evaluating API usage in the context of software ecosystems: a proof of concept. In: Gervasi, O., et al. (eds.) ICCSA 2020. LNCS, vol. 12254, pp. 335–350. Springer, Cham (2020). https://doi.org/10.1007/978-3-030-58817-5_26
3. Basili, V.R., Selby, R.W., Hutchens, D.H.: Experimentation in software engineering. IEEE Trans. Softw. Eng. **12**(7), 733–743 (1986). http://dl.acm.org/citation.cfm?id=9775.9777
4. Biffl, S., Winkler, D.: Value-based empirical research plan evaluation. In: First International Symposium on Empirical Software Engineering and Measurement (ESEM 2007), pp. 494–494, September 2007. https://doi.org/10.1109/ESEM.2007.50
5. Bykov, A., et al.: Towards non-invasive software measurement system: architecture and implementation. In: Ciancarini, P., Litvinov, S., Messina, A., Sillitti, A., Succi, G. (eds.) SEDA 2016. AISC, vol. 717, pp. 149–165. Springer, Cham (2018). https://doi.org/10.1007/978-3-319-70578-1_15
6. da Costa Araújo, I., da Silva, W.O., de Sousa Nunes, J.B., Neto, F.O.: ARRESTT: a framework to create reproducible experiments to evaluate software testing techniques. In: Proceedings of the 1st Brazilian Symposium on Systematic and Automated Software Testing. SAST, pp. 1:1–1:10. ACM, New York (2016). https://doi.org/10.1145/2993288.2993303
7. Ferreira, W., Baldassarre, M.T., Soares, S., Cartaxo, B., Visaggio, G.: A comparative study of model-driven approaches for scoping and planning experiments. In: Proceedings of the 21st International Conference on Evaluation and Assessment in Software Engineering. EASE 2017, pp. 78–87. ACM, New York (2017). https://doi.org/10.1145/3084226.3084258
8. Freire, M., et al.: A model-driven approach to specifying and monitoring controlled experiments in software engineering. In: Heidrich, J., Oivo, M., Jedlitschka, A., Baldassarre, M.T. (eds.) PROFES 2013. LNCS, vol. 7983, pp. 65–79. Springer, Heidelberg (2013). https://doi.org/10.1007/978-3-642-39259-7_8

9. Garcia, R.E., Höhn, E.N., Barbosa, E.F., Maldonado, J.C.: An ontology for controlled experiments on software engineering. In: Proceedings of the Twentieth International Conference on Software Engineering & Knowledge Engineering (SEKE 2008), San Francisco, CA, USA, 1–3 July 2008, pp. 685–690. Knowledge Systems Institute Graduate School (2008)
10. Häser, F., Felderer, M., Breu, R.: An integrated tool environment for experimentation in domain specific language engineering. In: Proceedings of the 20th International Conference on Evaluation and Assessment in Software Engineering. EASE 2016, pp. 20:1–20:5. ACM, New York (2016). https://doi.org/10.1145/2915970.2916010, http://doi.acm.org/10.1145/2915970.2916010
11. Hochstein, L., Nakamura, T., Shull, F., Zazworka, N., Basili, V.R., Zelkowitz, M.V.: An environment for conducting families of software engineering experiments. In: Software Development, Advances in Computers, vol. 74, pp. 175–200. Elsevier (2008). https://doi.org/10.1016/S0065-2458(08)00605-0
12. Jedlitschka, A., Ciolkowski, M., Pfahl, D.: Reporting experiments in software engineering. In: Shull, F., Singer, J., Sjøberg, D.I.K. (eds.) Guide to Advanced Empirical Software Engineering, pp. 201–228. Springer, London (2008). https://doi.org/10.1007/978-1-84800-044-5_8
13. Johnson, P.M.: Requirement and design trade-offs in Hackystat: an in-process software engineering measurement and analysis system. In: First International Symposium on Empirical Software Engineering and Measurement (ESEM 2007), pp. 81–90 (2007)
14. Karahasanoviæ, A., et al.: Collecting feedback during software engineering experiments. Empir. Softw. Eng. 10(2), 113–147 (2005)
15. Lemos, O.A.L., Ferrari, F.C., Silveira, F.F., Garcia, A.: Development of auxiliary functions: should you be agile? An empirical assessment of pair programming and test-first programming. In: 2012 34th International Conference on Software Engineering (ICSE), pp. 529–539, June 2012. https://doi.org/10.1109/ICSE.2012.6227163
16. Lemos, O.A.L., Ferrari, F.C., Silveira, F.F., Garcia, A.: Experience report: can software testing education lead to more reliable code? In: 2015 IEEE 26th International Symposium on Software Reliability Engineering (ISSRE), pp. 359–369, November 2015. https://doi.org/10.1109/ISSRE.2015.7381829
17. Lemos, O.A.L., Silveira, F.F., Ferrari, F.C., Garcia, A.: The impact of software testing education on code reliability: an empirical assessment. J. Syst. Softw. 137, 497–511 (2017)
18. Martin, R.C.: Clean Architecture: A Craftsman's Guide to Software Structure and Design. Robert C. Martin Series, Prentice Hall, Boston (2017)
19. Mendonça, M.G., et al.: A framework for software engineering experimental replications. In: 13th IEEE International Conference on Engineering of Complex Computer Systems (ICECCS 2008), pp. 203–212, March 2008. https://doi.org/10.1109/ICECCS.2008.38
20. Neto, J.P., Scatalon, L.P.: ExpTool: a tool to conduct, package and replicate controlled experiments in software engineering. In: Proceedings of the International Conference on Software Engineering Research and Practice (SERP), p. 1. The Steering Committee of The World Congress in Computer Science, Computer Engineering and Applied Computing (WorldComp) (2014)

21. de Oliveira Neto, F.G., Torkar, R., Machado, P.D.L.: An initiative to improve reproducibility and empirical evaluation of software testing techniques. In: Proceedings of the 37th International Conference on Software Engineering - Volume 2. ICSE 2015, pp. 575–578. IEEE Press, Piscataway (2015). http://dl.acm.org/citation.cfm?id=2819009.2819106

22. Richards, M.: Software Architecture Patterns. O'Reilly Media Inc., Sebastopol (2015)

23. Scotto, M., Sillitti, A., Succi, G., Vernazza, T.: A non-invasive approach to product metrics collection. J. Syst. Archit. **52**(11), 668–675 (2006). https://doi.org/10.1016/j.sysarc.2006.06.010. Agile Methodologies for Software Production

24. Sjoeberg, D.I.K., et al.: A survey of controlled experiments in software engineering. IEEE Trans. Softw. Eng. **31**(9), 733–753 (2005). https://doi.org/10.1109/TSE.2005.97

25. de Souza, I.E., Oliveira, P.H.L., Bispo Junior, E.L., Inocencio, A.C.G., Parreira, Junior, P.A.: TESE - an information system for management of experimental software engineering projects. In: Proceedings of the Annual Conference on Brazilian Symposium on Information Systems: Information Systems: A Computer Socio-Technical Perspective - Volume 1. SBSI 2015, pp. 75:563–75:570. Brazilian Computer Society, Porto Alegre (2015). http://dl.acm.org/citation.cfm?id=2814058.2814147

26. Stolee, K.T., Elbaum, S.: Exploring the use of crowdsourcing to support empirical studies in software engineering. In: Proceedings of the 2010 ACM-IEEE International Symposium on Empirical Software Engineering and Measurement. ESEM 2010, pp. 35:1–35:4. ACM, New York (2010). https://doi.org/10.1145/1852786.1852832

27. Torii, K., Matsumoto, K., Nakakoji, K., Takada, Y., Takada, S., Shima, K.: Ginger2: an environment for computer-aided empirical software engineering. IEEE Trans. Softw. Eng. **25**(4), 474–492 (1999). https://doi.org/10.1109/32.799942

28. Travassos, G.H., dos Santos, P.S.M., Mian, P.G., Neto, A.C.D., Biolchini, J.: An environment to support large scale experimentation in software engineering. In: 13th IEEE International Conference on Engineering of Complex Computer Systems (ICECCS 2008), pp. 193–202, March 2008. https://doi.org/10.1109/ICECCS.2008.30

29. Wohlin, C., Runeson, P., Höst, M., Ohlsson, M.C., Regnell, B., Wessln, A.: Experimentation in Software Engineering. Springer, Heidelberg (2012). https://doi.org/10.1007/978-3-642-29044-2

30. Yskout, K., Van Landuyt, D., Joosen, W.: Towards a platform for empirical software design studies. In: 2017 IEEE/ACM 1st International Workshop on Establishing the Community-Wide Infrastructure for Architecture-Based Software Engineering (ECASE), pp. 3–7 (2017). https://doi.org/10.1109/ECASE.2017.3

DevOps Job Roles: A Multivocal Literature Review

Muhammad Umar and Ricardo Colomo-Palacios[(✉)] [iD]

Østfold University College, BRA veien. 4, 1757 Halden, Norway
{muhammau,ricardo.colomo-palacios}@hiof.no

Abstract. DevOps bridges the gap between software development and operations to provide rapid deliveries and integrated collaboration. However, DevOps entails lots of factors and challenges involved in its implementation including technical, organizational and personnel aspects. Focusing on the last set of aspects, this paper identifies current DevOps job roles, an aspect that is crucial to implement and to support DevOps practices in organizations. It also highlights collaboration between different actors under different automation levels in DevOps to deliver software at high speed.

Keywords: Multivocal literature review · DevOps · Job roles · Software development

1 Introduction

As the world is moving swiftly towards technological advancements, software development operations are carried out at excessive rates to keep up with the required change [1]. However, these changes do not come easy, software development companies are working hard to keep up with demands of frequent changes, but as the software and applications become extensive, it becomes nearly impossible to deliver rapid updates to end users. Development team can implement these changes relatively quick as compared to the time it takes for actual deployment to end system [2].

Agile development techniques were adopted to speed up the development process as the waterfall model failed to provide frequent updates. Agile development techniques successfully solved problems related to longer development time by splitting requirements in short sprints, however, it raises problems for IT operations responsible for deployment of code [3]. With the code now coming fast from agile methods it becomes hard for IT operations to test and validate these changes and deploy new changes. In other words, in agile settings, the information circulating between development and operations teams was not faster or more frequent [4].

Apart from that it is also a time consuming and labor-intensive work to manually test and move changes to deployment [5]. Frequent changes in development would normally create bottleneck at IT operations function which can lead to longer delay in software releases to customers. So in order to minimize the gap between development and deployment a strong relation between Development and Operations needs to be

© Springer Nature Switzerland AG 2021
O. Gervasi et al. (Eds.): ICCSA 2021, LNCS 12957, pp. 247–256, 2021.
https://doi.org/10.1007/978-3-030-87013-3_19

established which is termed as "DevOps" [3]. DevOps is about end-to-end automation in software development and delivery [6]. Inside DevOps arena, microservices architectures [7] are one of the main enablers in the adoption of DevOps [8], given that DevOps is grounded in the cloud [4].

The origin DevOps can be traced back to 2008 at Agile Conference in which Debois pointed out the need to improve collaboration between development and operations teams in order to deliver rapid response time to customer demands [9].

DevOps follows the **CI/CD** pipeline (Constant Integration/Constant Delivery) towards software automation. After the pioneering adoptions by big companies, many software companies are increasingly switching to DevOps to support short feedback loops and automated processes. In a recent study [10], authors indicate that one of the main reasons behind the adoption of DevOps is the acceleration of time-to-market while delivering high-quality products. While there are many benefits to adopting DevOps, companies and organizations also face many challenges during the transition. A company may have to undergo cultural changes to achieve DevOps [1].

DevOps provides greatest job satisfaction than agile [11]. DevOps follow agile principles for collaborative work and further extend them to broader perimeters. Grouping development and operations team improved team satisfaction. DevOps required strong collaboration between team members of different expertise to reach common ground, many challenges arise during the process so it required both strong hard and soft skills [11]. In a scenario in which technical issues regarding DevOps automation are more studied, however, there is no consensus on how to effectively empower collaboration among departments and persons [12]. Literature reported poor team performance as one of the aspects to improve in DevOps projects [13] being close communication, integration and collaboration measures to tackle this problem. DevOps fosters the formation of cross-functional squads in which there is a need among team members to contemplate and forestall the job to be completed by other members [3].

DevOps capable and experienced team members are hard to find as DevOps is still in emerging phase [14]. Different DevOps job roles require a comprehensive collaboration among team members, and each role is not just limited to a specific task but intertwined with one another. However major responsibility of these roles include planning, building and running within a team [15]. Release Manager, Architect, Product Owner, Department/Project Manager and Production Engineer are key roles to any DevOps environment. Developer is also crucial to DevOps as they share knowledge and collaborate, but we will not discuss them during this study because there is no significant challenges for them moving toward DevOps [3]. There exists several other software engineering job roles such as business specialist, test managers, QA engineer, which are not included in this study as they don't directly influence DevOps environment [1].

The rest of this paper is structured as follows: Sect. 2 describes the study method followed by results presented in Sect. 3. Finally, Sect. 4 presents conclusions and future research directions are depicted in Sect. 5.

2 Research Approach

2.1 Multivocal Literature Review

This study helps to identify and analyze various DevOps job roles that can make a successful and functioning DevOps environment. It also identifies key responsibilities for each role and how these roles contribute to **CI/CD** pipeline. Academic literature on selected topic is quite limited and gray literature must be included to provide further insights. So, in order to achieve goals presented earlier, authors adopted a multivocal literature review (MLR) as the selected method. In MLRs academic literature and gray literature are combined, academic literature represents scientific literature whereas gray literature involves all other sources of information like blog, post, websites, newspaper articles, white papers etc. Research is piloted observing known guidelines for counting grey literature and performing MLRs in software engineering [16] as well as guidelines in paper writing in ICT related disciplines [17].

2.2 Research Questions

The goal of this study to understand different job roles in DevOps and their importance at different stages of development and deployment, so, in order to accomplish the aim of this paper, three research questions (RQs) are formulated. There are two researchers involved in this study, first author is responsible for the selection procedure and provide initial results while second author assessed the process, checked the results and supervised answers to research questions, the research questions are as follows:

- **RQ 1:** What are major DevOps Job Roles?
- **RQ 2:** What are different automation levels in DevOps?
- **RQ 3**: How different job roles collaborate at each automation level

2.3 Selection of Studies

This section illustrates all the phases required for collecting literature for reviews, including the selection of which online databases will be used for searching literature. This section also explains search strategy, inclusive and exclusive criteria to find relevant literature for review.

Databases
The listed databases were recommended by the library of Østfold University College for selecting academic literature on the topic under review in this study.

- ACM
- IEEE
- Springer
- Science Direct
- Google Scholar

Apart from the internal recommendations mentioned earlier, these sources were chosen given that they are among the most relevant sources of information in the broad computing field. Also, in order to find relevant grey literature, the following search engines are used.

- Google Search
- Bing

Search Terms

The first step towards building a search strategy is to identify potential keywords that can pin-point research to literature that is relevant to topic and helps to achieve the goals of this study.

After the initial screening the potential keywords for this study are identified. These keywords include "DevOps" and "Job Roles". These keywords are not case sensitive, so now only thing required is to rearrange keywords in a manner that it brings out relevant literature either gray or academic. After testing following search string is used to conduct this review:

("DevOps") AND ("Job Roles")

Inclusion and Exclusion Criteria

Once search results are obtained by applying the search query mentioned in previous step, a list of inclusive and exclusive criteria needs to be determined to limit content to fewer and relevant literature that aligns well with objective of this study.

Inclusion Criteria

- Papers that precisely deals with DevOps Job Roles.
- Literature that discusses major DevOps Job Roles.
- Literature that discusses advantages/benefits DevOps Job Roles.
- Literature that discusses challenges/limitations DevOps Job Roles.
- Literature only retrieved from the first 15 pages of Google Search & Bing.

Exclusion Criteria

- Papers that are not accessible.
- Studies that contain required keywords but are not relevant to this study.
- Duplicates found in Google Scholar.
- Literature not available in English.

2.4 Literature Retrieval

Literature retrieval involved finding the relevant literature in an efficient and organized way. Four stages were designed to achieve the goal, first stages documents all the papers that are returned by applying initial search string. Second stages filters papers based on the inclusive and exclusive criteria. Third stages involve reading of title, keywords and abstract to identify papers that are relevant to study. Fourth stage is an in-depth study of entire paper by a full text read to see how it can help to achieve the objectives of this study.

2.5 Data Storage

Retrieved literature is stored systematically in a reference manager, namely Zotero, Furthermore, important papers were color coded for references during this study in order to facilitate their classification in this study.

3 Results

In what follows, obtained results previous sections will be discussed to answer formulated RQs.

3.1 Studies Retrieved

In Table 1 authors show the quantity of papers and articles retrieved from different stages of literature retrieval, first stage shows the total number of papers returned after applying search query, second stage shows papers after applying inclusive and exclusive criteria, third stage shows relevance of papers based on title and abstract, and fourth stage shows paper with full depth analysis. Table 2 contains the final set of 11 papers selected indicating the reference and the title of each of these papers.

Table 1. Number of papers analyzed per stage

Source	1	2	3	4
ACM	7	2	1	1
IEEE	10	6	3	1
Springer	18	8	6	1
Science Direct	2	0	0	0
Google Scholar	149	45	24	3
Google	463,000	150	12	5
Bing	65,600	150	5	0
Total	**528,786**	**361**	**51**	**11**

Table 2. List of primary studies

#	Title	Reference
1	*A Large Agile Organization on Its Journey Towards DevOps*	[1]
2	*The Impacts of Digital Transformation, Agile, and DevOps on Future IT curricula*	[2]
3	*From Agile to DevOps: Smart Skills and Collaborations*	[3]
4	*DevOps for Developers*	[5]
5	*Orchestrating automation and sharing in DevOps teams: a revelatory case of job satisfaction factors, risk and work conditions*	[11]
6	*A Survey of DevOps in the South African Software Context*	[14]
7	*Are you ready for DevOps? Required skill set for DevOps teams*	[15]
8	*DevOps and the Product Owner - what changes?*	[18]
9	*DevOps Release Manager - Roles, responsibilities, and salary insights,*	[19]
10	*Cloud and DevOps: CI/CD and Market Analysis*	[20]
11	*DevOps Career Path: 6 Demanding & Diverse Roles*	[21]

3.2 RQ1: What are Major DevOps Job Roles?

Although everyone involved in Software Development and IT Operations is part of the DevOps functional chain, few roles play a crucial role in determining success and failure of DevOps. These roles are as follows:

- Product Owner
- Architect
- Production Engineer
- Department/Project Manager
- Release Manager

Developer is not part of major DevOps job roles because developer does not have any significant challenge in moving towards DevOps. These roles are identified as important by performing a 2 stage experiment process in a large European IT services firm [3]. However, other research articles discuss DevOps job roles and responsibilities but does not assign importance to any job role. The description of the roles in DevOps are as follows:

Product Owner
A product owner is responsible for representing client during the entire lifecycle from development to deployment. It is real operation role that links business to project management. And product owner is responsible for managing the product backlog. Product

owners understand the vision of project and responsible for deliveries, with fewer deliveries before DevOps, but now with DevOps they must move faster to keep up with instant updates. Product owners also needs to think in terms of system [18].

Architect
A crucial member of the team as they are responsible for setting up system and functional architecture. They must strongly communicate with project manager to exchange information. Architect is responsible for setting up smooth transition between development and operation functions [3]. Architect focus is towards setting up smooth CI part in the DevOps pipeline.

Production Engineers
Production Engineers are production integrators, they are also tester and responsible for productions. operations, incident monitoring, user support.

Department/Project Manager
Project managers are responsible for collaborating between all other actor, to debate budget, tracking and prioritization of items. Sometimes also work with functional architecture.

Release Manager
Release manager is a crucial member towards safeguarding success of project. They are responsible for handling Constant Delivery (CD) part of a DevOps pipeline [19].

3.3   RQ2: What are Different Automation Levels in DevOps?

There are three major automation levels in DevOps [3], they are listed as follows.

Automation Level 1 (Agile)
Automation level 1 represents traditional agile development life cycle in which development and operations are working in silos without any proper sharing, no automation in release so it's fine to say the DevOps is not realized during automation level 1.

Automation Level 2 Continuous Integration
The operation requests to be in line with development, during this automation process more focus is provided toward the integration part between development and operation, the reason behind is company policy toward rapid movement of code form development to production, performs unit testing, study shows that 53% of companies using DevOps prefer continuous integration [20].

Automation Level 3 Continuous Deployment
Fully automated DevOps pipeline performs integration testing, user testing, performance testing. Here the development needs to be aligned with operations. Greater the level of automation requires more sharing and mutual discussion.

3.4   RQ3: How Different Job Roles Collaborate at Each Automation Level?

In order to solve this RQ, we focus on a paper presenting a study conducted in a large European IT Services company with over 15000 employees. 12 teams were selected from the company which were following agile and DevOps techniques [3]. The study showed the collaboration between operation and development can be divided in three different automation levels.

Collaboration During Automation Level 1
During automation level 1 the development and operations has little collaboration between each other compared to communication within Development and also within Operations teams.

Collaboration During Automation Level 2
At this level, development and operations have almost equal communication with one another and among themselves, however internal communications can be a bit higher.

Collaboration During Automation Level 2
At this level, development and operations present a perfect balance in the communication both internally and externally.

4   Conclusion

In this paper, authors present a MLR devoted to analyze DevOps Job Roles. With the goal of identifying major DevOps job roles, how DevOps affects each role, different automation level in DevOps process and how different automation level increase or decrease collaboration between different job roles. Different literature databases and search engines were used for gathering literature used in this study.

DevOps is rapidly increasing field of software development [21], it's less about code and more about collaboration between individual to improve integration and delivery pipeline. DevOps expert requires diversity in skills as it requires knowledge of development and operations functions. It also addresses barriers in DevOps, various factors that impose problems for a new company to adopt DevOps [1].

5   Future Work

The research in this study is limited to few DevOps job roles and automation levels associated with them. However, DevOps is still evolving rapidly, so it is important that each software engineering role and process needs to be redefined to align with DevOps concepts. Also, there are several challenges involved for an organization to move towards DevOps from traditional development techniques because of insufficient technical skills existing within an organization. Research can be done towards mitigating these aspects. In order to help organizations in the adoption and implementation of DevOps, a recent paper provides guidance to adopt DevOps, including a generic process and a mapping of roles [22].Following this path, authors would like to map this approach with more stablished approaches. Finally, given the increasing importance of DevSecOps or SecDevOps [23], authors would like to perform research on job roles in this evolution of DevOps to check for specific job roles in the approach. Also, specific studies in line with [24] are planned to study competences and skills beyond roles.

References

1. Kuusinen, K., et al.: A large agile organization on its journey towards DevOps. In: 2018 44th Euromicro Conference on Software Engineering and Advanced Applications (SEAA), pp. 60–63 (2018). https://doi.org/10.1109/SEAA.2018.00019
2. Betz, C., Olagunju, A.O., Paulson, P.: The impacts of digital transformation, agile, and DevOps on future IT curricula. In: Proceedings of the 17th Annual Conference on Information Technology Education, p. 106. Association for Computing Machinery, New York (2016). https://doi.org/10.1145/2978192.2978205
3. Hemon, A., Lyonnet, B., Rowe, F., Fitzgerald, B.: From agile to DevOps: smart skills and collaborations. Inf. Syst. Front. 22(4), 927–945 (2019). https://doi.org/10.1007/s10796-019-09905-1
4. Gokarna, M., Singh, R.: DevOps: a historical review and future works. In: 2021 International Conference on Computing, Communication, and Intelligent Systems (ICCCIS), pp. 366–371 (2021). https://doi.org/10.1109/ICCCIS51004.2021.9397235
5. Hüttermann, M.: DevOps for Developers. Apress, New York (2012)
6. Ebert, C., Gallardo, G., Hernantes, J., Serrano, N.: DevOps. IEEE Softw. 33, 94–100 (2016). https://doi.org/10.1109/MS.2016.68
7. Larrucea, X., Santamaria, I., Colomo-Palacios, R., Ebert, C.: Microservices. IEEE Softw. 35, 96–100 (2018). https://doi.org/10.1109/MS.2018.2141030
8. Waseem, M., Liang, P., Shahin, M.: A systematic mapping study on microservices architecture in DevOps. J. Syst. Softw. 170, 110798 (2020). https://doi.org/10.1016/j.jss.2020.110798
9. Debois, P.: Agile infrastructure and operations: how infra-gile are you? In: Agile 2008 Conference, pp. 202–207 (2008). https://doi.org/10.1109/Agile.2008.42
10. Díaz, J., López-Fernández, D., Pérez, J., González-Prieto, Á.: Why are many businesses instilling a DevOps culture into their organization? Empir. Softw. Eng. 26(2), 1–50 (2021). https://doi.org/10.1007/s10664-020-09919-3
11. Hemon-Hildgen, A., Rowe, F., Monnier-Senicourt, L.: Orchestrating automation and sharing in DevOps teams: a revelatory case of job satisfaction factors, risk and work conditions. Eur. J. Inf. Syst. 29, 474–499 (2020). https://doi.org/10.1080/0960085X.2020.1782276
12. Leite, L., Rocha, C., Kon, F., Milojicic, D., Meirelles, P.: A survey of DevOps concepts and challenges. ACM Comput. Surv. 52, 127:1–127:35 (2019). https://doi.org/10.1145/3359981
13. Khan, A.A., Shameem, M.: Multicriteria decision-making taxonomy for DevOps challenging factors using analytical hierarchy process. J. Softw. Evol. Process. 32, e2263 (2020). https://doi.org/10.1002/smr.2263
14. Rowse, M., Cohen, J.: A survey of DevOps in the South African software context (2021). https://doi.org/10.24251/HICSS.2021.814
15. Wiedemann, A., Wiesche, M.: Are you ready for DevOps? Required skill set for DevOps teams. Inb: Research Papers (2018)
16. Garousi, V., Felderer, M., Mäntylä, M.V.: Guidelines for including grey literature and conducting multivocal literature reviews in software engineering. Inf. Softw. Technol. 106, 101–121 (2019). https://doi.org/10.1016/j.infsof.2018.09.006
17. Misra, S.: A Step by Step Guide for Choosing Project Topics and Writing Research Papers in ICT Related Disciplines. In: Misra, S., Muhammad-Bello, B. (eds.) ICTA 2020. CCIS, vol. 1350, pp. 727–744. Springer, Cham (2021). https://doi.org/10.1007/978-3-030-69143-1_55

18. DevOps and the Product Owner - What Changes?. https://amazicworld.com/devops-and-the-product-owner-what-changes/. Accessed 21 Apr 2021
19. Miller, E.: DevOps release manager - roles, responsibilities, and salary insights. https://www.invensislearning.com/blog/devops-release-manager-responsibilities-salary-insights/. Accessed 21 Apr 2021
20. Cloud and DevOps: CI/CD and Market Analysis. https://devops.com/cloud-and-devops-ci-cd-and-market-analysis/. Accessed 21 Apr 2021
21. DevOps Career Path: 6 Demanding & Diverse Roles. https://www.upgrad.com/blog/devops-career-path-job-roles/. Accessed 21 Apr 2021
22. Muñoz, M., Rodríguez, M.N.: A guidance to implement or reinforce a DevOps approach in organizations: a case study. J. Softw. Evol. Process. n/a, e2342. https://doi.org/10.1002/smr.2342
23. Sánchez-Gordón, M., Colomo-Palacios, R.: Security as culture: a systematic literature review of DevSecOps. In: Proceedings of the IEEE/ACM 42nd International Conference on Software Engineering Workshops, pp. 266–269. Association for Computing Machinery, New York (2020). https://doi.org/10.1145/3387940.3392233
24. Cano, C., Fernández-Sanz, L., Misra, S.: Featuring CIO: Roles Skills and Soft Skills. IJHCITP 4, 22–33 (2013). https://doi.org/10.4018/jhcitp.2013010103

Machine Learning Model for Recommending Suitable Courses of Study to Candidates in Nigerian Universities

Garba Aliyu[1], Usman Haruna[2], Idris Abdulmumin[1(✉)] [ID], Murtala Isma'il[2], Ibrahim Enesi Umar[1], and Shehu Adamu[3]

[1] Department of Computer Science, Ahmadu Bello University, Zaria, Nigeria
{algarba,iabdulmumin,ieumar}@abu.edu.ng
[2] Department of Computer Science, Yusuf Maitama Sule University, Kano, Nigeria
uharuna@yumsuk.edu.ng
[3] School of Information Technology & Computing, American University of Nigeria, Yola, Nigeria
shehu.adamu@aun.edu.ng

Abstract. The diversity of courses and complications of admission requirements are complex tasks particularly in Nigerian Universities where a number of parameters are used during the admission process. These courses may be wrongly assigned to applicants who have not met the minimum requirements. In a previous related work, a model was developed to address this issue. However, the model considered only seven subjects out of the mandatory nine subjects required of every senior secondary school student to register (O'Level). Such a decision may be to the detriment to the candidates because credits may be required from those subjects that were not considered. This paper tends to enhance the existing model to address all these issues. Grade of nine Secondary school subjects, the aggregate score of Unified Tertiary Matriculation Examination (UTME) and post-UTME, and catchment area are used as parameters in this study. The results were obtained when various reference classifiers were trained and tested using the processed dataset of the O'Level and JAMB results of candidates seeking admission into the university. Individual classifiers namely, Logistic Regression, Naive Bayes, Decision Tree, K-Nearest Neighbor, and Random Forest were trained and evaluated using reference performance metrics namely precision, recall, and f1-score. The resulting best classifier, the Random Forest, has shown to be correct 94.94% of the time and is capable of detecting correctly 94.17% of the classes. Since the precision and recall are similar in value, the f1-score tends to favor this classifier also with a value of 93.19%.

Keywords: Admission · Recommender system · Prediction · Classifiers · Machine learning

© Springer Nature Switzerland AG 2021
O. Gervasi et al. (Eds.): ICCSA 2021, LNCS 12957, pp. 257–271, 2021.
https://doi.org/10.1007/978-3-030-87013-3_20

1   Introduction

The rapid evolution of information technology has resulted in prompt developments across innumerable disciplines – education, healthcare, transportation, etc. The tools and resources that are used in this era are substituted nearly daily. Analogous to these changes, various ICT applications are substituting the traditional processes that aid teaching and learning activities [11]. Education has been acknowledged in Nigeria as the most dominant instrument of positive change and for national development [6]. For education to execute its part, recommending an alternative – or perhaps a more suitable – course of study to students is supreme [1]. Many students apply to different courses of their choice in different universities for their undergraduate study with their secondary school results as well as consistent test scores such as Unified Tertiary Matriculation Examination (UTME) and Post-UTME that helps determine their suitability or not for studying such choices. Institutions are expected to offer admission to suitable candidates based on their Senior Secondary Certificate Examination (SSCE or O'Level) results and other relevant test scores. However, in this whole route, while the course selection is the most critical phase for applying to undergraduate admission, it is difficult, time wasting and, in many instances, where students are not qualified for admission in their selected choice of courses, allocating alternatives to such students can be better improved.

Recommender systems are artificial intelligence-based systems that intelligently offer to users appropriate recommendations of items based on the previous interests of other people. They have been shown as very capable of serving users appropriately in online services, for marketing by eBay, Amazon, etc. [14], recommendation of words or phrases on platforms such as Google search, social media, and emailing service, in education, health, among other things. Most of the manufacturing industries have been advancing in many fields of data science by employing a recommender engine as a leading preference in their daily business. Academics have become aware of the tremendous potentialities offered by recommender systems and have adapt these systems to suggest courses especially by online classes administrators, e.g. Coursera, Lynda, etc. It is, consequently, critical that these systems are employed to traditional universities during the processes of admissions to help the students to study courses based on their capabilities. A knowledgeable analysis of the present-day system is need to be conducted to each theoretical study and practical tendencies of the recommendation systems [9]. Data mining techniques are very much useful to determine such kind of hidden knowledge from the important as well as composite data types [4].

In every new academic session, each university formulates diverse rules for admitting students who apply for admission. The challenge to that is determining which of the courses can be given to a particular student based on the admission requirements fulfilled. The recommended program may be the same as what the candidate applied for or contrary. The complexity of this is subject to many admission requirements criteria in SSCE, UTME score, Post-UTME, among other things. According to [6], beside each candidate's results, other requirements such as 45% strictly admitted based on merit, 20% from less

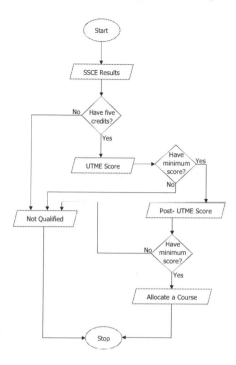

Fig. 1. Existing admission process.

educationally developed states (LEDs) to ensure equity, 20% from catchment areas, etc. further complicates the admission process. According to [13], university admission is a difficult decision process that goes beyond matching test scores and validation necessities. Most of the investigations carried out for university admission are based totally on the point of view of the universities who decide the most appropriate course to give to the candidate, and no longer at the interest of applicants who are either capable or not to study the program to administered and, therefore, making the choice of the course study to administer to the prospective students by the university a trivial problem every year [2].

The present way of assigning course of study to applicants in Nigerian universities – see illustration in Fig. 1 – needs reconsideration as allocating a suitable course is very sensitive to the candidates' performances in the higher institution of learning. In the start, the candidates are required to write for UTME. During the registration, each candidate indicates three subjects combination that are requisite for the course of study of their choice, with English being the fourth and compulsory. After obtaining the score in the UTME, the candidates are then requested to provide the grades, in each subject, they obtain in their SSCE. These subjects must include that which were registered in the UTME and, also, compulsorily passing Mathematics and English language. Most students sit for, and provide the grades of, nine subjects in their SSCE. As at the time of this study, the minimum UTME score to qualify for securing admission into any

Nigerian university is 160, based on the guidelines set by the Joint Admission and Matriculation Board (JAMB). However, most universities increase the score depending on the program the candidate applied and the availability of vacancies of each course [7]. Furthermore, some universities require a candidate to write a post-UTME examination, an examination that is conducted to further screen the candidates, provisional to the standards required by the administration of the university. After the scores of the UTME and post-UTME are aggregated and the SSCE is considered, the universities then assign courses to candidates first according to their choices and then according to the availability of slots in other courses, and this usually results in various problems.

The aim of this study is, therefore, to develop a model for recommending suitable and appropriate courses of study for prospective undergraduate students in Nigerian universities. This is despite the fact that some of these candidates may be recommended with a course different from what the they applied and may fail to accept the offer. This may then result in wasted slots. To reduce this, the model, therefore, takes into consideration and gives priority to the intended programs the candidates wished to study as long as they have met the minimum requirements and provides, alongside, a list of recommendations for other suitable programs. We explored the use of various classifiers such as Logistic Regression, Decision Trees (DT), K^{th} Nearest Neighbor (KNN), Naive Bayes (NB) and Random Forest (RF). Although previous work [6] have presented a tremendous contribution towards developing the course recommender system, the work focused only on the use of a relatively small number of dataset and few number of features (parameters) to automatically predict a suitable course to the student despite the fact that researches have shown that the more the number of data the better the accuracy [15,18]. Therefore, we extended the work in Isma'il et al. [6] by providing more datasets and using more features to automatically recommend a more appropriate course of study for the candidate. Nine subjects were considered in this work as opposed to seven subjects used in Isma'il et al. and, also, priority is given to the candidates' choice aside from other recommended courses that the candidate has met the requirements.

Thus, this work aims to address the following problems that are associated with admissions recommendation in Nigerian universities:

- courses given to candidates who may not best be suited for such courses or may even have some deficiencies in their SSCE,
- wrong assignment of candidates across disciplines, for example, candidates who applied for a particular discipline say in Science may be allocated courses in Engineering due to the similarity of requirements, Social Sciences to Art, etc.
- wastage of vacancy as students refuse to register into some courses allocated to them while others are looking for same.
- priority usually not given to the applicants' choice of courses which they have met the minimum requirements before exploring to recommend other relevant programs.

The rest of the paper is organized into the following sections. Section 2 reports the relevant related literatures. Section 3 describes, in detail, the proposed method for realizing the solutions to the identified problem. In Sect. 4, we discussed the results obtained after evaluating the recommendation systems. Finally, Sect. 5 presents the conclusion of the work and suggests future work.

2   Review of Related Literature

Many kinds of research exist on the recommendation systems in diverse fields such as hospitals, e-commerce, education, government among others. In several countries such as Nigeria, Saudi Arabia, India, China, among others, researches on admission recommender system have been carried out. This section discusses some of the related works in relation to building a recommender system for the university system of education.

In Swaminathan et al. [16], a recommender system was built using K^{th} Nearest Neighbors (KNN), Random Forest (RF), and Support Vector Machines (SVMs) to recommend Graduate Studies of a university to candidates. They used the candidates' profile and the university's perspective to decide if it is relevant and sufficient to secure admission. This helps the candidate to choose and secure admission from the most appropriate university upon the recommendation made by the model. However, the model was not built to recommend a course to prospective candidates who are seeking admission.

Similarly, Hassan et al. [4] built a recommender engine that lists N universities that matched the candidates' educational profile who are seeking a postgraduate admission. This uses the data of those candidates that have been given a chance to study abroad from different countries in the world to recommend to prospective candidates. Enough data is required to be generated, which has to emanate from students who have previously secured admission, for these models to make an excellent recommendation.

In Ragab et al. [13], a recommender system was built using a combination of knowledge discovery rules and data mining called a hybrid recommender engine to recommend college admission. The model was designed as a prototype, which was implemented and evaluated using active data accessible on the On-Demand University Services (ODUS-Plus) database sources, at King Abdulaziz University.

A similar study to Ragab et al. was conducted by Wakil et al. [17] which used the University of Human Development as the field of study for universities in Iraq. Decision Tree (**DT**) was used to classify the candidates into 10 groups with each group having a unique property, **NN** employed to fit the candidate to the available courses, and to find the most appropriate course. Furthermore, the work regarded grade point average (GPA), test score, candidates' interest, and desire jobs as decision parameters. A hybrid system approach using **NN**, **DT**, and Our Proposed Algorithm (**OPA**) were used.

A recommender system was trained in the study conducted by Ismail et al. The system takes a combination of the grades of seven subjects in their SSCE to recommend a suitable course of study for each candidate. The study, though, did not take into consideration and give priority to the actual choice of each candidate. It does not consider the whole of the nine subjects provided in the

SSCE results. It was also trained on less data with a small number of courses that can be allocated.

This work presents an extension to the work originally presented in International Conference in Mathematics, Computer Engineering and Computer Science by [6]. In this paper, we consider more subjects in the SSCE result of candidates (9 subjects vs the 7 subjects in [6]), more courses from additional faculties, catchment areas, and we give priority to the choice of applicants and then followed it by a list of other recommended courses if minimum requirements have been made. It is observed that some of the subjects that are required for Computer Science are not required for Accounting and vice versa. Furthermore, two or more courses may have the same requirement, for example, Computer Science and Physics, Accounting and Economics, etc. Nevertheless, our recommender engine is capable of recommending those possible courses but giving priority to the course applied if a candidate has met all the requirements. Different classification algorithms are used to build models and we choose the best that outperformed others in terms of standard performance metrics.

3   The Methodology

This section presents the step by step description of the proposed approach, including the admission recommendation process, the conceptual model for building the recommendation systems, data collection and algorithm selection.

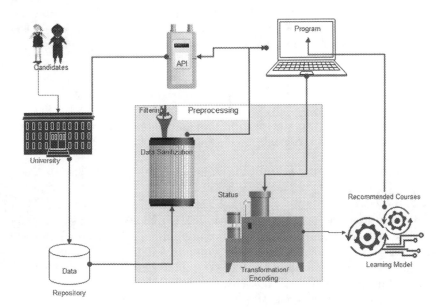

Fig. 2. Enhanced System Model

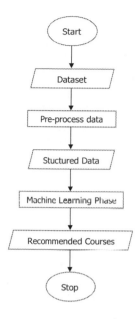

Fig. 3. Proposed admission process.

3.1 The Proposed Approach

The enhanced conceptual model adopted from [6] is shown in Fig. 2. The proposed approach, in contrast to the existing system (Fig. 1), is illustrated in Fig. 3. The first phase of data generation comes to the universities through the JAMB headquarters. The second phase of the data is generated by giving candidates access to the university portal to upload (SSCE results and other details). However, the subjects that every candidate is expected to write as Post-UTME (exam conducted by the university as entrance exam) is automatically added based on the course applied. All the relevant information necessary for the model is fetched as input to the model through an Application Programming Interface (API).

As an extension of the work of [6], this work takes into account the course applied by the candidates, asides from other possible courses that can be assigned. The data obtained is cleaned to eliminate all irregularities before transforming them into the categorical form that it can be fitted and processed by the classification models. The sanitized data then fed into the model for training, testing, and cross-validation to predict the likely courses from unforeseen data that can be given to a prospective candidate. It is worth mentioning that this recommender system make recommendations to the university. It is expected that instead of the existing process of randomly assigning available courses to prospective students, the proposed system make intelligent recommendations based on the candidates' abilities as presented in their academic records. The final decision to either accept the recommended course and assign to the students lies solely on the prerogative of the university based on the availability of admission vacancies, which varies every year.

This study is implemented in three phases in a pipeline fashion. This implies that the output of one phase serves as the input of the next phase. The first phase involves data collection and pre-processing. This is the most important phase because the outcome of this phase will determine the effectiveness of the subsequent phases. In the second phase, selected classifiers are trained, tested, and evaluated. Evaluation metrics used are precision, recall, accuracy, and F1-score. In the final phase, we compare these metrics. The following subsections describe each phase.

3.2   Data Collection

Generalization is a crucial feature required of a machine-learning model. Therefore, the resulting model must generalize well. To achieve that, sufficient data needs to be collected. More so, the data collected need to be representative of the cases we want to generalize. We identified various sources of data but settled on two prominent universities: Ahmadu Bello University (ABU) Zaria, Kaduna State and Bayero University Kano (BUK), Kano State both in Nigeria. Both universities are among the largest and most popular universities in Nigeria and West Africa. They both offer a wide variety of courses and have been doing a good job of managing their collection of data. The demography of students is highly diverse ranging from students from all parts of Nigeria to international students from all over the world. In ABU, we collected a dataset of three (3) sessions; 2015/2016, 2016/2017, and 2017/2018 while in BUK we were able to collect a dataset of 2 sessions; 2016/2017 and 2017/2018. This amounts to a total of 8,700 data instances. The dataset collected comprises 4 variables forming the information about the students. These are the UTME number and score, post-UTME score, and SSCE results.

Real-world datasets are highly affected by the presence of noise, missing values, inconsistent data, and duplicate records, and redundant features. We employed several data pre-processing techniques to eliminate these negative factors. Some of the pre-processing were done using spreadsheet application and python. We also prepared the data so that it is suitable for each of the selected classification algorithms. We then obtain a reduced representation of the data where necessary. Since we gathered our data from different sources, there is the need to merge the data into a single dataset. Fortunately, the dataset used for this research came in the same format (CSV). During data integration and exploration, redundant attributes were detected and eliminated from the resulting dataset. We achieved this by using the well-known Pearson's product-moment coefficient for numeric attributes and correlation test for nominal attributes. We then move forward to cleaning the dataset. During the early stage of pre-processing, the data was split into training and testing. 20% of the data was reserved for evaluation purposes.

The most challenging was encoding the SSCE results, where the transformation is done in a way that, for example, if a candidate is having a minimum of credit (C4, C5, C6, B2, B3, and A1) in say English Language, then a unique code is given to the grade and the subject as 21. The first digit refers to the subject code while the second (or last digit) corresponds to the grade code. This process continues in the same manner for all the nine-subjects considered in this work. Courses that candidates applied with other possible courses that can be given based on the course's requirements are coded in the same fashion as SSCE results.

3.3   Algorithm Selection

Machine learning algorithms are used in recommender systems to deliver reliable recommendations. There are numerous machine learning algorithms to choose from when building a recommender system. According to [12], the types of machine learning algorithms used in building recommender systems were listed in order of most commonly used to the least commonly used. It was observed that the majority of studies reviewed were based on the first seven machine learning algorithms. We then based our choice of algorithm on these sets. Specifically, in this study, we developed models for our recommender system using five algorithms - Naive Bayes, Linear regression, Decision tree, Random Forest, and K-Nearest Neighbour. We then compared their performance using various performance metrics.

Every algorithm has some unique capabilities and drawbacks thus, the need to explore and choose the best algorithm that suits the model [8,16]. According to Isinkaye et al. [5], DT fits regression and classification while selecting a tree structure. A decision tree is formed from a given dataset that is split into a smaller subset, which makes it eminent in decision-making problem. Naive Bayes is a machine learning algorithm that uses in a diversity of probabilistic nature of knowledge. Varying the value of one feature, which seems not undeviatingly alter or change the value of any of the rest of the features used in the algorithm, it is a powerful algorithm [10]. The classification applied in developing a recommendation system is critical that the system will not give very good recommendations if the model is not thoroughly built. The more the availability of data, the best for the model to learn and gather more experience to provide better, meaningful and more accurate information right from the onset [5].

It is important that these algorithms are trained with a sufficient amount of data that are representative of the problem domain. Luckily the data obtained were provided by Universities where such a solution will be of most importance. Even though the amount of data obtained from these universities is fairly large enough to get meaningful outcome from training with the selected algorithms, better result could be obtained if more data were available.

3.4   Model Training and Evaluation

In the previous subsections, we presented the process of dataset processing, feature selection, and the process of splitting the dataset for training and testing. In this subsection, we address the problem of selecting the best model for use in

Table 1. Comparison of model performances with respect to accuracy, precision, recall and F1 scores for various values for K-Fold. Values indicated in percentages (%). KEY: CV – *Cross Validation*, LR – *Logistic Regression*, NB – *Naive Bayes*, DT – *Decision Tree*, KNN – K^{th} *Nearest Neighbor*, RF – *Random Forest*.

Score	CV	LR	NB	DT	KNN	RF	Score	CV	LR	NB	DT	KNN	RF
Accuracy	5	89.11	83.46	90.42	93.11	94.12	*Recall*	5	89.11	83.05	90.42	93.10	94.15
	10	89.25	83.46	90.28	93.23	94.12		10	89.25	83.45	90.30	93.22	94.17
	20	89.21	83.46	90.23	93.11	94.22		20	89.20	83.45	90.20	93.34	94.17
	avg	89.19	83.46	90.31	93.15	94.15		avg	89.19	83.32	90.31	93.22	94.16
	s.d	7.21	0.00	9.85	6.93	5.77		s.d	7.09	23.09	11.01	12.00	1.15
Precision	5	87.40	88.85	90.56	92.75	94.91	*F1*	5	87.49	84.06	89.45	92.61	93.16
	10	87.23	88.85	90.46	92.80	94.93		10	87.62	84.06	89.45	92.72	93.10
	20	87.42	88.85	90.37	92.94	94.94		20	87.61	84.06	89.22	92.84	93.19
	avg	87.35	88.85	90.46	92.83	94.93		avg	87.57	84.06	89.34	92.72	93.15
	s.d.	10.44	0.00	9.50	9.85	1.53		s.d.	7.23	0.00	11.50	11.50	4.58

the recommender system. The main objective of this section is to train and test the individual reference classifiers mentioned in the research framework section with the same dataset. The implementation of this process was performed using Jupiter Notebook. Model evaluation was performed on the test data set aside earlier on. Each of the models is tested with the test set using cross-validation. GridSearch was also employed to determine the best hyper-parameters for each model. The performance was measured base on precision, recall, accuracy, and f1-score.

4   Results and Discussion

In this section, we compared the model performances using various metrics. In [6] – the conference paper submitted regarding this study – accuracy was used as the performance measure. However, it has been demonstrated in [3] that accuracy is not always the preferred metric for measuring the performance of classifiers. We therefore included other concise metrics such as precision, recall and f1-score.

Table 1 compares the accuracy, precision, recall and f1 scores of all reference classifiers used in this study. Corresponding charts of the results obtained are also shown in Fig. 4, 5, 6 and 7. In the table, the average of the scores and standard deviation were computed. It can be observed, from the table above, that the standard deviation values vary significantly among each classifier. This signifies that the choice of classifier is very crucial. Also, we observed from the scores in the table that among all performance measures, the **Random Forest** classifier produced the highest score. Figure 8 illustrates the standard deviation for accuracy and other evaluation metrics obtained from each reference classifier.

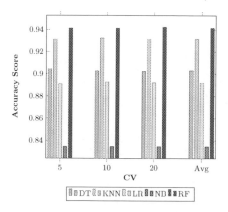

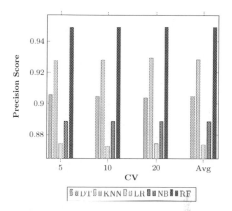

Fig. 4. Accuracy Score. KEY: CV – *Cross Validation*, LR – *Logistic Regression*, NB – *Naive Bayes*, DT – *Decision Tree*, KNN – K^{th} *Nearest Neighbor*, RF – *Random Forest*

Fig. 5. Precision Score. KEY: CV – *Cross Validation*, LR – *Logistic Regression*, NB – *Naive Bayes*, DT – *Decision Tree*, KNN – K^{th} *Nearest Neighbor*, RF – *Random Forest*

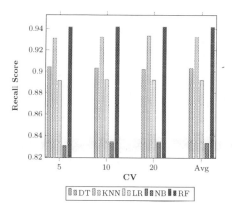

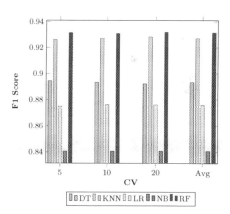

Fig. 6. Recall Score. KEY: CV – *Cross Validation*, LR – *Logistic Regression*, NB – *Naive Bayes*, DT – *Decision Tree*, KNN – K^{th} *Nearest Neighbor*, RF – *Random Forest*

Fig. 7. F1 Score. KEY: CV – *Cross Validation*, LR – *Logistic Regression*, NB – *Naive Bayes*, DT – *Decision Tree*, KNN – K^{th} *Nearest Neighbor*, RF – *Random Forest*

This work increased the number of SSCE results from seven in [6] to nine subjects. Even though universities require candidates to have a minimum of credit in only five relevant subjects, but in exactly which subjects is a major concern, because if, for example, a student registered nine subjects with a university, apart from Mathematics and English, there is maximum of $^{7}C_3 - 35$ – possible combination to choose the remaining three courses out of the seven subjects. Limiting the number of subjects to seven may be a detriment to the candidates. Some candidates do not register more than seven subjects; as such, the model

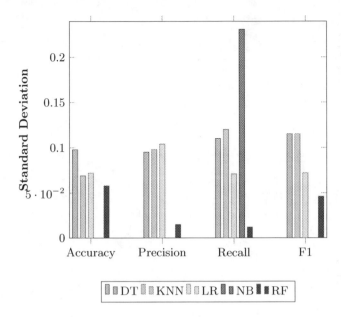

Fig. 8. Standard Deviations for the Accuracy, Precision, Recall and F1 Scores for the various classifiers

Table 2. Best classifier performance

Performance of random forest with CV = 20	
Performance Metric	Score
Precision	94.94%
Recall	94.17%
F1 Score	93.19%

was built with some null values to accommodate nine subjects, but it increases the chances for some candidates.

For each model trained, the performance metrics are presented in terms of precision, recall and F1-score. So we can conclude that random forest performs better than the other reference classifiers considered in this study. More so, the results obtained from the experiments showed that training random forest with a cross validation fold of 20 produces the best f1-score as shown in Fig. 7. We, thereby, extracted and presented the performance of the best classifier in Table 2. Finally, we discussed the result obtained from the comparison. The results obtained for the nine subjects considered in this work, which is 94.15% accuracy even though it is not better than for the seven subjects, which is 99.94% accuracy but because of the null entries for some candidates who do not have up to nine subjects, to some degree, it confuses the model and thus

Table 3. Result comparison between the previous and the current work

Model	Accuracy (%)	
	Previous work [6]	Current work
LR	–	89.25
NB	99.94	83.46
KNN	99.87	93.23
DT	98.01	90.42
RF	–	94.22

wrongly recommended courses to candidates. Consequently, 94.15% of accuracy was achieved as shown in Table 1.

The scores for accuracy obtained when each reference classifier was evaluated with various values for K. Observe that random forest with K=20 produced the highest value for accuracy and the highest average score for accuracy was obtained with random forest classifier. Moreover, the prioritization of candidate's choice reduces the wastage of admissions or blocking some slots that can be given to those who also qualified based on the requirements.

Table 3 shows the performance comparison between the models in [6] and the models trained in our work. It can be observed that the performances in this work under-performed that of the previous work. This is because the data features that were considered in the previous work was fewer than that used in training the models in this work. Despite this, we are confident that our model is able to generate more realistic recommendations based on the additional subjects scores provided – 7 to 9 subjects.

5   Conclusion and Future Work

This study presents a recommender system for helping the university admission process to assign more appropriate courses to prospective students based on prior performances in the O'Level, UTME and post-UTME examinations. Instead of the existing manual system that randomly assign courses based on the subjects combination and the availability of vacancies, it is intended that the proposed system will intelligently assign a more suitable course of study based on the capability of the students. The experimental results in this work were obtained when various reference classifiers were trained and evaluated using the processed dataset of the O'Level and JAMB results of candidates seeking admission into two Nigerian universities. Individual classifiers namely: Logistic Regression, Naive Bayes, Decision Tree, K-Nearest Neighbour, and Random Forest were trained and evaluated with reference performance metrics namely: accuracy, precision, recall, and f1-score. The resulting best classifier (Random Forest) was shown to be correct 94.94% of the time and is capable of detecting correctly 94.17% of the classes. Since the precision and recall are similar in value, the f1-score tends to favour this classifier also with a value of 93.19%.

The nine subjects considered in this study has its limitation because it is possible that an applicant will have five credits but few of which may not be part of those considered and, meanwhile, are part of the requirement for the applied program. Another limitation to this study is the scope of our validation. In future work, we plan to deploy our model in the Nigerian universities whose data was used in this work during the subsequent admission process so as to test and validate the model on new and unseen admission data. This work can be extended by looking at other subjects beyond nine subjects, even though the remaining subjects that are not considered in this study were found to be trivial, as such, they are avoided in order not to confuse the model with null values because few applicants have those subjects. The wastage of slots by candidates who are not usually accepting provisional admission simply because it is not their choice can be further looked into so that this wastage of admissions can further be reduced.

Acknowledgment. This research was carried out under the support of Ahmadu Bello University, Zaria, Yusuf Maitama Sule University, Kano, and Bayero University, Kano who provided us with datasets.

References

1. Bulkachuwa, A.S.: Availability and Utilization of Microteaching Laboratories and their Influence on Students' Teaching Practice Performances in Colleges of Education. Technical report, Kano (2017)
2. Fong, S., Buik-Aghai, R.P.: An automated university admission recommender system for secondary school students. In: The 6th International Conference on Information Technology and Applications (ICITA), China (2009)
3. Géron, A.: Hands-on Machine Learning with Scikit-Learn Keras, and TensorFlow, 2nd edn. O'Reilly Media Inc., Sebastopol (2019)
4. Hassan, M., Ahmed, S., Abdullah, D.M., Rahman, M.S.: Graduate school recommender system: assisting admission seekers to apply for graduate studies in appropriate graduate schools. In: 5th International Conference on Informatics, Electronics and Vision (ICIEV), p. 503. Institute of Electrical and Electronics Engineers (2016)
5. Isinkaye, F.O., Folajimi, Y.O., Ojokoh, B.A.: Recommendation systems: principles, methods and evaluation. Egypt. Inform. J. **16**, 261–273 (2015)
6. Isma'il, M., Usman, H., Aliyu, G., Abdulmumin, I., Shehu, A.: An autonomous courses recommender system for undergraduate using machine learning techniques. In: International Conference in Mathematics, Computer Engineering and Computer Science (ICMCECS). IEEE, Lagos, Nigeria (2020). https://doi.org/10.1109/ICMCECS47690.2020.240882
7. JAMB: Exam/jamb-cut-off-mark/ (2019). https://www.currentschoolnews.com/exam/jamb-cut-off-mark/
8. Jauro, F., Alhassan, B.B., Aliyu, G., Toro, M.S.: Predicting child delivery mode using data mining by considering maternal. Sci. Forum (J. Pure Appl. Sci.) **18**, 31–35 (2019)
9. Lu, J., Wu, D., Mao, M., Wang, W., Zhang, G.: Recommender system application developments: a survey. Decis. Supp. Syst. **74**(C), 12–32 (2015)

10. Machine Learning Plus: How Naive Bayes Algorithm Works? (with example and full code)—ML + (2018). https://www.machinelearningplus.com/predictive-modeling/how-naive-bayes-algorithm-works-with-example-and-full-code/
11. Muhammad, A.: Undergraduate students project supervision recommendation system, Technical report, Federal University, Dutsen-Ma, Katsina (2017)
12. Portugal, I., Alencar, P., Cowan, D.: The use of machine learning algorithms in recommender systems?: a systematic review. Expert Syst. Appl. **97**, 205–227 (2018)
13. Ragab, A.H.M., Mashat, A.F.S., Khedra, A.M.: Design and implementation of a hybrid recommender system for predicting college admission. Int. J. Comput. Inf. Syst. Ind. Manag. Appl. **6**, 35–44 (2014)
14. Said, A., Bellogin, A.: Comparative recommender system evaluation: benchmarking recommendation frameworks. In: Proceedings of the 8th ACM Conference on Recommender systems - RecSys '14, Foster City, Silicon Valley, California, USA, pp. 129–136 (2014). https://doi.org/10.1145/2645710.2645746. http://dl.acm.org/citation.cfm?doid=2645710.2645746
15. Salas, J.: Sanitizing and measuring privacy of large sparse datasets for recommender systems. J. Ambient Intell. Human. Comput. (2019). https://doi.org/10.1007/s12652-019-01391-2
16. Swaminathan, R., Gnanasekaran, J.M., Krishnakumar, S.: Recommender system for graduate studies in USA Suresh (2015). https://www.semanticscholar.org/paper/Recommender-System-for-Graduate-Studies-in-USA-Suresh
17. Wakil, K., Akram, B., Kamal, N., Safi, A.: Web recommender system for private universities' admission in Iraq: UHD case study. Int. J. e-Educ. e-Bus. e-Manag. e-Learn. **4**, 329–340 (2014)
18. Zubairu, M.J., et al.: Text normalization algorithm for Facebook chats in Hausa language. In: 2014 5th International Conference on Information and Communication Technology for The Muslim World (ICT4M), pp. 1–4. IEEE, Kuching (2014). https://doi.org/10.1109/ICT4M.2014.7020605. http://ieeexplore.ieee.org/document/7020605/

Team Topologies in Software Teams: A Multivocal Literature Review

Waqar Ahmed and Ricardo Colomo-Palacios(✉) ⓘ

Østfold University College, BRA veien. 4, 1757 Halden, Norway
{waqar.ahmed,ricardo.colomo-palacios}@hiof.no

Abstract. Team topologies have been frequently associated with organization's success for effective software delivery in the shape of right product. Achieving excellence for software development highly depends upon the team's coordination and communication between them. Team topologies are methodology helping an organization deliberately think about different teams' purposes (fundamental topologies) and how and when they should interact with each other (core interaction mode). Authors aim to investigate the concept and the impact of team topologies. Using a Multivocal Literature Review we found significant impact of team's goals over the individual's goal in an organization. As expected organization formed using fundamental topologies and core interaction mode lead to high success rate.

Keywords: Multivocal Literature Review · Team topologies · Team topology · Software engineering

1 Introduction

In almost any human activity, teams are used to perform tasks, particularly the ones that are more creative and complex. In spite analyses have revealed the benefits of diversity for team creativity, these benefits carry several challenges linked to diversity in teams [1]. Many organizations are making teams to divide the work in small parts such as developing and improving IT products or services [2].

For the intricate tasks, process models are also aspects to analyze. In creative processes in which its complicated nature is a fact, knowing the team topologies and how teaming process affects the team performance is interesting [3]. In software arena, global software development is a common approach to tackle higher pressures in time [4, 5]. In practice, the success of software development projects is dependent on the successful completion of its requirements engineering activities, which is challenging phase in software development [6]. Shared understanding is crucial and helpful in resolving conflicts and clearing ambiguities, it occurs when all the individuals working on a project have the same understanding of every requirement.

A team is collection of different individuals working in different organizations, to carry out different tasks in different fields of study. In virtual teams, team members work in different locations and their interaction is based and enabled by technology. In these

© Springer Nature Switzerland AG 2021
O. Gervasi et al. (Eds.): ICCSA 2021, LNCS 12957, pp. 272–282, 2021.
https://doi.org/10.1007/978-3-030-87013-3_21

environments, communication can be intricate, but, on the other hand, this environment could lead to fewer distractions [7]. Team topologies describe how teams are organized in an organization defining their responsibility limits and how they interact or communicate among teams [8]. In this regard, two important aspects must be considered: group coordination and group cohesiveness. Coordination refers to the task coordination by allocating roles to the team members and denoting to individual abilities, knowledge, skills and experience. Group cohesiveness is related to members' willingness to pertain to a given group. According to [9], group cohesiveness can be achieved by three main communication acts: informal talks, confirmation and appreciation. Informal talks are non-task related communication; appreciation is unambiguous information liking towards a contribution of team member and, finally, confirmation is the appreciation of a contribution. Preceding works underlines that performance within work groups is determined by the groups social network topologies [10]. Team topologies as a concept provides a lens which can help to structure an organization for effective collaborations, autonomy, delivery focus and product alignment [11]. Authors are not proposing that increasing connections among team members can increase the performance, however, it is true that some network structures determine performance. In the current scenario in which the introduction of agile methods moved the focus from the individual developer to the team [12], and, on the other hand, automation [13] and continuous software engineering [14], the need to adopt forms that can be applied in such scenarios is of paramount importance. One of the approaches designed to improve collaboration and improve the delivery of products is Team Topologies. This work is aimed to study the impact of this method in the literature. Given the novelty of the concept, but also its importance driven buy the key role of software in the world, authors develop this study to understand the concept and its implications.

The organization of this paper is as follows. Section 2 depicts the research methodology adopted in this paper. Section 3 presents the results of the study. Finally, Sect. 4 present and discuss the answers to the research questions and further research is depicted in Sect. 5.

2 Research Methodology

The main objective of this paper is to study and present in an organized way the state of art of team topologies. Consequently, the aim is to determine its meaning, identify trends and also to detect future work opportunities.

In order to perform the study, a Multivocal Literature Review (MLR) was conducted following the guidelines provided by [15]. A MLR is one of the forms of systematic literature reviews which, in this case, allows us to include primary, secondary as well as grey literature, including in this set videos, white papers or blog posts [15, 16]. Given the novelty of the concept, the amount of relevant studies in scientific literature is very limited, leading to MLR as a valid tool to investigate the concept.

In MLR we use certain criteria to evaluate the search and evaluation method in order to identify the group of primary studies from different databases. As [17] established, there are three stages that should be followed in this review; first, planning; second, conducting and, finally, reporting. In the first stage the planning protocol will be defined including the process for performing the review, including the definition of research questions (RQs), strategies regarding the search and assessment of studies, inclusion and exclusion criteria and other aspects.

2.1 Aims and RQs

In this section, authors will defined the aim of the study and from that, the set of RQs that will be answered in this work.

The main goal for this review is to review team topologies as a concept, examining its repercussion. Accordingly, the goals of this work are: (a) identify team purpose and responsibilities (b) to collect and analyze communication paths, and (c) to observe the perceived benefits of team topologies in software teams.

Inspired in these goals, authors defined the two RQs as follows:

- **RQ1:** What kind of teams and in which ways they operate under team topologies?
- **RQ2:** What are the different ways to communicate with other teams in team topologies?

2.2 Study Selection

In this section, authors outline search and evaluation strategies to discover and classify primary studies. In this regard, authors define search terms, based on them, build the search string as well as describe the process to guide study selection.

Databases: Authors used the set databases to identify scientific literature on the topic:

- ACM
- IEEE
- Springer
- Science Direct
- Google Scholar

The reason behind the selection of these databases is the popularity of the set in literature studies in the broad field of computing. Authors would like to mention that Google Scholar was selected as a source of scientific outputs that could be out of the previous four databases. Apart from this five databases retrieving scientific articles, Google Search was used to surf for relevant sources in grey literature.

Search Terms: Authors analyzed RQs with the intention of selecting general terms related to team topologies with the aim of gathering relevant works for this study. Therefore, as a results of this search terms will be "team topology" and "team topologies".

Search String Construction: Following Brereton et al. [18], in this work, authors tried in order to fine-tune the search string. The result of this process was a Boolean Expression " (A1 OR B1)" where search terms are is:

"Team Topologies" OR "Team Topology"

Inclusion and Exclusion Criteria: Our MLR identifies the studies that enlighten the importance of team topologies in IT sectors. So as to analyze the state of research of team topologies, authors decided not to limit publication periods.

Inclusion Criteria

- Studies that presents team topologies.
- Studies that explains the team topologies.
- Studies analyzing team topologies.

Exclusion Criteria

- Papers not specifically related to team topologies.
- Studies that presents the outcome of team topology but do not show any information about the IT sector.
- Papers with unobtainable abstract and the full text.
- Studies not written in English
- Duplicates.

2.3 Literature Retrieval

As stated before, authors selected the following databases: ACM Digital Library, Springer Link and Science Direct. These are the databases common in the set of published secondary studies in the field [19]. Also, in the search of grey literature, authors used Google Scholar, because its popularity and usefulness.

2.4 Scientific Selection Process

The search process allows us to select primary studies from the scientific literature in the previously presented databases. The process is comprised of four phases that follow a test-retest approach to reduce bias in the selection process. The same process was also con-ducted to identify grey literature on Google Search. The four phases are as follows:

Phase 1. Initial Search. The search string was applied to the search engines in order to identify the literature related to topic under review. Searches are limited to title, abstract, and keywords. In terms of timeline, our study was conducted in February 2021, and thus we included the papers published until that time.

Phase 2. Remove Duplicates. Studies identified during phase one of the selection process will be checked in order to remove the duplicates. If duplication is identified, papers providing detailed information such as an abstract or the full text of the paper, complete references of the publication will be selected.

Phase 3. First Selection Process. Studies selected in phase two will be evaluated with inclusion and exclusion criteria. In this phase, the title and abstract of each paper will be reviewed. If the papers are out of inclusion criteria papers will be completely discarded however if the papers fall under inclusion criteria, papers will be selected for the next phase.

Phase 4. Second Selection Process. Studies selected during phase three will be reviewed thoroughly. This stage will be done to ensure that publication contains the relevant information for the study under review. This approach helps in omitting irrelevant literature.

2.5 Grey Selection Process

The grey selection process allows selecting the primary studies from the grey literature. This process is composed of four phases that helps find the grey primary studies through a test-retest approach. The four phases of the grey selection process are the following:

Phase 1. Analyze References & Authors: In this phase, first forward and backward snowballing will be conducted on the scientific primary studies. Snowballing, in this context, refers to using the reference list of paper (backward snowballing) or the citations to the paper to identify additional papers (forward snowballing) [20]. Second, the researcher responsible of the searches will apply the search string to the list of works of each of the authors of the scientific primary studies. The aim of this search is to find all the works of each author related to the topic under review. At the end of this phase, a set of additional studies will be retrieved from the analysis of the grey literature.

Phase 2. Remove Duplicates: The studies retrieved during Phase 1 of the grey selection process will be checked in order to remove the duplicates, the studies that are clearly irrelevant to the topic under review and the papers that belongs to the scientific primary studies.

Phase 3. Second Selection Process: Once the duplicates have been removed, in this phase, the researcher responsible will carry out the same activities described in Phase 3 of the scientific selection process.

Phase 4. Second Selection Process: The work classified as possible selected papers (PS) during Phase 3 will be thoroughly analyzed by reading the full text. In this phase, the researcher responsible will carry out same activities described in Phase 4 of this scientific selection process.

In our MLR, we used Google Scholar for conducting the forward snowballing and the searches in the list of works of each of the authors of scientific primary studies.

2.6 Data Extraction

During the execution of the MLR, a substantial amount of data will be collected. There are two main sources of data: data collected during the search process and data collected during the extraction process. The data collected during search process allow collecting general data to identify the papers retrieved from both, scientific and grey selection process, support decision making of selecting the primary studies of the review and document the selection process. On the other hand, the data collected during the extraction process are the specific data needed to achieve the objectives of the study and answer the research questions under review.

2.7 Data Storage

All papers were organized in a systematic way in a reference manager namely Zotero. Additionally, an Excel sheet containing selected literature was employed to highlight the importance of each paper by means of a list of colors.

3 Results

This study was performed in February, March and April 2021. During this time, authors developed all aspects presented in section two and also conducted the study itself. The two researchers participated in the MLR: the first author conducted the MLR and the second author supervised the work, designed the approach, reviewed the process and verified the process and the results.

In what follows, authors present main results of this study, particularizing the explanation in scientific and grey literature extraction.

3.1 Scientific Selection Process Results

This process consist of four consecutive steps. In the first round, authors executed the query in the five selected databases. A set of 147 papers was identified. Subsequently, authors looked for duplicates. The result of this process was the removal of 6 duplicated papers. As a third stage, authors examined 141 title and abstracts assessing inclusion and exclusion criteria for each paper. The result of this process was the identification of 3 papers. In the last step, authors read the full text of the three papers in order to ensure the suitability of the set. One paper more was excluded leading to a final set of two papers in scientific databases. Table 1 depicts this four stage process.

3.2 Grey Selection Process Results

Authors followed similar approach on the grey studies selection process. In the first round, buy means of google search; we retrieved 865000 results.

The second round of grey selection process started with 865000 studies in Google search. Normally, the first pages in these search are relevant. Consequently, in this paper we adopted the approach in [21] to proceed further only if needed. So, $(n + 1)^{th}$ page was checked just in the case the result on n^{th} page was found relevant. After removing duplicates, authors carried out a 3rd round. At this stage, we analyzed the title and abstracts examining inclusion and exclusion criteria. Once the first selection process we excluded the 864999 studies from the set. Then authors faced the final step of grey selection process to analyze full text of the studies. At the end of this stage, authors identified just one study to take into account for the final set of studies.

3.3 Primary Studies

As the result of the four rounds, just 3 studies were found relevant. Figures for papers in each of the rounds are presented in Table 1.

Table 1. Papers analyzed per round

Database	First	Second	Third	Fourth
ACM	6	6	1	1
Springer	14	13	0	0
Science Direct	5	4	0	0
Google Scholar	122	118	2	1
TOTAL Scientific	*147*	*141*	*3*	*2*
Google search	865,000	864,991	1	1
TOTAL	***865,147***	***865,132***	***4***	***3***

4   Discussion

4.1   RQ1. What Kind of Teams and in Which Ways They Operate Under Team Topologies?

Within a team, the accent on accountability (individual and team) has turn out to be prevalent in the evaluation of task orientation factors [22]. A team's goal is a future state of affairs desired by enough members of a team to motivate the team to work toward its achievement. Tohidi [23] suggested that a team´s goal is more significant than individual goals. Still, it is also stated that the success of the company could be less important than team's success.

   It is reported that modern complex systems require effective team performance. In the software arena, the complexity, diversity, speed and frequency of change needed for modern software tools means that different development teams in software development are vital [8]. In particular, a research by Google on their own teams found that who is on team matters less than the team dynamics; and that when it comes to measuring performance, team matters more than individuals [24]. We must, therefore, start with team for effective software delivery.

Systems that are built by organizations are always questioned by users based on the previous agreed upon requirements. Values are always measured on the basis of the product delivery, excellence, and fast paced-evaluation of the systems, rapidly changing environment, changing requirement of customers, pressure of shorter time to market, and speedily advancement of IT. To overcome this state of affairs, agility and its practices bring flexibility, efficiency and speed [25]. Team topologies refer to the organizational capability to develop, communicate and learn. This brings operation the chance to build, evolve and refactor the systems design, developing the functionality, satisfying customers, and getting instant feedback from users to inform the next development cycle. Furthermore, the tools employed in different software development phases (analysis, coding, deployment…) must be aligned with rapid cycles.

We found four different types of teams:

- **Stream aligned teams:** Present an end to end responsibility on a new functionality or change, including operation roles in production.
- **Enabling teams:** They empower the previous type to upsurge their competences for a given time (new technology, new process…)
- **Complicated subsystem teams:** They are skilled specialists that would be hard to place into stream aligned teams because their dissimilarities.
- **Platform teams:** Platform specialists aimed to fast-track or make straightforward software delivery for the first group.

4.2 RQ2. What are Different Ways to Communicate with Other Teams in Team Topologies?

Velocity and efficiency are aspects crucial for the survival of software industry software organizations in their release process and product shipping [26]. Undeniably, continuous delivery is impacting organizations and their organizational structures, given that release activities encompasses many units of these organizations, typically Development and Operations in DevOps settings, but also others like security or business areas. Consequently, organizations adopting these approaches must adapt their toolchain but, just that, they need to find a way to better orchestrate their teams. We found three different ways for team topologies to interact with each other [27]:

- **Collaboration:** Teams collaboration must be effective to meet challenges of balancing speed and safety of software development.
- **X as a Service:** The organization must not restrict to optimize for top/down or bottom/up communication and reporting. Decision based on organization chart structure tends to optimize only part of an organization ignoring upstream/downstream effects. Local optimizations help the team directly involved, but they do not necessarily help improve overall delivery of value to the customer. For example, assigning task of infrastructure as a service (IaaS) to software as a service (SaaS). Thus, the group of teams should work in one domain to have high quality product.
- **Facilitate:** Facilitate refers to informal and value creation structure (interaction between people and team). Empowering the teams for better outcome of software

delivery. Addition to this, treating team as a fundamental building blocks and trust between the teams.

As a result, these are three main interaction modes that not only encourage teams to deliver high quality product but also overall help to an organization.

5   Future Work

Authors present a study towards a more detailed understanding of team topologies. Four different teams were found within the topic under review. In addition to this we also explained three different interaction modes which are basis of team topologies. The results of our MLR, including the perceived benefits identified allow us to conclude that team topologies have potential for organizations to help them in their endeavors. Nevertheless, the use of team topologies is an emergent research field in which researchers will work in the next future. However, authors call for further research and, in particular, experimental works to document the full potential of team topologies in the scope of software work.

In the near future, to properly execute the conclusion and ideas shared in this paper, some additional work has to be done. We want to devote time to investigate the connections and interlinks of team topologies with the increasing importance of automation in software work (DevOps and DevSecOps) and the new roles in these teams.

References

1. Tang, M., Schmidt, J.T.: Chapter 4 - Fostering creativity in interdisciplinary and intercultural teams: the importance of team building and team management. In: McKay, A.S., Reiter-Palmon, R., Kaufman, J.C. (eds.) Creative Success in Teams, pp. 55–79. Academic Press, Cambridge (2021). https://doi.org/10.1016/B978-0-12-819993-0.00004-7
2. Deeter-Schmelz, D.R., Ramsey, R.P.: An investigation of team information processing in service teams: exploring the link between teams and customers. J. Acad. Mark. Sci. **31**, 409–424 (2003). https://doi.org/10.1177/0092070303255382
3. Badke-schaub, D., Badke-schaub, P., Lauche, K., Neumann, A., Ahmed, S.: 1 Task – Team – Process: Assessment and Analysis of the Development of Shared Representations in an Engineering Team
4. Holtkamp, P., Pawlowski, J.M.: A competence-based view on the global software development process. J. Univ. Comput. Sci. **21**, 1385–1404 (2015)
5. Khan, A.A., Keung, J., Niazi, M., Hussain, S., Shameem, M.: GSEPIM: a roadmap for software process assessment and improvement in the domain of global software development. J. Softw. Evol. Process. **31**, e1988 (2019). https://doi.org/10.1002/smr.1988
6. Humayun, M., Gang, C.: An empirical study on improving shared understanding of requirements in GSD. Int. J. Softw. Eng. Appl. **7**, 14 (2013)
7. Klonek, F., Parker, S.K.: Designing SMART teamwork: how work design can boost performance in virtual teams. Organ. Dyn. **50**, 100841 (2021). https://doi.org/10.1016/j.orgdyn.2021.100841
8. Skelton, M., Pais, M.: Team topologies: organizing business and technology teams for fast flow. IT Revol. (2019)

9. Goodman, P.S., Ravlin, E., Schminke, M.: Understanding groups in organizations. Res. Organ. Behav. **9**, 121–173 (1987)

10. Wise, S.: Can a team have too much cohesion? The dark side to network density. Eur. Manag. J. **32**, 703–711 (2014). https://doi.org/10.1016/j.emj.2013.12.005

11. Manuel Pais on Team Topologies during COVID-19. https://www.infoq.com/news/2021/03/team-topologies-during-pandemic/. Accessed 20 Mar 2021

12. Lenberg, P., Feldt, R.: Psychological safety and norm clarity in software engineering teams. In: Proceedings of the 11th International Workshop on Cooperative and Human Aspects of Software Engineering, pp. 79–86. Association for Computing Machinery, New York (2018). https://doi.org/10.1145/3195836.3195847

13. Leite, L., Kon, F., Pinto, G., Meirelles, P.: Building a theory of software teams organization in a continuous delivery context. In: 2020 IEEE/ACM 42nd International Conference on Software Engineering: Companion Proceedings (ICSE-Companion), pp. 296–297 (2020)

14. Fitzgerald, B., Stol, K.-J.: Continuous software engineering: a roadmap and agenda. J. Syst. Softw. **123**, 176–189 (2017). https://doi.org/10.1016/j.jss.2015.06.063

15. Garousi, V., Felderer, M., Mäntylä, M.V.: Guidelines for including grey literature and conducting multivocal literature reviews in software engineering. Inf. Softw. Technol. **106**, 101–121 (2019)

16. Sánchez-Gordón, M., Colomo-Palacios, R.: A multivocal literature review on the use of DevOps for e-learning systems. In: Proceedings of the Sixth International Conference on Technological Ecosystems for Enhancing Multiculturality, pp. 883–888 (2018)

17. Calderón, A., Ruiz, M., O'Connor, R.V.: A multivocal literature review on serious games for software process standards education. Comput. Stand. Interfaces **57**, 36–48 (2018). https://doi.org/10.1016/j.csi.2017.11.003

18. Brereton, P., Kitchenham, B.A., Budgen, D., Turner, M., Khalil, M.: Lessons from applying the systematic literature review process within the software engineering domain. J. Syst. Softw. **80**, 571–583 (2007). https://doi.org/10.1016/j.jss.2006.07.009

19. MacDonell, S., Shepperd, M., Kitchenham, B., Mendes, E.: How reliable are systematic reviews in empirical software engineering? IEEE Trans. Softw. Eng. **36**, 676–687 (2010). https://doi.org/10.1109/TSE.2010.28

20. Wohlin, C.: Guidelines for snowballing in systematic literature studies and a replication in software engineering. In: Proceedings of the 18th International Conference on Evaluation and Assessment in Software Engineering - EASE 2014, pp. 1–10. ACM Press, London (2014).https://doi.org/10.1145/2601248.2601268

21. Garousi, V., Mäntylä, M.V.: A systematic literature review of literature reviews in software testing. Inf. Softw. Technol. **80**, 195–216 (2016)

22. Shameem, M., Kumar, C., Chandra, B.: A proposed framework for effective software team performance: a mapping study between the team members' personality and team climate. In: 2017 International Conference on Computing, Communication and Automation (ICCCA), pp. 912–917 (2017).https://doi.org/10.1109/CCAA.2017.8229936

23. Tohidi, H.: Teamwork productivity & effectiveness in an organization base on rewards, leadership, training, goals, wage, size, motivation, measurement and information technology. Procedia Comput. Sci. **3**, 1137–1146 (2011). https://doi.org/10.1016/j.procs.2010.12.185

24. Friedman, Z.: Google Says The Best Teams Have These 5 Things. https://www.forbes.com/sites/zackfriedman/2019/01/28/google-says-the-best-teams-have-these-5-things/. Accessed 11 Apr 2021

25. Konersmann, M., Fitzgerald, B., Goedicke, M., Holmström Olsson, H., Bosch, J., Krusche, S.: Rapid continuous software engineering - state of the practice and open research questions: report on the 6th international workshop on rapid continuous software engineering (RCoSE 2020). SIGSOFT Softw. Eng. Notes. **46**, 25–27 (2021). https://doi.org/10.1145/3437479.3437486

26. Leite, L., Pinto, G., Kon, F., Meirelles, P.: The organization of software teams in the quest for continuous delivery: a grounded theory approach. arXiv:2008.08652 [cs]. (2020)
27. Q&A on the Book Team Topologies. https://www.infoq.com/articles/book-review-team-top ologies/. Accessed 12 Apr 2021

Precision Shooting Training System Using Augmented Reality

Estefani Lucero-Urresta[1] , Jorge Buele[2]([✉]) , Patricio Córdova[1],
and José Varela-Aldás[2]

[1] Universidad Técnica de Ambato, Ambato 180206, Ecuador
{elucero9571,edgarpcordovac}@uta.edu.ec
[2] SISAu Research Group, Facultad de Ingeniería y Tecnologías de la Información y la
Comunicación, Universidad Tecnológica Indoamérica, Ambato 180103, Ecuador
jorgebuele@indoamerica.edu.ec, josevarela@uti.edu.ec

Abstract. Precision shooting training is conventionally done at outdoor shooting ranges. There are also virtual training grounds that use weapons and scenarios that do not provide a completely real experience. When the practitioner begins training, the waste of ammunition represents an economic inconvenience both for him and for the training center. For this reason, this research analyzes the factors and tactical strategies involved in precision shooting practices, developing a virtual augmented reality system that implements three-dimensional objects that facilitate training with short-range weapons. The panorama of vision in the sights of the weapons is expanded, to have a better alignment between the three key points that intervene in the shots. Thus, the training method is modernized, but the reactions caused by the recoil force generated by a shot are preserved, without affecting the practitioner's cognitive process. When acting within a combat environment, it is necessary to recreate a situational awareness that allows generating a perception, understanding, and anticipation of all the elements of the environment. Experimental tests show a 116.67% increase in effectiveness when compared to the traditional method. Thus, there is a reduction in the consumption of resources, making it a sustainable proposal.

Keywords: Augmented reality · Precision shooting · Tactical training

1 Introduction

Augmented reality (AR) allows the introduction of computer-generated elements into the natural environment, improving the ability to detect, recognize and process objects and situations [1]. The ability to communicate with other devices has been made part of the daily life of users and facilitates operation in various interdisciplinary applications [2]. The entertainment industry has been one of its forerunners, although its importance in industry and in the professional sphere can also be highlighted [3, 4]. Besides being a tool to motivate consumers, with various marketing strategies [5]. In the military field, these systems are used to generate skills and abilities in personnel undergoing training

O. Gervasi et al. (Eds.): ICCSA 2021, LNCS 12957, pp. 283–298, 2021.
https://doi.org/10.1007/978-3-030-87013-3_22

[6]. This highlights the work of [7], where surfaces are used in high terrain using AR during the training of cadets in military tactics, encouraging active participation.

The evolution of military technology has been developing as the needs in military confrontations have appeared. In this way, the use of firearms of all kinds has been part of the formative process of the soldiers, but over time, it is also a domain knowledge of the civilian personnel. For this reason, training grounds, known as firing ranges, are created all over the world. In these establishments, the skills of the practitioners are perfected through technical instruction, improving performance in the execution of precision shots and in reaction. Correct tactical shooting training includes mastery of drawing, grasping, and control of the weapon in rapid sequences and an adequate vision of the crosshairs. This last skill corresponds to the alignment of the weapon and the accuracy of the shot depends on it [8].

Conventional training is based on the practitioner's eyesight and considering that only one clearly visible reference point can be focused on at a time, a problem is created. The problem with the height of the reference sights of a short-range weapon is that the observer must pay attention to three key points to make a precision shot: the rear and front sight located on the weapon, plus the target at a distance [9]. This causes the entire surrounding environment to become diffuse so that the script becomes the main object of observation and an important point for taking a precision shot. With this, the effectiveness of the shot is focused on the view and posture of the user, which, at distances greater than 15 m generates inaccurate results and is one of the limitations when training progresses towards the practice of reaction shots [10]. The alignment of the crosshairs depends on the posture adopted, according to the situation in which he finds himself and the recoil caused in the body by the inertia of detonation.

As an alternative proposal that reduces the amount of ammunition used and additional expenses during practice, sessions at a physical firing range, laser-guided firing simulators, and virtual ranges are used. These commercial systems represent a high economic investment since having laser weapons, virtual target projection systems, and video cameras. For this reason, shooting simulators have been developed at a lower cost as part of research related to virtual reality (VR) [11]. In [12] the changes in the cardiovascular responses of police officers in the training routines of a virtual system are evidenced. While in the work of [13], the virtual environment includes a device for the feedback of forces, allowing to evaluate the generation of force, the firing reactions, and the experimental results. In [14] a prototype is created that replicates the properties of a commercial VR device (i.e., adjustable shape, weight, and force feedback) and evaluates the effects of these parameters on user performance, obtaining good results.

Although most applications are made using VR, augmented reality proves to be a valid technological tool for training and the educational process. In the work of [5], several bibliographic sources are reviewed and the usefulness of RA in education and sports training is described, as well as suggestions for the design of training scenarios. Military tactics also benefit from AR, in [15] a system is described that using three-dimensional objects and audiovisual resources, simulates the environment of a real war conflict. Applications involving the execution of shots are prevalent in entertainment, as shown in [16], where a mobile AR game is developed where the player can walk in any environment and hunt ghosts [17].

Although the literature review is found not relevant articles, which are made tactical training with augmented reality, which has led to the present research. In this context, it is proposed to develop a virtual system for the practice of precision shots using AR. In the hardware, a smartphone has been coupled to a helmet for military use, which is safe and non-invasive for the user. In software, Unity, Vuforia, Blender, Adobe Illustrator, and Visual Studio have been used for the development of three-dimensional objects. The functional tests validate this initial proposal.

The document consists of six sections, including the introduction (Sect. 1). Section 2 describes the previous context on the use of weapons and Sect. 3 the development of the proposal. The tests and results obtained are set out in Sect. 4 and Sect. 5 respectively. Finally, the conclusions are shown in Sect. 6.

2 Previous Context

A firearm is a mechanical or semi-automatic object that is always under the control of a wearer. For the development of this proposal the initial analysis, implementation, and experimental tests have been carried out in a private establishment. Different physical and technical factors go into the effectiveness and accuracy of a shot. These can be external environmental factors or at the same time tactical strategies that require constant correction and training.

2.1 External Factors

There are those physical factors that can affect or distort the trajectory of a projectile from the point of origin to the destination (target).

Distance. It is relevant in firing precision since the longer the projectile travels, additional factors such as gravity and wind direction must be taken into account. This when used long-range weapons such as rifles, ammunition that reach n up to 3000 m of track, while short - range weapons are considered negligible.

Moving Target. It is the factor of greatest difficulty in shooting since the speed and variable position of the final target intervenes. It is necessary to anticipate the position of the target by observing through the sights and thus establish the necessary compensation interval to bring the shot closer. This is done through the use of visual tracking techniques for short-range shots (ideal for airsoft) or momentary hold for longer ranges. For this case study, the objectives are static, so this factor is also neglected.

Wind. The force of the wind is not constant and could destabilize both the projectile and the shooter. The direction and intensity of it must be taken into account, and it is advisable to shoot downwind to gain distance. When taking a shooting position, to have an empirical measurement of wind speed, the following ranges are established. (i) imperceptible wind: less than 5 km/h; (ii) gentle breeze that is perceived on the face: 5–9 km/h; (iii) leaves constantly shaking: 9–12 km h; (iv) flight of leaves and dust: 12 to 20 km/h. (v) shrubs and small trees oscillating: 20–27 km/h.

It must be taken into account that the wind affects the flight direction of the projectile, having to make drift corrections for the shot. The 9:00 a.m. wind blows the bullet to the right and the 3:00 p.m. wind blows it to the left. The factor that is considered for distances greater than 50 m. During the practice, it must wait for the wind intensity to be as low as possible, and in this establishment due to the location, it is very low.

Brightness. The reflection of sunlight or artificial light can n have disruptive effects on the field of view and affect directly the alienation of view for shooting. Therefore, it is required to use sunglasses to reduce the unnecessary reflections and contrast in a change of environment.

2.2 Tactical Strategies

There are those techniques that facilitate and improve shooting training, establishing coordination between the elements that intervene when shooting. To achieve an effective interaction of the proposed system, the most relevant tactical aspects are analyzed and summarized in Table 1.

3 Proposal Development

With the implementation of a precision shooting training system using augmented reality, the aim is to totally reduce the waste of ammunition and take advantage of the instructional time. Training times would focus solely on rounds of fire, reducing instructor time by 40%. This percentage of the practice is destined for the training and correction of the shooting posture of the practitioner to achieve efficiency and precision in the shots.

1. The environmental conditions under which the system must operate correspond to those of an open field, with full exposure to natural light. This environment has a hot dry climate, with the presence of dust and without direct connections to electricity.
2. The system must not have elements that interfere or present an obstacle when performing target practice in any of its stages. This should not have immersive hardware, as it would alter the safety standards for the shooter.
3. Personal protection elements can be used for the system, complying with the ANSI standard. This includes elements of visual protection, hearing protection, or external elements that are to be used for the protection of the shooter.
4. The sighting, projection, and alignment images should conform to the generally used internationally used tactical shooting characteristics.
5. The training, performance tests, and validation will be under supervision.

Based on the analysis of external physical factors that influence the accuracy of the shot, the tactical strategies used, and information on the facilities, it is inferred that only the external factor of luminosity is taken into account. The other external factors are not considered since the variations are negligible at distances less than 30 m (distance from the runways).

Table 1. Analysis of tactical shooting strategies.

Strategy	Analysis in training	Conclusion
Position	There are established positions; however, the physical constitution of each shooter makes it impossible for them to be final. Every posture must provide to the shooter: stability, balance, flexibility, and comfort	The shooting instructor must have access to the field vis ion of the shooter to correct the posture and achieve better results
Grip	The grip of the weapon must cover the largest possible surface of the weapon, without leaving free spaces, with rigid and straight wrists. It must allow a correct alignment of sights and objectives	This is relevant to the effectiveness of the reaction shots, the control of the recoil movement and the alignment of sights
Alignment	Shooter must have accurate rear and front sight alignment. It is must focus solely on the front sight of the weapon to have a proper sighting frame with the dominant eye	It is key in a precision shot. This depends on the vision of the shooter and the ability to form a focus box between the view and the target
Breathing	The rib cage is in constant motion due to inhalation, and exhalation, so a relaxed breath should be maintained	It is recommended to take the shot at the moment of apnea so as not to affect the precision
Trigger control	Of this depends on most of the effectiveness of a shot. It is necessary to have an effective recovery after each execution, to shoot again	Works in conjunction with weapon alignment

Figure 1 shows the architecture of this proposal. Here it can be seen that the input corresponds to the gun, sight, and target alignment by the shooter. On the weapon and on the target there are augmented reality tags on which AR elements are superimposed aimed at providing a better focus on the sights of the weapon and the target to be shot. These are developed on different platforms and are viewed by both the shooter and the instructor on different screens so that erroneous postures can be corrected and thus improve the accuracy of the shot. This information is stored on a server to have a training history of the shooters.

It is essential that each shooter receives prior technical instruction on shooting fundamentals and tactical strategies to achieve precision shots. So that the student is related to the type of weapon to be used, positioning strategies, alignment of sights on the weapon, and current safety regulations. The system should not present obstacles in the development of the practice, therefore, the strategic points for the development are:

- Shooting targets located 20 m from the shooter's starting position.
- The targets to shoot are silhouette targets at the height of the average person.

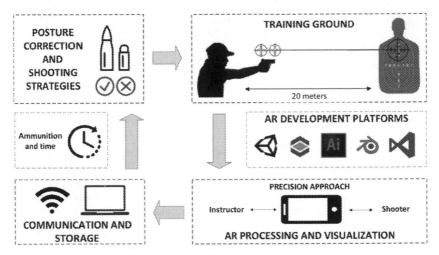

Fig. 1. General diagram of the system.

- The location of the shooter starts from an outdoor area with direct exposure to natural light, there are five training courts.
- The instructor's location is at a safe and prudent distance from the shooter, but adequate enough for him to appreciate the techniques used.
- The server is stored locally within the institution, in a secure area.

3.1 Hardware

Smart Device for AR System Visualization. It needs a display screen that is not invasive, that does not have problems with the brightness and dust of an open field. The use of augmented reality glasses because despite the good features in image quality, have discarded vibrations and software required paid. It is also considered that in the case of glasses, the location of the camera is not central, since there are two (one for each eye), which does not allow it to be used when handling short-range firearms. For this reason, it is decided to use a Smartphone, following strict visual safety regulations.

Smartphone. Quality graphics display depends directly on the smartphone where it will run the application. The intrinsic requirements of the application require a medium or high-end device, to guarantee visibility in an outdoor environment. In addition, since it is an application for a private institute, this system has been conditioned to the smartphones that the instructors of that place have. Therefore, technical analysis of each of the devices and satisfactory performance tests of the AR application is carried out.

Computer. To develop a system that uses AR requires the use of a computer with a graphics development engine and a compatible software development kit. Therefore, the computer where the system develops requires specific characteristics recommended for a good performance, avoiding slowdowns. These are:

- OS: Windows 10 64 bits.
- Android SDK Development Kit, Java (JDK), Vuforia SDK, Unity Hub.
- 16 GB RAM memory.
- CPU: Intel Core i7-7700HQ 2.8 GHz–3.8 GHz.
- 15.6″ (1920 × 1080) IPS LED screen.
- NVIDIA GTX 1050 Ti 4 GB Graphics Card.

In the case of the server, it must be on a local computer and since the amount of data is not that high, it does not require further considerations. It is recommended to install an OS: Windows 7 64 bits and an Intel Core i5-2450M @ 2.80 GHz 4 GB RAM processor.

Tactical Helmets. A fastening system is required to be attached to Safe Guard brand tactical incursion helmets, with security level IIIA ballistic protection. Thus, the absolute vision of the student is not obstructed and at the same time, it can have a screen where the alignment of sights is displayed.

Shooting Targets. Targets with human silhouettes, rings, and poppers are available. Taking into account that the system focuses on close-range shooting, silhouette targets have been chosen. These are the height of an average person locating the thorax.

Short-Range Weapons. The weapons made available for training and validation tests are Pietro Beretta and Glock model pistols. The projectiles are 9 mm caliber and the speed reached is 360 m/s. These are chosen for ergonomics, performance, and proper weight. It should be noted that the institution has the necessary permits for handling weapons.

3.2 Software

Unity. It is a graphics engine for the development of multiplatform videogames that has an integrated development environment (IDE). In the field of augmented reality, it offers tools to create fully enriched AR experiences, which interact intelligently with the real world and a unified workflow for all devices. The version used in this application is 2019.1.11 and for the installation, it is required to have previously Unity Hub. A desktop interface that streamlines the installation process and access to the different versions of Unity and its add-on packages. It also has compatibility with Vuforia.

Vuforia. It is a software development kit (SDK) for building mobile applications with AR. To do this, use the main camera of the mobile device and the screen to view the super-imposed objects. An application made in Vuforia consists of the following components: camera, image converter, tracker, and application code.

The most robust AR development platforms are Vuforia, ARKit, and ARCore. The latter is robust for the design of applications but has incompatibilities with certain smart-phones so it is ruled out. ARKit is focused on iOS, so the Vuforia SDK is chosen for its strengths and compatibility. As AR targets that are supported by Vuforia, Mult Target has been chosen, which works as an image target but with multiple images. These must be different for the system to recognize them.

Adobe Illustrator. It is a vector graphics editor, where the AR tags are developed for the development of the system. This software is used since these must be vectorized images with the best possible image quality.

Blender. It is a multiplatform software focused on modeling, lighting, rendering, animation, and the creation of three-dimensional graphics. In the development of the project, it allows to elaborating the 3D modeling of the silhouette that is superimposed on the target to be shot and the AR alignment sight as seen in Fig. 2.

Fig. 2. Developing three-dimensional elements in Blender.

Visual Studio. t is the software selected for the development of the programming code of the scripts. This program has a link with Unity to go to the code development interface from the inspector panel. It allows the creation of a script in several programming languages such as Java, C++, C#; In this case, C# programming has been used for image stabilization.

3.3   Interface Design

Initial Tests: Above the markers that are located in the scene panel, the 3D elements that are going to be visualized in the final mobile application must be placed. For this, 3D assets can be downloaded as packages from the Unity online store. As the system is applied in a real environment, the 3D elements are a crosshair whose tag is located on the front sight of the weapon and a silhouette with scores that are superimposed on the target located at a distance. Each element is modified in a blender, thus obtaining a file with a compatible *.blend extension. It is necessary to take into account the size of the elements, due to the distance at which the markers are located. This optimal size is adjusted according to observational and error tests.

At this point it is necessary to perform functional tests for the AR elements added through the Unity panel, using the computer camera for marker recognition. In this test, it is evident that the AR crosshair tends to be confused by the color of the final objective, so the design is changed to a more interactive green color without background with the firing center in a red tone. In this way, the precision point towards which the projectile is directed when the weapon is fired is distinguished. Figure 3 shows this change, which is the definitive one in terms of element design.

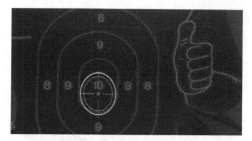

Fig. 3. Functional tests of AR elements in Unity.

To generate a mobile application in Unity through the use of the Vuforia SDK, the location and brightness parameters to which it is exposed must first be configured. Then the Android platform is added, as shown in the flow chart in Fig. 4. So that the system does not present problems when being rendered in an outdoor environment and with direct natural lighting. This object is configured in Unity in the inspector panel.

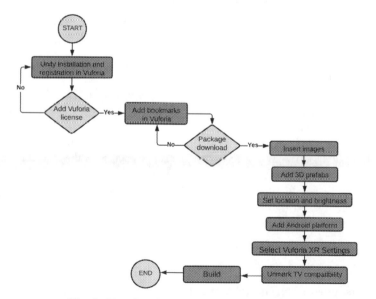

Fig. 4. Functional tests of AR elements in Unity.

Scripts Development. A script in Unity allows it to edit the source code of the elements placed in the scene to make the actions fit the user's needs. For this Unity has a partnership with Visual Studio for code editing. This is later attached to the project with the import of packages. The process for the development of a script is observed in the flow chart of Fig. 5. In the system, the luminosity is an important factor and the configuration of the directional light carried out and the AR elements are not enough. This involves using too many resources on the smartphone, causing overheating. For this reason, it proceeds to edit the scripts for the shooting silhouette and the crosshairs, to add luminosity to each one, independently. In addition, the general lighting conditions of the system are improved by increasing the brightness that Unity assigns to the application, changing the texture of the shooting silhouette that is superimposed on the target.

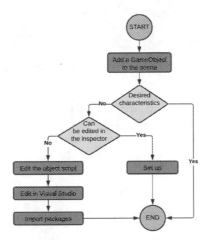

Fig. 5. Flowchart for developing a script.

The AR sight has a green tone, to make it clearer, editing the source code of the script that contains it, for it's clicked on the object and within the Unity inspector and add a Script type component. A new element is created within the inspector, to edit it in Visual Studio just open the script editing tab. All the parameters that want to be improved of each game object present in the scene can be edited through the use of scripts. Most of them already come with a source code, in which the exact variables must be edited. In case there is no direct script for necessary parameters such as texture, lighting, percentage of brightness, and optimal rendering with a low consumption level, the source code of the elements is edited. This programming is done in the C# language.

3.4 Dual Screen Display

The system requires that the instructor be able to have the vision of the shooter to correct misalignments and postures and achieve greater precision in the shot. Unity offers the ability to create a multiplayer environment, so in the augmented reality section, the camera of the second device is activated as well. For this proposal it is not ideal, that is why it's access to remote control of the Android device on which the application is running. In this way, the two screens display the same environment in real-time and the instructor can thus identify what the student is doing.

3.5 Server

The system requires that the videos of the use of the system in each training be stored on a computer. This way, it has a training history for each shooter and it can identify trends in the most frequent mistakes that are made. For this reason, an FTP server is implemented in the main computer of the establishment. (File Transfer Protocol). In the configuration, there is a port value assigned for instructors to connect to initiate the file transfer. Also has access to the stored videos of the practitioners, respecting the respective access codes granted to the sta.

All instructors are enabled to access the server and to add videos of each training to specific folders from smartphones, by connecting to the establishment's network. Through the AndFTP application (compatible with the server) they access only using a link with the IP address of the computer and a personal password. The server interface is shown in Fig. 6.

Fig. 6. Flowchart for developing a script.

4   Tests

Before starting the testing stage, the environmental conditions under which the system must operate are defined (which have already been mentioned previously). The system must not have elements that interfere or represent an obstacle when practicing, in any of its stages. Personal protection elements that comply with ANSI standards must be used, this includes elements of visual protection and hearing protection. Viewing, projection, and sight alignment images should conform to the tactical shooting characteristics used internationally and locally. Also, the physical characteristics of each of the five training courts and the signage present in the facilities.

Conventional shooting targets are used to assess the level of accuracy of the shooter. Scores are awarded, where the maximum is 10 points in the center, the contiguous areas with 9 and the most dispersed with 8 points respectively. When all shots that have not reached the target have a score of 0. There are integer values and very close precision data, obtaining variance is not justified. The number of wasted ammunition in the established series is reviewed and the percentage of efficiency is calculated. Figure 7 shows one of the targets used for the shooting session with the AR system and the instructor in the posture correction stage.

Fig. 7. Counting shots on target and posture correction.

Figure 8 shows the Safe Guard anti-ballistic helmet, which has additive support for mobile devices. It is made of metal alloys and presents an absolutely secure and stable grip for both the shooter and the smartphone. The design is adaptable according to the required size and has a fabric covering over the polymer to avoid scratches, without obstructing the view of the shooter. The measurement is exact so that the camera captures the augmented reality marker located in the front sight of the weapon to be shot when a stable shooting position is adopted.

Fig. 8. Ballistic protection helmet with support.

During practice, when acquiring a shooting stance, the shooter observes the super-position of two objects on the screen. First, the target to be shot with numbers for the proximity of the shots with the center of the thorax and then the firing point in green. This alignment is key to making precision shots since it represents the point that the projectile reaches when it is fired. Figure 9 shows the screen with the AR overlays, where the gun script contains the first marker and the firing target contains the second marker.

Fig. 9. Viewing AR items during testing.

5 Experimental Results

5.1 System Efficiency

To measure the effectiveness of the system, experimental tests have been carried out with three amateur shooters, a number reduced by the available budget. Series of five shots each are executed. First under the traditional instruction, to count the number of successful shots. After that, a new series of shots are fired, but this time using the proposed system together with the shooting instructor. The results are observed in Fig. 10. The arithmetic mean of the system's efficiency shows that there is an improvement of 116.67% when compared to conventional training.

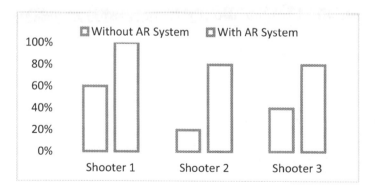

Fig. 10. Comparison chart of successful shots.

When using the AR system, hitting the target is much more likely to happen as the instructor has full access to the shooter's view and corrects misalignments and postures. In the first round, nine ammunition of the fifteen occupied is wasted, while in the second there are only two.

5.2 Subsequent Results

Then the closeness of the shots to the center of the board is evaluated, using the previously established scores. Figure 11 shows a comparison of the scores obtained according to the precision of each shot. The highest percentage of missed shots are directly related to the posture of the shooter, for which the instructor corrects it, adjusting them to a combat posture. After using the system, shooters improve posture and control of the weapon, in addition to reducing training time and ammunition used Practitioners show greater retention of the corrections made by the instructor, maintaining correct postures, even when no longer use the system.

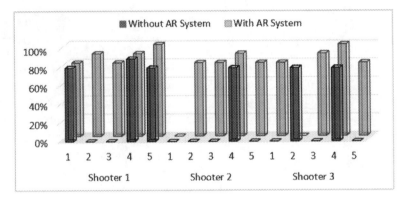

Fig. 11. Shot accuracy comparison chart.

5.3 Comparison with a Virtual Firing Range

When comparing the operation of this proposal with a virtual firing range, the conclusions shown below in Table 2 are obtained.

Table 2. Comparison of characteristics of the AR system with a virtual polygon.

Augmented reality system	Virtual shooting range
Allows the use of real weapons and ammunition	Air guns and ammunition are used, the characteristics of which do not resemble real conditions
The training can be in an outdoor environment, subject to climatic variations and in contact with the environment	The training takes place in a closed place, there is no interaction with external factors
The trajectory of the ammunition and recoil force of the weapon in the detonation is real and requires adequate tactical strategies	Lasers are often used to simulate the path of ammunition and there is no recoil force from a firearm
The vision and the environment are not completely invaded by virtual elements, but there are coupled in a non-invasive way	The environment becomes completely digitized, the immersion in a virtual system removes the real reaction conditions

6 Conclusions

During the analysis of external factors, tactical strategies, and information on the facilities used, it is inferred that the system must only take into account the external factor of luminosity. This since the system is constantly exposed to an outdoor environment with a dry hot climate. The other external factors are not considered, since the distance from the training tracks does not exceed 30 m. Variations in the trajectories of the 9 mm projectiles are also neglected since there are tiny when operating with a speed of 360 m/s.

The proposed system is non-invasive and makes up for the limitations that the shooter has at the moment of sight alignment. It supports tactical instruction and enables training under real physical conditions, which distinguishes it from a laser beam weapon present in virtual ranges. The practitioner should be trained in shooting fundamentals before using the system. Given these fundamentals: posture, alignment, and framing of sights.

During the tests, the instructor is located a few meters away, which allows for correcting erroneous shooting postures. Using the AR marker placed on the front sight improves the targeting focus for the ammo. This allows having a constant correction on the systematic errors that the shooter commits, due to the limitations of vision in a focus frame and inadequate shooting position. This is corroborated with the experimental tests that showed an increase of 116.67% of effectiveness when compared with the traditional method. Which shows that there is a reduction in the amount of wasted ammunition. This also improves the cognitive abilities of shooters, correcting the postures and precision after using the system, which allows time to be optimized.

Several proposals have been developed but in the field of VR, which shows that immersive environments are a trend that is increasing. By implementing this prototype, the use of AR in the field of tactical training can be appreciated. This research seeks to create a sustainable training process that reduces waste production, optimizes times, and offers lasting results over time. Finally, the authors of this document propose as future work to develop an improved version of this system, to improve the service provided.

References

1. You, X., Zhang, W., Ma, M., Deng, C., Yang, J.: Survey on urban warfare augmented reality. ISPRS Int. J. Geo-Inf. **7**, (2018). https://doi.org/10.3390/ijgi7020046
2. Soltani, P., Morice, A.H.P.: Augmented reality tools for sports education and training. Comput. Educ. **155**, 103923 (2020). https://doi.org/10.1016/j.compedu.2020.103923
3. Kasapakis, V., Gavalas, D.: Occlusion handling in outdoors augmented reality games. Multimedia Tools Appl. **76**(7), 9829–9854 (2016). https://doi.org/10.1007/s11042-016-3581-1
4. Gattullo, M., Scurati, G.W., Fiorentino, M., Uva, A.E., Ferrise, F., Bordegoni, M.: Towards augmented reality manuals for industry 4.0: a methodology. Robot. Comput. Integr. Manuf. (2019). https://doi.org/10.1016/j.rcim.2018.10.001
5. Tsai, S.: pei: Augmented reality enhancing place satisfaction for heritage tourism marketing. Curr. Issues Tour. **23**, 1078–1083 (2020). https://doi.org/10.1080/13683500.2019.1598950
6. Andersen, D., et al.: An augmented reality-based approach for surgical telementoring in austere environments. Mil. Med. (2017). https://doi.org/10.7205/milmed-d-16-00051
7. Boyce, M.W., et al.: The impact of surface projection on military tactics comprehension. Mil. Psychol. (2019). https://doi.org/10.1080/08995605.2018.1529487
8. Guven, S., Durukan, A.H.: Empty bullet-related ocular injuries during military shooting training: a 20-year review. Mil. Med. **185**, E799–E803 (2020). https://doi.org/10.1093/milmed/usz400
9. Kos, A., Umek, A., Marković, S., Dopsaj, M.: Sensor system for precision shooting evaluation and real-time biofeedback. Procedia Comput. Sci. 319–323 (2019). Elsevier B.V.. https://doi.org/10.1016/j.procs.2019.01.228
10. Ahir, K., Govani, K., Gajera, R., Shah, M.: Application on virtual reality for enhanced education learning, military training and sports. Aug. Hum. Res. **5**(1), 1–9 (2019). https://doi.org/10.1007/s41133-019-0025-2
11. Zhang, M., Li, X., Yu, Z., Chen, Z., Sun, Y., Li, Y.: Virtual range training based on virtual reality, 23 July 2019. https://doi.org/10.2991/iccessh-19.2019.339
12. Muñoz, J.E., Quintero, L., Stephens, C.L., Pope, A.T.: A psychophysiological model of firearms training in police officers: a virtual reality experiment for biocybernetic adaptation. Front. Psychol. (2020). https://doi.org/10.3389/fpsyg.2020.00683
13. Wei, L., Zhou, H., Nahavandi, S.: Haptically enabled simulation system for firearm shooting training. Virtual Real. **23**(3), 217–228 (2018). https://doi.org/10.1007/s10055-018-0349-0
14. Berna-Moya, J.L., Martinez-Plasencia, D.: Exploring the effects of replicating shape, weight and recoil effects on VR shooting controllers. In: Lamas, D., Loizides, F., Nacke, L., Petrie, H., Winckler, M., Zaphiris, P. (eds.) INTERACT 2019. LNCS, vol. 11746, pp. 763–782. Springer, Cham (2019). https://doi.org/10.1007/978-3-030-29381-9_45
15. Amaguaña, F., Collaguazo, B., Tituaña, J., Aguilar, W.G.: Simulation system based on augmented reality for optimization of training tactics on military operations. In: De Paolis, L.T., Bourdot, P. (eds.) AVR 2018. LNCS, vol. 10850, pp. 394–403. Springer, Cham (2018). https://doi.org/10.1007/978-3-319-95270-3_33
16. Armstrong, S., Morrand, K.: Ghost hunter – an augmented reality ghost busting game. In: Lackey, S., Shumaker, R. (eds.) VAMR 2016. LNCS, vol. 9740, pp. 671–678. Springer, Cham (2016). https://doi.org/10.1007/978-3-319-39907-2_64
17. Misra, S.: A step by step guide for choosing project topics and writing research papers in ICT related disciplines. In: Misra, S., Muhammad-Bello, B. (eds.) ICTA 2020. CCIS, vol. 1350, pp. 727–744. Springer, Cham (2021). https://doi.org/10.1007/978-3-030-69143-1_55

A Qualitative Study on SysML Based on Perceived Views from Industry Professionals

Tauany L. S. Santos[ID] and Michel S. Soares[(✉)][ID]

Federal University of Sergipe, São Cristóvão, Brazil
{tauany.lorene,michel}@dcomp.ufs.br

Abstract. SysML is a UML profile, proposed more than 15 years ago, as a systems modeling language supporting specification, design, development, verification and validation of a variety of complex systems and systems of systems which include elements such as processes, information, people, software and hardware. In the past years, SysML has been used in industry to support the development of systems in many domains. SysML shares diagrams and other constructions and elements with UML, which, at least in theory, makes it easy to learn for those who are already familiar with UML diagrams. However, there are few researches on the evaluation of what professionals in industry who are effectively using SysML in their daily tasks think about the language. This paper brings new reflections of a survey on what professionals think about SysML when used in practice. The survey received responses from 344 professionals from 38 different countries. 163 participants left their written general comments on SysML. After reading each one of the comments from the participants, these comments were divided into positive or negative for the language. In view of this, 70 responses were categorized as positive and 72 as negative. Based on this categorization of comments, we performed a qualitative analysis of the positive and negative responses, and then proposed a cloud word for each type of statement.

Keywords: SysML · Qualitative study

1 Introduction

SysML is a modeling language derived from UML to be applied to a variety of systems, supporting activities of specification, design, development, verification and validation. In the past years, SysML has been used in academia and industry to support the development of systems in many domains, including railway transportation [13], energy [8], automotive [10], and many others [25].

As a UML profile, SysML shares diagrams and other constructions and elements with UML, which, at least in theory, makes the language easy to learn for those who are already familiar with UML diagrams. There are studies on using UML and SysML together to solve a variety of problems [9,14,22]. However,

© Springer Nature Switzerland AG 2021
O. Gervasi et al. (Eds.): ICCSA 2021, LNCS 12957, pp. 299–310, 2021.
https://doi.org/10.1007/978-3-030-87013-3_23

there are few researches on the evaluation of what professionals in industry, who are effectively using SysML in their daily tasks, think about the language [4]. For instance, it would be interesting to know if SysML is really easier to use, understand and manage than UML, as first proposed by its creators [18]. In addition, research on drawbacks and weakness of SysML are rarely studied in practice, in systems engineering projects in industry, as most often industrial companies are not interested in publishing their results in detail.

From an industrial perspective, many aspects on the Verification and Validation of SysML models are presented in [4]. Verification and Validation activities accelerate the system development process with less time consumed on testing and system validation, which, in the end, improves the final quality of products and processes developed in industry [4]. However, these results are still incipient, and further analysis in industry are necessary.

Companies that are willing to use SysML in their projects in the near future may be interested in knowing what other professionals think about SysML in practice. Knowing what SysML really looks like for those who are responsible to design real products and systems in industry is an important issue, and can provide confidence for those who are thinking about investing resources for introducing SysML as a modeling language in their software and systems development processes. One can not neglect that industrial companies are interested in final results and not only academic research, in quality of products and processes and short time to market. Therefore, this paper describes positive and negative answers about SysML extracted from a survey from practitioners who work in their daily activities with SysML.

This paper brings new reflections of a survey on what professionals think about SysML when used in practice. The survey received written comments about what those professionals think about SysML. A total of 163 participants professionals from 38 different countries left their written general comments on SysML. After reading each one of the comments from the participants, these comments were divided into positive or negative for the language. In view of this, 70 responses were categorized as positive and 72 as negative. Based on this categorization of comments, we performed a qualitative analysis of the positive and negative responses, and then proposed a cloud word for each type of statement.

2   Basics on SysML

The Systems Modeling Language (SysML) is a standard from the Object Management Group (OMG) proposed more than 15 years ago. It is an extended subset of UML that provides a graphical modeling language for designing complex systems, considering software, people, processes, hardware parts and other systems elements. The current version of the OMG SysML specification is SysML version 1.6.

SysML supports the specification, analysis, design, verification, and validation of a broad range of systems, allowing one to model from different perspectives, such as behavior, structure or requirement [16]. According to the International Standard Document of the Systems Modeling Language [18], SysML diagrams contain elements named concrete syntax, which represents elements of the model such as activities, blocks and associations.

Different from UML, SysML involves modeling blocks instead of modeling classes, accordingly providing a vocabulary that is more suitable for Systems Engineering than considering only its software counterpart [15]. However, the compatibility between these two languages can facilitate the integration of the disciplines of Software Engineering and Systems [24].

SysML offers new language elements in relation to UML, such as value types, quantity types, as well as the opportunity to describe the functionality of continuous systems [3]. The fact that SysML establishes well-integrated architectural descriptions [12], makes it possible to define and visualize the complexity of a system from different, well-defined and restricted points of view, without losing sight of the complete whole or the need for details.

SysML provides 9 diagrams, 4 of them are similar with others from UML: Use Case, Sequence, State Machine and Package Diagram. Another 3 diagrams are modified to be consistent with the SysML extensions, they are Activity, Block Definition and Internal Block diagrams. Finally, 2 SysML diagrams are new in relation to UML, the Requirements and the Parameter Diagrams [18].

SysML consists of four pillars [26]: Structure, Behavior, Requirements and Parametric Diagram, which allow several views of the system design. The system structure view mainly describes the system hierarchy (Block Definition diagram) and the interconnections between its parts (Internal Block diagram). The Package diagram, which is used to organize a model, also belongs to the structure view. The Parametric diagram provides system property values, such as performance and reliability.

Behavior diagrams declare the sequence of events and activities that a system performs, which includes Use Case diagram, Activity diagram, Sequence diagram and State Machine diagram. Behavior diagrams integrate the specification and design model with engineering analysis models. The Requirements diagram captures requirements hierarchies and allows them to be linked to other parts of the model.

Relevant activities within the life cycle of the system in which SysML can be used are Communication with stakeholders, which can be performed through the Use Case and Requirements diagrams, where the requirements can be graphically visualized.

The effective use of SysML improves the knowledge of the system, through the application of visual models, facilitating the understanding and definition of patterns. Model execution and verification, which are made possible through transformations of semi-formal SysML diagrams (Sequence, State Machine, Activity Diagrams) to a formal model, mainly assisting in the discovery of design problems. SysML models are useful to document design decisions, which facilitates future maintenance to the system. Considering that changes in a system become necessary, the language becomes useful to meet such changes and even carry out the reengineering of legacy systems.

3   Motivation

Studies found in the literature about SysML bring in their discussions and considerations points considered as positive and negative for the language. However, most of these studies are specific to a domain, or only consider toy examples, or even do not evaluate SysML as a modeling language in their examples.

In [12], the authors claim that well-defined modeling languages such as SysML can increase the ability to assess systems engineering in general and thus provide support in a more accurate way of verifying its value. In addition, they consider that the maturity and breadth of SysML applications are still limited, even though the trend indicates the continuity for its increasing use.

As SysML diagrams do not follow strict formal semantics [2], the accuracy of the description of SysML models cannot be easily verified. Thus, at least two approaches can be followed here. First one is the formalization of SysML [1]. Second, is the combination and/or transformation of SysML diagrams to formal methods [19,20]. Both approaches have been followed by some researchers, but still need further evaluation.

In [6], the authors stated that, through a SysML profile, it is possible to have greater traceability and integration, in addition to greater consistency between safety information and system design information and can assist in communicating this information to interested parties.

As SysML is a language and not a methodology, it is expected that SysML can be incorporated into an organization's development process without much difficulty [24]. In addition, the authors point out as a facilitator the fact that SysML is based on UML, which is a popularly known and used language.

Although SysML is well established as a modeling language for designing, analyzing and verifying complex systems, many researchers customize the language for their purposes and therefore define their own profiles, since SysML seems still too generic for some domain-specific tasks. Nevertheless, SysML lacks operational semantics, although some approaches aim to bridge this gap by combining SysML with formal methods [11,27].

4   Methodology

The results of this research were obtained through a survey which main objective was to seek quantitative and qualitative information on the use of SysML all around the world. The survey was conducted online, through Google Forms, and was available between the months of November 2020 and February 2021.

To reach the largest possible number of SysML users, we first performed a search through Google Scholar to identify the 100 most relevant works in this research field. Therefore, after removing the repetitions, a survey was sent by email to each one of the authors of these articles. For another source of data, the questionnaire was published in groups of the social network LinkedIn which are related to SysML. The most important considered groups were INCOSE, SysML User Group and Systems Engineers.

The survey was also sent by direct message to professionals who present among the skills of their LinkedIn profile the term "SysML". In the message sent, we included the request for participants to invite other professionals from their network of friends and acquaintances, thus aiming to reach a new and larger network of invited people. That technique is known as Snowball Sampling [5].

Participants were asked to leave, in a non-mandatory way, a general comment on SysML. The comment sought to identify, from the point of view of industry professionals, what are their motivations for using SysML, expectations about SysML's future, in addition to the flaws and benefits perceived by them when using SysML.

5 Categorization of the Survey

The survey received responses from 344 professionals from 38 different countries. 163 participants left their written general comments on SysML. After reading each one of the comments from the participants, these comments were divided into positive or negative for the language. In view of this, 70 responses were categorized as positive and 72 as negative. Another 45 responses were discarded because they did not contain relevant information to the research. Based on this categorization of comments, we performed a qualitative analysis of the positive and negative responses.

Participants from the following 38 countries (Fig. 1): Argentina, Australia, Austria, Belgium, Brazil, Canada, China, Colombia, Czech Republic, England, France, Germany, Greece, India, Iran, Ireland, Italy, Japan, Luxembourg, Mexico, Norway, Pakistan, Poland, Portugal, Romania, Saudi Arabia, Singapore, South Africa, South Korea, Spain, Sweden, Switzerland, Thailand, The Netherlands, Tunisia, Turkey, United Kingdom and United States answered the survey.

The most common undergraduate degree among participants is Electrical or Electronic Engineering (29%), followed by Mechanical Engineering (14%) and Computer Science (9%). Computer Engineering (6%), Aerospace Engineering (6%) and Systems Engineering (5%), although to a lesser extent, were also mentioned.

Master's is the most popular academic degree, selected by 61% of the participants. Bachelor's and Doctor's degrees are also often mentioned, selected by 19%–17% of participants.

Most participants (34%) have at least 2 years of experience with SysML, while another 33% have 3 to 6 years of experience, 19% have 10+ years and 14% have 7 to 9 years of experience.

From the categorization of the survey responses, it is possible to identify common points in relation to the comments of professionals in the area in relation to SysML and, thus, perform a qualitative analysis of these data. Next, data will be presented by category, both positive or negative.

Europe	France	47
	Germany, United Kingdom	32
	The Netherlands	13
	England	11
	Spain	10
	Italy, Sweden	8
	Romania	6
	Poland	5
	Switzerland	4
	Portugal	2
	Austria, Belgium, Czech Republic, Greece, Ireland, Luxembourg, Norway	1
America	United States	41
	Brazil	22
	Canada	5
	Mexico	5
	Argentina	2
	Colombia	1
Asia	India	33
	Turkey	16
	Iran, Japan, South Corea	4
	Pakistan	3
	Singapore	2
	China, Saudi Arabia, Thailand	1
Oceania	Australia	11
Africa	South Africa, Tunisia	1

Fig. 1. Countries where the participants work.

5.1 Positive Comments

It is possible to identify, in most of the positive responses, statements about the usefulness and benefits of SysML. Most participants describe the language as powerful, detailed, consistent and broad.

Some of the interviewees point out the importance of SysML within the area of Systems Engineering. Modeling of systems architecture in SysML is pointed out by many as ideal. In addition, the Requirements Diagram also stands out for allowing requirements specification and traceability, enabling the identification of possible future design problems.

As for the modeling possibilities using SysML, most participants affirm that the language allows to model different types of systems, from software to hardware, which confirms SysML characteristics. It is also possible to model the system completely and in detail, covering the entire development life cycle and describing the system from different points of view.

Many of the comments describe the benefits of SysML in terms of team communication through the diagrams. It is reported among the participants that SysML is an unequivocal means for communication between stakeholders, in addition to facilitating the integration of new participants in the development

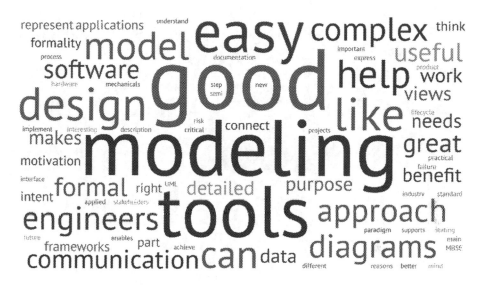

Fig. 2. Word cloud of positive comments.

team and allowing easy communication between professionals who have different functions.

Figure 2 depicts the word cloud for positive responses of the survey.

5.2 Negative Comments

Most of the participants highlighted the main negative point of SysML as its learning difficulty and complexity, especially for beginners and non-specialized people, with training in different areas of systems/software engineering. It was alleged that there is short experience in industry regarding to the language and that it requires a great amount of specific knowledge for its effective use, in addition to a steep learning curve.

Another highlight among the comments concerns the existing tools for modeling in SysML. Participants argue that the tools are expensive and difficult to use, in addition to having deficiencies such as the absence of design rules and support for analysis. There are still complaints about lack of updating in relation to the standard and lack of interchange of models between tools.

Simulation and validation of models in SysML were also criticized in some of the comments. Difficulties were identified in relation to the simulation and validation of the models. Respondents state that SysML's resources do not allow for the proper and efficient execution of these tasks. Some associate part of this difficulty also with limitations of the used tools.

For some participants, SysML diagrams can introduce many abstractions and complexity into a project, which are not needed. They also claim that a language such as SysML has an extensive and complicated set of rules to deal

Fig. 3. Word cloud of negative comments.

with and that the absence of a standardized modeling method has created many conflicting interpretations about the use of the language.

It is also noteworthy that many of SysML users are waiting for version 2.0. Some report that the expectation is that the new version will solve flaws and add improvements to the language, but some present concerns about migration to this new version.

Some other problems were pointed out to a lesser extent, such as difficulties with scalability, usability and traceability, flaws in parametric diagrams, lack of formality and adaptation to agile software models. In addition to impediments to its use in industry are the need for productivity and efficiency.

Figure 3 depicts the word cloud for negative responses of the survey.

6   Discussion

SysML has been increasingly used in academia and research environments in the past 15 years. A systematic mapping study on SysML was published recently, in which the authors present, among other results, the most prolific authors, most prominent conferences and scientific journals regarding the number of publications, most used SysML diagrams, and most common domains [29]. These results have mostly an academic focus.

Considering a systems life cycle, SysML has been considered as a modeling language for activities of Software/Systems Requirements Engineering [21–23] using both SysML Requirements and Use Cases diagrams, as well as for system design using SysML Block diagrams [28] and other behavioral diagrams [11]. SysML has also been considered as useful for Simulation [17]. There are even attempts on using SysML together with other modeling languages, tools and processes [7, 25].

This article carried out a qualitative analysis, through a survey, on what industry professionals think about SysML when used in practice. Through the collection and categorization of the comments received (positive and negative) it was possible to identify gaps and different perceptions about SysML.

Given the purpose of the language, the importance of SysML in the Systems Engineering area is recognized by the participants as ideal, and can be used to model different types of systems, in a complete and detailed way throughout the life cycle.

As an example, two comments considered positive are mentioned as follows.

"SysML is absolutely necessary to represent a system in all point of views. External analysis (needs architecture), functional architecture, logic architecture, and component architecture. This language is the most advanced I know to represent the way a system should work."

"SysML is one among the powerful languages existing to bring in the imagination of a systems engineer about the system and its corresponding interaction. It's more about the unfurl of the purpose of the system in accomplishing right goals and objectives, keeping in mind the perspective of not falling into the solution right away."

Because it is derived from UML, which is a widely known and used language, and shares some of its elements and diagrams, SysML is considered by many to be an easy-to-learn language, especially for users already familiar with UML. However, most comments were categorized as negative regarding this statement.

"Learning curve is too high for most engineers. Lack of standard frame work. Traceability between different stages of engineering as well as between different diagrams are a major concern."

"SysML is complex and hard to teach. To express simple concepts you often have to create lots of elements which is time consuming."

Therefore, further research should be performed on the subject of learning curve, effective use and every detail that can be considered when one wants to learn how to use SysML in a project. For future research, an evaluation can be performed on current books, tutorials, courses and so on.

Through the qualitative analysis carried out, it is possible to perceive that despite presenting great advantages in its use, SysML still presents some gaps that need to be studied and deepened so that the industry can expand its use and that more professionals recognize it as a valuable language.

There are even sentences with both positive and negative aspects. For instance, one individual wrote that "SysML as a modelling language is adequate to communicate the detailed system design though it is not easy to simulate a SysML model for quick validation. Maybe this is a flaw of the tools and not the language itself".

Sentences with positive and negative characterization are normal for SysML and also other modeling languages. It is common that, when using a modeling language for a project, one becomes an expert on the language. Thus, after an in depth knowledge of concepts, stereotypes, models and diagrams, one can characterize the benefits of using a modeling language, and can even avoid known flaws. For instance, in the mentioned case, it is clear that simulating SysML models is considered an issue, and then other modeling languages can be considered for simulation.

7   Conclusion

SysML has been considered as a modeling language for developing systems in the past 15 years, in many domains, both in industry and academia. From its first studies and applications, the language increased in popularity and importance. Currently in its 1.6 version, there are many books, courses, tools and case studies on SysML. Thus, a study such as the one described in this paper is necessary, in which the industry professionals describe what they think about using SysML in practice. Future works should also deal with comparison of SysML with other modeling languages in the context of systems engineering development.

In this paper, after distribution of a survey for 344 individuals who use SysML in industry, we received 163 responses on general comments about the use of SysML in industry. After reading all these comments, 142 were selected and further characterized as 70 positive and 72 negative responses. Based on these comments, we performed a qualitative analysis of the positive and negative responses, and then proposed a cloud word for each type of statement. Some entries in the survey bring positive comments, as well as negative aspects of SysML. In this case, each comment is counted two times, one as positive and one as negative.

One important result is that SysML, as a general purpose modeling language for systems applications, is considered useful for some activities and less important/useful for other activities. This means that SysML, as a modeling language, presents flaws and benefits, and is not different from many other modeling languages proposed in the past 50 years, As a matter of fact, well-known negative aspects of SysML such as, for instance, lack of formality or high complexity of models, can be addressed, for instance, by creating extensions and formal profiles for the language, as well as integrating SysML with other modeling languages.

Further research should be performed on the subject of difficulty of using SysML in practice, including its learning curve, comparison to other modeling languages, effective use and every detail that can be considered when one wants to learn how to use SysML in a project.

Acknowledgments. This study was financed by Fundação de Apoio à Pesquisa e à Inovação Tecnológica do Estado de Sergipe (FAPITEC/SE).

References

1. Ando, T., Yatsu, H., Kong, W., Hisazumi, K., Fukuda, A.: Formalization and model checking of SysML state machine diagrams by CSP#. In: Murgante, B., et al. (eds.) ICCSA 2013. LNCS, vol. 7973, pp. 114–127. Springer, Heidelberg (2013). https://doi.org/10.1007/978-3-642-39646-5_9
2. Ando, T., Yatsu, H., Kong, W., Hisazumi, K., Fukuda, A.: Translation rules of SysML state machine diagrams into CSP# toward formal model checking. Int. J. Web Inf. Syst. (2014)
3. Apvrille, L., de Saqui-Sannes, P.: Static analysis techniques to verify mutual exclusion situations within SysML models. In: Khendek, F., Toeroe, M., Gherbi, A., Reed, R. (eds.) SDL 2013. LNCS, vol. 7916, pp. 91–106. Springer, Heidelberg (2013). https://doi.org/10.1007/978-3-642-38911-5_6
4. Baduel, R., Chami, M., Bruel, J.-M., Ober, I.: SysML models verification and validation in an industrial context: challenges and experimentation. In: Pierantonio, A., Trujillo, S. (eds.) ECMFA 2018. LNCS, vol. 10890, pp. 132–146. Springer, Cham (2018). https://doi.org/10.1007/978-3-319-92997-2_9
5. Baltes, S., Ralph, P.: Sampling in software engineering research: a critical review and guidelines. CoRR abs/2002.07764 (2020)
6. Biggs, G., Sakamoto, T., Kotoku, T.: A profile and tool for modelling safety information with design information in SysML. Softw. Syst. Model. 15(1), 147–178 (2016). https://doi.org/10.1007/s10270-014-0400-x
7. Bouwman, M., Luttik, B., van der Wal, D.: A formalisation of SysML state machines in mCRL2. In: Peters, K., Willemse, T.A.C. (eds.) FORTE 2021. LNCS, vol. 12719, pp. 42–59. Springer, Cham (2021). https://doi.org/10.1007/978-3-030-78089-0_3
8. Cawasji, K.A., Baras, J.S.: SysML executable model of an energy-efficient house and trade-off analysis. In: 2018 IEEE International Systems Engineering Symposium (ISSE), pp. 1–8 (2018)
9. Gomez, C., DeAntoni, J., Mallet, F.: Multi-view power modeling based on UML, MARTE and SysML. In: 2012 38th Euromicro Conference on Software Engineering and Advanced Applications, pp. 17–20 (2012)
10. Gruber, K., Huemer, J., Zimmermann, A., Maschotta, R.: Integrated description of functional and non-functional requirements for automotive systems design using SysML. In: 2017 7th IEEE International Conference on System Engineering and Technology (ICSET), pp. 27–31 (2017)
11. Huang, E., McGinnis, L.F., Mitchell, S.W.: Verifying SysML activity diagrams using formal transformation to petri nets. Syst. Eng. 23(1), 118–135 (2020)
12. Huldt, T., Stenius, I.: State-of-practice survey of model-based systems engineering. Syst. Eng. 22(2), 134–145 (2019)
13. Kotronis, C., Nikolaidou, M., Kapos, G., Tsadimas, A., Dalakas, V., Anagnostopoulos, D.: Employing SysML to model and explore levels-of-service: the case of passenger comfort in railway transportation systems. Syst. Eng. 23(1), 82–99 (2020)
14. Kruus, H., Robal, T., Jervan, G.: Teaching modeling in SysML/UML and problems encountered. In: 2014 25th EAEEIE Annual Conference (EAEEIE), pp. 33–36 (2014)
15. Lopata, A., Ambraziūnas, M., Veitaitė, I., Masteika, S., Butleris, R.: SysML and UML models usage in knowledge based MDA process. Elektronika ir elektrotechnika 21(2), 50–57 (2015)

16. Mori, M., Ceccarelli, A., Lollini, P., Frömel, B., Brancati, F., Bondavalli, A.: Systems-of-systems modeling using a comprehensive viewpoint-based SysML profile. J. Softw.: Evol. Process **30**(3), e1878 (2018)

17. Nigischer, C., Bougain, S., Riegler, R., Stanek, H.P., Grafinger, M.: Multi-domain simulation utilizing SysML: state of the art and future perspectives. Procedia CIRP **100**, 319–324 (2021). 31st CIRP Design Conference 2021 (CIRP Design 2021)

18. OMG: OMG Systems Modeling Language (OMG SysML), Version 1.6 (2019)

19. Rahim, M., Boukala-Ioualalen, M., Hammad, A.: Hierarchical colored petri nets for the verification of SysML designs- activity-based slicing approach. In: Senouci, M.R., Boudaren, M.E.Y., Sebbak, F., Mataoui, M. (eds.) CSA 2020. LNNS, vol. 199, pp. 131–142. Springer, Cham (2021). https://doi.org/10.1007/978-3-030-69418-0_12

20. Rahim, M., Hammad, A., Boukala-Ioualalen, M.: Towards the formal verification of sysml specifications: translation of activity diagrams into modular petri nets. In: 2015 3rd International Conference on Applied Computing and Information Technology/2nd International Conference on Computational Science and Intelligence, pp. 509–516 (2015). https://doi.org/10.1109/ACIT-CSI.2015.97

21. Ribeiro, F.G.C., Misra, S., Soares, M.S.: Application of an extended SysML requirements diagram to model real-time control systems. In: Murgante, B., et al. (eds.) ICCSA 2013. LNCS, vol. 7973, pp. 70–81. Springer, Heidelberg (2013). https://doi.org/10.1007/978-3-642-39646-5_6

22. Ribeiro, F.G.C., Pereira, C.E., Rettberg, A., Soares, M.S.: Model-based requirements specification of real-time systems with UML. SysML MARTE. Softw. Syst. Model. **17**(1), 343–361 (2018). https://doi.org/10.1007/s10270-016-0525-1

23. Soares, M.S., Cioquetta, D.S.: Analysis of techniques for documenting user requirements. In: Murgante, B., Gervasi, O., Misra, S., Nedjah, N., Rocha, A.M.A.C., Taniar, D., Apduhan, B.O. (eds.) ICCSA 2012. LNCS, vol. 7336, pp. 16–28. Springer, Heidelberg (2012). https://doi.org/10.1007/978-3-642-31128-4_2

24. Soares, M.S., Vrancken, J.L.: Model-driven user requirements specification using SysML. JSW **3**(6), 57–68 (2008)

25. Souza, L.S., Misra, S., Soares, M.S.: SmartCitySysML: a SysML profile for smart cities applications. In: Gervasi, O., et al. (eds.) ICCSA 2020. LNCS, vol. 12254, pp. 383–397. Springer, Cham (2020). https://doi.org/10.1007/978-3-030-58817-5_29

26. Wan, W., Cheong, H., Li, W., Zeng, Y., Iorio, F.: Automated transformation of design text ROM diagram into SysML models. Adv. Eng. Inform. **30**(3), 585–603 (2016)

27. Wang, H., Zhong, D., Zhao, T., Ren, F.: Integrating model checking with SysML in complex system safety analysis. IEEE Access **7**, 16561–16571 (2019)

28. Waseem, M., Sadiq, M.U.: Application of model-based systems engineering in small satellite conceptual design-a SysML approach. IEEE Aerosp. Electron. Syst. Mag. **33**(4), 24–34 (2018)

29. Wolny, S., Mazak, A., Carpella, C., Geist, V., Wimmer, M.: Thirteen years of SysML: a systematic mapping study. Softw. Syst. Model. **19**(1), 111–169 (2020). https://doi.org/10.1007/s10270-019-00735-y

Data Selection as an Alternative to Quality Estimation in Self-Learning for Low Resource Neural Machine Translation

Idris Abdulmumin[1,2]([envelope]) [ORCID], Bashir Shehu Galadanci[2], Ibrahim Said Ahmad[2] [ORCID], and Rabiu Ibrahim Abdullahi[1]

[1] Ahmadu Bello University, Zaria, Kaduna, Nigeria
{iabdulmumin,raibrahim}@abu.edu.ng
[2] Bayero University, Kano, Kano, Nigeria
{bsgaladanci.se,isahmad.it}@buk.edu.ng

Abstract. For many languages, the lack of sufficient parallel data to train translation models have resulted in using the monolingual data, source and target, through self-learning and back-translation respectively. Most works that implemented the self-learning approach utilized a quality estimation system to ensure that the resulting additional training data is of sufficient quality to improve the model. However, the quality estimation system may not be available for many low resource languages, restricting the implementation of such approach to a very few. This work proposes the utilization of the data selection technique as an alternative to quality estimation. The approach will ensure that the models will learn only from the data that is closer to the domain of the test set, improving the performance of the translation models. While this approach is applicable to many, if not all, languages, we obtained similar and, in some implementations, even better results (+0.53 BLEU) than the self-training approach that was implemented using the quality estimation system on low resource IWSLT'14 English-German dataset. We also showed that the proposed approach can be used to improve the performance of the back-translation approach, gaining +1.79 and +0.23 over standard back-translation and self-learning with quality estimation enhanced back-translation respectively.

Keywords: Data selection · Self-learning · Quality estimation · Self-training · Neural machine translation · Machine translation

1 Introduction

Neural machine translation (NMT) [4,27,40] is the current state-of-the-art approach for building automatic translation systems [14,30]. Though it is simple,

This work is conducted as part of a PhD research supported by the NITDEF 2018.

O. Gervasi et al. (Eds.): ICCSA 2021, LNCS 12957, pp. 311–326, 2021.
https://doi.org/10.1007/978-3-030-87013-3_24

it out-performs other statistical machine translation approaches provided the parallel training data between the languages is sufficiently large [26,45]. The technique relies only on this huge parallel data to learn the probability of mapping sentences to the target language given a set of sentences in the source language [42]. This data is not only scarce between many languages but it is very expensive to create. This has influenced many research works that were aimed at investigating the possibility of applying other techniques and readily available resources to improve the performance of such translation models. These techniques include using other high resource languages through transfer learning [12,25,28,45] and the readily available large amounts of monolingual data through forward translation or self-training [2,37,43], dual learning [18] and back-translation [9,14,20,29,35].

The monolingual data in the source or target or both of the languages have been used in various studies to enhance the performance of models that are built for automatic machine translation, especially in settings that are considered low resource – where the training data is not sufficient to train models that are of acceptable standard. Currey et al. [11] proposed using a (moderately changed [8]) duplicate of the target sentences as the corresponding source sentences. Sennrich et al. [34] proposed using the back-translation of the target sentences that are generated with an intermediary reverse model while Ueffing [39] and Zhang and Zong [43] proposed using the forward translation approach to self-train the generating model. He et al. [18] used target and source language monolingual data through a dual learning approach and Gulcehre et al. [17] infused a language model that was trained on monolingual data to ensure that the decoder produce fluent translations.

The self-training (or self-learning) approach uses the translations of the monolingual source data to improve the performance of the generating model. The approach has been used in both phrase-based statistical [37,39] and neural machine translation systems [2,43]. The approach relies on the usually large amounts of readily available source language monolingual data to better translation models. The authentic parallel training data – which is scanty in low resource set-ups – is used to train a translation model. The additional pseudo-parallel training data is then used to generated by translating the available monolingual data using the model. The synthetic data is then paired with the available authentic data and the resulting large dataset is used to retrain an improved forward translation model. The synthetic data is often infested with mistakes. This is because the generating model is in itself not qualitative enough to generate error-free translations.

Earlier implementations of the approach, especially in [37,39], relied on a quality estimation system to ensure that the quality of the synthetic data that is generated is fit enough to improve the performance of the generating model. Although the work of Abdulmumin et al. [2] have shown that the generating model is capable of benefiting from the synthetic data even without estimating the quality, extensive studies by Abdulmumin et al. [3] (see implementation in Fig. 1) have found that models are better off when implemented with the

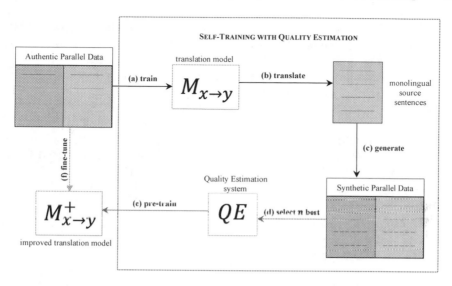

Fig. 1. Self-learning with quality estimation for improved machine translation models [3].

system. For most of low resource languages, the quality estimation system is not existent and so is the data for training such systems. This will, therefore, limit the application of the self-learning approach in such set-ups.

This work, therefore, proposes an alternative technique of generating a synthetic data that best benefits the generating model than the whole of the synthetic data. As with the principle of using the quality estimation to only select data that is considered best for the generating model, more (synthetic) data may not necessarily mean a better model [15]. The proposed approach utilizes a data selection algorithm to select a fraction of the monolingual data that is closest in domain to the source-side of the test set. This data is then translated and used as the additional data for the self-training approach. The approach is similar to the data selection described in Poncelas et al. [32] for back-translation but instead of comparing the domain of the synthetic data with that of the target-side of the test set (which can only be done after translating all of the available monolingual sentences), we compare the domain of the monolingual data with that of the source-side of the test set before translating. This will not only save translation time but it will also ensure that the domain match is as accurate as possible because all of the data used is authentic. Therefore, in this work, the following contributions are made:

- instead of relying on a quality estimation system that is only available for a few languages for implementing the more effective self-training approach, we propose a new alternative that relies on the more common data selection algorithms for selecting the more appropriate monolingual data,

– we applied data selection in self-learning in a way that ensures both the monolingual and source-side of the test data are natural, ensuring the domain match is as accurate as possible,
– we proposed a faster approach, ensuring that only a subset of the monolingual data is selected and translated instead of translating all of the available monolingual data and selecting only a subset for self-learning,
– we showed that the proposed technique is not only capable of producing comparable results with that of the self-training approach that is implemented with quality estimation but that in some implementations, it yielded better performances, and
– we successfully applied the proposed approach on low resource IWSLT 14 German- English data, improving over baseline and various implementations of the self-learning approaches.

2   Related Works

In this section, we present related works on self-training in automatic machine translation.

Ueffing [39] introduces self-learning in machine translation as an approach that utilizes the translations of a model for improving the performance of the generating model. In the proposed approach, sentences in the source language are translated and their quality is determined using a quality estimation system. The sentences whose quality is below a set minimum are discarded and then, the remaining generated parallel data is used to better the model.

Zhang and Zong [43] used the approach, naming it forward translation, in NMT for improving the encoder side of the model. The authors claimed that when the training data consists of an authentic source and synthetic target, only the model's encoder is improved because, they say, the impurities in the synthetic data will deteriorate the decoder's performance. To mitigate this, the authors freezes the parameters of the decoder when training on the synthetic data and only update them when the training instance is authentic.

Specia and Shah [37] propose an iterative version of [39]. Instead of discarding the low quality synthetic sentences, the monolingual source sentences whose translations are not selected during the self-learning approach are reserved and used in subsequent iterations to continue improving the model. The first iteration in this approach selects the top n translations using a quality estimation system for retrain the generating model. The rest of the iterations utilizes the same self-training approach but using the rest of the unselected monolingual sentences.

Abdulmumin et al. [2] investigated using the approach without data cleaning (quality estimation) to enhance the performance of an intermediary (backward) model in the back-translation approach. The proposed method was still found to benefit the model. But further studies in [3] has found that using quality estimation ensures a more effective self-learning approach.

The studies above showed benefits of using a quality estimation system to determine the synthetic data that is considered best for improving the performance of the generating model. The lack of such models can greatly affect the

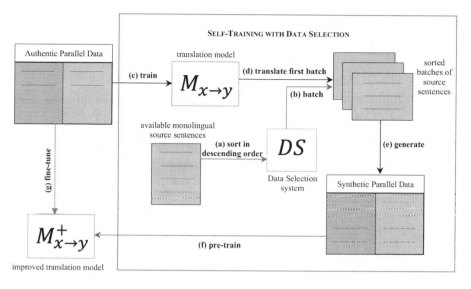

Fig. 2. Proposed self-learning with data selection for improved machine translation models.

rather efficient performance of such models. An alternative system that can produce similar or even better results is needed therefore in applying the self-learning approach especially in low resource languages.

3   Methodology

This section presents the proposed self-learning with data selection approach.

3.1   Overview of the Proposed Approach

The proposed approach is illustrated in Fig. 2 and presented in Algorithm 1. Our approach requires the monolingual source sentences, $X = \{(x^{(p)})\}_{p=1}^{P}$, the authentic parallel training data, $D = \{(x^{(q)}, y^{(q)})\}_{q=1}^{Q}$ and the test set, $T = \{(x^{(r)}, y^{(r)})\}_{r=1}^{R}$. Firstly, we used a data selection system to rank the monolingual source sentences according to how close their domain is to that of the source-side of the test set, $x^{(r)} \in T$. Afterwards, we selected the top a sentences from these sorted sentences. Secondly, a source-to-target model, $M_{x \rightarrow y}$, was trained on the authentic parallel data, D. Thirdly, the forward model was used to generate the synthetic parallel data, $D' = \{(x^{(a)}, y^{(a)})\}_{a=1}^{A}$, by translating the selected monolingual source data, X^a. Lastly, the resulting synthetic data is then used to enhance the performance of the forward model through pre-training and fine-tuning it on the synthetic and authentic data respectively. This method of training has been shown to best benefit any model that is trained on

---

Algorithm 1. Self-Learning with Data Selection

Input: Monolingual source data, $X = \{(x^{(p)})\}_{p=1}^{P}$, Authentic training data, $D = \{(x^{(q)}, y^{(q)})\}_{q=1}^{Q}$, and the Test set, $T = \{(x^{(r)}, y^{(r)})\}_{r=1}^{R}$.

1: **procedure** DATA SELECTION
2:    Using a Data Selection algorithm, sort X, from closest to farthest, based on how close the domain of $x^{(p)} \in X$ is to the domain of $x^{(r)} \in T$;
3:    Let X^a = the closest a monolingual source sentences;
4: **end procedure**
5: **procedure** SELF-LEARNING
6:    Train a forward model $M_{x \to y}$ on the authentic parallel data, D;
7:    Let $D' = \{(x^{(a)}, y^{(a)})\}_{a=1}^{A}$ = the synthetic data generated by $M_{x \to y}$, for all $x \in X^a$;
8:    Pretrain a model $M_{x \to y}^{+}$ on the synthetic parallel data, D';
9:    Finetune the forward model $M_{x \to y}^{+}$ on the authentic parallel data, D;
10: **end procedure**

Output: improved translation model, $M_{x \to y}$

---

synthetic and authentic data [2,3]. This approach is similar to the implementations of the self-learning approach in [3,39].

Alternatively, the self-learning with quality estimation was implemented in [37] to intelligently utilize all of the available data through an iterative process. As explained in Sect. 2, during the first iteration, the whole monolingual data is translated using a baseline model. Afterwards, a quality estimation model is used to select a subset (top n) of the monolingual data that is considered to be the most accurate. This data is then added to the training data to self-train an improved forward model. In the second iteration, the improved forward model is used to generate the synthetic data using all of the monolingual data whose translations were not previously selected and the best n of this batch are selected for the third iteration. This process is repeated until all of the monolingual data are used to train a better forward model. In this work, we implemented the same approach but instead of using the quality estimation system, we used the data selection algorithm to first sort and batch the monolingual data. The first batch was used for self-learning in the first iteration and subsequently, the remaining batches were used in each of the corresponding iterations to further improve the quality of the forward model.

We also implemented an iterative approach that uses only the closest (first) batch to continue to improve the forward model instead of all of the monolingual data. After self-training the forward model on the first batch, it was used to translate the same first batch and the process was repeated over some iterations. This was also implemented with the quality estimation system to compare the performances of both systems. The synthetic data that is estimated to be the best translated data was used in each of the iterations to further improve the model.

Table 1. The data used

Data	Train			Dev	Test
	Sentences	Words (vocab)			
IWSLT '14 German-English	153,348	En	De	6,970	6,750
		2,837,240 (50,045)	2,688,387 (103,796)		
WMT '14 German-English – Mono English	399,951	9,918,380 (266,640)		–	–

3.2 Data

The data used in this work is the IWSLT 2014 De-En (German-English) shared translation task [10]. We used the code provided by Ranzato et al. [33] for cleanup and splitting of the train, dev and test datasets. This resulted in 153,348, 6,970 and 6,750 parallel sentences respectively. The data statistics is shown in Table 1. For the additional monolingual data, we randomly selected and used 399,951 English monolingual sentences from the pre-processed [27] WMT 2014 German-English translation task [7]. For tokenization, we trained a byte pair encoding (BPE) [36] with 10,000 merge operations on the training dataset before applying it on the training, evaluation (dev) and test sets. For the self-training, a joint BPE is learned on the mixture of the synthetic and authentic parallel data. Afterwards, the training vocabulary was built on the mixed dataset.

3.3 Experimental Set-Up

In this work, a unidirectional Long Short-Term Memory (LSTM) [19], a recurrent neural network (RNN) machine translation (RNMT) architecture, with Luong attention [27] was used to built the encoder-decoder models. This architecture is summarized below. Our proposed method can be implemented using other architectures such as the Transformer [13,40] and the convolutional NMT (CNMT) [16,41]. The Neural Machine Translation (NMT), a sequence-to-sequence system, is made up of a neural encoder and another neural decoder for modeling the conditional probability of an output sentence given a sentence in the source language [4,27,38]. The encoder encodes the input sentence into a set of vectors while the decoder decodes these vectors and the previously predicted words into the desired output language, word by word, through an attention mechanism. Bahdanau et al. [4] proposed the attention mechanism for keeping track of context in longer sentences.

For building the models, we used the same settings as in [2]. This is the NMTSmallV1 configuration of the OpenNMT-tf [24] framework, which is implemented using the TensorFlow [1]. This consists of a 2-layer unidirectional LSTM encoder-decoder model with Luong attention [27]. Each of the encoder and decoder is made up of 512 hidden units. We used the Adam optimizer [23], a training batch size of 64 and a static learning rate of 0.0002. The models were

Table 2. Performances of the baseline and self-trained models with data selection and quality estimation for German-English NMT.

Checkpoint	Baseline	Self-training					
		+ synth-all [2]		+ synth-qe [3]		+ synth-ds	
		Pretrain	Finetune	Pretrain	Finetune	Pretrain	Finetune
Best	10.03	6.02	20.80	6.24	23.22	7.35	23.07
(training step)	(65k)	(75k)	(125k)	(65k)	(165k)	(55k)	(140k)
Average	10.25	6.01	21.31	6.23	23.66	7.16	23.34

evaluated, using the bi-lingual evaluation understudy (BLEU) [31], on the dev set after each 5,000 steps. The training of each model was stopped when the maximum improvement observed is not more than 0.2 BLEU after evaluating four successive checkpoints. Unless stated otherwise, the training of all of the models was discontinued after the stopping condition is reached and for getting the optimal performance in most of the models, the average model is computed on the last 8 checkpoints. Since a joint BPE was used and the vocabulary was learned on the mixture of the two data, only the training data is changed during fine-tuning.

For quality estimation, we used the pre-trained Predictor-Estimator [22] QE model that was provided in the OpenKiwi's [21] quality estimation tutorial for synthetic German sentences. The model is based on an RNN architecture that, for estimating the quality of synthetic sentences, uses multi-level task learning. The model was trained using a neural predictor and neural quality estimation models that were jointly learnt using stack propagation [44]. For implementing the monolingual data selection, the frequency decay algorithm, FDA [5,6], was used. This algorithm uses the source-side of the test set as seed to rank, according to n-grams, the monolingual sentences due to their closeness to the domain of the test set.

4   Experiments and Results

Firstly, we used the data selection algorithm to sort the monolingual data from the closest to the farthest in their domain to the test set. The closest one-third of the monolingual sentences were selected for implementing the proposed self-learning with data selection approach. We then trained a baseline forward model (En-De) on the available parallel data for 80,000 steps. This model achieved the best single-checkpoint performance of 10.03 BLEU at the $65,000^{th}$ step. The best performance was obtained after averaging the last 8 checkpoints – 10.25 BLEU. This, taken as the baseline model, was used to generate the synthetic data for implementing the self-learning approaches. The performances of these improved forward models and the baseline are shown in Table 2.

Table 3. Performances of the iterative self-training with quality estimation as implemented in [37] and the same implementation of the self-learning approach but with data selection, utilizing all of the monolingual data for English-German NMT.

Method	Iteration	Performance of best checkpoint (training step)		Average (last 8 checkpoints)	
		Pretrain	Finetune	Pretrain	Finetune
SL + QE [3]	0	6.24 (65k)	23.22 (165k)	6.23	23.66
	1	16.18 (105k)	23.41 (200k)	15.88	23.62
	2	19.59 (155k)	23.69 (210k)	19.83	24.05
SL + DS	0	7.35 (55k)	23.07 (140k)	7.16	23.34
	1	20.42 (115k)	24.01 (170k)	20.54	24.24
	2	21.39 (150k)	24.03 (215k)	21.45	24.31

After the selected data was translated using the baseline forward model, the resulting synthetic data was labeled *synth-ds*. The baseline model was also used to generate *synth-all*, by translating all of the available monolingual data. The quality estimation system was used to estimate the accuracy of *synth-all*. The best one-third of this synthetic data was selected and labeled *synth-qe*. Each of *synth-ds* and *synth-qe* consisted of 133,295 parallel sentences, with 45,212 sentences found in both. Finally, the authentic parallel data was used with each of the three synthetic data were used to self-train improved forward models.

For the forward model that uses *synth-all*, it stopped training during the first phase – pre-training – at the $85,000^{th}$ training step, achieving the best single-checkpoint performance of 6.02 BLEU and an average checkpoint with 6.01 BLEU. Fine-tuning on the authentic parallel data resulted in an improvement of +14.78 and +15.30 BLEUs (20.80 and 21.31 BLEUs) for best and average checkpoints respectively. Altogether, the model was trained for 165,000 training steps. This model achieved a better performance than the baseline by 11.06 BLEU.

With *synth-qe*, the forward translation model achieved the best performance of 23.66 BLEU after averaging the last 8 checkpoints. This translates to +2.35 BLEU improvement over the forward model that was self-trained on *synth-all*. However, using *synth-ds* resulted in the overall best performance of 23.34 BLEU. This −0.32 BLEU less than that of the former model that was trained using *synth-qe*.

The performances of the iterative approaches with quality estimation and data selection are presented in Table 3. It can be observed that although the implementation using the quality estimation system outperformed the data selection at the self-learning stage, the later catches up and even outperformed the former at all stages of the iterations, achieving +0.62 and +0.26 respectively after the first and second iterations. The implementation with data selection even

Table 4. Performances of the iterative self-training with quality estimation and data selection approaches, utilizing only the best monolingual data for English-German NMT.

Method	Iteration	Performance of best checkpoint (training step)		Average (last 8 checkpoints)	
		Pretrain	Finetune	Pretrain	Finetune
+ QE	0	6.24 (65k)	23.22 (165k)	6.23	23.66
	1	18.71 (105k)	23.84 (160k)	18.82	24.10
	2	19.94 (110k)	23.79 (185k)	19.90	24.09
+ DS	0	7.35 (55k)	23.07 (140k)	7.16	23.34
	1	20.51 (95k)	24.05 (155k)	20.51	24.33
	2	21.72 (115k)	24.23 (185k)	21.87	24.62

Table 5. Time taken to estimate synthetic data quality when using all of the monolingual data and when using only the best monolingual data vs the time taken for sorting the monolingual data based on the domain closeness to the test set.

Methods	Iteration	Time taken
QE (all)	sl	31 h, 1 min and 29 s
	1	22 h, 54 min and 53 s
	2	–
QE (best)	sl	31 h, 1 min and 29 s
	1	30 h, 28 min and 4 s
	2	34 h, 42 min and 38 s
DS	–	0 h, 1 min and 7 s

pre-trained a forward model on the synthetic data that outperformed (+0.08 BLEU) the forward model that was self-trained on *synth-all* – see Tables 2 and 3.

Having selected from the monolingual data the closest sentences in domain to the test set, the same set was used in all of the iterations. The same subset of the monolingual data that was selected as *synth-qe* was also re-translated using the improved forward models in all of the iterations to compare. The performances of the resulting forward models are shown in Table 4. It can be observed also that the self-learning that was implemented with data selection achieved superior performance in all of the iterations, gaining +0.23 and +0.53 after the first and second iterations respectively.

Although all of the approaches produced similar performances, Table 5 shows that using data selection was faster especially during the data selection vs the quality estimation stage. On a computer with 2.30GHz frequency Intel CPU and 12GB RAM, the time it took to estimate the quality of the synthetic sentences when implementing the approach that utilizes all of the available synthetic data was 53 h, 56 min and 22 s (well over 2 days), while the approach that utilizes only

Table 6. Performances of the various forward models with and without the standard or the various enhanced back-translation approaches for German-English NMT. All of the methods were implemented using the pre-training and fine-tuning except the baseline model which was just indicated to compare performance.

Method	Performance of best checkpoint (training step)		Average (last 8 checkpoints)	
	Pretrain	Finetune	Pretrain	Finetune
Baseline [3]	–	20.30 (75k)	–	20.95
Standard BT [3]	5.43 (60k)	28.31 (155k)	5.13	28.83
SL + QE [3]	19.38 (160k)	30.01 (225k)	19.37	30.39
SL + DS	19.62 (95k)	30.21 (170k)	19.31	30.42
Iterative SL + QE (all mono) [3]	17.97 (120k)	29.55 (185k)	18.09	30.05
Iterative SL + DS (all mono)	19.21 (135k)	30.15 (190k)	19.31	30.62
Iterative SL + QE (best mono)	19.43 (115k)	30.12 (185k)	19.65	30.15
Iterative SL + DS (best mono)	19.58 (150k)	29.93 (215k)	19.63	30.10

the best synthetic data was 96 h, 12 min and 11 s (just over 4 days), compared to the 1 min and 7 s for sorting the data, a best case scenario of more than two days compared to the just over a minute in data selection.

4.1 Back-Translation

The various models that are trained were then taken as backward models and used to generate synthetic data for training German-English forward models to implement the back-translation approach. The performances of these models are shown in Table 6. It can be observed that both the quality estimation and the data selection enhanced self-learning influenced the improved performance in their respective forward models. The scores can be said to be statically similar, having a range of 0.57 BLEU. For the one-off self-learning with quality estimation and data selection, the difference was just a paltry 0.03 BLEU, almost the same difference as when we used only the best monolingual (synthetic) data for the self-training (0.05 BLEU). The huge difference was observed when we used all of the monolingual data for self-learning, a difference of 0.57 BLEU. However, all of the approaches above were significantly better than the baseline and the standard back-translation models.

5   Discussion

Neural machine translation models cannot be relied upon to generate acceptable translations between languages when the training data is not sufficiently large. These category of languages are referred to as low resourced. Using the synthetic data – generated from a large collection of monolingual sentences – through self-learning has been investigated to improve the models' performances. The implementation of this approach has been shown to rely on quality estimation systems to better improve the models. But these quality estimation models are not available for many languages, especially those that are in the category of low resourced. Applying the self-learning approach without cleaning the synthetic data have also shown to be useful but not as effective. Also, the quality estimation systems expect that every sentence, no matter how large their number is, to be translated before estimating their quality and determining which are useful and which are not. This is not efficient.

This work, therefore, proposed the use of data selection to determine the sentences whose domain is closest to that of the test set to be used for self-learning. The approach has been used in back-translation to select from the synthetic data the sentences that share n-grams with the test set. Contrastingly, we select sentences from the authentic monolingual data before translation rather than from the synthetic sentences. The proposed approach achieved a performance that is similar but less than that of the current self-learning with quality estimation approach (−0.32 BLEU). But after the iterating the process, our proposed method reached the best performance of 24.31 BLEU, an improvement of +0.26 BLEU over the latter approach. We showed that even if the best of all of the available synthetic data was selected at each iteration, unlike in [37] where the best of the rest of the synthetic data is selected, implementing the iterative approach with data selection (using only the closest monolingual data) resulted in the best model – 24.10 vs 24.62 BLEUs respectively. The approach has not only shown to be just as effective (and even better), but that the number of monolingual sentences to be translated is the exact number that is needed for the self-learning approach. Determining the required sentences was also faster than estimating the quality of the synthetic data.

We also implemented the back-translation approach, taking all the previously trained models as backward models. The performances of the resulting forward models showed that the proposed approach can also be used to enhance the performance of the backward model in the back-translation method.

6   Conclusion and Future Work

In this work, we investigated using the monolingual data selection as an alternative to synthetic data quality estimation to improve self-learning in low resource neural machine translation. The approach was shown to be simpler and faster and can achieve a performance that is comparable or even better than using the quality estimation system. We showed, also, that the approach can be deployed in back-translation to enhance the performance of the backward model and that this improvement resulted in a better forward model.

For future work, we plan to study the efficacy of a hybrid of both quality estimation and data selection to further improve the performances of translation models. We plan, also, to study the applicability of the approach on rich-resourced languages.

References

1. Abadi, M., et al.: TensorFlow: a system for large-scale machine learning. In: Proceedings of the 12th USENIX Conference on Operating Systems Design and Implementation, OSDI'16, pp. 265–283. USENIX Association, Berkeley (2016). http://dl.acm.org/citation.cfm?id=3026877.3026899
2. Abdulmumin, I., Galadanci, B.S., Isa, A.: Enhanced back-translation for low resource neural machine translation using self-training. In: ICTA 2020. CCIS, vol. 1350, pp. 355–371. Springer, Cham (2021). https://doi.org/10.1007/978-3-030-69143-1_28
3. Abdulmumin, I., Galadanci, B.S., Isa, A., Sinan, I.I.: A hybrid approach for improved low resource neural machine translation using monolingual data. arXiv:2011.07403 (2021)
4. Bahdanau, D., Cho, K., Bengio, Y.: Neural machine translation by jointly learning to align and translate. In: Bengio, Y., LeCun, Y. (eds.) 3rd International Conference on Learning Representations, ICLR 2015, San Diego, CA, USA, 7–9 May 2015, Conference Track Proceedings (2015). http://arxiv.org/abs/1409.0473
5. Biçici, E., Yuret, D.: Instance selection for machine translation using feature decay algorithms. In: Proceedings of the 6th Workshop on Statistical Machine Translation, pp. 272–283. Asian Federation of Natural Language Processing, Edinburg (2011). https://pdfs.semanticscholar.org/14c6/731b2839d40b0c45f447b07afce1cc996de4.pdf
6. Biçici, E., Yuret, D., Bicici, E., Yuret, D.: Optimizing instance selection for statistical machine translation with feature decay algorithms. IEEE/ACM Trans. Audio Speech Lang. Process. **23**(2), 339–350 (2015). https://doi.org/10.1109/TASLP.2014.2381882
7. Bojar, O., et al.: Findings of the 2017 conference on machine translation (WMT17). In: Proceedings of the Second Conference on Machine Translation, Shared Task Papers, vol. 2, pp. 169–214. Association for Computational Linguistics, Copenhagen (2017). http://www.aclweb.org/anthology/W17-4717
8. Burlot, F., Yvon, F.F.: Using monolingual data in neural machine translation: a systematic study. In: Proceedings of the Third Conference on Machine Translation: Research Papers, pp. 144–155. Association for Computational Linguistics, Brussels (2018). https://doi.org/10.18653/v1/W18-6315. https://www.aclweb.org/anthology/W18-6315
9. Caswell, I., Chelba, C., Grangier, D.: Tagged back-translation. In: Proceedings of the Fourth Conference on Machine Translation (Volume 1: Research Papers), pp. 53–63. Association for Computational Linguistics, Florence (2019). https://doi.org/10.18653/v1/W19-5206. https://www.aclweb.org/anthology/W19-5206
10. Cettolo, M., Niehues, J., Stüker, S., Bentivogli, L., Federico, M.: Report on the 11th IWSLT evaluation campaign, IWSLT 2014. In: Proceedings of the 11th Workshop on Spoken Language Translation, Lake Tahoe, CA, USA, pp. 2–16 (2014)
11. Currey, A., Miceli Barone, A.V., Heafield, K.: Copied monolingual data improves low-resource neural machine translation. In: Proceedings of the Second Conference on Machine Translation, vol. 1, pp. 148–156. Association for Computational Linguistics, Copenhagen (2017). https://doi.org/10.18653/v1/W17-4715
12. Dabre, R., et al.: NICT's supervised neural machine translation systems for the WMT19 news translation task. In: Proceedings of the Fourth Conference on Machine Translation (WMT), Florence, Italy, vol. 2, pp. 168–174 (2019)

13. Dehghani, M., Gouws, S., Vinyals, O., Uszkoreit, J., Kaiser, Ł.: Universal transformers. In: ICLR, pp. 1–23 (2019). http://arxiv.org/abs/1807.03819
14. Edunov, S., Ott, M., Auli, M., Grangier, D.: Understanding back-translation at scale. In: Proceedings of the 2018 Conference on Empirical Methods in Natural Language Processing, pp. 489–500. Association for Computational Linguistics, Stroudsburg (2018). https://doi.org/10.18653/v1/D18-1045. http://aclweb.org/anthology/D18-1045
15. Gascó, G., Rocha, M.A., Sanchis-Trilles, G., Andrés-Ferrer, J., Casacuberta, F.: Does more data always yield better translations? In: EACL 2012–13th Conference of the European Chapter of the Association for Computational Linguistics, Proceedings, pp. 152–161 (2012)
16. Gehring, J., Michael, A., Grangier, D., Yarats, D., Dauphin, Y.N.: Convolutional sequence to sequence learning. In: Precup, D., Teh, Y.W. (eds.) Proceedings of the 34th International Conference on Machine Learning, vol. 70, pp. 1243–1252. PMLR, Sydney (2017). http://proceedings.mlr.press/v70/gehring17a.html
17. Gulcehre, C., Firat, O., Xu, K., Cho, K., Bengio, Y.: On integrating a language model into neural machine translation. Comput. Speech Lang. **45**(2017), 137–148 (2017). https://doi.org/10.1016/j.csl.2017.01.014
18. He, D., et al.: Dual learning for machine translation. In: Proceedings of the 30th International Conference on Neural Information Processing Systems, NIPS'16, pp. 820–828. Curran Associates Inc., USA (2016). http://dl.acm.org/citation.cfm?id=3157096.3157188
19. Hochreiter, S., Schmidhuber, J.: Long short-term memory. Neural Comput. **9**(8), 1735–1780 (1997)
20. Imamura, K., Fujita, A., Sumita, E.: Enhancement of encoder and attention using target monolingual corpora in neural machine translation. In: Proceedings of the 2nd Workshop on Neural Machine Translation and Generation, pp. 55–63. Association for Computational Linguistics, Melbourne (2018)
21. Kepler, F., Trénous, J., Treviso, M., Vera, M., Martins, A.F.T.: OpenKiwi: an open source framework for quality estimation. In: Proceedings of the 57th Annual Meeting of the Association for Computational Linguistics: System Demonstrations, pp. 117–122. Association for Computational Linguistics, Florence (2019)
22. Kim, H., Lee, J.H., Na, S.H.: Predictor-estimator using multilevel task learning with stack propagation for neural quality estimation. In: Proceedings of the Conference on Machine Translation (WMT), vol. 2, pp. 562–568. Association for Computational Linguistics, Copenhagen (2017). https://doi.org/10.18653/v1/w17-4763
23. Kingma, D.P., Ba, J.: Adam: a method for stochastic optimization. In: Bengio, Y., LeCun, Y. (eds.) 3rd International Conference on Learning Representations, ICLR 2015, Conference Track Proceedings, San Diego, CA, USA (2015). http://arxiv.org/abs/1412.6980
24. Klein, G., Kim, Y., Deng, Y., Senellart, J., Rush, A.: OpenNMT: open-source toolkit for neural machine translation. In: Proceedings of ACL 2017, System Demonstrations, pp. 67–72. Association for Computational Linguistics, Vancouver (2017). https://www.aclweb.org/anthology/P17-4012
25. Kocmi, T., Bojar, O.: CUNI submission for low-resource languages in WMT news 2019. In: Proceedings of the Fourth Conference on Machine Translation (WMT), Florence, Italy, vol. 2, pp. 234–240 (2019)
26. Koehn, P., Knowles, R.: Six challenges for neural machine translation. In: Proceedings of the First Workshop on Neural Machine Translation, pp. 28–39. Association for Computational Linguistics, Vancouver (2017). https://doi.org/10.18653/v1/w17-3204

27. Luong, T., Pham, H., Manning, C.D.: Effective approaches to attention-based neural machine translation. In: Proceedings of the 2015 Conference on Empirical Methods in Natural Language Processing, pp. 1412–1421. Association for Computational Linguistics, Stroudsburg (2015). https://doi.org/10.18653/v1/D15-1166. http://aclweb.org/anthology/D15-1166

28. Nguyen, T.Q., Chiang, D.: Transfer learning across low-resource, related languages for neural machine translation. In: Proceedings of the Eighth International Joint Conference on Natural Language Processing, vol. 2, pp. 296–301. Asian Federation of Natural Language Processing (2017)

29. Niu, X., Denkowski, M., Carpuat, M.: Bi-directional neural machine translation with synthetic parallel data. In: Proceedings of the 2nd Workshop on Neural Machine Translation and Generation. pp. 84–91. Association for Computational Linguistics, Melbourne (2018). https://doi.org/10.18653/v1/W18-2710. https://www.aclweb.org/anthology/W18-2710

30. Ott, M., Edunov, S., Grangier, D., Auli, M.: Scaling neural machine translation. In: Proceedings of the Third Conference on Machine Translation: Research Papers, pp. 1–9. Association for Computational Linguistics, Stroudsburg (2018). https://doi.org/10.18653/v1/W18-6301. http://aclweb.org/anthology/W18-6301

31. Papineni, K., Roukos, S., Ward, T., Zhu, W.J.: BLEU: a method for automatic evaluation of machine translation. In: Proceedings of the 40th Annual Meeting on Association for Computational Linguistics, ACL '02, pp. 311–318. Association for Computational Linguistics, Stroudsburg (2002). https://doi.org/10.3115/1073083.1073135

32. Poncelas, A., Maillette de Buy, G.W., Way, A.: Adaptation of machine translation models with back-translated data using transductive data selection methods. CoRR abs/1906.0 (2019). http://arxiv.org/abs/1906.07808

33. Ranzato, M., Chopra, S., Auli, M., Zaremba, W.: Sequence level training with recurrent neural networks. In: International Conference on Learning Representations (2016)

34. Sennrich, R., Haddow, B., Birch, A.: Edinburgh neural machine translation systems for WMT 16. In: Proceedings of the First Conference on Machine Translation, Shared Task Papers, vol. 2, pp. 371–376. Association for Computational Linguistics, Stroudsburg (2016). https://doi.org/10.18653/v1/W16-2323, http://aclweb.org/anthology/W16-2323

35. Sennrich, R., Haddow, B., Birch, A.: Improving neural machine translation models with monolingual data. In: Proceedings of the 54th Annual Meeting of the Association for Computational Linguistics, pp. 86–96. Association for Computational Linguistics, Berlin (2016)

36. Sennrich, R., Haddow, B., Birch, A.: Neural machine translation of rare words with subword units. In: Proceedings of the 54th Annual Meeting of the Association for Computational Linguistics (Volume 1: Long Papers), pp. 1715–1725. Association for Computational Linguistics, Stroudsburg (2016). https://doi.org/10.18653/v1/P16-1162. http://aclweb.org/anthology/P16-1162

37. Specia, L., Shah, K.: Machine translation quality estimation: applications and future perspectives. In: Moorkens, J., Castilho, S., Gaspari, F., Doherty, S. (eds.) Translation Quality Assessment. MTTA, vol. 1, pp. 201–235. Springer, Cham (2018). https://doi.org/10.1007/978-3-319-91241-7_10

38. Sutskever, I., Vinyals, O., Le, Q.V.: Sequence to sequence learning with neural networks. In: NIPS (2014)

39. Ueffing, N.: Using monolingual source-language data to improve MT performance. In: International Workshop on Spoken Language Translation, Kyoto, Japan, pp. 174–181 (2006)
40. Vaswani, A., et al.: Attention is all you need. In: 31st Conference on Neural Information Processing Systems, Long Beach, CA, USA (2017)
41. Wu, F., Fan, A., Baevski, A., Dauphin, Y.N., Auli, M.: Pay less attention with lightweight and dynamic convolutions. arXiv:1901.10430v2, pp. 1–14 (2019)
42. Yang, Z., Chen, W., Wang, F., Xu, B.: Effectively training neural machine translation models with monolingual data. Neurocomputing **333**, 240–247 (2019). https://doi.org/10.1016/j.neucom.2018.12.032
43. Zhang, J., Zong, C.: Exploiting source-side monolingual data in neural machine translation. In: Proceedings of the 2016 Conference on Empirical Methods in Natural Language Processing, pp. 1535–1545. Association for Computational Linguistics, Austin (2016). https://doi.org/10.18653/v1/d16-1160
44. Zhang, Y., Weiss, D.: Stackpropagation: improved representation learning for syntax. In: Proceedings of the 54th Annual Meeting of the Association for Computational Linguistics (Volume 1: Long Papers), pp. 1557–1566. Association for Computational Linguistics, Berlin (2016). http://www.aclweb.org/anthology/P16-1147
45. Zoph, B., Yuret, D., May, J., Knight, K.: Transfer learning for low-resource neural machine translation. In: Proceedings of the 2016 Conference on Empirical Methods in Natural Language Processing, pp. 1568–1575. Association for Computational Linguistics, Austin (2016). https://doi.org/10.18653/v1/D16-1163. https://www.aclweb.org/anthology/D16-1163

An Experimental Comparison of Algorithms for Nodes Clustering in a Neural Network of Caenorhabditis Elegans

Jorge Hernandez[ID] and Hector Florez[✉][ID]

Universidad Distrital Francisco Jose de Caldas, Bogota, Colombia
hrjorgee@correo.udistrital.edu.co, haflorezf@udistrital.edu.co

Abstract. Caenorhabditis Elegans (C. Elegans) is a worm, which has had several studies to search its nerve paths. In a neuronal network simulation, it is util to know which is the first weight to assign in each link if it is not presented to determine other characteristics (e.g. distances by weights). Normally, the weight is a heuristic to solve a problem. There is a data set about connections of C. Elegans which is a result of other authors. The weights by the connection are not set in the data set. In this work, we use the data set to determine experimental weights for each connection with four cluster algorithms. The weights are to use in future work. To compare the algorithms, we created several models for each algorithm. We used metrics to evaluate the results for each model. A spectral clustering algorithm was chosen how the better algorithm to generate the weights.

Keywords: Clustering · Caenorhabditis Elegans · MiniBatch K-means algorithm · DBSCAN algorithm · Spectral clustering algorithm · Clustering feature tree algorithm

1 Introduction

In animals, the inputs are received and managed in a neuronal network to make animal behavior. In comparison with machines, the behavior in robots is programmed previously by the human. There are several techniques and theories to calculate the movement in the machines [7,15,18]. The main purpose of robots is to simulate their behavior. In animals, movements are through external (environment) or internal stimulus and managed by the nervous system. In healthy conditions, the brain must be able to continuously maintain strict functional control between the inputs and outputs of the system [16,23]. Thus, the behavior is dynamic in comparison with the machines.

Creating neural networks based on real connections could allow us to understand how animal behavior works, thus, bio-inspired models for behavior in agents could be created. A neural network is formed with neuron cells that

O. Gervasi et al. (Eds.): ICCSA 2021, LNCS 12957, pp. 327–339, 2021.
https://doi.org/10.1007/978-3-030-87013-3_25

receive or apply the chemical or electrical stimulus. Caenorhabditis Elegans is a worm, which has two sexes: hermaphrodite and male. The map of the neuronal connections of C. Elegans is almost complete and was proposed by Sydney Brenner [19].

The nervous system of C. Elegans, which consists of 302 neurons with three types (sensory, inter, motor) is relatively small to be analyzed [11]. To represent its neural network with a computational approach, it is necessary to create a connections graph. To make a simulation network, it is necessary to know the weights of connections to calculate the distances between nodes for future calculations. The nodes are cells of neuronal networks of C. Elegans. In the C. Elegans neural network, connections are structured and weights can be based on its structure. In others applications, each edge of a graph has a numeric value that corresponds to the weight. At the initial stage, weights can be set with random values or using a custom approach. We propose a custom approach to set weights based on the better group of the neuronal network.

This work is focused on searching the weights of a neural network with clusters in nodes with four applied algorithms. Additionally, we discussed from a computing perspective a data set that represents the connections of C. Elegans. Based on the results, we use metrics for the models of algorithms. In addition, in this work, we used the names of neurons according to Brenner [19], which corresponds to more than 282 neurons names.

The paper is structured as follows. Section 2 presents the main concepts of C. Elegans and the data set. Section 3 presents the related work. Section 4 presents the applied algorithms. In Sect. 5, we illustrate the proposed approach. Section 6 presents the results. Finally, Sect. 7 concludes the paper.

2   Neural Network Data Set

Normally, C. Elegans feed on microorganisms, mainly bacteria. There have been different works to design and validate a neuronal map of C. Elegans [17]. The data set of connections used in this work can be downloaded at Wormatlas[1]. C. Elegans has few neurons in comparison with other animals, most neurons can be unambiguously identified by morphology and position [3]. In addition, according to Brennen, neurons have a name convention [19].

Supervised and unsupervised algorithms can be used in machines to simulate intelligence. Supervised search algorithms find the best node based on a heuristic. The deployment in a search algorithm represents the possible paths that an agent can take when trying to find the best solution [10]. In consequence, it is interesting to observe the process in animals for finding possible ways to make artificial intelligence.

Generally, applying a cluster in a group of elements serves a problem in which the total characteristics are not set yet. Clustering is a division of data into groups or similar objects [1]. As an unsupervised classification technique,

---

[1] https://www.wormatlas.org/.

clustering identifies some inherent structures present in a set of objects based on a measure of similarity [5]. Before of search the clusters in node connections, we applied a transformation in data to discretize and then use data in each algorithm.

2.1 Connection Details

The electrical stimulus is called gap junctions and works as a relation between neurons. Another process is chemical synapses between neurons that correspond to a receiver and transmitter a signal. Thus, neuron A can have various links with neuron B. Also, neuron B can have links with neuron A.

C. Elegans neurons can be classified into 118 classes by morphology, dendritic specialization, and connectivity. There are the following three categories based on functional and structural properties [11]:

- **Sensory**. It responds to environmental conditions.
- **Inter**. Interconnects with other neurons.
- **Motor**. It has neuromuscular junctions.

The data set presents the connectivity of neuronal connections. Thus, the data set presents the number of synapses per neuron, its synaptic partner, and synapse type (incoming chemical synapse, outgoing chemical synapse, electrical junction, or neuromuscular junction). The data set contains 6417 records, where each row contains three categorical attributes and one numeric attribute. Nevertheless, this work uses 6414 records because three rows were removed. Removed records are explained in the next sections. The categorical attributes are *Neuron A* that indicates the point of origin, *Neuron B* that indicates the target neuron, *Type of Synapses* and *Links (NBR)*. NBR is a number of synapses between neurons A and B.

2.2 Data Preparation and Transformation

The data does not have missing values and the numeric column *Links NBR* does not have out-of-range or abnormal values. To check the range of values in *NBR*, a limit was created and calculated using Eq. 1.

$$limit = mean \pm 3.4 * standard\_deviation \qquad (1)$$

The max limit was *13*, while the min limit was *-8*; however, negative values were abnormal values in this case. Then, the range was between *0* and *13* for *NBR*. The connections can be modeled as a network or directed graph.

To implement the algorithms, the categories (neuron name A and neuron name B) were converted to numbers. We implemented a transformer[2]. The transformer was an ordinal type, where the characteristics are converted into ordinal integers. The result is a single column of integers from 0 to $n-1$ features, where

---

[2] Sklearn Ordinal Encoder.

n is the number of features. Normally, machine learning algorithms tend to require numbers instead of strings as inputs [13]. So, we needed some methods of coding to convert categories to numbers.

2.3   Data Analysis

Figure 1 shows the structure of the network cell connections of C. Elegans, which has been generated using the dataset mentioned above. This network was created iterating each connection and connecting the nodes transmitters with the receivers. Furthermore, it shows that there are many neurons directed to the neuromuscular junction (NMJ) node. NMJ helps with the locomotive movement of C. Elegans.

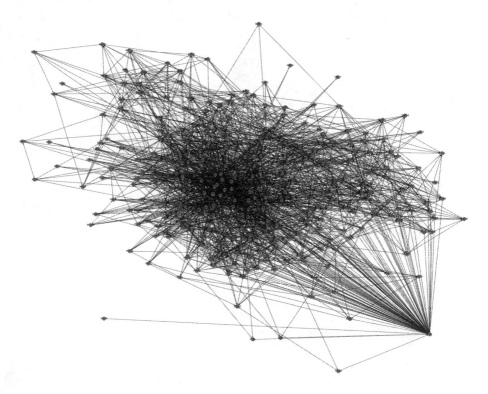

Fig. 1. Network connection structure

Same Origin. In the data set, the links that are connected to the same point were eliminated (i.e., point of origin is connected to the same point), since they will not generate additional characteristics. Table 1 shows the removed connections where the source node is equal to the end node. When the data was analyzed, these nodes do not represent additional features; therefore, the next neurons (RIBL, RIBR, and VA08) were removed. These removed nodes have elec-

Table 1. Deleted connections (A = B)

Node A	Type neuron	NBR
RIBL	EJ	1
RIBR	EJ	1
VA08	EJ	1

trical junctions (EJ). RIBL and RIBR are interneurons, while VA08 is a motor neuron.

Degree Centrality. The degree centrality of a node corresponds to the number of edges it has. The most central node is the one with a higher degree [8]. Centrality describes the importance of a node in the entire network. Thus, the degree centrality is a simple count of the total number of connections attached to a vertex. Figure 2, presents the degrees centrality of the nodes, where the highest peak is presented for the NMJ neuron node. In this figure, we can observe that the NMJ neuron is part of the core of the network since it is the most central node. In contrast, most of the other nodes have a degree of centrality between 0.05 and 0.10.

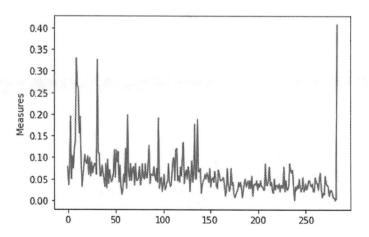

Fig. 2. Measures of centrality in the network

Isolated Nodes. Based on the graph, it is possible to find isolated nodes, which are those nodes that are not connected to the graph or network. In this case, two nodes were not connected to the network, which is neuron AVFL towards AVFR neuron. These nodes are neurons with type interneuron.

3   Related Work

Complex graph networks often represent relationships between sets of entities. One of the main questions in understanding a data set is knowing how many communities there and its memberships. [20]. As of the date of the article, we did not find an approach to generate the weights of the C. Elegans neural network. Next, we present related works about the analysis of C. Elegans neural network.

Bertin et al. [12] mapped a large fraction of the Caenorhabditis Elegans interactome network of protein-protein interaction. The authors examined the C. Elegans interactome network for the presence of highly connected neighborhoods by determining the mutual clustering coefficient between proteins in the network. C. Elegans is an ideal model for studying how protein networks relate to multicellularity. The authors analyzed the network of representing proteins and calculated the percentage of protein interaction pairs that share embryonic lethal phenotype.

Froese et al. [14] present a self-optimization process that has been replicated in various neural network formalisms. Nevertheless, it is not yet clear whether it can be applied to more biologically realistic network topologies and scale to larger networks. The authors demonstrated the self-optimization capacity for the C. Elegans connectome. In addition, they explored the possible beneficial effects of inhibitory connections between groups. They conclude that the self-optimization process can be applied to neural network topologies characterized by greater biological realism and that long-range inhibitory connections can facilitate the generalizability of the process.

Chen et al. [4] formulated an inference for graphs that represent a neural map of chemical and electrical connections. The formulation consists of a set of own graph inferences from the perspectives of the coincidence of graph matching (i.e., a set of edges that do not have a set of common vertices) and the classification of joint vertices. They concluded that jointly in the chemical and electrical connectivity maps, there is a conserved statistically significant similarity in the two synaptic connectome structures.

Bacik et al. [2] analyzed the weighted and directed C. Elegans connectome from a flow-based perspective. The authors' methods use graphical diffusion processes as a simple means of linking directed network characteristics and propagation dynamics. The analysis uses data from C. Elegans to represent the connectome of C. Elegans, we use the two-dimensional network design, that is, the neurons are placed in the plane according to their normalized Laplacian eigenvector (x-axis) and the processing depth (y-axis).

4   Algorithms

In this work, we created several models for each algorithm. Models are explained in Sect. 5. The models were created with Scikit Learn[3]. Scikit Learn is a software

---

[3] https://scikit-learn.org/.

tool package for Python[4] language. Scikit Learn permits the use of different algorithms related to data science.

4.1 Spectral Clustering

Spectral clustering has been successful in a wide variety of applications providing significant results at reasonable costs [22]. Spectral Clustering is used to group relevant data points. It also takes care of separating irrelevant data points. This algorithm is formulated like the partition of a graph, which is mapped by data points. It is called spectral since it is based on the theory of spectral graphs.

4.2 Density-Based Spatial Clustering (DBSCAN)

The DBSCAN algorithm is called a density-based spatial grouping for noisy data. It finds high-density core samples and expands groups from them. It is a successful algorithm for data containing groups of similar density [6].

DBSCAN looks at the clusters as areas that have high density and are separated by other areas that are of low density. It is the reason why the groups found by this algorithm can obtain the shape they want, unlike other algorithms, where their groups take a specific form. To define the word dense, we can include two parameters in the algorithm, which are $min\_samples$ and epsilon (EPS). EPS is the maximum distance to consider the neighborhood between two samples. Each one defines a density level, where $min\_samples$ is high and EPS is low indicating the density that is necessary to form a group.

The min_sample parameter is in charge of controlling the tolerance of the algorithm towards the noise, while the EPS parameter is in charge of choosing the data set and the function that determines the distance, which generally cannot take a default value. In addition, EPS controls the proximity of the points. When these points are chosen very small, most of the data cannot be grouped correctly, but if they are chosen very large, they tend to join with other clusters; then, all data is returned in a single cluster.

4.3 Mini Batch K-Means

Mini Batch is a variation of the K-Means algorithm that uses mini-batches to reduce computation time while trying to optimize the same objective function. Mini-batches are subsets of the input data obtained randomly in each training iteration. Mini batches drastically reduce the amount of convergence execution for a local solution.

4.4 Clustering Feature Tree (CFT)

This algorithm builds a tree called the Clustering Feature Tree (CFT) for the given data. The CFT algorithm has two parameters, the threshold, and the

---

[4] https://www.python.org/.

branching factor [21]. The branching factor limits the number of subgroups in a node and the threshold limits the distance between the incoming sample and existing subgroups. The algorithm creates subclusters called CF that contain the information necessary for clustering.

5   Proposed Approach

To implement these algorithms, different models were created to find the best grouping result. Six models were created for each algorithm varying the parameters according to each model. Table 2 presents 24 models and its parameters per algorithm. Each model was enumerated.

Table 2a presents the experimentation to find the best model for the data addressed. All DBSCAN models use the *ball tree* method to find point distances and to find the closest neighbors. *Ball tree* is a spatial partition data structure to organize points in a multidimensional space. The first parameter to vary is the maximum distance (EPS) between two samples for one to be considered in the vicinity of the other. The other parameter to vary is the number of samples (or total weight) in a neighborhood for a point to be considered as a central point. This includes the point itself.

Table 2b presents the experimentation to find the best model for the data approached with the Spectral Clustering algorithm. The parameter to be validated is the space that defines the dimension of the projection subspace. The

Table 2. Parameters in Models

Model	Max. Distance (EPS)	BDSCAN Weights
M1	0.2	10
M2	0.3	10
M3	0.4	10
M4	0.2	20
M5	0.3	20
M6	0.4	20

(a) BDSCAN

Model	Space	Neighbors
M7	28	20
M8	38	20
M9	48	20
M10	28	30
M11	38	30
M12	48	30

(b) Spectral Clustering

Model	Threshold	Branching factor
M13	0.2	40
M14	0.2	50
M15	0.5	60
M16	0.5	70
M17	0.8	80
M18	0.8	90

(c) CTF

Model	Num. clusters	Batch size
M19	3	20
M20	3	40
M21	8	20
M22	8	40
M23	10	20
M24	10	40

(d) MiniBatch K-Means

other parameter to vary is the number of neighbors to use when constructing the affinity matrix using the nearest neighbor method.

Table 2c presents the models for the CFT algorithm. Each model presented a variation in two parameters, the threshold, and the branching factor.

Table 2d presents the models for mini-batch K-Means. The parameters that varied were the number of clusters and the batch size. The initialization method k-means++ was used in each model, which selects the initial cluster centers for the clustering of k-mean in an automatic way to accelerate convergence.

5.1 Weights Calculations

With the best cluster model, the weights for edges were calculated. Equation 2 serves to make the weight calculations. M12 was chosen as the best model compared to the other models and based on the results of the metrics. The number of clusters for M12 is 48. Each cluster was given a score that corresponds to the total number of members in the cluster.

$$wi_j = 0.2 * cluster\_score + \frac{Tn}{Tf + NBR} \qquad (2)$$

In Eq. 2, NBR is the number of synapses, Tn is the number of appearances of that neuron in the connections, Tf is the total number of neurons or characteristics, and $O.2$ is a constant value associated with a fixed weight for each connection.

6 Results

In this section, the results of the models are presented. To compare each model, four metrics were established for the results of the groups. The chosen metrics do not need classes or target variables compared to forecasting algorithms. The four applied metrics are:

- **Silhouette coefficient**. It is calculated using the mean distance within group (a) and the closest mean distance to group (b) for each sample. The coefficient ranges from 1 to −1, where 1 is the best result.
- **Calinski harabasz**. It is known as the variance ratio criteria and defines the relationship between the sum of the dispersion between groups and the dispersion between groups for all groups, where the dispersion is defined as the sum of the squared distances. The highest value is the one chosen as the best.
- **Davies bouldin**. It stands for the average "similarity" between groups, where similarity is a measure that compares the distance between groups with the size of the groups. Values closest to zero perform the best.
- **Composed Density between and within clusters (CDBW)**. A reliable cluster validity index should match all "good" clustering requirements. This implies evaluating the cohesion of the groups, as well as the separation of the groups along with their compactness [9]. The lowest value is the one that performs best.

Table 3 presents the results of the metrics for each model. For the DBSCAN algorithm, the best model is M3, for the Spectral Clustering algorithm the best model is M12. CFT algorithm's best model is M13. Finally, in Mini Batch K-Means best model is M21.

Figure 3 represents the deployment of the nodes in the clusters for the best model chosen by an algorithm. The M12 model has a greater grouping. The sub-figures present a cluster grouping for each algorithm, where the nodes categories were transformed to ordinal numbers (i.e., the number associated with categories). Therefore, the X-axis can be seen as nodes A and the Y-axis as nodes B. Figure 3a presents a model M3 that has 6 clusters. Figure 3b presents a model M12 that has 48 clusters. Figure 3c presents a model M13 that has 3 clusters. Figure 3d presents a model M21 that has 8 clusters.

Table 3. Metrics results for models

Model	Silhouette	Calinski harabasz	Davies bouldin	CDBW
M1	−0.077	103.897	1.496	0.318
M2	−0.145	184.323	2.244	0.348
M3	0.046	554.804	3.337	0.821
M4	0.041	113.346	1.452	0.330
M5	−0.146	159.847	1.904	0.305
M6	−0.091	288.206	2.891	0.554
M7	0.191	1238.900	1.327	0.300
M8	0.236	1329.701	1.181	0.261
M9	0.253	1221.748	1.085	0.233
M10	0.198	1195.593	1.288	0.302
M11	0.250	1357.473	1.153	0.250
M12	0.285	1602.309	1.060	0.233
M13	0.247	2096.772	1.342	0.772
M14	0.245	1951.496	1.377	0.788
M15	0.271	2339.545	1.333	0.779
M16	0.271	2339.545	1.333	0.779
M17	0.271	2346.092	1.298	0.941
M18	0.271	2346.092	1.298	0.941
M19	0.265	2437.222	1.327	0.760
M20	0.297	2768.210	1.198	0.756
M21	0.301	2651.399	1.005	0.521
M22	0.295	2569.843	1.119	0.547
M23	0.296	2466.860	1.053	0.487
M24	0.289	2402.525	1.068	0.507

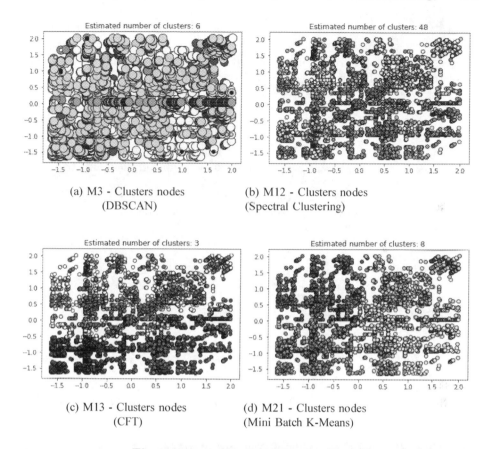

(a) M3 - Clusters nodes
(DBSCAN)

(b) M12 - Clusters nodes
(Spectral Clustering)

(c) M13 - Clusters nodes
(CFT)

(d) M21 - Clusters nodes
(Mini Batch K-Means)

Fig. 3. Best models chosen by algorithm

7 Conclusions and Future Work

C. Elegans is an animal model for implementing works about network cell structure with a computational perspective. Drawing network connections permits
showing a structure and analyzing the main connections and nodes. Thus, The
network can be represented as a directed graph.

In this work, we present an approach to calculate the weights of the connections according to the groupings between the connections. Thus, through grouping, the calculation of the weights was proposed. Different models were tested
before the final models were established. The results allow establishing that for
the case, the 6414 connections can be grouped according to their characteristics
in 48 clusters. For this problem and data set, it is observed that DBSCAN had
the worst results compared to the other algorithms. In our context, the CDBW
and the silhouette coefficient were the most determining metrics to establish
better models.

As future work, the weights might allow analyzing network structure. In addition, the future objective is to observe how the weights affect the propagation in a signal network of C. Elegans. Thus, we will create an interactive system that can allow seeing the structure of the network, the weights, and the propagation of the signals (chemical and/or electrical).

References

1. Abbas, O.A.: Comparisons between data clustering algorithms. Int. Arab J. Inf. Technol. (IAJIT) **5**(3) (2008)
2. Bacik, K.A., Schaub, M.T., Beguerisse-Díaz, M., Billeh, Y.N., Barahona, M.: Flow-based network analysis of the Caenorhabditis Elegans connectome. PLoS Comput. Biol. **12**(8), e1005055 (2016)
3. Bargmann, C.I., Horvitz, H.R.: Chemosensory neurons with overlapping functions direct chemotaxis to multiple chemicals in c. elegans. Neuron **7**(5), 729–742 (1991)
4. Chen, L., Vogelstein, J.T., Lyzinski, V., Priebe, C.E.: A joint graph inference case study: the c. elegans chemical and electrical connectomes. In: Worm, p. e1142041. Taylor & Francis (2016)
5. Du, K.L.: Clustering: a neural network approach. Neural Netw. **23**(1), 89–107 (2010)
6. Ester, M., Kriegel, H.P., Sander, J., Xu, X., et al.: A density-based algorithm for discovering clusters in large spatial databases with noise. In: KDD, pp. 226–231 (1996)
7. Florez, H., Cárdenas-Avendaño, A.: A computer-based approach to study the Gaussian moat problem. In: Florez, H., Misra, S. (eds.) ICAI 2020. CCIS, vol. 1277, pp. 481–492. Springer, Cham (2020). https://doi.org/10.1007/978-3-030-61702-8_33
8. Golbeck, J.: Analyzing the Social Web. Newnes (2013)
9. Halkidi, M., Vazirgiannis, M.: A density-based cluster validity approach using multi-representatives. Pattern Recogn. Lett. **29**(6), 773–786 (2008)
10. Hernandez, J., Daza, K., Florez, H.: Alpha-beta vs scout algorithms for the Othello game. In: CEUR Workshops Proceedings, vol. 2846 (2019)
11. Kim, J., Leahy, W., Shlizerman, E.: Neural interactome: interactive simulation of a neuronal system. Front. Comput. Neurosci. **13**, 8 (2019)
12. Li, S., et al.: A map of the interactome network of the metazoan C. elegans. Science **303**(5657), 540–543 (2004)
13. McGinnis, W.D., Siu, C., Andre, S., Huang, H.: Category encoders: a Scikit-learn-contrib package of transformers for encoding categorical data. J. Open Sour. Softw. **3**(21), 501 (2018)
14. Morales, A., Froese, T.: Unsupervised learning facilitates neural coordination across the functional clusters of the C. elegans connectome. Front. Robot. AI **7**, 40 (2020)
15. Sanchez, D., Florez, H.: Improving game modeling for the Quoridor game state using graph databases. In: Rocha, Á., Guarda, T. (eds.) ICITS 2018. AISC, vol. 721, pp. 333–342. Springer, Cham (2018). https://doi.org/10.1007/978-3-319-73450-7_32
16. Towlson, E.K.: Caenorhabditis elegans and the network control framework–FAQs. Philos. Trans. R. Soc. B: Biol. Sci. **373**(1758), 20170372 (2018)

17. Varshney, L.R., Chen, B.L., Paniagua, E., Hall, D.H., Chklovskii, D.B.: Structural properties of the Caenorhabditis elegans neuronal network. PLoS Comput. Biol. **7**(2), e1001066 (2011)
18. Velosa, F., Florez, H.: Edge solution with machine learning and open data to interpret signs for people with visual disability. In: CEUR Workshop Proceedings, vol. 2714, pp. 15–26 (2020)
19. White, J.G., Southgate, E., Thomson, J.N., Brenner, S.: The structure of the nervous system of the nematode Caenorhabditis elegans. Philos. Trans. R. Soc. Lond. B Biol. Sci. **314**(1165), 1–340 (1986)
20. White, S., Smyth, P.: A spectral clustering approach to finding communities in graphs. In: Proceedings of the 2005 SIAM International Conference on Data Mining, pp. 274–285. SIAM (2005)
21. Zhang, T., Ramakrishnan, R., Livny, M.: BIRCH: an efficient data clustering method for very large databases. ACM SIGMOD Rec. **25**(2), 103–114 (1996)
22. Zhuzhunashvili, D., Knyazev, A.: Preconditioned spectral clustering for stochastic block partition streaming graph challenge (preliminary version at arxiv.). In: 2017 IEEE High Performance Extreme Computing Conference (HPEC), pp. 1–6. IEEE (2017)
23. Zuluaga, J.Y., Yepes-Calderon, F.: Tensor domain averaging in diffusion imaging of small animals to generate reliable tractography. ParadigmPlus **2**(1), 1–19 (2021)

Classification Aspects of the Data Offloading Process Applied to Fog Computing

Sávio Melo[1]([✉])(iD), Cícero Silva[2](iD), and Gibeon Aquino[1](iD)

[1] Federal University of Rio Grande do Norte, Natal 59078-970, Brazil
`savio.melo.016@ufrn.edu.br`, `gibeon@dimap.ufrn.br`
[2] Federal Institute of Education, Science and Technology of Paraíba,
Catolé do Rocha 58884-000, Brazil
`cicero.alves@ifpb.edu.br`

Abstract. The process of data offloading in fog-based environments can offer advantages such as energy savings, freeing up storage space, reduction in decision-making time, network usage reduction, among others. Thus, it is important that the data offloading process must be governed by rules and policies which will define how and when the process will be executed in the solution. Therefore, it is necessary to know the aspects of the data offloading process and discover the importance of each one of them, aiming to select the best techniques for policies definition in fog-based systems. So, this paper presents an approach through structuring in the form of a taxonomy, which classifies and organizes the knowledge needed to develop policies governing the data offloading process. Overall, fourteen (14) aspects that influence decisions for the data offloading process were classified. Finally, a practical example of how this approach can be instantiated in real-world scenarios is provided.

Keywords: Data offloading · Fog computing · Taxonomy

1 Introduction

The term called fog computing was defined in 2014 by the CISCO [6]. It refers to a decentralized computing architecture that manages data and processing closer to the network's edge. In summary, fog computing extends cloud computing capabilities by enabling the development of applications for the Internet of Things. Fog computing works between the data source and the cloud, providing several advantages: latency reduction with minimized response times and data transmission reduction from edge servers to cloud. However, fog computing has some bottlenecks: storage and local processing power, which are mandatory requirements for this architecture to work adequately [4].

As fog computing is close to the data origin, it must consider its storage limitations since the archiving and treating of some data is done locally. Therefore, it is necessary to think about ways that can help mitigate the problems caused

O. Gervasi et al. (Eds.): ICCSA 2021, LNCS 12957, pp. 340–353, 2021.
https://doi.org/10.1007/978-3-030-87013-3_26

by these limitations. One alternative would be to transfer this data to entities with larger storage capacities, a strategy known as computational offloading. Offloading is performed when an entity cannot complete a specific task with its resources due to an infrastructure limitation. When this happens, the most common is that this task is transferred to another more robust entity such as the cloud. The cloud can be used effectively to store, analyze, and use accumulated process data [2]. Data offloading from the fog nodes to the cloud happens in several cases. The most common of them is when there is a need for longer-term storage [1].

Policies need to be defined to conduct the data transfer process between persistence entities on the data offloading task. These policies determine security factors, storage, timeout, and issues involving data management and privacy. Therefore, their correct elaboration can help develop more secure and efficient applications in fog computing environments.

The realization of the process of data offloading has several purposes. In [1], are listed some of them: load balancing, long-term storage, latency, data management, among others. In the same study, such goals are called "criteria for performing data offloading". However, since each criterion depends on the architecture and domain characteristics, defining a standard policy for data offloading in diverse scenarios would be a difficult task since there could be numerous policy possibilities that meet the various aspects to be considered.

Because of the onerousness of designing policies for data *offloading*, this paper suggests a way that facilitates the selection of essential concepts and techniques of the data offloading process, both from the data perspective and from the system infrastructure perspective. Thus, the main contribution of this work is to provide a classification structure that organizes aspects of the data offloading process, enabling policy development in fog-based solutions. Furthermore, such a framework systematizes knowledge about this process and supports its execution to be composed of the best techniques. Therefore, this serves as a support for the solutions in the fog environment to enjoy the benefits of data offloading, such as energy savings, freeing up storage space, decreased network usage, decreased decision-making time, among others.

The rest of this paper is organized as follows: In Sect. 2, the works related to the theme of this article are described. Section 3 discusses the approach in the form of a taxonomy. Section 4 demonstrates the application and instantiation of the proposed approach through a case study. Finally, Sect. 5 talks about the main findings and future work.

2   Related Works

Alelaiwi et al. [3] and Pisan et al. [22] use the data offloading process to meet their applications' requirements better. So, they consider strategies and policies that set the direction of such a process, serving to mitigate the limitations of the fog environment.

The process of data offloading in fog computing is a topic under discussion. Alelaiwi et al. [3] used machine learning algorithms that select data to be sent to the cloud. The data offloading from an edge platform is only performed after deep learning techniques are executed in this approach. Pisan et al. [22] consider data that needs to be balanced among the fog nodes as a way to decide the offloading execution according to the available storage. However, these studies do not discuss the volume and nature of data, such as size and criticality, respectively.

Aazam et al. [1] classify the existing types of offloading, defining different situations where the process can occur and showing its variations. Whereas, He et al. [13] ponder that security and load balancing aspects are significant in the data offloading process. However, neither paper relates the data properties and infrastructure.

Still dealing with security, He et al. [13] propose a security model for fog data storage, highlighting the possible vulnerabilities that these data may be subject. Among other points found, we can highlight the proposal of Verma et al. [29], which proposes an adaptive processing balancing model for the fog data context. However, the authors do not specify the techniques used in the processes and their possible impacts.

To summarize, several works in the literature propose solutions for the data offloading process in fog computing, which gather proposals for different problems. However, many of them do not consider the properties of the data: security, management, nature, and volume of the data, nor the characteristics of the infrastructure, such as network, storage, processing, and power. Thus, unlike other works, this study seeks to classify the aspects, concepts, techniques, and particularities involved in the process so that it is possible to define more substantiated policies that allow the execution of data offloading in fog-based solutions.

3   Taxonomy of Aspects of the Data Offloading Process

Offloading is a technique that aims to assist devices with limited capabilities by migrating processing and/or data from these devices to other entities with larger computational power and storage. In general, offloading occurs when the network situation is favorable and when there are gains in the migration of data or processing. On the other hand, when no connection is available between the device and the external entity, the storage is performed locally.

There are two types of offloading: processing and data [10]. Data offloading is a topic that has been discussed in the fog computing paradigm [1]. This happens due to the resource constraints of the distributed entities that usually form the fog. This process is governed by rules that dictate how it should occur, commonly called policies. Thus, its realization is conditioned to policies that describe how the data is managed during the procedure. Therefore, based on the criteria defined by Aazam et al. [1], a taxonomy was proposed to assist in the process of eliciting essential aspects for the definition of rules and policies for data offloading.

3.1   Taxonomy Organization

First, the defined aspects were divided into two perspectives for organizational reasons. Thus, the classes and subclasses from the taxonomy were organized according to the following views: data and infrastructure.

The **data** view represents the basis of the data offloading process in fog computing because of the properties of the data. For example, some studies suggest using deep learning techniques to recognize such properties [3], while others consider data size an essential element for executing the process [22]. Therefore, this view brings together the characteristics directly associated with the data being generated, transferred, and processed in the context of fog computing. The classes defined to detail this category were: *security, management, nature, and volume*

The **infrastructure** view was considered to represent the data offloading process because of the physical characteristics of the environment's infrastructure. In the study of Hao et al. [12], for example, the data offloading decision is based on the intensity of network resource utilization, while other studies only consider predetermined times as a parameter for the execution of the process. Thus, this category concerns the requirements of the environment where the data is located, that is, the properties to be considered in the nodes that form the fog. So, this category has only one class called *resources*.

3.2   Taxonomy Structure

Figure 1 presents a taxonomy that allows listing aspects to develop policies for data offloading in fog computing. The main goal of this taxonomy is to guide the development of policies for data offloading, providing the main criteria and aspects to be considered in the process. This way, industry and researchers could understand the importance of data offloading policy development. That said, the subsequent sections will detail the classes that form the proposed taxonomy.

3.3   Security

Many security problems in personal information can happen in distributed fog nodes. This happens due to incorrect approaches and the existence of malicious users [16]. However, the correct practice of the four pillars of information security (confidentiality, availability, integrity, and privacy) ensure the secure traffic of data generated in the fog environment, resulting in improving application security.

Aiming at data *confidentiality*, authentication protocols can be applied between the nodes in the fog to obtain the identity of the connected nodes [14]. The deployment of these protocols prevents unauthorized people from accessing the data traffic between these nodes. On the other hand, to ensure that the fog nodes or the cloud servers are always available, techniques that promote the *availability* of the data [14] must be applied. Thus, the use of techniques such as

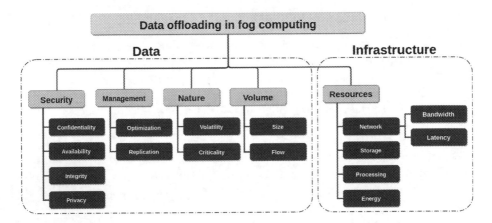

Fig. 1. Taxonomy for data offloading process in fog computing.

data replication and load balancing can help in this assurance. The work developed by Verma et al. [29], for example, uses the technique of data replication in conjunction with load balancing to decrease the environment's dependence on large cloud servers.

Data *integrity* ensures that any unauthorized attempts to modify transmitted or stored data are detected [14]. It is common to use the *blockchain* technique in addressing this vulnerability in fog computing [23,28]. Another property that helps in data preservation is *privacy*, which protects sensitive personal information [20]. Silva et al. [27] propose an approach based on *blockchain* to ensure the privacy of patient medical data in the context of fog computing. In the face of all these solutions, it is common to find approaches that use *blockchain* techniques, anonymization, and others.

3.4   Management

Data are commonly moved from one device to another in fog computing, so this flow requires appropriate data management [1]. The main motivation for considering management in the data offloading process is that the fog nodes are geographically distributed, making it somewhat challenging to identify the location of the data. Therefore, one of the first moments in the data management process is the data *optimization* task, followed by the data *replication* procedure. This set of techniques can distribute data among the nodes in the fog more efficiently since the requested data may not be available at nearby nodes.

The process of data size optimization is closely related to local storage and processing constraints, a feature quite common in fog computing [5]. According to Rahman et al. [24], two optimization techniques stand out in the fog layer: data filtering and data compression. Data filtering helps remove noise in the data acquisition phase, while the data compaction technique aims to reduce latency and the energy consumed during operations. Commonly, solutions use optimization techniques and data replication on their nodes, often aiming to reduce data size and promote data availability on nearby nodes. However, one should also consider that data replication can generate large data redundancy, which can compromise the storage factors of the fog nodes. Likewise, optimization techniques can require more processing from these nodes.

3.5 Nature

Fog computing environments generally do not use proprietary hardware or communication technologies, such as non-volatile storage devices [30]. Usually, resources such as storage and networking are leveraged from devices near the network's edge, such as smartphones, smart TVs, or connected vehicles. This implies a challenge which is the availability of resources that are on fog nodes, as it may not be continuous due to its volatile nature [15]. Therefore, these aspects of infrastructure in fog environments can lead to data taking on volatile and non-volatile natures.

Several applications also use fog computing to meet their real-time operation needs. Therefore, large computing infrastructures are increasingly dependent on critical data, which is also stored in databases arranged in the cloud [9]. So, when manipulating/transferring data generated by cloud layer devices, one must consider their different degrees of criticality. Critical data, for example, could be found in a scenario of monitoring the vital health information of a patient. In contrast, some other data in the same solution could be less relevant and even discarded. In this way, data generated at the edge of the network can also be volatile and/or critical.

3.6 Volume

The volume discusses metrics involving data centralization in fog computing, among one the *size* and *flow* of data stand out. [18]. These two metrics are the most common in the literature and the most relevant when there is the intention to work with data analysis at the nodes of the fog or external entities. Thus, identifying the volume of data in systems is advantageous because it allows the data to be integrated into more sophisticated analysis processes, providing better decision-making. Furthermore, the data volume analysis of the fog nodes allows the data offloading to the cloud to be performed only in opportune cases.

Regarding data size, it is understood how much data needs to be processed and stored in the fog environment. In some works, data size is discussed and related to the computational requirements [25]. Thus, such a property is considered aiming to mitigate the storage limitations of the fog. Another property associated with the volume of information between the fog and the cloud is data flow, which refers to the intensity with which data is sent from the source to the fog nodes. Such flow can be event-driven [17] or real-time [11]. Real-time data streams transmit data to storage at the fog nodes as they are generated, causing overload and high storage demands. Therefore, understanding the size and flow of data in fog systems is decisive in the data offloading process.

3.7   Resources

Fog computing is a very heterogeneous paradigm and has hardware constraints from its devices. However, cloud computing supports this paradigm by having almost unlimited capabilities and resources compared to the resources of fog computing-based environments. In this way, data offloading can support fog to take advantage of cloud capabilities.

Issues involving the communication *network* between devices are also pertinent for data offloading in fog computing. The fog is very heterogeneous and can be formed by different types of communication, approaches such as that of Zhou et al. [31] must be developed that propose a heterogeneous and hierarchical network architecture for fog enabling mobile communication networks in fog to achieve higher capacities than conventional communication networks. Issues like this are also related to *bandwidth* and decreasing *latency*, which are useful aspects of any fog application.

The *storage* in the fog computing paradigm is a topic already discussed in some studies [4, 26]. Despite offering many other features such as data management, eliminating unnecessary transactions, and minimizing latency times, fog computing has limited local data storage. In addition, such a paradigm also performs techniques involving *processing* [19], which, despite aiming to reduce the amount of data sent to the cloud, intensifies the infrastructure's processing constraint. Moreover, although the techniques that compress and process local data serve to mitigate the restrictions of the environment, it is worth remembering that in the fog, the devices that are in the network form the nodes and that most of them are powered by battery [7]. So, it is simple to say that the overload of these devices can worsen the energy autonomy of the fog infrastructure.

In summary, the evaluation of infrastructure resources is a requirement that helps when designing policies for data offloading because the availability of resources can decide whether the flow will follow normal or data offloading will be performed [8].

3.8   Taxonomy Discussion

The aspects listed in this section bring essential concepts involved in the data offloading process. It also highlights the main properties to be considered when developing rules, policies, and strategies for data offloading in the most diverse fog scenarios, considering the characteristic of the data and the infrastructure of the environments involved. Therefore, the study classifies and exemplifies some concepts about the data offloading process, as well as exemplifies and cites the main techniques used in such a process. Thus, this classification can serve as a basis for selecting techniques and aspects to define policies for data offloading since it provides many of the concepts needed for this definition. A summary of the main aspects and techniques used in data offloading process decisions is presented in Table 1. Finally, to show that the taxonomy is applicable, in the following section, a proof of concept is provided, in a typical cloud and fog computing scenario, that instantiates the classes specified by the taxonomy.

Table 1. Data offloading aspects and techniques summary

Aspects	Techniques
Confidentiality	- Authentication
Availability	- Replication; - Collaboration between fog nodes
Integrity	- *Blockchain*
Privacy	- *Blockchain*; - Anonymization policies
Optimization	- Data filtering; - Data Compression
Replication	- Data replication
Volatility	- Local processing
Criticality	- Data prioritization
Size	- Data distribution; - Data compression
Flow	- Event-driven; - Real-time
Network	- Network hierarchy architecture
Storage	- Data distribution; - Data compression; - Data filtering
Processing	- Load balancing
Energy	- Local processing

4 Proof of Concept

A healthcare scenario was instantiated to employ the taxonomy of classification of aspects for data offloading proposed in this work. It was analyzed under the aspects listed by the taxonomy, demonstrating its use and assisting in the process of specifying policies for data offloading for this example. Finally, this section performs an adaptation of OpenFog [21] and considers that the scenario is constituted by an environment based on fog and cloud paradigms.

4.1 Patient Monitoring

This scenario focuses on the analysis of cases where the health of patients needs to be continuously monitored. For example, people with diabetes, heart disease, and hypertension usually have more intense medical monitoring, and after surgical procedures, they need even more care. One of the intelligent monitoring techniques is Patient-Controlled Analgesia (PCA), a procedure to control post-operative pain in patients through self-administration of analgesics. An overview of this scenario can be seen in Fig. 2.

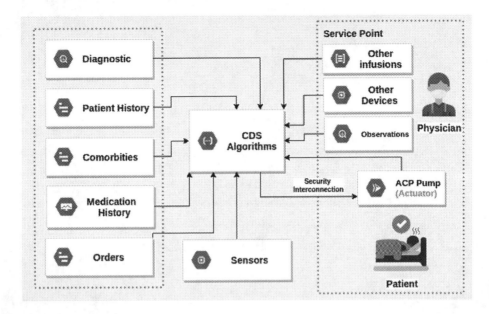

Fig. 2. Patient monitoring scenario overview.

In the fog computing environment of this scenario, data from the devices is integrated into and utilized by Clinical Decision Support (CDS) applications. This information is provided to healthcare professionals, wherever and whenever they need it. In addition, the systems have several alerting mechanisms, generating automatic responses if any anomaly is identified. The most common procedures are monitoring vital signs and stopping infusions until a healthcare professional can verify the patient's condition.

The architecture design of healthcare fog computing infrastructures must consider points that ensure the secure operation of the applications. The main ones are exemplified through the instance of the taxonomy proposed in this work presented in Fig. 3. The classes and aspects assigned for this scenario are described in the following.

4.2   Security

Healthcare fog computing environments must meet specifications that guard patient data, protecting it from unauthorized access. Aimed at this protection, the *confidentiality* of patient data can usually be provided through encryption and the use of data authentication approaches.

Another requirement of medical systems is to ensure that sensitive patient data is not exposed. For this assurance, the systems must allow the patient to control what information will be shared between the nodes and cloud, ensuring their *privacy* and preserving their personal and intimate data. Another guarantee that must implement in this type of application is the *integrity* of the data

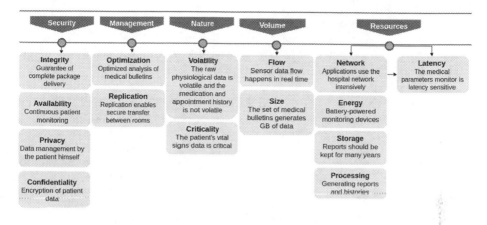

Fig. 3. Taxonomy applied to the patient monitoring scenario.

because fatal problems can happen if they are tampered with or lost, so the validation of data from offloading must be done.

Patient monitoring is a continuous action, so essential data must be available on the medical parameters monitor at all times. To ensure this *availability*, replication and load balancing techniques must be used to balance the work between the nodes and prevent the system from shutting down at critical times.

4.3 Management

In large hospitals, the data that is in fog may be geographically distributed, creating the need to use data management techniques between nodes. These environments must match data flow to patients even as the physical location and network changes during transfers between rooms. Therefore, one strategy that allows this information to be available regardless of location is *replication*, which will allow the information not to depend on the environment in which the patient is located. However, the data replication technique can harm the storage resources, so another aspect needs to be addressed, namely data optimization. Optimization will allow only essential data to be kept. So, only essential patient data will be kept in the fog environment after performing techniques such as data filtering and compression.

4.4 Nature

The nature of the data in this scenario can assume moments of *volatility*. Health care applications collect raw physiological data, which can be requested from the source and analyzed without the need for storage (*volatile*) or even synthesized in anamnesis procedures. However, data used in diagnostic parameters and patient health histories (*non-volatile*) must be kept in long-term storage infrastructures such as the cloud. This scenario also addresses the *critical* nature of the data, as monitoring operates on patients' vital signs, i.e., data considered *critical*. When missing, this information can compromise the system's overall functioning and lead to the patient's death. Therefore, data offloading must occur adaptively. This adaptivity allows transactions to happen according to the criticality of the data. For example, in cardiac patient monitoring, the system must adapt the request priorities to heart-related parameters when detecting abnormalities. Therefore, adaptive data offloading can improve the sensitivity of these systems for critical data.

4.5   Volume

The intense *flow* of data generated by sensors arranged in the environment and on the patients happens in real-time. This fact is known to aggravate the storage constraints of the devices that form the nodes of the cloud. Therefore, the intensity with which the data will be transferred to the cloud must be well managed to avoid damage to these devices. In addition, in cases involving critical data in the medical environment, almost all the information collected from patient monitoring is accumulated, generating patient health reports. When accumulated in a hospital, these reports can have sizes that reach many gigabytes of data, therefore overloading fog nodes with storage constraints. So, these two aspects also impact how data offloading should proceed in these cases.

4.6   Resources

The connection between devices, fog nodes, and proprietary data is responsible for overloading the *network* of hospitals. The use of the hospital network can be heavy due to a large number of patients, rooms, and emergency centers. Therefore, data offloading should be restricted to essential situations, preventing the network transmission capacity from being affected by the execution of non-essential tasks.

Another aspect to consider in this scenario is its *storage* limitation. Patient reports and histories must be kept for many years, further limiting the storage environment of the fog nodes. However, this fact enables the data offloading process, which can transfer such data to external entities and free up local space. Another resource constraint in the fog is that of *processing*. However, offloading allows specific processing to be performed in the cloud. Finally, given that currently, many wireless devices used in patient monitoring are battery-powered. Knowing that recharging opportunity is not always favorable, data offloading also allows the *energy* consumption on these devices to be reduced.

In monitoring scenarios like this, *latency* requirements are critical. The delay the network generates to exchange data elements can mean the death of a patient. Integration with emergency room data, for example, must provide essential information parameters for patient care, i.e., *latency* communication between devices can cost severe consequences to patient health. Therefore, the data offloading process must always choose the best node to store and retrieve the data.

4.7   Discussion

In fog scenarios like these, the elicitation of aspects pertinent to the data offloading process is very important. Through these, it is possible to make faster decisions at critical moments and efficiently take advantage of all the resources of the fog and cloud environments. To this end, the instantiation of the taxonomy allows the useful aspects of the scenario to be selected and the choice of techniques to be employed in the solution to be made with criteria and not in an empirical way. Therefore, this selection aims to ensure that the data offloading process of the solution is improved to reduce future problems. However, the financial and effort costs of this activity must be considered. The main cost identified in the applicability of this approach is related to the time and effort devoted to the selection and implementation of techniques, i.e., the most significant impact is in the requirements elicitation phase.

5   Conclusion

This paper proposes an approach to classifying aspects of the fog data offloading process through a taxonomy. The taxonomy was instantiated in a healthcare scenario and allowed prior surveys of aspects to provide the necessary background for future policy implementations. Thus, with this study, we believe that the creation of a taxonomy for understanding the aspects of data offloading provides better conditions for choosing the most appropriate techniques for the offloading process, allowing optimized data management, faster decision making, efficient use of resources, and above all, the construction of safer solutions for the fog and cloud paradigms. The work also showed that the taxonomy is instantiable, evidencing that it is helpful in fog computing scenarios. As future work, it is intended to build a guidance mechanism for policy implementation, including instantiation examples in other scenarios.

Acknowledgments. This study was financed in part by the Coordenação de Aperfeiçoamento de Pessoal de Nível Superior - Brasil (CAPES) - Finance Code 001.

References

1. Aazam, M., Zeadally, S., Harras, K.A.: Offloading in fog computing for IoT: review, enabling technologies, and research opportunities. Future Gener. Comput. Syst. **87**, 278–289 (2018)
2. Ahn, D.J., Jeong, J., Lee, S.: A novel cloud-fog computing network architecture for big-data applications in smart factory environments. In: Gervasi, O., et al. (eds.) ICCSA 2018. LNCS, vol. 10964, pp. 520–530. Springer, Cham (2018). https://doi.org/10.1007/978-3-319-95174-4_41
3. Alelaiwi, A.: An efficient method of computation offloading in an edge cloud platform. J. Parallel Distrib. Comput. **127**, 58–64 (2019)

4. Azimi, I., Anzanpour, A., Rahmani, A.M., Liljeberg, P., Salakoski, T.: Medical warning system based on internet of things using fog computing. In: 2016 International Workshop on Big Data and Information Security (IWBIS), pp. 19–24. IEEE (2016)

5. Bonomi, F., Milito, R., Zhu, J., Addepalli, S.: Fog computing and its role in the internet of things. In: Proceedings of the First Edition of the MCC Workshop on Mobile Cloud Computing, pp. 13–16. ACM (2012)

6. Cisco, A.: Fog computing and the internet of things: extend the cloud to where the things are. [Electronic resource] (2015). https://www.cisco.com/c/dam/en_us/solutions/trends/iot/docs/computing-overview.pdf. Accessed 10 Mar 2019

7. Dubey, H., Yang, J., Constant, N., Amiri, A.M., Yang, Q., Makodiya, K.: Fog data: enhancing telehealth big data through fog computing. In: 2015 Proceedings of the ASE Bigdata & Social Informatics, pp. 1–6. Proceedings of the ASE bigdata (2015)

8. Enzai, N.I.M., Tang, M.: A taxonomy of computation offloading in mobile cloud computing. In: 2014 2nd IEEE International Conference on Mobile Cloud Computing, Services, and Engineering, pp. 19–28. IEEE (2014)

9. Esteves, S., Silva, J., Veiga, L.: Quality-of-service for consistency of data geo-replication in cloud computing. In: Kaklamanis, C., Papatheodorou, T., Spirakis, P.G. (eds.) Euro-Par 2012. LNCS, vol. 7484, pp. 285–297. Springer, Heidelberg (2012). https://doi.org/10.1007/978-3-642-32820-6_29

10. Fernando, N., Loke, S.W., Rahayu, W.: Mobile cloud computing: a survey. Future Gener. Comput. Syst. 29(1), 84–106 (2013)

11. Giang, N.K., Blackstock, M., Lea, R., Leung, V.C.: Developing IoT applications in the fog: a distributed dataflow approach. In: 2015 5th International Conference on the Internet of Things (IOT), pp. 155–162. IEEE (2015)

12. Hao, Z., Novak, E., Yi, S., Li, Q.: Challenges and software architecture for fog computing. IEEE Internet Comput. 21(2), 44–53 (2017)

13. He, S., Cheng, B., Wang, H., Xiao, X., Cao, Y., Chen, J.: Data security storage model for fog computing in large-scale IoT application. In: IEEE INFOCOM 2018-IEEE Conference on Computer Communications Workshops (INFOCOM WKSHPS), pp. 39–44. IEEE (2018)

14. Huang, C., Lu, R., Choo, K.K.R.: Vehicular fog computing: architecture, use case, and security and forensic challenges. IEEE Commun. Mag. 55(11), 105–111 (2017)

15. Kuo, P.H., et al.: An integrated edge and fog system for future communication networks. In: 2018 IEEE Wireless Communications and Networking Conference Workshops (WCNCW), pp. 338–343. IEEE (2018)

16. Lee, K., Kim, D., Ha, D., Rajput, U., Oh, H.: On security and privacy issues of fog computing supported internet of things environment. In: 2015 6th International Conference on the Network of the Future (NOF), pp. 1–3. IEEE (2015)

17. Lee, W., Nam, K., Roh, H.G., Kim, S.H.: A gateway based fog computing architecture for wireless sensors and actuator networks. In: 2016 18th International Conference on Advanced Communication Technology (ICACT), pp. 210–213. IEEE (2016)

18. Mahmud, R., Kotagiri, R., Buyya, R.: Fog computing: a taxonomy, survey and future directions. In: Di Martino, B., Li, K.-C., Yang, L.T., Esposito, A. (eds.) Internet of Everything. IT, pp. 103–130. Springer, Singapore (2018). https://doi.org/10.1007/978-981-10-5861-5_5

19. Maksimović, M.: Improving computing issues in internet of things driven e-health systems. In: Proceedings of the International Conference for Young Researchers in Informatics, Mathematics and Engineering 2017, pp. 14–17 (2017)

20. Moysiadis, V., Sarigiannidis, P., Moscholios, I.: Towards distributed data management in fog computing. Wirel. Commun. Mob. Comput. **2018**, 1–14 (2018). https://doi.org/10.1155/2018/7597686
21. OpenFog: Openfog use cases (2020). http://openfogconsortium.org/
22. Pisani, F., do Rosario, V.M., Borin, E.: Fog vs. cloud computing: should i stay or should i go? Future Internet **11**(2), 34 (2019)
23. Podsevalov, I., Iakushkin, O., Kurbangaliev, R., Korkhov, V.: Blockchain as a platform for fog computing. In: Misra, S., et al. (eds.) ICCSA 2019. LNCS, vol. 11620, pp. 596–605. Springer, Cham (2019). https://doi.org/10.1007/978-3-030-24296-1_48
24. Rahmani, A.M., et al.: Exploiting smart e-health gateways at the edge of healthcare internet-of-things: a fog computing approach. Future Gener. Comput. Syst. **78**, 641–658 (2018)
25. Shi, H., Chen, N., Deters, R.: Combining mobile and fog computing: using CoAP to link mobile device clouds with fog computing. In: 2015 IEEE International Conference on Data Science and Data Intensive Systems, pp. 564–571. IEEE (2015)
26. Silva, C.A., de Aquino Júnior, G.S.: Fog computing in healthcare: a review. In: 2018 IEEE Symposium on Computers and Communications (ISCC), pp. 1126–1131. IEEE (2018)
27. Silva, C.A., de Aquino Júnior, G.S., Melo, S.R.M.: A blockchain-based approach for privacy control of patient's medical records in the fog layer. In: Anais Principais do XXV Simpósio Brasileiro de Multimídia e Web, pp. 133–136. SBC, Porto Alegre (2019). https://sol.sbc.org.br/index.php/webmedia/article/view/8011
28. Tuli, S., Mahmud, R., Tuli, S., Buyya, R.: FogBus: a blockchain-based lightweight framework for edge and fog computing. J. Syst. Softw. **154**, 22–36 (2019)
29. Verma, S., Yadav, A.K., Motwani, D., Raw, R., Singh, H.K.: An efficient data replication and load balancing technique for fog computing environment. In: 2016 3rd International Conference on Computing for Sustainable Global Development (INDIACom), pp. 2888–2895. IEEE (2016)
30. Yousefpour, A., et al.: All one needs to know about fog computing and related edge computing paradigms: a complete survey. J. Syst. Archit. (2019)
31. Zhou, Y., Tian, L., Liu, L., Qi, Y.: Fog computing enabled future mobile communication networks: a convergence of communication and computing. IEEE Commun. Mag. **57**(5), 20–27 (2019)

Artificial Intelligence and Data Science in the Detection, Diagnosis, and Control of COVID-19: A Systematic Mapping Study

Verónica Tintín[1] and Hector Florez[2(✉)] [iD]

[1] Universidad de las Fuerzas Armadas ESPE, Sangolquí, Ecuador
[2] Universidad Distrital Francisco Jose de Caldas, Bogota, Colombia
haflorezf@udistrital.edu.co

Abstract. On March 11 2020, the World Health Organization (WHO) announced that the new COVID-19 disease, caused by the SARS-CoV2 could be considered a pandemic. Both this new virus and the disease it causes were unknown before the outbreak in Wuhan (China) in December 2019. Since then, the number of infections has grown exponentially causing the collapse of health-care systems, as well as socio-economic structures of countries around the world. The objective of this study is to give an overview of the application of Artificial Intelligence and Data Science in the control of the pandemic through a systematic mapping of scientific literature that determines the nature, scope and quantity of published primary studies. The research was carried out using the databases Scopus, IEEE Xplore, PubMed Central and the global research database of the World Health Organization. Thus, 372 studies were identified that met the inclusion criteria. The application of artificial intelligence techniques was observed, such as neural networks, deep learning, and machine learning in some areas including detection and imaging diagnosis, prediction of new outbreaks and mortality, social distancing, among others. In data analysis, artificial intelligence has become an important tool in the fight against COVID-19 and this study may be useful for the scientific community to direct future research into less-investigated areas.

Keywords: Artificial intelligence · Data science · COVID-19 · Deep learning · Machine learning

1 Introduction

The COVID-19 epidemic was declared by the World Health Organization (WHO) as a public health emergency of international concern on January 30 2020, and on March 11 2020, this organization announced that the new COVID-19 could be characterized as a pandemic [26,55,56].

In this pandemic crisis, the scarcity of resources and medical personnel has caused major problems in the health systems [14,36], and a negative impact on

© Springer Nature Switzerland AG 2021
O. Gervasi et al. (Eds.): ICCSA 2021, LNCS 12957, pp. 354–368, 2021.
https://doi.org/10.1007/978-3-030-87013-3_27

the socioeconomic structures of all countries around the world. Due to this, the COVID-19 pandemic poses a series of challenges for the artificial intelligence community. Among these challenges there are the tracking and predicting of the spread of the infection, conducting diagnoses and forecasting, social control, search for treatments and vaccines, among others [43].

As the virus advances at pandemic speed, scientists have been working and publishing their research on the application of artificial intelligence and data science by combining traditional mathematical and statistical models with sophisticated models from Machine Learning and Deep Learning, including the use of technologies such as the Internet of Things (IoT) and Big Data [58].

Recent studies have revealed that Machine Learning, Deep Learning and Artificial Intelligence are promising technologies used by various healthcare providers, as they allow to improve scale, accelerate processing capacity, be reliable and even outperform humans in tasks specific healthcare [39]. Therefore, healthcare industries and physicians around the world are employing these technologies to cope with the COVID-19 pandemic and provide decision support tools on what has been modeled.

In this study, a systematic mapping of scientific literature is carried out using the databases of Scopus, IEEE Xplore, PubMed and the global research database of the World Health Organization to collect the most recent information from peer reviewed articles published in scientific journals and international conference proceedings, which demonstrate the use of artificial intelligence techniques and data science in the context of the COVID-19 pandemic.

2 Method

2.1 Systematic Mapping Study

A systematic mapping study is a method that consists of a literature survey on an area of interest, in order to determine the nature, scope, and quantity of published primary studies, as well as to give an overview of the area under study through the classification and counting of literary contributions [46]. The fundamental objective is to identify, categorize, and analyze in the existing literature what is relevant to a given research topic. The steps of the systematic mapping process are: request questions, search strategy, selection of primary studies, data extraction, analysis, classification, and verification.

2.2 Research Questions

The structure of this study follows the guidelines established in the Petersen guidelines for conducting systematic studies in software engineering in order to answer the following research questions:

- RQ1: How many studies have been reported identifying artificial intelligence and data science techniques for the detection and control of COVID-19?

- RQ2: Which artificial intelligence and data science techniques are being used for the detection and control of COVID-19?
- RQ3: What are the characteristics of the techniques found and in which areas are they being applied?
- RQ4: What is the effectiveness of the techniques found in the detection and control of COVID-19?

The research questions were developed with the purpose of giving an overview of the research that has being carried out to combat COVID-19 in the field of data science and artificial intelligence. In this context, techniques and tools used are identified for diagnosis, prediction, outbreak control, sentiment analysis, contact tracing, drug development, fake news, etc.

2.3   Search Strategy

For the design of the research strategy, the PICO strategy was used, which identifies four key components: Population, Intervention, Comparison, and Outcome [35,46]. This strategy allows adjustment of the appropriate terms to structure the search chain in the different bibliographic sources and answer the research questions posed. In this study, no empirical comparison was made. Thus, the terms determined are: *Population*: `coronavirus`, `COVID-19`, or `SARS-CoV-2`; *Intervention*: `data science`, `data analytics`, or `artificial intelligence`; and *Outcome*: `prediction`, `diagnosis`, `forecast`, `detection`, or `forecasting`. Since no empirical comparison is made between the intervention alternatives, this component as well as the results are omitted as a relevant consequence of interest.

Four bibliographic databases were used for the selection of the primary studies: IEEE Xplore, Scopus, MEDLINE, which can be accessed via PubMed Central, and the World Health Organization global research database that compiles the latest research reports on COVID-19. The world documentation cited in the WHO COVID-19 database is updated daily from searches of bibliographic databases, manual searches, and other scientific articles referred by experts.

Definition of the Search String. The search string was constructed based on the structuring of regular expressions formed with keywords determined in the PICO strategy, linked with the logical AND/OR connectors and applied to the titles and abstracts. For each base the following search string was defined:

- IEEE Xplore: ((("Document Title": "coronavirus" OR "Document Title": "COVID-19" OR "Full Text Only": "SARS-CoV-2") AND ("Full Text Only": "data science" OR "Full Text Only": "data analytics" OR "Full Text Only": "artificial intelligence") AND ("Full Text Only": prediction OR "Full Text Only": "diagnosis" OR "Full Text Only": "forecast" OR "Full Text Only": "forecasting" OR "Full Text Only": "detection"))
- Scopus: (TITLE-ABS-KEY ("coronavirus") OR TITLE-ABS-KEY (COVID-19) OR TITLE-ABS-KEY ("data science")) AND (TITLE-ABS-KEY ("data analytics") OR TITLE-ABS-KEY ("SARS-CoV-2") OR TITLE-ABS-KEY

("artificial intelligence")) AND (TITLE-ABS-KEY (prediction) OR TITLE-ABS-KEY (diagnosis) OR TITLE-ABS-KEY (forecast) OR TITLE-ABS-KEY (detection) OR TITLE-ABS-KEY (forecasting))

- PubMed(("coronavirus" [Abstract] OR "COVID-19" [Abstract] OR "SARS-CoV-2" [Abstract]) AND ("data science" [Abstract] OR "data analytics" [Abstract] OR "artificial intelligence" [Abstract]) AND ("prediction" [Abstract] OR "diagnosis" [Abstract] OR "forecast" [Abstract] OR "forecasting" [Abstract] OR "detection" [Abstract]))
- WHO: (tw:("COVID-19") OR tw:("SARS-CoV-2") OR tw:("coronavirus")) AND (tw:("artificial intelligence") OR tw:("data science") OR tw:("data analytics")) AND (tw:("prediction") OR tw:("diagnosis") OR tw:("forecast") OR tw:("forecasting") OR tw:("detection"))

The Mendeley tool was used for the management of bibliographic references and the reference period for the search was from January 2020 to the second week of February 2021. The number of results for each database are: IEEE Xplore: 264, Scopus: 340, PubMed: 193, and WHO: 262.

2.4   Selection of Primary Studies

The Backward Snowball Sampling Method was used for the selection of studies. Articles that did not meet the criteria of basic language, period of publication type, and peer review were excluded. Duplicate articles were eliminated. The inclusion and exclusion criteria were applied to titles and abstracts. Many of them were not clearly identifiable, so the full text was read. The following inclusion and exclusion criteria were applied:

Inclusion Criteria

- Studies in English peer-reviewed in conferences, journals and included in the COVID-19 Open Research Dataset, published from January 2020 to the second week of February 2021.
- Studies in which the application of artificial intelligence in the diagnosis, detection, and control of COVID-19 is identified.
- Studies in which the application of data science in the detection and control of COVID-19 is identified.
- Studies that demonstrate the effectiveness of artificial intelligence and data science in the detection and control of Covid-19, either in case studies or proofs of concept.

Exclusion Criteria

- Studies that are not written in the English language in full text and that have not been peer reviewed.
- Secondary studies corresponding to third-party studies.

The number of included articles during the study selection process are: apply search on databases: 1059 results, remove duplicates: 730 results, apply inclusion/exclusion criteria: 478 results, and full text reading: 372 results.

2.5   Data Extraction

From the total of selected main studies, it was necessary to extract the relevant information to determine the number of studies that answer the research questions. The bibliographic manager made it possible to extract the relevant information from each publication and generate a report with the data shown in Table 1:

Table 1. Data extraction form.

Data item	Value
Type	Type of article, conference article or journal article
Author	Names of the authors of the document
Date	Date of document
DOI	Digital Object Identifier
Library Catalog	DataBase where the article is hosted
Conference	Conference Name
Abstract	Article Summary
Keywords	Author keywords
Url	Resource locator
Files	Full text file

2.6   Analysis, Classification and Validity Verification

The analysis and classification was carried out using the SciMAT software (Science Mapping Analysis Software Tool). SciMAT is an open source tool that performs a scientific mapping analysis of bibliography under a longitudinal framework to analyze and track the conceptual, intellectual or social evolution of a research field over consecutive periods of time [16]. Strategic diagrams, cluster networks, and areas of evolution were used to better understand the results and to identify the thematic areas that are the object of this research.

The verification of the studies quality was carried out by reading the abstracts of the documents. The full text was read of incomplete documents to verify that the selected studies meet the following quality criteria:

- Does the selected study contribute to answering the research questions?
- Does the selected study contain references to studies published in journals or conferences?
- Is the study based on research: case study or proof of concept?
- Is there a clear statement of the research objectives?
- Is there a clear statement of the results?

3   Results and Discussion

3.1   Frequency of Publication (RQ1)

The number of selected articles published in 2020 were 306, while the number of selected articles published in 2021 were 66. Moreover, the number of selected article published in journals were 218, while the number of selected articles published in conferences were 154.

From the 218 selected articles published in journals, 23 were published in the IEEE Access journal, which is an open access scientific journal with continuous publication frequency and impact factor of 3,745. From the 154 articles published in conferences, 44 were published at conferences sponsored by IEEE, a global organization dedicated to the advancement of technology. Table 2 shows the main scientific journals of the selected articles. In general, it can be observed that the IEEE journals are preferred.

Table 2. Targeted Venues.

Journal/Conference	Articles
IEEE Access	23
IEEE Internet of Things Journal	9
Chaos, Solitons and Fractals	8
IEEE Journal of Biomedical and Health Informatics	7
Computers, Materials and Continua	6
Scientific Reports	5
Applied Intelligence	4
Journal of Medical Internet Research	4
European Radiology	4
Medical Image Analysis	4
IEEE Transactions on Medical Imaging	4
PLoS ONE	3
Informatics in Medicine Unlocked	3
Process Safety and Environmental Protection	3
Radiology	3
IEEE Sensors Journal	3
IEEE Transactions on Industrial Informatics	3
IEEE Transactions on Computational Social Systems	3
Applied Sciences (Switzerland)	3
Others	116
Total	**218**
IEEE Advancing Technology for Humanity	44
ACM International Conference Proceeding Series	4
Advances in Intelligent Systems and Computing	4
Others	102
Total	**154**

3.2   Identified Techniques (RQ2)

From the selected papers, we identified supervised classification and regression algorithms as well as unsupervised clustering algorithms. 66.13% of the papers uses Neural Networks, 6.45% uses Support Vector Machine, 5.38% uses Long Short Term Memory, 4.03% uses Random Forest, 3.76% uses Decision Tree, 3.23% uses Naive Bayes, 2.42% uses Logistic Regression, 2.42% uses Gaussian Process Regression, 2.15% uses Fuzzy C-Means, 1.88% uses K Nearest Neighbors, 0.81% uses K Means Clustering, 0.81% uses Linear Regression, 0.27% uses Hidden Markov Model, and 0.27% uses Support Vector Machine Regression.

The aforementioned algorithms were used in combination with other algorithms, techniques, statistical models and mathematical models, such as those shown in Table 3 to optimize and balance the prediction models in several studies:

Table 3. Additional algorithms, techniques and models used.

Item	Reference
ADAptive SYNthetic (ADASYN)	[9]
Differential Evolution (DE)	[60]
Particle Swarm Optimization (PSO)	[8, 23, 27, 44, 52]
Principle Component Analysis (PCA)	[8]
Sequential Minimal Optimization (SMO)	[1]
AdaBoost	[28, 31]
Prophet	[4]
ARIMA	[4, 15, 20, 25, 38, 49, 50, 54]
Stacked Long Short-Term Memory (SLSTM)	[20]
Marine Predators Algorithm (MPA)	[2]
Single Shot Detector (SSD)	[40, 57]
Guided Whale Optimization Algorithm	[23]
Stochastic Fractal Search (SFS)	[23]
Epidemiological models: SEIR – SIR – SIRQ - SIRD	[4, 6, 12, 34, 45, 60–62, 64]
Time Series	[13, 17, 24, 32, 38, 42, 48, 52, 54]

According to [5], the convergence between data science, Big Data, advanced analytics, artificial intelligence, among others present various research and development options to combat COVID-19. In the same way, [18] states that data science is the most imperative part of medical science and is contributing significantly to finding solutions to the greatest existing obstacles in the face of the pandemic. Some of the traditional models mentioned in Table 3 have been used in the past and have given reliable prediction results, but due to the increasing complexity of COVID-19 data sets, it is necessary to combine them with recent trends in data science, including big data and the Internet of Things [44].

With many success stories, Machine Learning (ML) and Deep Learning (DL) have been widely used in our everyday lives in various ways. They have also been instrumental in addressing the Coronavirus (COVID-19) outbreak, which has been occurring around the world.

In addition, based on the approach of how machines can learn, two approaches are a subset of artificial intelligence which is being widely used to address the COVID-19 outbreak [3]. The results show the following percentages: Machine Learning (43.72%) and Deep Learning (56.28%).

3.3   Topics and Features (RQ3)

372 studies have been identified exploring different areas in which Artificial Intelligence and Data Science have been shown to be effective in the fight against COVID-19. The percentage of studies according to the areas of application are: Diagnostic imaging (50.92%), Analysis and prediction of the spread (18.45%), Detection of masks by facial recognition (4.06%), Social distancing (4.06%), Mortality prediction (3.69%), Precision diagnosis (3.69%), Cough/voice recognition diagnosis (2.21%), Contact tracing (2.21%), Drug development and reuse (1.85%), Blocking, quarantine and self-isolation (1.48%), Prediction of protein structure (1.48%), Tracking of travelers and mobility profiles (1.48%), Vaccine development (1.48%), Sentiment analysis (1.11%), Environmental intelligence (1.11%), Sanitation/Disinfection (0.37%), and Mental Health (0.37%).

The publications have shown that the main area of application of Artificial Intelligence and Data Science is diagnostic imaging. Said diagnostic test is based on X-ray images (CXR) and computed tomography (CT). Chest imaging is generally used by physicians to diagnose disease, while awaiting RT-PCR results or when RT-PCR results are negative and the person has symptoms of COVID-19 [51]. Computed tomography is considered the gold standard in diagnostic tests and is the most commonly used in studies for a more accurate diagnosis, since it is faster and cheaper [10].

Regarding the analysis and prediction of new outbreaks, several studies are being carried out. In the study by [6], a model is proposed that combines Machine Learning with traditional susceptible-infected prediction models- recovered (SIR) and susceptible-exposed-infectious-recovered (SEIR). The combination is an effective tool for outbreak modeling. Similarly, the study by [33] shows an outbreak analysis model using continuous variable quantum neural networks and the quantum backpropagation multilayer perceptron (QBMLP) thus demonstrating that there is a promising future with the use of the quantum machine learning.

Social distancing is a control measure that was implemented with the aim of reducing the spread of COVID-19. In the research presented by [53], an artificial intelligence system was proposed for the classification of social distancing using images acquired through thermal cameras to establish a complete system for tracking people, classifying social distancing, and monitoring body temperature. In the study by [41], a model created for the detection of distances and objects was trained with the OpenCV library. This model detects objects in video streams in real time, calculates their distance, generates analytical reports, and sends notifications of safe areas. In the two mentioned studies, a state-of-the-art Machine Learning algorithm called YOLO was used.

Medical researchers from around the world have provided evidence that COVID-19 and pandemic diseases are transmitted through respiratory droplets, hence the use of a mask is an infection control measure. Few research studies have been found on the detection of face masks based on artificial intelligence technology and image processing. In the study by [22], the use of MobileNet Mask, a multiphase face mask detection model based on Deep Learning to prevent virus transmission, was proposed. However, in [59], deep convolutional neural networks (CNN) such as ResNet-50 were used for the construction of the model, which notably improved the classification of images.

The use of Machine Learning and Artificial Intelligence to predict SARS-CoV-2 infection from complete blood counts is a useful tool for precision diagnosis. In the study by [11] several Machine Learning models like Random Forest were used as classifiers. They fit a traditional logistic model, but instead of using all the predictors, they use a regularized path to select the most important variables for logistic regression. Furthermore, they define artificial neural network models.

In the study by [37] in-hospital blood samples were taken from patients at the time of admission and used for the prediction of mortality. A model was trained with the information from 28 blood biomarkers including age and gender of patients. The approach combined 5-layer Deep Neural Network (DNN) models and Random Forest in conjunction with tools such as TensorFlow, NumPy, Pandas, and Matplotlib to build the model and analyze the results. Additionally a web application (BeatCOVID19) is available so that anyone can record their laboratory tests.

3.4   Effectiveness of Artificial Intelligence and Data Science Techniques (RQ4)

Although computed tomography is considered a higher precision test, in study conducted in October 2020, a diagnostic model with X-ray images was developed. This model is based on a neural network and shows an accuracy of 99.49% for diagnosis of COVID-19 in suspected patients. It is important to indicate that this process is carried out in less than 5 min [29]. In another study by the same author [30], they propose a model that includes Deep Learning and Convolutional Neural Network (CNN) algorithms with a precision of 99.9%. Similarly, in the study by [19] the proposed model showed a 99.96% accuracy.

Regarding diagnostic tests with computed tomography, in the study by [36], a Deep Learning model was trained with a dataset of 3993 images which includes low-quality images. The model ResNet-50 showed excellent diagnostic performance (sensitivity of 99.58%, specificity of 100.00% and precision of 99.87%), being one of the models that has shown the best results. Methodologies based on Artificial Intelligence (AI) can be useful to predict, control and prevent the spread of new outbreaks. In the study by [63], a predictive framework was proposed, which incorporates vector support machines (SVM) in anticipation of a possible COVID-19 outbreak. The results indicate that the suggested system outperformed the more advanced approaches, with 98.88% and 96.79% of results in terms of accuracy during training and training validation respectively. In another study, the assembly of decision trees and logistic regression demonstrated a model with an improved interaction effect, especially in the predictions of continuous response variables [44]. This model included swarm optimization of particles (PSO) for the adjustment of the parameters and incorporated the modeling of time series, providing levels of prediction precision of 99%.

In the study by [7], a model for tracking travelers and mobility profiles was proposed to classify daily passengers on trains according to age groups. The data set was compared to several Machine Learning algorithms and the vector support machine mobility prediction classification (SVM) reached an accuracy of up to 86.43% and 81.96% in the age groups 16 to 59 years and over 60 years.

In the model by [21] called MobileNet Mask, two different data sets of face masks have been used together with more than 5200 images to train and test the Deep Learning model. This model detects people with and without face masks from the images and the video stream. The results of the experiment show that with 770 validation samples MobileNet Mask has achieved 93% precision, while with 276 validation samples it achieved an accuracy of almost 100%. Similarly, in the study by [47], a Deep Learning model was trained with a data set of images of people with and without masks collected from various sources. The trained architecture reached 98.7% precision in distinguishing people with and without a face masks.

In the model by [37] for the prediction of in-hospital mortality based on routine blood samples, the EDRnet model based on Deep Neural Networks and Random Forest was proposed, which provided a high 100% sensitivity, 91% specificity, 92% precision, and 96% balanced precision. The training times were 796 and 126 s respectively, and the total calculation time for the EDRnet test was 72 s. This indicates that the trained model is very effective in predicting mortality. To expand the number of patient data points, a web application (Beat-COVID19) was developed in which anyone can access the model to predict mortality and can record their own blood lab results.

4   Conclusions

This study shows that, in the literature, there is a large number of research carried out in the context of the COVID-19. Artificial Intelligence and Data Analytics constitute elements of great support in several areas of application, mainly in diagnostic imaging, analysis and prediction of spread, prediction of mortality, etc.

Due to the strong impact which the pandemic has had on the health and economy of the world, there are a large number of scientific studies in the area of diagnostic imaging with excellent results. However, there are still areas that need more attention, such as ambient intelligence which allows people to safely return to educational, commercial, and work activities, mainly in safe environments.

In diagnostic imaging, studies indicate that chest x-ray and computed tomography may be appropriate tests to confirm the diagnosis of COVID-19, mainly in people who have been diagnosed with the disease by other tests with unreliable results.

In data analysis, Artificial Intelligence has become an important tool in the fight against COVID-19. Deep Learning and Machine Learning models for pandemic prediction have shown greater precision than mathematical and statistical models previously used by epidemiologists.

Finally, it can be concluded that this study may be useful to direct the scientific community to research areas in the future which receive less attention, but are of the same level of importance, since it is necessary to carry out research that contributes to the recovery of the economy in the countries that have been the most affected by the effects of the pandemic.

References

1. Al Mahmoud, R.H., Omar, E., Taha, K., Al-Sharif, M., Aref, A.: Covid-19 global spread analyzer: an ML-based attempt. J. Comput. Sci. **16**(9), 1291–1305 (2020)
2. Al-qaness, M.A.A., et al.: Efficient artificial intelligence forecasting models for COVID-19 outbreak in Russia and Brazil. Process Saf. Environ. Prot. **149**, 399–409 (2021)
3. Alafif, T., Tehame, A.M., Bajaba, S., Barnawi, A., Zia, S.: Machine and deep learning towards COVID-19 diagnosis and treatment: survey, challenges, and future directions. Int. J. Environ. Res. Public Health **18**(3), 1117 (2021). Number: 3
4. Alazab, M., Awajan, A., Mesleh, A., Abraham, A., Jatana, V., Alhyari, S.: COVID-19 prediction and detection using deep learning. Int. J. Comput. Inf. Syst. Ind. Manag. Appl. **12**, 168–181 (2020)
5. Alwaeli, Z.A.A., Ibrahim, A.A.: Predicting COVID-19 trajectory using machine learning. In: 2020 4th International Symposium on Multidisciplinary Studies and Innovative Technologies (ISMSIT), pp. 1–4. Institute of Electrical and Electronics Engineers Inc., October 2020
6. Ardabili, S.F., et al.: COVID-19 outbreak prediction with machine learning. Algorithms **13**(10), 249 (2020)
7. Asad, S.M., Dashtipour, K., Hussain, S., Abbasi, Q.H., Imran, M.A.: Travelers-tracing and mobility profiling using machine learning in railway systems. In: 2020 International Conference on UK-China Emerging Technologies (UCET), pp. 1–4. Institute of Electrical and Electronics Engineers Inc., August 2020
8. Asghar, M.A., Razzaq, S., Rasheed, S., Fawad: A robust technique for detecting SARS-CoV-2 from X-ray image using 2D convolutional neural network and particle swarm optimization. In: 2020 14th International Conference on Open Source Systems and Technologies (ICOSST), pp. 1–6 (2020)
9. Awal, M.A., Masud, M., Hossain, M.S., Bulbul, A.A.M., Mahmud, S.M.H., Bairagi, A.K.: A novel Bayesian optimization-based machine learning framework for COVID-19 detection from inpatient facility data. IEEE Access **9**, 10263–10281 (2021)

10. Babukarthik, R.G., et al.: Prediction of COVID-19 using genetic deep learning convolutional neural network (GDCNN). IEEE Access **8**, 177647–177666 (2020)
11. Banerjee, A., et al.: Use of Machine Learning and Artificial Intelligence to predict SARS-CoV-2 infection from Full Blood Counts in a population. Int. Immunopharmacol. **86**, 106705 (2020)
12. Bannur, N., Maheshwari, H., Jain, S., Shetty, S., Merugu, S., Raval, A.: Adaptive COVID-19 forecasting via Bayesian optimization. In: ACM International Conference Proceeding Series, p. 432. Association for Computing Machinery, January 2020
13. Bodapati, S., Bandarupally, H., Trupthi, M.: COVID-19 time series forecasting of daily cases, deaths caused and recovered cases using long short term memory networks. In: 2020 IEEE 5th International Conference on Computing Communication and Automation (ICCCA), pp. 525–530 (2020)
14. Butt, S.A., Misra, S., Anjum, M.W., Hassan, S.A.: Agile project development issues during COVID-19. In: Przybyłek, A., Miler, J., Poth, A., Riel, A. (eds.) LASD 2021. LNBIP, vol. 408, pp. 59–70. Springer, Cham (2021). https://doi.org/10.1007/978-3-030-67084-9_4
15. Chatterjee, A., Gerdes, M.W., Martinez, S.G.: Statistical explorations and univariate timeseries analysis on covid-19 datasets to understand the trend of disease spreading and death. Sensors (Switzerland) **20**(11), 3089 (2020)
16. Cobo, M.J., López-Herrera, A.G., Herrera-Viedma, E., Herrera, F.: SciMAT: a new science mapping analysis software tool. J. Am. Soc. Inf. Sci. Technol. **63**(8), 1609–1630 (2012)
17. Dandekar, R., Rackauckas, C., Barbastathis, G.: A machine learning-aided global diagnostic and comparative tool to assess effect of quarantine control in COVID-19 spread. Patterns **1**(9), 100145 (2020)
18. Darapaneni, N., et al.: COVID 19 severity of pneumonia analysis using chest X Rays. In: 2020 IEEE 15th International Conference on Industrial and Information Systems (ICIIS), pp. 381–386 (2020)
19. Das, D., Santosh, K.C., Pal, U.: Truncated inception net: COVID-19 outbreak screening using chest X-rays. Phys. Eng. Sci. Med. **43**(3), 915–925 (2020). https://doi.org/10.1007/s13246-020-00888-x
20. Devaraj, J., et al.: Forecasting of COVID-19 cases using deep learning models: is it reliable and practically significant? Results Phys. **21**, 103817 (2021)
21. Dey, S.K., Howlader, A., Deb, C.: MobileNet mask: a multi-phase face mask detection model to prevent person-to-person transmission of SARS-CoV-2. In: Kaiser, M.S., Bandyopadhyay, A., Mahmud, M., Ray, K. (eds.) Proceedings of International Conference on Trends in Computational and Cognitive Engineering. AISC, vol. 1309, pp. 603–613. Springer, Singapore (2021). https://doi.org/10.1007/978-981-33-4673-4_49
22. Dey, S., Biswas, S., Nandi, S., Nath, S., Das, I.: Deep greedy network: a tool for medical diagnosis on exiguous dataset of COVID-19. In: 2020 IEEE International Conference for Convergence in Engineering, ICCE 2020 - Proceedings, pp. 340–344. Institute of Electrical and Electronics Engineers Inc., September 2020
23. El-Kenawy, E.S.M., Ibrahim, A., Mirjalili, S., Eid, M.M., Hussein, S.E.: Novel feature selection and voting classifier algorithms for COVID-19 classification in CT images. IEEE Access **8**, 179317–179335 (2020)
24. El Mouden, Z.A., Jakimi, A., Taj, R.M., Hajar, M.: A graph-based methodology for tracking covid-19 in time series datasets. In: 2020 IEEE 2nd International Conference on Electronics, Control, Optimization and Computer Science, ICECOCS 2020. Institute of Electrical and Electronics Engineers Inc., December 2020

25. Elsheikh, A.H., et al.: Deep learning-based forecasting model for COVID-19 outbreak in Saudi Arabia. Process Saf. Environ. Prot. **149**, 223–233 (2021)
26. Florez, H., Singh, S.: Online dashboard and data analysis approach for assessing covid-19 case and death data. F1000Research **9**, 570 (2020)
27. Gupta, H., et al.: Data analytics and mathematical modeling for simulating the dynamics of COVID-19 epidemic-a case study of India. Electronics (Switzerland) **10**(2), 1–21 (2021)
28. Hamida, S., Gannour, O.E., Cherradi, B., Ouajji, H., Raihani, A.: Optimization of machine learning algorithms hyper-parameters for improving the prediction of patients infected with COVID-19. In: 2020 IEEE 2nd International Conference on Electronics, Control, Optimization and Computer Science (ICECOCS), pp. 1–6 (2020)
29. Haritha, D., Pranathi, M.K., Reethika, M.: COVID detection from chest X-rays with DeepLearning: CheXNet. In: 2020 5th International Conference on Computing, Communication and Security (ICCCS), pp. 1–5 (2020)
30. Haritha, D., Praneeth, Ch., Krishna Pranathi, M.: Covid prediction from x-ray images. In: Proceedings of the 2020 International Conference on Computing, Communication and Security, ICCCS 2020. Institute of Electrical and Electronics Engineers Inc., October 2020
31. Iwendi, C., et al.: COVID-19 patient health prediction using boosted random forest algorithm. Front. Public Health **8**, 357 (2020)
32. Johnsen, T.K., Gao, J.Z.: Elastic net to forecast COVID-19 cases. In: 2020 International Conference on Innovation and Intelligence for Informatics, Computing and Technologies (3ICT), pp. 1–6 (2020)
33. Kairon, P., Bhattacharyya, S.: COVID-19 outbreak prediction using quantum neural networks. In: Bhattacharyya, S., Dutta, P., Datta, K. (eds.) Intelligence Enabled Research. AISC, vol. 1279, pp. 113–123. Springer, Singapore (2021). https://doi.org/10.1007/978-981-15-9290-4_12 ISSN 21945365
34. Kerdvibulvech, C., Chen, L.L.: The power of augmented reality and artificial intelligence during the Covid-19 outbreak. In: Stephanidis, C., Kurosu, M., Degen, H., Reinerman-Jones, L. (eds.) HCII 2020. LNCS, vol. 12424, pp. 467–476. Springer, Cham (2020). https://doi.org/10.1007/978-3-030-60117-1_34 ISSN 16113349
35. Kitchenham, B.: Guidelines for performing Systematic Literature Reviews in Software Engineering (2007)
36. Ko, H., et al.: COVID-19 pneumonia diagnosis using a simple 2D deep learning framework with a single chest CT image: model development and validation. J. Med. Internet Res. **22**(6), e19569 (2020)
37. Ko, H., et al.: An artificial intelligence model to predict the mortality of COVID-19 patients at hospital admission time using routine blood samples: development and validation of an ensemble model. J. Med. Internet Res. **22**(12), e25442 (2020)
38. Kumar, N., Susan, S.: COVID-19 pandemic prediction using time series forecasting models. In: 2020 11th International Conference on Computing, Communication and Networking Technologies (ICCCNT), pp. 1–7 (2020)
39. Lalmuanawma, S., Hussain, J., Chhakchhuak, L.: Applications of machine learning and artificial intelligence for Covid-19 (SARS-CoV-2) pandemic: a review. Chaos Solitons Fractals **139**, 110059 (2020)
40. Liu, J., Zhang, Z., Zu, L., Wang, H., Zhong, Y.: Intelligent detection for CT image of COVID-19 using deep learning. In: 2020 13th International Congress on Image and Signal Processing, BioMedical Engineering and Informatics (CISP-BMEI), pp. 76–81. Institute of Electrical and Electronics Engineers Inc., October 2020

41. Melenli, S., Topkaya, A.: Real-time maintaining of social distance in Covid-19 environment using image processing and big data. In: 2020 Innovations in Intelligent Systems and Applications Conference (ASYU), pp. 1–5 (2020)

42. Mirri, S., Roccetti, M., Delnevo, G.: The New York City covid-19 spread in the 2020 spring: a study on the potential role of particulate using time series analysis and machine learning. Appl. Sci. (Switzerland) **11**(3), 1–19 (2021)

43. Naudé, W.: Artificial intelligence vs COVID-19: limitations, constraints and pitfalls. AI Soc. **35**(3), 761–765 (2020). https://doi.org/10.1007/s00146-020-00978-0

44. Ngie, H.M., Nderu, L., Mwigereri, D.G.: Tree-based regressor ensemble for viral infectious diseases spread prediction. In: CEUR Workshop Proceedings, vol. 2689. CEUR-WS (2020). ISSN 16130073

45. Nie, Q., Liu, Y., Zhang, D., Jiang, H.: Dynamical SEIR model with information entropy using COVID-19 as a case study. IEEE Trans. Comput. Soc. Syst. **8**(4), 1–9 (2021)

46. Petersen, K., Vakkalanka, S., Kuzniarz, L.: Guidelines for conducting systematic mapping studies in software engineering: an update. Inf. Softw. Technol. **64**, 1–18 (2015)

47. Rahman, M.M., Manik, M.M.H., Islam, M.M., Mahmud, S., Kim, J.H.: An automated system to limit COVID-19 using facial mask detection in smart city network. In: 2020 IEEE International IOT, Electronics and Mechatronics Conference (IEMTRONICS), pp. 1–5 (2020)

48. Ren, J., et al.: A novel intelligent computational approach to model epidemiological trends and assess the impact of non-pharmacological interventions for COVID-19. IEEE J. Biomed. Health Inform. **24**(12), 3551–3563 (2020)

49. Saba, A.I., Elsheikh, A.H.: Forecasting the prevalence of COVID-19 outbreak in Egypt using nonlinear autoregressive artificial neural networks. Process Saf. Environ. Prot. **141**, 1–8 (2020)

50. Sadasivuni, S.T., Zhang, Y.: Using gradient methods to predict Twitter users' mental health with both COVID-19 growth patterns and tweets. In: Proceedings - 2020 IEEE International Conference on Humanized Computing and Communication with Artificial Intelligence, HCCAI 2020, pp. 65–66. Institute of Electrical and Electronics Engineers Inc., September 2020

51. Salameh, J.-P., et al.: Thoracic imaging tests for the diagnosis of COVID-19. Cochrane Database Syst. Rev. **9**, CD013639 (2020)

52. Salgotra, R., Gandomi, M., Gandomi, A.H.: Evolutionary modelling of the COVID-19 pandemic in fifteen most affected countries. Chaos Solitons Fractals **140**, 110118 (2020)

53. Saponara, S., Elhanashi, A., Gagliardi, A.: Implementing a real-time, AI-based, people detection and social distancing measuring system for Covid-19. J. Real-Time Image Process. (2021)

54. Sharma, R.R., Kumar, M., Maheshwari, S., Ray, K.P.: EVDHM-ARIMA-based time series forecasting model and its application for COVID-19 cases. IEEE Trans. Instrum. Meas. **70**, 1–10 (2021)

55. Singh, S., Florez, H.: Bioinformatic study to discover natural molecules with activity against covid-19. F1000Research **9**, 1203 (2020)

56. Singh, S., Florez, H.: Coronavirus disease 2019 drug discovery through molecular docking. F1000Research **9**, 502 (2020)

57. Szczepanek, R.: Analysis of pedestrian activity before and during COVID-19 lockdown, using webcam time-lapse from Cracow and machine learning. PeerJ **8**, e10132 (2020)

58. Vaishya, R., Javaid, M., Khan, I.H., Haleem, A.: Artificial Intelligence (AI) applications for COVID-19 pandemic. Diabetes Metab. Syndr. **14**(4), 337–339 (2020)
59. Venkateswarlu, I.B., Kakarla, J., Prakash, S.: Face mask detection using MobileNet and global pooling block. In: 2020 IEEE 4th Conference on Information & Communication Technology (CICT), pp. 1–5 (2020)
60. Wang, D., Sun, Y., Song, J., Huang, Y.: A SEIR model optimization using the differential evolution. In: Chen, X., Yan, H., Yan, Q., Zhang, X. (eds.) ML4CS 2020. LNCS, vol. 12487, pp. 384–392. Springer, Cham (2020). https://doi.org/10.1007/978-3-030-62460-6_34 ISSN: 16113349
61. Wang, S., Fang, H., Ma, Z., Wang, X.: Forecasting the 2019-ncov epidemic in Wuhan by SEIR and cellular automata model. In: Journal of Physics: Conference Series, vol. 1533. Institute of Physics Publishing, June 2020. ISSN 17426596, Issue: 4
62. Yang, Z., et al.: Modified SEIR and AI prediction of the epidemics trend of COVID-19 in China under public health interventions. J. Thorac. Dis. **12**(3), 165–174 (2020)
63. Zagrouba, R., et al.: Modelling and simulation of COVID-19 outbreak prediction using supervised machine learning. Comput. Mater. Contin. **66**(3), 2397–2407 (2020)
64. Zhan, C., Tse, C.K., Lai, Z., Hao, T., Su, J.: Prediction of COVID-19 spreading profiles in South Korea, Italy and Iran by data-driven coding. PLoS One **15**(7), e0234763–e0234763 (2020)

Wireless Protocols in Device Communication in the Industrial Internet of Things: Systematic Review

Walter L. Neto(ID), Itamir de M. Barroca Filho(✉)(ID),
Philipy A. Silveira de Brito(✉)(ID), Inácia F. da Costa Neta(✉)(ID),
Larissa K. de Menezes Silva(✉)(ID), and Denis R. Ramalho Orozco(✉)(ID)

Digital Metropolis Institute, Federal University of Rio Grande do Norte,
Natal 59078970, Brazil
walter.lopes@ifrn.edu.br, itamir.filho@imd.ufrn.br

Abstract. The technological revolution proposed by the Internet of Things (IoT) allows interconnections between users, devices, and the internet. Regarding Industries, the interconnection between devices, industrial applications, and computer networks is called the Industrial Internet of Things (IIoT). Industrial environments present a particular scenario regarding the difficulties faced concerning wireless data exchange between devices. This article proposes an examination of the state of the art of wireless communication protocols used in industry 4.0 through the systematic literature review (SLR), where 10 papers were selected (from 179) to answer the research questions. As the main results of this review, we can mention the summary of the main characteristics of wireless communication protocols applied in the industry, an overview of the principal authors in this area (43 authors), and a summary of the main challenges. Among the main challenges are the optimization problem related to interference and noise in the different industrial environments, the impact on communication between wireless devices due to physical obstacles, and the natural restriction of resources concerning IoT and IIoT devices. Another challenge is the few protocols aimed at the industry that support IPV6. In this review, we identified a tendency to increase interest in this field of research as well as present open fields and opportunities, such as the development of lightweight protocols for devices with severe resource limitations, the need for solutions aimed at observability IIoT devices, and strategies aimed at minimizing the impacts of interference in wireless IIoT communications.

Keywords: Industrial Internet of Things (IIoT) · Industry 4.0 · Systematic literature review (SLR) · Wireless

1 Introduction

As Its name suggests, IIoT concerns the possible applications of IoT for the industrial area. This application of the IoT predicts the decentralization of indus-

© Springer Nature Switzerland AG 2021
O. Gervasi et al. (Eds.): ICCSA 2021, LNCS 12957, pp. 369–381, 2021.
https://doi.org/10.1007/978-3-030-87013-3_28

trial processes while requiring an interconnection of these systems [10]. Thus, to proposing to carry applications in IoT to Industrial context, must be necessary to consider the increase in complexity related to specific industrial processes considering the needs related to scalability, according to the industry's growth itself [10]. So, It's important to think about a real impact in terms of resources and capital.

Nevertheless, IIoT should not be restricted to traditional data collection or simple automation, but be a means for exponentiating processes by also using more accurate real-time data analysis for industry and business [10]. On therms of accurate, real-time analysis of production, will be working based on data collected at the moment and thus generate up-to-orientated production data. The benefits of this type of industry are also understood by the production of traceable objects, whose raw materials are localized, as well as its defects and causes of low quality [10].

In this sense, it is observed that not only a physical structure in the sense of machinery or human resources but the need to think at a network structure that enables the realization of the IoT industry model is created. Based on changes in industry requirements and in huge demand for bandwidth, speed, data consumption, data analysis, and use of this data, at the level of great industries and its production it is necessary to implement protocols and technologies that can cover the needs of the market, since the connection with wires, in this proportion, is unthinkable [8]. During the systematic review, some challenges were found in the area of IIoT, among them, is the lack of compatibility between protocols used in the industry environment with Internet Protocol version 6 (IPv6). In this sense, the article [13] brings a proposal to develop a new solution with hardware that does the translation from IPv6 to Industrial Wireless networks that cannot communicate through this protocol.

Using this solution, it's possible to improve the communication and monitoring of applications within the network and make it compatible with networks that use the IPv6 protocol. Another challenge faced it's about identifier security related issues in wireless protocols in natural restriction of resources concerning IoT and IIoT devices, [7] proposes a Lightweight & Secure Industrial IoT Communications via the MQ Telemetry Transport Protocol, where Message Queue Telemetry Transport (MQTT) is used as a lightweight protocol suitable for the industrial domain. Then are evaluated different security mechanisms used to protect the MQTT-enabled interactions on a real testbed of wireless sensor motes.

Also, we identified the most frequent challenge presented is related to interference and noise problems in the different industrial environments. In this sense, [1] shows some challenges and issues in a real implementation for smart production in the context of Wireless connectivity in Industrial sensor and control networks. They propose an implementation of a LoRaWAN, a low-cost solution for the industry with a wireless solution.

This paper presents a systematic literature review (SLR), aiming to understand state of the art and related trends as wireless communication protocols in the context of the Industrial Internet of Things (IIoT). Section 2 presents the main aspects of the methodology, adopted for the present review, while Sect. 3 presents the results of the review method. The results are discussed in Sect. 3. Finally, Section 4 presents the conclusions, limitations, and future work.

2   Methodology

This study proposes a systematic literature review (SLR), for which the conduction was carried according to the process that Kitchenham [8] proposed. The SLR was conducted aiming to identify and analyze the state of the art of wireless protocols used in the communication of IIoT devices. The steps to carry out this research was as follow: defined the guiding questions, defined a search string, set criteria for inclusion and exclude studies according to a quality assessment (of what is sought), and, finally, put the steps into practice for the collection and selection of articles in the area in question. Then, the detailed explanation of the steps taken follows:

2.1   Research Questions

The following research questions guided this review:

- RQ1. What are the main characteristics of IIoT-based wireless communication protocols in the industry?
- RQ2. What are the challenges and opportunities related to IoT-based monitoring applications in the industry?
- RQ3. Who are the main authors of works in the area of wireless communication protocols in IIoT?

The main characteristics investigated in RQ1 were to identify the protocols used in the link and application layers and the communication architectures used specifically in wireless communication. RQ2 allowed the analysis of the relevance of the considered works and, in this sense, understanding of the demands that are still needing investigation in the area. On the other hand, RQ3 allowed the development of a more accurate study about the context to the analysis of the articles was not superficial and without foundation.

2.2   Search Process

The database used for the selection of studies was Scopus (Elsevier), once it indexes the main databases in the computing area.

To define the search string the terms collected through the exploratory stage of the search were used. The main objective was to obtain the largest number of papers related to the application of wireless communications in the industry. Thus, the search string used was (("protocol" OR "protocols") AND ("iiot" OR "industrial internet of things") AND "wireless").

2.3   Inclusion and Exclusion Criteria

This investigation included researches published from 2017 to 2021, fully available in the searched databases, peer-reviewed, and whose abstract has presented all the following items: context, objective, method, and results. The research excluded papers published as short articles, studies with unclear research questions, process, and also unclear data extraction process. In addition to that, it also excluded duplicate studies, studies in languages other than English, papers not accessible from free of charge, and those studies that did not identify the protocols used in wireless communication.

2.4   Quality Assessment

The studies were analyzed according to the quality assessment criteria defined according to Dyba [4] guidelines. The quality assessment criteria were described below.

- QA1. Is there a clear statement of the aims of the research?
- QA2. Is there an adequate description of the context in which the research was carried out?
- QA3. Is the study of value for research or practice?
- QA4. Is there a clear statement of findings?

Each study was evaluated from the perspective of the 4 assessment questions cited receiving the following score: 0 if the study does not meet the criteria, 0.5 if the article partially satisfies the criteria, and 1 if the study completely meets the criteria.

2.5   Data Collection

The principal data extracted from the studies were: title, authors, objectives, application protocols, wireless protocols applied, hardware platform, network topology, challenges, opportunities, and additional comments.

3   Results

This section presents the main results of the review, a summary of the studies used to answer the research questions, and the results of the quality assessment of the studies.

3.1   Search Results

Since the search string was applied in the Scopus database, 179 papers (stage 1) resulted. We read titles (stage 2), of which we adhered to 57 titles. In stage 3, we read abstracts, in which 10 studies returned. Finally, the 10 studies returned in stage 4 were read in full to answer the research questions.

Figure 1 demonstrates the selection process. The results of the data extraction of the 10 studies are presented in https://cutt.ly/MlpZdkn. Table 1 shows the studies considered useful to answer the research questions (Stage 4).

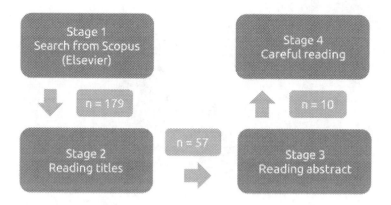

Fig. 1. Stages of the selection process.

Table 1. 10 studies object of step 4 - Careful reading.

Id	Author	Year	Venue
T1	Van Leemput D., et al.	2021	Journal
T2	Seo H., et al.	2021	Journal
T3	Hermeto R.T., et al.	2019	Journal
T4	Lino M. T. et al.	2020	Journal
T5	Ahmed A., et al.	2020	Conference Paper
T6	Karaagac A, L. et al.	2020	Journal
T7	Suresh Babu B, X. et al.	2020	Journal
T8	Wei M., et al.	2020	Conference Paper
T9	Wu H.-T., et al.	2019	Conference Paper
T10	Katsikeas S., et al.	2017	Conference Paper

3.2 Overview of Studies

Considering the origin of the selected studies, 60% of them were from journals and 40% from conferences.

Figure 2 shows that there is a tendency to increase interest in publications.

Figure 3 presents the main technology stack wireless communication standards identified in the included papers. The technology view was organized into three layers based on TCP/IP model: i) Application layer, ii) Communication layer, iii) Device layer.

Discussion

In this section, answers to research questions and review limitations will be discussed.

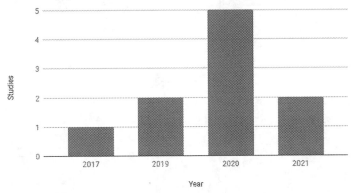

Fig. 2. Stages of the selection process.

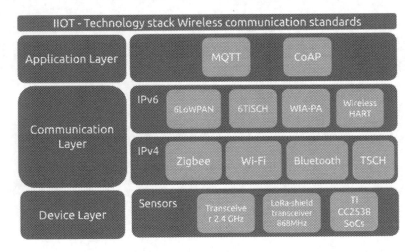

Fig. 3. Technology stack wireless communication standards.

3.3   RQ1. What are the Main Characteristics of IIoT-Based Wireless Comunication Protocols in the Industry?

According to Damasevicius [3], IoT applications have brought great advances in several segments, including in the industrial area. These IoT devices, in general, are adopted as a means of data transmission by the use of some wireless communication protocols. In Table 2, we can see the protocols that are currently used by IoT applications according to Damasevicius [3].

Table 2. Communication protocols used in IoT applications.

1	Wireless Fidelity (WiFi)
2	Near Field Communication (NFC)
3	ZigBee
4	Z-Wave
5	Bluetooth
6	Radio Frequency Identification (RFID)

Next, we can observe the application and communication protocols that are most used in IIoT-based applications

Application Protocols. Regarding the application protocols used, Whei [13] uses CoAP (Constrained Application Protocol) to demonstrate an IEEE 802.15.4-2015 TSCH industrial IoT implementation. Wu [14] uses Highlights the Message Queue Telemetry Transport (MQTT) to evaluate different security mechanisms while Ahmed [1] proposes the implementation of a LoRaWAN through a low-cost solution for the industry.

Wireless and Communication Protocols. About the wireless communication protocols used in the studies, 70% of the articles use variations of the Zigbee IEEE 802.15.4 protocol with time Slotted Channel Hopping(TSCH). In [5] Hermeto uses Zigbee IEEE 802.15.4 with 6TiSCH. Table 3 shows the frequency of occurrence of wireless protocols in the studies indicated.

Proposed Algorithms and Protocols. Among the 10 articles analyzed, 8 of them had new implementations of solutions. These solutions are divided between applications with hardware and communication protocols. For the applications, two of the studies worked on development: in the first one, proposed by Ahmed [1], we have a factory monitoring using Arduinos with sensors connected to it, wherein its infrastructure communicates through LoRa-Shields sending its data to a Raspberry Pi, which acts as a gateway to send data to the application server. In the second application, proposed by Wei [13], the hardware developed allows wireless IIoT networks to communicate with the application servers through the Internet Protocol version 6 (IPv6). For the new protocols developed, we have the following solution: Van Leemput [12] brings the creation of TSCH MAC, which modifies an existing protocol TSCH, implementing a new Multi-PHY transmission. Seo [11] proposes a new distributed consensus protocol that is more tolerant of transmission failures. For Lino [9] we have a new communication model (DyRET algorithm), using the Load-SDA algorithm and CSMA-CA protocol. Karaagac [6] brings an implementation proposal based on In-Band Network Telemetry and applicable, mainly, to the 6TiSCH protocol, but it can also be used in 802.15.4e-like TSCH-based. Finally, Babu [2] proposes

Table 3. Frequency of occurrence of wireless protocols.

Protocol	Studies	Frequency
802.15.4	T1, T3, T4, T6, T7, T9, T10	7
LoRaWAN	T5, 10	2
WirelessHART	T8	1
WIA-PA	T8	1
Bluetooth	T2	1

a new algorithm "REES Model" associated with the TSCH protocol, which can provide high traffic applications without affecting the power consumption of devices on a MANET network, with the ability to activate or deactivate additional slots dynamically, without the need to rearrange new schedules according to the protocol.

Hardware Platforms. Seo H. [11] uses a platform with Bluetooth-based communication. Ahmed [1] uses a hardware platform based on Arduino-Uno and LoRa-shield transceiver. Karaagac [6] proposes a solution based on In-Band Network Telemetry and applicable to the 6TiSCH protocol using the Zolertia Remote platform through ZigBee.

Communication Topologies. The main communication topologies identified in this review were 1) Wireless communication between sensors and a central node [1,2,4,6] e [13] and Peer-to-peer [5] e [6].

3.4 RQ2. What are the Challenges and Opportunities Related to IoT-Based Monitoring Applications in the Industry?

In general, there was a great need for studies and implementations in the area, given the diverse nature of the difficulties encountered. They extend from the communication of industry bodies with *business*, focusing on monitoring; the improvement of collected data, and ways of using that data, in addition to improvements on the internet within the industry itself. Such diversity shows that the problems are multiple and dispersed.

As for the difficulties from which the works arose, there are more general challenges such as the optimization of problematic factors in the different environments. 30% of the studies were concerned with this issue, while 20% of which focused on factories, or, still, on development network structure based on IPV6. Emphasizing that every research is in the scope of improving the forms of the wireless connection in IIoT.

Article [6] when dealing with the challenges that the non-IP industrial wireless network faces when trying to access IPV6, presents one of the challenges that are quite different from the others. In it, the author cites the problem that few protocols aimed at the industry support IPV6, although there are efforts to overcome this barrier. In this sense, the main challenges for this purpose are listed, namely: the difficulty of carrying out both the development and the implementation of systems for wireless networks for IPV6 at the industrial level, due to the scarcity of wireless networks with IPv6 IoT; the difficulty of obtaining gateways for industrial wireless networks and the impossibility of IPv6 access "in the northbound"; and, yet, the possible inconsistency of deterministic data on the IPv6 internet. Although the future proposals are clear in this case, two different results were obtained for the challenge in question.

Articles [5] and [6] will focus on difficulties within the scope of monitoring what happens in the industry, with IIoT techniques both for disaster prevention and for better monitoring of production - respectively. Thus, while article I3 is part of the search for greater resource savings, [6] is part of articles [1,9,12, 14] when seeking to improve performance. Article [5] proposes for future work an improvement in the mechanism on which it is based, suggesting that the network be stabilized by merging or integrating data. On the other hand, [6] offers a less punctual proposal when suggesting the development of network management systems in search of a more flexible and reconfigurable industrial wireless solution.

The research presented in [5] aims to monitor IoT devices, taking into account the focus in terms of security. Article [7], on the other hand, is focused on applying the security of the network itself and not physical spaces. This same article points out the limitation of resources in embedded devices, which justifies the difficulty of finding alternatives for secure wireless protocols. Furthermore, it also cites interoperability, due to the unified character of the IoT, as one of the main challenges.

Table 4 summarizes the main challenges of the subject found in this review, as well as some of the solutions presented:

3.5   RQ3. Who are the Main Authors of Works in the Area of Wireless Communication Protocols in IIoT?

In this review, 43 authors working in the area of wireless protocols for IIoT were identified. Of these, 3 authors (Poorter E; Hoebeke J; and Li C.) appear more frequently (2 papers each). Of the articles included, the article [7] Katsikeas S. was the one with the highest number of citations (34) (Fig. 4).

The distribution of articles published by the institution was: Université de Strasbourg (4), CNRS Center National de la Recherche Scientifique (2), INRIA Institut National de Recherche en Informatique et en Automatique (2), Universiteit Gent (2), Center for Wireless Communications Finland (1), National Taipei University of Technology (1), Oulun Yliopisto (1), Seoul National University (1), Infineon Technologies AG, Austria (1), Deakin University (1), Foundation for Research and Technology-Hellas (1), Technical University of Munich (1), Technical University of Crete (1), Institut de Recherche en Informatique et Systèmes Aléatoires (1), Korea Advanced Institute of Science & Technology (1),

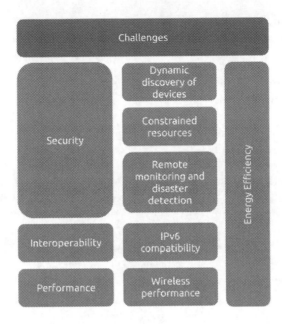

Fig. 4. Main challenges.

Table 4. Challenges summary

Challenges summary	
Challenges	Solutions
IIoT wireless communication systems vulnerable to interference due to heterogeneous environments	Implementation of a low-cost solution for the industry with a wireless solution and evaluating the stability of the performance of different protocols
IoT devices that are resource-constrained and do not support security implementations, such as using commonly used protocols	Implementation of lightweight variants of security protocols
Efficient and remote monitoring in industrial wireless sensor networks, including at the time of critical events	Design of a flexible, intelligent and efficient architecture for IIoT monitoring. Telemetry solution with powerful bandwidth, minimized use of resources and communication overhead
Interoperability and optimization of communication link between devices	Implement new protocols; automatically adaptable link layer between channels
IPv6 compatibility	Develop a protocol for IIoT networks that supports IPv6
Implementation of dynamic discovery of devices with limited resources	Large-scale dynamic reconfiguration for ZigBee-based wireless sensor cluster tree networks

IMT Atlantique (1), International Hellenic University (1). The institution that published the most was the Université de Strasbourg, appearing 4 times.

Figure 5 represents the distribution of articles between countries.

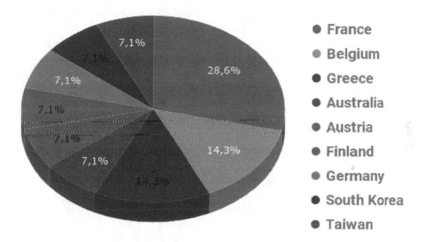

Fig. 5. Distribution of publications by country of origin.

3.6   Limitations of This Review

The main related limitations of this review include bias during the study selection and data extraction steps. As a way to remove the bias from these processes, we strictly followed the protocol described in Sect. 2 and did the review with 5 reviewers. Another limitation of this research was the inclusion of studies in English only since publications made only in other languages may have been omitted. As a final limitation of this review, we can mention the time of conducting the review, in which some new publications may have been made and not included.

4   Conclusions and Future Work

This research presented a systematic review of the literature carried out to identify the main applications of wireless communication protocols in the context of the industrial internet of things as well as the main challenges and gaps. For this, the steps described in Sect. 2 were strictly followed, in which 179 studies were returned from the search string. After the selection processes, data were extracted from the careful reading of 10 complete searches between articles in journals and conferences. Based on the extracted data, we were able to answer the research questions summarizing the main characteristics of wireless communications and protocols used in IIoT, as well as the main challenges in this field and which the main authors are researching in this area. In this review, 43 authors working in the area of wireless protocols for IIoT were identified. About the wireless communication protocols used in the papers, 70% of the articles use variations of the Zigbee IEEE 802.15.4. From the distribution of studies per year, it was possible to infer that there is a continuous trend of increasing interest in research in this area. As main contributions, we can mention the compilation of the main challenges and the development of a technology view that summarizes the main standards and protocols used. In future work, we will present the development of a solution that addresses the mentioned challenge of dynamic discovery of IIoT devices safely and efficiently in terms of energy consumption.

References

1. Ahmed, A., Valtiner, D., Thomos, C., Dielacher, F.: Wireless connectivity in industrial sensor and control networks: challenges and issues in a real implementation for a smart production use-case. In: 2020 25th IEEE International Conference on Emerging Technologies and Factory Automation (ETFA), vol. 1, pp. 302–309. IEEE (2020)
2. Babu, B., Hussain, D.A., Mirza, M.A.: Reliable and energy efficient scheduling model for TSCH enabled mobile adhoc network. Int. J. Sci. Technol. Res. **9**, 2202–2207 (2020)
3. Damasevicius, R., Maskeliunas, R., Oluranti, J.: Internet of things: applications, adoptions and components-a conceptual overview
4. Dybå, T., Dingsøyr, T.: Empirical studies of agile software development: a systematic review. Inf. Softw. Technol. **50**(9–10), 833–859 (2008)
5. Hermeto, R.T., Gallais, A., Theoleyre, F.: Experimental in-depth study of the dynamics of an indoor industrial low power lossy network. Ad Hoc Netw. **93**, 101914 (2019)
6. Karaagac, A., De Poorter, E., Hoebeke, J.: In-band network telemetry in industrial wireless sensor networks. IEEE Trans. Netw. Serv. Manage. **17**(1), 517–531 (2019)
7. Katsikeas, S., et al.: Lightweight & secure industrial IoT communications via the MQ telemetry transport protocol. In: 2017 IEEE Symposium on Computers and Communications (ISCC), pp. 1193–1200. IEEE (2017)
8. Keele, S., et al.: Guidelines for performing systematic literature reviews in software engineering. Technical report, Citeseer (2007)
9. Lino, M., Leão, E., Soares, A., Montez, C., Vasques, F., Moraes, R.: Dynamic reconfiguration of cluster-tree wireless sensor networks to handle communication overloads in disaster-related situations. Sensors **20**(17), 4707 (2020)
10. Sadeghi, A.R., Wachsmann, C., Waidner, M.: Security and privacy challenges in industrial internet of things. In: 2015 52nd ACM/EDAC/IEEE Design Automation Conference (DAC), pp. 1–6. IEEE (2015)
11. Seo, H., Park, J., Bennis, M., Choi, W.: Communication and consensus co-design for distributed, low-latency and reliable wireless systems. IEEE Internet Things J. **8**, 129–143 (2020)
12. Van Leemput, D., Bauwens, J., Elsas, R., Hoebeke, J., Joseph, W., De Poorter, E.: Adaptive multi-PHY IEEE802. 15.4 TSCH in sub-GHz industrial wireless networks. Ad Hoc Netw. **111**, 102330 (2021)

13. Wei, M., Li, C., Li, C.: An IPv6 internet accessing architecture and approach for industrial wireless network. In: 2020 14th International Conference on Ubiquitous Information Management and Communication (IMCOM), pp. 1–6. IEEE (2020)
14. Wu, H.T., et al.: The implementation of wireless industrial internet of things (IIoT) based upon IEEE 802.15. 4–2015 TSCH access mode. In: 2019 IEEE International Conference on Dependable, Autonomic and Secure Computing, International Conference on Pervasive Intelligence and Computing, International Conference on Cloud and Big Data Computing, International Conference on Cyber Science and Technology Congress (DASC/PiCom/CBDCom/CyberSciTech), pp. 367–369. IEEE (2019)

Data Extraction of Charts with Hybrid Deep Learning Model

Kirill Sviatov[1]([⊠]) [iD], Nadezhda Yarushkina[1], and Sergey Sukhov[2]

[1] Ulyanovsk State Technical University, Ulyanovsk, Russia
{k.svyatov,jng,y.lapshov}@ulstu.ru
[2] Ulyanovsk Branch of the Institute of Radio Engineering
and Electronics. V. A. Kotelnikov of Russian Academy of Science, Ulyanovsk, Russia

Abstract. This article describes an approach to automatic recognition of charts images using neural networks with hybrid deep learning model, which allows to extract data from an image and use this data to quickly find information, as well as to describe charts for visually impaired people. The key feature of this approach is the model of the recognition process, which includes classical algorithms for image analysis and deep learning models with flexible model tuning to improve the key quality indicators of recognition software.

Currently, the problem of chart recognition is usually solved in an interactive mode, which makes it possible to recognize in a semi-automatic way with a gradual refinement of the recognized data: "end-to-end" models of neural networks or pure computer vision algorithms cannot be used for complete recognition. This article describes an approach and models that use both deep learning models with attention and computer vision algorithms to accurately extract data from charts. This article describes an approach to recognizing only function charts with continuous lines, not pie or histograms. The resulting accuracy of using a deep learning network for localizing parts of charts is 72%, this is enough for recognition since post-processing algorithms significantly improve the final recognition accuracy.

Keywords: Artificial intelligence · Neural networks · Machine learning · Computer vision · Attention networks · Data extraction

1 Introduction

Currently, there are many scientific and technical events with video broadcasting, recordings of which are published in video services, materials in articles, and social networks without source codes of programs and data. When conducting research based on such materials, there is a problem of reproduction in terms of writing program code, as well as finding the data used, which is often presented in the form of function diagrams. Code and data publishing initiatives, such as "Papers with code" [24], are widespread among a narrow circle of researchers and are not widely used.

One of the ways to simplify the solution of the reproducibility problem is automatic graph recognition, which can also be used for visually impaired people when reading

© Springer Nature Switzerland AG 2021
O. Gervasi et al. (Eds.): ICCSA 2021, LNCS 12957, pp. 382–393, 2021.
https://doi.org/10.1007/978-3-030-87013-3_29

articles. Additional motivation for writing this article is the need to develop technology that will allow visually impaired people to understand the meaning and data presented in the images.

In this paper, we consider the solution of five tasks for data extraction from the chart:

1. Automatic detection of the number of human-readable chart color. This task is important because to highlight the graph lines, it is important to use a separate color for each line. At the same time, upon a detailed examination of the graphs on video or from a camera, it often turns out that the same color can be represented by several colors. In this task, it is necessary to calculate how many human-readable colors are in the image. The following task is a color quantization of the source image.
2. After reducing the number of colors, it is necessary to find charts corresponding to a certain color.
3. Image text recognition. It is used to recognize all chart parts separately: title, labels, legend, axis scales.
4. Detection of the image components location. In this task, it is necessary to detect the position of the parts of the chart images in the coordinate system of the original image: axis labels, title, data labels, and data axes.
5. Chart recognition. It is a way to combine all the previously obtained analysis data in order to obtain a dataset describing the original cha image.

Chart classification, detection of the image, and perspective correction are outside the scope of this work. We only extract data from the image of a chart.

2   Literature Review

Despite the success of using neural networks in image processing, they usually perform only certain processing steps: object detection, localization in the image, and class prediction. It is also possible to determine all available objects in the image for subsequent analysis, for example, a geometric assessment of the relative position of objects, their size, and shape [29]. Despite these possibilities, there is a lot of information in the task of extracting data from charts, which makes the end-to-end approach inapplicable.

Automated data extraction from charts has been studied for many years, and this can be solved with four steps: localization of the chart on the image, chart classification, text detection, and data reconstruction. Our project focuses on the last two steps. In 2007, Prasad et al. [1] have described a classical computer vision method to classify charts in five categories, based on the Histograms of Oriented Gradients and the Scale Invariant Feature Transform descriptors for feature extraction and Support Vector Machine (SVM) for classification. Savva et al. [2] created a system called Revision to recognize charts, which includes chart classification, data extraction, and visualization. Low-level image features are extracted for chart classification by SVMs. There are automatic chart data extraction algorithms based on image processing and machine learning to extract data from chart images [8–11].

ReVision [12] is a tool that makes automatic classification of chart types (ten types) and extracts data from a chart image. iVoLVER [14] is also a tool that allows to extracts data from an image. It relies on users inputs in both specifying data types (e.g., text, colors, shapes, etc.) and sampling data points in the image. Thus, it requires a relatively large number of interactions to extract data accurately from a chart image. DataThief [15] is a tool that extracts data from line charts. Users have to run it multiple times for a chart with multiple lines because it can extract one line at a time. People also have to specify six points (origin point, end-points of x-y axis, start- and end-point of the target line, and a point on the line).

WebPlotDigitizer [13] is a web-based tool that extracts data from four chart types (bar and line charts, polar and ternary diagrams) in automatic and manual modes. In the manual mode, people have to provide information for data extraction: labels, axis, and other chart components positions. Ycasd [16] is a tool for line chart data extraction with a manual technique similar to WebPlotDigitizer with which people have to specify all the data points in a line chart. In the task of chart recognition, there are many works done with regular computer vision technologies. Zhou et al. [3] use Hough lines transform and boundary detection to recognize bars. Huang et al. [4] use rules with edge maps. Deep learning models allow detect all the texts and chart components automatically with different models for each part of a model: Cliche et al. [5] use three object detection models. Poco et al. [6] use a CNN model to classify each pixel of an image as text or not and then exclude all non-text pixels.

The next step is data reconstruction. It also can be divided into two stages: text recognition and numerical data extraction. All detected texts are extracted by a text recognition model. Tick labels are combined with the coordinate positions to predict the coordinate-value relation. But another problem appears: matching objects between different categories, which has been studied by a few researchers. In the work of Siegel and Farhadi [7], this task is formulated as an optimal-path-finding problem with features combined from CNN model and pixels. The attention mechanism in neural networks [17] is popular now among researchers [18], because it allows us to interpret the results of the models and perform selection according to positions of objects in feature maps. Despite the fact that the technology appeared only several years ago, the range of applications is very wide [19, 28].

In this regard, it is necessary to use a hybrid approach for graph recognition: deep learning models use for chart elements localization, text extraction, and classical image analysis algorithms for data extraction.

In our work, an attention recurrent U-Net deep neural net is built to predict all objects locations. To recognize texts and numbers, Tesseract OCR software library was used. We also introduce brand new concepts and approaches to make the final data extraction.

3 Offered Approach

We offer a hybrid approach that uses different models for different stages of analysis. The common data flow structure is presented in the Fig. 1.

In the first step, the type of image is determined, one of several: bar graph - 1, chart - 2, block diagram - 3, line chart - 4 (the type of charts considered in this article), growth graph - 5, pie chart - 6, table - 7, just images - 0. This problem is solved using a neural network with the Resnet-152 architecture [25], the solution is based on the proposed solution [26].

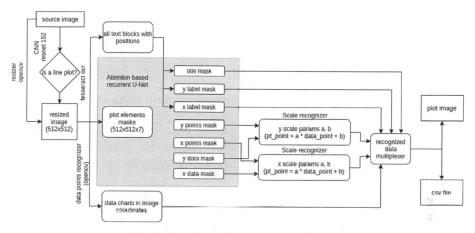

Fig. 1. Data flow of the recognition process

Second, the picture is resized by 512×512 pixels. The scale coefficient is calculated by the formula:

$$scale = \frac{512}{\max(width,\ height)}$$

where width and height are the original sizes of the source image. After that scaling, a new empty 512×512-pixel image is created and combine with the newly obtained.

The following 3 steps are performed in parallel mode:

- Text recognizing.
- Chart elements position detection.
- Chart data extraction in image coordinates.

4 Text Recognizing

This step is performed with Tesseract OCR software module which allow to extract data in the following format:

$$result = image\_to\_data(image, config),$$

Where *image* – source image, *result* – resulting dictionary, containing texts and their location on the source image, *config* – configuration parameters of the tesseract software.

After this recognition, we combine closely located words in single phrases. It is important for titles and labels.

5 Chart Components Localization

Chart components localization is very important part of the recognition process. It allows determining a location of all parts of the image: title, data, and labels for both horizontal and vertical axes, tick points for horizontal and vertical axes, located on the lines. Without this location, important data cannot be extracted.

We use several models to detect the location of the most important parts of a chart: U-Net, Fast R-CNN, Attention Recurrent Residial U-Net (AR2U-Net) [27]. All models don't show meaningful results except Attention AR2U-Net model. It can generalize training set images. An example of such recognition is shown in Fig. 2.

The deep learning model performs the following transformation:

$$mask = recognize(image)$$
$$mask = <Tm, Xd, Yd, Xl, Yl, Xt, Yt>$$

The mask is the result of the recognition process by Attention recurrent AR2U-Net model. It is a set of masks, where Tm – title mask, Xd – horizontal data location, Yd – vertical data location, Xl – labels for horizontal axis, YL – labels for vertical axis, Xt – tick points for horizontal axis, Yt – tick points for vertical axis.

The example of the resulting mask is shown on the Fig. 2.

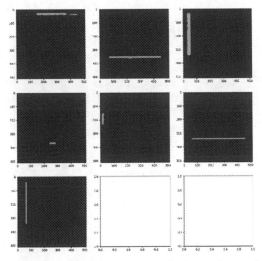

Fig. 2. Result of the inference process for image decomposition

The work [17] describes the problem of recognizing the relationship between objects in the image. The authors note that the variability of relations between objects is too large, therefore it is very difficult to create a one-hot sample to solve a similar problem. They offer an approach based on the search for patterns in textual descriptions of images. Such a network output can be considered weakly formalized, because human speech also has great variability, although textual descriptions of images are much easier to find [23]. The authors use a recursive network that iteratively analyzes objects in the scene and words in the text. However, to solve such a complex problem, the authors use the preliminary extraction of features from the image, namely, they select objects and spatial information between them.

The categorical cross-entropy loss function has a value of 72%, and this is a good result because very precise masking is not required for this task: post-processing algorithms significantly improve the final recognition accuracy.

6 Dataset Collection

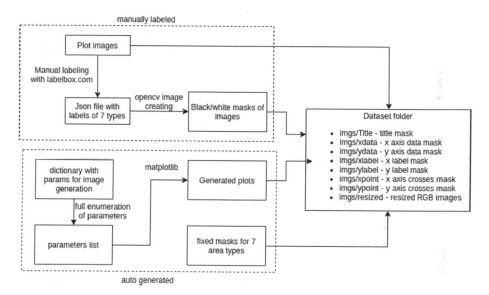

Fig. 3. Dataset generation and labeling process

To prepare the dataset, two sources were used: manually collected data, labeled using the Labelbox tool, and also automatically generated data using the Matplotlib library. The process of data generation and transformation is shown in the Fig. 3. As a result, the final dataset contains 10000 images with 10000 × 7 mask images, where 2000 images and masks was used for validation, 2000 images and masks for testing and 6000 for training.

7 Chart Scale Recognition

It is very important step to automatically convert the coordinates of the image to the coordinates of the target graph of the function. To do this, it is necessary to recognize ticks on the axis lines, then select the text that refers to the signature of these axes, then filter these values for more accurate recognition, then solve a simple linear equation to further transform the coordinates of the image into the coordinates of the objective function for each of the axes. The resulting process is shown in the Fig. 4.

Tick detection is performed as follows. First, on the area of the image corresponding to the axis line in the mask, the longest line is searched for using the hough lines transform method from the OpenCV library. This line counts as the axis line. Then, all ticks are localized on this line using the sliding window method. At the next stage, the text is searched for, the position of which corresponds to the axis data mask. The found text is filtered according to two rules. The first is to exclude all texts that do not contain numbers. The second allows to include dot symbol to numbers like "025", and then the number is converted to a real type.

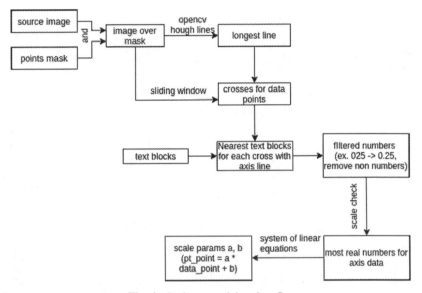

Fig. 4. Scale recognizing data flow

In the next step, the nearest filtered text is selected for each tick. Then, for each pair of ticks and their corresponding numerical values, an extrapolated value is determined for all other ticks. If the number of matches is maximum for the selected pair, then such a pair is used to calculate the coefficients of the linear equation for transferring coordinates from the image coordinate system to the coordinate system of the target function of the chart.

As a result of solving a system of linear equations, coefficients a and b are obtained, which are used to transform the coordinates of points from the image coordinate system to the coordinate system of the target function of the chart by the formulas

$$x_i' = (x_i - b_x)/a_x$$

$$y_i' = (y_i - b_y)/a_y$$

where a and b are coefficients of the linear functions for horizontal and vertical axes. Example of recognized ticks is presented on the Fig. 5.

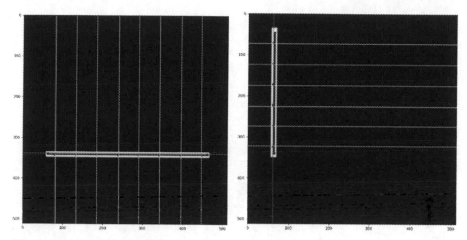

Fig. 5. Example of the axis tick recognition for horizontal axis (left) and vertical axis (right)

8   Data Extraction

The process of extracting data in the image coordinate system is performed by classical algorithms for image analysis without the use of machine learning. The overall process is shown in the Fig. 6.

In the first step, the image is color quantized by k-means clustering to reduce the number of colors. To determine the target value for the number of colors, the following transformations are performed.

First, the image is converted to a HSV palette. Then a HSV (hue, saturation, value) histogram is generated, in which the abscissa axis is the Hue channel (in the interval from 0 to 255), and the ordinate axis is the number of pixels that have a given color on the Hue channel. Then this data is gone through a double filter with a low-pass filter according to the formula

$$O_n = O_{n-1} + \alpha(I_n - O_{n-1})$$

where O_n is a predicted value, O_{n-1} – previous calculated value, I_n – real value, α – regularization term (the best value is selected experimentally).

After double filtering, the number of peaks of the histogram data corresponds to the number of human-readable colors, which is used for color quantization.

An example of such recognition is shown in Fig. 7. For peak detection, we use find_peak method from scipy.signal package.

The task of color quantization is important to the following selection of color lines of the chart.

In the next step, the color masks of the image corresponding to the found number of colors are extracted from the source image and the contours are determined in each part using the canny edge detector. For a found contours, then its area and the area of its bounding rectangle are calculated. If the ratio of these areas is small enough, then we can assume that the contour limits a line, which can be considered a chart of the function.

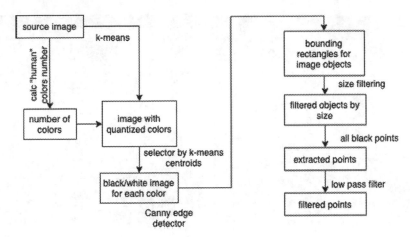

Fig. 6. Data extraction in image coordinates

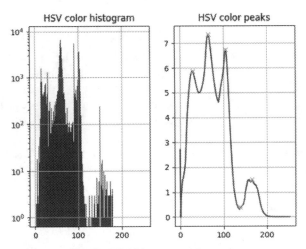

Fig. 7. HSV histogram color peaks

At the final step, the points are extracted from the found contour and the data array is generated in the coordinate system of the image size for each of the color channels. An example of the result of this process is shown in the Fig. 8.

9   Data Complexing

At the final step, the data is converted from the image coordinate system into the coordinate system of the objective function for each graph. A data table is generated with the corresponding signatures of the signs, the data header. The data obtained can be used in the future in the form of tables or text descriptions. We implement the plotting of a function chart for each line. An example is shown in the Fig. 8.

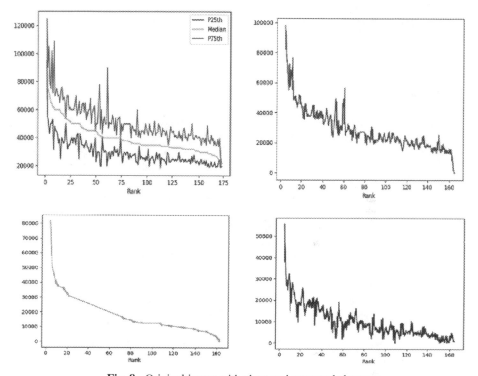

Fig. 8. Original image with chart and extracted charts

10   Conclusion

In some cases, it is not very precise, but it can be improved in the next research. The hybrid architecture of the designed software allows to improve and replace independent modules without changes in other modules:

- Data extraction in the coordinates of the original image can be performed by other methods of filtering.
- Text recognition can use deep learning models taking into account the context of the image.
- Generating data for a dataset can make the data more diverse.
- The mask for detecting image components can be more accurate.
- Applications for recognized data can be broader.

The result of using a deep learning network for localizing parts of charts is 72%, this is enough for recognition since post-processing algorithms significantly improve the final recognition accuracy. The proposed approach and the framework can extract data with good quality and it can be improved with the next steps of work.

Acknowledgments. This study was supported Ministry of Education and Science of Russia in framework of project № 075-00233-20-05 from 03.11.2020 «Research of intelligent predictive multimodal analysis of big data, and the extraction of knowledge from different sources» and RFBR grant 18-47-732004 p_мк.

References

1. Prasad, V.S.N., Siddiquie, B., Golbeck, J., Davis, L.S.: Classifying computer generated charts. In: Content-Based Multimedia Indexing Workshop, pp. 85–92 (2007)
2. Savva, M., Kong, N., Chhajta, A., Fei-Fei, L., Agrawala, M., Heer, J.: Revision: automated classification, analysis and redesign of chart images. In: Proceedings of the 24th Annual ACM Symposium on User Interface Software and Technology, pp. 393–402 (2011)
3. Zhou, Y., Tan, C.L.: Hough-based model for recognizing bar charts in document images. In: SPIE, pp. 333–341 (2000)
4. Huang, W., Tan, C.L.: A system for understanding imaged infographics and its applications. In: ACM Symposium on Document Engineering, pp. 9–18 (2007)
5. Cliche, M., Rosenberg, D. Madeka, D., Yee, C.: Scatter-act: automated extraction of data from scatter plots. In: Joint European Conference on Machine Learning and Knowledge Discovery in Databases, pp. 135–150 (2017)
6. Poco, J., Heer, J.: Reverse-engineering visualizations: recovering visual encodings from chart images. In: Computer Graphics Forum, pp. 353–363 (2017)
7. Siegel, N., Horvitz, Z., Levin, R., Divvala, S., Farhadi, A.: FigureSeer: parsing result-figures in research papers. In: Leibe, B., Matas, J., Sebe, N., Welling, M. (eds.) ECCV 2016. LNCS, vol. 9911, pp. 664–680. Springer, Cham (2016). https://doi.org/10.1007/978-3-319-46478-7_41
8. Gao, J., Zhou, Y., Barner, K.E.:. View: visual information extraction widget for improving chart images accessibility. In: Proceedings of the 19th IEEE International Conference on Image Processing (ICIP 2012), 2865–2868 (2012)
9. Huang, W., Tan, C.L., Leow, W.K.: Model-based chart image recognition. In: Lladós, J., Kwon, Y.-B. (eds.) GREC 2003. LNCS, vol. 3088, pp. 87–99. Springer, Heidelberg (2004). https://doi.org/10.1007/978-3-540-25977-0_8
10. Huang, W., Liu, R., Tan, C.L.: Extraction of vectorized graphical information from scientific chart images. In: Proceedings of the 9th International Conference on Document Analysis and Recognition (ICDAR 2007), pp. 521–525 (2007)
11. Shao, M., Futrelle, R.P.: Recognition and classification of figures in PDF documents. In: Liu, W., Lladós, J. (eds.) GREC 2005. LNCS, vol. 3926, pp. 231–242. Springer, Heidelberg (2006). https://doi.org/10.1007/11767978_21
12. Savva, M., Kong, N., Chhajta, A., Fei-Fei, L., Agrawala, M., Heer, J.: ReVision: automated classification, analysis and redesign of chart images (2011). http://vis.stanford.edu/papers/revision
13. Rohatgi, A.: WebPlotDigitizer, Version 3.8 (2015). http://arohatgi.info/WebPlotDigitizer. Accessed 22 Sept 2015
14. Méndez, G.G., Nacenta, M.A., Vandenheste, S.: iVoLVER: interactive visual language for visualization extraction and reconstruction. In: Proceedings of the SIGCHI Conference on Human Factors in Computing Systems (CHI 2016), pp. 4073–4085 (2016)
15. Tummers, B.: DataThief III (2015). http://www.datathief.org/. Accessed 22 Sept 2015
16. Gross, A., Schirm, S., Scholz, M.: Ycasd–a tool for capturing and scaling data from graphical representations. BMC Bioinform. 15(1), 219 (2014)
17. Liu, X., Klabjan, D., Bless, P.N.: Data extraction from charts via single deep neural network. https://arxiv.org/abs/1906.11906

18. Girshick, R.: Fast R-CNN. https://arxiv.org/pdf/1504.08083.pdf

19. Zhao, Z.-Q., Zheng, P., Xu, S., Wu, X.: Object detection with deep learning: a review. https://arxiv.org/pdf/1807.05511.pdf

20. Xu, K., et al.: Show, attend and tell: neural image caption generation with visual attention. https://arxiv.org/pdf/1502.03044.pdf

21. Wang, W., et al.: Learning unsupervised video object segmentation through visual attention. http://openaccess.thecvf.com/content_CVPR_2019/papers/Wang_Learning_Unsupervised_Video_Object_Segmentation_Through_Visual_Attention_CVPR_2019_paper.pdf

22. Sun, J., Darbehani, F., Zaidi, M., Wang, B.: SAUNet: shape attentive U-net for interpretable medical image segmentation. https://arxiv.org/pdf/2001.07645v3.pdf

23. Sviatov, K., Miheev, A., Kanin, D., Sukhov, S., Tronin, V.: Scenes segmentation in self-driving car navigation system using neural network models with attention. In: Misra, S., et al. (eds.) ICCSA 2019. LNCS, vol. 11623, pp. 278–289. Springer, Cham (2019). https://doi.org/10.1007/978-3-030-24308-1_23

24. Papers with code. https://paperswithcode.com/

25. He, K., Zhang, X., Ren, S., Sun, J.: Deep residual learning for image recognition. https://www.cv-foundation.org/openaccess/content_cvpr_2016/papers/He_Deep_Residual_Learning_CVPR_2016_paper.pdf

26. Graph-and-Chart-Recognition.   https://github.com/Grigorii-24/Graph-and-Chart-Recognition

27. Oktay, O., et al.: Attention U-net: learning where to look for the pancreas. https://arxiv.org/abs/1804.03999

28. Behera, R.K., Shukla, S., Rath, S.K., Misra, S.: Software reliability assessment using machine learning technique. In: Gervasi, O., et al. (eds.) ICCSA 2018. LNCS, vol. 10964, pp. 403–411. Springer, Cham (2018). https://doi.org/10.1007/978-3-319-95174-4_32

29. Abayomi-Alli, A., et al.: Facial image quality assessment using an ensemble of pre-trained deep learning models (EFQnet). In: 2020 20th International Conference on Computational Science and Its Applications (ICCSA). IEEE (2020)

Middleware for Healthcare Systems: A Systematic Mapping

Ramon Santos Malaquias and Itamir Morais Barroca Filho[✉]

Digital Metropolis Institute, Federal University of Rio Grande do Norte,
Natal 59078970, Brazil
{malaquias,itamir.filho}@imd.ufrn.br

Abstract. The improvement of technological applications focused on the health context is growing. Different types of applications, such as Health Information Systems (HIS), Electronic Health Records (EHR), and e-Health and m-Health applications, are being developed. With the increasing use of technological solutions in this context, there is a need to integrate the data collected, stored, and processed in these systems. However, the heterogeneity of the data is a factor that makes this integration difficult. To mitigate this problem, middleware appears as an option. This paper aims to understand the current state and future trends of middleware for healthcare applications. To do so, we carried out systematic mapping of the literature on middleware for healthcare systems. This Systematic Mapping initially collected 1162 works, which after the execution of its stages, 34 works were selected for careful reading and, as a result, we present answers to the defined research questions, collected from a careful reading of the selected works. Finally, we concluded that, although there are several middleware solutions in the literature, there is no standard among these solutions, and they end up being limited to solving the problem in a specific context in the health area.

Keywords: Healthcare · Middleware · Interoperability · e-Health · m-Health

With the advancement of technological applications focused on the health context, there is a need to store, process, and extract information from the data used in the health area to support decisions and optimize processes, aiming to improve the service provided. In this sense, Health Information Systems (HIS) emerge, which, according to Fatima et al. [1], can be defined as "a set of interrelated components that collect, process, store and distribute information to support the decision-making process and assist in the control of health organizations."

HIS use medical information in digital format, also known as Electronic Health Records (EHR). Iakovids [2] defines EHR as "health information stored digitally about an individual's life to support the continuity of care, education, and research, ensuring confidentiality at all times." Thus, the use of EHR systems allows the clinical team to quickly access patients information without the

© Springer Nature Switzerland AG 2021
O. Gervasi et al. (Eds.): ICCSA 2021, LNCS 12957, pp. 394–409, 2021.
https://doi.org/10.1007/978-3-030-87013-3_30

need to ask them personally [3], bringing a series of advantages, such as reducing costs and increasing efficiency in the management and recovery of patient data, in addition to enabling centralization and remote access to the patient's health information [4,5].

Another concept related to the context of technologies for the health area is that of e-Health. E-Health is the field that emerges as an intersection between medical informatics, public health, and business, referring to health services that are improved through the use of technologies that operate through the internet [6]. Also, the advancement of mobile communications, which currently supports 3G, 4G, and even 5G mobile networks for data transport, means that mobile computing promotes numerous possibilities for creating solutions for m-Health [3,7]. M-Health consists of the use of mobile computing and communication technologies in health [8]. Systems based on m-Health can support clinical and administrative data management, systems for monitoring vital signs and sending alerts, predictive systems, and medication management [9].

The e-Health, m-Health, and SIS applications have resources that can provide solutions for different contexts in the health field. These solutions can support everything from EHRs to solutions for detecting and monitoring patient vital signs, including solutions for test management, hospital and clinic management data, and epidemiological data. These different solutions that can be used in the health context generate heterogeneous data, which, if integrated, better support clinical decision-making and patient care, providing meaningful and current information [10]. However, integration becomes a challenge since the data generated is increasingly heterogeneous [11]. In this sense, the degree to which two or more systems can exchange information through interfaces in a specific context is called interoperability. Therefore, in the context of healthcare applications, where data is highly heterogeneous, interoperability becomes a critical requirement to be met, and, for that, the proposal of developing a middleware can be a good option.

According to Atzori et al. [12], middleware is "the layer or set of sub-layers of a software interposed between the technological and application levels." Middleware allows the low-level development details to be abstracted, facilitating development and enabling the programmer to focus on the system's functional requirements [12,13]. Thus, the proposal of developing a middleware based on an open standard for health data interoperability, such as HL7 Health Level - 7 (HL7) that meets the interoperability requirements can facilitate the development and decrease the cost of promoting integration between different types of technological health solutions. HL7 is an international standard based on layer 7 of the Open System for Intercommunication (OSI) model, which contains a set of standards for transferring clinical and administrative data between software applications used by healthcare organizations [14].

Considering the advancements in the use of technologies in the health context, the heterogeneity of data in this context, and the challenge of integration between different healthcare systems, it is necessary to investigate the use of middleware on this challenge. Therefore, this article aims to describe a review to understand the current state and future trends of middlewares for e-Health and m-Health applications and find areas for further investigation. For this, a study was carried out based on the Systematic Mapping Study methodology [15].

The paper is organized as follows: Sect. 1 deals with the methodology used in developing the research. The third section presents an analysis of the results found in the articles selected. Finally, we concluded the work dealing with general discussions and future works.

1   Methodology

According to Kitchenham et al. [16], Systematic Mapping is a type of secondary study that aims to identify existing research related to a specific topic, that is, to answer broader questions related to the evolution of the investigation, which can be classified as exploratory. This research was carried out based on the guidelines recommended by Kitchenham et al. [16]. In this section, the most important details of the protocol defined and validated for the Systematic Mapping are presented.

1.1   Objective and Research Questions

This Systematic Mapping aimed to understand the current state and future trends of middleware for e-Health and m-Health applications and find areas for future investigations. For this, the following Research Questions (**RQ**) were defined and used in the investigation of the articles:

- **RQ1:** What are the existing middlewares for healthcare systems?
  RQ1 aims to identify the main middleware solutions for healthcare systems described in the literature and understand how they promote interoperability.
- **RQ2:** What are the main characteristics of middleware for healthcare systems?
  RQ2 aims to map the main characteristics and requirements that middleware solutions for the healthcare area must meet.
- **RQ3:** How are middlewares evaluated in the works analyzed?
  Through RQ3, we intend to understand under which metrics middlewares are evaluated from the point of view of quality attributes such as performance and availability to identify possible obstacles in developing middleware for the health area.
- **RQ4:** What are the challenges and opportunities to develop middleware for healthcare systems?
  RQ4 aims to analyze the main challenges present in the development of middleware for healthcare solutions and, through this, to identify opportunities and gaps for future investigations and the development of healthcare middleware solutions.

1.2   Research Process

The search engine established for selecting the studies was the Elsevier's Scopus Platform [17]. This Platform indexes the main bases of scientific studies in the area of Computer Science, such as the ACM Digital Library [18], the IEEExplorer [19], the Science Direct [20], and the Springer Link [21]. For this reason, it was chosen to execute the search string defined in the protocol and perform the collection of the works.

The search string was built from the concatenation of terms present in the research questions, and, for search purposes, the titles, abstracts, and keywords of the works were considered. Therefore, in this Systematic Mapping, the following search string was used: "Middleware" AND ("Health" OR "Health-care").

1.3   Inclusion and Exclusion Criteria

In this Systematic Mapping, studies published in any year, provided they are written in the English language, were included. The Exclusion Criteria (EC) defined were:

EC1: Duplicate papers;
- **EC2:** Articles derived from the same author and research;
- **EC3:** Works that do not present middleware solutions;
- **EC4:** Works that do not present middleware solutions for healthcare systems;
- **EC5:** Works not available for download;
- **EC6:** Papers that do not answer any research question.

1.4   Quality Assessment

Each study selected was evaluated according to the following Quality Assessment (QA) questions:

- **QA1:** Does the work have a clear statement of the research objectives?
- **QA2:** Does the work describe well the context in which the research was carried out?
- **QA3:** Are the results obtained clear?

The quality assessment questions were scored as follows: -1 in case of non-compliance with the criteria; 0 in case of partial fulfillment of the criteria; and 1 if it fully met the criteria. The evaluation is available in the spreadsheet that can be accessed through the following link: http://bit.ly/mapeamento-sistematico.

1.5   Extraction, Analysis, and Selection of the Articles

The data extracted from each study were: year of publication, link to access, number of citations, title, abstract, characteristics and requirements of the proposed solution, protocols used, challenges, and additional comments. Thus, the process of extracting, analyzing, and selecting the articles included three phases, described below:

- Phase 1 - Execution of the search string in the search engine: in this phase, the search on the Scopus Platform returned 1,162 papers;
- Phase 2 - Analysis of the titles and abstracts of the papers obtained in Phase 1: the analysis was performed based on the inclusion and exclusion criteria defined. After completing this phase, 142 articles were selected;
- Phase 3 - Analysis of the introduction and conclusion of the articles selected in Phase 2: the articles selected in Phase 2 were read to identify and select those that answered at least two research questions defined in the protocol. In this phase, 34 articles were selected for detailed reading and final analysis.

Figure 1 shows the process of extracting, analyzing, and selecting the articles and the number of works that were picked after the execution of each phase.

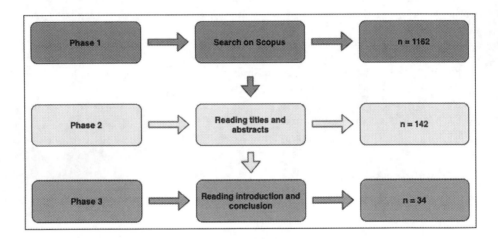

Fig. 1. Process of extracting, analyzing, and selecting the articles.

2   Results

Phase 3 of the data extraction and analysis process resulted in 34 articles, which were read in a detailed and attentive manner to understand how each work answers the research questions defined in the research protocol. This section reports the analysis of these articles from the point of view of each research question defined. An online spreadsheet was used to control better the analysis of the works, which is available at the following link: http://bit.ly/mapeamento-sistematico.

2.1   RQ1: What Are the Existing Middlewares for Healthcare Systems?

Many middleware-based solution proposals were found in the analyzed papers, as well as a series of analyses of the existing middleware. In general, as an alternative to promote interoperability between health systems, Pervez et al. [22] cite Device Interoperability Middleware (DIM), stating that these solutions have shown potential to solve such a problem. Also, Message Oriented Middleware (MOM) is used as well [23].

Solutions based on the $HL7$ standard [24] are mentioned as options for the development of middleware for healthcare systems [25]. In Zhang et al. [26], some solutions referred to as "standard" by the authors are cited, such as the "Medical Telemonitoring System," which consists of a method for sending physiological and medical information remotely over the internet to an analysis and diagnosis center, and the middleware described in the article itself, the "Mobile Context and Ontology-based Reasoning/Feedback ($MCOM$)," a system that monitors the health status of patients using the smartphone.

In Alonso et al.'s work [27], a study including several middlewares was carried out, among which was the Kura, a middleware proposed by the Eclipse consortium, which was designed to be installed on gateways; the AllJoyn, proposed by the Linux Foundation, which provides a version for restricted features, as well as different APIs for developers; and the Macchina.io, which, according to the author, is modular and extensible, implementing a messaging protocol based on the publication/subscription model. In the line of applications that use this model, Almadani et al. [28] propose a Middleware Real-Time Publish-Subscribe ($RTPS$), while Singh et al. [29] present a middleware model to control information sharing in a publication/subscription-based environment.

The $My-AHA$, described by Madureira et al. [30], is a multiplatform middleware designed to perfectly integrate different health and active aging solutions, aiming at well-being. According to the authors, the architecture proposed for the $My-AHA$ is a multi-module system architecture, fully scalable and easily implementable, focusing on helping caregivers and the elderly themselves improve their current condition, considering changes in cognitive, physical, social, and psychological parameters.

A framework for the interoperability between health systems is proposed by Ryan et al. [31]. The Health Service Bus (HSB) is a solution based on the Enterprise Service Bus (ESB) middleware software architecture, which provides a loosely coupled and highly distributed approach for enterprise systems integration. Along the same lines, Ayeni et al. [32] describes a framework for overcoming integration barriers between Nigerian health systems and improving health care delivery in Nigeria [10]. Another example of middleware is the SALSA, proposed by Rodriguez et al. [33], which allows developers to create autonomous agents that react to the medical environment's contextual elements and communicate with other agents, users, and services available in the environment.

The *POStCODE* (POstmarket SurveillanCe Of DEvices) is a middleware proposed by Chaudhry et al. [34] that provides the devices' operational details directly to the manufacturers, being careful to exclude private patient data, thus enabling the monitoring and maintenance of medical devices by the manufacturers. In the line of synchronization of medical data, we also have the solution proposed by Lomotey et al. [35], a middleware for the m-Health (mobile health) that facilitates the efficient process of synchronizing medical data with minimal latency.

The *SBUS* is a middleware presented by Singh et al. [36]. It is a solution that allows multiple forms of communication that are dynamically reconfigurable. It ensures that the terminals' message types match and that each transmission (message) conforms to the type scheme. Also, the *SBUS* supports several communication methods, including client-server (request-response and RPC) and streaming of push/pull messages.

Some initiatives used to promote interoperability between health systems continent or country-wise have also been identified in the literature. For example, Ferrara [37] proposes the DHE (Distributed Healthcare Environment), a middleware that follows the European Standard Health Information System Architecture proposal, implementing a distributed repository for all clinical, organizational, and management information of the healthcare structure, making them available when and where needed for all applications in the health information system. AlZghoul et al. [38] describe a middleware architecture to help healthcare providers in Jordan access electronic health data residing in a national health database.

Healthcare applications deal with a series of multimedia files, mainly tests in image format. In this sense, Kallepalli et al. [39] describe a security middleware for DICOM images that provide refined access control, policy management, demographic filtering, and record-keeping restricted to the Canadian-Manitoban PHIA and the DICOM standard. Another middleware solution proposed for use in healthcare data environments is the CORBA (Common Object Request Broker Architecture), which was used in Murshed et al. [40], Waluyo et al. [41], and Blobel and Holena [42]'s work.

Many technologies, systems, and standards are used by Hsieh et al. [43] to characterize a middleware solution, such as a Single Sign-On Server (SSOS) in a Healthcare Enterprise Information Portal (HEIP) and in a Health Information System (HIS). This set of solutions was implemented in the network infrastructure of the National Taiwan University Hospital (NTUH).

Finally, a series of middlewares were mentioned in the analyzed works, such as the *MiThrilNGN*, the *MyHearth* and the *X73uHealth* [44], the *ANGELAH* (AssistiNG ELders At Home) - proposed in Taleb et al. [45] - and the HYDRA, a solution that allows different devices to be incorporated into applications through a simple service interface.

Table 1 summarizes the main middleware for health systems proposed in the analyzed studies, indicating the authors and a brief description of each solution.

2.2   RQ2: What Are the Main Characteristics of Middleware for Healthcare Systems?

The analyzed papers cite the main characteristics of middleware for health systems. Rodriguez and Favela [33] state that the main characteristics of middleware for health are to provide data integration between different devices and artifacts, data mobility between doctors, patients, and users, and the mobility of documents and equipment.

In Alonso et al. [27]'s work, a set of middleware requirements based on an analysis of Structural Health Monitoring (SHM) deployments and desirable middleware resources is defined, bringing the following items: heterogeneity, high abstraction level, energy optimization, scalability, security, Quality of Service (QoS), reliability and fault tolerance.

According to Ferrara [37], middleware for healthcare systems must (i) provide optimized support to the specific needs of individual centers and units (which are intrinsically different from an organizational, clinical, and logistical point of view), allowing different suppliers to offer specialized applications and enabling users to select the most effective solutions for their needs; and (ii) allow the different centers and units to cooperate based on a substantial functional and informational consistency, capable of ensuring the general consistency of the health organization, which is necessary to increase the effectiveness and reliability of the clinical, administrative, epidemiological and management activities carried out at both local and territorial levels.

Data integration is one of the main characteristics cited for creating middleware for healthcare systems. In this sense, Taleb et al. [45] mention that middleware for healthcare systems must ensure that the integration of devices and middleware enables rapid response action to ensure user safety. Oliveira et al. [46] complement and state that middleware should be able to provide sharing and integration of information between third-party applications, provide support for data collection and be able to integrate with other mobile devices and applications. Furthermore, Martíez et al. [47] cites the need for transparency in data integration, that is, the integration needs to happen without being too costly for the integrated applications, conserving the business details of each application.

Concerning integration with other devices, the flexibility and dynamism characteristics emerge. That means that new components can be added or removed without modifying the existing application in different contexts and environments, reducing the burden of developing new resources [26,39]. The importance of this characteristic is also stated by Pereira et al. [48], who says that middleware must be able to provide flexibility, adaptability, and security for monitoring health devices.

Adaptability is an essential feature for healthcare middleware. According to Kliem et al. [49], such solutions must be able to handle standard and proprietary devices; quickly handle change in requirements; handle all existing medical devices, and preserve interoperability at the application level if they are replaced (extending the integration with a migration challenge).

According to Waluyo et al. [41], the characteristics that the middleware should provide are related to data acquisition, dynamic plug-and-play system,

Table 1. Middleware solutions for healthcare systems.

Author	Middleware	Description
Zhang et al. [26]	Mobile Context and Ontology-based Reasoning/Feedback (MCOM)	System for monitoring the patients' health status using the smartphone
Alonso et al. [27]	Kura	Proposed by the Eclipse consortium and designed to be installed on gateways
	AllJoyn	Proposed by the Linux Foundation, it provides a version for restricted features and different APIs for developers
	Macchina.io	Middleware that implements a publishing/subscription-based messaging protocol
Almadani et al. [28]	*RTPS*	It presents a middleware model to control information sharing in a publication/subscription-based environment
Singh et al. [29]	Publish/subscribe-based middleware for policy-based information sharing	Defines a template for defining and enforcing refined information sharing policies in an active notification environment. The model was described based on a publish/subscribe middleware
Madureira et al. [30]	*My − AHA*	Multiplatform solution based on multi-module system architecture for the integration of different health and active aging solutions
Ryan et al. [31]	Health Service Bus (*HSB*)	Solution based on the Enterprise Service Bus (ESB) middleware software architecture, which provides a loosely coupled and highly distributed approach for enterprise systems integration
Rodriguez and Favela [33]	*SALSA*	Solution based on the creation of autonomous agents that react to the contextual elements of the medical environment and communicate with other agents, users, and services available in the environment
Chaudhry et al. [34]	*POStCODE* (POstmarket SurveillanCe Of DEvices)	Middleware that provides operational details, being careful to delete private patient data from devices directly to manufacturers
Lomotey et al. [35]	Middleware for m-Health	Solution-focused on the data synchronization process and on reducing latency
Singh et al. [36]	*SBUS*	A solution that allows multiple forms of communication that are dynamically reconfigurable, supporting various communication methods, such as client-server and message streaming
Ferrara [37]	*DHE*® (Distributed Healthcare Environment)	Middleware following the European Standard Health Information System Architecture proposal, implementing a distributed repository for all clinical, organizational, and management information of the health structure
Kallepalli et al. [39]	Security middleware for DICOM images	Provides refined access control, policy management, demographic filtering, and record-keeping restricted to the Canadian-Manitoban PHIA and the DICOM standard

security, being light and easy to reconfigure, and having resource control management. Prados-Suarez et al. [50] cite, in addition to integration, access control. In this sense, the authors include an access control layer that guarantees privacy protection and adaptation and compliance with standards. Also, it has an access layer specially designed to facilitate the development of external access functions based on the principle of reuse. The need to control access to data is also mentioned by Singh et al. [29], making clear the need for these data to be available to those providing care, but the sensitivity of medical information means that it must also be protected. Also regarding safety, AlZghoul et al. [38] say that Electronic Health Data Record Systems contain private data that must be protected from any unwanted access and that separating the personal data database from the medical data database can preserve the patient's data and maintain the useful medical data without affecting privacy. Thus, providing solutions for access control in middleware is an important feature [37].

Finally, Table 2 summarizes the main requirements for health systems pointed out in the analyzed studies.

Table 2. Main requirements for middleware for healthcare systems.

Requirement	Description	References
Transparent data integration	Enable transparent data integration between different devices and mobile applications; data mobility between doctors, patients, users; and mobility of documents and equipment	[27, 33, 45–47, 50]
Data heterogeneity	Provide ways to treat heterogeneous data with a high level of abstraction, flexibility, and dynamics in different contexts and environments	[26, 27, 37, 39, 48]
Flexibility and dynamism	Provide optimized and flexible support to the specific needs of each center and unit	[26, 27, 37, 39, 48]
Scalability	Provide means where applications can scale without compromising the Quality of Service (QoS)	[27, 29, 37, 38, 41, 49, 50]
Reliability	Allow data from different centers and units to be integrated, ensuring the reliability of the data involved	[27, 37]
Security	Ensure the protection and privacy of the data used by doctors, patients, and users, mainly through access control	[29, 37, 38, 41, 49, 50]

2.3   RQ3: How are Middlewares Evaluated in the Works Analyzed?

The middlewares are mainly evaluated from the point of view of performance, direct and indirect costs, and effectiveness. The *ANGELAH*, for example, was evaluated based on metrics from performance evaluation systems, which used probabilistic calculations and determined a satisfactory result for the prototype developed [45].

The middleware proposed in Lomotey et al. [51] is used by a mobile application and was evaluated from two perspectives: (i) the processing time of the clinical transactions, which are reported from the users' devices; and (ii) the indirect communication cost. In the second case, the evaluation is made by studying the data collected in three different categories: 1) less load, 2) average load, and 3) maximum load. The categorization is based on the use of the Health Information System (HIS).

The Device Nimbus had its performance evaluated through a series of tests that used different data sources and reached data collection, integration, and analysis expectations [46]. In Almadani et al. [28]'s work, to evaluate the middleware, a model of practice tests with devices consuming and sending data to the middleware was used to check the response time, the quality of the response, and the data in different scenarios.

In Waluyo et al. [41], the middleware was evaluated for its performance in wireless data transmission time, real-time performance (with and without security), and waiting in line. The *BioMIMS*, on the other hand, was validated by researchers from the Rizzoli Orthopedic Institute, in which researchers analyzed data provided by themselves regarding two types of diseases (Multiple Osteochondromas - MO and Osteogenesis Imperfecta - OI). Through empirical analysis, the researchers proved the effectiveness of using the solution [23].

In Pervez et al. [22], a probabilistic model tester called PRISM was used to analyze the reliability and performance of the systems. The Markov Decision Process (MDP) was used to find the probability of failures, while the Markov Continuous Time Chain (MCTC) was used to model the workflow and evaluate the probability of failures in real-time. The study concluded that this reliability analysis approach is more scalable than the analysis techniques based on traditional simulations.

Kim et al. [52] set up a test environment for the evaluation of the proposed middleware. The following items were evaluated through tests: the service start time on a public network, the average jitter (delay between packets with the increase in the number of receiving terminals), and the connectivity on a private network.

Finally, in general, from the performance point of view, it is evident that the main metrics investigated are transmission time and data processing in real-time (with and without security). Regarding costs, direct and indirect costs are considered; and concerning effectiveness, middleware is evaluated mainly through empirical analysis and probabilistic approaches to analyze the reliability and performance of the solutions, for example, evaluating the probability of failures in real-time.

2.4   RQ4: What are the Challenges and Opportunities to Develop Middleware for Healthcare Systems?

The general health scenario is currently characterized by many different, heterogeneous, and mutually incompatible applications, which are already installed and operational in individual centers, to support the particular needs of specific groups of users [37].

According to Schweiger et al. [53], the integration of standalone applications is a difficult task as they often represent similar information in different data schemas and any communication requires an agreement between the sender and recipient on a common data representation, this challenge is also cited by Soyemi et al. [54], which says that it is necessary to standardize the data that enables the communication between solutions implemented with different software languages, allowing the automation of processes and services in this sense.

On the other hand, Kliem et al. [49] say that semantic interoperability is an important challenge for integrating middleware and the e-Health domain in general since it allows the integration of all types of medical devices using different protocols and data formats. The diversity of sensor protocols is also one of the challenges for developing middleware for healthcare systems [44].

Therefore, Prados-Suarez et al. [50] state that several sources of information, not just from medical institutions, should be integrated, generating the need for a homogeneous access point for all of this data, with the capacity to adapt (to adequate itself to new systems, standards, and needs), but without the need to transfer data ownership. Also, according to Prados-Suarez et al. [50], promoting accessibility is also a challenge in developing these solutions since there are different access needs with different requirements - personal use, medical use, research purposes - especially regarding the protection of data privacy.

According to Lomotey et al. [51], the high latency in the m-Health system when sending data between the cell phone and the computing facilities in the hospital can make transferring medical data very slowly, bringing up the challenge of decreasing the data latency considering different network conditions.

Concerning safety and reliability, Arunachalan et al. [55] reinforce that the transmission of critical data, such as demographic data and vital signs, using wireless network infrastructure presents different requirements for the middleware solution. Besides, the authors pay attention to legal and privacy issues related to patient care data, which the middleware solution should consider.

Regarding handling images by digital means in the health area (such as tests, for example), Kallepalli et al. [39] mention that protecting and providing refined access control for Digital Imaging and Communication in Medicine (DICOM) based on the Personal Health Information Act (PHIA) is one of the biggest challenges in image uploading and sharing systems, which can also be applied for healthcare middleware solutions. Finally, Shand et al. [56] claim that as messaging middleware technology matures, users are increasingly demanding resources, leading to modular middleware architectures. However, the extra complexity increases the risk of a security breach.

We noticed that there are several challenges involved in the process of developing middleware for health systems. Among the main ones, it is possible to mention the heterogeneity of the data; the different means of communication between devices, sensors, and systems; reliability; and data security. Therefore, investigation and research opportunities arise regarding middleware solutions that use open standards, such as $HL7$ [24], that can meet the requirements of developing middleware for health systems while overcoming the challenges present in the development.

3   Conclusion

This work presented an analysis of the state the art of research on the use of middleware to solve the problem of interoperability between health systems to understand how the works available in the literature answer the defined Research Questions (RQ), as well as identify future trends in the development of middleware for e-Health and m-Health applications.

Therefore, a Systematic Mapping [15, 16] was carried out, in which 1,162 articles were explored. After the extraction, analysis, and selection of the articles, 34 works were selected for analysis and data extraction. The analysis showed us that there is a large amount of middleware developed for the health area. However, they are not entirely flexible and applicable in different contexts in the area and, therefore, do not meet all of the essential requirements for middleware solutions for the health field. Given this, the opportunity to create middleware for health data that uses open standards, such as $HL7$, for integration and interoperability between different health solutions and that meet the requirements presented in this work is still open.

We understand that the corporate Electronic Health Records systems, as well as solutions based on mobile computing, are being increasingly used in the health context and, therefore, as future work, we intend to propose the architecture of a middleware that meets all of the requirements presented in this work, as well as carrying out the implementation and analysis of a case study of the developed solution.

References

1. de Fátima Marin, H.: Sistemas de informação em saúde: considerações gerais. J. Health Inform. **2**(1) (2010)
2. Iakovidis, I.: Towards personal health record: current situation, obstacles and trends in implementation of electronic healthcare record in Europe. Int. J. Med. Informatics **52**(1–3), 105–115 (1998)
3. Silva, B.M., Rodrigues, J.J., de la Torre Díez, I., López-Coronado, M., Saleem, K.: Mobile-health: a review of current state in 2015. J. Biomed. Inform. **56**, 265–272 (2015)
4. Zandieh, S.O., Yoon-Flannery, K., Kuperman, G.J., Langsam, D.J., Hyman, D., Kaushal, R.: Challenges to EHR implementation in electronic-versus paper-based office practices. J. Gen. Intern. Med. **23**(6), 755–761 (2008). https://doi.org/10.1007/s11606-008-0573-5

5. Devkota, B., Devkota, A.: Electronic health records: advantages of use and barriers to adoption. Health Renaiss. **11**(3), 181–184 (2013)
6. Eysenbach, G.: What is e-health? J. Med. Internet Res. **3**, e20 (2001)
7. de Mattos, W.D., Gondim, P.R.: M-health solutions using 5G networks and M2M communications. IT Prof. **18**(3), 24–29 (2016)
8. Free, C., Phillips, G., Felix, L., Galli, L., Patel, V., Edwards, P.: The effectiveness of m-health technologies for improving health and health services: a systematic review protocol. BMC Res. Notes **3**(1), 1–7 (2010)
9. Zuehlke, P., Li, J., Talaei-Khoei, A., Ray, P.: A functional specification for mobile eHealth (mHealth) systems. In: 2009 11th International Conference on e-Health Networking, Applications and Services (Healthcom), pp. 74–78. IEEE (2009)
10. Ayeni, F., Omogbadegun, Z., Omoregbe, N.A., Misra, S., Garg, L.: Overcoming barriers to healthcare access and delivery. EAI Endorsed Trans. Pervasive Health Technol. **4**(15), e2 (2018)
11. Jayaratne, M., et al.: A data integration platform for patient-centered e-healthcare and clinical decision support. Future Gener. Comput. Syst. **92**, 996–1008 (2019)
12. Atzori, L., Iera, A., Morabito, G.: The internet of things: a survey. Comput. Netw. **54**(15), 2787–2805 (2010)
13. Bruneo, D., Puliafito, A., Scarpa, M.: Mobile middleware: definition and motivations. In: The Handbook of Mobile Middleware, pp. 145–167 (2007)
14. Bezerra, C.A.C., de Araújo, A.M.C., UNITPAC-Araguaína, T.: Especificando um middleware para a interoperabilidade do registro eletrônico em saúde
15. Petersen, K., Feldt, R., Mujtaba, S., Mattsson, M.: Systematic mapping studies in software engineering. In: 12th International Conference on Evaluation and Assessment in Software Engineering (EASE) 12, pp. 1–10 (2008)
16. Kitchenham, B., Brereton, O.P., Budgen, D., Turner, M., Bailey, J., Linkman, S.: Systematic literature reviews in software engineering-a systematic literature review. Inf. Softw. Technol. **51**(1), 7–15 (2009)
17. Boyle, F., Sherman, D.: ScopusTM: the product and its development. Ser. Libr. **49**(3), 147–153 (2006)
18. ACM Digital Library: ACM digital library home page (2021). https://dl.acm.org/. Accessed 15 Mar 2021
19. Durniak, A.: Welcome to IEEE Xplore. IEEE Power Eng. Rev. **20**(11), 12 (2000)
20. ScienceDirect: Science direct home page (2021). https://www.sciencedirect.com/. Accessed 15 Mar 2021
21. Springer Nature Switzerland AG. Part of Springer Nature. Springer link home page (2021). https://link.springer.com/. Accessed 15 Mar 2021
22. Pervez, U., Mahmood, A., Hasan, O., Latif, K., Gawanmeh, A.: Improvement strategies for device interoperability middleware using formal reliability analysis. Scalable Comput.: Pract. Exp. **17**(3), 150–170 (2016)
23. Melament, A., et al.: Biomims-soa platform for research of rare hereditary diseases. In: 2011 Annual SRII Global Conference, pp. 83–90. IEEE (2011)
24. H. F. Foundation: HL7 FHIR foundation about page (2021). http://fhir.org/about. html. Accessed 15 Mar 2021
25. Liu, L., Huang, Q.: An extensible HL7 middleware for heterogeneous healthcare information exchange. In: 2012 5th International Conference on BioMedical Engineering and Informatics, pp. 1045–1048. IEEE (2012)
26. Zhang, W., Thurow, K., Stoll, R.: A knowledge-based telemonitoring platform for application in remote healthcare. Int. J. Comput. Commun. Control **9**(5), 644–654 (2014)

27. Alonso, L., Barbarán, J., Chen, J., Díaz, M., Llopis, L., Rubio, B.: Middleware and communication technologies for structural health monitoring of critical infrastructures: A survey. Comput. Stand. Interfaces **56**, 83–100 (2018)
28. Almadani, B., Saeed, B., Alroubaiy, A.: Healthcare systems integration using real time publish subscribe (RTPS) middleware. Comput. Electr. Eng. **50**, 67–78 (2016)
29. Singh, J., Vargas, L., Bacon, J., Moody, K.: Policy-based information sharing in publish/subscribe middleware. In: 2008 IEEE Workshop on Policies for Distributed Systems and Networks, pp. 137–144. IEEE (2008)
30. Madureira, P., Cardoso, N., Sousa, F., Moreira, W.: My-AHA: middleware platform to sustain active and healthy ageing. In: 2019 International Conference on Wireless and Mobile Computing, Networking and Communications (WiMob), pp. 21–26. IEEE (2019)
31. Ryan, A., Eklund, P.W.: The health service bus: an architecture and case study in achieving interoperability in healthcare (2010)
32. Ayeni, F., Misra, S.: Overcoming barriers of effective health care delivery and electronic health records in Nigeria using socialized medicine. In: 2014 11th International Conference on Electronics, Computer and Computation (ICECCO), pp. 1–4. IEEE (2014)
33. Rodriguez, M.D., Favela, J.: An agent middleware for ubiquitous computing in healthcare. In: Sordo, M., Vaidya, S., Jain, L.C. (eds.) Advanced Computational Intelligence Paradigms in Healthcare - 3. Studies in Computational Intelligence, vol. 107, pp. 117–149. Springer, Heidelberg (2008). https://doi.org/10.1007/978-3-540-77662-8_6
34. Chaudhry, J., Valli, C., Crowley, M., Haass, J., Roberts, P.: Postcode middleware for post-market surveillance of medical devices for cyber security in medical and healthcare sector in Australia. In: 2018 12th International Symposium on Medical Information and Communication Technology (ISMICT), pp. 1–10. IEEE (2018)
35. Lomotey, R.K., Nilson, J., Mulder, K., Wittmeier, K., Schachter, C., Deters, R.: Mobile medical data synchronization on cloud-powered middleware platform. IEEE Trans. Serv. Comput. **9**(5), 757–770 (2016)
36. Singh, J., Bacon, J.: Managing health information flows with a reconfigurable component-based middleware. In: 2011 IEEE 12th International Conference on Mobile Data Management, vol. 2, pp. 52–54. IEEE (2011)
37. Ferrara, F.M.: The standard 'healthcare information systems architecture' and the DHE middleware. Int. J. Med. Informatics **52**(1–3), 39–51 (1998)
38. AlZghoul, M.M., Al-Taee, M.A., Al-Taee, A.M.: Towards nationwide electronic health record system in Jordan. In: 2016 13th International Multi-Conference on Systems, Signals & Devices (SSD), pp. 650–655. IEEE (2016)
39. Kallepalli, V.N., Ehikioya, S.A., Camorlinga, S., Rueda, J.A.: Security middleware infrastructure for DICOM images in health information systems. J. Digit. Imaging **16**(4), 356–364 (2003). https://doi.org/10.1007/s10278-003-1710-7
40. Murshed, A.N., Almansoori, W., Xylogiannopoulos, K.F., Elzohbi, M., Alhajj, R., Rokne, J.: Developing an efficient health clinical application: IIOP distributed objects framework. In: 2012 IEEE/ACM International Conference on Advances in Social Networks Analysis and Mining, pp. 759–764. IEEE (2012)
41. Waluyo, A.B., Pek, I., Chen, X., Yeoh, W.-S.: Design and evaluation of lightweight middleware for personal wireless body area network. Pers. Ubiquit. Comput. **13**(7), 509–525 (2009)
42. Blobel, B., Holena, M.: Comparing middleware concepts for advanced healthcare system architectures. Int. J. Med. Informatics **46**(2), 69–85 (1997)

43. Hsieh, S.-L., et al.: An integrated healthcare enterprise information portal and healthcare information system framework. In: 2006 International Conference of the IEEE Engineering in Medicine and Biology Society, pp. 4731–4734. IEEE (2006)
44. Ji, Z., Ganchev, I., O'Droma, M., Zhang, X., Zhang, X.: A cloud-based x73 ubiquitous mobile healthcare system: design and implementation. Sci. World J. **2014** (2014)
45. Taleb, T., Bottazzi, D., Guizani, M., Nait-Charif, H.: ANGELAH: a framework for assisting elders at home. IEEE J. Sel. Areas Commun. **27**(4), 480–494 (2009)
46. Oliveira, E.A., Kirley, M., Fonseca, J.C., Gama, K.: Device nimbus: an intelligent middleware for smarter services for health and fitness. Int. J. Distrib. Sens. Netw. **11**(8), 454626 (2015)
47. Martíez, I., et al.: Seamless integration of ISO/IEEE11073 personal health devices and ISO/EN13606 electronic health records into an end-to-end interoperable solution. Telemed. e-Health **16**(10), 993–1004 (2010)
48. Pereira, R., Barros, C., Pereira, S., Mendes, P.M., Silva, C.: A middleware for intelligent environments in ambient assisted living. In: 2014 36th Annual International Conference of the IEEE Engineering in Medicine and Biology Society, pp. 5924–5927. IEEE (2014)
49. Kliem, A., Boelke, A., Grohnert, A., Traeder, N.: Self-adaptive middleware for ubiquitous medical device integration. In: 2014 IEEE 16th International Conference on e-Health Networking, Applications and Services (Healthcom), pp. 298–304. IEEE (2014)
50. Prados-Suarez, B., Molina, C., Peña-Yañez, C.: Providing an integrated access to EHR using electronic health records aggregators. Stud. Health Technol. Inform. **270**, 402–406 (2020)
51. Lomotey, R.K., et al.: Using cloud-based middleware to enable mobile medical data management. In: 2016 IEEE International Conference on Mobile Services (MS), pp. 142–149. IEEE (2016)
52. Kim, H.H., Jo, H.G., Kang, S.J.: Self-organizing peer-to-peer middleware for healthcare monitoring in real-time. Sensors **17**(11), 2650 (2017)
53. Schweiger, R., Bürkle, T., Dudeck, J.: Post-integration of a tumor documentation system into a his via middleware. Stud. Health Technol. Inform. **43**, 6–9 (1997)
54. Soyemi, J., Misra, S., Nicholas, O.: Towards e-healthcare deployment in Nigeria: the open issues. In: Intan, R., Chi, C.-H., Palit, H.N., Santoso, L.W. (eds.) ICSIIT 2015. CCIS, vol. 516, pp. 588–599. Springer, Heidelberg (2015). https://doi.org/10.1007/978-3-662-46742-8_54
55. Arunachalan, B., Light, J.: Middleware architecture for patient care data transmission using wireless networks. In: Proceedings of the 2007 International Conference on Wireless Communications and Mobile Computing, pp. 182–185 (2007)
56. Shand, B., Rashbass, J.: Security for middleware extensions: event meta-data for enforcing security policy. In: Proceedings of the 2008 Workshop on Middleware Security, pp. 31–33 (2008)

Determining the Impact of Perspex Obstacles on Bluetooth Transmission Paths Within a Simulated Office Environment for More Accurate Location Determination

Jay Pancham[1]([✉]), Richard C. Millham[1]([✉]), and Simon James Fong[1,2]([✉])

[1] Durban University of Technology, Durban, South Africa
{panchamj,richardm1}@dut.ac.za
[2] University of Macau, Taipa, Macau SAR, China
ccfong@umac.mo

Abstract. Research on Real-Time Location Systems (RTLS) for indoor environments establishes Bluetooth Low Energy as a promising technological low-cost solution for various environments. However, in indoor environments, there are numerous obstacles such as furniture, walls, partitions, etc. that will cause obstructions to Bluetooth signals. This research established the effect of Perspex on Bluetooth transmission in an indoor environment. This research extends on our previous research which evaluated RTLS technologies, RTLS constraints, and an energy efficient design model for sensor detection in indoor environments. Perspex was chosen for this research as it is used as a common shield used to minimize COVID transmission in an office environment. In general, the 3 mm and 5 mm Perspex did not have a significant impact on Bluetooth transmission.

Keywords: BLE · Bluetooth Low Energy · RSSI · Real-Time Location System · Obstacle · Obstruction · Perspex

1 Introduction

During the past few decades, with the proliferation and availability of indoor positioning hardware, this RTLS realm has developed into a significant research area, inviting interest from a variety of researchers [1]. The interest in location services provided by the Internet of Things (IoT) technologies identified a critical period for indoor real-time location [2]. Our eventual intention is to design an efficient and cost-effective RTLS taking into consideration the constraints documented in research work [3] for an office environment. Authors in [4] also explored the technologies relating to indoor RTLS and went further to determine the different methods that could be used in calculating locations. This research determines the impact of obstructions in particular Perspex in the path of Bluetooth transmission of Low Power Nodes (LPN) to gateways. Perspex is a clear acrylic sheet that is used as a screen to reduce transmission of COVID in office environments. Various

© Springer Nature Switzerland AG 2021
O. Gervasi et al. (Eds.): ICCSA 2021, LNCS 12957, pp. 410–420, 2021.
https://doi.org/10.1007/978-3-030-87013-3_31

thicknesses of this material are available, but the most popular thicknesses used are the 3 mm and 5 mm. These are used to partition spaces between employees or between employees and customers.

This paper is arranged as follows: Sect. 2 discusses the underlying principles of indoor location and Bluetooth technology, Sect. 3 defines the methodology used to conduct the experiments to evaluate the impact of Bluetooth signals through the obstacle Perspex, Sect. 4, presents the results obtained from the research, Sect. 5 discusses the results obtained from the experiment and Sect. 6 concludes and recommends future work.

2 Literature Review

2.1 RTLS Technologies

Research to track assets and people indoors has been conducted for many decades. More recently research on the implementation of indoor tracking technologies are being conducted on visible light positioning [5], Ultra Wide Band (UWB) [6–8], BLE [9], Wi-Fi [10], and visualization from video recordings [11]. Furthermore, the advancement and development of new hardware have delivered new solutions that have inspired new research in the field of indoor localization and navigation. Global Navigation Satellite Systems (GNSS) provides a feasible technology for tracking both people and objects outdoors. Similarly, many indoor applications necessitate the need for localization of both people and objects. In case of an emergency, the location of objects and people indoors needs to be determined at real time. Indoor environmental constraints require additional designs to provide a reasonable degree of accuracy. Using GPS technology [12] it is not possible to determine real time positioning indoors as the devices used for tracking require a direct line of sight to the different satellites [13] to triangulate the position. Therefore, alternative design models with different technologies must be used in real-world systems for indoor locations. According to [14], an RTLS constitutes a "combination of software and hardware that is used to repeatedly calculate and furnish the location of assets at real time to resources that are designed to operate with the system".

Various solutions used in RTLS have been evaluated. However, the advancement in technologies warrants the most appropriate solutions to be designed taking into account constraints of an indoor RTLS. [4] appraised prominent technologies of RTLS that were published in peer reviewed research articles. This research used the most common attributes in terms of RTLS within the healthcare exemplar and literature to assess these technologies. The evaluation process included data from 23 US hospitals [15] together with the exemplar of a hospital survey. In an earlier paper [3], we evaluated technologies such as RFID, Wi-Fi, and Bluetooth and determined evaluation criteria viz. cost [16], energy consumption [17], accuracy [18], detection range [16], and form factor. This preliminary research determines the effects of obstacles in particular Perspex on Bluetooth signals before data can be processed for accurate prediction of locations.

[19] used a single fixed distance of one meter to compare BLE and ZigBee technologies. However, they did not have compelling results that indicated which of the two technologies is superior as wireless transmission is largely affected by interferences in a realistic environment. Hence our research to more accurately determine the effects of one of the obstacles on Bluetooth in an office environment. Furthermore, their research did not provide measurements for throughput or RSSI beyond this fixed distance to report on the effects of the signals. Our research expands on their work to extend the 1 m range to cover an office as a more realistic environment for indoor location and tracking.

Bluetooth Local Infotainment Point (BLIP) [20] is an example of a Bluetooth system that offers access to LAN/WAN via Bluetooth [21]. Several BLIP nodes are required for such a network to allow the Bluetooth devices to connect due to Bluetooth's limited range. Due to the advancements of BLE the number nodes required will be decreased.

Bluetooth classic's limitation in densely populated areas due to interference and signal attenuation. Bluetooth classic can send large amounts of data, but depletes battery power quickly and is more expensive than Bluetooth LE or other indoor localization technology [22]. Furthermore, for increased accuracy for RTLS, there will be an increased form factor, increased power consumption, etc. With the advances in technology, Bluetooth LE emerged as a more suitable technology to transfer small packets of data whilst consuming lower energy and at a lower cost.

2.2 Bluetooth Low Energy

Bluetooth Low Energy (BLE) is designed for the Internet of Things (IoT) making it most suitable for equipment to work for long periods on power sources, such as energy-harvesting devices or coin cell batteries [23]. One of the key features is BLE can transmit small packets of data whilst significantly reducing the power consumption when compared to the previous version of Bluetooth [17]. A BLE RTLS typically consists of a tag, a stationery anchor to detect the tags, and the location engine to calculate the location of the tags [24]. BLE offers several advantages such as extended coverage, lower cost, and smaller form factor. The point-to-point nature of the communication of BLE nodes has limited coverage. Hence the proposal of a possible solution by [25] to extend this limited coverage by using a wireless mesh network that uses multiple hops to enable routing of packets from multiple nodes (sensors) to facilitate communication among the nodes.

The introduction of Bluetooth® 5 in 2016 provided the industry with increased speed and broadcasting capacity. Both BLE and Bluetooth Classic use 2.4 GHz in the unlicensed industrial, scientific, and medical (ISM) band. BLE uses 40 channels with 2 MHz spacing whilst Bluetooth Classic uses 79 channels with 1 MHz spacing, see Fig. 1. The increased 2402 MHz wider channels can provide higher transmission speeds as compared to the Bluetooth classic. Furthermore, the higher transmission frequency allows for increased data transmission.

With the rapid rise in COVID cases in 2020 and 2021 and the need for employees and customers to interact in an office environment it became necessary to install screens to act as a protective shield between people. These shields provided additional protection against the spreading of the virus while enabling a functioning office working environment. The most commonly used material for shields, in this case, is 3 mm and 5 mm

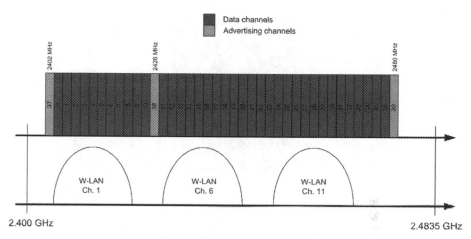

Fig. 1. Bluetooth LE channels.

Perspex as it is clear, lightweight, and easy to install. Such screens either hang from the ceilings or is installed directly on the desks or work surfaces. Bluetooth is used by various devices in an office environment and in particular for real time location. The impact of these screens on RSSI levels needed to be investigated. This led to setting up the experiment to study this impact in an office environment and report on the results.

3 Methodology

The focus of this research is to establish the received of RSSI values from Low Power Nodes when passed through obstacles, and transmitted with obstructions, and Gateways. Because Bluetooth transmission is affected by obstructions we simulate an office environment by using Perspex as screens separating workspaces. The intention is to establish the impact Perspex will have on Bluetooth transmission. The data must be derived from a reliable source thereby minimizing any error when the location is calculated. The hardware uses the latest Bluetooth technology available ie. Bluetooth 5 and the module is powered by 2 AAA batteries. The firmware has been developed to broadcast messages containing the device UUID and the message identifier at regular intervals. The research entails the setup of the hardware, setup of the screens, and capture of data from LPN's to a server for processing.

3.1 Hardware Selection and Software Configuration

In this experiment, we used Skylab's SKB501 solution shown in Fig. 2 as the Low Power Node (LPN). This solution used Nordics NRF52840 Bluetooth® 5 System on Chip (SOC) hardware. The hardware takes uses the feature advancements of Bluetooth® 5 such as increased performance capabilities, long-range and high throughput modes.

Fig. 2. SKB501 – LPN top view

The gateway setup for this experiment is a Raspberry Pi 4 with Ubuntu V18.04 as its operating system. The gateway acts as the bridge between the low power nodes and the server. BlueZ is used on the Raspberry Pi to provide support for the core Bluetooth layers and protocols. It is selected as the preferred choice as its flexible, efficient, and uses a modular implementation. The gateway software listens for broadcasts on the Bluetooth interface and translates messages to be sent to the server via the Wi-Fi network port. This application is written in C# and uses the UDP protocol to send the messages from the gateway to the server. The server is installed with the Ubuntu server as the Operating System and PostgreSQL to store the data from the low power nodes. The software to receive the message from the gateway continuously monitors for UDP messages. The software written in C# writes these messages to a data table residing in a PostgreSQL database. The LPN, gateway, and server architecture are depicted in Fig. 3.

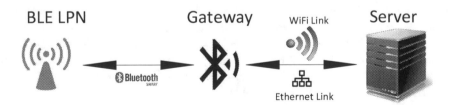

Fig. 3. Architecture

3.2 Data Collection

The LPN firmware was set up to broadcast the transmit RSSI level, LPN identifier, and unique message identifier every 100 ms. Each gateway transmitted its unique identifier. Both the gateway and LPN mac_address were initially saved so that they could be uniquely identified on the network. The unique message identifier can be used to analyze the receipt of messages at each of the gateways. This experiment simulated an office environment where workspaces are separated by partitions. In this case, we used Perspex as the partition to evaluate the impact it has on Bluetooth transmission. The obstruction used were two sheets of Perspex measuring 1.2 m × 0.6 m × 3 mm and 1.2 m × 0.6 m × 5 mm (m = meters, mm = millimeters). The readings were observed with no obstruction, with 3 mm Perspex obstruction, 5 mm Perspex obstruction, and both 3 mm and 5 mm sheets placed side by side as the obstruction. Each test was conducted for a 5 min duration and this was repeated three times i.e. test 1, test 2, test 3. The tests were repeated to monitor and evaluate the consistency in the measurements taken across the tests.

The gateways labeled GW-001 to GW-004 were arranged 2 m apart at (x, y) positions (0, 2; 2, 2; 4, 1; and 6, 2). LPN001 was placed between GW-001 and GW-002 at position (1, 2) whilst LPN002 was placed between GW-003 and GW-004 at position (5, 2). This layout resulted in a 1 m distance between LPN001 and GW-001 and GW-002 and a 1 m distance between LPN002 and GW-003 and GW-004. This layout is depicted in Fig. 4. The mean RSSI values received by the gateways from the LPNs are also shown in the figure.

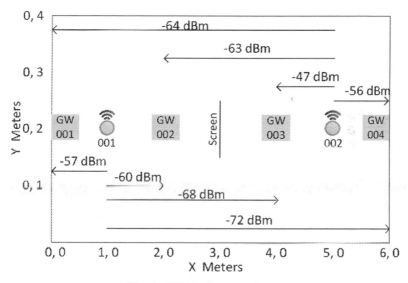

Fig. 4. LPN and gateway layout

An application was used to configure the positions of the gateways and LPNs, set the duration of the test, and start the test. The session name and session ID (automatically generated) are used to identify the data set collected for each test. The positions of the gateways and LPNs are saved for each test. Figure 5 shows the interface for the data collection.

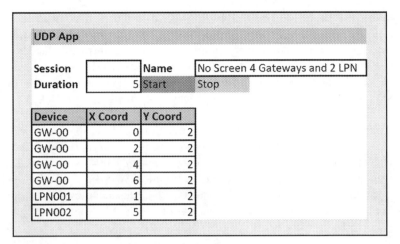

Fig. 5. UDP application for data capture

4   Results

4.1   Data Collection

An average of 28522 messages was processed by the gateways from the two LPNs over the 5 min for the tests. Each gateway processed approximately 7100 messages whilst each LPN broadcast approximately 300 messages. All details of the test, messages and locations of the gateways and LPNs were saved to the PostgreSQL database.

4.2   Aggregation of Data

After analysis of the RSSI levels received and the number of messages received at each RSSI level by the gateway from each LPN, it was found that about 70% of the messages received were at 3 RSSI levels as depicted in column "J" in Table 1. Subsequent RSSI levels had significantly lower count message counts. Therefore it was decided to use the 3 RSSI levels that had the most message counts and thereafter calculate the mean which is an accepted metric for the evaluation of RSSI levels. An extract of the data received is depicted in Table 1.

An average of these three RSSI levels received by each gateway from each LPN was calculated as listed in the column "I", "Q", "Y' and "AG" in Table 2.

Table 1. Extract of data collected

	A	B	C	D	E	F	G	H	I	J
1			No Screens							
2			Test 1		Test 2		Test3		Avg	%Count
3	GW	LPN	Count	Level	Count	Level	Count	Level		295
4	GW-001	LPN001	85	-60	111	-59	110	-59	-57	75
5	GW-001	LPN001	73	-55	81	-55	86	-55		92
6	GW-001	LPN001	62	-58	78	-58	57	-58		86
7	GW-001	LPN002	83	-64	97	-64	86	-64	-64	68
8	GW-001	LPN002	65	-60	55	-61	65	-67		69
9	GW-001	LPN002	52	-67	52	-67	52	-61		69
10	GW-002	LPN001	98	-56	102	-56	87	-56	-60	73
11	GW-002	LPN001	61	-70	62	-54	80	-54		68
12	GW-002	LPN001	55	-54	37	-69	48	-69		73

Table 2. Aggregated data

	A	B	I	Q	Y	AG
1			No Screens	3 mm Screen	5 mm Screen	3 and 5 mm Screen
2			Avg	Avg	Avg	Avg
3	GW	LPN				
4	GW-001	LPN001	-57	-57	-57	-56
5	GW-001	LPN001				
6	GW-001	LPN001				
7	GW-001	LPN002	-64	-64	-61	-64
8	GW-001	LPN002				
9	GW-001	LPN002				
10	GW-002	LPN001	-60	-57	-57	-58
11	GW-002	LPN001				
12	GW-002	LPN001				
13	GW-002	LPN002	-63	-63	-63	-62
14	GW-002	LPN002				
15	GW-002	LPN002				
16	GW-003	LPN001	-68	-68	-68	-69
17	GW-003	LPN001				
18	GW-003	LPN001				
19	GW-003	LPN002	-47	-47	-47	-47
20	GW-003	LPN002				
21	GW-003	LPN002				
22	GW-004	LPN001	-72	-71	-74	-73
23	GW-004	LPN001				
24	GW-004	LPN001				
25	GW-004	LPN002	-56	-62	-56	-56
26	GW-004	LPN002				
27	GW-004	LPN002				

5   Discussion of Results

Table 2 shows the average RSSI calculated from the selected received levels. The average RSSI level is consistent across the different tests conducted for no screen, 3 mm screen, 5 mm screen, and a combination of both 3 mm and 5 mm screens. The average RSSI levels between GW-001, GW-002, and LPN001 range between −60 and −56, RSSI levels between GW-003 and LPN002 were consistent at −47, and RSSI levels between GW-004 and LPN002 range between −62 and −56. This was expected as no screens were placed between the Gateway and the LPN. However, a difference in levels was noted between the GW-003, GW-004, and LPN 4 as the distance was 1 m.

The average RSSI levels between GW-001, GW-002, and LPN002 range between −64 and −61, whilst the average RSSI levels between GW-003, GW-004, and LPN001 range between −74 and −68. No significant difference levels were noted with both the Perspex obstructions placed between GW-002 and GW-003. We can therefore conclude that 3 mm and 5 mm Perspex commonly used as COVID shields will have little or no effect on Bluetooth messages transmitted at a level of 0 dBm. Although we initially tried to determine the effect of obstructions on RSSI signals which would subsequently affect how our location determination algorithm we would proceed to take into account the results to update a footprint regularly so that they can be used for location determination.

Results show that generally the further away from the LPN the lower the level. This observation is expected as the levels drop as distance increases. These results expand on research work done by [19] where measurements were done within a meter range. Measurements of received RSSI values were recorded with and without the obstruction Perspex to establish the effect it has on Bluetooth Transmission.

6   Conclusion and Future Work

This research established the effect of using Perspex as an obstruction on Bluetooth signals between LPNs and Gateways. Using 4 Gateways, 2 LPNs, 3 mm and 5 mm Perspex the experiment was conducted in a 6 m by 4 m office. In general, the 3 mm and 5 mm Perspex did not have a significant impact on the Bluetooth signal. Although these results were not as expected these are experimental results. Our concern is to obtain the RSSI signal strength for accurate location determination taking into account a specific common indoor scenario, i.e. office environment where Perspex is used as a screen/partition that could lower the signal strength. Our work indicates that BLE signals are not affected by these common obstacles and the RSSI levels can be used for location determination.

Future research will include establishing and testing an increased number of LPNs and Gateways in the same environment. Another variation that will be tested is to set up screens to cover a wider width and then test the impact of the screens on the transmission between the LPNs and the gateways to determine if obstacles do play a part in RSSI signal strength transmission, which is relied upon for location determination. We started our experiment with the most common obstacle, Perspex, and are moving to less common but frequently found items like metal cabinets and shelving. The findings of this future research will be presented in subsequent articles.

References

1. Wang, Y., Ye, Q., Cheng, J., Wang, L.: RSSI-based bluetooth indoor localization. In: 11th International Conference on Mobile Ad-hoc and Sensor Networks (MSN), pp. 165–171. IEEE (2015)
2. Thaljaoui, A., Val, T., Nasri, N., Brulin, D.: BLE localization using RSSI measurements and iRingLA. In: 2015 IEEE International Conference on Industrial Technology (ICIT), pp. 2178–2183. IEEE (2015)
3. Pancham, J., Millham, R., Fong, S.J.: Assessment of feasible methods used by the health care industry for real time location. In: Federated Conference on Computer Science and Information Systems (2017)
4. Pancham, J., Millham, R., Fong, S.J.: Evaluation of real time location system technologies in the health care sector. In: 17th International Conference on Computational Science and its Applications (ICCSA), pp. 1–7. IEEE (2017)
5. Liang, Q., Lin, J., Liu, M.: Towards robust visible light positioning under LED shortage by visual-inertial fusion. In: 2019 International Conference on Indoor Positioning and Indoor Navigation (IPIN), pp. 1–8. IEEE (2019)
6. Schroeer, G.: A real-time UWB multi-channel indoor positioning system for industrial scenarios. In: 2018 International Conference on Indoor Positioning and Indoor Navigation (IPIN), pp. 1–5. IEEE (2018)
7. Risset, T., Goursaud, C., Brun, X., Marquet, K., Meyer, F.: UWB ranging for rapid movements. In: 2018 International Conference on Indoor Positioning and Indoor Navigation (IPIN), pp. 1–8. IEEE (2018)
8. Martinelli, A., Jayousi, S., Caputo, S., Mucchi, L.: UWB positioning for industrial applications: the galvanic plating case study. In: 2019 International Conference on Indoor Positioning and Indoor Navigation (IPIN), pp. 1–7. IEEE (2019)
9. Naghdi, S., O'Keefe, K.: Trilateration with BLE RSSI accounting for pathloss due to human obstacles. In: International Conference on Indoor Positioning and Indoor Navigation (IPIN), pp. 1–8. IEEE (2019)
10. Moreira, A., Silva, I., Meneses, F., Nicolau, M.J., Pendao, C., Torres Sospedra, J.: Multiple simultaneous Wi-Fi measurements in fingerprinting indoor positioning. In: 2017 International Conference on Indoor Positioning and Indoor Navigation (IPIN), pp. 1–8. IEEE (2017)
11. Kim, C., Bhatt, C., Patel, M., Kimber, D., Tjahjadi, Y.: InFo: indoor localization using fusion of visual information from static and dynamic cameras. In: 2019 International Conference on Indoor Positioning and Indoor Navigation (IPIN), pp. 1–8. IEEE (2019)
12. Kim, S., Ha, S., Saad, A., Kim, J.: Indoor positioning system techniques and security. In: Fourth International Conference on e-Technologies and Networks for Development (ICeND), pp. 1–4. IEEE (2015)
13. Sato, A., Nakajima, M., Kohtake, N.: Rapid BLE beacon localization with range-only EKF-SLAM using beacon interval constraint. In: 2019 International Conference on Indoor Positioning and Indoor Navigation (IPIN), pp. 1–8. IEEE (2019)
14. International Standards Organization (ISO): Information Technology - Automatic Identification and Data Capture (AIDC) Techniques - Harmonized Vocabulary - Part 5: Locating Systems, vol. ISO/IEC 19762-5. ISO, Geneva (2007)
15. Fisher, J.A., Monahan, T.: Evaluation of real-time location systems in their hospital contexts. Int. J. Med. Inform. **81**, 705–712 (2012)
16. Tsang, P., Wu, C., Ip, W., Ho, G., Tse, Y.: A bluetooth-based indoor positioning system: a simple and rapid approach. Annu. J. IIE (HK) **35**, 11–26 (2015)
17. Yu, B., Xu, L., Li, Y.: Bluetooth low energy (BLE) based mobile electrocardiogram monitoring system. In: International Conference on Information and Automation (ICIA), pp. 763–767. IEEE (2012)

18. Deng, Z.Y., Yu, Y., Yuan, X., Wan, N., Yang, L.: Situation and development tendency of indoor positioning. China Commun. **10**, 42–55 (2013)
19. Lee, J.-S., Dong, M.-F., Sun, Y.-H.: A preliminary study of low power wireless technologies: ZigBee and bluetooth low energy. In: 10th Conference on Industrial Electronics and Applications (ICIEA), pp. 135–139. IEEE (2015)
20. Kolodziej, K.W., Hjelm, J.: Local Positioning Systems: LBS Applications and Services. CRC Press, Boca Raton (2017)
21. Deak, G., Curran, K., Condell, J.: A survey of active and passive indoor localisation systems. Comput. Commun. **35**, 1939–1954 (2012)
22. Zaim, D., Bellafkih, M.: Bluetooth low energy (BLE) based geomarketing system. In: 11th International Conference on Intelligent Systems: Theories and Applications (SITA), pp. 1–6. IEEE (2016)
23. https://www.bluetooth.com/what-is-bluetooth-technology/how-it-works/low-energy
24. Han, G.K., Gudrun, J., Ostler, D., Schneider, A.: Testing a proximity-based location tracking system with bluetooth low energy tags for future use in the OR. In: 2015 17th International Conference on E-Health Networking, Application & Services (HealthCom), pp. 17–21. IEEE (2015)
25. Raza, S., Misra, P., He, Z., Voigt, T.: Building the internet of things with bluetooth smart. Ad Hoc Netw. **57**, 19–31 (2016)

Multi-level Fault Tolerance Approach for IoT Systems

Mário Melo[1]($\boxtimes$) and Gibeon Aquino[2]

[1] Federal Institute of Rio Grande do Norte, Natal, Brazil
mario.melo@ifrn.edu.br
[2] Federal University of Rio Grande do Norte, Natal, Brazil
gibeon@dimap.ufrn.br

Abstract. The presence of faults is inevitable in the Internet of Things (IoT) systems. However, fault Tolerance in IoT systems is a challenge to overcome due to their size, complexity, dynamicity, and level of heterogeneity, especially error detection and error recovery and continued service. Thus, it is impractical to consider a unified fault tolerance technique for an entire system. The purpose of this study is to propose a multi-level fault tolerance approach granting interconnection among IoT system levels allowing information exchange and collaboration in order to attain the dependability property. Therefore, we define an event-driven framework called FaTEMa (Fault Tolerance Event Manager), creating a dedicated fault-related communication channel to propagate events among system levels. The implemented framework acted to assist error detection and continued service. Also, it offers extension points to support heterogeneous communication protocols and evolves to new capabilities. Our empirical results show that the FaTEMa introduction has improved error detection and error resolution time, consequently improving system availability. In addition, the use of FaTEMa demonstrates a reliability improvement and a reduction in the number of failures produced.

Keywords: Fault tolerance · Dependability · IoT · Multi-level

1 Introduction

Internet of Things has emerged as a framework of technologies and paradigms for the future of the internet [1]. The term Internet of Things (IoT) has attracted attention by projecting the vision of a global network of physical objects, enabling connectivity anytime, anyplace, for anything and anyone [10,11,16]. IoT made everyday life more pervasive, personal and intimate through technology [17]. However, this came with a price: failures on those systems can cause fatal accidents, undermining their trustworthiness in the public eye [19]. For this reason, the dependability of IoT systems has become crucial in many contexts, particularly in critical domains [4,20]. Although much progress has been made in the systems, hardware, approaches, and networks, several challenges still need to be appropriately addressed [18,23].

© Springer Nature Switzerland AG 2021
O. Gervasi et al. (Eds.): ICCSA 2021, LNCS 12957, pp. 421–436, 2021.
https://doi.org/10.1007/978-3-030-87013-3_32

Current implementations of FT mechanisms in IoT are static, tightly coupled, and inflexible. For example: (1) they are designed for a specific architecture and application [5,22]; (2) they do not scale beyond small (decentralized) solutions [12]; and (3) they provide solutions to specific faults, such as link failures [8], device failures [9]. These concerns are problematic because IoT systems are expected to continuously evolve to support new services, capabilities, and devices and add at runtime. Thus, FT mechanisms should evolve along with the system needs. Also, IoT FT mechanisms are concerned with handling faults at a single level point of view or do not raise concerns about heterogeneity and collaboration [2,3,5]. However, it is hard to adopt a unified, effective fault tolerance mechanism in complex and heterogeneous systems such as IoT systems.

The objective of the present study is to propose a novel mechanism that supports multi-level fault tolerance. This approach allows information exchange between different fault tolerance strategies, especially for error detection, error recovery, and continued service. The term "multi-level fault tolerance" indicates that two or more system abstraction levels pass information or are adapted to each other (at design time or runtime) to reduce error occurrence and error propagation through system levels. Thus, the goal is to minimize the effort in terms of hardware, software, and network resources through this information exchange and adaption compared to the case where the levels are optimized without being aware of fault tolerance events or applied means at the others levels.

We implemented our approach in the framework called FaTEMa (Fault Tolerance Event Manager). This framework uses an event-driven architecture providing extension points that enable ways to meet each level's inherent needs and enable heterogeneous intercommunication. In addition, it acts as a dedicated channel for the transversal communication of information regarding failures and their implications. Using an event-based architecture limits the system intrusion to send and receive information through events. Therefore, it does not act directly in the tolerance of the failures in the levels. To evaluate the FaTEMa feasibility, especially efficiency and effectiveness, we design an experiment to empirically compare a system implementation with a well-known fault tolerance technique using the multi-level fault tolerance approach and not using it.

Our experiment simulates a smart home system injecting two faults to measure and analyze each scenario regarding error detection and resolution, availability, failure occurrence, and error detection effectiveness. Our results indicate that using the multi-level fault tolerance approach has better efficiency and reached a greater degree of effectiveness. Consequently, there was an improvement in the system availability, which can improve the overall system dependability.

The contributions of this paper are summarized as follows:

- We introduce a novel mechanism that supports multi-level fault tolerance that supports information exchange between different fault tolerance strategies, especially for error detection, error recovery, and continued service.
- We implemented a novel framework called FaTEMa. This framework uses an event-driven architecture providing extension points to provide ways to meet

the inherent needs of each level and enable heterogeneous intercommunication.

– We report on an empirical study comparing a smart home system under two scenarios using and not using a multi-level fault tolerance approach.

The remainder of the article is organized as follows: in Sect. 2, we revise related works pointing its weakness and strengths. In Sect. 3, we present the novel multi-level fault tolerance approach and the FaTEMa framework in detail. Section 4, presents the results and discussion of the empirical evaluation of the proposed approach by comparing two smart home system scenarios, using the FaTEMa framework and not using it. Finally, we discuss the paper findings presenting future research gaps and concluding the paper in Sect. 5.

2 Related Work

IoT systems are used in a wide variety of domains. In some of these domains, the occurrence of failures is acceptable or causes only discomfort. In others, on the contrary, the damage can be disastrous. Thus, several works have contributed to the area, including those reported below directly related to this work.

In Su et al. [21], a fault tolerance mechanism for IoT middleware is developed. Their work aims to provide a way to overcome component failures by reaching the tolerance levels defined by the developers. The proposed mechanism can detect, recover from failures, and reconfigure the system autonomously. The mechanism uses each node to replicate several components to guarantee these characteristics and uses a monitoring chain through heartbeat messages from each node. Thus, when a failure occurs, the node that perceives the failure informs the others so that everyone keeps their replicas consistent and ends by reconfiguring the nodes and removing dead nodes from monitoring.

Woo et al. [22] proposes a layered IoT system for personal health devices based on the oneM2M communication protocol. To guarantee the reliability of the proposed solution, the authors define an algorithm for fault tolerance. This algorithm acts on the gateways present in each layer of the system. The same layer's gateways form a chain, and each of them has a backup copy of the previous gateway in the chain, forming a fault tolerance strategy in each layer. Furthermore, the upper layer gateways are connected to the lower layer, thus managing the lower layer gateways.

The proposal by Li et al. [14] aims to solve the problem of complexity in the management of end-to-end communication failures in IoT. To this end, the authors propose a flexible, feasible, and layered approach to perform fault detection, localization, and correction efficiently. Fault management is divided into two layers. The upper layer is responsible for adaptively detecting and locating faults using observers at different transmission networks. These observers collect information about traffic and abnormal events, so prediction models are introduced (cognitive map fuzzy and semi-Markov). The lower layer executes the failure recovery strategy. This strategy varies according to each type of network used in the system.

In the work of Celesti et al. [2], a watchdog service for IoT monitoring is proposed, which allows checking the status of microservice applications, detecting faults, and repairing them. This service operates on each IoT device, synchronizing with each other using rsync and Network Time Protocol (NTP). Henceforth, microservices have replicas spread over network nodes when a watchdog detects a failure, the instance that is failing is removed, and a new replica is started on another device. Data from each device and microservice are stored on a shared database in the cloud. This database is available for all resources.

Javed et al. [7] propose an architecture for the edge and cloud designed to tolerate failures, called CEFIoT. This architecture's main objective is to enable fault tolerance at the edge nodes, especially when processing operations are moved from the cloud to the edge. Thus, there must be local strategies to preserve the system's state, especially in scenarios of node failure or connectivity problems. The proposed architecture is divided into three layers. The first layer is application isolation, where individual containerized processes in a single application from source to destination. The data is transported through a publish/subscribe framework in the second layer, whose data is replicated through the architecture nodes. At last, the cluster management layer responsible for monitoring and managing the operations of the previous two layers. Thus, to guarantee fault tolerance, data replication is used to process this information in several edge devices, reconfiguring whenever a failure occurs.

3   Multi-level Fault Tolerance Approach

The multi-level fault tolerance approach provides a communication channel that allows the exchange of events related to dependability and fault tolerance aspects. This dedicated channel should not interfere with the functioning of the system, assisting and allowing the collaboration of the different fault tolerance strategies to obtain an increase in the dependability of the systems. To provide this intercommunication channel, we develop a framework called FaTEMa (Fault Tolerance Event Manager) that consists of a set of extensible components to handle external fault tolerance events and propagate them among levels of an IoT system. It acts as a mediator, enabling communication between IoT system levels to assist fault tolerance mechanisms, aiming for failure avoidance. Thus, it facilitates information exchange between local or distributed techniques providing interoperability between them to improve systems' dependability.

By general means, fault tolerance can be implemented to prevent faults from leading to system failures. Fault tolerance has four constituent phases: error detection, damage confinement and assessment, error recovery, fault treatment, and continued system service [13]. The FaTEMa focused on assisting error detection and fault treatment techniques and continued system service, especially resuming a system to normal service. The success of any fault tolerance technique depends on the effectiveness with which it can detect errors. Thus, the initial stage of any technique is the error detection step. Therefore, the more errors are detected, the better system dependability will be. Once the errors are detected, the appropriate techniques can be applied to prevent the system from failing. For this reason, the use of FaTEMa allows the propagation of information regarding error detection allowing different levels and techniques to act in order to recover from those errors, which could eventually avoid a system failure.

Once an error is detected and recovered, it is necessary to return a system to its normal operation. Consequently, components could be resumed or restart, others can be reconfigured, and some can be terminated. Thus, FaTEMa acts to assist continued service techniques to communicate to other entities and levels measures to the resumption of an IoT system's normal operation.

However, FaTEMa, by itself, does not contain any fault tolerance mechanism. The FaTEMa framework's vision is to enable intercommunication between the various levels of abstraction, enabling efficient and effective error detection and continued service, improving an IoT system's dependability. Also, the proposed framework aims to be a technology, hardware, or operating system agnostic, facilitating the development of new solutions for fault tolerance.

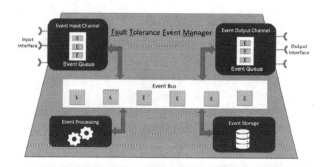

Fig. 1. Fault Tolerance Event Manager (FaTEMa) architecture

3.1   Architecture

Figure 1 depicts FaTEMa framework architecture. This framework has five components: Event Input Channel, Event Processing, Event Storage, Event Output Channel, and Event Bus. Each component acts independently, separating responsibilities. The communication between components occurs through the use of asynchronous messages posted and received at the EventBus. This interaction between the components and the EventBus occurs using the Publish-Subscribe messaging pattern. Thus, the components subscribe on the bus to certain types of events. Once these events are detected, the component is notified and receives the specific event. Also, each component can send events to the EventBus. However, there are two special cases: EventInput Channel and EventOutput Channel. The first one can only post external events received at the entrance of the framework in the bus. The second is only allowed to receive events posted on the bus and make them available externally. These events are triggered and consumed by the local fault tolerance strategies.

Additionally, each component has an interface that makes it possible to implement new behaviors. The framework uses the Observer pattern allowing the extensions to indicate in what are the events of interest. Once the component receives an event, it verifies if there is a valid observer extension point. If it is true, the event is passed to the extension point.

Event Input Channel: Acts as an event broker, providing an external communication interface to receive events. In order to support heterogeneous communication, the component provides an extensible interface allowing the implementation of different communication protocols. However, due to the heterogeneity of technologies in IoT, this component defines a standard event ensuring interoperability between protocols.

Event Processing: This component acts by providing event processing capabilities. It supports extensions that register interest in specific events to perform its computation. These processing rules must avoid using specific systems processing rules since the FaTEMa is a distributed component by nature. Thus, rules regarding system-specific fault tolerance (error detection and recovery) should not be placed at FaTEMa components. Some examples of processing are device registration, system metrics, system state, FaTEMa fault tolerance, among others.

Event Storage: It is responsible for store e recover data from and for the event processing. The data can be stored locally or distributed. The size should be set according to the domain or system need. However, it is not a mandatory component once certain devices could have processing and storage limitations.

Event Output Channel: It is responsible for providing events to the external environment. Like the Event Input Channel component, this component provides an extensible interface to support different communication protocols. The data sent follows the event structured, and the receiver must treat them according. Thus, support heterogeneous technologies and provides interoperability between them, creating a multi-level communication channel for fault tolerance.

3.2   FaTEMa Operation

The proposed framework creates a "virtual" communication channel between the different levels of abstraction, as depicted in Fig. 2. This channel acts by facilitating information exchange through local fault tolerance mechanisms (Local FT) present in system levels. Each level is subjected to specific types of uncertainty and different types of faults that have to be detected and recovered, ideally in a coordinated manner. Local fault tolerance mechanisms are responsible for handle faults in a specific level or scenario without shares a global system vision. Additionally, as IoT systems grow in size, complexity, speed, and heterogeneity level, it becomes impractical to assume that a single fault tolerance mechanism can access the entire system's information. Therefore, the FaTEMa integrates system levels enabling information exchange between fault tolerance approaches.

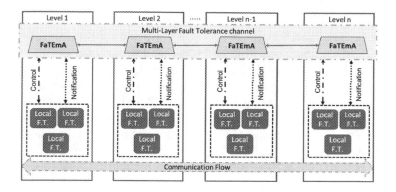

Fig. 2. Generic IoT system using the FaTEMa and multi-level fault tolerance channel

The framework acts to reduce the complexity in the implementation of multi-level fault tolerance techniques. Although the complexity introduced by these techniques could decrease system dependability, the FaTEMa is designed does not reduce, rather than increase, the dependability. The framework does not directly interfere in the functioning of fault tolerance techniques. It enables distributed intercommunication between fault tolerance techniques through its communication channel. On this channel, there are two types of generic events: Control and Notification. Control Event messages are related to fault-tolerance measures and treatments. Notification Event messages carry information about the system's current state, system administrative information, or metrics regarding system utilization information.

The flow of communication occurs in both directions. Higher-level fault tolerance techniques can communicate with lower levels and vice versa. Also, FT techniques can use the framework to collaborate in the measures against errors at the same level. However, to enable this intercommunication, there must be at least one FaTEMa instance at each level. FaTEMa allows instance replication in order to assure availability and avoid single failure points. Each instance acts isolated. However, it is possible to configure a distributed database to replicate the stored information between instances. These functionalities are available by default. Furthermore, all internal or external communication carried out by FaTEMa is done asynchronously. Thus, to send or receive FaTEMa events, each local FT must register in the framework's input and output channels.

4   Experiment Evaluation

Aiming to evaluate the framework's efficiency and effectiveness to assist error detection and continued service, we implemented a smart home system prototype. This system was designed to involve monitoring various devices in a home, such as security cameras, temperature, pressure, humidity sensors, various equipment (such as TVs, microwaves, refrigerators).

The system architecture consists of four levels of abstraction. The perception level is directly related to the device monitoring and actuation in the smart home. This level contains a set of appliances connected to the monitored devices making it possible to manage them. All information generated or obtained by the house devices flows through a gateway that concentrates the information of a certain set of houses, connecting them to the upper levels. The service level provides a cloud middleware that enables the treatment, processing, and storage of a high volume of information. Finally, a mobile app that interacts with the devices managing them is available at the application level.

The smart home contains several devices (D) sensing and acting over the environment in order to facilitate a user life experience. These devices are linked to an appliance (AP) responsible for monitoring and connection distribution. The appliances are responsible for having a physical connection with devices providing efficient communication with the rest of the system. The access to devices and appliances must happen through a gateway (GW) responsible for centralizing the information of several instances of houses and transferring them to the upper levels. In addition, it receives requests directed to devices and identifies which paths the requests will follow. The Cloud middleware (CM) has a high computational power to process and store all the information transferred. Furthermore, it implements fault tolerance mechanisms in order to prevent system failures. The mobile application (MA) interacts with the CM, sending and receiving information to the devices.

In this execution, an omission fault was injected into a device (temperature sensor), which results in an error when activated. This experiment evaluates the efficiency of detecting error occurrences and their efficiency in decreasing failure occurrences using the proposed approach. Also, it is essential to assess the impact that the use of the framework will have on the system's general use. To attain these objectives, we define two questions to answer.

RQ1 – An IoT system using the multi-level fault tolerance approach is more efficient in detecting an error and resume the system to its normal operation than a system using fault tolerance techniques at each level?

RQ2 – An IoT system using the multi-level fault tolerance approach is more effective than a system using fault tolerance techniques at each level?

Efficiency in this context is measured by error detection time and error resolution time. The smaller the time to detect and resolve errors are, the more efficient it is considered. Effectiveness is measured by the rate of failures (Failure per second), Handled Error Rate (Total of Errors per Total of Failures), and Detected Error Rate (Total of Detected Errors per Total Errors). The effectiveness successfully achieves the desired results, reduces the number of failures, and leads to improved dependability attributes.

4.1   Experiment Design

In order to carry out this evaluation, we compared the use of the system from two scenarios, Scenario #1 (S#1) - using FaTEMa and the multi-level fault tolerance

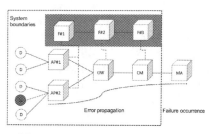
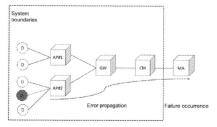

(a) Scenario #1 – Using FaTEMa   (b) Scenario #2 – Not using FaTEMa

Fig. 3. Experiment scenarios

channel and Scenario #2 (S#2) - not using FaTEMa. Both scenarios use the exact implementation and fault tolerance strategies. The fault tolerance (FT) mechanism is activated when they obtain the information in response to a request to an unavailable device (Df). The implemented FT mechanism was the Bounded Retries [6]. This mechanism deals with transient errors by restricting the number of retries to a faulty entity. It typically takes an exponential backoff function to control the retrying process to avoid massives requests to fail. Then, the CM starts an asynchronous check using a retry strategy with exponential backoff, checking if the unavailable device is active again. While the device is unavailable, incoming requests to the faulty device are intercepted and returned, informing its unavailability in order to avoid failure occurrence. When the asynchronous check detects the faulty device has resumed its continuous operation, the retry process is interrupted, and CM stops intercepting requests to the unavailable device (Fig. 3).

In both scenarios, the APs are responsible for identifying that the device has failed. Therefore, they perform device monitoring in order to identify possible faults. If a fault is identified in a given device, the subsequent request is returned to the sender with the device's unavailability information. Once the APs identify that the device has returned to continued service, the following response is carried out normally. In scenario S#1, in addition to the described fault notification, when an AP identifies that a device is not working correctly, a control event is sent to FaTEMa. Likewise, if a device that was not in regular operation resumes service continuation, a control event is sent to FaTEMA.

4.2 Experiment Execution

In order to answer the research questions, this experiment injects two omission faults in the system at specifics intervals. The faults occur in a device (temperature sensor) connected to AP#2, occurring according to the following pair (start, duration): Fault Activation 1 (15,15) and Fault Activation 2 (40,30). The start time means the instant of fault activation, initiating the omission errors. The duration is the amount of time the error occurrence lasts (both expressed in seconds). The values of request timeout and the maximum throughput were

200 ms and 20 req/s, respectively. At the beginning of the test, a setup phase was executed to minimize the resource initialization effects. This procedure took approximately 5 s, and only after this, the simulated mobile application started to send requests for 70 s. Each scenario was executed 12 times, and in each one, all requests are randomly generated. Thus, measures obtained and analyzed are the average of these executions.

4.3   Efficiency Results

The detection of an error occurs when the manifestation of a fault is detected [13]. In this study, an erroneous state is considered detected when is detected by the CM. The same principle is applied to error resolution that a system will be considered error-free when the CM enables the system to continue providing its services. Table 1 presents measurements obtained regarding error detection and error resolution time. The average error detection time in scenario 1 resulted in over 30% higher than scenario 2. It is possible to notice a significant difference in the detection time, greater than 25%, for the two fault injections.

Table 1. Error detection time and error resolution time measurements

		Metrics	
		Error detection (ms)	Error resolution (ms)
S#1	Fault injection 1	667.42	637.83
	Fault injection 2	648.08	601.25
	Average	657.75	619.54
S#2	Fault injection 1	727.50	3573.63
	Fault injection 2	691.58	8804.72
	Average	709.54	6189.18

Similarly, the average error resolution time in scenario 1 obtained a result 90% lower than scenario 2. In this case, the system returns to its regular operation 90% faster in scenario 1 when compared to scenario 2. These results indicate a better efficiency in detect errors and resuming the system's continuous operation in scenario 1. This assertion is mainly supported since the communication channel used by the FaTEMas for propagating information does not require active CM interaction. Once the recovery event is launched on the Multi-Level Fault Tolerance Channel, all interested parties, regardless of level, will receive the information passively. Thus, in scenario 1, the faulty level actively propagates F.T. information, contrary to scenario 2, where the C.M. actively requests the appliances for error detection and error resolution.

The availability of a system can be defined as the fraction of time this system is in a functioning condition [15]. In this study, we measure the Df availability adopted the ratio TA/TE, where TA means the amount of time the device is available and operating according to its specifications, and TE the duration of the experiment. Independent of the scenarios, the Df availability was fixed based on the experiment configuration (TA = 70 − 10 − 20, TE = 70, and consequently, availability = 57.14%). However, CM availability is influenced by the F.T. mechanism applied. Thus, it is necessary to consider error detection time and error resolution time to calculate system availability. Thus, we adopted the ratio TAs = (TA − TD − TR)/Te, where TAs is the system availability, TD is the sum of the errors detection time, Tr = sum of the errors resolution time. Table 2 shows the system availability in each scenario. In S#1, the system availability is 86,12% higher than in S#2. Hence, it indicates that the use of FaTEMa provided a superior effective system availability, demonstrating that S#1 performs more efficiently compared to S#2. The error detection time and error resolution time metrics also support this assertion.

Table 2. Measurements related to device and system availability for each scenario

Scenario	Metrics					
	TE (s)	TA (s)	DA	TD (s)	TR (s)	TSa
S#1	70	40	57.14%	1.31	1.23	53.51%
S#2				1.41	12.37	37.46%

4.4   Effectiveness Results

To assess the effectiveness of using FaTEMa mechanisms combined with the fault tolerance strategies, we collect measurements regarding the requests received at the C.M. and classifies them according to the produced response. In other words, the effectiveness of using FaTEMa as a dedicated channel for fault tolerance information was assessed under the C.M. perspective. Thus, if a request sent to the C.M. does not produce one of the expected responses, a failure occurs. The C.M. is the component responsible for protecting the system from failing, implementing fault tolerance strategies. Moreover, produce responses that indicate that the system cannot respond to the request at the moment, informing that the selected resource is unavailable or successfully provides the selected resource.

Table 3 presents the collected measurement for the C.M. responses from the mobile application requests. The average of total requests sent to C.M. resulting in a difference of about 1.20%. This difference was expected given the experiment's random nature, and it is unlikely that the same amount of requests were produced and responded. However, this metric points out that despite FaTEMa introduction at each system level in S#1, that there was a low impact on the overall system functioning. Nevertheless, S#1 successful responses were 77.41% higher than S#2. Also, it produces about 31% fewer failure responses. As for the total of handled requests, S#2 produces more than 36% responses compared to S#1. This difference is explained due to the higher error resolution time measured in S#2 compared to S#1.

Figure 4 represents the average of requests responded by the C.M. over experiment time. There is a considerable difference in the error detection time and the number of failures produced until the system responds adequately to that failure when the scenarios are compared, shown in Fig. 4b. Also, the two fault injections produce similar results, the number of failures produced and error detection time for both scenarios. Thus, this result indicates that the adoption of FaTEMa provided a more efficient response to the injection of a fault, reducing the error detection, leading to a reduction in the number of failures produced by the system. Similar behavior is identified in the handled requests as shown in Fig. 4c, in which S#1 identifies error recovery occurrence has been corrected firstly compared to S#2. This difference between scenarios was produced because instead of waiting for the tolerance strategy identifies that the requested resource is available again, the use of FaTEMa in S#1 allowed a proactive sharing of fault tolerance and recovery events, allowing without a need for new requests to handle failures or continued service. This situation directly impacts the successful responses (Fig. 4a) because while the CM does not deactivate the FT mechanisms, the responses produced will continue to indicate that there is still an error in progress.

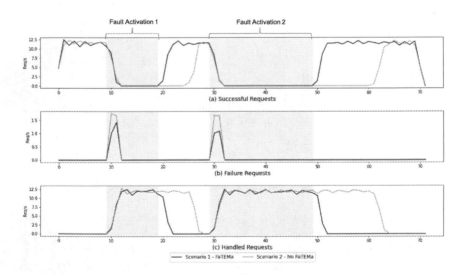

Fig. 4. C.M. responses over time

The impact of FaTEMa usage requires the use of metrics related to dependability property. We establish the measures of Failure Rate defined by the total of failures over second, Handled Error Rate is defined as the total of failures over a total of errors, and Detection Error Rate which is adopted as the total of detected errors over a total of errors, which are typical metrics to assess reliability and fault tolerance effectiveness. Regarding the Failure Rate metric, S#1 demonstrates an inferior occurrence of failures per unit of time than S#2, having a rate of 31,52% fewer failures than S#2. In other words, 93,88% of error requests produces failures. Consequently, the use of FaTEMa demonstrates a positive effect on the system reliability, and consequently, its dependability. The Handled Error Rate and Detection Error Rate metrics are complementary and demonstrate how effective a fault tolerance strategy concerns the total of failures and detected errors. The use of FaTEMa (S#1) provided a decrease of about 14% in the number of failures produced and increased the Detection Error Rate by more than 20% compared to S#2.

Table 3. Measurements related to the responses sent by the C.M. to the mobile application during the experiment for all scenarios.

Metric	Scenarios	
	S#1	S#2
Total	895.83	906.75
Successful	497.33	280.33
Handled	393.25	618.75
Error	6.58	8.17
Failures	5.25	7.67
Detected error	1.33	0.50
Failure rate	0.08	0.11
Handled error rate	79.75%	93.88%
Detected error rate	25.40%	6.52%

4.5   Discussion

The FaTEMa introduction allowed the information propagation related to fault through the levels of the system detailed in the experiment. In addition, the usage of FaTEMa demonstrates to assist in identifying the occurrence of an error and returning the system to the continued service. A highlighted aspect perceived by the results is that the introduction of FaTEMa made it possible to use proactive communication in error detection and resolution stages without adding additional complexity to the system. Thus, the reactive communication model for detecting and resolving errors remained active but could be combined with that one. Therefore, the evidence collected and presented in Tables 2 and 3 reveals that with the multi-level fault tolerance strategy, it was possible to reduce the time to detect the fault activation by 7.8% and reduce the time taken to propagate an error resolved 93.28%. Consequently, the use of FaTEMa improved system availability by about 86%. In just 3.63% of the time that the error was happening, the system was responding erroneously. This time represents about 2.5 s of the total experiment to propagate FT information regarding error detection and error resolution. Thus, the FaTEMa introduction contributed to the error detection and resolution to operate quickly and efficiently in an organized way, increasing system dependability.

Related to the effectiveness of using a multi-level fault-tolerance approach is possible to verify a reduction of more than 31% in the number of failures in S#1 when compared to the use of the fault tolerance strategy with only local treatment (S#2). In addition, we found that the average error detection rate was 2.5× higher in S#1, which demonstrates the importance of error detection occurring as promptly as possible. Because lower detection time tends to be, it could reduce the number of errors and failures. This fact is directly linked to the rate of failures, which is a well-established metric used to assess the reliability of a system. Thus, S#1 reduced the failure rate by about 27%, leading to an improvement in reliability and dependability. In addition, S#1 revealed that the use of FaTEMa in S#1 improved the rate of errors handled, meaning that they did not become failures at a rate greater than 14% compared to S#2. In the same way, in S#1, there was a substantial increase, more than 4x, the rate of errors detected concerning the total errors produced by the system. Therefore, the use of FaTEMa is considered more effective because they successfully achieved an increase in system reliability, reducing the failure rate and increasing error detection.

Although the use of the communication channel for multi-level fault tolerance introduces an increase in CPU processing and network bandwidth, no negative impact was perceived on the system's overall functioning. On the contrary, the average difference in the total number of requests answered between scenarios is 1.2%. This difference can be explained due to the difference of more than 2x responding successful requests by S#1. Successful requests require more time between source-destination-source as they need to go through the entire system. Also, the results presented in this experiment demonstrate the efficiency and effectiveness of using a dedicated channel for transmitting events related to fault tolerance, only two scenarios were considered. However, it was evidenced that the exchange of collaborative messages about tolerance between the levels of the IoT system can help and improve dependability attributes. By creating a channel that permeates all levels, solutions can collaborate, promoting end-to-end fault tolerance within an IoT system.

5   Conclusion and Future Work

This paper proposes a framework to enable the propagation of fault tolerance events between system levels. It acts as a mediator, enabling communication to collaborate between levels and its local fault tolerance aiming to improve the steps of error detection and continued service. Thus, the FaTEMa focused on assisting error detection and fault treatment and continued service, especially to resuming a system to normal service. Because the success of any fault tolerance technique depends on its effectiveness, it can detect errors. This multi-layer approach provides an end-to-end communication channel that facilitates FT event exchange to minimize fault occurrence and propagation effects. Also, the framework facilitates system levels interoperability by providing extensible interfaces for heterogeneous communication protocols.

The empirical evaluation was accomplished by conducting an experiment to compare two scenarios: a system using FaTEMa and the multi-level fault tolerance approach; and a system not using FaTEMa. The implemented system used in the experiment uses a well-known fault tolerance approach and uses the exact implementation in both scenarios. Overall, the results show that the scenario using the multi-level fault tolerance had a better efficiency in error detection and error resolution. Also, it was observed that in the scenario using FaTEMa, the system had a greater availability when compared to the other scenario leading to an increase in dependability attributes. This behavior was expected because once an error is detected as soon as possible, it will be conceivable to activate measures to tolerate and recover faults. Equally important is the time to resume system operation once a fault is recovered. The use of FaTEMa demonstrated a high capacity to propagate the recovery event between levels, enabling a more efficient resumption of the system's normal functioning, leading to improved availability.

As future work, we plan to extend the empirical evaluation to a real-world scenario. Furthermore, the present study investigated the applicability e effectivity of fault tolerance multi-level in one IoT System. However, IoT is an ecosystem, and thus, we plan to extend the study to investigate the feasibility of applying a multi-systems fault tolerance approach. Also, we plan to expand FaTEMa event processing to handle complex events and contextual information.

References

1. Atzori, L., Iera, A., Morabito, G.: The internet of things: a survey. Comput. Netw. **54**(15), 2787–2805 (2010)
2. Celesti, A., Carnevale, L., Galletta, A., Fazio, M., Villari, M.: A watchdog service making container-based micro-services reliable in IoT clouds. In: 2017 IEEE 5th International Conference on Future Internet of Things and Cloud (FiCloud), pp. 372–378. IEEE (2017)
3. Choi, J., Jeoung, H., Kim, J., Ko, Y., Jung, W., Kim, H., Kim, J.: Detecting and identifying faulty IoT devices in smart home with context extraction. In: 2018 48th Annual IEEE/IFIP International Conference on Dependable Systems and Networks (DSN), pp. 610–621. IEEE (2018)
4. Ciccozzi, F., Crnkovic, I., Di Ruscio, D., Malavolta, I., Pelliccione, P., Spalazzese, R.: Model-driven engineering for mission-critical IoT systems. IEEE Softw. **34**(1), 46–53 (2017)
5. Gia, T.N., Rahmani, A.M., Westerlund, T., Liljeberg, P., Tenhunen, H.: Fault tolerant and scalable IoT-based architecture for health monitoring. In: 2015 IEEE Sensors Applications Symposium (SAS), pp. 1–6. IEEE (2015)
6. Homer, A., Sharp, J., Brader, L., Narumoto, M., Swanson, T.: Cloud Design Patterns: Prescriptive Architecture Guidance for Cloud Applications. Microsoft Patterns & Practices, CreateSpace, Scotts Valley (2014)

7. Javed, A., Heljanko, K., Buda, A., Främling, K.: CEFIoT: a fault-tolerant IoT architecture for edge and cloud. In: 2018 IEEE 4th World Forum on Internet of Things (WF-IoT), pp. 813–818. IEEE (2018)
8. Karthikeya, S.A., Vijeth, J., Murthy, C.S.R.: Leveraging solution-specific gateways for cost-effective and fault-tolerant IoT networking. In: 2016 IEEE Wireless Communications and Networking Conference, pp. 1–6. IEEE (2016)
9. Khan, F.I., Hameed, S.: Understanding security requirements and challenges in Internet of Things (IoTs): a review. arXiv preprint arXiv:1808.10529 (2018)
10. Kosmatos, E.A., Tselikas, N.D., Boucouvalas, A.C.: Integrating RFIDs and smart objects into a unified internet of things architecture. Adv. Internet Things $1(01)$, 5 (2011)
11. Kubler, S., Främling, K., Buda, A.: A standardized approach to deal with firewall and mobility policies in the IoT. Pervasive Mob. Comput. **20**, 100–114 (2015)
12. La Marra, A., Martinelli, F., Mori, P., Saracino, A.: Implementing usage control in internet of things: a smart home use case. In: 2017 IEEE Trustcom/BigDataSE/ICESS, pp. 1056–1063. IEEE (2017)
13. Lee, P.A., Anderson, T.: Fault tolerance. In: Fault Tolerance. Dependable Computing and Fault-Tolerant Systems, vol. 3, pp. 51–77. Springer, Vienna (1990). https://doi.org/10.1007/978-3-7091-8990-0_3
14. Li, X., Ji, H., Li, Y.: Layered fault management scheme for end-to-end transmission in internet of things. Mob. Netw. Appl. **18**(2), 195–205 (2013)
15. Lyu, M.R.: Software reliability engineering: a roadmap. In: Future of Software Engineering (FOSE 2007), pp. 153–170. IEEE (2007)
16. Madakam, S., Ramaswamy, R., Tripathi, S.: Internet of things (IoT): a literature review. J. Comput. Commun. **3**(05), 10 (2015)
17. Miraz, M.H., Ali, M., Excell, P.S., Picking, R.: A review on Internet of Things (IoT), Internet of Everything (IoE) and Internet of Nano Things (IoNT). In: 2015 Internet Technologies and Applications (ITA), pp. 219–224 (2015). https://doi.org/10.1109/ITechA.2015.7317398
18. Ojie, E., Pereira, E.: Exploring dependability issues in IoT applications. In: Proceedings of the Second International Conference on Internet of things, Data and Cloud Computing, p. 123. ACM (2017)
19. Ratasich, D., Khalid, F., Geißler, F., Grosu, R., Shafique, M., Bartocci, E.: A roadmap toward the resilient internet of things for cyber-physical systems. IEEE Access **7**, 13260–13283 (2019). https://doi.org/10.1109/ACCESS.2019.2891969
20. Ştefan, V.K., Otto, P., Alexandrina, P.M.: Considerations regarding the dependability of internet of things. In: 2017 14th International Conference on Engineering of Modern Electric Systems (EMES), pp. 145–148. IEEE (2017)
21. Su, P.H., Shih, C.S., Hsu, J.Y.J., Lin, K.J., Wang, Y.C.: Decentralized fault tolerance mechanism for intelligent IoT/M2M middleware. In: 2014 IEEE World Forum on Internet of Things (WF-IoT), pp. 45–50. IEEE (2014)
22. Woo, M.W., Lee, J., Park, K.: A reliable IoT system for personal healthcare devices. Futur. Gener. Comput. Syst. **78**, 626–640 (2018)
23. Xing, L., Zhao, G., Wang, Y., Mandava, L.: Competing failure analysis in IoT systems with cascading functional dependence. In: 2018 Annual Reliability and Maintainability Symposium (RAMS), pp. 1–6. IEEE (2018)

The Pathology of Failures in IoT Systems

Mário Melo[1](✉) and Gibeon Aquino[2]

[1] Federal Institute of Rio Grande do Norte, Natal, Brazil
mario.melo@ifrn.edu.br
[2] Federal University of Rio Grande do Norte, Natal, Brazil
gibeon@dimap.ufrn.br

Abstract. The presence of faults is inevitable in the Internet of Things (IoT) systems. Dependability in these systems is challenging due to the increasing level of dynamicity, heterogeneity, and complexity. IoT connects anything, anytime, and everywhere, introducing a complex relationship of interdependence, generating an increase in the susceptibility of the propagation of failures. The purpose of this study is to propose a pathology of failure in IoT Systems, exploring and characterizing faults, errors, failures, and their effects. This study investigates and classifies the source of faults, defines a taxonomy of the types of faults prone to happen, and defines the failure propagation model. As a result, the pathology establishes a common reference for fault, errors, and failures to be used by researchers and practitioners to improve tools for fault detection, fault diagnosis, fault tolerance, and fault handling in IoT Systems. This paper also proposes a failure propagation model for IoT systems that identify different combinations, paths, and fault-failure propagation effects.

Keywords: IoT · Dependability · Pathology · Taxonomy · Fault type · Fault source · Failure propagation

1 Introduction

Internet of Things (IoT) has attracted attention by projecting the vision of a global network of physical objects, enabling connectivity anytime, anyplace, for anything and anyone [18]. Nevertheless, this technological evolution came with a price: failures can cause fatal accidents, undermining their trustworthiness in the public eye [30]. For this reason, the dependability of IoT applications and infrastructures has become crucial in many contexts, particularly in critical domains [7,32]. Therefore, among the comprehensive variety of challenges when designing and deploying IoT systems, like their complexity, heterogeneity of the elements involved, and interoperability between different application domains, dependability is an open issue [9,26,38].

Fault management plays an essential role in maintaining system regular operation and decreasing faults, errors, and failures, leading to increased dependability property [14]. IoT systems often have particular requirements regarding fault

© Springer Nature Switzerland AG 2021
O. Gervasi et al. (Eds.): ICCSA 2021, LNCS 12957, pp. 437–452, 2021.
https://doi.org/10.1007/978-3-030-87013-3_33

managing schemes, including specific fault characteristics due to their heterogeneity and complexity [11, 19]. Although significant attention has been given to dependability aspects in IoT systems, no comprehensive, consistent, generally adopted fault characterization explains its cause and effects [23, 29, 30, 40].

The objective of the present study is to propose a pathology of failures in IoT systems providing standard definitions and characterizations to assist researchers and practitioners in developing appropriate fault management solutions. To this aim, we focused on identifying the cause of faults, what are fault and error manifestation types, and a failure propagation behavior. Thus, the causal relationship between faults, errors, and failures is extended to identify which source of faults, the types of errors that can be activated, and how failure propagation occurs in IoT systems.

The term "pathology of failures" involves the creation and manifestation mechanisms of faults, errors, and failures displaying the causal relationship between them [4]. This concept can be generically interpreted: An active fault causes an error, and by propagation, many errors can be activated before a failure occurs. However, in medical science, pathology is a field of study primarily concerning the cause, origin, and nature of diseases. Similarly, a dependence among two systems could result in a pathological process that can develop along "linkage or connection" among them characterized by the activation of faults, the propagation of errors, and the occurrence of failures [4]. Thus, this research aims to establish the characterization, origin, and behavior of faults, errors, and failures that compose the pathology of failures in IoT systems.

The main contribution of this paper is to propose a pathology of failures for IoT systems establishing the context for the steps of the causal relationship. This contribution is composed of the pathological steps, which characterize the fundamental of the chain of dependability threats. The fault origin step identifies the sources of faults in order to provide a general view of fault distribution in IoT systems. Therefore, the fault origin distribution classification is established considering components and levels of abstraction present in IoT systems. The examination of the type of faults step identifies the causes of error occurrence, types of fault activation. Aiming to characterizes and classifies these types of faults and errors, we propose an IoT fault taxonomy to be used as a reference by researchers, developers, integrators, and developers for fault management solutions. The failure propagation behavior step establishes a failure propagation model considering the relation between levels of abstraction, systems, and the environment existing in IoT ecosystems.

As defined in this paper, the pathology of failures is useful for researchers, developers, and IoT practitioners, establishing the origin of threats to IoT systems, allowing the design of solutions that contemplate means to tolerate possible failures. In addition, it discusses a classification indicating the types of faults, establishing a common understanding, and describes its nature. Finally, this pathology supports researchers and practitioners in designing systems considering the interdependence between layers, systems, and the environment in which it is inserted.

The remainder of the article is organized as follows: The pathology of failure and the pathological step to define it are present in Sect. 2. In Sect. 3, the first step of the pathological process is presented, classifying the source of faults. Section 4 discusses and characterizes the types of faults defining a taxonomy. The failure propagation model is presented in Sect. 5. Finally, in Sect. 6, we conclude the paper and discuss future works.

2   The Pathology of Failures

In any given system, there is a causal relationship among faults, errors, and failures. This relationship is materialized when the fault-failure chain is activated, which includes the creation and activation mechanisms of faults, errors, and failures. A generic interpretation is that error only occurs when a fault is activated, and by propagation, can generate several errors before a failure occurs. Thus, this propagation, and chain instantiation, can occur via interaction between components, elements, and systems. These manifestations and relationships between dependability impairments are called the pathology of failures.

To define how pathology is instantiated in an IoT system, it is necessary to identify and classify a set of steps. Figure 1 shows the pathology steps in an IoT system. The Fault source identification step classifies where are the sources of threats. In order to achieve dependable systems, one effective way is to identify the source of faults and mitigate them timely, aiming to prevent failure propagation from causing significant in an IoT system and its dependents. The fault/Error taxonomy step defines a classification for the types of faults. Thus, identifying and establishing a comprehensive body of knowledge of faults and errors prone to happen in IoT systems will help researchers and practitioners propose suitable fault management strategies to mitigate these threats. A taxonomy of faults and errors describing characteristics, nature, and exemplification of faults and errors is proposed to this aim.

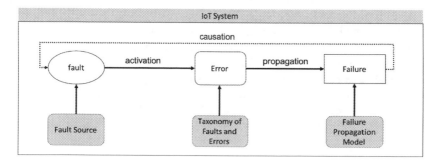

Fig. 1. Pathology of failures in IoT systems (adapted from [4])

IoT systems are composed of interrelated devices, which operate collaboratively and autonomously to deliver a service. If faults and errors were not handled properly due to the interactions and dependencies between different devices in function or structure, propagation and cascading failures require understanding and investigation.

This paper considers an IoT system as a system composed of levels and components that deliver services to other systems. According to a given structure, the components of an IoT system can be physical or logical, which, in sequence, are composed by other systems recursively. Examples of physical components are sensors, actuators, gateway, cloud servers, routers, among others. Logically, the components can be embedded software systems, control and management software, and applications for end-users. At every level, all of these components act to deliver service of the level. From a more general perspective, all IoT System levels cooperate to deliver services to other external systems. There are different architecture models of IoT systems. We consider a four-level architecture to facilitate discussions of dependability and faults in this paper. The four generic levels include the perception level (e.g., sensors, actuators, and sensor networks), the communication or transport level (e.g., wired and wireless networks), the service or support level (e.g., cloud computing, storage area networks), and the application level (e.g., smart home, smart healthcare).

3   Sources of Faults

The first measure, usually necessary for a system to tolerate faults, is to detect them briefly. However, designers and developers should consider the causes of failures to assemble efficient fault tolerance strategies. Fault source classification is defined according to the system boundaries being internal and external [4]. These faults are related to the origin of the fault in relation to the system boundaries. Internal faults occur within the system boundaries and external faults outside system boundaries. However, this classification is too broad and does not go into the specifics and restrictions present in IoT systems. Therefore, understand and characterize these faults from an IoT systems viewpoint is essential to build effective dependability measures.

Aiming to identify fault sources and causes in IoT systems, we conduct an extensive analysis of the literature and state-of-the-art dependability related to IoT systems. As a result, we identified a comprehensive set of sources and causes through this investigation, which was subsequently organized into an IoT system levels viewpoint such as Perception Level, Communication Level, Service Level, and Application Level.

3.1   Perception Level

At this level, the causes of faults are directly related to obtaining and extracting the data associated with physical devices. The devices are typically different sensor nodes deployed to perform different measurements (e.g., temperature, humidity, ECG, EMG) and actuation. These sensor nodes are heterogeneous with diverse sensing and actuation mechanisms, processing, and communication.

Thus, this classification organizes the level in four major components, usually available in IoT devices, such as Sensors/Actuators, Processing Units, Network interfaces, Embedded Software. However, we know that some devices may not have any components or have other types of components not contemplated in this classification.

Sensors/Actuators. Physical components such as sensors, actuators, mobile devices, and mechanical components can produce faults. Some examples of faults are physical stress on components, inadequate enclosures, harsh environment deployment, and low energy could cause physical devices to malfunction. Furthermore, devices placed in hostile environments are vulnerable to faults related to disruption, direct intervention, or destruction. These types of faults are usually permanent, requiring manual intervention and replacement. Another fault type faced by physical objects is eletromagnetical interference. As the number of connected devices increases, radiation increases. This situation may influence measurements, transmitted messages, or control signals [37,39].

Faults that cause miss calibration may occur to the drift throughout the network lifetimes, which decreases the accuracy of sensor measurements. In addition, the calibration errors can produce specific faults such as offset faults (sensor measurements offset from the initial value by a constant quantity), gain faults (the rate of change of the measured data does not match with expectations over time), and drift faults (performance may drift away from the original calibration measurements) [21].

Processing Unit. This source of faults encompasses sensor nodes processing related components, such as memory, battery, and microprocessor. Faults on processing components could affect the quality or consistency of the stored data or their operations. For instance, memory bit flips or specific registers can corrupt the stored data. Limited memory fault or memory errors (memory leak, memory violation) can cause a system to crash or operate in degraded mode [1]. For energy supply, high battery temperature causes battery degradation leading to power outage. Likewise, battery low voltage may lead to data faults [21].

Network Communication. The form of communication utilized to connect devices can be wireless or wired, and each one can suffer different types of faults. For example, wireless communications are normally prone to interference (e.g., ambient noise, channel noise, multipath fading, radio frequency interference). Wired communication is vulnerable to a broken connector, material decay, and environmental effects on physical components (e.g., dirtying) [27,30].

Embedded Software. At sensor nodes, the software acts to processing and routing collected measurements. Thus, data processing faults can occur if data acquisition is not performed appropriately if the underlying sensors provide incorrect readings [36]. For example, an error in data aggregation can lead to erroneous data to the upper levels. A typical data aggregation approach calculates the average correlated measured values of variables, sending only one message to the upper levels. If this level generates incorrect data, data aggregation results can lead to divergences from the real value. Software bugs are widespread, and some of them can generate cascading failures. Some generic examples are incorrect design specification, architectural faults, software design faults, incorrect algorithms [20].

3.2   Communication Level

The communication level is responsible for providing internetworking communication for the perception level. Specifically, the communication level transmits the sensed/aggregated data from the perception level to the upper levels through wired and wireless networks. The possibles causes of faults are a collision of messages, communication protocol violation, host environments, interference, dynamic changes in the network topology, and congestion. Therefore, we organize the faults in this level as Link and Connectivity.

Link. IoT communication links are established through wired and wireless communication mediums. Wired links have a constant rate of messages and tend to be more stable; however, there is exposition to disruption. On the other hand, wireless links are highly volatile and do not always yield the same message delivery rate [34]. Link instability can lead to faults in the routing paths [31]. Another fault related to both types of communication links is interference. If a communication link has heavy traffic, it could cause unavailability or message collision [34].

Moreover, devices can move to different locations where they become unreachable, resulting in complete data loss. For example, autonomous vehicles going to underground tunnels or places without cellular towers. Links also may fail when permanently or temporarily obstructed by an external object or environmental condition [27].

Connectivity. Connectivity faults could cause unacceptable delays and dropped or misguided messages [10]. Bugs at the connectivity routing network could cause incorrect destination message delivery, affecting several system paths and other collaborative systems. Routing is a fundamental feature for IoT systems [13, 22]. Similar to the interference fault, the number of communicating devices might trigger connectivity faults, e.g., collisions or an overload of the network resulting in message collision. Another connectivity fault is protocol violation due to wrong message content due to different protocol versions or protocol mismatch.

3.3   Service Level

The service level is mainly qualified for storing and processing mass data in IoT systems [33]. At this level are cloud computing strategies, complex event processing systems (CEP), and storage area networks (SAN). Faults originated from this level are linked mainly to hardware and software threats. Examples of hardware faults could be a hard disk that degrades its function due to temperature fluctuations, network connectivity issues, and service unavailability [25]. Software faults are related to contextual situations such as the wrong collection, erroneous inference, or the loss of events. Also, faults may be related to system control restrictions, such as input errors, deadline miss, and aging effects. Another probable cause is data fault, which involves threats due to data corruption, missing source data, and other flaws in the data [12]. Computation faults involve several types of hardware and infrastructure that could lead the system to fail due to storage access exceptions, server overload, network congestion, and software bugs [6].

3.4 Application Level

The faults related to this abstraction are related to application crashes due to bugs, operating system errors, unhandled exceptions, and incorrect usage [6]. However, the faults here have a higher amplitude than in the other abstractions since they can vary according to the applications' requirements. These faults are that most perceptible to the final users of an IoT system.

4 Taxonomy of Faults

Maintaining a dependable IoT system, even in the presence of faults, is a significant challenge. Therefore, understanding and characterizing these faults is vital for building solutions and strategies to attain dependability in these systems. Several aspects are significant for understanding and characterizing fault occurrence, particularly identifying fault types, origins, and probable causes. Thus, aiming to identify fault types in IoT systems, we conduct an extensive analysis of the literature and state of the art on faults, fault management, and dependability aspects in this domain. Through this analysis, we were able to identify a comprehensive set of classes and types, as presented in Fig. 2.

This proposed fault taxonomy has the purpose of being used as a reference by researchers, developers, system designers, and users, eliminating ambiguity and, eventually, enabling the use of a standard and comprehensible understanding of IoT faults. Furthermore, it will help system designers provide better fault management strategies to mitigate these faults to attain the dependability property.

This taxonomy organizes the faults by following the following classification: Duration, Location, Semantics, Behavior, Dimension, and Source Level (Detailed and Presented in Sect. 3). Although Azivienis et al. [4] and Raposo et al. [29] present and detail a taxonomy of faults, the first is to present a generic classification applicable to any system. The second extends this rating, including new views for the WSN domain, which is is part of the IoT domain. However, these presented fault taxonomy considers the few characteristics of WSN technologies, but their work provides insufficient information about current research trends, issues, and challenges, especially related to IoT systems faults.

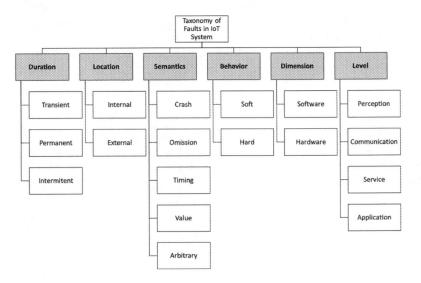

Fig. 2. Taxonomy of faults in IoT system

Duration. Another important type of fault is related to the duration of a fault. Hence, based on the period of the fault, faults can be further classified into persistent, permanent, and transient [4, 17, 21, 23, 24, 29, 30].

Transient. Transient faults are temporary faults that occur due to certain circumstances such as network congestion, changing climate conditions, among others. They occur for a short period and automatically rectify but may develop again. So, it is difficult to diagnose and manage transient faults. Some fault examples are radiation, input mistakes, security breaches.

Permanent Permanent faults that always produce errors. Some permanent faults examples are design faults, broken connectors, noise, system crashing, and aging effects.

Intermittent. Intermittent faults are developed in a longer period compared with transient faults. They may occur in an intermittent interval and have a specific frequency. Generally, intermittent faults cause behavior alteration in a system for some time duration and normal behavior at other times. This type of fault could occur in logical components (software) or physical components (hardware). Faults examples are effects of temperature on hardware, a transient fault like a short in the circuit activated by a specific input, reconfiguration faults, electromagnetic interference fault, incorrect computation fault.

4.1 Location

Each system has its boundary limit, delimiting the frontier between the system and the external environment. Consequently, faults can occur inside a system or external systems (i.e., environment or other systems). Thus, faults can be classified based on the location which occurs. Regarding system limits, faults are classified as internal or external [4, 23, 29].

Internal. Internal faults may be originated from faulty physical components (e.g., broken device or connector) or introduced by design [30]. This type of fault generally affects a small number of components [24, 29]. However, the lack of proper measures to rectify internal faults could cause fault propagation leading to external faults [23].

External. External faults originate from the environment (e.g., noise, radiation), other systems (e.g., system collaboration), or inputs (e.g., wrong or malicious usage of the system) [30]. Some causes of failure are channel noise, radiation, electromagnetic interference, operator mistakes, and environmental conditions [29]. External faults could propagate to internal systems generating internal faults. Furthermore, this type of fault may produce several types of errors and, consequently, system and component failures [4, 29].

4.2   Semantics

This classification organizes the faults according to the behavior produced by the system when it is activated. Consequently, practitioners and researchers can understand the likely faults a system might exhibit to develop relevant fault tolerance strategies. They are as follows:

Crash. A crash fault occurs when an entity loses its internal state and cannot respond to the requests. Natural phenomena can cause this type of fault without human participation. Some reasons are battery depletion, message loss, power down, physical damage [2, 8, 10, 21, 28, 40].

Omission. An omission fault is determined by a service eventually not responding to requests. Then, when a service fails to respond to incoming messages, caused by faults to send or receive messages in proper time. For instance, some reasons are radio interference, collision, channel overflow [8, 10, 21, 28, 40]. The malicious fault could also be considered an omission fault introduced by a human with a malicious objective or a natural fault [4].

Timing. A timing fault occurs when a service responds to a request out of the time interval. So, this fault happens when an entity response contains the correct value, but the response is received too late or too early. Timing failures will only occur if the application has timing constraints [2, 8, 10, 21, 28, 40]. For example, even if the information is received correctly in real-time systems, it must be received within the maximum time defined in its restrictions. Thus, an overloaded sensor node that produces correct values with an excessive delay suffers from a timing failure.

Value. A fault value is produced when a service sends a timely response to a request with an inaccurate delivered value or an incorrect state transition.

For instance, a service performing aggregation of data generated by diverse sensor nodes could forward a result value to a gateway that does not correctly reflect the input data. Such situations could be caused by malfunctioning software, hardware, corrupt messages, or even security breaches generating incorrect data [2,21].

Arbitrary. Arbitrary faults include all previous types that cannot be classified in the described categories. This type of fault is also called Byzantine fault. In general, the cause of this fault may be a malicious service that behaves erroneously and fails to behave when interacting with other services and systems consistently. Some causes of this type of fault are security attacks, such as censorship, freeloading, misrouting, and data corruption [8,10,21,40].

4.3   Behavior

A fault occurrence could change the behavior of a system. In an IoT system, a fault could be classified according to system functioning after fault occurrence. So, based on a faulty IoT system's behavior, faults are classified as hard and soft [21,23,24,40].

Soft. When a system is subject to a soft fault continues operating with altered behavior. Some examples are offset faults that indicate a deviation in sensed data by an additive constant from the required data. Another fault type is the data loss fault produced when sensed data is missing from the time series for a given node.

Hard. Once it occurs causes general inactivity in the system. Some examples are depletion of the batteries leading to inaccurate data transmission or no transmission [34,35]. Other fault types are related to communication and hardware devices malfunction or breakage that require replacing faulty hardware.

4.4   Dimension

IoT system components can be simplified in two dimensions: first, they consist of hardware parts that physically support their operation and, second, they involve software/firmware modules that logically determine their functionality. Consequently, faults at any level can be classified in hardware or software [4,29].

Hardware. These are faults that originate in or affect IoT physical components and systems. Hardware faults examples are manufacturing imperfections, design errors, aging effects, disruption, environmental influence, electromagnetic interference.

Software. Classifies faults that directly or indirectly affect software components (i.e., programs or data). T This classification includes all faults generated in the development process and all software faults resulting from interaction with other systems. Examples of faults are software bugs, software aging, and security faults.

5   Failure Propagation

An IoT system could be defined as a large collection of independent and inter-connected computing elements that cooperate to achieve a common goal [15]. These elements are organized in levels of abstraction, grouping elements with the same goal. If one of these elements could not handle its faults, another element inside its abstraction level must be handled, or a failure occurs. Avizienis et al. [4] define this behavior as a chain of threats that demonstrates a causal relationship between faults, errors, and failures. This chain could be, generically, interpreted as: when a fault is activated, it becomes a possible cause of an error. An error is a deviation of the system state that, through propagation, may lead to its subsequent failure. The propagation of failures in a system occurs if an abstraction level can not handle the failure, by itself or by a lower abstraction level, then propagated to upper abstraction levels.

IoT systems are an interrelated set of devices and entities that work collaboratively in obtaining data and processing that information. Thus, this interdependence could lead to a cascading failure when a propagated failure originating from a dependent component may have dynamic impacts, dependent on its occurrence time. Such sequence-dependent and dynamic effects pose a unique challenge [16]. Moreover, IoT systems are directly associated with the physical environment, so the context information affects system operation and environment. Therefore, failure propagation in IoT systems should consider the importance of context-awareness and ubiquity present in these systems and the impacts of failure propagation over them [3, 28].

In order to model the propagation of failures in a system, we establish a causal relationship and dependence between the levels of abstraction and elements in IoT systems. We extend the cause-effect chain proposed by Bernardi et al. [5]] to an IoT System. Figure 3 exhibits the cause-effect relationship model for IoT systems. The diagram captures relationships between faults, errors, and failures according to its corresponding level of abstraction element. So a fault could affect an element (hardware, software, or communication unit), an error could affect a level of abstraction service performed by the faulty element or a faulty Level communication service, and, in general, a failure could affect the entire level of abstraction if errors are not recovered in due time. If an error reaches level boundaries, a failure is generated, affecting the service provided by the level.

Moreover, suppose an element service is affected by an error. In that case, this error can be propagated to another element service either delivered by the same element (internal propagation) or by another element communicating with the previous (external propagation). The Ecause-Eeffect association represents this error propagation.

In the context of IoT systems, a level of abstraction offers services that correspond to the delivered service by its element services or element communication service. So, faults are associated with the elements, while errors associated with the element service can potentially deliver. Thus, failure of a level of abstraction can be interpreted as an error not properly handle in the element communication service, causing an error propagation to the element service related to the

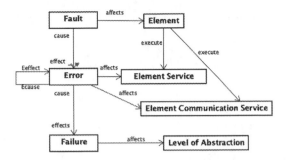

Fig. 3. IoT system cause-effect model

former or the failure of the faulty element, which is still unable to carry out any of its services, is perceived as an external fault by other interacting elements. In both cases, a failure may impact the entire level of abstraction, the system, and be observed as an external fault by other IoT systems interacting with the previous.

Although the cause-effect diagram illustrates the causal relationship between IoT elements, levels of abstraction, and threats, it lacks to describe a model for failure propagation considering systems and environment interaction. Considering this gap, we define a failure propagation model for IoT systems based on levels, systems, and environment interaction. Figure 4 depicts this model.

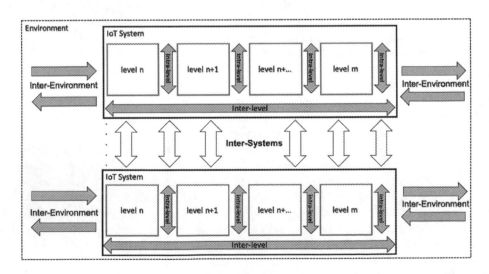

Fig. 4. Failure propagation model in IoT systems

IoT systems are formed by a set of abstraction levels providing services interacting with each other. However, each level has its own set of elements that interact with each other, providing and depending on services. Thus, a faulty element can cause a succession of errors that, if not appropriately treated, could propagate internally into a certain level resulting in an intra-level propagation. However, if this failure crosses the abstraction level boundaries and reaches other levels, inter-level propagation occurs. These propagations could lead an entire system to fail. In the IoT domain, systems are inserted into an ecosystem that collaborates to provide common objectives. These linkages between systems could occasion the propagation of failures leading to inter-system propagation. This inter-system dependence reveals failure propagation into different types that eventually manifest as hazards due to the interaction with the physical world. Thus, it generates a failure propagation flow between the environment and IoT systems.

This model provides an IoT system viewpoint in which direction a failure propagation is probable to occur. Consequently, it provides a useful way of evaluating how errors propagate from one element to another due to their interactions. These interactions are complex due to the IoT system nature and increase with the number and type of interactions, resulting in emergent behaviors, including failure propagation, which is very difficult to predict. Thus, an important part of the system design is the analysis of failure propagation. This analysis increases the ability to project systems capable of limit the damage caused by any failure of their elements. Propagating a culture of evaluating scenarios of failures seems an essential part of improving dependability aspects.

To illustrate the applicability of the failure propagation model, we will use a smart home system as an example. This system includes several sensors and actuators such as temperature, presence, smart locks, video surveillance, and smart objects. All devices send the measurements to a gateway that collects and sends the data a cloud middleware. Each user can use a mobile app to monitor the house devices. A service provided by the perception level is that if a temperature sensor reaches a certain data threshold, the air conditioner is notified to decrease the house's temperature. If there is an incorrect computation fault in the gateway that calculates the house temperature, then an error occurs, and if the air conditioner remains off, a failure has occurred (intra-level propagation).

At the cloud level, a service provided is to unlock the using door using the mobile device. However, due to a bug fault introduced by a programmer, an error is raised and propagates and becomes a failure reaching the perception level by not open the required door (inter-level propagation). The communication internet communication is realized wirelessly through a set of antennas placed on the house's roof. However, the house is lashed with high-speed wind and rain, causing interference leading to data loss failing to obtain real-time data (inter-environment propagation). During a storm, a smart city disaster monitoring system sends incorrect information to the houses, informing only a short rain. However, an incorrect information fault has occurred, the houses should be warned to prepare for a massive hurricane, and due to this failure, people's lives are in danger (inter-system propagation).

6   Conclusion and Future Work

Faults in IoT systems, if they are not treated properly and become system failures, may interfere with user's everyday life or even lead to danger in their lives. However, to develop efficient fault management strategies, we define a pathology of failures for IoT systems. The pathology is divided into three steps: identifying fault sources, error/fault type definition, and failure propagation model.

The identification of fault source step classifies the fault origin classification for IoT systems organizing the faults at the level of probable occurrence. The defined levels are perception, communication, service, and application. On the error/fault type definition step, a taxonomy of faults was proposed. This taxonomy classifies the faults in the following classes: Duration, Location, Semantics, Behavior, Dimension, and Level. This taxonomy can be used by IoT researchers, developers, practitioners, and users. While presenting the taxonomy, examples of several faults and errors were given, and state-of-art references were provided. The failure propagation model step characterizes the fault-failure chain and the implications of failure propagation in an IoT system. Finally, the propagation model was established considering that an IoT system is a composition of levels of abstraction that interact with other systems and the environment. Thus, a failure propagates intra-level, inter-level, and inter-system and inter-environment failures.

In future research, we intend to propose a novel fault management framework for IoT Systems, which can manage fault-failures considering the level of interdependence and propagation.

References

1. Ali, A., Tixeuil, S.: Advanced faults patterns for WSN dependability benchmarking. In: Proceedings of the 13th ACM International Conference on Modeling, Analysis, and Simulation of Wireless and Mobile Systems, pp. 39–48. ACM (2010)
2. Alrajei, N., Fu, H., Zhu, Y.: A survey on fault tolerance in wireless sensor networks. In: 2014 American Society For Engineering Education North Central Section Conference ASEE NCS Conference April, vol. 4 (2014)
3. Andrade, R.M.C., Carvalho, R.M., de Araújo, I.L., Oliveira, K.M., Maia, M.E.F.: What changes from ubiquitous computing to internet of things in interaction evaluation? In: Streitz, N., Markopoulos, P. (eds.) DAPI 2017. LNCS, vol. 10291, pp. 3–21. Springer, Cham (2017). https://doi.org/10.1007/978-3-319-58697-7_1
4. Avizienis, A., Laprie, J.C., Randell, B., Landwehr, C.: Basic concepts and taxonomy of dependable and secure computing. IEEE Trans. Dependable Secur. Comput. **1**(1), 11–33 (2004)
5. Bernardi, S., Donatelli, S., Dondossola, G.: Towards a methodological approach to specification and analysis of dependable automation systems. In: Lakhnech, Y., Yovine, S. (eds.) FORMATS/FTRTFT -2004. LNCS, vol. 3253, pp. 36–51. Springer, Heidelberg (2004). https://doi.org/10.1007/978-3-540-30206-3_5
6. Chetan, S., Ranganathan, A., Campbell, R.: Towards fault tolerance pervasive computing. IEEE Technol. Soc. Mag. **24**(1), 38–44 (2005). https://doi.org/10.1109/MTAS.2005.1407746

7. Ciccozzi, F., Crnkovic, I., Di Ruscio, D., Malavolta, I., Pelliccione, P., Spalazzese, R.: Model-driven engineering for mission-critical iot systems. IEEE Softw. **34**(1), 46–53 (2017)
8. Cristian, F.: Understanding fault-tolerant distributed systems. Commun. ACM **34**(2), 56–79 (1991)
9. Dar, K.S., Taherkordi, A., Eliassen, F.: Enhancing dependability of cloud-based IoT services through virtualization. In: 2016 IEEE First International Conference on Internet-of-Things Design and Implementation (IoTDI), pp. 106–116. IEEE (2016)
10. De Souza, L.M.S., Vogt, H., Beigl, M.: A survey on fault tolerance in wireless sensor networks. Interner Bericht. Fakultät für Informatik, Universität Karlsruhe (2007)
11. Denker, G., Dutt, N., Mehrotra, S., Stehr, M.-O., Talcott, C., Venkatasubramanian, N.: Resilient dependable cyber-physical systems: a middleware perspective. J. Internet Serv. Appl. **3**(1), 41–49 (2012). https://doi.org/10.1007/s13174-011-0057-4
12. Ganesh, A., Sandhya, M., Shankar, S.: A study on fault tolerance methods in cloud computing. In: 2014 IEEE International Advance Computing Conference (IACC), pp. 844–849. IEEE (2014)
13. Gia, T.N., Rahmani, A.M., Westerlund, T., Liljeberg, P., Tenhunen, H.: Fault tolerant and scalable IoT-based architecture for health monitoring. In: 2015 IEEE Sensors Applications Symposium (SAS), pp. 1–6. IEEE (2015)
14. Huangshui, H., Guihe, Q.: Fault management frameworks in wireless sensor networks. In: 2011 Fourth International Conference on Intelligent Computation Technology and Automation, vol. 2, pp. 1093–1096. IEEE (2011)
15. Iwanicki, K.: A distributed systems perspective on industrial IoT. In: 2018 IEEE 38th International Conference on Distributed Computing Systems (ICDCS), pp. 1164–1170 (2018). https://doi.org/10.1109/ICDCS.2018.00116
16. Khan, F.I., Hameed, S.: Understanding security requirements and challenges in internet of things (IoTs): A review. arXiv preprint arXiv:1808.10529 (2018)
17. Khan, M.Z., Merabti, M., Askwith, B.: Design considerations for fault management in wireless sensor networks. In: 10th Annual Conference on the Convergence of Telecommunications, Networking and Broadcasting, Liverpool, UK (2009)
18. Kubler, S., Främling, K., Buda, A.: A standardized approach to deal with firewall and mobility policies in the iot. Pervasive Mob. Comput. **20**, 100–114 (2015)
19. Li, X., Ji, H., Li, Y.: Layered fault management scheme for end-to-end transmission in internet of things. Mob. Netw. Appl. **18**(2), 195–205 (2013)
20. Ma, R., Xing, L., Michel, H.E.: Fault-intrusion tolerant techniques in wireless sensor networks. In: 2006 2nd IEEE International Symposium on Dependable, Autonomic and Secure Computing, pp. 85–94. IEEE (2006)
21. Mahapatro, A., Khilar, P.M.: Fault diagnosis in wireless sensor networks: a survey. IEEE Commun. Surv. Tutor. **15**(4), 2000–2026 (2013)
22. Misra, S., Gupta, A., Krishna, P.V., Agarwal, H., Obaidat, M.S.: An adaptive learning approach for fault-tolerant routing in internet of things. In: 2012 IEEE Wireless Communications and Networking Conference (WCNC), pp. 815–819. IEEE (2012)
23. Moridi, E., Haghparast, M., Hosseinzadeh, M., Jassbi, S.J.: Fault management frameworks in wireless sensor networks: a survey. Comput. Commun. **155**(March), 205–226 (2020). https://doi.org/10.1016/j.comcom.2020.03.011
24. Muhammed, T., Shaikh, R.A.: An analysis of fault detection strategies in wireless sensor networks. J. Netw. Comput. Appl. **78**, 267–287 (2017). https://doi.org/10.1016/j.jnca.2016.10.019. (November 2016)

25. Mukwevho, M.A., Celik, T.: Toward a smart cloud: a review of fault-tolerance methods in cloud systems. IEEE Trans. Serv. Comput. **14**(2), 589–605 (2018)
26. Ojie, E., Pereira, E.: Exploring dependability issues in IoT applications. In: Proceedings of the Second International Conference on Internet of things, Data and Cloud Computing, p. 123. ACM (2017)
27. Paradis, L., Han, Q.: A survey of fault management in wireless sensor networks. J. Netw. Syst. Manag. **15**(2), 171–190 (2007)
28. Power, A., Kotonya, G.: Complex patterns of failure: fault tolerance via complex event processing for IoT systems. In: Proceedings - 2019 IEEE International Congress on Cybermatics: 12th IEEE International Conference on Internet of Things, 15th IEEE International Conference on Green Computing and Communications, 12th IEEE International Conference on Cyber, Physical and So, pp. 986–993 (2019). https://doi.org/10.1109/iThings/GreenCom/CPSCom/SmartData.2019.00173
29. Raposo, D., Rodrigues, A., Silva, J.S., Boavida, F.: A taxonomy of faults for wireless sensor networks. J. Netw. Syst. Manag. **25**(3), 591–611 (2017)
30. Ratasich, D., Khalid, F., Geißler, F., Grosu, R., Shafique, M., Bartocci, E.: A roadmap toward the resilient internet of things for cyber-physical systems. IEEE Access **7**, 13260–13283 (2019). https://doi.org/10.1109/ACCESS.2019.2891969
31. Schmid, T., Dubois-Ferriere, H., Vetterli, M.: Sensorscope: experiences with a wireless building monitoring sensor network. In: Workshop on Real-World Wireless Sensor Networks (REALWSN 2005). No. CONF (2005)
32. Ştefan, V.K., Otto, P., Alexandrina, P.M.: Considerations regarding the dependability of internet of things. In: 2017 14th International Conference on Engineering of Modern Electric Systems (EMES), pp. 145–148. IEEE (2017)
33. Suo, H., Wan, J., Zou, C., Liu, J.: Security in the internet of things: a review. In: 2012 International Conference on Computer Science and Electronics Engineering, vol. 3, pp. 648–651. IEEE (2012)
34. Szewczyk, R., Polastre, J., Mainwaring, A., Culler, D.: Lessons from a sensor network expedition. In: Karl, H., Wolisz, A., Willig, A. (eds.) EWSN 2004. LNCS, vol. 2920, pp. 307–322. Springer, Heidelberg (2004). https://doi.org/10.1007/978-3-540-24606-0_21
35. Tolle, G., et al.: A macroscope in the redwoods. In: Proceedings of the 3rd International Conference on Embedded Networked Sensor Systems, pp. 51–63. ACM (2005)
36. Warriach, E.U., Aiello, M., Tei, K.: A machine learning approach for identifying and classifying faults in wireless sensor network. In: 2012 IEEE 15th International Conference on Computational Science and Engineering, pp. 618–625. IEEE (2012)
37. Xing, L., Li, H., Michel, H.E.: Fault-tolerance and reliability analysis for wireless sensor networks. Int. J. Perform. Eng. **5**(5), 419–431 (2009)
38. Xing, L., Zhao, G., Wang, Y., Mandava, L.: Competing failure analysis in iot systems with cascading functional dependence. In: 2018 Annual Reliability and Maintainability Symposium (RAMS), pp. 1–6. IEEE (2018)
39. Yaqoob, I., et al.: Internet of things architecture: recent advances, taxonomy, requirements, and open challenges. IEEE Wirel. Commun. **24**(3), 10–16 (2017)
40. Zhang, Z., Mehmood, A., Shu, L., Huo, Z., Zhang, Y., Mukherjee, M.: A survey on fault diagnosis in wireless sensor networks. IEEE Access **6**, 11349–11364 (2018). https://doi.org/10.1109/ACCESS.2018.2794519

Method to Convert UML State Chart Diagram to the Virtual Object Mock-Up

N. N. Voit$^{(\boxtimes)}$ ⓘ and S. I. Bochkov$^{(\boxtimes)}$ ⓘ

Ulyanovsk State Technical University, Ulyanovsk, Russia
n.voit@ulstu.ru

Abstract. Virtual reality technology in engineering is one of the most effective tools of solutions of various tasks in product development: prototyping, modeling, modifying. Since VR objects tend to fully simulate the behavior of real products, the volume of project documentation tremendously arises, therefore it becomes hard to model VR objects being based upon it. In this paper, the authors propose a method converting the UML state chart formal description of the product to the virtual object model. The key feature of the method is the mapping event function which connects input signals and user actions. The method is hardware-free, so it is not attached to a certain VR platform. Authors have tested it on the concrete technical object, namely measurement device, output data is also given in the article.

Keywords: Virtual reality · UML · State chart · Diagram

1 Introduction

Nowadays most industrial enterprises [1–4] successfully use virtual reality technology (VR) to solve a variety of different tasks: personnel training and retraining on the workplace, modeling of assembled products, complex physical processes taking place inside products, and on the manufacturing line.

VR is used throughout the entire product lifecycle: from the early design stages, errors identification, ergonomics checking, to the production process organization, the development of maintenance, repair, and modernization processes [5].

In manufacturing, VR technology is widely used to simulate the installation of new equipment simultaneously with the manufacturing line design. In parallel, it becomes possible to train future operators of designed equipment on the VR prototypes. Thus, when opening the updated site, employees will be able to immediately get down to work and not waste time on training. Time saved can also come in handy when setting up factory lines. Production speed and the quality of the manufactured products play a leading role in the success of the enterprise, therefore it is so important to save time on parallel processes.

VR allows simulating emergencies [6]. Often, it is either dangerous or too expensive to reproduce such cases in reality, because the staff only knows in theory how to get out of a difficult or emergency. Equipped with VR, staff can be prepared to handle any challenge.

Demonstrating the future product to customers even before production with the VR allows the client to see a life-size item and touch it.

It becomes evident that one of the keys to a successful VR software product is the design process and design solutions in form of documentation. The process should be as short as possible, and project solutions, in turn, must contain a detailed description of the developed object. In other words, project solutions should be clear for every member of the design team and adaptive under new requirements.

Complex technical systems, including those using VR technology, are designed using diagrammatic models, which are the artifacts of the visual graphic languages such as AADL, BPMN, SysML, UML, IDEF, Simulink, and others [7]. They significantly increase the efficiency and quality of design procedures by unifying the language of interaction between process participants including developers and client representatives, thorough documentation of design and architectural solutions, formal methods of checking diagrams for correctness. However, the larger the diagram and the more types of them are engaged the more complex system becomes. As a result, the visual system prototype is hard to understand and maintain.

Automata models (automata), or (finite) state machines are the most common means of representing systems at a high level of abstraction, which gives developers the most complete understanding of the software system principles. There is a wide range of reverse engineering techniques - getting a state machine from source code - to obtain concise and up-to-date documentation on how the system works.

UML 2.0 modeling language [8] is de facto the standard in object-oriented modeling and design. It is considered the most popular language for modeling reactive systems [9]. It is intended for designing, documenting, modeling the behavior of system artifacts [10, 11] and is widely used in technology and industry [12].

UML State Chart diagrams are of particular interest. They model the system behavior depending on external actions, or input signals, which are, in fact, analogous to state machine models.

Thus, combining UML State Chart diagrams and state machines to automatically synthesize virtual objects or *virtual mock-ups*, allows expecting reducing time and resource costs in this task. A large number of virtual mock-ups exists but there is no unified approach transforming descriptive models especially in above mentioned visual languages to the ones which can be applied in virtual reality.

This work is aimed to create an effective method for transforming a formal description of the UML State Chart diagram into a programmable model of an object that changes in time according to the principle of a state machine. The structure of the article is the following. Section 2 provides an overview of the work on the automated design of complex technical systems in virtual reality, as well as the design of systems using the UML State Chart. In Sect. 3 short UML review is given. The authors' models of the UML State Chart diagram and a virtual dynamic object, which is a VR representation of an automaton model, and events mapping function are described in Sect. 4. In Sect. 5 the method is given which converts a UML model into a VR one, which will be further used for program code generation. An example of converting is in Sect. 6.

2   Related Works

Authors investigated not only scientific and research works but also the software solutions supporting diagram-to-code transformation. There are few works containing not only applicable but also scientific results in generating virtual mock-ups models, therefore, firstly, we will consider software tools.

Visual Paradigm [13] is a CASE tool supporting UML, SysML, and BPMN languages developed by Visual Paradigm International Ltd. It has a good interface and supports various types of diagrams. Visual Paradigm provides reverse engineering procedures, demo online environment. Also, Visual Paradigm provides code generation from diagrams to C++, C#, Java. However, the tool has a proprietary license and in most cases generates a huge and bulky program code.

Software Ideas Modeler [14] is a smart CASE tool and diagram software that supports various diagram types. It is developed by Software Ideas company. Apart from UML, it works with ERD, BPMN, ArchiMate. Software Ideas Modeler has an interface similar to Microsoft products (Office and Visual Studio) consisting of tabbed ribbon with groups, toggled side panels. The tool supports the export of diagrams to more than 10 languages, and import from C#, C++, Java, etc. The free version has little functionality available which does not solve the problem described in the article. Also, the generated code contains a lot of extra classes and interfaces so it is hard to maintain.

Atmani et al. [15] generate virtual mock-ups of human bones in case of surgical operations. Authors compare several modeling methods and based on requirements they choose a simple-form method where objects are represented with quadrics, planes, etc. 14 parameters are involved in the virtual model synthesis, data is extracted from the radiological images. However, the method errors and in modeling. The method is also highly specialized.

Al-Fedaghi [16] describes a method that converts the UML model to the thinging machine (TM) model and back. Inspired by Heidegger's works, the author offers a specific all-in-one model which should solve problems of UML by internal cross-diagram integration. TM is built as a one-category ontology. TM consists of stages such as creation, process, release, input and output. The conversion process is based on [17] and the following five diagram types are involved: activity, use case, sequence, class and state ones.

3   UML Review

3.1   Shortly About UML

UML diagrams can be divided into structural and behavioral diagram groups [10]. Structural diagrams show the static structure of a system and its components at various levels of abstraction and implementation, as well as the relations between components. Behavioral diagrams simulate the principles of the system and its components in dynamics, thereby showing changes in the system at certain timestamps.

UML State Chart diagram is of particular interest in theory and practice. This diagram type simulates the dynamics of systems, highlighting the control flow following from one state to another. Essentially, a state chart is a special case of a state machine that models behavior determining a sequence of states over the course of an object's existence. This sequence is considered to be the response to events and includes feedback to those events.

3.2 UML State Chart Diagrams

Consider main UML State Chart diagrams concepts [18]. Any UML state machine consists of regions, containing vertices and transitions between them. A vertex is either a state which may have a complex hierarchical structure of regions or a pseudo-state, regulating how transitions are compound in execution. Transitions have input and output states. They are executed with events (input signals or triggers), thus forming an area of possible state changes. The state is called simple if it has no regions; a complex state has two or more regions and is called orthogonal if it contains several regions visually divided dotted line. A region can contain simple states as well as complex ones. If the current state is not on the top level of the automaton, it should include at least one from the region. It is obvious that a complex state and states recursively layered into it form states tree.

In real automata, a designer works with parallel states; therefore, the transitions contained in them activate not only the target state but also indirect ones. The same can be said for deactivated states. On the contrary, a state can be activated/deactivated not only by a direct "near" transition but also by an indirect "far" transition.

4   Objects Formal Description

4.1   UML State Chart Model

UML State Chart diagram can be expressed via extended finite state machine (eFSM) with the following model [19–26]:

$$A = (S, X, S_0, C, TT, Fstart),$$

where:

- $S = S_{simple} \cup S_{complex}$ is states set, where:

  - $S_{simple} = s_{s1}, s_{s2}, \ldots, s_{sm}$ is simple (atomic) states set,
  - $S_{complex} = s_{c1}, s_{c2}, \ldots, s_{cn}$ is complex states set, $s_{ci} = \{R_{ij} | j \in \mathbb{N}\}$, where $R_{ij} \subset S \backslash s_{ci}$ is a region.

- X is input signals set,
- C is guard conditions set,
- S_0 is an initial state $S_0 \in S_{simple}$,
- $Fstart : R \rightarrow S_{simple}$ is initial state function,
- $TT = \{t_i | i \in \mathbb{N}\}$ is transitions table, $t_i = (src, dst, x, cond)$, $src, dst \in S, x \in X, cond \in C \cup \emptyset$.

Define the function $parent : S \rightarrow S$ which takes s_{child} as argument and returns state s_{parent} so that $\exists s_{parent}, r | r \in s_{parent} \cap s_{child} \in r$; if s_{child} has no parent state, the function returns A.

4.2 Virtual Mock-Up Model

Virtual environment consists of objects the user interacts with. Assume such objects as *virtual objects,* or *virtual mock-ups* and formalize them with the following view:

$$VO = (Ctrls, Events, F, CE, S, S_0),$$

where:

- *Ctrls* is controlers set,
- *Events* is events set,
- *F* is virtual object functions set, $F = \{f_i | f_i = (src_i, dst_i)\}$, $src_i \in S$, $dst_i \in S$,
- *CE* is a function mapping, $CE = \{ce_i | ce_i : Ctrls \times Events \to F\}$,
- $S = \{(Name, Values, CurrentValue)\}$ is states set, $CurrentValue \in Values$;
- S_0 is an initial state.

4.3 Mapping Functions

Introduce the *events mapping function* which maps each eFSM input signal from X to the couple of event type from *Events* and controller from *Ctrls*. It has one-to-one relation and thus the following formal description:$fEventsMap : X \to Events \times Ctrls$. The function is purposed to model human-computer interaction.

Also introduce the states map which links eFSM and virtual object states: $Map_S = \{(S_{Ai}, S_{VOj}), S_{Ai} \in A[S], S_{VOj} \in VO[S]\}$. Functions to find corresponding states are the following:$fgetSA(s_{VO}) = s_A | (s_A, s_{VO}) \in Map_S, fgetSVO(s_A) = s_{VO} | (s_{VO}, s_A) \in Map_S$.

5 Conversion Method

Method converting state chart model to the virtual dynamic object model is the following.

Copy All States

1. For each s in $A[S_{simple}]$:

   a. Insert s' in $VO[S]$ and (s, s') into Map_S.

2. For each s in $A[S_{complex}]$:

   a. Create empty state s'_c.
   b. For each r in s:

      (1) Create values set vs, initial state s_0.
      (2) For each s' in r:

         i. If $s' \in A[S_{simple}]$ go to step ii else go step v.
         ii. Insert s' into vs.

        iii. If $s' = A[Fstart(r)]$, assign s' to s_0.

        iv. Continue.

        v. Go to step (2) and replace $A\left[S_{complex}\right]$ with s'.

    (3)   Insert (r, vs, s_0) into s'_c.

c.   Insert s'_c in $VO[S]$ and (s, s') into Map_S.

Copy All Transitions

1. For each t in $A[TT]$:

    a.   Get $src = t[src]$, $dst = t[dst]$.

    b.   Get $srcExternal = P(parent(src) == A)$, $dstExternal = P(parent(dst) == A)$.

    c.   If $srcExternal$ $\wedge$ $dstExternal$ insert $f = (fgetSVO(src), fgetSVO(dst), fEventsMap(t[x]))$ into $VO[F]$.

    d.   Else if $\neg srcExternal \wedge \neg dstExternal$:

        (1)   Create $src' = fgetSVO(src)$.

        (2)   Create $dst' = fgetSVO(dst)$.

        (3)   Update $src'[CurrentValue] = x \in src'[Values] | x \equiv src'[CurrentValue]$.

        (4)   Update $dst'[CurrentValue] = x \in dst'[Values] | x \equiv dst'[CurrentValue]$.

        (5)   Insert $f = (src', dst', fEventsMap(t[x]))$ to the F.

    e.   Else if $srcExternal \wedge \neg dstExternal$:

        (1)   Create $dst' = fgetSVO(dst)$.

        (2)   Update $dst'[CurrentValue] = x \in dst'[Values] | x \equiv dst'[CurrentValue]$.

        (3)   Insert $f = (src, dst', fEventsMap(t[x]))$ to the F.

    f.   Else if $\neg srcExternal \wedge dstExternal$:

        (1)   Create $src' = fgetSVO(src)$.

        (2)   Update $src'[CurrentValue] = x \in src'[Values] | x \equiv src'[CurrentValue]$.

        (3)   Insert $f = (src', dst, fEventsMap(t[x]))$ to the F.

6 Virtual Object Example

Consider the generation method on the (fragment) example of the oscilloscope S1-116 [27].

The UML state chart model of the device is structured below:

- Input signals: X = {powerOn, Polarity2Click, switchClick, VTClick, FClick, FLongClick, ScanA, ScanSettings},
- Guard conditions: C = {Fbutton}
- States: S = {Off, Introduction, WorkState = {ChannelI, ChannelII = {Norm, Inv}, View1, View2, View1 + 2, VTOff, VTQueue, VTDiscrete, ScanA, ScanAhighlight, ScanB, ScanMix}}
- Initial state: S_0 = *Off*

Transitions are visualized on the UML state chart diagram shown in the Fig. 1. Entities above are also shown on the diagram.

After the method application the VR model will be structured as shown below:

- Controlers: *Ctrls* = {Switch button, Scan view button, VT mode button, Change polarity button, Scan A settings button, Scan select button, Scan settings button, Channel I input, Channel I Y-scale switch, Channel II Y-scale switch, Channel II input},
- Event types: *Events* = {trigger click, trigger click and move, trigger double click, trigger click and hold},
- States: see "States" in the UML model structure above,
- Initial state: S_0 = *Off*.

Events mapping function for this device is given in the Table 1. 'Input signal' column stands for X set, 'Event type' – for *Events* set.

The virtual mock-up of the device is shown in Fig. 2. Controlers in visual form are given in the Table 2.

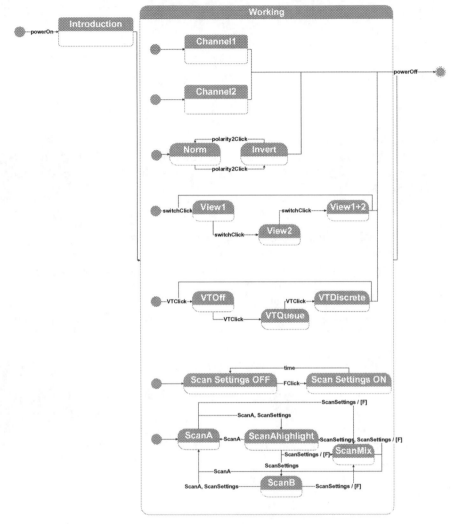

Fig. 1. S1–116 oscilloscope UML state chart diagram.

Table 1. Events mapping function

Input signal	Event type
powerOn	Trigger click
Polarity2Click	Trigger click
switchClick	Trigger click
VTClick	Trigger click
FClick	Trigger click
FLongClick	Trigger click and hold
ScanA	Trigger click
ScanSettings	Trigger click

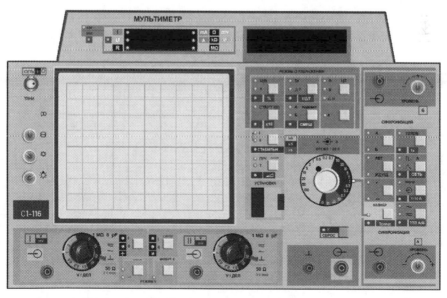

Fig. 2. S1-116 virtual mock-up

Table 2. Controllers of virtual mock-up

Graphical view	Name
	Switch button
	Scan view button
	VT mode button
	Change polarity button
	Scan A settings button
	Scan select button
	Scan settings button
	Channel I input
	Channel I Y-scale switch
	Channel II Y-scale switch
	Channel II input

7   Conclusion

Authors have developed method converting UML State Chart model to the virtual mock-up. It differs in the use of events mapping function forming human-computer interaction scheme. The method uses state chart model developed in accordance with UML 2.0. Generated virtual mockup reflects its behavior features depending on external triggers.

The method is hardware free and can be applied in generation of the program code modelling object behavior in VR.

The next research topics are the following: extending the method for the multi-object dynamic systems, development and analysis of virtual environment using other UML diagram models such as use case, sequence etc.

References

1. Bider, I., Jalali, A.: Agile business process development: why, how and when—applying Nonaka's theory of knowledge transformation to business process development. Inf. Syst. e-Bus. Manag. **14**(4), 693–731 (2014). https://doi.org/10.1007/s10257-014-0256-1
2. Sherehiy, B., Karwowski, W., Layer, J.K.: A review of enterprise agility: concepts, frameworks, and attributes. Int. J. Ind. Ergon. **37**, 445–460 (2007)
3. A global Swiss company offering advanced intelligent application software for multiple business sectors. http://whitestein.com/
4. Abidi, M.-A., Lyonnet, B., Chevaillier, P., Toscano, R., Baert, P.: Simulation of manufacturing processes via virtual reality. In: Virtual and Augmented Reality: Concepts, Methodologies, Tools, and Applications, pp. 918–953 (2018). https://doi.org/10.4018/978-1-5225-5469-1.ch044
5. Connect WIT, vol. 10, October 2019
6. Dozortsev, V.: Virtual reality technology in teaching operators of technological processes. Autom. Remote. Control. **6**, 42–50 (2018)
7. Liu, B., Zhang, Y.-R., et al.: A survey of model-driven techniques and tools for cyber-physical systems. Front. Inform. Technol. Electron. Eng. **21**(11), 1567–1590 (2020). https://doi.org/10.1631/FITEE.2000311
8. UML 2.0: https://www.omg.org/spec/UML/2.0/About-UML/
9. UML State Machine Diagrams. https://www.uml-diagrams.org/state-machine-diagrams.html. Accessed 10 Nov 2020
10. Maklaev, V.A, Sosnin, P.I.: Creation and usage of automatized design organization experience base. UlSTU, Ulyanovsk (2012)
11. Fowler, M.: UML Distilled: A Brief Guide to the Standard Object Modeling Language, 3rd edn. Pearson Education, Inc., London (2004)
12. Binder, R.V.: Testing object-oriented software: a software testing verification reliability, **6**(3/4), 125–252 (1996)
13. Ideal Modeling & Diagramming Tool for Agile Team Collaboration: https://www.visual-paradigm.com/
14. Diagram CASE Tool for Software Modeling & Analysis - UML, BPMN, ERD. https://www.softwareideas.net/
15. Atmani, H., Merienne, F., Fofi, D., Trouilloud, P.: From medical data to simple virtual mock-up of scapulo-humeral joint. In: Proceedings of Eighth International Conference on Quality Control by Artificial Vision, vol. 6356. https://doi.org/10.1117/12.736712
16. Al-Fedaghi, S.: UML modeling to TM modeling and back. Int. J. Comput. Sci. Netw. Secur. **1**(21), 84–96 (2021)

17. Sommerville, I.: Software Engineering, 10th edn. Pearson Education Limited, Essex (2016)
18. About the Unified Modeling Language Specification Version 2.5.1. https://www.omg.org/spec/UML/2.5.1
19. Afanasyev, A., Voit, N., Ukhanova, M., Ionova, I., Epifanov, V.: Analysis of the design and technological workflow in a large radio engineering enterprise. Radioengineering **6**, 49–58 (2017)
20. Afanasyev, A., Voit, N., Kirillov S.: Development of RYT-grammar for analysis and control dynamic workflows. In: Proceedings of International Conference on Computing Networking and Informatics (ICCNI 2017), pp. 1–4. IEEE (2017)
21. Afanasyev, A., Voit, N.: Grammar-algebraic approach to the analysis and synthesis diagrammatically models of hybrid dynamic design workflows. Inf. Meas. Contr. Syst. **15**(12), 69–78 (2017)
22. Voit, N.: Development of timed RT-grammars for controlling processes in cyber-physical systems. In: Proceedings of the 13th International Conference on Interactive Systems: Problems of Human-Computer Interaction, pp. 87–91. UlSTU, Ulyanovsk (2017)
23. Afanasyev, A., Voit, N., Ukhanova, M.: Control and analysis of denotative and significant semantic errors diagrammatic models of design flows in designing automated systems. Radioengineering **6**, 84–92 (2018)
24. Afanasyev, A., Voit, N.: Grammar-algebraic approach to the analysis of hybrid dynamic design workflows. In: Maschenko, E. (ed.) Information Technologies and Information Security in Science, Technique and Education "INFOTECH-2017", pp. 43–48 (2017)
25. Kirillov, S., Voit, N., Molotov, R., Stepanov, A., Voevodin, E., Brigadnov, S.: Development and research of methods for analysis and control of semantic integrity and consistency of dynamic distributed workflows diagrammatic models based on temporary RV-grammarIn: 9th All-Russian school-Seminar for Graduate Students, Students and Young Scientists "Information Systems and CAD 2017", pp.135–139. UlSTU, Ulyanovsk (2017)
26. Voit, N.: Automated methods and software for designing of workflows. Inf. Meas. Contr. Syst. **16**(11), 84–89 (2018)
27. Bochkov, S.: Development of S1-116 oscilloscope virtual simulator. In: Tolok, A.V. (ed.) CAD/CAM/PDM–2017 Proceedings, pp. 249–251. Trapeznikov Institue of Control Sciences RAS, Moscow (2017)

Using Edge-to-Cloud Analytics IoT Dumpsite Monitor for Proactive Waste Management

E. S. Mbonu, K. C. Okafor, G. A. Chukwudebe$^{(\boxtimes)}$, C. O. Ikerionwu, and E. C. Amadi

Federal University of Technology Owerri, Owerri, Nigeria
{ekene.mbonu,kennedy.okafor,gloria.chukwudebe,
charles.ikerionwu}@futo.edu.ng

Abstract. In this work, an Edge-to-Cloud Analytics architecture model for Waste Management and Hazard Alert system is developed for prompt management of waste dumpsites. The system enables IoT smart nodes to monitor dumpsites and generate alerts on the detection of gas emissions, smoke, and fire. The custom-designed IoT dumpsite edge aggregator module is achieved using MQ-7 (carbon monoxide), MQ-2 (smoke/methane), MQ-135 (CO_2, benzene, NH_3, NOx), and flame sensors for proactive detection of environmental hazards. The scalable Edge-to-Cloud Analytics architectural model produces efficient data stream uploading from the IoT sensor nodes into the cloud domain with an MKR-1000 Edge Controller used to achieve edge-to-fog gateway processing. Three algorithms developed for the system include IoT node characterization, sensor reading/calibration, and data transmission to remote servers using Simultaneous Wireless Information Power Transfer (SWIPT). A proof of concept was demonstrated by building three IoT dumpsite nodes that were used for testing. The Testbed deployment with visualization patterns is observed on Open Source ThingSpeak Cloud-native platform. The key contributions to knowledge include the use of Edge-to-Cloud analytics for dumpsite monitoring and prompt evacuation, the introduction of SWIPT to conserve energy for optimized valued-insights and the development of an architectural model that allows lower computer-storage resources at the edge. This is very good since a single IoT device only serves a small geographic area. Future work will investigate throughput and latency minimization, API containerization for light deployments using Docker Swarm and Kubernetes. Since most dumpsites are remarkably close to end-users, edge to cloud (IoT) analytics is recommended for a sustainable solution to waste management in Nigeria.

Keywords: Software engineering · Cloud computing · IoT applications · Edge-to-cloud analytics · Dumpsite monitoring · Waste management systems

1 Introduction

Environmental sustainability has greatly suffered enormous setbacks because of the potential risks emanating from unsustainable waste disposal systems in Nigeria. Most towns and cities have several open dumpsites existing close to residential areas as well as business domains. Some of the wastes are dumped where they block access roads and drainage systems which empty into rivers that communities use for domestic purposes

© Springer Nature Switzerland AG 2021
O. Gervasi et al. (Eds.): ICCSA 2021, LNCS 12957, pp. 465–480, 2021.
https://doi.org/10.1007/978-3-030-87013-3_35

(Fig. 1a). Sometimes, waste collectors set fire at dumpsites, such fires release hazardous gases to neighboring communities and at times the fire can spread to destroy farms and individual properties.

Sadly, the Nigerian population continues to increase at 2.6% annually without any robust waste evacuation and management system in place [1]. The amount of waste generated in a city grows in similar proportion to the economic engagements and population growth rate. The glaring consequence of unattended waste disposal and management systems is that it leads to environmental hazards to the human populace [2]. To date, the regulations governing solid waste management in Nigeria are not adequately enforced by appropriate authorities [3]. Hence, many Nigerians do not appreciate the idea of efficient waste management since many people get away with the indiscriminate dumping of refuse. In Nigerian cities today, the aggregate waste generation rate is estimated at 0.65–0.95 kg/capita/day [3].

(a)

(b)

Fig. 1. a. Wste dumpsite in Umuosu Community, Naze, Owerri, Imo State. b. Waste Site Nekede Community, Owerri, Imo State, *Source*: (Author's field Photo, March 2020)

Although recently, the informal sector has started waste collection and recycling in most cities in Nigeria (Fig. 1b), the effort is grossly inadequate because about 42 million tons of wastes are generated annually in the country, monitoring, and channeling these wastes presently constitute huge economic concerns [4].

Today, some of the lingering issues associated with waste management systems in the country include limited waste collection systems, unsustainable collection services, and weak disposal procedures. The health and environmental consequences are randomly huge, cutting across several African countries. Despite the various organizations involved in the waste management value chain in Nigeria, very little success rate has been recorded, the predominate indiscriminate disposal of wastes is still a serious environmental and public health challenge.

Software engineering, IoT and cloud computing technologies can be introduced to resolve this challenge as is done in advanced countries. This work is part of a Waste Management and Hazard Alert System (WM-HAS) research project for use of ICT and innovative business model to create a synergy amongst stakeholders in the waste management supply chain, waste generators, evacuators, and recycling companies. The project involved the setting up of a waste management Network Operating Center (NOC) that will house network equipment and database repositories. The focus of this aspect of WM-HAS research is on the integration of smart IoT sensor nodes at selected dumpsites (both legal and illegal) where hazardous materials are likely to be generated. Software design processes with best practices from software engineering will be utilizing for implementation of the IoT and Edge-cloud architecture. The major activities include field study to gather requirements, programming, software testing, integration, and deployment. The Software development process employed is the Agile approach. This relies on various software configuration management to govern changes in both the IoT, and Cloud algorithm designs as well as their integrity, traceability, and code design.

The primary objective of this research is to introduce state-of-the art proactive technology to avert hazards from dumpsites using IoT Smart Sensors and cloud-based predictive visualizations. Given the challenges of utilizing real-time data from several smart IoT nodes, Edge to Cloud Analytics (ECA), and a computing model that involves real-time data analysis in which data streams (incoming) are processed and analyzed at both non-central locations as well as the Cloud space will be considered. This is inspired by some previous work involving Cloud-connected devices [5–7]. Additionally, because of electricity power inadequacies at dumpsites, this work will explore Simultaneous Wireless Information and Power Transfer (SWIPT) [8]. A prototype IoT system with ECA technology and Simultaneous Wireless Information and Power Transfer will be developed for real-time monitoring of dumpsites for mitigation of hazardous gases or fire.

The remainder of this paper is organized as follows: a review of closely related works is presented in Sect. 2. The edge-cloud computing architecture and implementation of the prototype IoT Dumpsite monitor system are described in Sect. 3. Section 4 presents the system simulation and evaluation. Section 5 presents the results and discussion. Section 6 concludes the paper with future directions and recommendations.

2 Review of Related Literature

The Internet of Things (IoT) refers to a system of internet-connected objects that can collect and transfer data over a wireless network without human intervention. IoT ecosystems are driven by data collected from devices that sense and interface with the physical world. Presently, IoT is inspiring the latest Industrial 4.0 applications and increasing pro- ductivity in agriculture, transportation, manufacturing, electric grids, and many more. With successes from some of these sectors, researchers are beginning to explore IoT applications for improved waste management. So far, the most common IoT applica- tion in waste management operations currently is the automated route optimization of garbage pickup trucks. These trucks generally follow a specific route every day to collect trash, the drivers generally do not know how full a trash bin is before they get to it, this results in a lot of wasted time and fuel. With a user interface revealing the locations and fill levels of all bins, waste collector trucks can get an automated route planned for them that has prioritized areas in urgent need of cleanup and avoid bins that are yet to get filled up [9].

The authors in [10–12] discussed IoT designs for smart-city projects using integrated ICT as well as highlighting existing IoT platforms for achieving smart city applications. The authors in [13] focused on a sustainable strategy for municipal solid waste manage- ment in Nigeria, especially for power generation. In [14], the researchers developed an agent-based waste management system and simulated the system behavior under various conditions. The work in [15] identified the major problems in waste management such as lack of waste segregation at source, low rate of house-to-house collections, use of open vans, and proposed an online management information system to optimize daily oper- ating resource allotment to make the system effective and sustainable. The work in [16] focused on decision support systems using Geographic Information System for waste disposal. Other technology-enabled approaches to waste management were studied in [5, 17–20], and [21]. Some other literature surveys carried out were on the power chal- lenges of IoT systems. The Simultaneous Wireless Information Power Transfer (SWIPT) in the energy-constrained environment for wireless devices was found promising for IoT nodes.

The major research gaps identified in the literature include:

i.   Non-existent tech solutions for dumpsite monitoring to mitigate potential hazards.
ii. Non-existent solutions for power challenges of IoT deployments in remote environments without electricity grid.
iii. Non-deployment of Edge analytics in process automation of waste management systems.

Because of these gaps, this research work explored the utilization of edge-to-cloud analytics and SWIPT for the development of IoT nodes for monitoring dumpsites to improve waste management systems. This is novel and will improve waste management in developing countries.

3   Methodology

The conceptual diagram for the Waste Management and Hazard Alert System (WM-HAS) is shown in Fig. 2. The Web and Mobile modules have been developed by a different team (wm-has.org.ng), while the work of IoT team is presented in this paper.

The IoT team visited various dumpsites, informal recyclers, and waste collectors in Imo and Anambra state in Nigeria. The team took into consideration the findings from

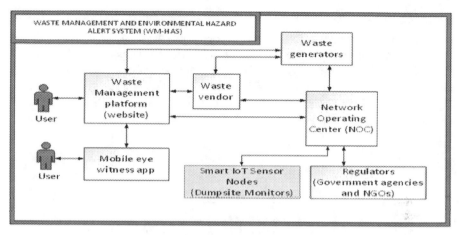

Fig. 2. The conceptual diagram for WM-HAS.

field surveys and literature reviews to develop an IoT Smart Node system for monitoring dumpsites. The block diagram model for a node of the IoT Dumpsite Monitor is shown in Fig. 3. The system is designed to be scalable so that it can have any number of IoT nodes for dumpsite monitoring. Each node system contains sensors for detecting smoke, flame, and gases (carbon dioxide, carbon monoxide, and nitrogen).

The system involves physical sensing of these parameters from dumpsites and transmission in real-time for online analytics. The detected parameters are used for decision-making for both frontend/backend activities. The other contents of the Node include the IoT controller, power supply, and IoT wireless gateway (Fig. 3). Each independent system located at a dumpsite transmits detected parameters to the central Server. The IoT controller manages the sensing and energy algorithms and implements the communication algorithm responsible for the transmission of the collected data streams into the Cloud server that runs the analytics.

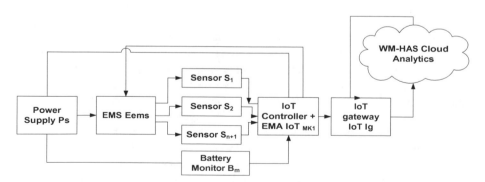

Fig. 3. IoT dumpsite monitor node.

The Energy Management System (EMS) in Fig. 3 is implemented with a bank of relays that energize the controller to activate (switch on) the sensors only at the sampling time. This then optimizes the power consumption of the whole system. Furthermore, the IoT gateway is active only when the system is ready to transmit data. The concept of full-duplex, dual-hop decode with SWIPT was implemented for the system. The power supply module P_s is DC, comprising the battery and solar panel. This is monitored via the IoT controller which pushes the output into the cloud. Figure 4 shows the state diagram.

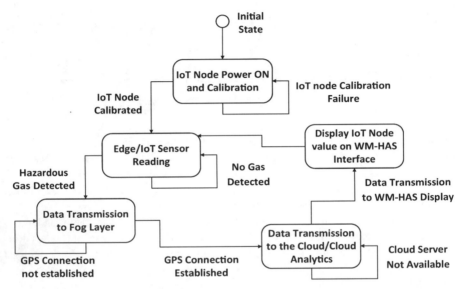

Fig. 4. IoT dumpsite node state diagram.

3.1 System Architecture

A key part of any IoT strategy design is figuring out where to process and analyze the data being generated, which analytics are best to use for maximum benefit, edge or cloud, or hybrid. This decision determines the system architecture to use for any solution. Edge analytics enables data analysis closer to the data source rather than having to send raw data to the cloud for analysis [6]. This reduces the huge costs associated with traditional big data analytics. Some of the other benefits of edge analytics are real-time analysis of data which helps with reliability, maintainability, and scalability because each device analyzes its data since the computational workload is distributed across devices [7].

For this work, a hybrid Edge-to-Cloud Analytics (ECA) architecture used is shown in Fig. 5. The dumpsites are deployed with IoT nodes $i, j, k, \ldots, z_{n+1}$ interacting with the IoT gateway. These are linked to wireless transmission gateway as Fog layer. Data analytics, storage, IoT dumpsite reputation management are handled at the Edge I/O data stream database. Device discovery management, mobility management, sampling mode management, sensing scope management, and energy management are handled at the cloud network layer (Edge APIs and Orchestrators) while the Edge controllers handle the sensor nodes, data preprocessing, and upward migration into the cloud.

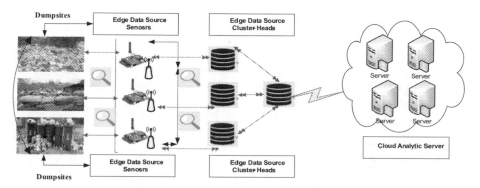

Fig. 5. IoT dumpsite monitor system architecture.

The Edge-to- Cloud analytics architecture used is an enhanced N-Tier architecture comprising:

i. Edge controllers (MKR 1000) for edge to Fog cluster-head (gateway) processing.
ii. Cloud APIs for full-duplex communication (i.e., edge to cloud and cloud to edge). Also, the Orchestrator (Logical) is deployed with the analytics server (pod cluster) for the management of data streams.
iii. Cloud I/O data stream database located in the pod cluster servers.

3.2 System Algorithm Design

In this Section, three software algorithms were derived based on the design requirements in Fig. 5. These are needed to successfully measure dumpsite environmental parameters and transfer the same to the cloud server. These include the IoT node characterization and setup algorithms I, sensor reading and calibration Algorithm II, and data transmission to remote server Algorithm III. From the software Algorithm I, IoT stream data is sent to the Server in Fig. 5 as a concatenated string made up of flame data, smoke data, gas data, and battery level data. In Algorithm II and III, address mapping, instantiations and the control loop decisions are synthesized in the Agile designs.

Algorithm I: IoT Node Characterization and Setup

    Input: IoT node physical addresses, PINs, and data type
    Output: mode classification of Testbed physical addresses, PINs
    Begin procedure ( )
    Data_type Flame_route_address = address _number;
    Data_type Smoke_route_address = address _number;
    Data_type Gas_route_address = address _number;
    Data_type GPRS_route_address = address _number;;
    Data_type battery_route_address = address _number
    Data_type Flame_data_label;
    Data_type Smoke_data_label;
    Data_type gas_data_label;
    Data_type battery_data_label;
    While (Crypt_round = 1) **do**
           void setup ( )
           { gprsSerial.begin(data_baudrate);
             pinMode(Flame_route_address, state_mode);
             pinMode(Smoke_route_address, state_mode);
             pinMode(Gas_route_address, state_mode);
             pinMode(GPRS_route_address state_mode);
             pinMode(battery_route_address, state_mode);
        }
           Until round = Ran ( );
    End
    Return *Input*

Algorithm II: Sensor reading and Calibration

    Input: Sensor Physical address
    Output: sensor real data value
    Begin procedure ( )
    For (sensor_address=0; sensor_address<4; sensor_address++)
      {Data_type sensor_value = analogRead(sensor_address);
       Data_type   sensor_real_value = (sensor_value *maximum ADC voltage)/adc_resolution;
         sensor real data value = map(sensor_value, R1, R2, M1, M2);
    While (Crypt_round = 1) **do**
           void setup ( )
           M1 is the minimum rated value the sensor can read in part per million(ppm)
           // M2 is the maximum rated value the sensor can read in part per million(ppm)
           // R1 is the actual reading of the sensor in the absence of test signal)
           // R2 is the actual reading of the sensor when subjected to the maximum concentration of the //test signal)
         }
           Until round = Ran ( );
    Endif
    Return *Input*

Algorithm III: Data Transmission to Remote Server

  Input: AT command of GPRS modem, APN, and API address of the remote server ( )

  Output: concatenated data comprising flame, smoke, gas, and battery levels ()

  Begin procedure ( )

  gprsSerial.println("set of AT_Commands for GPRS configuration");

  gprsSerial.println("AT+CSTT=\"APN_address of GPRS modem\"");

  gprsSerial.println("AT+CIPSTART=\"TCP\",\" APN_address of remote server\",\"port_number of the server\"");

  String str="GET https://api.thingspeak.com/update?api_key=API_addres_of_the_server&field1=" + String(flame_level) +"&field2="+String(smoke_level) +"&field3="+String(gas_level) +"&field4="+String(battery_level);

  Serial.println(str);

  gprsSerial.println(str);

  While (Crypt_round = 1) **do**

    void setup ( )

      Until round = Ran (str);

  Endif

  Return *Input*

3.3 Mathematical Formulations

In this section, the mathematical representation of the GPRS transmitted datastreams into the hybrid analytics cloud is described.

Consider the string of data, S_d transmitted to the online server O_s from the IoT node. The transmitted data Tx_d is a function of Flame level F_m, Smoke level S_k, Gas level G_s, and Battery level B_t. So mathematically,

$$S_d = F(F_m, S_k, G_s, B_t,) \tag{1}$$

Let $\oplus$ be the factor that concatenates the four variables. It follows then that

$$S_d = F_m \oplus S_k \oplus G_s \oplus B_t \tag{2}$$

But flame, smoke, gas, and battery levels are measurable quantities.

If F_{mo} is the analog output of the flame sensor (in volts), and the resolution of the analog to digital converter (ADC) interfaced to the IoT controller is V_{res}, then the digital equivalent, F_{md} of the flame sensor output is given by Eq. (3)

$$F_{md} = \frac{F_{mo}}{V_{res}} * V_{cc} \tag{3}$$

Where V_{cc} is the maximum voltage used in powering the ADC, [22].
Similarly

$$S_{kd} = \frac{S_{ko}}{V_{res}} * V_{cc} \tag{4}$$

$$G_{sd} = \frac{G_{so}}{V_{res}} * V_{cc} \tag{5}$$

$$B_{td} = \frac{B_{to}}{V_{res}} * V_{cc} \tag{6}$$

Where S_{kd} *and* S_{Ko} are digital equivalents and analog equivalents of the smoke sensor's output, respectively.

Also G_{sd} *and* G_{so} are digital equivalents and analog equivalents of the gas sensor's output respectively, just as B_{td} *and* B_{to} are digital equivalents and analog equivalents of the battery sensor's output, respectively.

F_{md}, S_{kd}, G_{sd} B_{td} are digital values in binary format.

Let *str* be a function that converts binary data to string equivalent. It follows then that.

$$F_m = str(F_{md}) \tag{7}$$

$$S_k = str(S_{kd}) \tag{8}$$

$$G_s = str(G_{sd}) \tag{9}$$

$$B_t = str(B_{td}) \tag{10}$$

By combining Eqs. 1 to 10, this gives the mathematical representation for IoT GPRS data transmission from IoT node (Figs. 5).

$$S_d = str(F_{md}) \oplus str(S_{kd}) \oplus str(G_{sd}) \oplus str(B_{td}) \tag{11}$$

4   System Simulation and Evaluation

The system was designed and simulated with Proteus in Fig. 6 and Fig. 7. Equation (11) was used to assemble the production setup. The materials utilized for the design include MKR 1000 Core Controller, Lithium-Ion Battery (5300 mA), Gas sensors (MQ-7 and MQ-2), Flame Detectors, transceiver, Lion Battery Charger, 100 W–12 V solar panel, API Analytics (ThingSpeak). C++ Domain-Specific Scripts (DSS) was employed for coordinating node to core deployments as well as the API interactions. The work used IoT datasheet specifications for the composite edge design. The DSS supported instance-based parameter passing to MKR-1000 core. This allowed for fine-grained customization for IoT module decoupling from the cloud. Hence, with any API script, the nodes can be activated for deployment. The PoC layout including edge to cloud orchestration activities were captured in the complete implementation. Although, EC gives lower compute-storage resources at the edge, it hardly affects the system as a single IoT device only serves a small geographic area. These constraints have been previously discussed in [23–31] which presented an improved orchestration platform for edge to cloud analytics in Smart City waste management.

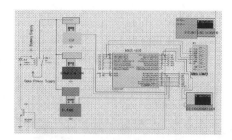

Fig. 6. Dumpsite IoT monitor node.

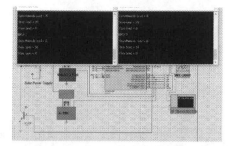

Fig. 7. Dumpsite monitor simulation.

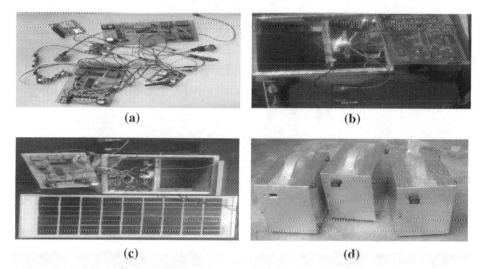

Fig. 8. a. IoT Edge Dumpsite Monitor circuit. b. Dumpsite Monitor with battery. c. Dumpsite Monitor with Solar panel. d. Dumpsite monitor prototypes.

Figure 8 (a–d) shows the prototype construction for the testbed used for moving data streams from the dumpsite into the cloud.

For the simulation testbed (Fig. 9), the following were utilized namely: OS Platform/NetC, Cloud Power-Edge C6420, Cisco WS-C3650-24TS-L 24 Port Switch, Microsoft Server 2019 for Cloud cores.

5   Results and Discussions

The work done in [27, 28] was employed for analysis of WM-HAS results. Figure 10 shows the generated API key by the server (Thingspeak). This API key is the optimized service used to push data to the server from the IoT sensor nodes. Also, high-level security end-to-end encryption was explored. At the cloud, the various sensed IoT parameters were streamed using the Opensource ThingSpeak IoT analytics platform. The prototype PoC fully supports the WM-HAS API service during the testing.

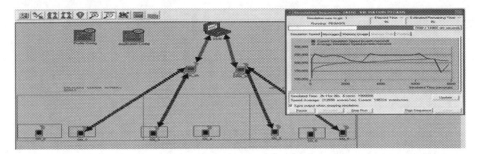

Fig. 9. Simulation compilation.

Fig. 10. API key generated by the Server (ThingSpeak server).

The API key (CN8J0L0CV9PESFNI) generated by the server as shown in Fig. 10 is embedded in the communication algorithm resident in MKR 1000 controller chip interfaced with the GPRS gateway. This enables the sensor node to transmit real-time data to the server. The server also generates an automatic timestamp for every data it receives. The screen captures from Thinkspeak for detected parameters are shown in Fig. 11(a–d). Figure 11a shows the received status of the IoT node battery resident at dumpsite A. It was transmitted via the GPRS gateway and received at the ThingSpeak server. From Fig. 11a, it is seen that a total of 18 data values were transmitted at an interval of about 5 min for 90 min. The integrity of the developed IoT sensor node was very good because no data was lost during the time under consideration, and the exact values of the battery voltage (13 V) as measured with a multimeter, was transmitted.

Figures 11b–11d show the sensors' data received from dumpsite A at an interval of 5 min for 90 min. The sensors were subjected to real-time variations of specific physical quantities they are supposed to measure. For example, the gas level sensor was tested by varying the concentration of a cooking gas within the dumpsite; Physical smoke was initiated by burning some waste materials at the dumpsite, while the flame sensor was tested by bringing an ignited gas lighter in the close range of the sensor. It was observed that the gas level sensor gave the highest reading when the nob of the cooking gas was fully opened. The smoke level sensor gave its highest reading when the smoke coming out of waste materials being burnt was thickest. The sensor reading declined as the waste materials went into real flame; the sharp rise observed in Fig. 10d is an exceptional data. The flame sensor showed a sharp rise in its reading when it was brought close to a physical

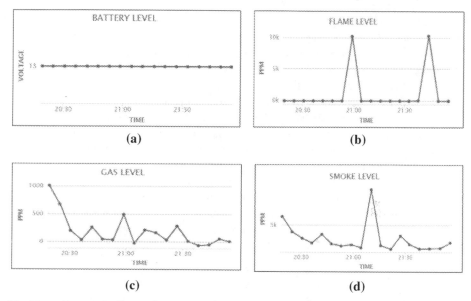

Fig. 11. a. Battery level sample at Dumpsite A. b. Flame sample level at Dumpsite A. c. Gas sample level at Dumpsite A. d. Flame sample level at Dumpsite A.

flame, otherwise, it showed a steady reading as shown in Fig. 11b. The Edge-to-Cloud Analytics used for the design and implementation of the IoT Dumpsite monitor of WM-HAS provided task computational off-loading from IoT enabled dumpsites into Fog and Cloud layers, respectively. This is because most tasks may not be feasible to carry out at the edge layer. The architecture model used, reduced latency when pushing out notifications-alerts to IoT sinks, especially in real-time usage contexts. The test results showed the tasks of sensing and reporting hazardous solutions at dumpsites in real-time. The solution addressed interoperability at Edge-sensor installations covering different locations, data sharing between multiple dumpsites by uses of edge computing systems with unified interfaces, open API standards, and standardized protocols. Furthermore, energy scheduling algorithms for IoT devices minimized energy consumption.

6   Conclusion

An Edge-to-Cloud Analytics architecture model for Waste Management and Hazard Alert system is developed in this paper for prompt management of waste dumpsites. The system utilizes IoT smart nodes to monitor dumpsites and generate alerts on the detection of hazardous gas emissions, smoke, and fire. The scalable Edge-to-Cloud Analytics architectural model produces efficient data stream uploading from the IoT sensor nodes into the cloud domain with an MKR-1000 Edge Controller used to achieve edge-to-fog gateway processing. Clearly, the IoT edge devices offered, lower compute-storage resources at the edge. Efficient data transmission to remote servers used SWIPT technique. The role of the ECA engine and its architecture was validated using a scenario-based simulation. A proof of concept was demonstrated by building three IoT dumpsite nodes that were used for testing. The Testbed deployment with visualization patterns observed on Open Source ThingSpeak Cloud-native platform confirmed very good performance and results when compared with measured values. The key contributions to knowledge include the use of Edge-to-Cloud analytics for dumpsite monitoring and prompt evacuation, the introduction of SWIPT to conserve energy for optimized valued-insights and the development of an architectural model that allows lower computer-storage resources at the edge. This is very good since a single IoT device only serves a small geographic area. Furthermore, unlike existing systems, the proposed system uses analytics for dumpsite monitoring and evacuation. The proposed system in a production scenario can facilitate and coordinate waste evacuation from both legal and illegal dumpsites. The design considered cost overhead requirements for distributed computer power and communication resources using a lightweight API service. Future work will study API containerization for light deployments using Docker Swarm and Kubernetes. Also, the service throughput and latency profiles of the IoT dumpsite monitors will be investigated to test performance at full deployments. Since most dumpsites are remarkably close to end-users, Edge (IoT) analytics is recommended for a sustainable model to waste management in Nigeria.

Acknowledgment. The authors wish to acknowledge and appreciate the Tertiary Education Trust Fund (TETFUND), Nigeria for funding the Waste Management and Hazard Alert System in 2019 and the Federal University of Technology Owerri management for providing a conducive environment for the research.

Conflicts of Interest. The IoT researchers assert no conflict of interest. The funding sponsors are not involved with any role in the conceptualization, study design, data collection, data analysis, manuscript writing, and results in publication.

References

1. Onu, B., Price, T., Surendran, S.S., Ebie, S.: Solid waste management: a critique of Nigeria's waste management policy. Int. J. Knowl. Cult. Change Manag. (12) (2012)
2. Bose, B.K.: Global warming: energy, environmental pollution, and the impact of power electronics. IEEE Ind. Electron. Mag. **4**(1), 6–17 (2010)
3. Thompson, A.F., Afolayan, A.H., Ibidunmoye, E.O.: Application of geographic information system to solid waste management. In: 2013 Pan African International Conference on Information Science, Computing & Telecommunications (PACT), Lusaka, pp. 206–211 (2013)
4. Ike, C.C., Ezeibe, C.C., Anijiofor, S.C., Daud, N.N.: Solid waste management in Nigeria: problems, prospects, and policies. J. Solid Waste Tech. Manag. **44**(2), 163–172 (2018)
5. Ogundokun, R.O., Awotunde, J.B., Misra, S., Abikoye, O.C., Folarin, O.: Application of machine learning for Ransomware detection in IoT devices. In: Misra, S., Kumar Tyagi, A. (eds.) Artificial Intelligence for Cyber Security: Methods, Issues and Possible Horizons or Opportunities. SCI, vol. 972, pp. 393–420. Springer, Cham (2021). https://doi.org/10.1007/978-3-030-72236-4_16
6. Hernandez, J., Daza, K., Florez, H., Misra, S.: Dynamic interface and access model by dead token for IoT systems. In: Florez, H., Leon, M., Diaz-Nafria, J.M., Belli, S. (eds.) ICAI 2019. CCIS, vol. 1051, pp. 485–498. Springer, Cham (2019). https://doi.org/10.1007/978-3-030-32475-9_35

7. What is Edge Analytics, Sisense (2020). https://www.sisense.com/glossary/edge-analytics/#lbf-680. Accessed 8 Mar 2020

8. Choi, K.W., et al.: Simultaneous wireless information and power transfer (SWIPT) for Internet of Things: novel receiver design and experimental validation. IEEE Internet of Things J. **7**(4), 2996–3012 (2020)

9. Erçin, M., Köse, M., Atasoy, A.: Route optimization for waste collection process through IoT supported waste management system, Technical report, January 2021

10. Özmen, G., Özsoy, A.: Waste management optimization by using IoT. Project Research Report

11. Mehmood, Y., Ahmad, F., Yaqoob, I., Adnane, A., Imran, M., Guizani, S.: Internet-of-Things-based smart cities: recent advances and challenges. IEEE Commun. Mag. **55**(9), 16–24 (2017)

12. Patil, S., Mohite, S.: IoT based smart waste management system for smart city. Int. J. Adv. Res. Comput. Sci. Softw. Eng. **7**(4), 1–4 (2017). ISSN 2277 128X

13. Adeola, A.M., Othman, M.: An overview of ICT waste management: suggestions of best practices from developed countries to developing nations (Nigeria). In: 7th International Conference on Networked Computing, Gyeongsangbuk-do, pp. 109–115 (2011)

14. Udoakah, Y.N., Akpan, U.S.: A sustainable approach to municipal solid waste management in southern Nigeria. In: IEEE Global Humanitarian Technology Conference (GHTC), San Jose, CA, pp. 321–325 (2013)

15. Guihong, B., Hua, W., Qiang, L., Yan, H.: Agent-based model for solid waste management and policy simulating analysis. In: 27th Chinese Control Conference on Kunming, pp. 768–773 (2008). https://doi.org/10.1109/CHICC.2008.4605156

16. Bhattacharya, B.K., Das, S.: A holistic approach for integrated solid waste management system of Kolkata municipality corporation area. In: IEEE 18th International Conference on Industrial Engineering and Engineering Management, Changchun, pp. 1999–2003 (2011)

17. Zeeshan, S., Shahid, Z., Khan, S., Shaikh, F.A.: Solid waste management in Korangi District of Karachi using GPS and GIS: a case study. In: 7th International Conference on Computer and Communication Engineering (ICCCE), Kuala Lumpur, pp. 1–4 (2018)

18. Vasagade, T.S., Tamboli, S.S., Shinde, A.D.: Dynamic solid waste collection and management system based on sensors, elevator and GSM. In: 2017 International Conference on Inventive Communication and Computational Technologies (ICICCT), Coimbatore, pp. 263–267 (2017)

19. Rumyantseva, N.V., Doronin, A.S., Primak, E.A.: Improvement of the system of selective collection of household waste in Latvia. In: 2018 IEEE International Conference on Management of Municipal Waste as an Important Factor of Sustainable Urban Development (WASTE), St. Petersburg, pp. 14–16 (2018)

20. Labib, S.M.: Volunteer GIS (VGIS) based waste management: a conceptual design and use of web 2.0 for smart waste management in Dhaka City. In: Third International Conference on Research in Computational Intelligence and Communication Networks (ICRCICN), Kolkata, pp. 137–141 (2017)

21. Ravi, S., Jawahar, T.: Smart city solid waste management leveraging semantic based collaboration. In: 2017 International Conference on Computational Intelligence in Data Science, Chennai, pp. 1–4 (2017)

22. Le Bin, T.W., Rondeau, J.H., Reed, C.: Analog-to-digital converters. IEEE Signal Process. Mag. **22**(6), 69–77 (2005). https://doi.org/10.1109/MSP.2005.1550190

23. Okafor, K.C.: Dynamic reliability modelling of cyber-physical edge computing network. Int. J. Comput. Appl. (IJCA) **42**, 1–10 (2019). SI-Sustainable Computing for Intelligent Systems

24. Okafor, K.C., Ononiwu, G.C., Goundar, S., Chijindu, V.C., Udeze, C.C.: Towards complex dynamic fog network orchestration using embedded neural switch. Int. J. Comput. Appl. (IJCA) **40**(4), 1–18 (2018). SI-Internet of Everything, Networks, Application, and Computing Systems

25. Okafor, K.C., Achumba, I., Chukwudebe, G., Ononiwu, G.: Leveraging fog computing for scalable IoT datacenter using spine-leaf network topology. J. Electr. Comput. Eng. **2017**, 1–11 (2017). https://doi.org/10.1155/2017/2363240

26. Atayero, A.A., Popoola, S.I., Williams, R., Badejo, J.A., Misra, S.: Smart city waste management system using Internet of Things and cloud computing. In: Abraham, A., Siarry, P., Ma, K., Kaklauskas, A. (eds.) ISDA 2019. AISC, vol. 1181, pp. 601–611. Springer, Cham (2021). https://doi.org/10.1007/978-3-030-49342-4_58

27. Misra, S.: A step by step guide for choosing project topics and writing research papers in ICT related disciplines. In: Misra, S., Muhammad-Bello, B. (eds.) Information and Communication Technology and Applications, ICTA 2020, pp. 727–744. Springer, Cham (2021). https://doi.org/10.1007/978-3-030-69143-1_55

28. Odun-Ayo, I., Geteloma, V., Misra, S., Ahuja, R., Damasevicius, R.: Systematic mapping study of utility-driven platforms for clouds. In: Singh, P.K., Panigrahi, B.K., Suryadevara, N.K., Sharma, S.K., Singh, A.P. (eds.) Proceedings of ICETIT 2019. LNEE, vol. 605, pp. 762–774. Springer, Cham (2020). https://doi.org/10.1007/978-3-030-30577-2_68

29. Samuel, V., Misra, S., Nicholas, O.: Internet of Things (IoTs) and its application to road navigation and usage problem. In: IEEE Asia-Pacific World Congress on Computer Science and Engineering, pp. 1–5 (2014)

30. Abiodun, M.K., et al.: Cloud and big data: a mutual benefit for organization development. In: Journal of Physics: Conference Series, vol. 1767, no. 1, p. 012020. IOP Publishing (2021)

31. Olowu, M., Yinka-Banjo, C., Misra, S., Florez, H.: A secured private-cloud computing system. In: Florez, H., Leon, M., Diaz-Nafria, J.M., Belli, S. (eds.) ICAI 2019. CCIS, vol. 1051, pp. 373–384. Springer, Cham (2019). https://doi.org/10.1007/978-3-030-32475-9_27

Predicting Student Academic Performance Using Machine Learning

Opeyemi Ojajuni[1], Foluso Ayeni[2]([✉]), Olagunju Akodu[3], Femi Ekanoye[4],
Samson Adewole[4], Timothy Ayo[4], Sanjay Misra[5], and Victor Mbarika[6]

[1] Department of Science and Mathematics Education, Southern University and A&M College,
Baton Rouge, USA
Opeyemi_ojajuni_00@subr.edu
[2] Department of Information Systems and Quantitative Analysis, University of Nebraska,
Omaha, USA
fayeni@unomaha.edu
[3] Department of Electrical and Electronics Engineering, Southern University and A&M
College, Baton Rouge, USA
olagunju_akodu_00@subr.edu
[4] Global Technology Management and Policy Research Group, Southern University and A&M
College, Baton Rouge, USA
femi_ekanoye@subr.edu, oluwadamilaresam@gmail.com,
timothyayo99@gmail.com
[5] Department of Information and Communication Engineering, Covenant University,
Ota, Nigeria
sanjay.misra@covenantuniversity.edu.ng
[6] Department of Management Information Systems, East Carolina University, Greenville, USA
mbarikav20@ecu.edu

Abstract The introduction of the Internet of Things (IoT), Artificial Intelligence
(AI), Machine Learning (ML), Deep Learning (DL), and Big Data have paved the
way for research focused on improving the student learning experience and help
to address challenges faced by the education system. Machine Learning technology analyzes data to recognize patterns and use them to make predictions. This
paper introduces a ML model that classify and predict student academic success by utilizing supervised ML algorithms like Random Forest, Support Vector
Machines, Gradient boosting, Decision Tree, Logistic Regression, Regression,
Extreme Gradient Boosting (XGBoost), and Deep Learning. This paper aims to
predict student's academic success based on historical data and identify the key
factors that affect student academic success. Thus, the proposed approach offers
a solution to predict student academic performance efficiently and accurately by
comparing several ML models to the Deep Learning model. Results show that the
Extreme Gradient Boosting (XGBoost) can predict student academic performance
with an accuracy of 97.12%. Furthermore, results showed significant social and
demographic features that affect student academic success. This study concludes
that applying Machine Learning technology in the classroom will help educators
identify gaps in student learning and enable early detection of underperforming
students, thus empowering educators with informed decision-making.

© Springer Nature Switzerland AG 2021
O. Gervasi et al. (Eds.): ICCSA 2021, LNCS 12957, pp. 481–491, 2021.
https://doi.org/10.1007/978-3-030-87013-3_36

Keywords: Machine learning · Deep learning · Student academic performance · Educational data mining · Data analytics · Convolutional Neutral Networks (CNN)

1 Introduction

Educational data mining (EDM) applies data mining, machine learning, and deep learning to data generated in an academic setting to improve student learning experiences [1, 2, 3]. The interaction of students with learning platforms and materials creates large amounts of data [4, 5]. Analyzing this data provides insight into the student learning process and student achievement. Further analysis can identify academic, demographic, and social factors affecting student academic success. Student academic success is measured by assessing student performance across academic subjects. Teachers measure student academic performance from different approaches, ranging from students' final grades, Grade Point Average (GPA), and Standardized Tests. According to reports from the United States of America Department of Education and National Assessment of Educational Progress (NAEP), the education system suffers from several challenges like student academic underachievement, increased university dropout rates, graduation delays, and inadequate student workforce readiness. Over the years, student academic success has continued to decline, even more prevalent amongst minority students [6, 7, 8]. Education technology advancements such as Artificial Intelligence (AI), Virtual Reality (VR), 3D printing, smart multimedia devices, Internet of Things (IoT), and Machine Learning are beginning to improve the student learning process and management [9].

Machine Learning analyzes data to recognize patterns and use those patterns to make predictions. Applying ML in the classroom will enable educators to identify critical factors affecting student's success. Furthermore, ML will allow educators to identify underperforming students, thus empowering educators with informed decision-making. Several tools such as R Software, Python Scikit-learn, TensorFlow are currently used in ML technology. A wide range of ML algorithms is also available for predicting student academic performance. These algorithms include Random Forest, Support Vector Machines (SVM), AdaBoost, Decision Tree, Naive Bayes, and K-nearest Neighbors.

In this research work, we aim to use historical education data on student academic performance collected from the UC Irvine Machine Learning Repository to identify the key factors that affect student academic achievement. Furthermore, the research intends to predict future student academic success by recognizing patterns in the historical dataset and using the patterns to make predictions. The research objectives addressed in this research work are listed below:

1. What are the factors that have significant effect on students' academic success?
2. How can these factors predict student academic performance using machine learning?

The research paper is organized under the following subheading: Related research work, methods and implementation, results, and conclusion.

2   Related Research Work

Learning management systems have empowered education institutions with interactive learning tools such as game-based, simulation applications, virtual reality, and e-learning systems. These platforms have allowed researchers to collect and analyze student data [2, 5]. The authors [9] applied the Decision Tree, Neural Network, and Support Vector Machine (SVM) classification ML algorithm to predict academic performance from student internet usage behaviors. Their results showed that student internet usage behaviors effectively predict academic performance with an accuracy of 71%–76%; however, the authors only considered accuracy as the performance metric. In [10] work, the authors proposed a system that uses ML algorithms trained to predict students' academic performance by classifying them into bad or good. The model was trained on data gathered from a university source and implemented using the K-nearest neighbor and Decision tree classifier. The result showed that the Decision tree classifier has 94.44% accuracy, but the author considered only accuracy as its performance metrics.

Similarly, the authors [2] proposed a classification ML model using SVM and Logistic regression classifiers to predict students' academic performance. The model extracted features from the preprocessed dataset obtained from an online educational platform to classify student academic performance as bad, average, or good. The result showed that the SVM produced an accuracy of 79%, which was higher than the logistic regression. The authors considered accuracy, recall, precision, and f1-score using confusion box metrics to evaluate the system's performance. The authors [1] used Naïve Bayes, Random Forest classifier, and Ensemble learners classification ML model to predict student academic performance using a dataset comprising 887 instances of 19 attributes of first-year students. The Random Forest classifier outperformed other models with an accuracy of 93%. Evaluation metrics of recall, precision, and f1-score using confusion box metrics was employed in evaluating the model performance. Research on ML in education is still in its preliminary stages, there are still many challenges such as prediction accuracy, overfitting, underfitting, deployment of the model that need attention. Thus, our proposed approach offers an efficient and accurate student academic performance by comparing several ML models to deep learning models. Generally, deep learning models have better accuracy because they extract features from the dataset in an incremental manner. ML algorithms are applied to the dataset to analyze and identify features that significantly impacted student academic performance. Finally, leveraging these features, several ML models are trained to classify and predict student academic performance category, and we also compared the model's performance based on accuracy score and cross-validation score.

3   Material and Methods

3.1   Tools

The experiments were conducted on a computer running MacOS Big Sur operating system with the specification of 2.3 GHz Dual-Core Intel Core i5 with 8 Gigabytes memory. Python programming language was used along with Scikit-learn, and TensorFlow ML libraries to implement algorithms, build ML model, and obtain statistical results [11, 12].

3.2 Dataset

The dataset used in this study was from the UC Irvine Machine Learning repository
[13]. The dataset consists of 1044 student's academic performance in two high schools.
The data attributes include demographic, social, and academic related features. Table 1
shows the summary of our dataset attributes.

Table 1. Dataset [13] attributes

Feature category	Name of the attributes	Description	Attribute type
Demographical features	School	Student's school	Categorical
	Sex	Student's sex	Categorical
	Age	Student's age	Numeric
	Address	Student's home address type	Categorical
	Famsize	Family size	Categorical
	Pstatus	Parent's cohabitation status	Categorical
	Medu	Mother's education	Numeric
	Fedu	Fedu - father's education	Numeric
	Mjob	Mother's job	Categorical
	Fjob	Father's job	Categorical
	Reason	Reason to choose this school	Categorical
	Guardian	Guardian - student's guardian	Categorical
Social features	Internet	Internet access at home	Categorical
	Romantic	With a romantic relationship	Categorical
	Famrel	Quality of family relationships	Numeric
	Freetime	Free time after school	Numeric
	Goout	Going out with friends	Numeric
	Dalc	Workday alcohol consumption	Numeric
	Walc	Weekend alcohol consumption	Numeric

(*continued*)

Table 1. (*continued*)

Feature category	Name of the attributes	Description	Attribute type
	Health	Current health status	Numeric
Academic related features	Absences	Number of school absences	Numeric
	Traveltime	Home to school travel time	Numeric
	Studytime	Weekly study time	Numeric
	Failures	Number of past class failures	Numeric
	Schoolsup	Extra educational support	Categorical
	Famsup	Family educational support	Categorical
	Paid	Number of past class failures	Numeric
	Activities	Extra-curricular activities	Categorical
	Nursery	Attended nursery school	Categorical
	Higher	Wants to take higher education	Categorical
	Final grade	Final grade	Numeric

3.3 Data Preprocessing and Feature Engineering

Data preprocessing is done on the dataset to check for null values, duplicates, and invalid values. Fortunately, our dataset is clean and ready for encoding. The final grade was converted into multiclass categories- "excellent, good, satisfactory, poor, and failure" under the following conditions:

- Excellent – final grade score is between 45–60
- Good– final grade score is between 36–44
- Satisfactory– final grade score is between 24–35
- Poor – final grade score is between 20–23
- Failure – final grade score is between 0–23

ML models require all input and output data to be attributed to numeric values. Any data that is not numeric must be encoded to numeric values before fitting it into a ML model. Several attributes are non-numeric and categorical in our dataset, as seen in Table 1. This study employs the One-Hot-encoding in Python's Scikit-Learn to encode and normalize non-numeric and categorical data attribute type [11]. Feature engineering techniques help in extracting important features from the dataset.

3.4 Machine Learning Classification Model

Solving problems with ML is grouped into supervised and unsupervised learning. Unsupervised ML works with unstructured data, while supervised ML works with a structured dataset where the input variables are mapped with the output variables. Supervised ML problems are grouped into regression and classification problems [14]. Regression problems involve predicting a continuous, discrete value, for example, predicting student final grade score. ML classification refers to the process of predicting a category from input data points. The category output can be binary classification - "fail" or "pass" or multiclass classification- "excellent, good, satisfactory, poor, and failure". ML classification is a supervised ML where input data is labeled and mapped with the output data; the ML model lis trained to predict the output from input. Implementing a ML classifier requires importing the necessary ML module package, then loading the dataset [14]. Data preprocessing and cleaning are done on the dataset to check for null values, duplicates, invalid values and encode non-numeric and category data attribute types.

After successful data preprocessing, the feature engineering technique explores the dataset to understand the correlation relationship between variables to identify features that significantly impact the output variable. This enabled us to improve the model's accuracy by removing attributes that significantly impact the output variable (final student grade) but not an essential feature in predicting student academic performance. The refined dataset is then split into training & testing sets. The training dataset trains the model, and the testing dataset measures the model's performance based on accuracy and cross-validation. Figure 1 shows this study ML model flowchart. This study built and trained the following ML classification algorithms: Random Forest, Support Vector Machine classifier, Stochastic Gradient Descent, Decision Tree, Adaptive Boosting, Logistic Regression, and Deep Learning. Deep learning is a technique that uses neural network concepts to build and train ML models. Deep learning consists of the input layer (receives the input data), hidden layer (incrementally extracts important features), and the output layer [15]. Deep learning consisting of a Convolutional Neural Network (CNN) model with four hidden layers is suitable for our research objectives.

3.5   Machine Learning Model Performance Evaluation

ML uses the testing dataset to measure the performance of the model. Accuracy, cross-validation, precision, recall, F1-score, confusion matrix, log loss, Receiver Operating Characteristic (ROC), and Area Under Curve (AUC) are some of the performance metrics used to evaluate ML classification model [16]. This research employs accuracy and cross-validation as performance metrics to evaluate the ML classification models. The CNN model's performance was evaluated using a confusion matrix to calculate the model's accuracy, precision, and sensitivity. Accuracy is the total number of correct predictions out of the total number of predictions [7]. Cross-validation assesses how effective the model will work on a new dataset. The confusion matrix is an error matrix that virtualizes ML model performance. The confusion matrix is used to calculate the accuracy, precision, and sensitivity of the model. Precision is the ratio of correctly predicted values to total predicted values. Sensitivity evaluates the proportion of correct prediction the model gets right [7].

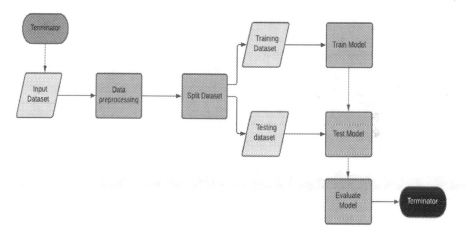

Fig. 1. ML model flowchart

4   Implementation and Result

The "plot_importance" function in Scikit-learn library help in plotting the important features that affect student final grade. In predicting student academic performances, the order of importance of features and its score can be seen in Fig. 2. The number of school absences has the highest importance score. This indicates that students who miss school are more likely to have poor academic performance. Current health status, going out with friends, free time after school, quality of family relationships are major social features that affect student academic performance. Mother's job, father's job, Parent's cohabitation status, student's home address type, and reason to choose this school are the most minor features that affect student academic performance.

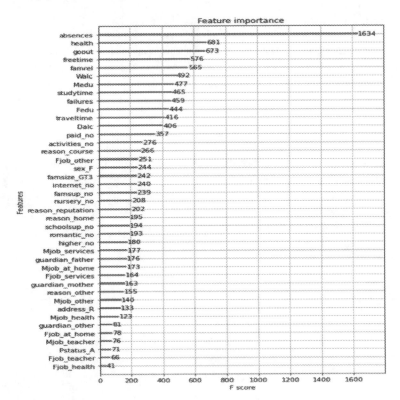

Fig. 2. Important features and its score

To get an accurate evaluation of our model, the dataset containing 1044 students is split into train and test dataset in 70% to 30% ratio using the 'train_test_split' function in sci-kit learn. After building and training the ML model, the cross-validation function 'cross_val_score' helped compute the model's average accuracy on the test dataset. The cross-validation function divides the test dataset into smaller subsets. The subsets are then fit into the model and compute the accuracy score five times with different subsets each time [17]. After applying various classification models to the dataset, different accuracy and cross-validation score were obtained for each model. Table 2 shows the accuracy and cross-validation scores for each model. The Deep Learning model gave an accuracy of 72.74%, precision of 30.31%, and sensitivity of 31.38% . Figure 3 shows the confusion matrix used in calculating the performance matrix. The Extreme Gradient Boosting (XGBoost) model outperforms other models in predicting student academic performance. XGBoost Model gave 97.12% accuracy and 35.67% cross-validation. Since the XGBoost model gave the best accuracy, this indicates that the XGBoost ML model is the most suitable ML model considering the nature of our dataset and research objectives.

Table 2. Comparison of Machine Learning models

ML classifier	Accuracy (%)	Cross validation (%)
Decision Tree Model	47.95	30.89
Random Forest Model	92.60	35.66
Support Vector Classifier Model	42.88	34.39
Logistic Regression Model	40.96	36.62
Ada Boost Model	35.75	32.48
Stochastic Gradient Descent	33.69	33.121
XGBoost Model	97.12	35.67
Deep Learning (CNN)	72.22	Precision – 30.31 Sensitivity = 31.38

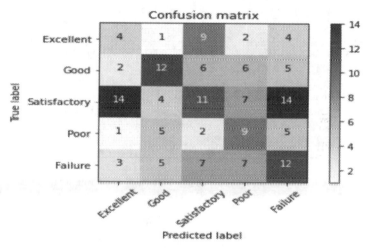

Fig. 3. Deep Learning confusion matrix

5 Conclusion and Future Work

This study has strengthened and explored how Machine learning can empower educators with informed decision-making. Predicting student academic performance or success is an essential concept in tackling the student academic performance crisis. This study used several ML classification models to predict student academic performance. Results showed a range of accuracy from 33% to 98% and a range of cross-validation from 30% to 37%. The XGBoost Model is the most suitable ML model by achieving 97.12% accuracy and 35.67% cross-validation. Furthermore, results showed that the number of school absences, current health status, going out with friends, free time after school, quality of family relationships is significant features that affect student academic performance. This study concludes that this research work can help educators identify gaps in student learning and enable early detection of underachieving students, thus empowering educators with informed decision-making, ultimately improving student academic success and learning process.

References

1. Jayaprakash, S., Krishnan, S., Jaiganesh, V.: Predicting students academic performance using an improved random forest classifier. In: 2020 International Conference on Emerging Smart Computing and Informatics (ESCI), Pune, India, pp. 238–243, March 2020. https://doi.org/10.1109/ESCI48226.2020.9167547
2. Bhutto, E.S., Siddiqui, I.F., Arain, Q.A., Anwar, M.: Predicting students' academic performance through supervised machine learning. In: 2020 International Conference on Information Science and Communication Technology (ICISCT), Karachi, Pakistan, pp. 1–6, February 2020. https://doi.org/10.1109/ICISCT49550.2020.9080033
3. Jacob, J., Jha, K., Kotak, P., Puthran, S.: Educational data mining techniques and their applications. In: 2015 International Conference on Green Computing and Internet of Things (ICGCIoT), pp. 1344–1348, October 2015. https://doi.org/10.1109/ICGCIoT.2015.7380675
4. Al Mayahi, K., Al-Bahri, M.: Machine learning based predicting student academic success. In: 2020 12th International Congress on Ultra Modern Telecommunications and Control Systems and Workshops (ICUMT), Brno, Czech Republic, pp. 264–268, October 2020. https://doi.org/10.1109/ICUMT51630.2020.9222435
5. Olaperi, Y., Fernandez-Sanz, L., Medina, J., Misra, S.: Framework for academic advice through mobile applications (2016)
6. Statement from Secretary DeVos on 2019 NAEP Results. U.S. Department of Education. https://www.ed.gov/news/press-releases/statement-secretary-devos-2019-naep-results. Accessed 24 Feb 2021
7. Rimadana, M.R., Kusumawardani, S.S., Santosa, P.I., Erwianda, M.S.F.: Predicting student academic performance using machine learning and time management skill data. In: 2019 International Seminar on Research of Information Technology and Intelligent Systems (ISRITI), Yogyakarta, Indonesia, pp. 511–515, December 2019. https://doi.org/10.1109/ISRITI48646.2019.9034585
8. bin Mohd Nasir, M.A.H., bin Asmuni, M.H., Salleh, N., Misra, S.: A review of student attendance system using near-field communication (NFC) technology. In: Gervasi, O., et al. (eds.) ICCSA 2015. LNCS, vol. 9158, pp. 738–749. Springer, Cham (2015). https://doi.org/10.1007/978-3-319-21410-8_56
9. Xu, X., Wang, J., Peng, H., Wu, R.: Prediction of academic performance associated with internet usage behaviors using machine learning algorithms. Comput. Hum. Behav. **98**, 166–173 (2019). https://doi.org/10.1016/j.chb.2019.04.015
10. Hasan, H.M.R., Rabby, A.S.A., Islam, M.T., Hossain, S.A.: Machine learning algorithm for student's performance prediction. In: 2019 10th International Conference on Computing, Communication and Networking Technologies (ICCCNT), Kanpur, India, pp. 1–7, July 2019. https://doi.org/10.1109/ICCCNT45670.2019.8944629
11. Scikit-learn: machine learning in Python—scikit-learn 0.24.2 documentation. https://scikit-learn.org/stable/. Accessed 04 May 2021
12. TensorFlow. https://www.tensorflow.org/. Accessed 04 May 2021
13. UCI Machine Learning Repository. https://archive.ics.uci.edu/ml/index.php. Accessed 28 Feb 2021
14. Nurafifah, M.S., Abdul-Rahman, S., Mutalib, S., Hamid, N.H.A., Malik, A.M.A.: Review on predicting students' graduation time using machine learning algorithms. Int. J. Mod. Educ. Comput. Sci. **11**(7), 1 (2019). https://doi.org/10.5815/ijmecs.2019.07.01

15. Lye, C.-T., Ng, L.-N., Hassan, M.D., Goh, W.-W., Law, C.-Y., Ismail, N.: Predicting pre-university student's mathematics achievement. Procedia. Soc. Behav. Sci. **8**, 299–306 (2010). https://doi.org/10.1016/j.sbspro.2010.12.041
16. Vijayalakshmi, V., Venkatachalapathy, K.: Comparison of predicting student's performance using machine learning algorithms. Int. J. Intell. Syst. Appl. **11**(12), 34 (2019). https://doi.org/10.5815/ijisa.2019.12.04
17. 3.1. Cross-validation: evaluating estimator performance—scikit-learn 0.24.2 documentation. https://scikit-learn.org/stable/modules/cross_validation.html. Accessed 04 May 2021

A Comprehensive Review of Nature-Inspired Search Techniques Used in Estimating Optimal Configuration Size, Cost, and Reliability of a Mini-grid HRES: A Systemic Review

Samuel Ofori Frimpong(✉) [iD], Richard C. Millham[iD], and Israel Edem Agbehadji[iD]

ICT and Society Research Group, Department of Information Technology, Durban University of Technology, Durban, South Africa

Abstract. Nature-inspired algorithms use random exploration and exploitation tactics as a searching strategy to explore a search space. These two searching schemes are harmonized in nature-inspired search techniques to solve any optimization problem. Although several traditional approaches have been applied to the design of optimal HRES, there is still a challenge of finding a near-optimal approach to estimate the configuration size, cost, and reliability of mini-grid HRES. In this paper, we reviewed the state-of-the-art optimization approaches that have been applied in estimating the configuration size, cost, and reliability of mini-grid HRES. A desktop-based research method was adopted in which a total of 49 scholarly articles which tie well to the topic was selected for a thorough review. Various nature-inspired search methods proposed and/or applied in the last 5 years (2016–2021) by different researchers in solving the optimization problem of HRES were showcased in this paper. The review suggested that the optimal design of HRES in most cases seeks to minimize a cost function and maximizes the reliability of the system to meet the load requirement. Again, based on the diverse scenarios and increasing complexities of HRES, nature-inspired algorithms promise better near-optimal solutions than their competitors. Furthermore, the review suggested that nature-inspired search techniques have been applied extensively in HRES optimization. Moreover, several studies have also hybridized two or more algorithms to improve the searching strategies for better performance of HRES. These findings among others suggest opportunities for future research in the design of near-optimal HRES. The review holds salient implications for researchers and industry professionals. It elucidates the chances to design a reliable, cost-efficient, and effective mini-grid HRES yet have economic benefits to the users.

Keywords: Nature-inspired search method · Optimization technique · Hybrid renewable energy system · Algorithms · Mini-grid

1 Introduction

The use of renewable energy resources to produce useful energy supply such as electricity is receiving reasonable attention in the global energy economy as the world strives to

© Springer Nature Switzerland AG 2021
O. Gervasi et al. (Eds.): ICCSA 2021, LNCS 12957, pp. 492–507, 2021.
https://doi.org/10.1007/978-3-030-87013-3_37

achieve a net-zero greenhouse gas emission by the end of this century [1, 2]. Renewable energy sources namely, sun, wind, biomass, hydro, etc. abound in nature, and they have the potential of generating energy for industrial, commercial, and domestic consumption [3–6]. Energy derived from these sources are clean, so they have little or no environmental consequences unlike fossil fuel products [7]. Moreover, a renewable energy system accrues economic benefits if the system is optimally designed and configured on the backdrop of economic objectives [8, 9]. They can operate in isolated, or grid-connected mode making its adoption easier for rural settlement and dispersed or cluster communities far-reaching with the grid [10]. These benefits of a renewable energy system do not come without challenges; renewable power production complexity is inherent in the resources used in their generation [11, 12]. The challenges of renewable source of energy and their advantages in power generation are outlined in Table 1. Due to their limitations, combining two or more renewable power generation units into a hybrid energy production system improves the system reliability in supplying power to the attached load [13, 14]. Hybridizing multiple resources to generate sufficient power to match a given load requires a thorough feasibility analysis at the system inception phase; this analysis is to ascertain proper sizing of the hybrid system components and their economic value [15].

Accordingly, an optimal configuration of HRES includes but not limited to maximizing the power generated from the system at a minimum cost. The need to configure HRES optimally is crucial for the economic management of the system as well as satisfying end users' demand. However, the HRES optimization problem is modelled as a nonlinear problem [16], and the difficult nature and complexities in solving such real-world optimization problems with exact methods fail to address the problem within a reasonable time [17] and space. Therefore approximation algorithms have become attractive alternatives to deal with this class of problem [18]. Though they may not find the optimal result, approximate algorithms have greater chances of finding a globally optimal solution. Approximation algorithms, also known as metaheuristics, are more generic approaches to solving a wide range of NP-hard optimization problem in a reasonable time to get a near-optimal solution. One benefit of metaheuristic algorithms is that they are simple to design and implement besides being robust algorithm [19]. Metaheuristic algorithms have wide applications in HRES optimization.

The optimization process involves several steps that result in finding a better solution usually by maximizing or minimizing an objective function of a modelled problem whiles satisfying certain restrictions of variables been considered. Optimizing HRES involves the formulation of a mathematical model to estimate the optimal configuration size of renewable energy technologies, the system reliability, and the economic benefit of the system. In the process, renewable resources availability, load profile, technical data of the power production units, and economic information are supplied to the optimization machinery to determine the optimum result. The dominating method adopted by scientists in this area of study continues to be a nature-inspired algorithm (NIA) [20, 21]. In these regards, the focus of this review is directed to analyzing the advancement in research concerning nature-inspired (metaheuristic) algorithms in dealing with HRES optimization problems.

HRES design is influenced by various factors, such as the availability of energy sources at specific sites as well as technical and social constraints; these factors directly affect the power production arrangements of the system with financial repercussion. In this context, an optimal sizing combination is a vital factor to achieve higher reliability with the least cost of the system [22]. The optimal design of HRESs is a complicated task since the configuration depends on the knowledge of energy sources, technical specifications, environmental conditions, and load profiles [23]. Table 1 shows the types of renewable energy resources vis-à-vis their merits and demerits.

Table 1. Advantages and disadvantages of renewable resources in power generation

Renewable resource	Demerit	Merit
Hydro	Demographic oriented with rivers playing the major role Seasonal factors such as rainfall affect its use for power production	The leading contributor of renewable power generation Hydropower is relatively cheap compared to fossil fuel
Wind	Intermittent source of energy. The power source of wind is variable seasonally and demographically	Free resource No pollution hence environmentally friendly
Solar	Not available at night and cloudy days	Available anywhere almost all year round Free resource Environmentally friendly
Geothermal	Limited to geothermal power extraction points (tectonic plate boundaries)	Efficient power supply or backup during hot springs
Biomass	Although feedstock can be free there is an inherent logistic cost to convey raw material to power generation sites Availability of some raw materials are seasonally affected and might compete with human needs	For biomass, several technology options focus on a variety of feedstocks. These options can be used to meet a wide range of energy requirements, from large-scale industrial installations to small-scale rural applications. Biofuels are environmentally safer

It is imperative to determine the economic benefit of the energy system against the alternatives choices in making an informed decision. Moreover, an HRES reliability highly depends on the system's component, therefore proper analysis of an energy system power supply reliability is significant for its adoption. Generally, the capital investment for 100% HRES is high when compared to the grid tide power system operating on fossil fuel/natural gas or diesel generator, but the long-term benefit of HRES includes not only the economic advantage but a cleaner environment [22, 24]. An in-depth analysis of the recent trend of optimization techniques namely, NIAs or metaheuristics is conducted to bring to light a comprehensive knowledge of the methodology used in optimizing hybrid renewable energy systems.

The contributions of this paper are in three folds:

1. It presents a comprehensive assessment and the trending analysis of nature-inspired search techniques for optimization of mini-grid HRES in recent studies.
2. A succinct account of useful designing and implementation techniques of NIAs for optimization of HRES.
3. Lastly, we discuss open challenges and research opportunities for further studies in a mini-grid renewable-based hybrid system.

1.1 Methodology

In the methodology, we explain the criteria used to select and analyze scholarly works on the developments of nature-inspired search techniques in the optimization of mini-grid HRES. Keywords in the subject domain: nature-inspired algorithms and hybrid renewable energy system were searched in Web of Science, Scopus, and Google scholar databases. To narrowed down the scope of the articles of relevance to the study, some combinations of the keywords were used during the search. For example, "hybrid renewable energy system", "nature-inspired algorithm", "bio-inspired", "metaheuristic algorithm", "mini-grid", "microgrid", "optimization algorithm". By using the Keyword criterion, the relevant articles were excluded or included for detailed review. Based on the date of publication of the article available online from 2016 and later were selected from the search results. The candidate articles were chosen based on their close ties to hybrid renewable energy system optimization and nature-inspired search strategies. Initially, 300 research articles were downloaded from online sources, in which the Keyword and date of article publication criteria were applied. A total of 49 related articles were selected for detailed review. Other references are related to the algorithm's details, previous review studies, HRES background, and related articles for future research directions.

1.2 Paper Organization

The rest of the paper is organized as follows: Sect. 2 presents an overview of mini-grid HRES and the requirements for optimizing HRES; Sect. 3 provides a taxonomy of optimization algorithms with analysis of their advantages and disadvantages; Sect. 4 discusses comprehensively the advancements of nature-inspired search methods for optimizing HRES, and Sect. 5 concludes the study with recommendations for scientist and energy stakeholders.

2 Overview of Mini-grid Hybrid Renewable Energy System Optimization

A mini-grid (MG) is a locally-based electricity provider that uses distributed energy infrastructure to lower energy costs and emissions. MGs are preferred alternatives to supplying power in isolated communities or rural settlements where the conventional grid is not economically a viable option. The wide adoption of MG in developing countries particularly in Africa and Asia can increase electricity coverage, as one of the goals of

Sustainable Development Goal (SDG) 7, equitable access to energy is part of the global development agenda [25]. In different parts of the developing world, MGs will play a critical role in closing the electricity gap. The configuration of grid-independent MG must account for the optimal sizing of the system components to derive the economic benefits without compromising on the reliability [26] of power supplied by the system. In an MG, Photovoltaic (PV), wind turbines (WT), and energy storage system (ESS) are more likely to be hybridized to always meet the load demand at both peak and off-peak times [26]. It is crucial, therefore, to select an optimal sizing of power units for a specific goal or objective to be met by the MG. The challenges of meeting all the system constraints yet production adequate power have resulted in many studies investigating the optimization of MG hybrid renewable energy system.

The rest of this section is devoted to MG optimization requirements and procedure for designing, assessing, and performing techno-economic analysis of HRESs. Figure 1 showcases a flow chart of the optimization process of HRES; it starts by identifying the ideal combination of renewable technologies which will be suitable for the set-up within the locality. By using meteorological data such as solar irradiation, ambient temperature, wind speed, and the assessment of load to be served by the system, the optimal sizing of a renewable-based hybrid system can be estimated.

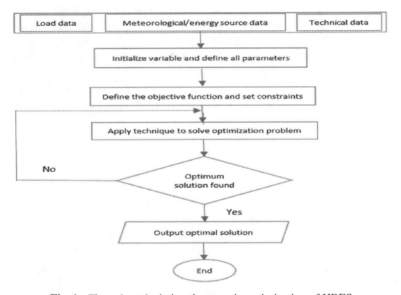

Fig. 1. Flow chart depicting the steps in optimization of HRES

2.1 Requirement for HRES Optimization

An HRES can be designed efficiently to achieve the specified objectives of users [27], here the HRES need an optimum component sizing before its configuration [26, 28]. The requirements for the optimization process are briefly discussed.

Data Requirement. Most importantly, the availability of renewable energy source on the site where the system is to be set up is paramount to realizing the optimal HRES configuration. To achieve the optimization objective(s), a study of the location's meteorological data characteristics is needed. If meteorological records of data are not obtainable for a given area, then satellite-based data or projected data may be used instead [27]. Another critical input data needed for optimal configuration of MG HRES is the electric load characteristics and profile. Since it is extremely difficult to determine and analyze actual load demand for all minute variations, hourly or daily estimates of load demand are commonly used for design optimization [27]. Finally, the specifications on the energy generation units provided by the vendors are equally important. This information details the device performance and efficiencies under various conditions. The permutation of the meteorological data with the device specifications gives a good estimate for the optimal configuration of the HRES. In the absence of actual device data, the web or scholarly literature could provide good representation of that information. With the set of information required for the configuration, the optimal decision can be deduced with the help of well-defined mathematical models. The data serve as input for the models; some of these models are examined in the next subsection.

Energy System Model. The performance of a mini-grid renewable-based hybrid system is highly dependent on components. The proper sizing of the component is usually determined with aid of mathematical models. Energy system models are mathematical models that have been developed to reliably represent various energy-related problems. These models are used in a variety of computing systems to identify and solve problems. For optimization, the accuracy of the developed models for a hybrid system component is critical. As a result, all required variables affecting energy conversion must be included in these models. These mathematical models should be based on simple principles, but in many situations, the sophistication of the model increases, or the researcher may overlook important variables, resulting in inaccuracy. Thereafter, the co-efficient of equations involving the hybrid system components which have been expressed as decision variables are evaluated to meet the optimization objective.

Objective Function. The problem of HRES optimization is generally posed in both economic and technological metrics when designing an optimal hybrid system. These two indices are used to determine the optimum system equipment sizing for a cost-effective and reliable system. The goal of the design issue is to reduce the cost feature, reduce CO_2 emissions, or increase system reliability. Cases of HRES optimization problems and the objective functions that needed to be solved are shown in Table 2. Since a technical evaluation should be performed for the mini-grid hybrid system to satisfy the load demand, reliability indices such as power supply probability (PSP), loss of power supply probability (LPSP), and loss of load probability (LLP) are frequently presented as reliability constraints (technical design index) in design studies for renewable energy systems.

Accordingly, the result of the HRES optimization problem revolves around the objective function and the defined constraints if any, to accurately estimate the co-efficient of all decision variables. The optimization results must be precise enough to avoid surplus or deficit power, and this is achieved if the data requirements for the proposed system and the corresponding equipment specifications are met.

Table 2. Sample cases of recent MG HRES optimization using AI methods

Ref	Year	Components/Energy sources	Optimization Algorithm	Objective	Optimization result
[29]	2020	PV, WT, DG and Battery,	NSGAII, NSGA III and MOPSO	Multi-objective: minimize LPSP, COE and maximize RF	NSGA II outperform the competitors with a minimum COE of 0.0588 $/kWh and a maximum of 0.14611 $/kWh
[30]	2020	PV, WT, micro-hydro turbines, fuel cell, electrolyser, hydrogen tank, compressors, power converters, supercapacitors (SCs), biopower plant	MFOA, DA, SSA, ALO, GWO, GOA	Optimal sizing of HRES components	MFOA found to result in a significant reduction in NPC, and it outperformed GA and PSO in terms of solution quality by 2.1% and 3.2% respectively
[31]	2021	PV, WT, and battery	Hybrid GWO and GA (HGWOGA)	Minimize annual cost	HGWOGA, GA and GWO found the optimal solution to be $ 5 572.01
[32]	2021	WT, PV, DG, and batteries	NSGA-II	Multi-objective model to size HRES	the renewable energy efficiency of 80% is achievable for the chosen climate
[33]	2021	PV, WT, FC, water electrolyser and Hydrogen gas tank	IAEO	Minimizing the Cost of Energy (COE), the reliability index presented by the Loss of Power Supply Probability (LPSP), and excess energy	the estimation of each energy component with the NPC of the system was deduced as: PV (17%), WT (20%), electrolyze (23%), hydrogen tank (32%), FC (2%) and inverter (6%)

(continued)

Table 2. *(continued)*

Ref	Year	Components/Energy sources	Optimization Algorithm	Objective	Optimization result
[34]	2020	PV, DG and FC	Modified CSA	Optimal sizing	CSA adaptive-AP found the optimal solution
[35]	2021	PV, WT, DG, and battery	PSO and ε-constraint method	Minimize the cost of energy (COE) and maximizing system reliability and RF	different optimal configurations were found for various sites
[36]	2020	PV, DG, and battery	cEHO	Minimize loss of load probability, CO_2 emissions value, and the annualized cost of the system	the initial capital of \$48,680 can provide reliable supplementary energy for the load demand such that the PV penetration has an impact of 97.9% to emit 1735 kg/year of CO_2 less than the result of PSO and HOMER
[37]	2021	PV, WT, DG, and battery	EO	Minimize the net present cost (NPC)	the best NPC, LCOE, and LPSP are obtained via EO achieving 74327 \$, 0.0917 \$/kWh, and 0.0489, respectively

In addition, an accurate mathematical model can positively influence the HRES optimal result. However, central to the optimization processes is the approach or technique for optimizing. In the next section, we will discuss in detail the techniques which have been applied to the HRES optimization problems.

3 Optimization Techniques for HRES

Algorithms for computing the maximum or minimum of mathematical functions are known as optimization algorithms. When designing a mini-grid HRES, it is crucial to consider the efficiency of its components. The key aim is to improve efficiency while lowering costs. These objectives can be met by optimizing the system model as described in the previous section. To achieve this goal an optimization technique is employed to solving the problem. There are several approaches to optimizing MG HRES. Classical, Computational/Artificial Intelligence and hybrid approaches are the three most widely used techniques for mini-grid hybrid systems.

3.1 Classical Techniques

The classical optimization methods are also referred to as analytical, traditional, or conventional methods. These optimization methods find the solution to an HRES optimization problem by utilizing information such as gradient or derivative of functions [38, 39]. The most widely used classical method for HRES optimization includes linear programming (LP), mixed-integer linear programming (MILP), Iterative Approach, Trade-off Approach. Some studies on HRES have been carried out their advantages and disadvantages have been thoroughly discussed in [39, 40].

Even though these methods are easier to use, understand, and have a wide variety of applications, these methods have a high risk of being stuck in the local optimum rather than the global optimum [27]. Table 3 summarizes the merits and demerits of the commonly used classical optimization techniques employed to solving MG HRES optimization problems.

3.2 AI Methods

The design of algorithmic models to solve increasingly complex problems is the focus of the algorithmic progress. These models may be based on mathematical models or they may be modelled on natural intelligence has resulted in what is known as Nature-inspired or meta-heuristic algorithms, which have had enormous success [39, 41, 42]. Evolutionary computation, swarm intelligence, artificial immune systems, are examples of these nature-inspired algorithms. These algorithms are part of the field of Artificial Intelligence (AI), and their application in HRES optimization have advanced the field. Several studies have applied AI techniques including particle swarm optimization (PSO), genetic algorithm (GA), ant colony optimization (ACO), biogeography based optimizations (BBO), differential evolution (DE), evolutionary programming (EP), evolution strategies (ES), artificial bee colony (ABC), honey bee mating optimization (HBMO), artificial immune system (AIS), harmony search (HS), and combinations of them.

The techniques here have some major disadvantages and advantages, some of which have been outlined in Table 4. Complex optimization problem, many of the algorithms fail to find out the optimal solution. In Table 4.

3.3 Hybrid Algorithms

The premature convergence affects most evolutionary computational techniques. These strategies take a long time to emerge from the local maxima or minima. By combining two or more optimization search techniques into a hybrid algorithm, these techniques can be used to solve a wide range of optimization problems. Hybrid techniques can overcome

Table 3. Advantages and disadvantages of classical optimization techniques for MG HRES adopted from [27]

Technique	Highlights	Strength	Weakness
Graphical	Provides a graphical representation of the solution to the optimization problem	Easy to visualize, understand, and simple to use	Cannot model several decision variables, and certain details cannot be captured
Probabilistic	Based on the random effects upon the performance of the system	Simple and straightforward to use	Difficult representing the dynamic changes and performances of hybrid systems
Iterative	It is a recursive process that stops when the best configuration is reached as per the design specifications	Easy to understand Tracks defects at early stages	Each iteration phase is rigid and does not overlap to accommodate any intermediaries
Linear programming	Model mathematical relationships of the system based on linear equations and inequalities	Best for solving a complex problem that can be express linearly, simple to implement, flexible, it can solve a wide range of problems	Linearity about variables, assumptions of linear programming are also unrealistic, there is a change in the relation between input, output gain, loss etc.
Trade-off	Based on a situation that involves losing one quality or accepting something in return for gaining another quality or aspect	Easy to understand	Application in renewable energy is limited

the limitations of individual techniques, resulting in more effective and reliable HRES solutions. In recent years, there has been a lot of interest in hybrid technique research [47].

While hybrid optimization techniques improve overall optimization performance, they may have drawbacks. For example, the hybrid MCS-partial PSO's optimism, hybrid iterative/suboptimal GA's solutions, random adjusting of the evolutionary algorithm's inertia weight, and optimization coding complexity [49].

Table 4. Advantages and disadvantages of some nature-inspired algorithms for MG HRES optimization

Algorithm	Advantage	Disadvantage	Ref
PSO	Simple to code; high convergence speed; minimum storage requirement	It converges prematurely. Difficult to design the parameters, it may be trapped in local optimum	[43]
GA	Can solve problems with multiple solutions; available in MATLAB toolbox	Fitness function calculation is repeated for each generation. It may not converge on global optimum if it is not carefully and properly implemented	[42, 44, 45]
ABC	Algorithms have both local and global search abilities; it is easy to use	With more decision variables the convergence rate is slow, and a global optimum may not be found	[31, 46]
ACO	Performs well in both local and global search; a vast range of application domain	The algorithm has several parameters that must be tuned. Initialization is done randomly	[27]
HGWOGA	blends the strength of GWO and GA to improve the searching strategy; MATLAB code is available for testing	Designing complexity and difficult to implement. It has so many parameters	[31, 46]
BBO	Good convergence	It may result in many infeasible solutions	[47]
HS	Requires few parameters value setting, and it can solve continuous and discontinuous function; it has good exploitation and exploration abilities	It has a complex solving process; not easy to implement	[48]

4   Advancements of Nature-Inspired Search Methods for Optimizing HRES

The application of NIAs in HRES optimization has taken a huge leap in recent times with a high success rate of finding an optimal/near-optimal solution. This high growth rate of NIA is attributed to many factors includes flexibility and robustness in solving complex scientific and engineering optimization problem. The complex nature of designing an optimal mini-grid hybrid energy architecture whiles incorporating multiple energy sources with several decision variables and constraints has given rise to the high usage of NIA for renewable energy optimization. Although NIA has wide application in HRES optimization it has extensively been applied to solar PV and wind energy optimization, but it has less coverage on geothermal, ocean-based renewable energy and biomass (biofuel). Moreover, the latter resource has shown greater potential [6] of alleviating the recurring energy crisis confronting most developing countries [4]. These renewable resources have varying decision variables, for instance, geothermal is continuous and ocean-based energy is periodic. An enhancement of NIA to accommodate these special situations would improve the optimal solution as well as management of the power system. In the advent of the massive improvements of NIA, it would be necessary for scientists to explore further the other renewable resources to augment the power supply industry. Here, NIA comes in handy.

New, enhanced, stochastic, advanced or hybrid optimization algorithms are proposed yearly to be solving various optimization problems. There is no single algorithm that supersedes all others in every problem. Therefore, identifying the appropriate search method for any optimization task addresses a scientific quest in making an informed decision. Table 5 summarizes the major optimization techniques employed in MG-HRES with their advantages and disadvantages.

Table 5. Advantages and disadvantages of optimization techniques

Optimization Technique	Advantages	Disadvantages
Classical Methods	Very simple (intuitive) to understand the logical flow of instructions and the analysis It is easy to write the code It has wider application areas	Computational time complexity is very high due to several mathematical or analytical operations Application in constraint satisfactory problem is problematic: does not handle constraints satisfactory High tendencies of been trapped in local optimum rather than global optimum
CI Methods	Ability to escape local minima or local maxima to finding a global optimum It achieves the global optimum with relatively low computational complexity Good computational time More efficient and robust Ability to handle several constraints Suitable for a wide range of decision variables Applicable in many areas of study Literature is readily available, and it is expanding at a high pace	May converge prematurely Can take a long time to leave the local optimum Not easy to code complex problems For a large set of decision variables and constraints, the response time could be very high

(continued)

Table 5. (*continued*)

Optimization Technique	Advantages	Disadvantages
Hybrid Methods	Better convergence Harnesses the strength of individual techniques to be more competitive	It has a complicated structure It is difficult to analyse
Software tools	Freely and commercially application programs easy to use suitable for multi-objective and mono-objective optimization problem on the fly techno-economic analysis of the system Can include many system components	Limited to a specific application domain Codes are not accessible for analysis or evaluations

5 Conclusion and Future Research

This paper presents an updated literature review of optimization techniques including hybrid algorithms used in mini-grid hybrid renewable energy system research, focusing on recent metaheuristic techniques which have been employed to solve the MG HRES optimization problem. It is found in the last few years several more non-conventional approaches have been implemented in renewable-based MG HRESs for system sizing, reliability and techno-economic analysis. In the past few years, a new trend has been observed in the growth of meta-heuristic particularly, swarm intelligence-based optimization algorithms. Although new algorithms are being developed, studies on hybridizing two or more techniques to solving MG HRES optimization is on the rise in the current literature. Moreover, different optimization methods used have varying performance efficiency when compared with other algorithms in some other studies, as no single method showed superiority in all comparative studies. Therefore, the selection of a suitable optimization technique may depend on several factors that will invariably inform the objective function result. Future studies could focus on improving the self-adaptive nature of metaheuristic algorithms to accommodate the marginalised renewable resources such as biomass, ocean-based energy etc. which have a high potential of mitigating the energy crisis in most developing economies. Finally, a data collection and analysis framework based on advanced IoT analytics viz hybrid renewable energy system optimization needs more attention to streamline the scientific frontiers for real-time data to predict or generate power to meet a changing load.

References

1. Committee on Climate Change: Net Zero Technical Report (2019). https://www.theccc.org.uk/publication/net-zero-technical-report/

2. Quarton, C.J., et al.: The curious case of the conflicting roles of hydrogen in global energy scenarios. Sustain. Energy Fuels **4**(80), 80–95 (2020). https://doi.org/10.1039/c9se00833k

3. Frank, C., Fiedler, S., Crewell, S.: Balancing potential of natural variability and extremes in photovoltaic and wind energy production for European countries Christopher. Renew. Energy (2020). https://doi.org/10.1016/j.renene.2020.07.103

4. Mugodo, K., Magama, P.P., Dhavu, K.: Biogas production potential from agricultural and agro-processing waste in South Africa. Waste Biomass Valor. **8**(7), 2383–2392 (2017). https://doi.org/10.1007/s12649-017-9923-z

5. Votteler, R., Brent, A.: A literature review on the potential of renewable electricity sources for mining operations in South Africa. J. Energy Southern Africa **27**(2), 1–21 (2016)

6. Adesanya, A., Misra, S., Maskeliunas, R., Damasevicius, R.: Prospects of ocean-based renewable energy for West Africa's sustainable energy future. Smart Sustain. Built Environ. **10**(1), 37–50 (2021) https://doi.org/10.1108/SASBE-05-2019-0066

7. Ghenai, C., Salameh, T., Merabet, A.: Technico-economic analysis of off grid solar PV/Fuel cell energy system for residential community in desert region. Int. J. Hydrogen Energy **45**(20), 11460–11470 (2020). https://doi.org/10.1016/j.ijhydene.2018.05.110

8. Singh, S., Singh, M., Kaushik, S.C.: Feasibility study of an islanded microgrid in rural area consisting of PV, wind, biomass and battery energy storage system. Energy Convers. Manag. **128**, 178–190 (2016). https://doi.org/10.1016/j.enconman.2016.09.046

9. Zafar, A., Shafique, A., Nazir, Z., Zia, M.F.: A comparison of optimization techniques for energy scheduling of hybrid power generation system. In: Proceedings 21st International Multi Topic Conference INMIC 2018, no. June 2019, pp. 1–6 (2018). https://doi.org/10.1109/INMIC.2018.8595665

10. Khezri, R., Mahmoudi, A.: Review on the state-of-the-art multi-objective optimisation of hybrid standalone/gridconnected energy systems. IET Gener. Transm. Distrib. **14**(20), 4285–4300 (2020). https://doi.org/10.1049/iet-gtd.2020.0453

11. Hou, R., Yang, Y., Yuan, Q., Chen, Y.: Research and application of hybrid wind-energy forecasting models based on cuckoo search optimization. pp. 1–18 (2019)

12. Lu, J., Wang, W., Zhang, Y., Cheng, S.: Hybrid energy system using entropy weight method (2017). https://doi.org/10.3390/en10101664

13. Donado, K., Navarro, L., Christian, G., Quintero, M., Pardo, M.: HYRES: a multi-objective optimization tool for proper configuration of renewable hybrid energy systems. Energies **13**(1), 26 (2019). https://doi.org/10.3390/en13010026

14. Yong, Z., Shaowu, L.: Economic evaluation and configuration optimization strategy of hybrid renewable energy generation system: a review. In: Proceedings 32nd Chinese Control and Decision Conference (CCDC) 2020, pp. 729–734 (2020). https://doi.org/10.1109/CCDC49329.2020.9164560

15. Torres-madroñero, J.L., Nieto-londoño, C.: Hybrid energy systems sizing for the colombian context : a genetic algorithm and particle swarm, pp. 1–30 (2020). https://doi.org/10.3390/en13215648

16. Urbanucci, L., Ettorre, F.D., Testi, D.: A comprehensive methodology for the integrated optimal sizing and operation of cogeneration systems with thermal energy storage (2019). https://doi.org/10.3390/en12050875

17. Nguyen, T., Nguyen, L.V., Jung, J.J., Agbehadji, I.E.: Bio-inspired approaches for smart energy management : state of the art and challenges, pp. 1–24 (2020). https://doi.org/10.3390/su12208495

18. Khan, A., et al.: Enhanced evolutionary sizing algorithms for optimal sizing of a stand-alone PV-WT-battery hybrid system. Appl. Sci. **9**(23), 5197 (2019). https://doi.org/10.3390/app9235197

19. Frimpong, S.O.: Nature-inspired search method for cost optimization of hybrid renewable energy generation at the edge (2020)

20. Alzahrani, A., Zohdy, M., Yan, B.: An overview of optimization approaches for operation of hybrid distributed energy systems with photovoltaic and diesel turbine generator. Electric Power Syst. Res. **191**, 106877 (2021). https://doi.org/10.1016/j.epsr.2020.106877
21. Diab, A.A.Z., Sultan, H.M., Kuznetsov, O.N.: Optimal sizing of hybrid solar/wind/hydroelectric pumped storage energy system in Egypt based on different meta-heuristic techniques. Environ. Sci. Pollut. Res. **27**(26), 32318–32340 (2019). https://doi.org/10.1007/s11356-019-06566-0
22. Das, B., Hassan, R., Mohammad Shahed, H.K., Tushar, F., Hasan, M., Das, P.: Techno-economic and environmental assessment of a hybrid renewable energy system using multi-objective genetic algorithm: a case study for remote Island in Bangladesh. Energy Convers. Manag. **230**, 113823 (2021). https://doi.org/10.1016/j.enconman.2020.113823
23. Clarke, D.P., Al-Abdeli, Y.M., Kothapalli, G.: Multi-objective optimisation of renewable hybrid energy systems with desalination. Energy **88**, 457–468 (2015). https://doi.org/10.1016/j.energy.2015.05.065
24. Barakat, S., Ibrahim, H., Elbaset, A.A.: Multi-objective optimization of grid-connected pv-wind hybrid system considering reliability, cost, and environmental aspects. Sustain. Cities Soc. **60**, 102178 (2020). https://doi.org/10.1016/j.scs.2020.102178
25. Micangeli, A., Duenas-Martinez, P.: Optimal design of isolated mini-grids with deterministic methods: matching predictive operating strategies with low computational requirements. Energies **13**(16), 4214 (2020). https://doi.org/10.3390/en13164214
26. Khan, F.A., Pal, N., Saeed, S.H.: Review of solar photovoltaic and wind hybrid energy systems for sizing strategies optimization techniques and cost analysis methodologies. Renew. Sustain. Energy Rev. **92**(March), 937–947 (2018). https://doi.org/10.1016/j.rser.2018.04.107
27. Sinha, S., Chandel, S.S.: Review of recent trends in optimization techniques for solar photovoltaic – wind based hybrid energy systems. Renew. Sustain. Energy Rev. **50**, 755–769 (2015). https://doi.org/10.1016/j.rser.2015.05.040
28. Eriksson, E.L.V., Gray, E.M.: Optimization and integration of hybrid renewable energy hydrogen fuel cell energy systems – a critical review. Appl. Energy **202**, 348–364 (2017). https://doi.org/10.1016/j.apenergy.2017.03.132
29. Husain, S., Shrivastava, N.A.: A comparative analysis of multi-objective optimization algorithms for stand-alone hybrid renewable energy system. In: ICIMIA, pp. 255–260 (2020)
30. Mohseni, S., Brent, A.C., Burmester, D.: A comparison of metaheuristics for the optimal capacity planning of an isolated, battery-less, hydrogen-based micro-grid. Appl. Energy **259**, 114224 (2020). https://doi.org/10.1016/j.apenergy.2019.114224
31. Geleta, D.K., Manshahia, M.S.: A hybrid of grey wolf optimization and genetic algorithm for optimization of hybrid wind and solar renewable energy system. J. Oper. Res. Soc. China (2021). https://doi.org/10.1007/s40305-021-00341-0
32. Ebrahimi, A., Attar, S., Farhang-Moghaddam, B.: A multi-objective decision model for residential building energy optimization based on hybrid renewable energy systems. Int. J. Green Energy, 1–18 (2021). https://doi.org/10.1080/15435075.2021.1880911
33. Sultan, H.M., Menesy, A.S., Kamel, S., Korashy, A., Almohaimeed, S.A., Abdel-Akher, M.: An improved artificial ecosystem optimization algorithm for optimal configuration of a hybrid PV/WT/FC energy system. Alexandria Eng. J. **60**(1), 1001–1025 (2021). https://doi.org/10.1016/j.aej.2020.10.027
34. Ghaffari, A., Askarzadeh, A.: Design optimization of a hybrid system subject to reliability level and renewable energy penetration. Energy **193**, 116754 (2020). https://doi.org/10.1016/j.energy.2019.116754
35. Mokhtara, C., Negrou, B., Settou, N., Settou, B., Samy, M.M.: Design optimization of off-grid hybrid renewable energy systems considering the effects of building energy performance and climate change: case study of Algeria. Energy **219**, 119605 (2021). https://doi.org/10.1016/j.energy.2020.119605

36. Ashraf, M.A., Liu, Z., Alizadeh, A., Nojavan, S., Jermsittiparsert, K., Zhang, D.: Designing an optimized configuration for a hybrid PV/Diesel/battery energy system based on metaheuristics: a case study on Gobi desert. J. Clean. Prod. **270**, 122467 (2020). https://doi.org/10.1016/j.jclepro.2020.122467

37. Kharrich, M., Kamel, S., Abdeen, M., Mohammed, O.H., Akherraz, M.: Developed approach based on equilibrium optimizer for optimal design of hybrid PV/Wind/Diesel/Battery Microgrid in Dakhla, Morocco, pp. 13655–13670 (2021). https://doi.org/10.1109/ACCESS.2021.3051573

38. Ganguly, P., Kalam, A., Zayegh, A.: Solar–wind hybrid renewable energy system: current status of research on configurations, control, and sizing methodologies. In: Hybrid-Renewable Energy Systems in Microgrids, Elsevier Ltd., pp. 219–248 (2018)

39. Twaha, S., Ramli, M.A.M.: A review of optimization approaches for hybrid distributed energy generation systems: off-grid and grid-connected systems. Sustain. Cities Soc. **41**(April), 320–331 (2018). https://doi.org/10.1016/j.scs.2018.05.027

40. Theo, W.L., Lim, J.S., Ho, W.S., Hashim, H., Lee, C.T.: Review of distributed generation (DG) system planning and optimisation techniques: comparison of numerical and mathematical modelling methods. Renew. Sustain. Energy Rev. **67**, 531–573 (2017). https://doi.org/10.1016/j.rser.2016.09.063

41. Zahraee, S.M., Khalaji Assadi, M., Saidur, R.: Application of artificial intelligence methods for hybrid energy system optimization. Renew. Sustain. Energy Rev. **66**, 617–630 (2016). https://doi.org/10.1016/j.rser.2016.08.028

42. Mohamed, M.A., Eltamaly, A.M., Alolah, A.I.: Swarm intelligence-based optimization of grid-dependent hybrid renewable energy systems. Renew. Sustain. Energy Rev. **77**, 515–524 (2017). https://doi.org/10.1016/j.rser.2017.04.048

43. Tezer, T., Yaman, R., Yaman, Gül.şen: Evaluation of approaches used for optimization of stand-alone hybrid renewable energy systems. Renew. Sustain. Energy Rev. **73**, 840–853 (2017). https://doi.org/10.1016/j.rser.2017.01.118

44. Xiao, H., Pei, W., Dong, Z., Kong, L., Wang, D.: Application and comparison of metaheuristic and new metamodel based global optimization. https://doi.org/10.3390/en11010085

45. Mandal, S.: Modeling of photovoltaic systems using modified elephant swarm water search algorithm. Int. J. Modell. Simul. **40**(6), 436–455 (2020). https://doi.org/10.1080/02286203.2019.1650488

46. El-salam, M., Beshr, E., Eteiba, M.: A new hybrid technique for minimizing power losses in a distribution system by optimal sizing and siting of distributed generators with network reconfiguration. Energies **11**(12), 3351 (2018). https://doi.org/10.3390/en11123351

47. Aala Kalananda, V.K.R., Komanapalli, V.L.N.: Nature-inspired optimization algorithms for renewable energy generation, distribution and management—a comprehensive review. In: Vinoth Kumar, B., Sivakumar, P., Rajan Singaravel, M. M., Vijayakumar, K. (eds.) Intelligent Paradigms for Smart Grid and Renewable Energy Systems. AIS, pp. 139–226. Springer, Singapore (2021). https://doi.org/10.1007/978-981-15-9968-2_6

48. Nazari-heris, M., Mohammadi-ivatloo, B., Asadi, S., Kim, H., Geem, Z.W.: Harmony search algorithm for energy system applications: an updated review and analysis. J. Exp. Theor. Artif. Intell. **31**(5), 723–749 (2019). https://doi.org/10.1080/0952813X.2018.1550814

49. Ashraf, M.M., Malik, T.N.: A hybrid teaching–learning-based optimizer with novel radix-5 mapping procedure for minimum cost power generation planning considering renewable energy sources and reducing emission. Electr. Eng. **102**(4), 2567–2582 (2020). https://doi.org/10.1007/s00202-020-01044-0

COVID-19 Diagnosis from Chest X-Ray Images Using Convolutional Neural Networks and Effects of Data Poisoning

Karthika Menon[✉], V. Khushi Bohra, Lakshana Murugan,
Kavya Jaganathan, and Chamundeswari Arumugam

Department of Computer Science and Engineering, Sri Sivasubramaniya Nadar
College of Engineering, Chennai 603110, India
{karthika18070,khushibohra18075,lakshana18082,
kavya17074}@cse.ssn.edu.in, chamundeswaria@ssn.edu.in

Abstract. At the end of 2019, a new type of virus called SARS-CoV-2 began spreading resulting in a global pandemic. As of June 2021, almost 175 million people were affected worldwide. Symptom-wise, it is very difficult to diagnose if a person has Covid or just a viral infection. But, taking a close look at chest X-Rays is extremely helpful in the diagnostic process. The proposed methodology in this paper helps in classification of chest X-Ray images into 3 categories: 'Covid', 'Viral' and 'Normal'. The dataset was created by integrating 3 pre-existing evergrowing datasets and the ResNet-18 model was adopted to train it. The experimental results show that the classification of the chest X-Ray images was done with an accuracy of 0.9648. An adversarial machine learning approach was employed to poison the train data after which the classification accuracy dropped to 0.8711.

Keywords: COVID-19 · Pneumonia · Chest X-Rays · Machine learning · CNN · ResNet-18 · Image classification · Medical imaging · Data poisoning · Data security

1 Introduction

The COVID-19 pandemic is one of the greatest health crises this world has faced till date. As of June 2021, around 175 million people have been affected by COVID-19 and 3.86 million people have lost their lives. Most patients who are suspected to have COVID-19 have symptoms like cough, fever, fatigue, anorexia, shortness of breath, and sputum production. Chest x-ray is the first diagnostic technique that has a significant role in COVID diagnosis. With the unfortunate spread of COVID 19, rapid imaging analysis will allow for quick digital detection of cases and prevent spread, eliminating the time required to generate radiological reports.

Nowadays, deep learning concepts are developing at a very fast rate. Deep Learning is a combination of machine learning methods mainly focused on feature

© Springer Nature Switzerland AG 2021
O. Gervasi et al. (Eds.): ICCSA 2021, LNCS 12957, pp. 508–521, 2021.
https://doi.org/10.1007/978-3-030-87013-3_38

extraction and image classification. Deep learning uses the process of convolution where a deep convolutional neural network is used for feature extraction. The network uses multiple layers that process non-linear information. Each layer involves a transformation of the data into a higher and more abstract level. More complex information is learned as the network is traversed deeper. Higher layers contain the information that is used for segregation and classification.

The continuous growth of COVID chest x-ray dataset allows us to use deep learning models to train and learn to detect COVID from these x-rays. Further, more information can be learned with regards to severity depending on scores and features learned from the training. One of the major issues about COVID diagnosis is that the symptoms of pneumonia and COVID-19 are almost the same. Image analysis of chest x-ray images aid doctors and healthcare workers significantly in differentiating between a COVID infection and pneumonia.

The purpose of this research is to segregate the chest x-Rays present in the dataset using the pre-trained convolutional neural network, ResNet-18. Classification is done into 3 classes namely- 'Normal', 'Viral', 'COVID'. The results are extremely encouraging and demonstrate how effective deep learning and transfer learning applications are, with CNNs for detection of abnormal X-ray images from normal ones and identifying which chest x-rays actually show signs of COVID-19.

Data poisoning is a method to corrupt or weaken the machine learning system by attacking it. The attack was performed in the form of data manipulation where the pre-existing training data was changed. In doing this, the system classifies wrong data into desired classes. This is done because tampering with the training data impacts the model's ability to classify data into correct classes. Since the dataset used to conduct this research is public, it is prone to manipulation by various sources. Hence, data poisoning was done to demonstrate the vulnerability of this model in case data poisoning occurs. In this paper, data manipulation of the dataset was employed as part of a data poisoning approach which resulted in a significant drop in test accuracy.

2   Literature Survey

COVID-19 detection using x-ray images would help physicians accelerate the diagnosis to a considerable extent and hence it is an active field of research. The following are few existing works related to this area of study.

COVID-19 pneumonia detection in chest x-ray images using transfer learning of convolutional neural networks [1] by Manop Phankokkruad chose VGG16, Xception, and Inception-Resnet-V2 pre-trained models for transfer learning. The comparative results drawn from this study indicate that VGG16 produced the highest training accuracy of 97.19%. Pneumonia diagnosis using chest x-ray images and machine learning [2] developed by Sara Lee Kit Yee et al. have evaluated the performance of the three classifiers namely kNN,SVM and NN. The study concluded that the accuracy of SVM turned out to be the highest with 93.1%. Automated pneumonia diagnosis using a customized sequential convolutional neural network [3] by Raheel Siddiqi used an 18 layer customised CNN model to classify the dataset into two classes- 'Normal' and 'Pneumonia'. This customised CNN model had an accuracy of 0.9375 which proved to be greater than the state-of-the-art model.

YU-net lung segment image preprocess methods used for common chest diseases prediction [4] proposed by Haoxiong Yu et al. have developed a novel method to improve the accuracy of CNN models using YU-net cleaned data. COVID-19 detection from chest x-ray images using deep learning and convolutional neural networks [5] developed by Antonios Makris et al. classified the images into 3 classes- 'Normal' ,'Covid' and 'Pneumonia'. The model applied Transfer Learning and evaluated 9 well known pre-trained CNN models out of which VGG16 obtained the highest overall accuracy of about 0.9588. COVID-19 chest radiography images analysis based on integration of image preprocess, guided grad-CAM,machine learning and risk management [6] by Tsung-Chieh Lin et al. proves that ensemble approach improves the accuracy compared to individual CNN models.

A neuro-heuristic approach for recognition of lung diseases from X-ray images [7] proposed by Qiao Ke et al. uses simplified image descriptors to detect degenerated lung tissues in x-ray images and predict respiratory diseases. Bio-inspired methods modeled for respiratory disease detection from medical images [8] by Marcin Woźniak et al. proposed a bio-inspired methodology search for areas in x-ray image where diseased tissues are likely to appear and hence detect respiratory diseases from that. Small Lung Nodules Detection Based on Fuzzy-Logic and Probabilistic Neural Network With Bioinspired Reinforcement Learning [9] by Giacomo Capizzi et al. presented an evaluation model based on a composition of fuzzy system combined with a neural network. The results show high performances with sensitivity and specificity reaching almost 0.95 and 0.90, respectively, with an accuracy of 0.9256.

3   Methodology

3.1   Proposed Model

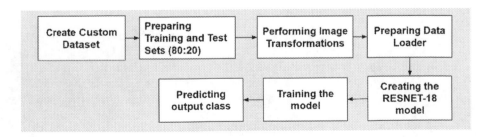

Fig. 1. Proposed model

The proposed model for solving the image classification problem in this paper is as detailed in Fig. 1. A custom dataset is first created by integrating 3 open source datasets (2 Kaggle and 1 GitHub) and then augmenting the images to obtain a balanced, more expansive database. Once the dataset is created, it is split into training and test sets applying an 80:20 train-to-test ratio. Python torchvision image transformations are then performed on the images to resize and customize them to desired dimensions before feeding them into the ResNet-18 model for training. The transformed images are imported into the data loader. The ResNet-18 model is then created and trained using the images in the train set by setting the hyperparameters. Finally, the model is tested using the images in the test set and the output classes are predicted i.e., Covid-19, Viral pneumonia or normal.

3.2   Data Description

The dataset used to build the model is a combination of 3 datasets. These include kaggle's COVID-19 radiography database [10], comprising 10,192 normal images, 3,616 COVID-19 images and 1,345 viral pneumonia images. The second dataset used is IEEE8023's covid chestxray dataset [11] from which 562 COVID-19 images, 40 viral pneumonia images and 18 normal images were incorporated into the dataset. The final dataset used is Kaggle's COVID-19 x-rays [12] dataset which consists of 71 COVID-19 images and 7 Normal images. In total they make up a dataset comprising 15,851 images i.e., 10,217 normal images, 4249 COVID-19 images and 1,385 viral pneumonia images (refer Fig. 2, 3, 4 for sample chest x-ray images).

Several modules of the python library imgaug.augmenters including Fliplr (horizontal flip), Flipud (vertical flip), Gaussian Blur, Dropout, AdditiveGaussianNoise were applied to augment the dataset. The dataset after augmentation comprises 7940 covid-19 images, 8192 normal images and 7366 viral pneumonia images which make up a total of 23,498 images in the dataset. Python torchvision image transformation functions such as Resize, Normalize, ToTensor etc. were applied in order to customize the images to the necessary input specification (224 × 224) before feeding into the pretrained ResNet-18 model.

The data loader was prepared to obtain training and test datasets. The training dataset has a total of 23,488 images comprising 8192 normal images, 7366 viral examples and 7940 covid-19 samples. The test dataset has a total of 6000 images, consisting 2000 image samples from each of the 3 classes.

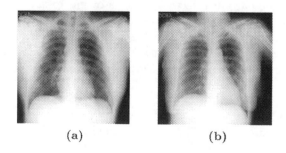

(a)   (b)

Fig. 2. Examples of COVID-19 chest x-ray images

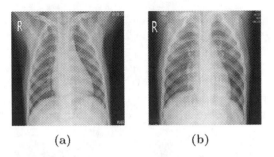

(a)   (b)

Fig. 3. Examples of viral pneumonia chest x-ray images

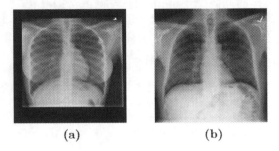

(a)   (b)

Fig. 4. Examples of normal chest x-ray images

3.3   Classification Method

A transfer learning approach of extracting features from a base convolutional neural network, and re-purposing feature maps learned previously on a larger dataset was employed to perform the classification task. The feature extraction task in this model was carried out using the convolutional layers of a pretrained ResNet-18 network.

The ResNet-18 architecture comprises alternating sequential convolutional layers, batch normalization layers and pooling layers. The convolutional layer generates feature maps based on the concentration of white regions in the chest x-ray indicating presence of infection. This is owing to the fact that the lungs of a covid-19 patient are full of water and sputum, hence more radiation is absorbed causing the affected region to appear in white or grey. Covid-19 and viral pneumonia chest x-rays differ in the distribution of lesions around the lungs. An axial distribution of lesions in the peripheral zone is observed in case of covid images, whereas a more random and diffuse distribution is observed in case of pneumonia x-rays.

The activation function applied to introduce non-linearity in the feature maps outputted by the convolutional layer is Rectified Linear Unit (RELU). In addition pooling layers are included to down sample the feature maps and prevent overfitting of the model, by making the model invariant to modulations in images brought forth by different lighting/positions. This improves the generalization of the model. Both max pooling and average pooling techniques were employed to achieve the same. A total of 512 in-features were applied in the creation of the model. The final connected dense layers, output the predicted class based on the features extracted from the previous sequential layers, which in this case is a total of 3 out-features i,e. COVID-19, viral pneumonia and normal.

The code was executed on a Jupyter notebook. The steps involved in the implementation process were namely, (1) Creating a custom dataset by augmenting images, (2) Preparing the training and test sets, (3) Performing image transformations to customise model input (4) Preparing the data loader, (5) Data visualization, (6) Creating the model, (7) Training the model and finally (8) Classifying images and showing predictions.

3.4 Training

The decision on which architecture is most suitable to train the dataset was made based on repeated experimentation. A few of the prominent pre-trained network architectures for image classification tasks are as tabulated in Table 1.

Table 1. Pre-trained network architectures for image classification tasks

VGG16	AlexNet	ResNet-18
The input to this network is an image of dimensions 224*224*3	The network has an input image size of 227*227*3	The image input size is of 224*224
It has 16 convolution layers and consists of 138 million parameters	The total parameters in this architecture is 62.3 million	ResNet-18 is a convolution neural network that consists of 18 layers with around 11 million trainable parameters
It has 16 convolution layers and consists of 138 million parameters. It uses multiple layers that include kernels of 3*3 dimension for convolution and 2*2 size for max pool	The AlexNet architecture consists of 8 layers among which 5 are convolution layers with a combination of max pooling followed by 3 fully connected layers. ReLU activation is used in each layer except the output layer	It has convolution layers with filters of size 3*3 and 2 pooling layers

Among the 3, the ResNet-18 model proved to be easier to train owing to fewer trainable parameters as compared to the other pretrained networks. In addition, it gave optimum accuracy results at the end of training.

As part of the transfer learning approach of feature extraction, once the ResNet-18 model is created, the last fully connected (FC) layer of the pre-trained model is modified. The pretrained ResNet-18 model has a total of 512 input features and 1000 output features, however in this particular case only 3 classes are outputted i.e., Covid-19, Viral Pneumonia and Normal. Hence, the FC layer is modified to have 3 output features.

The hyper parameters used for training the model are as mentioned in Table 2.

Table 2. Hyper-parameters used for the CNN training

Hyper-parameters	Values
Learning Rate	0.01
Loss Function	Cross Entropy Loss
Batch Size (training)	3917
Batch Size (testing)	1000
Optimizer	Adam
Number of Epochs	1
Steps per Epoch	340

The hyperparameters were decided upon by continuous experimentation and tuning. Cross entropy was decided as the loss function since the model tries to solve a multi classification problem. Adam is an efficient optimizer that proves to be useful in handling sparse gradients, and was chosen over other gradient based optimizers such as SGD and adagrad since it produced greater training accuracy on the ResNet-18 model. The learning rate of adam is 0.01, and this default rate is employed in training the model.

The ResNet18 model is initially set to training phase and gradients are first set to zero before starting to perform backpropragation. Loss is generated from the network parameters and the gradients are computed. After this, loss is optimized by updating the parameters based on the current gradient values. This process is iterated over all images in the train set. At every 20nth iteration, the model is set to evaluation phase where the validation loss and accuracy are computed. The model is trained until the validation loss stops dropping for several consecutive iterations i.e., after one epoch of 340 steps which witnessed a minimum validation loss of 0.12.

3.5 Data Poisoning

An adversarial machine learning approach of poisoning the dataset was applied in misguiding the model by providing malicious input. In this paper, the data poisoning approach of data manipulation was employed to manipulate the train data and cause the model to make false predictions. Out of the 7940 covid examples in the train data, 3400 of the images were overlaid with normal chest X-ray images which resulted in manipulated images as shown in Fig. 5. The overlaying of images was performed using Python Imaging Library (PIL) modules in a Jupyter notebook. The corrupted dataset was then used to train the

ResNet-18 model, keeping the hyperparameters the same as before. Training was performed for a single epoch of 340 steps after which the model was tested using the images in the test dataset. The testing accuracy underwent a significant drop of 9% from 0.9648 to 0.8711 indicating the magnitude of the threat that data poisoning imposes on machine learning models.

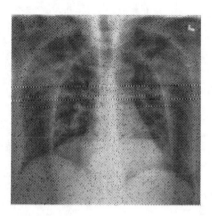

Fig. 5. Manipulated image after overlaying a normal x-ray over a covid-19 x-ray

4   Results

Table 3 shows a comparative analysis of the performance of three different pre-trained networks i.e., ResNet-18, AlexNet and VGG16 after training and testing.

Table 3. Comparative analysis of the performance of 3 models

Value	ResNet-18	AlexNet	VGG16
Validation Accuracy	0.9672	0.9040	0.8748
Validation Loss	0.1236	0.2940	0.3642
Test Accuracy	0.9648	0.9037	0.8552

The classification reports of the three models are as represented in Fig. 6. It can be understood that the ResNet-18 model performs better than the other two pre-trained networks since it delivers optimum precision, recall and f1-score values. The accuracy obtained after testing is 0.9648 which is higher than most state-of-the-art models.

	precision	recall	f1-score	support
0	0.93	0.98	0.96	497
1	0.99	0.97	0.98	474
2	0.97	0.94	0.95	535
accuracy			0.96	1506
macro avg	0.96	0.96	0.96	1506
weighted avg	0.96	0.96	0.96	1506

(a) ResNet-18

	precision	recall	f1-score	support
0	0.84	0.96	0.89	525
1	0.96	0.93	0.94	486
2	0.94	0.83	0.88	495
accuracy			0.90	1506
macro avg	0.91	0.90	0.90	1506
weighted avg	0.91	0.90	0.90	1506

(b) AlexNet

	precision	recall	f1-score	support
0	0.78	0.88	0.82	487
1	0.91	0.95	0.93	491
2	0.89	0.75	0.81	528
accuracy			0.86	1506
macro avg	0.86	0.86	0.86	1506
weighted avg	0.86	0.86	0.85	1506

(c) VGG16

Fig. 6. Classification report

The confusion matrices are plotted as shown in Fig. 7. Testing was performed by selecting a pool of 1500 images (approximately 500 from each of the classes) arbitrarily from the test dataset comprising 6000 images (2000 from each class). The colour scale in the figures suggest that the darker regions depict 400+ images, the lighter regions less than 100 images, while the mid-range colours on the scale denote 100–400 images.

Hence, it can be inferred from the confusion matrix of the ResNet-18 model, that over 450 images from each of the classes were correctly classified while the misclassifications were extremely minimal (less than 30 images per class). Furthermore, it is understood that the AlexNet model does reasonably well in correctly classifying images i.e., above 400 images per class, followed by VGG16 which correctly classifies above 350 images per class. The misclassification rates are considerable low in both the models. i.e., less than 100 images per class.

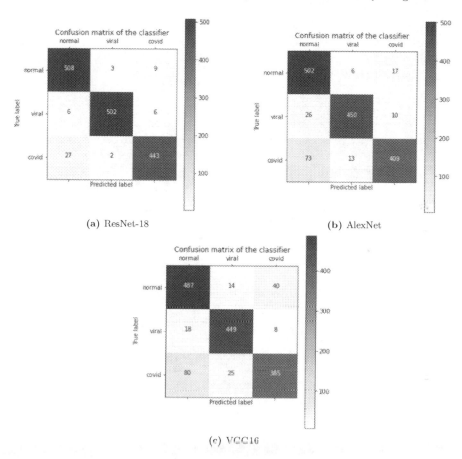

(a) ResNet-18

(b) AlexNet

(c) VGG16

Fig. 7. Confusion matrix

The model accuracy curves are as plotted in Fig. 8. As seen, the curves increase exponentially over time which is desirable during training. The accuracy curves plotted here are on the validation data i.e. steps per epoch vs validation accuracy. It can be inferred that the ResNet-18 curve reaches a maximum validation accuracy of 0.9672, followed by 0.9040 for AlexNet and 0.8748 for VGG16. It can also be noted that the increase in accuracy is seemingly smooth for the ResNet-18 curve, while the other two curves are considerably erratic in their progression.

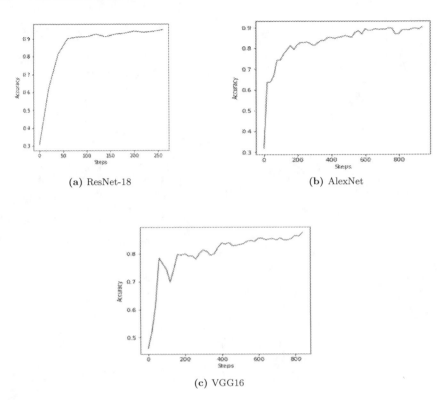

(a) ResNet-18

(b) AlexNet

(c) VGG16

Fig. 8. Accuracy curves

The model loss curves are as plotted in Fig. 9. Here, the curves decrease exponentially over time which is ideal while training the model. The loss curves plotted here are on the validation data i.e. steps per epoch vs validation loss. It can inferred that the ResNet-18 curve touches a minimum validation loss of 0.1236, followed by 0.2940 for AlexNet and 0.3642 for VGG16. The curves show a reasonably smooth decline for all three models.

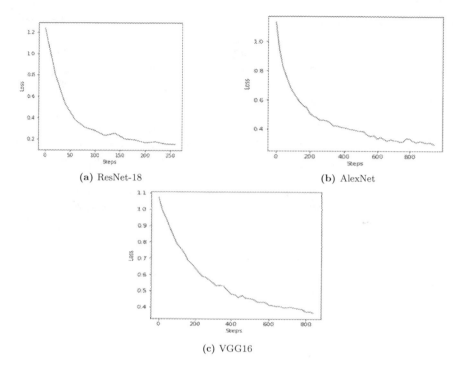

(a) ResNet-18   (b) AlexNet

(c) VGG16

Fig. 9. Loss curves

Figure 10 demonstrates the classification report of the ResNet-18 model after data poisoning. As seen there is a significant drop in the accuracy rate from 0.9648 (before poisoning) to 0.8711.

	precision	recall	f1-score	support
0	0.96	0.94	0.95	494
1	0.78	0.97	0.86	507
2	0.92	0.70	0.79	505
accuracy			0.87	1506
macro avg	0.88	0.87	0.87	1506
weighted avg	0.88	0.87	0.87	1506

Fig. 10. Classification report of ResNet-18 after data poisoning

Table 4 summarizes a comparative analysis of the performance of the ResNet-18 model before and after data poisoning.

Table 4. Comparative analysis of the ResNet-18 model before and after data poisoning.

Value	Before Data Poisoning	After Data Poisoning
Train data	8192 normal examples, 7366 viral examples, 7940 covid examples	8192 normal examples, 7366 viral examples, 7933 covid examples 3400 covid images were overlaid with normal images as part of a data manipulation poisoning attack
Test data	2000 normal examples, 2000 viral examples, 2000 covid examples.	2000 normal examples, 2000 viral examples, 2000 covid examples
Validation Accuracy	0.9672	0.8818
Validation Loss	0.1236	0.2973
Test Accuracy	0.9648	0.8711

5   Conclusion and Future Work

Detection of COVID-19 using chest x-rays can help in advancing its diagnosis. This paper details the approach that has been employed in achieving the classification task, and also rationalizes the different implementation choices made such as selection of hyper parameters and model architecture. The ResNet-18 model detailed here shows an optimum accuracy result of 0.9648 which is higher than most state-of-the-art models. A comparative analysis of the model's performance with other pre-trained networks proved that the ResNet-18 model delivered better classification results. The results obtained from data poisoning (9% drop in accuracy from 0.9648 to 0.8711) indicate that it poses a realistic threat to machine learning models, thereby making it extremely easy for an adversary to insert benign looking files and corrupt machine learning models. By expanding the dataset and fine tuning the parameters used, the classification accuracy can be increased even further, which is a scope for future study. The implementation of a Covid-19 CT-severity score in the model is another area of future analysis.

References

1. Phankokkruad, M.: COVID-19 pneumonia detection in chest x-ray images using transfer learning of convolutional neural networks. In: MDSIT 2020: Proceedings of the 3rd International Conference on Data Science and Information Technology, pp. 147–152 (July 2020)
2. Yee, S.L.K., Raymond, W.J.K.: Pneumonia diagnosis using chest x-ray images and machine learning. In: ICBET 2020: Proceedings of the 2020 10th International Conference on Biomedical Engineering and Technology, pp. 101–105 (September 2020)

3. Siddiqi, R.: Automated pneumonia diagnosis using a customized sequential convolutional neural network. In: ICDLT 2019: Proceedings of the 2019 3rd International Conference on Deep Learning Technologies, pp. 64–70 (July 2019)

4. Yu, H., Xu, X., Zhao, Z., Li, D.: YU-net lung segment image preprocess methods used for common chest diseases prediction. In: ICMLT 2020: Proceedings of the 2020 5th International Conference on Machine Learning Technologies, pp. 68–71 (June 2020)

5. Makris, A., Kontopoulos, I., Tserpes, K.: COVID-19 detection from chest x-ray images using deep learning and convolutional neural networks. In: SETN 2020: 11th Hellenic Conference on Artificial Intelligence, pp. 60–66 (September 2020)

6. Lin, T.C., Lee, H.C.: COVID-19 chest radiography images analysis based on integration of image preprocess, guided grad-cam, machine learning and risk management. In: ICMHI 2020: Proceedings of the 4th International Conference on Medical and Health Informatics, pp. 281–288 (August 2020)

7. Ke, Q., et al.: A neuro-heuristic approach for recognition of lung diseases from x-ray images. Expert Syst. Appl. **126**, 218–232 (2019)

8. Woźniak, M., Połap, D.: Bio-inspired methods modeled for respiratory disease detection from medical images. Expert Syst. Appl. **41**, 69–96 (2018)

9. Capizzi, G., Sciuto, G.L., Napoli, C., Połap, D., Woźniak, M.: Small lung nodules detection based on fuzzy-logic and probabilistic neural network with bioinspired reinforcement learning. IEEE Trans. Fuzzy Syst. **28**(6), 1178–1189 (2020). https://doi.org/10.1109/TFUZZ.2019.2952831

10. Kaggle's COVID-19 Radiography Database. https://www.kaggle.com/tawsifurrahman/covid19-radiography-database

11. IEEE8023's Covid ChestXray Dataset. https://github.com/ieee8023/covid-chestxray-dataset

12. Kaggle's COVID-19 X rays. https://www.kaggle.com/andrewmvd/convid19-X-rays

Conceptual Modeling Interacts with Machine Learning – A Systematic Literature Review

Moayid Ali Zaidi[✉]

Østfold University College, Halden, Norway

Abstract. Due to the advancement in the digital world, society's expectation towards Machine Learning is very high, especially in Conceptual Modeling. However, the relationship between Machine Learning and Conceptual models are very interesting. Literature in this field has identified the relationship and interaction between Machine Learning and Conceptual Models. However, to the best of our knowledge, there is not a Systematic Literature Review devoted to studying in deep the interaction of these two fields. In this paper, the authors conduct a Systematic Literature Review to get to know how Machine Learning is used in Conceptual Modeling. Results show the deep connection of Machine Learning with Conceptual Models in a solid way, as well as providing challenges and opportunities for future research.

Keywords: Machine Learning · Conceptual Modeling · Systematic Literature Review

1 Introduction

Conceptual Modeling advances the diagrammatic representation of the concepts converges from a broad concept to a very specific point. The goal is to simplify complex information visually. It reduces the gap between planning and requirements to solve the problem. It is the finest way to show how business goals align with the user's expectations visually. Having a long history, Conceptual Modeling has been conducted in the internal organizational settings [1]. The research and practice of the conceptual modeling assumed that the organizations develop these models to support comprehensive and stable internal requirements [2]. Rapid changes occurred in the Information systems (IS) over the last decade, including big data technologies, social media, business analytics, sensors, artificial intelligence, and the internet of things. These variations transformed how the IS designed and used. There is a necessity to innovate new approaches that support these developments in befitting manner [3]. Machine Learning plays a key role in the organizational competitive advantages within the business context [4]. Machine Learning is considered to have an ability to transform organizations and the society in general [5]. Machine Learning is one of the "three trends that

© Springer Nature Switzerland AG 2021
O. Gervasi et al. (Eds.): ICCSA 2021, LNCS 12957, pp. 522–532, 2021.
https://doi.org/10.1007/978-3-030-87013-3_39

organizations must track to gain a competitive advantage" according to Gartner's Hype Cycle for Emerging Technologies 2016 [6]. Machine Learning works without the support of external knowledge; for instance, domain models relies on the learning algorithm and training data. Current research is exploring new ways to scramble the semantics so that rules do not have to be learned from data (training data) [7]. Without external assistant from the users, it mainly focuses on infusing of a learning algorithm. Several issues have been reported working with Machine Learning algorithms and data. The quality of the data is crucial while performing Machine Learning techniques [8]. There is a dire need to improve the ability of Machine Learning techniques to explain the decisions and predictions of the models in effective manner [9]. Historically speaking, the main focus of Artificial Intelligence was symbolic representation while using logical formalism [10]. The first engineering requisite rules such as semantic networks were used to develop AI applications. With the excessive amount of data AI shifted its focus to computationally intensive data-driven approaches (Machine Learning) [11]. Machine Learning iterates over the data to detect the complex relationship among target and input variables. This type of approach is not easily understood by humans. In the contribution of the model's decision some methods give importance to the weight of input features. This type of technique has local interpretable model agnostic explanations with a focus on precise features but it fails to abstract the higher-level concept [12]. Roman [13] proposed the new approach based upon the concept of conceptual modeling, where he used the ML model agnostic approach. This approach can complement existing approaches [14] by combining the knowledge form the application domain and the Machine Learning model. It can deliver the cognitive benefits that facilitate understanding and explanation of the model. Considering the ever-increasing importance of the topic, the authors present the systematic literature review devoted to investigating the intersection of these two fields. To best our knowledge there is no systematic literature review on Machine Learning interacting with conceptual modeling. Our approach provides new insight on this topic. The rest of the paper is organized as follows: Sect. 2 discusses the background and research questions. Section 3 discusses the Research Methods and Research Questions. Section 4 described the review protocol, data sources and search strategy). Section 5 focused on Analysis and Discussion. Finally, Sect. 6 described the conclusion and recommendations for future work.

2   Background

In the development of an Information System (IS), conceptual modeling is the major phase that captures the requirements from the users to support the development of Information Systems. It has led to several kinds of conceptual models including process model, data model, models of business activities, models of enterprise, and system architecture [15]. These models are diagrams that hold graphics and text which are massively used in the development of IS to facilitate communication, improve understanding and guide the activities such as user interface design, database design, and programming [16]. The conceptual model plays a vital role in the designing of databases, where the Entity-Relationship model has become a standard to represent the structured data. The benefits of conceptual models for information development have been investigated by the researchers. Three basic needs through which the conceptual model arises [17].

2.1   Need to Cope with Complexity

It reduces the complexity of the development of the Information System by concentrating on the relevant aspects, organizing, and structuring the requirements.

2.2   Need for Shared Understanding

In the development of Information Systems, involve many peoples with different backgrounds, expertise, beliefs, and training. That type of diversity creates conflicts and may lead to project failure if it is left unresolved. So they are designed by the general objectives [18].

2.3   Need to Solve Problems

Information Systems are designed to address the organizational and societal needs, although it is very difficult to design a system that has several options. Conceptual modeling supports precise design solutions and analysis. These three needs to be studied in the development of an Information System and Machine Learning. Therefore, these techniques might be useful in resolving challenges, adoption, and development. The potential to apply conceptual modeling to Machine Learning seems to be missing while the existing efforts focused on specific issue.

3   Research Method and Research Questions

The purpose of this study is to structure and characterize the state of the practice on the usage of Conceptual Modeling in Machine Learning. A systematic literature review is used as a research method. The systematic literature review is the means of interpretation, identification, and evaluation of the research relevant to the specific subject or research question. Thus, the main research question driving this study is: What is the state of the practice of the use of Conceptual Modeling in Machine Learning? To address the goal of the paper, three research questions were formulated by the authors. RQ1: How conceptual modeling is used in Machine Learning? RQ2: What are the reported challenges and opportunities in the use of conceptual models in Machine Learning? RQ3: How can Machine Learning facilitate in the conceptual modeling? In the first research question, we discuss which aspects and features in Machine Learning have been reported by the conceptual modeling, while in the second, we examine the potential challenges and opportunities and third describe how ML can facilitate in the Conceptual Modeling.

4   Review Protocol

A review protocol describes the duty that needs to be completed to answer the research questions in a systematic literature review. To find viable literature, the authors used six popular academic databases.

- Google Scholar (https://scholar.google.com/)
- SpringerLink (https://link.springer.com/)
- ScienceDirect (https://www.sciencedirect.com/)
- IEEE Explore (https://ieeexplore.ieee.org/)
- ACM Digital Library (https://dl.acm.org/)
- Wiley Online Library (https://onlinelibrary.wiley.com/)

These databases were chosen because they are among the most relevant source of articles within the extensive field of computing and they are also accessible using institutional accounts.

4.1   Search Strategy

While managing the literature search, it is required to describe the search strategy to find the similar search result. After brainstorming the different terms, the author constructed the search string according to the research questions. To cover the exact topic the string should be simple and comprehensive. The author uses the Boolean operator AND to concatenate the major terms. Hence the resulting query is: ("Conceptual Modeling") AND ("Machine Learning") Zotero was used as a reference management tool to avoid duplication. After the search string, the author chose to filter out the paper based on the inclusion and exclusion criteria. Once the initial results were retrieved, the inclusion and exclusion procedures were applied. The scope of the time in this SLR is set from 2015 to September 2020.

Inclusion criteria

- Papers that are based on the discussion on conceptual modeling and ML. Papers, which covers the research questions
- Papers were published in the period 2015 to 2020
- Papers which are written in English

Exclusion Criteria

- Papers contain no relevant data to answer the research question
- The Paper's full text is not available
- Papers that are more than 5 years old
- Duplicated Studies

4.2   Data Extraction

The studies and articles gathered were recorded and stored in a reference manager. This made it simpler to filter different elements based on results. The selection process was recorded as well, and Excel was used to get an additional overview of the selected studies. This made it feasible to attain quantitative data to answer the research questions.

4.3 Selected Primary Studies

The search query provided a total of 3991 results. 25 papers were selected based on their titles, keywords, and abstracts. The papers were filtered by the inclusion and exclusion criteria for this paper. During the filtering process () papers were eliminated because they were not relevant in terms of Research questions and the aim of the paper. Out of 25 results which were selected based on titles, keywords, and abstracts. One is removed because of duplicate. Other discarded because of a lack of connection to the research questions. Although it was approved and used in this paper to answer the questions. The filtering process of the papers is described in Table 1 sorted by their databases.

Table 1. Paper filtering phase

Library	Number of hits	Abstract	Full text
Google Scholar	3050	20	8
ScienceDirect	72	0	0
Springer Link	754	3	2
Wiley Online Library	39	0	0
IEEE Xplore	5	1	0
ACM	71	1	0
Total	3991	25	10

5 Analysis and Discussion

This section deals with answer and findings of research questions. The literature will be compared and discussed, concerning each research question. First, RQ1 will be discussed which feature in Machine Learning have been stated as conceptual modeling. Second, RQ2 investigate the challenges and opportunities. Finally, RQ3 provides a narrow approach to how Machine Learning facilitates conceptual modeling.

RQ1: How conceptual modeling is used in Machine Learning? Conceptual modeling can be used as the standard and effective activity in the different phases of Machine Learning. It can be valuable to improve the understanding of training data, rise the performance and accuracy of Machine Learning algorithms, and recognizing the specific problem. The conceptual modeling benefits in different stages of the Cross-Industry Standard Process for Data Mining for instance understanding of the business, data understanding, modeling, deployment, and evaluation [19, 20]. Models are also used to define the experience which is gained by solving Machine Learning tasks [21]. The first phase of CRISP-DM [6] is to understand the requirements and objectives of the project. Conceptual Modeling is used to support this phase. The specific goals cannot be achieved without understanding the business objectives in Machine Learning projects. Conceptual models describe the goals and objectives of Machine Learning projects. It can assist the managers and other parties to identify the processes which are affected by the Machine Learning. Roman [20] proposed the following steps for conceptual modeling research in Machine Learning.

5.1   Data Understanding

This phase starts with the acquisition of data that is suitable for business problem identification. Modelers review the data, overcome the quality issues, and prepare it for the Machine Learning software. Common notations and modeling grammars such as ER, UML support this phase and well suited for the understanding and modeling of data.

5.2   Data Preparation

This phase involves all the activities which are used to construct the final version of the dataset for the learning algorithms. It includes a different transformation of data by performing the ETL (Extract-Transform-Load) procedure. Previous research in the field of conceptual modeling described the use of process models such as EPCs and BPMN to document the ETL process [20,22]. Conceptual modeling grammar can graphically communicate and better reflect the needs of the Machine Learning process.

5.3   Modeling

In this stage, the dataset emerges from the prior stage is supplied to Machine Learning algorithms for learning, training, and validation. A conceptual model can be used to assist the modeling process and Machine Learning algorithm. For instance, if there is some important information, the modeler may select the inputs manually to ensure that the algorithm examines these inputs. It is accomplished by hard coding some of the data inputs and could also improve the performance of the algorithm.

5.4   Evaluation

This stage includes the interpretation of results of the model generated by the algorithm into the language which is convenient to business users. The conceptual model can highlight the inputs which are necessary for the training model and left the other attributes that exist in the domain. It enhances the understandability of complex Machine Learning models. The notable concern regarding the usage of the Machine Learning algorithm is the lack of transparency i.e. neural networks, random forests, and support vector machines. In the critical and sensitive applications, the "black box" property of these models is a barrier to the wider adoption of Machine Learning [20,23].

5.5   Deployment

The building of the model is not the end of the Machine Learning project. The performance of the model needs to be sufficient if it addresses the business objectives. If the model is working sufficiently then it is introduced into the real world. For instance, to prioritize the case of interest neural networks serve as the decision support tool. Table 2 presents the use of CM for Machine Learning based on the CRISP-DM phases [6].

Table 2. Conceptual modeling and machine learning [6]

Phase	How CM can contribute to the phase	Suggested grammar
Business understanding	Represent, identify boundary objects	i*, BPMN, UML, BIM
Data understanding	Modeling scripts, extending	ER, UM
Data preparation	Attribute selection, transformation	BPMN, EPCs
Modeling	Representation of domain models	UML, ERD
Evaluation	Transparency, understandability	UML, enterprise model
Deployment	Documentation	i*, BPMN, UML

The conceptual model is used to document the goals and objectives of phase 1. When the deployment occurs, the user can refer to phase 1 for the original goals and objectives. The deployment of Machine Learning in business may occur some changes in the business process. Various models like the process model and enterprise model document these changes and consult with the stakeholders about the effect of the business process [20]. Another interesting approach is one taken by Datameer, a data analytics platform that allows us to define and refine the visual representation of pipeline, while the SKYMIND allows us to translate the Machine Learning models into a set of tasks [24].

RQ2: What are the reported challenges and opportunities in the usage of conceptual models in Machine Learning? The different approach is the usage of deep learning, which is based on the data that represent previously observed process instances. One important drawback of using Deep Learning is that the artificial neural network cannot be easily understood in terms of traditional theory elements, such as causes and constructs [21]. Hossain [25] described that the restricted natural language can serve as a high-level language for conceptual modeling particularly for entity-relationship models, and also mentioned that this approach has the potential to bridge between informal specification and formal representation of conceptual modeling. It involves different aspects such as on front end, natural language understanding; on back end scene generation technology and it also mapping the discrete data to continuous data of the graphic scene [26]. Conceptual Modeling addresses the issue related to handling data integration and curation [27]. The limitation of conceptual modeling in data manipulation via Machine Learning is that it does not focus on the limitation of conceptual modeling methods or grammars and thus, it does not directly contribute to the progress in conceptual modeling research [28]. There is a dearth of research in designing processes to express deploying Machine Learning for business applications, it is because applying conceptual modeling in Machine Learning is different from traditional Information Systems [29].

RQ3: How can Machine Learning facilitate in the conceptual modeling? Machine Learning introduces the natural path to help modeling systems that are inherently involved with data of high complexity. It could automate or semi-automate the process of knowledge capturing. It can be beneficial where the behavioral aspect of the real system is hard to express in equations analytically or simply as data distribution. With the help of Machine Learning, it is possible to learn and illustrate the vast number of datasets. Machine Learning models were also used to learn the complex patterns of flowing crowds. The necessary point to consider is a mechanism of integration. The development of models is an iterative process from conceptual modeling to implementation (Fig. 1). The preliminary concern is to identify the stages where Machine Learning could be applicable or useful. The main point is that Machine Learning can be utilized at different stages of modeling in different ways as follow [30].

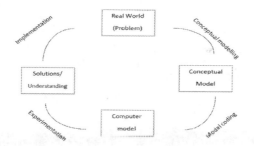

Fig. 1. Key stages of simulation modeling [30]

Sterman [30] consistently stated the importance of developing assistive tools that can understand the complexity and also support the process of learning about systems. At the early stages of problem formulation unsupervised Machine Learning serve as the purpose of knowledge elicitation. For the conceptualization of the system's behavior or structure, unsupervised techniques could be used during the conceptual modeling phase. In the context of the feedback loop, mental models supported the data-driven knowledge learned by Machine Learning. Figure 2 shows the idea, where new data is considered as a form of feedback produced by the new system states. The models continuously re-fitted to the feedback loops to demonstrate the new conditions. In this way, the new states can be learned based on Machine Learning models. While dealing with the large-scale datasets data-driven prediction could be less biased compared to the human modeler.

Using Machine Learning at the process of conceptualization can contribute to lowering the bias of human-based knowledge elicitation. Further, the Machine

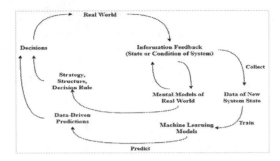

Fig. 2. Data-driven feedback loops; system modeling aided by ML [30]

Learning guided simulation can also help to attain a higher level of model realism. There is a dire need for constructing a high-fidelity representation of real-world problems that brings up new practical aspects for taking advantage of Machine Learning potentials.

6   Conclusion

The future holds many exciting opportunities for assimilating the practice of Machine Learning and Conceptual Modeling. The main motivation for this work was to examine how Conceptual Modeling used in Machine Learning and how Machine Learning interacts with Conceptual modeling. Result show the importance of these two fields paving the way to the new research efforts. Conclusion to our work also identifies the opportunities and challenges in the topic. In addition, many fascinating challenges for Machine Learning and Conceptual Modeling exists which have to be more deeply explored in future.

References

1. Liew, C.F., DeLatte, D., Takeishi, N., Yairi, T.: Recent developments in aerial robotics: a survey and prototypes overview. arXiv:1711.10085 cs, November 2017
2. Castellanos, A., Tremblay, M.C., Lukyanenko, R., Samuel, B.: Basic classes in conceptual modeling: theory and practical guidelines. J. Assoc. Inf. Syst. **21**, 44 (2020)
3. Eckerson, W.W.: Data warehousing special report: data quality and the bottom line. Appl. Dev. Trends **1**, 1–9 (2002)
4. Sabegh, M.A.J., Lukyanenko, R., Recker, J., Samuel, B., Castellanos, A.: Conceptual modeling research in information systems: what we now know and what we still do not know, p. 11 (2017)
5. Khatri, V., Samuel, B.M.: Analytics for managerial work. Commun. ACM **62**(4), 100 (2019). https://doi.org/10.1145/3274277
6. Jones, N.: Using massive amounts of data to recognize photos and speech, deep-learning computers are taking a big step towards true artificial intelligence. Nature **505**, 1–3 (2014)

7. Lukyanenko, R., Parsons, J., Storey, V.C.: Modeling matters: can conceptual modeling support machine learning?, p. 11 (2018)
8. Tsymbal, A., Zillner, S., Huber, M.: Ontology – supported machine learning and decision support in biomedicine. In: Cohen-Boulakia, S., Tannen, V. (eds.) DILS 2007. LNCS, vol. 4544, pp. 156–171. Springer, Heidelberg (2007). https://doi.org/10.1007/978-3-540-73255-6_14
9. Alonso, O.: Challenges with label quality for supervised learning. J. Data Inf. Qual. **6**(1), 1–3 (2015). https://doi.org/10.1145/2724721
10. Castelvecchi, D.: Machine learning is becoming ubiquitous in basic research as well as in industry. But for scientists to trust it, they first need to understand what the machines are doing, p. 4
11. Crevier, D.: AI: The Tumultuous History of the Search for Artificial Intelligence. Basic Books, New York (1993)
12. Cerf, V.G.: AI is not an excuse! Commun. ACM **62**(10), 7 (2019). https://doi.org/10.1145/3359332
13. Ribeiro, M.T., Singh, S., Guestrin, C.: 'Why should i trust you?': explaining the predictions of any classifier. In: Proceedings of the 22nd ACM SIGKDD International Conference on Knowledge Discovery and Data Mining, San Francisco, CA, USA, pp. 1135–1144, August 2016. https://doi.org/10.1145/2939672.2939778
14. Lukyanenko, R., Castellanos, A., Storey, V.C., Castillo, A., Tremblay, M.C., Parsons, J.: Superimposition: augmenting machine learning outputs with conceptual models for explainable AI. In: Grossmann, G., Ram, S. (eds.) ER 2020. LNCS, vol. 12584, pp. 26–34. Springer, Cham (2020). https://doi.org/10.1007/978-3-030-65847-2_3
15. Henelius, A., Puolamäki, K., Boström, H., Asker, L., Papapetrou, P.: A peek into the black box: exploring classifiers by randomization. Data Min. Knowl. Discov. **28**, 1503–1529 (2014). https://doi.org/10.1007/s10618-014-0368-8
16. Azevedo, C.L.B., Iacob, M.-E., Almeida, J.P.A., van Sinderen, M., Pires, L.F., Guizzardi, G.: Modeling resources and capabilities in enterprise architecture: a well-founded ontology-based proposal for ArchiMate. Inf. Syst. **54**, 235–262 (2015). https://doi.org/10.1016/j.is.2015.04.008
17. Aguirre-Urreta, M.I., Marakas, G.M.: Comparing conceptual modeling techniques: a critical review of the EER vs. OO empirical literature. SIGMIS Database **39**(2), 9–32 (2008). https://doi.org/10.1145/1364636.1364640
18. Lukyanenko, R.: Rethinking the role of conceptual modeling in the introductory IS curriculum, p. 10 (2019)
19. Mark, G., Lyytinen, K., Bergman, M.: Boundary objects in design: an ecological view of design artifacts. J. Assoc. Inf. Syst. **8**(11), 34 (2007). https://doi.org/10.17705/1jais.00144
20. Jackson, J.: Data mining; a conceptual overview. CAIS **8**, 19 (2002). https://doi.org/10.17705/1CAIS.00819
21. Lukyanenko, R., Castellanos, A., Parsons, J., Chiarini, T.M., Storey, V.C.: Using conceptual modeling to support machine learning. In: Cappiello, C., Ruiz, M. (eds.) CAiSE 2019. LNBIP, vol. 350, pp. 170–181. Springer, Cham (2019). https://doi.org/10.1007/978-3-030-21297-1_15
22. Fettke, P.: Conceptual modelling and artificial intelligence (2020)
23. Song, I.-Y., Liddle, S.W., Ling, T.-W., Scheuermann, P. (eds.): ER 2003. LNCS, vol. 2813. Springer, Heidelberg (2003). https://doi.org/10.1007/b13244
24. Hall, P., Gill, N.: An Introduction to Machine Learning Interpretability, 2nd edn., p. 62. O'Reilly, Boston (2019)

25. Damiani, E., Frati, F.: Towards conceptual models for machine learning computations. In: Trujillo, J.C., et al. (eds.) ER 2018. LNCS, vol. 11157, pp. 3–9. Springer, Cham (2018). https://doi.org/10.1007/978-3-030-00847-5_1
26. Hossain, B.A., Schwitter, R.: Specifying conceptual models using restricted natural language (2018)
27. Wang, J.: Research on spatial conceptual modeling of natural language processing based on deep learning algorithms. J. Phys. Conf. Ser. **1345**, 042090 (2019). https://doi.org/10.1088/1742-6596/1345/4/042090
28. Storey, V.C., Song, I.-Y.: Big data technologies and management: what conceptual modeling can do. Data Knowl. Eng. **108**, 50–67 (2017). https://doi.org/10.1016/j.datak.2017.01.001
29. Lukyanenko, R., Parsons, J., Wiersma, Y., Wachinger, G., Huber, B., Meldt, R.: Representing crowd knowledge: guidelines for conceptual modeling of user-generated content. JAIS **18**(4), 297–339 (2017). https://doi.org/10.17705/1jais.00456
30. Sothilingam, R., Yu, E., Senderovich, A.: Towards higher maturity for machine learning: a conceptual modelling approach. iJournal Grad. Stud. J. Faculty Inf. **5**(1), Art. no. 1 (2019). https://doi.org/10.33137/ijournal.v5i1.33476
31. Elbattah, M.: How can machine learning support the practice of modeling and simulation? – a review and directions for future research. In: 2019 IEEE/ACM 23rd International Symposium on Distributed Simulation and Real Time Applications (DS-RT), Cosenza, Italy, October 2019, pp. 1–7. https://doi.org/10.1109/DS-RT47707.2019.8958703

An Adaptive Multi-layered Approach for DoS Detection and Mitigation

Sowmya Ramesh⬤, Subhiksha Selvarayan⬤, Kanishq Sunil⬤,
and Chamundeswari Arumugam⁽✉⁾⬤

Department of Computer Science and Engineering,
Sri Sivasubramaniya Nadar College of Engineering, Chennai, India
{sowmya18159,subhiksha18172,kanishq17069}@cse.ssn.edu.in,
chamundeswaria@ssn.edu.in

Abstract. A Denial of Service (DoS) attack imposes a heavy load on a system rendering it unavailable to the benign traffic. One of the most popular approaches to carry out the attack is to send a multitude of requests to the targeted site or network, causing the host or network to become unable to reply to the benign traffic or to respond slowly. The complexity and frequency of these attacks have been increasing in recent years. Hence, there is a need to design an efficient system that would detect any suspicious activity in the network and dispatch a timely and appropriate response to counter the same. In this paper, different design models and implementations of contemporary intrusion detection systems have been reviewed and analyzed for shortcomings. A multi-level design for an Intrusion Detection and Prevention System (IDPS) that aims to efficiently detect the DoS attack with minimal response time and high accuracy has been proposed. A UDP flood is simulated inside a virtual network environment to emulate the attack and the results demonstrate the successful detection and mitigation of the DoS attack.

Keywords: Denial of Service (DoS) · UDP flood attack · Intrusion Detection System · IDPS · Virtual network

1 Introduction

The Internet has transformed the way people communicate today. The facilities they provide are easy to use even though a large number of people are using them for their day-to-day activities [1]. The services they provide have extended to banking transactions, medicine, education, research, etc. The exponential growth in technology has also made them the primary targets for cyberattacks [2]. Security is a sensitive issue for all organizations and institutions as malicious users can exploit the design weaknesses of the network and steal confidential information making the organization lose millions of dollars [3]. Security threats like Denial of Service (DoS) attacks have profound effects on the server. They work by overwhelming the target's resources, making it unavailable to provide its intended

© Springer Nature Switzerland AG 2021
O. Gervasi et al. (Eds.): ICCSA 2021, LNCS 12957, pp. 533–545, 2021.
https://doi.org/10.1007/978-3-030-87013-3_40

services for legitimate users [4]. Different open-source software and toolkits are made available to attack the target with fewer resources [5]. The attack is often challenging and complex to detect as they mimic legitimate traffic and downgrade the server [6]. Thus, a secure network is essential to uphold the safety and security of all services provided through the Internet. An Intrusion Detection Prevention System(IDPS) is a combination of both IDS(Intrusion Detection System) and IPS (Intrusion Prevention System). An IDS is a system that identifies suspicious network traffic, which cannot be detected by the traditional firewall, based on available data about previous attack history [7,8]. The attacks can be adversarial intrusions against IDS or simply a set of actions that violate the security policies associated with the IDS itself [9]. The IPS system can block the attack/threat in addition to detecting them [10].

The four common types of IDPS: Network-Based, Wireless, Network Behaviour Analysis System, and Host-Based IDPS are discussed in detail in [11]. A signature-based IDPS matches the signature of known attacks that have already been stored in the database and then identifies the attacks [12]. An anomaly-based IDPS first records the incoming traffic and details of normal traffic of the system [13].

A host-based IDPS system has been implemented that uses signature-based methods to detect abnormalities. The IDPS presented in this paper is capable of efficiently detecting and mitigating the attack. The type of DoS attack demonstrated in this paper is the User Datagram Protocol(UDP) flood attack. This volumetric DoS attack floods the server with UDP packets on either random or specified ports [14]. The server soon exhausts its resources by trying to process and reply to the overwhelming requests making it impossible to process legitimate traffic. The solution also compares the results with various previous solutions.

The rest of the paper has been organized as follows: Sect. 2 reviews the existing work and research done in this field. Section 3 presents the proposed methodology for the implementation of the Intrusion Detection and Prevention System. Section 4 presents the experimental results and performance evaluation of the proposed work. Finally, Sect. 5 provides the concluding remarks and gives some insight into future work.

2   Literature Survey

M. Nenova et al. [15] proposed a design for an IDS system based on some open-source IDS and IPS systems and they have tested the system designed against two common attacks, SQL injection and SYN flood attack. They have also performed bandwidth traffic analysis on the snort IDS and analyzed different firewall policies. They have used snort IDS and IPS software blade integrated with check point security Gateway to provide another layer of security in addition to the check point firewall technology. They have simulated the attack using web servers and FTP servers to carry out the tests. The signature for an SYN flood attack had been included in the IPS system and they have thus succeeded in preventing the DOS attack as soon as it is detected. This solution relies heavily on the firewall system and the open-source technologies being used here since all the incoming packets are routed through the firewall using NAT. A successful attack on the firewall entry point or any downtime could lay the network bare to malicious activity.

M. M. Shurman et al. [16] proposed a hybrid design that combines a signature-based IDS and an anomaly-based IDS which monitors user behavior and classifies the network packets to detect DoS attacks as soon as it commences. The hybrid approach has a lot of benefits since signature-based IDS has a fast detection period but it can't detect unknown attacks like the anomaly-based IDS. Signature-based IDS also compensates for the high false-positive rate of the anomaly-based system. In their system, they relay the incoming traffic to the anomaly-based detector only if the incoming traffic pattern does not match any known attack signatures. The anomaly-based detector also adds the signature of an attack that it detects to the database thus enabling the system to detect the attack sooner the next time it repeats. As mentioned before, the anomaly-based detector could cause the overpopulation of the database with false-positive signatures and prevent valid attack signatures from getting stored in the database.

A. A. Titorenko et al. [17] examined the influence of different DoS attacks on Network Intrusion Detection Systems (NIDS) and proposed methods for strengthening the resistance to these attacks. As DoS and DDoS attacks are unpredictable, they complicate the development of prompt countermeasures. To improve the functioning of the IDS, they collected the percentage distribution of different kinds of attacks against IDS snort with default settings. Based on the received data, they proposed a mathematical model capable of selecting the configuration which will maximize the probability of successful attack detection and minimize false positives. The model was developed based on game theory which uses Hurwitz and Wald criterion for making decisions. They have also developed and presented the criteria for evaluating attack detection performance. If the necessary statistical data related to a particular situation is available, then the model developed will significantly increase the performance and fault tolerance of the IDS.

M. T. Kurniawan et al. [18] proposed a signature-based IDS that adopts a blocking approach that blocks all the packets from the attacker until the attacker cannot generate more packets. They implemented the IDS on a Wireless Sensor Network (WSN) that is vulnerable to DoS attacks. They have adopted the RREQ_RATELIMIT (Route Limit) calculation scheme for the implementation and blocking approach. The attack packet gets dropped when there is a DoS attack, then the RREQ (Route Request) request exceeds RREQ_RATELIMIT, which is 10 packages per second based on RFC. An RREQ_ACCEPT_LIMIT is set to not change the RREQ_RATELIMIT to a higher value. When RREQ exceeds RATE_ACCEPT_LIMIT, the request gets rejected. They have used the Quality of Service (QoS): delay, packet loss, throughput, and energy to determine the performance of the WSN in different scenarios.

Researchers have also worked on extending the protection offered by IDS to the cloud. This area has seen designs for various hybrid systems that combine signature-based and anomaly-based detection strategies come up. Kumar et al. [19] proposed a hybrid system that employs a packet sniffer, a feature extractor, and an SVM classifier to detect different flood-based DoS attacks in virtual machines hosted in a cloud environment. In his paper [20], Shubhra Dwivedi has proposed an IDS system which they called GOIDS. It selects features using Grasshopper Optimization Algorithm(GOA) and passes them to different classifiers to classify the attack. They have evaluated their model on the KDD and CIC-IDS datasets, widely used by many researchers working on anomaly-based detection strategies. Odusami et al. [21] proposed an anomaly-based detection strategy using LSTM to detect DDoS attacks on web servers. Another work that uses an LSTM based approach [22], where a hybrid model combined with CNN for weights training has been employed. Abushwereb et al. [23] compared the performance of various machine learning classifiers in detecting different types of DoS attacks. Kim et al. [24] proposed a way to create attack images by transforming numerical features like destination port and protocol type into grayscale and RGB images. Further, they employed a CNN model to classify the attacks based on the attack image.

Table 1 summarizes the existing work related to IDS. Extensive research has also been done to identify the shortcomings of the IDS system. One of the most commonly reported problems is that the system goes into action well after the system/service performance degrades or after it has become unavailable. Dos attack, in particular, is a huge threat because it is hard to determine the scale of the attack and take necessary measures to prevent it.

Table 1. Comparison of existing works and their detection methodology

Paper	SIDS	AIDS	Hybrid IDS	Detection strategy
M. Nenova et al. (2019)	✓	✗	✗	Signature based IPS system that uses open source intrusion detection software and tested against SQL injection and SYN flood attacks
M. M. Shurman et al. (2019)	✓	✓	✓	Incoming traffic is sent to the anomaly detector only if no matches are found in the known attack signature database
M. T. Kurniawan et al. (2020)	✓	✗	✗	Implemented a blocking approach based on RREQ rate limit to mitigate DoS attacks on a Wireless sensor network
Dwivedi et al. (2020)	✗	✓	✗	Anomaly based IDS that uses grasshopper optimization algorithm along with the C4.5 decision tree classifier
M Odusami et al. (2019)	✗	✓	✗	Proposed an LSTM based detection model to detect both low rate and high rate layer seven DDoS attacks with high accuracy and low false positive rate
Kim et al. (2020)	✗	✓	✗	CCN based detection model that performs binary and multi-class classification
Abushwereb et al. (2020)	✗	✓	✗	Compared the detection rate of various machine learning classifiers in detecting different attacks.TCP-SYN attacks were found to have the lowest detection rate
Smys et al. (2020)	✗	✓	✗	Proposed a hybrid model that combines an LSTM and CNN model to achieve a detection accuracy of 98%

3   Proposed Methodology

This paper proposes a new type of IDPS system that takes into consideration a lot of factors before disallowing access to the source host of a packet. The experiment has been carried out on an Ubuntu 20.04 Long Term Support (LTS) virtual machine. The hypervisor that was used for the experiment is VirtualBox and a network emulator, mininet, was used as the testbed to simulate different variations of the DoS attack. The IDS system has been tuned to an optimal configuration based on the results of the experiment. All experiments have been tested on 3 hosts + Switch configuration. Figure 1 shows the network topology configured in mininet.

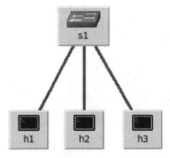

Fig. 1. Simulated network topology using mininet

The above topology has been simulated using mininet, which allows for rapid prototyping and experimentation of network configurations through its light virtualization technology. The virtual networking components and hosts support OpenFlow protocol for advanced routing use cases, but the experiments carried out in this paper use the legacy switch. Figure 2 shows the IP address of the host h3 being set. It also provides various other customization options like delay, bandwidth, loss %, and maximum queue size.

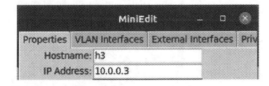

Fig. 2. Setting IP address for a host in the virtual network

The 3 hosts in the network topology have 3 different roles. Host node, h1, is the attacker. h2 takes on the role of the victim node and h3, which is of interest to us, is where the IDPS system is set up to act as a firewall. All packets that need to be sent to the victim node have to be routed through the IDPS system which allows us to perform packet filtering and analysis at h3. Figure 3 shows the high-level overview of the proposed IDPS.

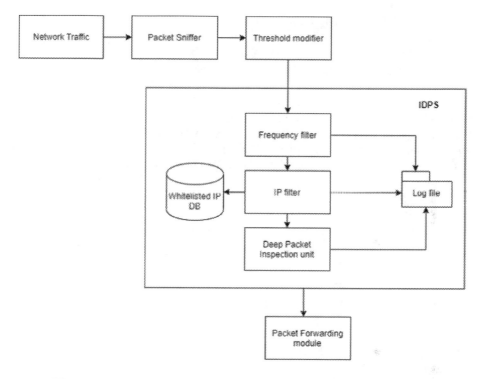

Fig. 3. Proposed design of intrusion detection and prevention system

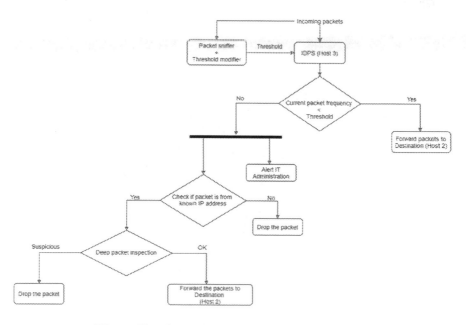

Fig. 4. Flowchart of adaptive multi-level approach

Figure 4 represents the flow of control within the IDPS system. The threshold modifier component calculates the incoming packet frequency at predefined intervals of time and updates the value for the allowed frequency threshold in the IDPS configuration. Since DoS detection by inspecting the frequency parameter alone can be inflexible and inaccurate at times, this dynamic threshold calculator will help to make adjustments according to a system's peak and off-peak hours, making the system adaptive to its network environment. If the frequency exceeds the set threshold, an alert is sent to the IT administrator and the packet undergoes further inspection. The source IP address of the packet is compared against a whitelist consisting of known and trusted IP addresses. On the occasion that it does not match, the packet gets dropped and the particular IP address is blocked until the administrator reviews the log file and decides on the further course of action. But if a match is found, it further undergoes Deep Packet Inspection (DPI) where the packet's header information and the payload are scrutinized thoroughly. If it gets classified as suspicious, the packet gets dropped, else it is forwarded to its destination.

4   Results and Discussion

After all the configurations have been made to the mininet virtual network, the python script for the IDPS is run on host 3, and the script for simulation of DoS attack is run on host 1. The attacker uses the packet manipulation library in python, scapy, to carry out the DoS attack by sending a flood of UDP packets. Scapy allows us to specify an "inter" parameter which represents the waiting time between two successive attack packets. The attack is simulated by varying this parameter.

Figure 5 illustrates the results observed when the DoS interval was varied over 6 iterations. Here, the DoS time refers to the amount of time (in seconds) it takes to reach 100% CPU utilization. It can be observed from the figure that as the interval decreases, the DoS time slumps for the interval - 0.0001 after which further decrease leads to erratic results as can be seen from the graph for the case of the last interval of 0.00001. Thus, the interval for the UDP flood has been set to the optimum value of 0.0001 after experimenting with different values.

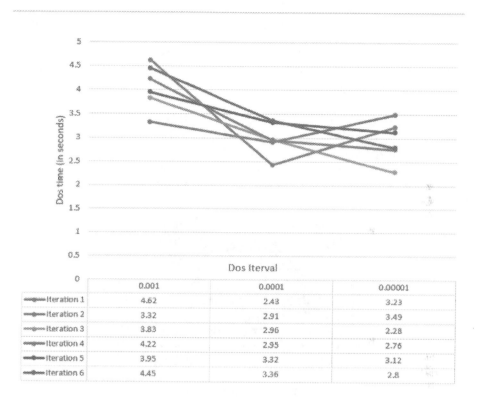

	0.001	0.0001	0.00001
Iteration 1	4.62	2.48	3.23
Iteration 2	3.32	2.91	3.49
Iteration 3	3.83	2.96	2.28
Iteration 4	4.22	2.95	2.76
Iteration 5	3.95	3.32	3.12
Iteration 6	4.45	3.36	2.8

Fig. 5. Variation of DoS time with respect to DoS interval

Fig. 6. IDPS attack detection

Figure 6 shows packets from the source routed to the destination through the IDPS (host 3). The IDPS checks if the frequency of the incoming packets is lesser than the threshold. The packets forwarded to the destination are the ones with frequency lesser than the threshold. If the frequency is higher, the IDPS flags the packet and sends it to the second level for further processing. It was observed that the dynamic frequency filter was able to adjust well to the different proportions of traffic. Around 60–70% of the malicious packets flagged by the first level were blocked successfully in the whitelisted IP filtering level. Only very few packets that employed IP spoofing techniques were able to make it to the final level. And in the final level, the packets get inspected thoroughly to detect whether it is malicious or not. The packets that get flagged as malicious are dropped and the IDPS system is successful in breaking the communication between the attacker and the victim.

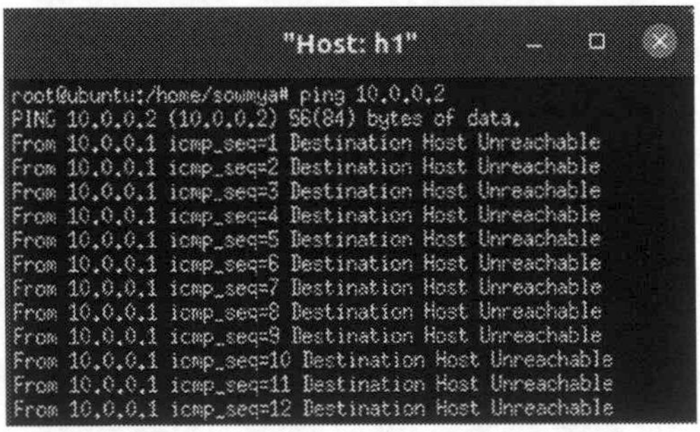

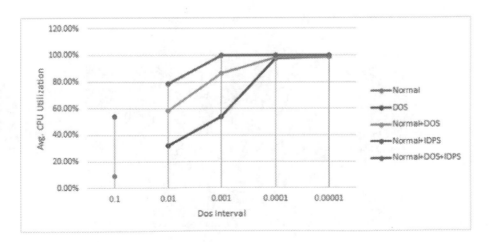

Fig. 7. Blocking of attacker's IP address

As it can be seen from Fig. 7, host h1's IP address has been blocked and it's now unable to send packets to the victim node.

Fig. 8. The average CPU utilization of different levels of network traffic recorded for varying DoS intervals

Figure 8 depicts how the average CPU utilization varies for different combinations of traffic and usage against different DoS intervals. The CPU utilization has been measured using the htop command-line utility. It can be seen that the CPU utilization is just above 0% for normal traffic. With the simulation of the DoS attack, it is evident that the utilization increases from 30% and reaches maximum utilization when the interval is 0.0001, which is the optimal DoS interval for this experimental setup as mentioned previously. The utilization is higher when both normal and DoS traffic are fed into the system.

Table 2. High level overview of performance metrics of the proposed approach compared against generic IDS types.

Detection techniques	Accuracy	False positive Rate	False negative rate	Resource utilization	Detection rate for new attacks
Anomaly-based	Varies	High	Low	High	High
Signature-based	High	Low	High	Low	Low
Proposed model	High	Low	Low	Low	Moderate

Table 2 shows an overview of the performance comparison for different DoS detection techniques. The proposed methodology attributes its high accuracy and low false-positive rate to its innate quality of being a signature-based IDS. A packet gets flagged as suspicious only after multiple tests, and it does not try to guess the behavior or intention of the traffic like an anomaly-based system does. The proposed multi-level approach helps to reduce the false-positive rate significantly especially since a whitelisting strategy is used instead of a blacklisting one. Also, when compared to anomaly-based intrusion detection systems, the proposed signature-based IDPS has lower resource demand.

5 Conclusion

In this paper, an experimental approach to building an IDPS system that can successfully detect and prevent a DoS attack has been presented. The experimental proceedings show that the IDPS installed was successful in detecting the DoS attack and interrupting the communication between the attacker and the server by dropping all the malicious packets. It is also possible to configure the IDPS system by adjusting the frequency threshold based on the peak value when the attack happens. In this solution, three main levels are involved: the frequency-based filtering level, the whitelisted IP matching level, and the deep packet inspection level. The proposed method uses a signature-based detection system in the second level of the inspection hierarchy and although it provides appreciable results in terms of detection rate, it is still slightly vulnerable to IP spoofing even with deep packet inspection. This provides more room for improvement, and one way to solve this problem would be to consider shifting to the more secure IPv6 protocol, which is inherently more reliable due to its encryption and authentication standards. As the transition to IPv6 might take a while, anomaly-based detection strategies could be integrated with the proposed system to form a hybrid IDPS to harden the system against zero-day attacks.

References

1. Damasevicius, R., Maskeliunas, R., Misra, S., Salaudeen, B., Azeez, N.: Identifying phishing attacks in communication networks using URL consistency features. Int. J. Electron. Secur. Digit. Forensics **12**, 200 (2020). https://doi.org/10.1504/IJESDF.2020.10027595
2. Fidele, K., Syafei, W.S.: Denial of service (dos) attack identification and analyse using sniffing technique in the network environment. E3S Web Conf. 202, 15003 (2020). https://doi.org/10.1051/e3sconf/202020215003
3. Farooq, U.: Network security challenges (2018). https://doi.org/10.13140/RG.2.2.27478.34885
4. Madhuri, A., Ramana, A.L.: Attack patterns for detecting and preventing DDOS and replay attacks. Int. J. Eng. Sci. Technol. **2**, 4850–4859 (2010)
5. Zlomislić, V., Fertalj, K., Sruk, V.: Denial of service attacks, defences and research challenges. Clust. Comput. **20**(1), 661–671 (2017). https://doi.org/10.1007/s10586-017-0730-x
6. Odusami, M., Misra, S., Abayomi-Alli, O., Adebayo, A.A., Fernandez-Sanz, L.: A survey and meta-analysis of application-layer distributed denial-of-service attack. Int. J. Commun. Syst. 33 (2020). https://doi.org/10.1002/dac.4603
7. Khraisat, A., Gondal, I., Vamplew, P., Kamruzzaman, J.: Survey of intrusion detection systems: techniques, datasets and challenges. Cybersecurity **2**(1), 1–22 (2019). https://doi.org/10.1186/s42400-019-0038-7
8. Titorenko, A.A., Frolov, A.A.: Analysis of modern intrusion detection system. In: 2018 IEEE Conference of Russian Young Researchers in Electrical and Electronic Engineering (EIConRus), pp. 142–143. IEEE (2018)
9. Anwar, S., Mohamad Zain, J., Zolkipli, M.F., Inayat, Z., Khan, S., Anthony, B., Chang, V.: From intrusion detection to an intrusion response system: fundamentals, requirements, and future directions. Algorithms **10**(2), 39 (2017)
10. Yousufi, R.M., Lalwani, P., Potdar, M.: A network-based intrusion detection and prevention system with multi-mode counteractions. In: 2017 International Conference on Innovations in Information, Embedded and Communication Systems (ICIIECS), pp. 1–6. IEEE (2017)
11. Scarfone, K., Mell, P., et al.: Guide to intrusion detection and prevention systems (idps). NIST Spec. Publ. **800**(2007), 94 (2007)
12. Acharya, A.A., Arpitha, K., Kumar, B.S.: An intrusion detection system against UDP flood attack and ping of death attack (DDOS) in manet. Int. J. Eng. Technol. (IJET), **8**(2) (2016)
13. Barbhuiya, S., Kilpatrick, P., Nikolopoulos, D.S.: Droidlight: lightweight anomaly-based intrusion detection system for smartphone devices. In: Proceedings of the 21st International Conference on Distributed Computing and Networking, pp. 1–10 (2020)

14. Xiaoming, L., Sejdini, V., Chowdhury, H.: Denial of Service (DoS) Attack with UDP Flood. University of Windsor, Canada, School of Computer Science (2010)
15. Nenova, M., Atanasov, D., Kassev, K., Nenov, A.: Intrusion detection system model implementation against ddos attacks. In: 2019 IEEE International Conference on Microwaves, Antennas, Communications and Electronic Systems (COMCAS), pp. 1–4. IEEE (2019)
16. Shurman, M.M., Khrais, R.M., Yateem, A.A.: IoT denial-of-service attack detection and prevention using hybrid IDS. In: 2019 International Arab Conference on Information Technology (ACIT), pp. 252–254. IEEE (2019)
17. Titorenko, A.A., Goncharov, D.E.: Influence of dos attacks on intrusion detection systems. In: 2018 IEEE Conference of Russian Young Researchers in Electrical and Electronic Engineering (EIConRus), pp. 144–146. IEEE (2018)
18. Kurniawan, M.T., Yazid, S.: Mitigation and detection strategy of dos attack on wireless sensor network using blocking approach and intrusion detection system. In: 2020 International Conference on Electrical, Communication, and Computer Engineering (ICECCE), pp. 1–5. IEEE (2020)
19. Kumar, R., Lal, S.P., Sharma, A.: Detecting denial of service attacks in the cloud. In: 2016 IEEE 14th International Conference on Dependable, Autonomic and Secure Computing, 14th International Conference on Pervasive Intelligence and Computing, 2nd International Conference on Big Data Intelligence and Computing and Cyber Science and Technology Congress (DASC/PiCom/DataCom/CyberSciTech), pp. 309–316. IEEE (2016)
20. Dwivedi, S., Vardhan, M., Tripathi, S.: Defense against distributed dos attack detection by using intelligent evolutionary algorithm. Int. J. Comput. Appl. 1–11 (2020). https://doi.org/10.1080/1206212X.2020.1720951
21. Odusami, M., Misra, S., Adetiba, E., Abayomi-Alli, O., Damasevicius, R., Ahuja, R.: An improved model for alleviating layer seven distributed denial of service intrusion on webserver. J. Phys: Conf. Ser. **1235**, 012020 (2019). https://doi.org/10.1088/1742-6596/1235/1/012020
22. Smys, S., Basar, D., Wang, D.: Hybrid intrusion detection system for internet of things (IoT). J. ISMAC **2**, 190 199 (2020). https://doi.org/10.36548/jismac.2020.4.002
23. Abushwereb, M., Mustafa, M., Alkasassbeh, M., Qasaimeh, M.: Attack based dos attack detection using multiple classifier (2020)
24. Kim, J., Kim, J., Kim, H., Shim, M., Choi, E.: CNN-based network intrusion detection against denial-of-service attack. Electronics **9**, 916 (2020). https://doi.org/10.3390/electronics9060916

Windows Firewall Bypassing Techniques: An Overview of HTTP Tunneling and Nmap Evasion

O. Igbekele Emmanuel[1]([⊠]) [iD], A. Adebiyi Ayodele[1] [iD], A. Marion Adebiyi[1] [iD], and B. Francis Osang[2]

[1] Landmark University, Omu-Aran, Kwara, Nigeria
{igbekele.emmanuel,ayo.adebiyi,marion.adebiyi}@lmu.edu.ng
[2] National Open University, Abuja, Nigeria
fosang@noun.edu.ng

Abstract. Internet technology has brought about significant improvement in economical drive thereby making automated processes the new norm. With this new technological drive comes the upsurge in criminal activities as technology has proved to be a densely crime-perpetrated territory. Operating Systems (OS) have had their fair share of this debacle with significant updates being pushed out regularly to mitigate threats. Particularly, the windows OS has the firewall feature which has been a huge success in Intrusion Prevention and Detection systems. The Windows 10 version of the OS will always have significant patches and updates regularly to mitigate security threats. However, there have been several techniques and experiments that proves that firewalls are not sufficient enough for system protection. Advanced techniques in firewall evasions are new generation firewall mechanisms with a combination of techniques usually used to bypass standard security tools, such as intrusion detection and prevention systems, which might detect a protection mechanism. This singular fact that the use of multiple combinations of simpler components is possible, hundreds of thousands of potential Advanced Evasion Techniques exists. This paper therefore takes an overview two of the most significant techniques when it comes to bypassing firewalls - HTTP Tunneling and Nmap Evasion. A comparative study of both techniques helps us look at their similarities and differences and future works.

Keywords: IDS/IPS · OS · Firewalls · HTTP tunneling · Nmap

1 Introduction

1.1 Background

Modern day technological wave has overtime incorporated essential services to further strengthen the concept of security within its usage [1, 2]. The Operating Systems (OS) upon which these services are layered also possess their own security layer which gives users without in-depth knowledge of security protection a level of safety with its usage. The Windows OS has enjoyed wide and significant acceptability because of its

O. Gervasi et al. (Eds.): ICCSA 2021, LNCS 12957, pp. 546–556, 2021.
https://doi.org/10.1007/978-3-030-87013-3_41

user-friendly environment, but this has made the OS the target of security vulnerability explorers. Connectivity of computing systems has brought security of operating systems under intense scrutiny [3]. Windows 10, most recent version of the Microsoft OS was released in 2015, precisely on July 29 to succeed Windows 8. It is described to be the most secure version of Windows. Most of the numerous challenges that faces Windows 10 ranges from privacy challenges to usability challenges as well as psychological challenges all categorized as either technical or non-technical challenge [4].

While these challenges have been prevalent over the years, different measures, in form of services are being released in updates that seeks to further reduce these risks. Windows 10 has incorporated some of these services believing that privacy is a fundamental right of everyone using their product [5] as well as requirements and maintaining user productivity and data protection [6].

Services ranging from anti-virus, network monitoring, firewall protection, and wireless security are some of the essential services on the Windows 10 OS that helps form extra layers of defense leading to an effective protection strategy. The importance of having a standard network system being protected using a firewall is a necessity, and effectively determines the happenings within the system network. It also can be the difference between safety of the network and possibility of being vulnerable to hacking [7].

Even with the vast reach of innovation, new applications and handsets, the industry technology can be often ignored and become the nest of vipers, and gaining access to mobile networks has always been a honeypot for attackers [8]. The bulk of the research on evasions focuses on how these bypassing techniques and their implementations act within a network. The actual effectiveness of evasion techniques against network defenses has been less explored.

2 Literature Review

2.1 Conceptual Issues

One of the sole aim of network hackers is to be on the lookout for users with little or no security measure in place and therefore making them vulnerable. They use this as a channel to enter networks by processes such as IP spoofing to steal data. There have been several identified ways through which these attackers get packets through firewalls, with IP addresses spoofing being a major channel [9]. With access to network traffic, they can cause a lot of damage ranging from password hijacking attacks, Trojan attacks, registry attacks, and so on, which can be disastrous for any organizations' network.

2.2 Windows 10 Security Issues

As with most OS, Windows 10 has had its share of vulnerabilities in the past. No sooner than its launch, it became the cybercriminals choice for carrying out their attacks. Some of these vulnerabilities include:

Information Disclosure. In exploiting this vulnerability, an attacker simply tricks a user into surfing a malicious website and clicking on some links [10].

Cold Boot Attack. This attack thrives by gaining physical access to the computer's hardware tools. For individuals who store highly-sensitive information on their personal computers, or for high-ranked government officials or top businessmen, the effect of this can be catastrophic.

Remote Code Execution. This vulnerability surfaced as a result of improper input validation by Microsoft.NET framework. This attack is not geographically bound as attacker gain remote access to user's computer without being physically present.

Privilege Elevation. This vulnerability exists as a weakness in authentication requests on the Windows OS. It usually comes into fore when the Windows kernel improperly handles objects in memory [11] (Table 1).

Table 1. Summary of Windows 10 vulnerability impact based on the CIA triad.

Criteria	Confidentiality breach	Integrity breach	Availability breach
Information disclosure	*Partial*	*None*	*None*
Code boot	*Complete*	*Complete*	*Partial*
Remote code execution	*Complete*	*Complete*	*Complete*
Privilege elevation	*Partial*	*Partial*	*Partial*

2.3 Firewalls

Firewalls are defense mechanisms designed with the sole aim of preventing unauthorized access into or from a network. They can be implemented either software or hardware, or a combination of both. Essentially, owners of private networks using the internet utilize firewalls to block unauthorized access to such networks, especially intranets (Fig. 1).

Firewalls are implemented in three basic forms:

- Packet Filters: sieves network access by controlling inbound and outbound network packets
- Stateful Inspection: analyses packet headers and the current state of the packets at the network layer of OSI
- Proxy Servers: acts as message filters in the application layer of the OSI.

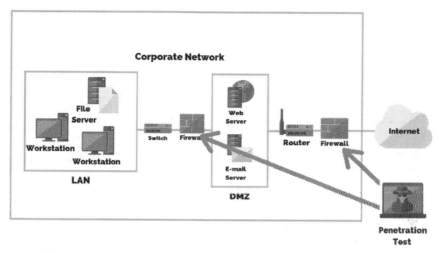

Fig. 1. Corporate Network Architecture showing firewall placements [12]

Firewall bypassing is a technique used by attackers in manipulating the attack sequence to mask themselves over the network to avoid being detected by the underlying security firewall [13]. Usually, firewalls operates on some predefined set of rules, and by extensive skills, such an attacker can bypass the firewall by exploring various firewall bypassing techniques.

Previous works of authors such as [14–17] have focused solely on firewall security as well as that of VPNs, leaving out attack mechanisms or threats on firewalls. The work of [18] was very extensive as regards the loopholes that have been overlooked in years past as regards firewalls. The authors highlighted packet-filtering, application proxy and stateful inspection as the major working principles on which firewalls thrive.

[19] identified some weaknesses in firewalls as displayed in the table below (Table 2)

Table 2. Five kinds of firewalls and their weaknesses [20]

SN	Firewall Type	Security Weakness
1	Personal Firewall	Inability to control and observe multiple communication simultaneously
2	Web Application Firewall	Restricted user range
3	Packet-filtering Firewall	Very difficult in its configuration
4	Network address Firewall	Helpless against attacks and threats from within the system
5	Dynamic detection Firewall	Causes delays in network connection

Although firewalls have weaknesses, they are very much active in protecting users from various forms of attack some of which are listed below from the in-exhaustive list [21]:

- Eavesdropping
- Password Guessing
- Service Denial
- Host Attacks
- Social Engineering
- Protocol Based attacks

These therefore signify the strengths of firewalls especially as it concerns places and organizations. Private networks that are connected to a public network will require firewall protection [22]. Also, individuals connected through the use of Internet modems to will require a personal firewall software. Dial-up internet users usually assume they are safe from illegitimate users, however, these users have fallen victim of attacks and in the process losing significant data [23]. Firewall is also required by these users to avoid such attacks.

[24] posited that next generation firewalls will incorporate integrated signature-based intrusion prevention system mechanism which particularly filters the intrusions received for its reporting system. Also, these firewalls will possess the ability to embed information from outside the system, including white records, index based arrangements, etc.

2.4 Tunneling

Tunneling, just as it appears in real world, is a passage way created where there exists none. It is a method of data transfer over a network protocol that is naturally not supported by the network. This method thrives by embedding small pieces of data inside other packets for reassembling at the destination in a process known as encapsulation. Often used in Virtual Private Networks, tunneling also helps set up secure and efficient connections between networks allowing users to bypass firewalls. This technique allows users to remotely access and connect to various network resources in form of Corporate Home Gateways or Internet Service Providers through external networks. Generally, tunnels established through these external network are done though a multipoint passage and connects a remote user to some resource at the far end of the tunnel.

There are basically four (4) Tunneling protocols, they are:

1. Point-to-point Tunneling protocol (PPTP)
2. Secure Socket Tunneling Protocol (SSTP)
3. Layer 2 Tunneling Protocol (L2TP)
4. Virtual Extensible Local Area Network (VxLAN)

HTTP Tunneling is a relatively more efficient technique involving the use of HTTP. It is a known fact that network administrators usually grant HTTP traffic access through their network boundaries albeit with the aid of application level proxies and a firewall.

The wide acceptance of this evasion technique is largely due to its effectiveness which makes it easy for users with legitimate motives, or worse still, spyware, adware and viruses, ability to bypass the established network security policies implemented at the proxy/firewall. This is done by incorporating just any protocol into what looks like a normal web browsing activity. What is essentially needed is an external host accepting HTTP connections, configured as a tunnel exit point and redirecting packets to the "true" destination, i.e., to the actual destination of the protocol.

2.5 Nmap

Network Mapper, commonly referred to as Nmap is a free, open source tool, available under Unix GPL as published by the Free Software Foundation. It is a network admin-istration tool used by IT security professionals to scan enterprise networks, looking for live hosts, specific services, or specific operating systems details. Nmap was created with firewall subversion purpose and it has always been a very useful tool in staying abreast of network and operating systems updates that impact the scanning capabilities of the tool.

Usually activated from the command-line, Nmap works simply by calling the appli-cation (nmap or nmap.exe) and padding the command with the appropriate parameters or switches. Also, new network users use the tool for advanced configuration having the help instructions close-by. These can be easily accessed from the command-line by typing nmap –h.

3 Procedural Comparison

3.1 HTTP Tunneling

It is common knowledge that attackers are always on the lookout for users whose account and access can be easily compromised, so that they tailgate into the networks using IP spoofing for the purpose of data theft. Attackers can readily access data packets through firewalls using this spoofing method [25]. If successful, damage can be perpetrated by causing Trojan attacks, password hijacking attacks, amongst many others, which can be disastrous for organizations' network. A simple HTTP Tunneling attack undergoes some of these procedures:

1. Ensure firewall is turned on in the target machine
2. Ensure the Internet Information Service (IIS) admin and WWW Publishing services are disabled on the target machine
3. Install any HTTP tunneling software (e.g. HTThost) on the target machine
4. After successfully blocking the attack machine IP address, leave target machine running and navigate to the attack machine
5. On target machine, ensure all FTP sites are stopped
6. Open Control Panel and Launch Firewall settings
7. Ensure firewall is turned on and set outbound rules to block all remote Ports and Protocols

8. Test rule by disabling and testing the ftp site on the target machine (ftp IP Address) – Access will be granted
9. Now, re-enable rule and check to see that access is denied.
10. Next, we perform tunneling using an application called HTTPort to establish a connection with the FTP site located on our target machine.
11. After successful installation, on the HTTPort main window, on the Proxy tab, enter the Host name or IP address of the target machine where HTThost is running. Enter the Port number 80.
12. Under Miscellaneous options, Bypass mode, select Remote host from the drop-down list. Under Use personal remote host at (blank = use public), re-enter the IP address of target machine and port number 80.
13. Select the Port mapping tab, and click Add to create a New Mapping, right-click the New Mapping node, and click Edit. Right-click the node below Local port, then click Edit, and enter the port value as 21. Right-click the node below Remote host, click Edit, and rename it as attack machine IP Address. Right-click the node below Remote port, then click Edit, and enter the port value as 21.
14. Now, switch to HTTPort Proxy tab and click Start to begin the HTTP tunneling. HTTPort intercepts the ftp request to the local host and tunnels through it. HTTHost installed in the target machine to connect you to the attack machine. This means you may not access ftp site directly by issuing ftp IP Address in the command prompt, but you will be able to access it through the local host by issuing the command ftp 127.0.0.1.

HTTP Tunneling Risks. Tunnels are very herculean to detect essentially because they work by bypassing HTTPS traffic, whereas HTTPS traffic should naturally undergo end-to-end encryption thereby preventing inspection [26]. This singular mechanism gives rise to a whole lot of risks, some of which are:

- Service interruptions when an insider uses internet bandwidth for personal or inappropriate gains.
- Tunneling allows behaviors or conduct outside of the security or organizational polices.
- Law suit risks when organizational network is used to access copyrighted materials.
- Intellectual property rights issues

3.2 Nmap Evasion

Nmap has achieved global acceptance from both systems and network administrators, security and network engineers, firewall administrators, incident response teams, pen-testers, desktop administrators, and indeed anyone who works around systems and networks in a secure environment. Job function that revolves around locating a system, looking out for open ports, determining what services running on a given port, or identifying the operating system that a particular server uses, has looked to Nmap to help fulfill these service needs [27]. A simple Nmap Evasion attack undergoes some of these procedures:

1. Ensure firewall is turned on on the target machine
2. Open Control Panel and Launch Firewall settings
3. Ensure firewall is turned on and set inbound rules to block all remote Ports and Protocols and IP Address of the attack machine
4. On attack machine, perform a different kinds of network scans (Basic nmap scan e.g. nmap IP Address, SYN scan e.g. nmap -sS IP Address, INTENSE scan e.g. nmap -T4 -A IP Address) – Result: No access as all scanned ports are filtered due to firewall restrictions.
5. However, a PING Sweep scan on the network subnet (e.g. nmap -sP IP Address/24) – Result: A revelation of the live machines on the network is returned.
6. Finally, a Zombie scan on any of the detected live hosts on the network will reveal the open ports on the network.

Nmap Evasion Risks. Although with proper usage, Nmap is a formidable network security against invaders, however with improper usage, Nmap can (in rare cases) result in complicated legal issues. Hence, it is important to reduce risks by reading available legal guides before using Nmap. This singular mechanism gives rise to a whole lot of risks, some of which are:

- Scanning a network without permission
- Loose scans not tightly targeted
- Doing controversial things using your organization's network
- Performing scans without any legitimate reasons.
- Using version scanning on portly written applications
- Scanning multiple ports and machines on a network

3.3 Similarities in Both HTTP Tunneling and Nmap Evasion Techniques

While both processes and procedures as firewall evasion techniques are distinct, there exist a measure of similarities between them [28], some of which are listed below:

1. They both use the pcap library routines in providing an interface which enables applications detect raw packets from the network.
2. They both have a software that helps with user interface to monitor network packets
3. They both possess network scanning capabilities which helps in discovering active hosts, ports, services, and operating systems on which the target system operates.
4. No server modification required for its operations.

3.4 Differences Between HTTP Tunneling and Nmap Evasion

The following Table gives a comparison of the significant differences between both techniques (Table 3).

Table 3. Differences between HTTP tunneling and Nmap evasion.

Criteria	HTTP tunneling	Nmap evasion
Operating Systems Platform	Windows Platform	Platform Independent
Scanning Option	Direct and Concise	Varying options available – in-depth knowledge is needed
Client Modification	Modification to help wrap the connection with the HTTP header	No additional modification required after installation
Multiple Connections	Each connection to a remote TCP port requires a distinct tunnel	A single connection can carry out multiple activities
Variances	Simple, VPN, etc. are variances	No variance of Nmap
Integrated timing policies	No timing policy integrated	Integrated timing policies that vary from T0 (very, very slow) to T5 (extremely fast)
DNS resolution issues	Cannot perform DNS resolution	The –n option allows this action to be performed

4   Conclusion

In this study, an overview has been done on firewalls and its components with a special focus on techniques that aids bypassing the security layer. It is clear and evident that firewalls on its own is not a guaranteed security layer as the concept of absolute security has been thwarted overtime. HTTP Tunneling and Nmap Evasion techniques were the two firewall evasion techniques compared and although there are a couple of similarities in their deployment mode, there also exists a few difference in their setup and inadvertently, their mode of operation.

The study reveals that although firewalls as a form of Intrusion Detection/Prevention Systems is widely accepted in systems deployment, its workability, performance, accuracy and security is not solely based on the rules and specifications put to use, but also a function of the additional security layer harnessed with the system and how the hybrid techniques are combined. This paper would create an awareness on the weakness of firewalls as a singular IPS and possible improvements on some of the existing evasion techniques.

The next-generation firewalls will require an improved detection of encrypted applications and inclusion of prevention services, hence modern threats like application-layer attacks or web-based malware attacks have an unignorably negative effect on these threat areas [29]. Moving forward, it is the best network security systems that can be used to block and quarantine attacks/threats according to the security policies [30].

References

1. Ansalem Ez, A., Igbekele, E.: Cloud computing research in Nigeria: a bibliometric and content analysis. Asian J. Sci. Res. **12**(1), 41–53 (2019). https://doi.org/10.3923/ajsr.2019.41.53
2. Khu-Smith, V.: Enhancing the security of electronic commerce transactions (2003). http://dig irep.rhul.ac.uk/items/e42a99f4-78e1-69a3-87fd-6ac743f828ca/1/
3. Alhazmi, O., Malaiya, Y., Ray, I.: Vulnerabilities in Major Operating Systems (2004)
4. Goretsky, A.: Microsoft Windows 10 Security and Privacy. An ESET White Paper, pp. 1–34 (2017). https://www.welivesecurity.com/wp-content/uploads/2016/06/windows-10-security-privacy.pdf
5. Microsoft: Windows and the GDPR: Information for IT Administrators and Decision Makers, 05 October 2018. https://docs.microsoft.com/en-us/windows/privacy/gdpr-it-guidance
6. Rogers, M.: Windows resources to help support your GDPR compliance, 5 September 2017. https://blogs.windows.com/windowsexperience/2017/09/25/windows-resources-to-help-support-your-gdpr-compliance/#17Jy0ZeZXv4dH6Gl.97
7. Igbekele, E., Adebiyi A., Ibikunle, F., Adebiyi, M., Olugbara, O.: Research trends on CAPTCHA: a systematic literature review. Int. J. Electr. Comput. Eng. (IJECE), **11**(5), 4300–4312 (2021). https://doi.org/10.11591/ijece.v11i5
8. R. Roaming Consulting Company Ltd.: Signalling Firewall Vendor Performance Report 2018, pp. 1–31 (2018)
9. EC-Council: Ethical Hacking and Countermeasures. Reproduction, pp. 1–19 (2008)
10. NIST: National Vulnerability Database. Published January 2019. https://nvd.nist.gov/vuln/detail/CVE-2019-0582
11. CVE Details: Microsoft Windows 10: List of security vulnerabilities - CVE Details. https://www.cvedetails.com/vulnerability-list/vendor_id-26/product_id-32238/Microsoft-Windows-10.html
12. Stankovic, S.: Firewall Penetration Testing: Steps, Methods, & Tools (2019). https://purplesec.us/firewall-penetration-testing/
13. Jiang, C.: Research on computer network security technology and firewall technology. Ability Wisdom 235 (2017)
14. Sun, K.: Concrete application of firewall technology in computer network security. Sci. Technol. Econ. Guide **17**, 38 (2017)
15. Sahin, M., Sogukpinar, I.: An efficient firewall for web applications (EFWA). In: 2017 International Conference on Computer Science and Engineering (UBMK), pp. 1150–1155 (2017)
16. Ma, L., Liang, H.: Application of firewall technology in computer network security. Comput. Knowl. Technol. **10**, 3743–3745 (2014)
17. Su, J., Yuan, J.: Firewall technology and its development. Computer Eng. Appl. 147–149 (2004)
18. Yang, Z., Cheng, Q.: Research of immune-based technology for the firewall system security. Microcomput. Inf. **21**, 9–3
19. Boukari, N., Aljane, A.: Security and auditing of VPN. In: Proceedings of Third International Workshop on Services in Distributed and Networked Environments, pp. 132–138, 6 Aug 1996
20. Jingyao, S., Chandel, S., Yunnan, Y., Jingji, Z., Zhipeng, Z.: Securing a network: how effective using firewalls and VPNs are? In: Arai, K., Bhatia, R. (eds.) FICC 2019. LNNS, vol. 70, pp. 1050–1068. Springer, Cham (2020). https://doi.org/10.1007/978-3-030-12385-7_71
21. Zhang, T.: Design and implementation of firewall based on content filtering software. University of Electronic Science and Technology (2012)

556   O. I. Emmanuel et al.

22. Zeng-gang, X., Xue-min, Z.: Research and design on distributed firewall based on LAN. In: Computer and Automation Engineering (ICCAE), pp. 517–520. IEEE, Singapore (2010). E-ISBN 978-1-4244-5586-7, Print ISBN 978-1-4244-5585-0, INSPEC Accession Number: 11259785. https://doi.org/10.1109/ICCAE.2010.5451596
23. Chopra, A.: Security issues of firewall. Int. J. P2P Netw. Trends Technol. **22**(1), 4–9 (2016). https://doi.org/10.14445/22492615/ijptt-v22p402
24. Chakravarthi, M.R., Meenakshi, N.: Next generation firewall- a review. Int. J. Comput. Sci. Inf. Technol. **7**(3), 1212–1215 (2016)
25. Alman, D.: Information Security Reading Room HTTP Tunnels Though Proxies (2021)
26. Pack, D.J., Streilein, W., Webster, S., Cunningham, R.: Detecting HTTP tunneling activities. In: Proceedings of the 2002 IEEE Workshop on Information Assurance, pp. 1–8 (2002)
27. Nmap: Chapter 2 Introducing Nmap Solutions in this chapter (2013). http://scitechconnect. elsevier.com/wp-content/uploads/2013/09/Introducing-Nmap.pdf
28. EC Council: Certified Network Defense (CND) Outline, pp. 1–26 (2021)
29. Saurav, P.J.: A brief survey on next generation firewall systems over traditional firewall systems. Int. J. Sci. Eng. Res. **11**(1), 795–800 (2020). http://www.ijser.org
30. Next-generation firewalls: Imperial J. Interdiscip. Res. (IJIR) 2(5) (2016). ISSN 2454-1362

International Workshop on Sustainability Performance Assessment: Models, Approaches and Applications Toward Interdisciplinary and Integrated Solutions (SPA 2021)

Expert System that Assists the Cultivation of Mandacaru Aimed at the Production of Water and Food in the Interior of Northeastern Brazil

Juliana Vieira de Carvalho[1]([✉]) [iD], Caique Zaneti Kirilo[1]([✉]) [iD],
Marcelo Nogueira[1,2]([✉]) [iD], Luiz Lozano[1]([✉]) [iD], Alvaro Prado[1]([✉]) [iD],
Jessica Santo[1]([✉]) [iD], Nuno Santos[2,3]([✉]) [iD], and Ricardo J. Machado[2,3]([✉]) [iD]

[1] Software Engineering Research Group, Paulista University,
UNIP, Campus Tatuapé, São Paulo, Brazil
marcelo@noginfo.com.br
[2] ALGORITMI Centre, School of Engineering, Universityof Minho, Guimarães, Portugal
nunosantos1983@iol.pt, rmac@dsi.uminho.pt
[3] CCG/ZGDV Institute, Guimarães, Portugal

Abstract. The purpose of this research is to provide more comfort in the life of the Northeasterners, more precisely those who live in the interior of the Northeast, using resources already present in their daily lives with the help of technology, and for that, the cactaceae will be studied and used. mandacaru (cereus jamacaru), a wild card from the hinterland and can be used in various ways for food, medicinal or even for handicrafts. The interior of the northeast is composed almost exclusively by the semiarid region, but also has the caatinga, both biomes where the heat is predominant practically throughout the year. The absence of rain in recent years has left the situation severe for many regions and especially for many residents, as the interior of the northeast is isolated from large centers, many places do not have running water, often even basic sanitation, which makes them dependent rainwater or water trucks that go very rarely to them. As an alternative for farmers who have their families and take care of livestock and the countryside, mandacaru comes as a relief to many, since it is not today that many animals die from drought and families are in need since there is no water to grow and generate food. But one solution is the assisted monitoring of the mandacaru, which can mitigate the conditions in which the Northeasterners and the animals find themselves.

Keywords: Cereus Jamacaru · IOT · Notheast · Paraconsistent logic

1 Introduction

This work presents an applied research that seeks to generate knowledge for practical application; with a quantitative approach, which tends to emphasize deductive reasoning, emphasizing the dynamic, comprehensive aspects focused on social and survival experiences. This type of research uses structured procedures with formal instruments for data collection, whose purpose is the collection and analysis of data. The exploratory

O. Gervasi et al. (Eds.): ICCSA 2021, LNCS 12957, pp. 559–573, 2021.
https://doi.org/10.1007/978-3-030-87013-3_42

objective of this study aims to provide familiarity with the problem and build the central hypothesis that is the use of the Paraconsistent Decision Method, thus developing a practical solution in the form of a functional prototype.

It is not just today that the Northeast of Brazil has been suffering from drought and forgetfulness, but even though large cities have resources and even places that are automated, the countryside suffers without any forecast of improvement, in some places there is no sanitation or even energy for homes. So how to open a company to generate jobs or how to automate processes when most of them are not even literate, or have access to education even with social advances [1]? People's livelihoods are provided by the government's agricultural assistance, which is approximately R$ 100.00 per farmer , but the main source of income comes from what they produce, the food plantation, the cattle they raise or even an embroidery that makes and manages to sell, this becomes a variable for many to leave schools, when it gets bigger, it is necessary to help with income in some way,

But sometimes living on the fields and livestock can be very difficult, both due to manual labor, but mainly because the Northeast has been suffering from a severe drought for some years [2], so finding a way to obtaining the provision for yourself and your family, feeding the cattle and taking care of the plantation can be an arduous task (Fig. 1).

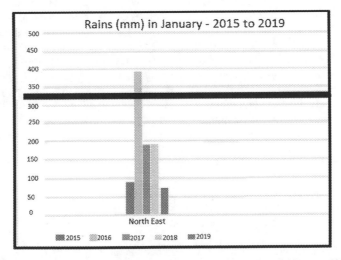

Fig. 1. Cutout of graph: average rainfall in Northeast Brazil [Source: [3]]

And then, as an alternative we use Cereus Jamacaru, which, although it has a slow growth compared to other flowers and cactaceae, it is possible to grow and develop anywhere, there are reports from residents who tell about mandacaru that grew even on top from the house, on the roofs. And because it does not need that much care, mandacaru is perfect for these regions, because, unlike other plants, it does not need a lot of water or constant irrigation, this, in fact, can cause damage to mandacaru, since one of its main pests is humidity.

In the northeast, Cereus Jamacaru is a symbol of resistance, as it remains firmly dry and has water storage as one of its main characteristics, which can make it resist years without the need for water. Its structure helps it to survive beyond the drought to the cold climate also true, not only droughts, but also to the cold climate, however the mandacaru found mostly in the Northeast due to the dry climate.

The physical characteristics of the Cereus Jamacaru are its long thorns, although the cactaceae has a variation without thorns, the thorns serve as a protection by acting so that no predator approaches the Cereus Jamacaru or its fruit. Its size varies, but it can reach up to six meters in height, possessing an edible stem and interior with a lot of liquid due to the storage of water, it is very well-known flower and present even in the local folklore for blooming at night and withering at dawn. day has medicinal properties, in addition to the regeneration ability that the mandacaru has, it has a fruit that has a characteristic abundance of water in addition to being very sweet, it is usually protected by the thorns of the Cereus Jamacaru, making the only animals that have access to be small birds, which eat the fruits and end up spreading the seeds, which helps in the multiplication of Cereus Jamacaru. These elements present in everyday life that can help in the life of the Northeast.

When the time comes to use Cereus Jamacaru (with thorns) and you need to remove it, sometimes they occur by burning the Cereus Jamacaru, where only the thorns are affected, or by cutting off a piece of Cereus Jamacaru together with the thorns, as they can serve by hand (Fig. 2).

Fig. 2. Cereus Jamacaru [Source: [4]]

The research will act to make his life easier, the Cereus Jamacaru can provide wonderful things for the population, using the paraconsistent logic and the IOT we will be able to reach an average of time that the Cereus Jamacaru develops, or the percentage of water it stores so that thus, let us have an average so that the population always has everything mandacaru has to offer.

2 Social Impact

By retaining water, in the driest season it becomes essential for the feeding of animals, because, when given, in addition to quenching hunger, it can quench thirst as well. Another way of using Cereus Jamacaru is in the medicinal area, and the roots and stem are commonly attributed to diuretic action and benefit from heart, respiratory and kidney diseases. The entire plant is used for scurvy and for respiratory tract disorders. Its flowers can also be used for the treatment of headache and body.

Cereus Jamacaru can contribute to the improvement of the quality of life of the people of the interior of northeastern Brazil, when it is possible to make a living through planting, many who live on it do not know how to continue taking care of cattle now that there are no resources to use as food or how to buy food for him and when using Cereus Jamacaru for this, the need to buy food for cattle does not exist, thus preventing the sale of the same or even that the cattle die of hunger.

3 Internet of Things (IoT) in Agriculture

The Internet of Things (IoT) can transform the world in which we live; more efficient industries, connected cars and smarter cities are all components of the IoT equation. However, the application of technology such as the internet of things in agriculture can have the greatest impact. The global population is expected to reach 9.6 billion by 2050. Thus, to feed this population, the agricultural industry has adopted the internet of things [5].

The challenges, such as extreme weather conditions and increasing climate change, and the environmental impact resulting from intensive agricultural practices, the demand for more food needs to be met. Intelligent agriculture, based on IoT technologies, will allow producers and farmers to reduce waste and increase productivity, from the amount of fertilizer used to the number of trips that agricultural vehicles have produced [5].

Smart farming is a capital-intensive, high-tech system for growing food cleanly and sustainably for the masses. It is the application of modern ICT (Information and Communication Technologies) in agriculture. In intelligent agriculture based on the internet of things, a system is built to monitor the crop field with the help of sensors (light, air humidity, temperature, soil moisture etc.) and automate the irrigation system. Farmers can monitor field conditions from anywhere [5].

The applications of intelligent IoT-based agriculture are not only intended for large conventional agricultural operations but can also be new levers to raise other common or growing trends in agriculture such as organic farming, family farming (complex or small spaces, private livestock and/or cultivation, preservation of particular or high-quality varieties, etc.), and to improve highly transparent agriculture [5].

4 Method

The process of developing this research was divided into three parts (Fig. 3).

The first stage had the objective of designing how the prototype would be monitored. For this purpose, mandacaru was planted from the seeds, with the chosen locations it

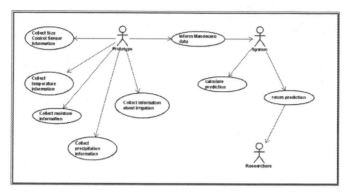

Fig. 3. Use case [Source: Authors]

will be possible to follow how growth occurs with Cereus Jamacaru exposed to different climates (Fig. 4).

Fig. 4. Description of the first phase [Source: Authors by cacoo]

After the seedlings are placed, manual monitoring is started, it consists of noting the average temperature of the day, if there was rain or sun and if they received water during the day (either from rain or irrigation) [5] (Fig. 5).

With the factors already extracted, in the second stage the seeds will be accompanied by sensors to validate phase 1, and calibrate the sensors more efficiently, already making it possible to remotely observe the samples using prototyping plates (Arduino) interconnected through a system via internet, using Wi-Fi module and being observed by a web observation system (Fig. 6).

With the sensors calibrated and the data starting to be obtained and stored in the previous phases. Phase three will consist of collecting the data and making a prediction of the mandacaru, using the paraconsistent logic of the average that each seed in each

Date D/M/Y:	Average temperature of the day	Sun:	Rain:	Water:
22/03/2020	20,5°C	Yes	No	No
23/03/2020	21,5°C	Yes	No	No
24/03/2020	20,5°C	Yes	No	No
25/03/2020	20,0°C	Yes	No	No
26/03/2020	21,0°C	Yes	No	No
27/03/2020	22,5°C	Yes	No	No
28/03/2020	23,0°C	Yes	No	Yes
29/03/2020	23,5°C	Yes	Yes	Yes
30/03/2020	23,0°C	Yes	No	No
31/03/2020	23,5°C	Yes	No	No
01/04/2020	23,5°C	Yes	No	No
02/04/2020	24,5°C	Yes	No	No
03/04/2020	22,5°C	Yes	No	No
04/04/2020	20,0°C	Yes	No	Yes
05/04/2020	21,5°C	Yes	No	No
06/04/2020	24,0°C	Yes	No	No
07/04/2020	20,5°C	Yes	No	No
08/04/2020	17,0°C	No	No	No
09/04/2020	18,0°C	No	No	No

Fig. 5. Manual Monitoring [Source: Authors]

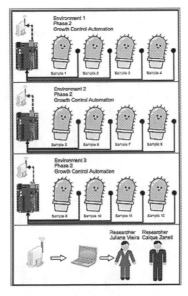

Fig. 6. Description of the second phase [Source: Authors by cacoo]

environment took to arrive at the right moment and with a significant amount of water, thus predicting how the future of the plant, in terms of the amount of water in it, age of the plant, frequency of the fruit and flower, size control and obtain data on humidity, rainfall and temperature at which it is found. The information will be presented on a dashboard to better illustrate the situation (Fig. 7).

And then, as all the steps done, and calibrated sensors will be possible to estimate the amount of food and water that the population will have in each period.

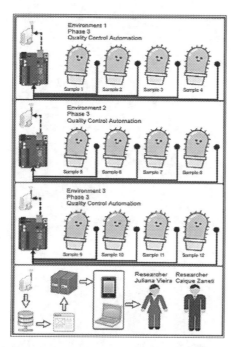

Fig. 7. Descriptive third phase [Source: Authors by cacoo]

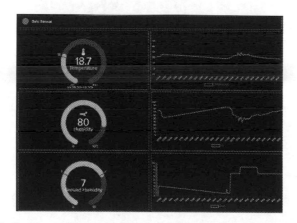

Fig. 8. Dashboard for monitoring [Source: Authors by Adafruit Platform

You can access Mandacaru's real-time tracking. A prototype was assembled, which has a Wi-Fi connection that, together with sensors, collects information and communicates with the Adafruit interface (Fig. 9).

By reading the Qr Code it is possible to access the research Dashboard and monitor the growth control and the climate situation in real time (Fig. 10).

The prototype was assembled using the ESP8266 which is a microcontroller just like the Arduino, however, it also has an integrated wifi card for communication and

Fig. 9. Qr code dashboard [Source: Authors]

Fig. 10. Prototype in state of the work [Source: Authors]

different from the Arduino too, it only has an analog port which resulted in a change in our plans using two hygrometers, being used one to measure soil moisture and the other rain. The DHT11 sensor was also used, which collects information about the current temperature of the environment and also has an air humidity sensor, communicating with the dashboard via a wifi module as shown in the Fig. 8 (Fig. 11).

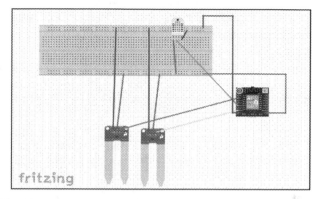

Fig. 11. Electrical scheme prototype [Source: Authors by Fritzing]

5 Paraconsistent Logic

The Paraconsistent Decision Method was developed by the study by Carvalho [6], with the objective of identifying factors that influence the success or failure of an enterprise, that is, that end up influencing the decision to carry out certain projects or not. Its analysis made it possible to identify that the attributes may, in some cases, indicate favorable conditions, in others, unfavorable and, in others, indifferent. These factors can be of different orders: economic, social, legal, environmental, technical, political, among others [7] (Fig. 12).

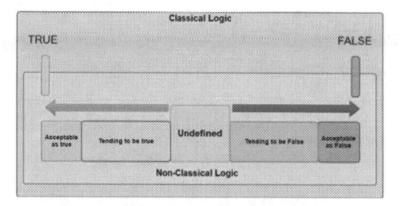

Fig. 12. Classical logic versus non-classical logic [Source: [8]]

The paraconsistent logic uses as input the experience of the participants in the decision-making process, the so-called experts, as a fundamental assessment tool on a given issue, making any situation feasible or unfeasible.

Starting from a problem, question or note, which receives the name of proposition, the method determines the need to end the so-called factors that, as the name says, are the factors that impact on the viability or unfeasibility of the present proposition [7].

The factors can be sectioned, to increase the accuracy of the analysis of a given factor. The created sections can extract more of the knowledge of the specialists who are evaluating them.

The paraconsistent logic, as an aid tool in decision making based on paraconsistent logic, has a fundamental role in the treatment of the opinions of its participants, considering its contradictions, which, in certain cases, is of extreme importance for more informed decision making exact [8] (Fig. 13).

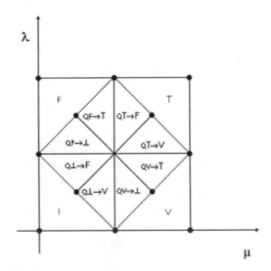

Fig. 13. Extreme and non-extreme States [Source: [9]]

6   Result and Discussion

Even with the slow growth of Cereus Jamacaru from the seed it is possible to observe that even though it is in a small size (about five centimeters), it stores a significant amount of water for its size.

As much as technology is advancing exponentially worldwide and processes that previously took a long time and a lot of labor, are now being carried out quickly and with less or even no labor, in the interior of the Northeast in Brazil this is something very scarce, it seems that the place has been forgotten. Simple resources of large cities can become difficult for people who still live in the countryside and livestock.

The research is still being developed slowly, her current situation is step two of the procedure, all data was collected manually, and the prototype is being developed, the growth of Cereus Jamacaru from seedling and seed is being monitored up close, but because it is a plant that has a firm structure to resist a long time without water it takes a while to develop (Fig. 14).

Because the research is not being developed precisely in the climate and native region of the Cereus Jamacaru, he ends up suffering more from the plagues that he normally would suffer in the northeast.

Fig. 14. Photo collage, Cereus Jamacaru before and after almost eight months [Source: Authors]

Like mealybugs, which occur when the mandacaru is exposed to too much moisture (Fig. 15).

Fig. 15. Appearance of mealybugs [Source: Authors]

The mealybug looks like dirt in the mandacaru, which leads us to think it could be that or earth, but it is a fungus that corrodes the mandacaru, sucking its nutrients, leaving it yellow and weak, so that the mandacaru will rot and release all the water stores and withers (Fig. 16).

This is not the only pest that affects the Cereus Jamacaru, there is also Phytophthora spp, a pest that reaches the roots and causes color and rot in the mandacaru, among others that affect it negatively, where the only way to save the Cereus Jamacaru is cutting out the diseased piece, but sometimes even that is not enough.

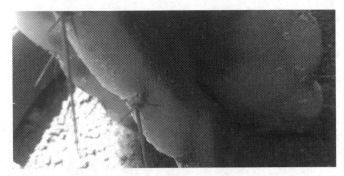

Fig. 16. Cereus Jamacaru rotting through chowchillas. [Source: Authors]

A study on the main pests and how they act is also being raised, so that in the future, in a way to increase the prototype, using image recognition, it can effectively the main pests, bringing less damage to the mandacaru.

7   Besides Mandacaru

This topic aims to present variations on how this project can be implemented, bringing ease to the daily lives of other people and regions.

7.1   Opuntia Cochenillifera

The research initially focused solely on Cereus Jamacaru, but could be extended to other categories of cacti that, like the mandacaru, develop better in hot weather and can take advantage of this same monitoring and pre-collected data, the Opuntia cochenillifera known in the region like Palma, very common in northeastern Brazil, it is also versatile in their daily lives (Fig. 17).

Fig. 17. Opuntia Cochenillifera [Source: [10]]

In addition to this species, it is possible to list other species in which few or any changes to the prototype would be necessary to be successful, considering that all the cactuses that will be accompanied by the prototype have the same purpose of supplying hunger and thirst for people and animals.

7.2 Pilosocereus Polygonus

Another option for the hot and dry climate is the Pilosocereus polygonus, known locally as xique-xique, which features branches that drag along the ground resembling a crown, as well as the Cereus Jamacaru also has a flower and fruit and can be used for food for people and animals (Fig. 18).

Fig. 18. Pilosocereus polygonus [Source: [11]]

The adaptation of the prototype for this kind would be simple, given the huge similarities between them, with the one of the few differences in the form of development because the Cereus Jamacaru grows vertically and Pilosocereus polygonus develop in scattered form, as said.

7.3 Pilosocereus Magnificus

An option that goes beyond the dry climate and is part of a more humid climate, the pilosocereus magnificus, regionally known as Blue cactus, is named for the bluish green color it has, this color is due to Anthocyanin, being a pigment of plant tissue, which can protect the plant from external environmental factors, due to this fact its development is facilitated in more humid climates. Anthocyanin can be found in blackberries, blueberries, cherries, juçara fruits and many other foods (Fig. 19).

In this case the prototype could fit well too, but with some adjustments, as it is found in wetter climates, it may need a little more water than the others, but that doesn't change the fact that it's still a cactus, and as a cactus, it enjoys the sun and needs it for its development.

The real benefit of the prototype is not just for the cultivation of mandacaru, as the intention of this project is above all to improve the quality of life of the inhabitants of northeastern regions in Brazil specifically, that is, in its development the productive factor was taken into account not imagining financial profits, but environmental and social benefits, which meant that low-cost materials were chosen (given that it is a region by definition more lacking in financial resources), low environmental impact with high-durability devices that use natural resources in a conscious way and return maximum positive results for the environment.

Fig. 19. Pilosocereus Magnificus [Source: [12]]

One of the concerns was also not to impact the environment in a predatory way, that is, so that there is no risk of turning into a worrying and fragile monoculture, since it will be possible to use it in a mixed plantation.

8   Conclusion

In short, although it has the capacity to regenerate, as it was said, it grows slowly, so it is necessary a large space to plant the Cereus Jamacaru so that it can have in greater quantity to supply the needs in greater quantity, because, as was said. In addition to being important to people, Cereus Jamacaru may be even more necessary for farmers who would not need to pay money that would be used for food for the family or something to plant.

The project is still in production more precisely in the second phase, where the software is being produced, so that it acts as a comparison of the information obtained in the manual monitoring with that collected by the sensors, although it is already possible to observe the water inside the mandacaru by unless it is, manual monitoring is of great importance for parameters for the prototype that will perform the procedure alone.

In a cost-effective manner, the purpose of the prototype is to be able to assist non-governmental organizations that operate in the northeast, so that it brings better planning to them and helps them better serve the population, and even, it can be used by people from the countryside, using the dashboard will make the interpretation of the presented data easier.

Acknowledgements. This work has been supported by FCT – Fundação para a Ciência e Tecnologia within the R&D Units Project Scope: UIDB/00319/2020.

References

1. IBGE: Conheça o Brasil - População – Educação. 12 July 2017. https://educa.ibge.gov.br/jov ens/conheca-o-rasil/populacao/18317-educacao.html#:~:text=A%20Regi%C3%A3o%20N ordeste%20apresentou%20a,Oeste%2C%204%2C9%25
2. Campos, J.N.B., Studart, T.M.D.C.: O Desastre Seca No Nordeste Brasileiro. In: Universidade Federal do Ceará, Ceara (2001)
3. Redação: Abaixo da média: Belo Horizonte pode ter o menor volume de chuva em janeiro desde 2015, 22 February 2019. https://www.itatiaia.com.br/noticia/abaixo-da-media-belo-hor izonte-pode-ter-o-men
4. Rural, C.: Canal rural, 13 December 2014. https://www.canalrural.com.br/noticias/conheca-caracteristicas-terra-roxa-terra-vermelha-53932/
5. Massruhá, S.M.F.S., de Andrade Leite, M.A.: Agricultura digital. Rev. Eletron. Compet. Digit. Para Agric. Familiar **2**, 72–88 (2016)
6. de Carvalho, F.R., Abe, J.M.: Method. Simplified version of the fuzzy decision method and its comparison with the paraconsistent decision. In: AIP Conference Proceedings, pp. 216–235 (2010)
7. Abe, J.M.: Lógica Paraconsistente Evidencial Et. Monografia (2009)
8. Kirilo, C.Z.: Método paraconsistente de decisão aplicado ao seis sigma. Universidade Paulista, São Paulo (2017)
9. Kirilo, C.Z., Abe, J.M., Lozano, L.C.M., Nogueira, M., Nakamatsu, K., de Lima, L.A.: Evaluation of adherence to the model six sigma. Innov. Intell. Syst. Appl. (INISTA) **1**(1), 7 (2018)
10. Portal DBO: Versatilidade da palma forrageira sustenta dieta do gado no Nordeste. http://ruralpecuaria.com.br/tecnologia-e-manejo/alimentacao-bovina/versatilidade-da-palma-for rageira-sustenta-dieta-do-gado-no-nordeste.html?fbclid=IwAR3drqQ-ICsGvxR4f27XdcY yflpg_OO237eTMJsaRntiwMT3E7ac0DtKA3U
11. Guia das suculentas: Cacto xique-xique saiba tudo sobre essa planta. https://guiadassucul entas.com/cacto-xique-xique-saiba-tudo-sobre-essa-planta/
12. PlantaSonya: PlantaSonya - Como cultivar o Cacto-azul (Pilosocereus Mangnificus), 19 October 2009. http://www.plantasonya.com.br/cactos-e-suculentas/como-cultivar-o-cacto-azul-pilosocereus-pachycladus.html

Systemic Approach for the Integration of Energy and Climate Planning in Urban Management

Luigi Santopietro$^{(\boxtimes)}$ ⓘ and Francesco Scorza ⓘ

School of Engineering, Laboratory of Urban and Regional Systems Engineering (LISUT),
University of Basilicata, Viale dell'Ateneo Lucano 10, 85100 Potenza, Italy
{luigi.santopietro,francesco.scorza}@unibas.it

Abstract. The voluntary-based initiative Covenant of Mayors (CoM) by 2016, through the Sustainable Energy and Climate Action Plans (SECAPs) has focused on the active role of local authorities and increased its targets in terms of GHG reduction from 20% to 40% by 2030. Considering SECAP as an urban planning tool, it can improve the resilience of the EU Municipalities to climate-change, developing adaptation/mitigation actions and increasing the "environmental awareness" of the involved actors. From a planning perspective, the CoM started a new season of urban planning in Europe covering the planning demand in the domain of implementing sustainable territorial development objectives. However, we may affirm that the SECAP is based on a sectorial approach, and it misses an integrated urban vision that represents a pre-requisite for an effective urban planning practice. Thus, in this research we suggest a methodological proposal to exploit this widespread of SECAPs among EU, including the systemic strategic planning approach in the process of SECAP design and ensuring an integrated vision of city development over the list of actions per sectors required by Global CoM procedures.

Keywords: Energy planning · SECAP · Covenant of mayors · Urban planning · Climate-change · European climate policies

1 Introduction

The Covenant of Mayors (CoM) in June 2016 increased its targets in terms of greenhouse gases (GHG) reduction from 20% to 40% by 2030 and adopted an integrated approach: energy and climate change mitigation/adaptation. It was the result of the join with another city initiative, the Compact of Mayors which is an agreement among city networks to support the reduction of city-level emissions and to reduce vulnerability to climate change by developing resilient cities [1–3].

Indeed, the Compact of Mayors is an agreement between city networks aimed to:

- undertake a supportive approach to reduce city-level emissions,
- reduce vulnerability and to enhance resilience to climate change, in a consistent and complimentary manner with respect to national level climate protection efforts.

© Springer Nature Switzerland AG 2021
O. Gervasi et al. (Eds.): ICCSA 2021, LNCS 12957, pp. 574–581, 2021.
https://doi.org/10.1007/978-3-030-87013-3_43

The Compact of Mayors builds on the ongoing efforts of the mayors that represents a city administration and may agree to such a commitment that increasingly sets ambitious, voluntary city climate commitments or targets for greenhouse gas (GHG) emission reduction and to address climate risk. They report on progress towards achieving those targets by meeting robust, rigorous and consistent reporting standards (as established through City Networks); and make that information publicly available by reporting through a recognized city platform, such as carbon Cities Climate Registry, CDP Cities.

The resulting "Global Covenant of Mayors for Climate and Energy" (G-CoM) represents the second implementation phase after the first phase (2008–2020) focused mainly to the energy efficiency and CO_2 emission reduction. Currently the G-CoM is the largest movement of local governments committed towards going beyond their own national climate and energy objectives and it is fully in line with the UN Sustainable Development Goals [4]. Every Signatory of G-CoM in the first phase developed a Sustainable Energy Action Plan (SEAP) while in the second phase upgraded the SEAPs to Sustainable Energy and Climate Action Plans, coupling the energy efficiency and the climate adaptation/mitigation actions. The Fig. 1 shows the energy and climate components that build the SECAP structure.

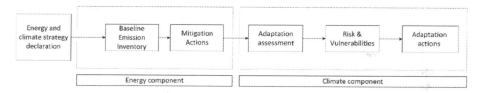

Fig. 1. The SECAP structure

SEAPs and SECAPs started a new season of urban and territorial planning in Europe according to a volunteer approach in developing planning tools out of any normative obligation deriving from any planning law (national/regional). In the perspective of the authors, these urban planning tools enriched the institutional planning framework through: effective practices, useful technical contributions in selecting intervention priorities, design of feasible project frameworks for public and private investments (also promoting EU Cohesion Policies by Regional Operational Programs). Indeed, SECAP has to be considered an urban planning tool, because climate adaptation planning *"is well suited to local levels of governments, as citizens can participate in creating targeted adaptation strategies that address the important regional impacts, and these strategies will provide tangible benefits to local residents"* [5].

Starting from recent researches [6–10] it has been highlighted a generalized success of the G-CoM policy both in terms of an effective contribution towards achieving the UE 2020 emission targets and in terms of commitment of local administrations and local communities towards EU policies objectives.

After a critical analysis of the SECAP methodological approach (in Sect. 2) that identifies the strengths and weaknesses of the G-CoM in terms of process rationality,

Sect. 3 provides a methodological proposal aimed at overcoming the SECAP sectorial approach towards a cross-system approach. Section 4 is related to the conclusions, highlighting the main results of this research.

2   The Strictly Sectorial Approach of SECAP

Experiences from European CoM Municipalities [11–16], reported a sectorial approach in the SECAP design process as a distinctive feature of it. This distinctive feature in our point of view, represents the main weakness of the SECAP approach, separating urban components such as transport, environment, energy, water management etc., without offering any integration between actions that covering multiple sectors. SECAP official Guidebook [17] requires to every CoM Signatory "*A cross-sector and holistic territorial approach*", but finally SECAP lists a number of actions, divided in sectors and without any assessment of the potential integration in terms of benefit in multiple sectors. Thus, we can affirm that the SECAP is based on a sectorial approach, and it lacks an integrated urban vision that represents a prerequisite for an effective urban planning practice. SECAP design is basically build on the development of actions according to a pre-defined standard set of sectors, preferring the implementation of specific actions related to sectors in a one-on-one relation and neglecting the possible impacts of the single actions (positive or negative) on the whole urban system. However, the flexibility of the SECAP approach intended as a decision-making process, compared to other institutional planning processes could fill the gap of traditional urban planning tools concerning the objectives of GHG reduction and climate adaptation/mitigation. In the perspective of the authors, cities should be considered as a set of systems (such as green spaces, waterproofed soils, energy system [18], active mobility [19] (Scorza and Fortunato, in print)etc.) where the implemented actions could affect several systems, according to an integrated urban vision. In the following section, is suggested a methodological proposal oriented towards a systemic approach to integrate the SECAP sectors through an integrated urban vision based on a cross-sectorial assessment of effects of selected actions.

3   A Methodological Proposal for SECAP: The Cross-System Assessment

Every CoM Signatory compiles a SECAP worksheet composed of the following parts: energy and climate strategy declaration, emission inventories, mitigation actions, risks and vulnerability and adaptation actions. Thus, the SECAP process design seems to be only a check between the proposed actions and the SECAP sectors, appearing as a weak process from a territorial point of view. Furthermore, it does not highlight the relations between actions and territorial context and facilitate the forward monitoring phase. The planning knowledge happens per territorial systems (i.e. mapping activities, data collections, spatial analysis) while SECAP approach organizes the plan in standard sectors that are subsets of the planning systems. Thus, is necessary to structure the relations between planning systems and SECAP sectors, reminding that those relations are strictly bounded to the local context characteristics. The methodological proposal of the authors is based on four steps:

1. Knowledge of the city based on its natural and artificial components such as water, soil, air, waterproofed soils or infrastructures. This first step allows to evaluate suitable areas for interventions looking to multiple critical issues (natural or not). Results of this step are Suitability Maps (SM), that support the process of defining territorial objectives and actions (mitigation, adaptation or other).
2. Starting from the SM, it can be defining the overall territorial objectives and typologies of actions which represent homogeneous groups of interventions related to the territorial objective.
3. On every SM the "territorial target" has to be identified, i.e. real elements of the city on which the planned actions are implemented. These territorial targets need to joined to a set of objectively verifiable indicators in order to measure, over time, the results obtained.
4. Defining the adaptation actions for territorial targets. Each action specifies intervention typology, territorial target and accountability variables of the design (budget, timeframe, stakeholders, etc.). These actions identified by the methodological proposal, will be included and detailed in the SECAP sections: "Mitigation Actions" and "Adaptation Actions".

Steps 1 and 2 represent the core of the whole proposal, because they support the decision-making process, establishing objectives and intervention priorities on the areas afflicted by the highest vulnerability (natural or not). The knowledge of the city happens through the Main Urban Systems (MUS), allowing to achieve a comprehensive vision of the city where the relations among different systems are clear and easier to understand. This aspect is the breakthrough, and let to overcame the sectorial SECAP approach towards a vision by systems.

In step 3 have been added innovative elements to the SECAP methodology: the "territorial targets". They are real elements or parts of the city that are recognizable into the MUS, on which it is possible to fit the actions. The usefulness of the "territorial targets" is further explicit considering the relation between the territorial dimension [20–24] and SECAP interventions.

Step 4 is the "conservative" step of the proposal. Indeed, the proposal is oriented to reinforcing the SECAP approach with the urban planning discipline principles (systemic approach), instead to dismantle nor replace it.

At last, the "territorial targets" are oriented to improve the achievement of an integrated urban vision.

Relations between SEAP sectors and systems identified for the case study Potenza Municipality deriving from previous researches [25–30] are presented in Fig. 2.

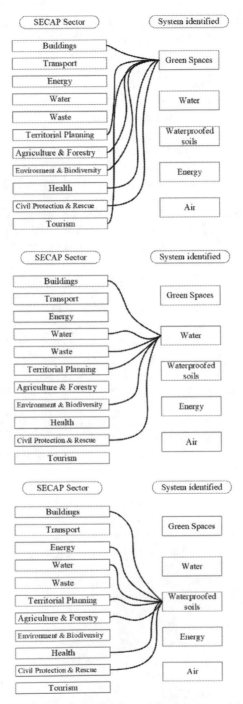

Fig. 2. Relations between SEAP sectors and systems identified

4 Conclusions

The CoM has opened a new season of urban and territorial planning in Europe, according to a voluntary approach and out of any normative obligations or planning law. This is the demonstration of the increasing planning demand oriented to the sustainable territorial development objectives [3, 4, 31, 32].

The introduction of "territorial target" represents an innovative element to explain the "spatialization" of the SECAP interventions provided.

Data availability still remains a weakness for assessing territorial policies [33, 34] but CoM database shows that among the Signatories (at April 2021) the 67,38% of the whole CoM Municipalities are "small" Municipalities (i.e. under 10000 inhabitants)., that look to SECAP as tool facing the climate-change. These are eligible case studies where apply the methodological proposal, in a promising perspective.

These "small" Municipalities could be the specific context where design better and implement strategies and actions related to the application of the methodological proposal. On this track, the methodological proposal highlights new scenarios of territorial planning: coupling the climate challenges with the energy efficiency. Among the forthcoming generation of planning tools, the SECAP could be a favourite candidate for the EU Municipalities [35].

An interesting component for further developments of this research is the engagement of stakeholders and the involvement of the citizens through participation methods such as public consultation, working groups, forums, workshops [36–39].

References

1. Longo, D., Boeri, A., Gianfrate, V., Palumbo, E., Boulanger, S.: Resilient cities: Mitigation measures for urban districts. A feasibility study. Int. J. Sustain. Dev. Plan. **13**(05), 734–745 (2018). https://doi.org/10.2495/SDP-V13-N5-734-745
2. Guerrieri, M., Schibel, K.: Mayors Adapt – Diventare Resilienti Localmente in Europa. In: Stato dell'Ambiente 54/14, pp. 211–218, Roma (2014)
3. Las Casas, G., Scorza, F., Murgante, B.: New urban agenda and open challenges for urban and regional planning. In: Calabrò, F., Della Spina, L., Bevilacqua, C. (eds.) ISHT 2018. SIST, vol. 100, pp. 282–288. Springer, Cham (2019). https://doi.org/10.1007/978-3-319-92099-3_33
4. United Nations: transforming our world: the 2030 Agenda for Sustainable Development. In: Sustainable Development Goals, pp. 333–374. Wiley (2019). https://doi.org/10.1002/978111 9541851.app1
5. Picketts, I.M., Déry, S.J., Curry, J.A.: Incorporating climate change adaptation into local plans. J. Environ. Plan. Manag. **57**, 984–1002 (2014). https://doi.org/10.1080/09640568.2013. 776951
6. Santopietro, L., Scorza, F.: The Italian experience of the covenant of mayors: a territorial evaluation. Sustainability **13**, 1289 (2021). https://doi.org/10.3390/su13031289
7. Abarca-Alvarez, F.J., Navarro-Ligero, M.L., Valenzuela-Montes, L.M., Campos-Sánchez, F.S.: European strategies for adaptation to climate change with the mayors adapt initiative by self-organizing maps. Appl. Sci. **9**, 3859 (2019). https://doi.org/10.3390/app9183859
8. Reckien, D., et al.: Climate change response in Europe: what's the reality? Analysis of adaptation and mitigation plans from 200 urban areas in 11 countries. Clim. Change **122**(1–2), 331–340 (2013). https://doi.org/10.1007/s10584-013-0989-8

9. Reckien, D., et al.: How are cities planning to respond to climate change? Assessment of local climate plans from 885 cities in the EU-28. J. Clean. Prod. **191**, 207–219 (2018). https://doi.org/10.1016/j.jclepro.2018.03.220

10. Coelho, S., Russo, M., Oliveira, R., Monteiro, A., Lopes, M., Borrego, C.: Sustainable energy action plans at city level: A Portuguese experience and perception. J. Clean. Prod. **176**, 1223–1230 (2018). https://doi.org/10.1016/j.jclepro.2017.11.247

11. Baró, F., Calderón-Argelich, A., Langemeyer, J., Connolly, J.J.T.: Under one canopy? Assessing the distributional environmental justice implications of street tree benefits in Barcelona. Environ. Sci. Policy. **102**, 54–64 (2019). https://doi.org/10.1016/j.envsci.2019.08.016

12. Madsen, H.M., Mikkelsen, P.S., Blok, A.: Framing professional climate risk knowledge: extreme weather events as drivers of adaptation innovation in Copenhagen. Denmark. Environ. Sci. Policy. **98**, 30–38 (2019). https://doi.org/10.1016/j.envsci.2019.04.004

13. Bohman, A., Glaas, E., Karlson, M.: Integrating sustainable stormwater management in urban planning: ways forward towards institutional change and collaborative action. Water (Switzerland). **12**, 203 (2020). https://doi.org/10.3390/w12010203

14. Rosenzweig, B., et al.: Developing knowledge systems for urban resilience to cloudburst rain events. Environ. Sci. Policy **99**, 150–159 (2019). https://doi.org/10.1016/j.envsci.2019.05.020

15. Martinez, G.S., et al.: Heat and health in Antwerp under climate change: projected impacts and implications for prevention. Environ. Int. **111**, 135–143 (2018). https://doi.org/10.1016/j.envint.2017.11.012

16. Verdonck, M.-L., et al.: The potential of local climate zones maps as a heat stress assessment tool, supported by simulated air temperature data (2018). https://doi.org/10.1016/j.landurbplan.2018.06.004

17. Bertoldi, P. (ed.): Guidebook "How to develop a Sustainable Energy and Climate Action Plan (SECAP)" (2018). https://doi.org/10.2760/223399

18. Scorza, F.: Towards self energy-management and sustainable citizens' engagement in local energy efficiency agenda. Int. J. Agric. Environ. Inf. Syst. **7**, 44–53 (2016). https://doi.org/10.4018/IJAEIS.2016010103

19. Scorza, F., Fortunato, G.: Cyclable cities: building feasible scenario through urban space-morphology assessment. J. Urban Plan. Dev. https://doi.org/10.1061/(ASCE)UP.1943-5444.0000713

20. Barca, F.: A place-based approach to meeting European Union challenges and expectations, Bruxelles (2009)

21. Scorza, F., Fortunato, G., Carbone, R., Murgante, B., Pontrandolfi, P.: Increasing urban walkability through citizens' participation processes. Sustainability. **13**, 5835 (2021). https://doi.org/10.3390/su13115835

22. Fortunato, G., Scorza, F., Murgante, B.: Hybrid oriented sustainable urban development: a pattern of low-carbon access to schools in the city of Potenza. In: Gervasi, O., et al. (eds.) ICCSA 2020. LNCS, vol. 12255, pp. 193–205. Springer, Cham (2020). https://doi.org/10.1007/978-3-030-58820-5_15

23. Campagna, M., Di Cesare, E.A., Matta, A., Serra, M.: Bridging the gap between strategic environmental assessment and planning: a geodesign perspective. In: Environmental Information Systems: Concepts, Methodologies, Tools, and Applications. pp. 569–589. IGI Global (2018). https://doi.org/10.4018/978-1-5225-7033-2.ch024

24. Torre, C.M., Selicato, M.: The support of multidimensional approaches in integrate monitoring for SEA: a case of study. Earth Syst. Dyn. **4**, 51–61 (2013). https://doi.org/10.5194/esd-4-51-2013

25. Corrado, S., Giannini, B., Santopietro, L., Oliveto, G., Scorza, F.: water management and municipal climate adaptation plans: a preliminary assessment for flood risks management at urban scale. In: Gervasi, O., et al. (eds.) ICCSA 2020. LNCS, vol. 12255, pp. 184–192. Springer, Cham (2020). https://doi.org/10.1007/978-3-030-58820-5_14

26. Santopietro, L., Scorza, F.: A place-based approach for the SECAP of potenza municipality: the case of green spaces system. In: Gervasi, O., et al. (eds.) ICCSA 2020. LNCS, vol. 12255, pp. 226–234. Springer, Cham (2020). https://doi.org/10.1007/978-3-030-58820-5_18

27. Santopietro, L., et al.: Geovisualization for energy planning. In: Gervasi, O., et al. (eds.) ICCSA 2020. LNCS, vol. 12252, pp. 479–487. Springer, Cham (2020). https://doi.org/10.1007/978-3-030-58811-3_35

28. Danese, M., Nolè, G., Murgante, B.: Visual impact assessment in urban planning. In: Murgante, B., Borruso, G., Lapucci, A. (eds.) Geocomputation and Urban Planning, pp. 133–146. Springer, Heidelberg (2009). https://doi.org/10.1007/978-3-540-89930-3_8

29. Orlando, G., Selicato, F., Torre, C.M.: The use of gis as tool to support risk assessment. In: van Oosterom, P., Zlatanova, S., Fendel, E.M. (eds.) Geo-information for Disaster Management, pp. 1381–1399. Springer, Heidelberg (2005). https://doi.org/10.1007/3-540-27468-5_95

30. Murgante, B., Las Casas, G., Sansone, A.: A spatial rough set for extracting the periurban fringe. In: Extraction et Gestion des Connaissances, EGC 2008, pp. 101–126 (2008)

31. Amorim, E.V.: Sustainable energy action plans: project management intercomparison. Procedia Technol. 16, 1183–1189 (2014). https://doi.org/10.1016/j.protcy.2014.10.133

32. European Commission: Urban agenda for the EU - Pact of Amsterdam, Amsterdam (2016)

33. Campagna, M., Deplano, G.: Evaluating geographic information provision within public administration websites. Environ. Plan. B Plan. Des. 31, 21–37 (2004). https://doi.org/10.1068/b12966

34. Crooks, A., Malleson, N., Wise, S., Heppenstall, A.: Big data, agents and the city. In: Big Data for Regional Science. pp. 204–213. Routledge (2018). https://doi.org/10.4324/9781315270838-17

35. Scorza, F., Santopietro, L.: A systemic perspective for the sustainable energy and climate action plan (SECAP). Eur. Plan. Stud. (2021)

36. Garau, C.: Processi di Piano e partecipazione (2013)

37. Scorza, F.: Sustainable urban regeneration in Gravina in Puglia, Italy. In: Fisher, T., Orland, B., Steinitz, C. (eds.) The International Geodesign Collaboration. Changing Geography by Design, pp. 112–113. ESRI Press, Redlands (2020)

38. Scorza, F.: Training decision-makers: GEODESIGN workshop paving the way for new urban agenda. In: Gervasi, O., et al. (eds.) ICCSA 2020. LNCS, vol. 12252, pp. 310–316. Springer, Cham (2020). https://doi.org/10.1007/978-3-030-58811-3_22

39. Gu, Y., Deal, B., Orland, B., Campagna, M.: Evaluating practical implementation of geodesign and its impacts on resilience. J. Digit. Landsc. Archit. 2020, 467–475 (2020). https://doi.org/10.14627/537690048

Monitoring SEAPs: Mismatching in Italian Implementation of Sustainable Energy Planning

Luigi Santopietro$^{(\boxtimes)}$ ⓘ and Francesco Scorza ⓘ

School of Engineering, Laboratory of Urban and Regional Systems Engineering (LISUT),
University of Basilicata, Viale dell'Ateneo Lucano 10, 85100 Potenza, Italy
{luigi.santopietro,francesco.scorza}@unibas.it

Abstract. European climate policy, since the 1990s, has developed incrementally and supported programs, plans and actions for sustainable, clean and secure energy. The Covenant of Mayors (CoM), a volunteer movement of local administrators established in 2008, set a target of a 20% reduction in CO_2 emissions by 2020. The CoM has launched a new season on energy planning in Europe based on Sustainable Energy Action Plans (SEAPs), defining actions for selected intervention sectors. The aim of the work was to evaluate after the 2020 deadline, the state of the implementation of Italian CoM signatories, assessing results achieved in terms of the Municipalities involved (CoM signatories), SEAPs developed and Monitoring Reports submitted. Specifically, the analysis of the Monitoring Reports data represents a relevant step needed in order to formulate some critical appraisals concerning the performance level of CoM adoption at a national scale, in terms of the commitment levels, goals achieved and actions completed or in progress. The paper also remarks the recurring issue of mismatching between Italian SEAPs submitted and their Monitoring Reports. This critical step is not allowed to know the real number of CoM Signatories on track or not with their commitments. Therefore, a realistic framework of Monitoring Reports represents a useful tool for interpreting the targets achieved in terms of CO_2 reduction and for improving the current Global Covenant of Mayors for Climate and Energy (GCoM) adoption procedures.

Keywords: SEAP · Covenant of mayors · Energy plans · Voluntary-based planning · European policies · CO_2 emission reduction

1 Introduction

The Covenant of Mayors (CoM) was launched in 2008 in Europe fostering the ambition to gather local governments voluntarily and committed to achieving and exceeding the EU climate and energy targets [1]. In October 2015, the new Covenant of Mayors for Climate & Energy was launched. Its goals were defined with cities through a consultation

This article is extracted from: Santopietro, Luigi, and Francesco Scorza. 2021. "The Italian Experience of the Covenant of Mayors: A Territorial Evaluation." *Sustainability* 13 (3). Multidisciplinary Digital Publishing Institute: 1289. https://doi.org/10.3390/su13031289.

O. Gervasi et al. (Eds.): ICCSA 2021, LNCS 12957, pp. 582–590, 2021.
https://doi.org/10.1007/978-3-030-87013-3_44

process and are ambitious and broad-ranging: signatory cities are now commit to actively supporting the implementation of the EU 40% GHG-reduction target by 2030 and agree to adopt an integrated approach to climate change mitigation and adaptation and ensure access to secure, sustainable and affordable energy for all. In the same year, the EU signed the Paris Agreements [2]. This global strategy integrates energy and climate policies including the so-called 20/20/20 targets [3], namely the reduction of carbon dioxide (CO_2) emissions by 20%, the increase of the market share of renewable energy to 20%, and a 20% increase in energy efficiency. In June 2016, the Covenant of Mayors entered a relevant new phase of its history joining with another city initiative, the Compact of Mayors.

The resulting "Global Covenant of Mayors for Climate and Energy" (GCoM) is currently the largest movement of local governments committed to going beyond their own national climate and energy objectives.

With an annual emissions reduction expected to reach 4.2 billion tons of CO_2eq in 2050, GCoM cities are showcasing the massive urban opportunity that national governments can harness to accelerate action and progress towards the Paris Agreement goals – simultaneously safeguarding the health and prosperity of their citizens. Fully in line with the UN Sustainable Development Goals such as affordable and clean energy, climate action and sustainable cities/communities [4, 5], the GCoM will tackle three key issues:

- climate change mitigation,
- adaptation to the adverse effects of climate change,
- universal access to secure, clean and affordable energy.

In May 2021 the Covenant of Mayors for Europe counted 10628 Signatories but only 7551 Signatories adopted a Sustainable Energy Action Plan (SEAP). All Signatories are able to develop a Sustainable Energy and Climate Action Plan (SECAP) with new ambitious goals: the EU 40% greenhouse gas-reduction target by 2030 and the adoption of a joint approach to tackling mitigation and adaptation to climate change [6, 7]. The research focuses on the Italian SEAPs looking to the implementation of the monitoring reports, often considered a quantitative step and not an evaluation of performance reached by the SEAP processes supporting the smart city planning [8–10].

The research in Sect. 2 explains some interesting features of the Italian SEAP MR from CoM website database while the Sect. 3 tackles the theme of the mismatching between SEAPs and Monitoring Reports. The conclusions in Sect. 4 highlight the main outcomes and future perspectives of the research.

2   Features from Italian SEAP Monitoring Reports

The official CoM website offers a database where have been collected Signatories and their SEAPs classified by various features as Commitment or Country. Thus, using as filter the commitment "2020" and Italy as "Country", 3224 Italian Signatories have been found with a submitted SEAP. After the deadline of 2020 (the first period of commitment), the work explores how the Municipalities have progressed through their planned interventions, analyzing the SEAP sectors covered and the overall CO_2 emission reduction target. This step also allows to know Signatories working on their SEAPs, that develop and implement them. In 2021, the Monitoring Reports (MRs) submitted to CoM database are 1030 compared to 3224 SEAPs, only the 32% of the whole SEAPs submitted. Analyzing the MRs, we calculated the occurrences of the SEAP sectors (industry, local electricity production, local heat/cold production, municipal buildings, equipment/facilities, public lighting, residential buildings, tertiary buildings, equipment/facilities, transport, and others). In Table 1 are suggested the occurrences of the SEAP sectors and the related percentage on total MRs.

Table 1. Occurrences of the SEAP's sectors among the Monitoring Reports submitted

SEAP Sector	Occurrence of sector on total MRs	Percentage of sector on total MRs
Agriculture	7	1%
Industry	298	29%
Local electricity production	921	89%
Local heat cold production	448	43%
Municipal buildings equipment facilities	949	92%
Others	802	78%
Public lighting	933	91%
Residential buildings	944	92%
Tertiary buildings equipment facilities	671	65%
Transport	946	92%

Another relevant data is related to the overall CO_2 emission reduction target, sets at the beginning to 20% (according to 20/20/20 target) and then upgraded to higher percentage. Among the 1030 MRs the range 20–25% of the overall CO_2 emission reduction target (see Table 2) gathers 796 Signatories (i.e. 77%), while only 233 have moved toward more ambitious targets over 25%.

Significant differences between SEAPs and MRs in terms of occurrences of sectors mean that in the implementation phase, occurred many changes in the overall strategy [11]. This can reflect a double perspective:

- the flexibility of the SEAP as an urban development program in adapting the implementation based on local issues that emerge in a specific implementation sector [12–15];

Table 2. Number of MRs per overall CO_2 emission reduction target

Overall CO_2 emission reduction target set	Number of MRs	Overall CO_2 emission reduction target set	Number of MRs
20%	295	29%	16
21%	182	30%	26
22%	115	0,31%–0,40%	52
23%	77	>40%	54
24%	61		
25%	66		
26%	39		
27%	28		
28%	18		

- a lack of robustness of the ex-ante evaluation and planning phases [13], based mainly on the BEI assessment and targets but not considering the relationship of such a framework with the contextual feasibility of the envisaged actions

From a spatial point of view, the geographical distribution of the MRs is suggested in Fig. 1, while in Table 3 have been counted the MRs currently available on CoM database divided per NUTS1 areas. NUTS1 classification subdivides Italy in 5 areas:

ITC - NORTH-WEST
ITH - NORTH-EAST
ITI - CENTRE (IT)
ITF - SOUTH
ITG – ISLANDS

Data from Table 3 compared to data of previous research [11], shows that among CoM Signatories only in ITC-NUTS1 Area there was a low process of implementation of SEAPs submitted. In the other NUTS1 Areas the high number of SEAP submitted (i.e. ITG NUTS1 Area with 472 SEAPs submitted on 767 Municipalities) have not followed by the same percentage in term of MRs.

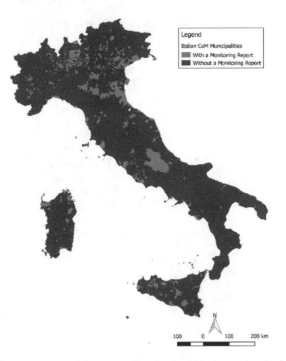

Fig. 1. Italian CoM Municipalities with or without a MR submitted

Table 3. Monitoring Reports classified per NUTS1 Areas

2016 NUTS1	Number of Monitoring Reports [No.]	Percentage on total MRs [%]
ITC	524	50
ITH	239	23
ITI	63	6
ITF	155	15
ITG	71	7

3   The Mismatching of Implementation Between SEAPs Submitted and Monitoring Reports

The implementation of SEAPs submitted with MRs is a critical step that allows to known how much progress has been achieved in term of CO_2 emissions reduction set. Thus, the Municipalities develop their MRs, but often the lack of support to the Municipalities uploading data on the CoM website forces them to do not upgrade data. This is the case of the Italian Basilicata Region, where among 84 SEAPs submitted by Municipalities on official CoM website, only one has the MR uploaded. It is not the true reality, considering that other Municipalities such as Melfi, Castelsaraceno or the Basilicata regional capital Potenza, have developed their MRs but have not uploaded them on CoM official website.

Another critical issue regards the changes in the institutional structures: in the last decade a lot of Municipalities were born from the joining of two or more small Municipalities. In this perspective, some Municipalities that submitted a SEAP as only-one, in the MRs are signed as the new Municipality born. This is a recurrent condition of many Italian Northern Municipalities, where among CoM Signatories 44 Municipalities from 2016 have become 9. The majority of them have signed up as single one as SEAP, while in MRs as new Municipality. Furthermore, the CoM classification does not take into account the fact that the population size of the signatories in Italy could refer either to a single municipality or to a group of Municipalities. This is the case for unions/associations of small Municipalities with populations under 5000 inhabitants, called "piccoli comuni" by the National Association of Italian Municipalities. This represents a discrepancy between the number of signatories on the CoM website and the actual number of Municipalities that are committed to the SEAP implementation: we have a number of Municipalities committed in the CoM implementation larger than the number of the submitted SEAPs. In the Italian case, we have 3299 CoM signatories, which include 104 unions/associations of Municipalities. The Municipalities included in those 104 unions/associations comprise 706 small Municipalities (representing 21% of the total CoM signatories). Among them, an example could be the "Comunità Montana Valle Sabbia" a mountain community built up by 25 Municipalities, that in term of SEAP Signatories is only-one. This last remark is a positive side of the mismatching: the real number of the CoM Signatories is higher than the official data on CoM website. The negative side of the mismatching is related to the lack of the MRs developed by the Municipalities but not uploaded on the CoM website, this represents basically the field where analyze the progresses achieved and build furthermore considerations or scenarios.

4 A Comforting Vision for the Future?

Mismatching at least can return a comforting vision of the CoM experience among the European Municipalities, considering the real widespread of Signatories. Indeed, the success of the CoM experience should be seen from the perspective of the engagement of the Municipalities and not only in term of Signatories count but mainly as an engagement process supported by effective participatory framework [18, 19]. This point of view changes the vision of the MR considered until now as a necessary step to continue the pathway of the SEAP process. Clearly, the MRs are basically tools to manage and perform the SEAPs, and through a step-by-step process go to the direction of the Sustainable Energy and Climate Action Plans (SECAPs), coupling the CO_2 reduction with the climate adaptation/mitigation actions [20]. Notwithstanding this positive aspect of the mismatching some critical issues remain unsolved:

1. The lack of technical support to the Municipalities during the uploading process to CoM official website of the MRs developed. This may affect the effectiveness of the entire process of CoM implementation at a local level;
2. The missing evaluation of the performance and the results in term of CO_2 reduction achieved by the interventions provided in the SEAP where the MRs have not developed,

3. The opportunity of increase the number of citizens and stakeholders engaged in the SEAP processes through the MRs in order to support the improvement of the environmental sustainability and quality of life [16, 21]

These issues are eligible topic of future developments, considering the fact that MRs represent a key component from a planning point of view. Additionally, profitable perspective for SECAP implementation goes in the direction to achieve effective green infrastructure planning [22, 23], reducing land take and urban sprawl [24–28]. Another critical domain regards urban mobility [29, 30] considered a support to improve urban quality [31]. MRs and SEAPs are tools that started a new season of urban and territorial planning in Europe according to a volunteer approach in developing planning tools [16, 32]. This is representative of the high planning demand in the domain of implementing sustainable territorial development objectives [4, 6, 33, 34]. At the same time, it is a measure of the unsuitability of the current normative framework concerning urban development and management to express required performances in promoting actions and tools (the "plans"), oriented towards applying sustainable development principles and climate adaptation/mitigation.

References

1. Kern, K., Bulkeley, H.: Cities, Europeanization and multi-level governance: governing climate change through transnational municipal networks. JCMS J. Common Mark. Stud. **47**, 309–332 (2009). https://doi.org/10.1111/j.1468-5965.2009.00806.x
2. United Nations: Paris Agreement. In: Conference of the Parties on its Twenty-First Session. p. 32, Paris (2015)
3. European Commission: EUROPE 2020 a strategy for smart, sustainable and inclusive growth. Publications Office of the European Union, Brussels (2010)
4. United Nations: Transforming our world: the 2030 agenda for sustainable development. In: Sustainable Development Goals. pp. 333–374. Wiley (2019). https://doi.org/10.1002/9781119541851.app1
5. Pielke, R.A.: Misdefining "climate change": consequences for science and action. Environ. Sci. Policy. **8**, 548–561 (2005). https://doi.org/10.1016/j.envsci.2005.06.013
6. Amorim, E.V.: Sustainable energy action plans: project management intercomparison. Procedia Technol. **16**, 1183–1189 (2014). https://doi.org/10.1016/j.protcy.2014.10.133
7. Abarca-Alvarez, F.J., Navarro-Ligero, M.L., Valenzuela-Montes, L.M., Campos-Sánchez, F.S.: European strategies for adaptation to climate change with the mayors adapt initiative by self-organizing maps. Appl. Sci. **9**, 3859 (2019). https://doi.org/10.3390/app9183859
8. Garau, C., Desogus, G., Coni, M.: Fostering and planning a smart governance strategy for evaluating the urban polarities of the Sardinian island (Italy). Sustain. **11**, 4962 (2019). https://doi.org/10.3390/su11184962
9. Garau, C., Annunziata, A.: Smart city governance and children's agency: an assessment of the green infrastructure impact on children's activities in Cagliari (Italy) with the tool "Opportunities for Children in Urban Spaces (OCUS)." Sustain. **11**, 4848 (2019). https://doi.org/10.3390/su11184848
10. Las Casas, G., Murgante, B., Scorza, F.: Regional local development strategies benefiting from open data and open tools and an outlook on the renewable energy sources contribution. In: Papa, R., Fistola, R. (eds.) Smart Energy in the Smart City. GET, pp. 275–290. Springer, Cham (2016). https://doi.org/10.1007/978-3-319-31157-9_14

11. Santopietro, L., Scorza, F.: The Italian experience of the covenant of mayors: a territorial evaluation. Sustainability **13**, 1289 (2021). https://doi.org/10.3390/su13031289
12. Scorza, F., Santopietro, L., Giuzio, B., Amato, F., Murgante, B., Casas, G.L.: Conflicts between environmental protection and energy regeneration of the historic heritage in the case of the city of Matera: tools for assessing and dimensioning of sustainable energy action plans (SEAP). In: Gervasi, O., et al. (eds.) ICCSA 2017. LNCS, vol. 10409, pp. 527–539. Springer, Cham (2017). https://doi.org/10.1007/978-3-319-62407-5_37
13. Santopietro, L., et al.: Geovisualization for energy planning. In: Gervasi, O., et al. (eds.) ICCSA 2020. LNCS, vol. 12252, pp. 479–487. Springer, Cham (2020). https://doi.org/10.1007/978-3-030-58811-3_35
14. Corrado, S., Giannini, B., Santopietro, L., Oliveto, G., Scorza, F.: Water management and municipal climate adaptation plans: a preliminary assessment for flood risks management at urban scale. In: Gervasi, O., et al. (eds.) ICCSA 2020. LNCS, vol. 12255, pp. 184–192. Springer, Cham (2020). https://doi.org/10.1007/978-3-030-58820-5_14
15. Santopietro, L., Scorza, F.: A place-based approach for the SECAP of Potenza municipality: the case of green spaces system. In: Gervasi, O., et al. (eds.) ICCSA 2020. LNCS, vol. 12255, pp. 226–234. Springer, Cham (2020). https://doi.org/10.1007/978-3-030-58820-5_18
16. Casas, G.L., Scorza, F.: Sustainable planning: a methodological toolkit. In: Gervasi, O., et al. (eds.) ICCSA 2016. LNCS, vol. 9786, pp. 627–635. Springer, Cham (2016). https://doi.org/10.1007/978-3-319-42085-1_53
17. Las Casas, G., Scorza, F.: Comprehensive evaluation and context based approach for the future of european regional operative programming. In: ERSA 48th European Regional Science Association Congress (2008)
18. Gu, Y., Deal, B., Orland, B., Campagna, M.: Evaluating practical implementation of geodesign and its impacts on resilience. J. Digit. Landsc. Archit. **2020**, 467–475 (2020). https://doi.org/10.14627/537690048
19. Scorza, F.: Training decision-makers: GEODESIGN workshop paving the way for new urban agenda. In: Gervasi, O., et al. (eds.) ICCSA 2020. LNCS, vol. 12252, pp. 310–316. Springer, Cham (2020). https://doi.org/10.1007/978-3-030-58811-3_22
20. Scorza, F., Santopietro, L.: A systemic perspective for the Sustainable Energy and Climate Action Plan (SECAP). Eur. Plan. Stud. (2021)
21. Pontrandolfi, P., Scorza, F.: Sustainable urban regeneration policy making: inclusive participation practice. In: Gervasi, O., et al. (eds.) ICCSA 2016. LNCS, vol. 9788, pp. 552–560. Springer, Cham (2016). https://doi.org/10.1007/978-3-319-42111-7_44
22. Lai, S., Leone, F., Zoppi, C.: Assessment of municipal masterplans aimed at identifying and fostering green infrastructure: a study concerning three towns of the metropolitan area of Cagliari, Italy. Sustain. **11**, 1470 (2019). https://doi.org/10.3390/su11051470
23. Lai, S., Leone, F., Zoppi, C.: Implementing green infrastructures beyond protected areas. Sustain **10**, 3544 (2018). https://doi.org/10.3390/su10103544
24. Zoppi, C., Lai, S.: Determinants of land take at the regional scale: a study concerning Sardinia (Italy). Environ. Impact Assess. Rev. **55**, 1 (2015). https://doi.org/10.1016/j.eiar.2015.06.002
25. Lai, S., Lombardini, G.: Regional drivers of land take: a comparative analysis in two Italian regions. Land Use Policy **56**, 262–273 (2016). https://doi.org/10.1016/j.landusepol.2016.05.003
26. Saganeiti, L., Pilogallo, A., Scorza, F., Mussuto, G., Murgante, B.: Spatial indicators to evaluate urban fragmentation in Basilicata region. In: Gervasi, O., et al. (eds.) ICCSA 2018. LNCS, vol. 10964, pp. 100–112. Springer, Cham (2018). https://doi.org/10.1007/978-3-319-95174-4_8
27. Saganeiti, L., Pilogallo, A., Faruolo, G., Scorza, F., Murgante, B.: Territorial fragmentation and renewable energy source plants: which relationship? Sustainability **12**, 1828 (2020). https://doi.org/10.3390/su12051828

28. Scorza, F., Saganeiti, L., Pilogallo, A., Murgante, B.: GHOST PLANNING: the inefficiency of energy sector policies in a low population density region. Arch. DI Stud. URBANI E Reg. (2020)
29. Scorza, F., Fortunato, G.: Cyclable cities: building feasible scenario through urban space-morphology assessment. J. Urban Plan. Dev. https://doi.org/10.1061/(ASCE)UP.1943-5444. 0000713
30. Scorza, F., Fortunato, G., Carbone, R., Murgante, B., Pontrandolfi, P.: Increasing urban walkability through citizens' participation processes. Sustainability 13, 5835 (2021). https://doi. org/10.3390/su13115835
31. Garau, C., Pavan, V.M.: Evaluating urban quality: indicators and assessment tools for smart sustainable cities. Sustainability 10, 575 (2018). https://doi.org/10.3390/su10030575
32. Las Casas, G., Scorza, F.: A renewed rational approach from liquid society towards anti-fragile planning. In: Gervasi, O., et al. (eds.) ICCSA 2017. LNCS, vol. 10409, pp. 517–526. Springer, Cham (2017). https://doi.org/10.1007/978-3-319-62407-5_36
33. European Commission: Urban agenda for the EU - Pact of Amsterdam, Amsterdam (2016)
34. Las Casas, G., Scorza, F., Murgante, B.: New urban agenda and open challenges for urban and regional planning. In: Calabrò, F., Della Spina, L., Bevilacqua, C. (eds.) ISHT 2018. SIST, vol. 100, pp. 282–288. Springer, Cham (2019). https://doi.org/10.1007/978-3-319-92099-3_33

Enhancing Effectiveness in Planning: An Innovative Approach to Implement the 2030 Agenda at the Local Scale

Francesca Leccis$^{(\boxtimes)}$ ⓘ

Università degli Studi di Cagliari, via Marengo 2, 09123 Cagliari, Italy
francescaleccis@unica.it

Abstract. The 2030 Agenda for Sustainable Development, signed by the 193 Member Countries of the United Nations in 2015, established 17 Sustainable Development Goals and 169 targets, which balance the economic, social and environmental dimensions of sustainable development. These are assumed to inform national and regional development strategies as well as local plans. To this purpose, Italy approved the law 221/2015, which implemented the National Sustainable Development Strategy. Italian Regions, in turn, are called to define a Regional Strategy for Sustainable Development, which has to contribute to the achievement of the objectives of the National Strategy. Such strategies need to be operationalized in terms of administrative actions. This requires new and innovative procedures able to adequately place plans and programs within the framework of the aforementioned key aspects of sustainability. This paper proposes an innovative approach to harmonize local plans with Sardinia's Regional Strategy for Sustainable Development. The illustrated procedure provides a new tool, which integrates the objectives of the Regional Strategy for Sustainable Development into local plans and programs and simultaneously assesses the efficiency of these strategies in the related territorial context. In this way, environmental concerns are complemented with social and economic issues according to a new approach to sustainable and inclusive territorial development, which requires a distinct governance model characterized by close cooperation with the public, private and voluntary sectors as well as with organizations of the civil society.

Keywords: Sustainable and inclusive planning · National sustainable development strategy · Regional strategy for sustainable development

1 Introduction

In the last decade, the concept of sustainable development shifted from the one of the Millennium Development Goals, with a major focus on environmental sustainability, to the global vision defined by the 2030 Agenda, which considers a variety of sustainabilities across different dimensions, with the aim of building an environmentally, economically and socially sustainable world. In this context, the planning practice is the tool most frequently identified by international organizations to achieve expected goals (Dvarioniene, et al. 2017). Therefore, the 2030 Agenda provides cities with a policy framework

© Springer Nature Switzerland AG 2021
O. Gervasi et al. (Eds.): ICCSA 2021, LNCS 12957, pp. 591–604, 2021.
https://doi.org/10.1007/978-3-030-87013-3_45

that leads them towards holistic approaches to development, collaborative partnerships with the private sector and result measurability and accountability (Fernández de Losada 2020). It was signed on 25th September 2015 by the 193 Member Countries of the United Nations, which committed to "end poverty and hunger everywhere; to combat inequalities within and among countries; to build peaceful, just and inclusive societies; to protect human rights and promote gender equality and the empowerment of women and girls; and to ensure the lasting protection of the planet and its natural resources. [...] to create conditions for sustainable, inclusive and sustained economic growth, shared prosperity and decent work for all, taking into account different levels of national development and capacities" (UNGA 2015). This new concept of sustainable development relies on the following five critical dimensions: people, prosperity, planet, partnership and peace (Fig. 1) (UNSSC 2017).

Fig. 1. The five dimensions of the 2030 Agenda (Wessa 2016).

In order to ensure the viability of such an ambitious vision, the five pillars are articulated across 17 Sustainable Development Goals (SDGs) (Fig. 2), further structured in 169 targets. Targets are defined as "the real working parts of the Goals" (Project everyone 2018), because they provide practical challenges that can be declined at a national and local level within the fields of action defined by the Goals.

Targets are "integrated and indivisible, global in nature and universally applicable, taking into account different national realities, capacities and levels of development and respecting national policies and priorities" (UNGA 2015). Each target is associated with one or more indicators, in order to ensure their monitoring and assessment. The set of indicators is composed by a global indicator framework defined by a specific

Inter-Agency and Expert Group and complemented by regional and national indicators, established by member states (UNSD, n.d.).

Fig. 2. The seventeen Sustainable Development Goals (AER 2019).

The 2030 Agenda represents a common framework to face economic, social and environmental challenges, which require cooperation among national, regional and local entities called to define complex processes of planning in terms of coordination among different government levels and institutions and with regard to consistency of objectives over time (Cavalli 2018). For this reason, regional and local authorities play a preeminent role in efficiently applying the 2030 Agenda and in involving citizens and stakeholders in order to coordinate planning processes at national, regional and local level (MiTE 2021). More precisely, National Governments are called to develop National Sustainable Development Strategies (NSDS), Administrative Regions are appointed to define Regional Strategies for Sustainable Development (RSSD) and Local Governments are expected to implement the Strategies at local level (OECD 2021).

Principles, objectives and targets of the 2030 Agenda have been attuned to the Italian context through the NSDS, approved on 22nd December 2017 (MiTE 2021). The participatory process for its definition focused on three aspects: (I) the analysis of the Italian framework, (II) the identification of strengths and weaknesses and (III) the definition of the national strategic objectives (MiTE 2021). Adopting the structure devised by the 2030 Agenda, the NSDS is organized into the same five dimensions (people, prosperity, planet, partnership and peace), while Strategic National Objectives are formulated on the basis of the Agenda targets and monitored through a set of national indicators defined by the Italian National Institute of Statistics (ISTAT) (Ibid.).

Sustainability strategies and objectives need to be contextualized to local realities. This operation is conferred by the Italian legislative decree 152/2006 to administrative regions and local governments. In particular, according to art. 34, fourth paragraph, Regions define RSSD consistently with the themes and priorities identified in the NSDS, while Local Governments implement policy instruments able to pursue the objectives of the RSSD. Therefore, new methodological tools are needed in order to properly design local plans and programs within the framework of both the NSDS and the RSSD.

In response to this need, this paper illustrates an innovative approach to local planning developed by the DICAAR research group within the project SOSLabs, directed to the implementation of the NSDS into local plans and programs. To this end, an original procedure to integrate economic, social and environmental dimensions of sustainable development into plans and programs is defined. In particular, the new methodology serves the purpose to integrate the objectives of the Regional Strategy for Sustainable Development into local plans and programs and to simultaneously assess the efficiency of these strategies in the related territorial context. Examples referred to Sardinia's RSSD help to better illustrate the process.

The paper is structured as follows. This introduction is followed by the description of Sardinia's RSSD. In the second section, methodology is illustrated. In the third section results are discussed and examples are reported. In the fourth section conclusions are drawn.

Fig. 3. Italy map. In red the Autonomous Region of Sardinia (Author's elaboration).

1.1   Sardinia's Regional Strategy for Sustainable Development

Sardinia is an Administrative Region in Italy, one of the five Italian Autonomous Regions, the second largest island in the Mediterranean Sea, located west of the Italian peninsula (Fig. 3).

The Autonomous Region of Sardinia is currently working on the definition of the RSSD. In order to gear the National Strategic Objectives to the Sardinian context, the regional administration has, first of all, implemented a "positioning analysis", which maps the current progress towards the SDGs in the island. The analysis is carried out by investigating a set of indicators able to highlight strengths and weaknesses related to each goal, with reference to other Italian regions as well as to the national average (Fig. 4). In this way, the RSSD can focus on the most pressing issues and thus adequately steer its efforts (RAS 2021).

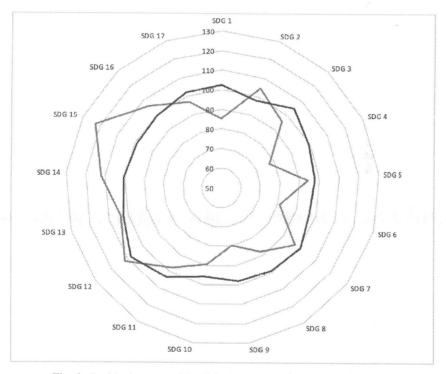

Fig. 4. Positioning map of Sardinia (red) and Italy (blue) (RAS 2021).

Accordingly, Sardinia identified five strategic themes to lean sustainable development in the region, following the European proposal for a Common Provisions Regulation, which delivered a common set of basic rules for seven European funds (European Parliament 2018). The themes are named as follows: (I) A smarter, more innovative and IT-oriented Sardinia; (II) A greener Sardinia: people, enterprises and institutions; (III) A more connected and accessible Sardinia; (IV) A more social, educated and prosperous Sardinia; (V) Sardinia closer to citizens, welcoming and with a stronger identity.

For each theme, critical issues have been identified and Strategic Regional Objectives (SROs) have been formulated on this basis. In order to reach the SROs, macro-actions and actions have been determined (RAS 2021). In December 2020, a Preliminary Document collecting the positioning analysis, the SROs and the actions was uploaded to the Regional Administration official website in order to boost public participation for its implementation (RAS 2020). In this regard, the Region organized two public meetings with institutions and the civil society, respectively, and five thematic workshops, one for each strategic theme, during the months of March and April 2021 (RAS 2021).

2 Methodology

The methodological approach developed by the DICAAR research group, aiming at integrating the objectives of the RSSD into local plans and programs and at simultaneously evaluating the efficiency of these strategies in the related territorial context, stems from the Logical Framework Approach (LFA).

The LFA has become a widespread tool in planning practices (Aune 2000), since it demonstrated to be a valuable method for project blueprint and assessment (Couillard et al. 2009). Thanks to its plain and simple structure, it supports the logic organization of plan activities (Las Casas and Scorza 2016) and emphasizes relations between project components and external aspects, thus highlighting the strategy dimension and allowing for continuous monitoring (NORAD 1999).

"It is objective-centered, it sketches out the resources required to attain the objectives and the main fields in which these will be used, and it seeks to clarify critical aspects of the interface between the development effort and its environment" (Dale 2003, p. 58).

It illustrates the reasons and purposes of the project, identifies fundamental requirements for project development, defines outputs or end results of the project and related necessary inputs (Couillard et al. 2009) and defines procedures for project success evaluation (NORAD 1999).

The implementation of the LFA led to a four-column and n-line matrix (Table 1), called the Objective tree. The four columns are: Sustainability Objectives (SO), Specific Objectives (SpO), Operational Objectives (OO) and Actions (A). The number of matrix lines is variable and depends on the objective and action counts.

Sustainability objectives are defined on the basis of both the SWOT analysis conducted in the local context, and of the SROs identified in the RSSD.

However, not all the SROs are relevant to local plans and programs. Indeed, many of them can be pursued through different initiatives and tools, but cannot be addressed by regional or local plans.

For this reason, the first fundamental step to integrate the SROs into local plans and programs is the selection of the ones that are pertinent to planning practices, irrespective of the governance scale. The identification is guided by the actions that the RAS associated with each objective, because they clarify the field of action of the objectives through the expected impact they might exert.

This methodology is adopted in the next section, where results are reported and discussed through some examples.

Table 1. The objective tree.

Sustainability Objectives	Specific Objectives	Operational Objectives	Actions
SO.1	SpO.1	OO.1	A.1
			A.2
		OO.2	A.3
			A.4
	SpO.2	OO.3	A.5
			A.6
		OO.4	A.7
			...
...	...	...	...

3   Results and Discussion

In order to identify and select the SROs pertinent to planning practices, all the 36 SROs defined in the RSSD are reported in a table together with the related actions. A specific additional column houses the output of the evaluation. In particular, the corresponding

Table 2. Selection of strategic regional objectives.

SROs	Actions	Evaluation
Guarantee sustainable beach fruition.	Discipline urban infrastructure and contrast urban sprawl along the coast.	
	Actions to safeguard extremely valuable communal areas.	
	Actions to combat coastal erosion.	
	Promotion of effective planning and implementation of policies and programs to efficiently manage communal spaces.	
	Monitoring and assessment of impacts on coastal areas and on their littoral ecosystems.	
	Definition of guidelines for coastal management.	
Improve digital accessibility and to enrich the delivery of on-line public services.	Increase and update of computer equipment.	
	Financial support for covering family connectivity costs.	
	Promotion of information literacy programs to improve digital competencies of the population.	
	Promotion of smart working as an ordinary way of working in order to enhance work productivity, support families and reduce employee journeys.	

cell is colored in green when the objective is considered pertinent to planning initiatives, whereas it is colored in red when it is evaluated not relevant (Table 2).

As it can be seen, the first SRO in Table 2 is colored in green because all the related actions can be implemented through a planning tool; whereas the second SRO is colored in red, because its actions concern aspects that are out of the scope of planning practices. The same reasoning is applied to all the 36 SROs of the RSSD.

At the end of this evaluation process, 27 objectives out of 36 are selected to be potentially included in the Objective tree of urban and regional plans and programs. However, their inclusion can never be taken for granted, but requires a case-by-case examination on the basis of the particular context and of the specific plan or program that is being defined.

The second step of the methodology is the association between the selected SROs with one or more NSDS objectives, which are, in turn, linked to a set of national strategic choices. Table 3 displays an example of these connections, related to the green-colored SRO in Table 2.

Table 3. Connections between SRO, NSDS objectives and 2030 Strategic choices.

SRO	NSDS objectives	2030 Strategic choices
Guarantee sustainable beach fruition	Safeguard and improve the conservation status of species and habitats in terrestrial and aquatic ecosystems	Halt the loss of biodiversity
	Ensure the development of potential and the sustainable management of territories, landscapes and cultural heritage	Create resilient communities and territories, protect landscapes and cultural heritage
	Promote the demand and increase the supply of sustainable tourism	Ensure sustainable production and consumption patterns

Table 3 shows that the SRO is linked to three NSDS objectives, which concern different aspects of sustainability. The first one is associated because it aims at safeguarding and improving habitats in terrestrial ecosystems, of which beaches clearly are a key component. The second one regards the development of potential and the sustainable management of territories and landscapes; thus, it includes sustainable beach fruition. The third one seeks the increase in the supply of sustainable tourism, which obviously comprises beach fruition. The association of 2030 Strategic choices is not part of this work, but provided by the NSDS and here reported to explicate logical connections.

The third step of the methodology is the acquisition of the association of the NSDS objectives with the Local Planning Strategic Actions (LPSAs), and related indicators, agreed by four Italian Regions (Marche, Umbria, Liguria and Piedmont) as part of a collaboration project. Table 4 shows three local planning strategic actions, and their related indicators, linked to the same number of NSDS objectives.

Table 4. Connections between NSDS objectives, LPSAs and related indicators.

NSDS objectives	LPSAs	Indicators
Protect and restore genetic resources and natural ecosystems linked to farming, forestry and aquaculture	Protection of agricultural sectors and of natural elements, which characterize them	Utilized agricultural area
		Land used for organic farming
		High-quality agricultural areas
		New residential, industrial and commercial developments or infrastructure
		Land used for organic farming and high-quality agricultural areas interested by new residential, industrial and commercial developments or infrastructure
Ensure ecosystems restoration and defragmentation, strengthen ecological urban-rural connections	Interventions for the realization and maintenance of Green Corridors	Green space fragmentation index
	Increase of urban green areas	Realization of new linear infrastructure
		New residential, industrial and commercial developments
		Actions oriented to the development of the ecological network
		Number of interruptions of the ecological network
		Faunal underpasses/overpasses
		Land covered by new developments in areas characterized by low or very low green fragmentation index

(*continued*)

Table 4. (*continued*)

NSDS objectives	LPSAs	Indicators
Ensure the development of potential and the sustainable management of territories, landscapes and cultural heritage	Conservation and enhancement actions on existing historic heritage	Number of Listed Buildings and Conservation Areas
	Actions oriented to landscape maintenance and protection	Archeological areas (m2)
		Buildings located in the historic city center that are renovated or refurbished
		Actions oriented to landscape maintenance and protection
		Listed Buildings and Conservation Areas in good conservation status
		Archeological areas in good conservation status

The fourth step of the methodology is the association of the NSDS objectives with the suited Indicators defined by the Italian National Institute of Statistics (ISTAT). Table 5 presents ISTAT indicators related to the same NSDS objectives reported as examples in Table 4.

Table 5. Connections between NSDS objectives and ISTAT indicators.

NSDS objectives	Indicators
Protect and restore genetic resources and natural ecosystems linked to farming, forestry and aquaculture	Rate of land used for organic farming
	Fertilizers distributed in agriculture
	Plant protection products distributed in agriculture
	Annual growth rate of organic farming
	Rate of forest area covered by protected areas established by law
	Ammonia emissions from the agricultural sector
	Index of forest areas
	Annual growth rate of forest areas

(*continued*)

Table 5. (*continued*)

NSDS objectives	Indicators
	Forest biomass in the forest area
Ensure ecosystems restoration and defragmentation, strengthen ecological urban-rural connections	Protected areas
	Rate of green areas in urban areas
	Index of forest areas
	Average coverage of protected areas in Key biodiversity Areas (KbAs)
	Fragmentation index of natural and agricultural areas
Ensure the development of potential and the sustainable management of territories, landscapes and cultural heritage	Illegal building
	Soil consumption and soil sealing
	Annual growth rate of organic farming

Lastly, descriptions of indicators, reported in Table 6, clarify which changes have to be measured over time and guide data gathering and analysis.

Table 6. Indicator descriptions.

Indicators	Indicator descriptions
Rate of land used for organic farming	Fraction of utilized agricultural area that is used for organic farming
Fertilizers distributed in agriculture	Quantity of fertilizers (fertilizers, soil conditioners and liming materials) distributed for agricultural use, in Kgs per hectare that can be fertilized
Plant protection products distributed in agriculture	Quantity of plant protection distributed for agricultural use, in Kgs per hectare that can be treated
Annual growth rate of organic farming	Ratio between land used for organic farming in two consecutive years, %
Rate of forest area covered by protected areas established by law	Rate of forest area included in protected areas established by law
Ammonia emissions from the agricultural sector	Ammonia emissions produced by the agricultural sector, tons x 1000
Index of forest areas	Ratio between forest areas and land surface, %
Annual growth rate of forest areas	Average annual growth rate of forest areas, as defined in the FAO Global Forest Resources Assessment

(*continued*)

Table 6. (*continued*)

Indicators	Indicator descriptions
Forest biomass in the forest area	Organic matter living on the soil surface in forest areas, including logs, stumps, bark, branches and leaves, measured in tons per hectare
Protected areas	Percentage of land area covered by terrestrial natural areas included in the official list of protected areas (Euap) or in Natura 2000 network
Rate of green areas in urban areas	Ratio between green areas and urban areas. Green areas include: historic green areas, municipal parks, green equipped areas, school gardens, urban gardens, outdoor sport areas, urban forests, zoos, cemeteries and other typologies of green areas
Index of forest areas	Ratio between forest areas and land surface, %
Average coverage of protected areas in Key biodiversity Areas (KbAs) in fresh water environments	Average coverage of protected areas in Key biodiversity Areas (KbAs) in fresh water environments
Fragmentation index of natural and agricultural areas	Ratio of natural or agricultural areas characterized by high or very high fragmentation
Illegal building	Number of illegal buildings erected in a year every 100 authorized buildings
Soil consumption and soil sealing	Square meters of annually sealed soil per inhabitant
Annual growth rate of organic farming	Ratio between land used for organic farming in two consecutive years, %

At this point, once the selected 27 SROs have been associated with NSDS objectives, 2030 Strategic choices, LPSAs and related Indicators, it is possible to compare them to the objectives deriving from the SWOT analysis and to consequently define the objectives to be included in the Objective tree. The objectives can be either transposed in the Objective tree according to the original formulation they had in the RSSD or in the SWOT analysis or rather rephrased by combining the two.

4 Conclusion

This paper addresses the need of including economic, social and environmental dimensions of sustainability in planning practices, by proposing an innovative procedure of urban planning that allows for the integration of the RSSD in urban and regional planning practices.

The developed methodology stems from the LFA and it is structured into five steps:

1. Selection of Strategic Regional Objectives pertinent to planning initiatives.
2. Connections between SROs, NSDS objectives and 2030 Strategic choices.
3. Connections between NSDS objectives, LPSAs and related Indicators.
4. Connections between NSDS objectives and ISTAT Indicators.
5. Description of ISTAT Indicators.

At the end of this process the identified objectives can be compared with those previously defined on the basis of the SWOT analysis. This comparison can lead to a combination of the two, that implies a rephrasing of the two objectives into a single one, or to the adoption in the Objective tree of both the objectives according to their original formulation.

In this way, objectives, actions and indicators included in the LF take into account social and economic issues alongside environmental concerns. Hence the purpose of the 2030 Agenda of building an environmentally, economically and socially sustainable world is pursued through the coherent strategies and the effective actions provided by local and sectoral plans.

Further development of this research envisages applying the illustrated methodology to two Sardinian case studies, in order to define a Local plan for the Municipality of Cagliari, and a Park plan for the Regional park of Tepilora, respectively.

Funding. This research is implemented within the research project SOSLabs. Laboratori di ricerca-azione per la Sostenibilità urbana" [SOSLabs. Research-action laboratories for urban sustainability], financed by the Ministry of the Environment and of the Protection of the Territory and the Sea of the Italian Government within the "Bando per la promozione di progetti di ricerca a supporto dell'attuazione della Strategia Nazionale per lo Sviluppo Sostenibile - Bando Snsvs 2" ["Public selection for the promotion of research projects focusing on the implementation of the National Strategy for sustainable development – Public selection Snsvs 2"].

References

AER (Assembly of European Regions) Homepage. https://aer.eu/. Accessed 26 March 2021

Aune, J.B.: Logical framework approach and PRA – mutually exclusive or complementary tools for project planning? Dev. Pract. **10**(5), 687–690 (2000)

Cavalli, L.: Agenda 2030 da globale a locale. FEEM, Milano (2018)

Couillard, J., Garon, S., Riznic, J.: The logical framework approach-millennium. Proj. Manag. J. **40**(4), 31–44 (2009)

Dale, R.: The logical framework: an easy escape, a straitjacket, or a useful planning tool? Dev. Pract. **13**(1), 57–70 (2003)

Dvarioniene, J., Grecu, V., Lai, S., Scorza, F.: Four perspectives of applied sustainability: research implications and possible integrations. In: Gervasi, O. et al. (eds.) Computational Science and Its Applications – ICCSA 2017. ICCSA 2017. Lecture Notes in Computer Science, vol. 10409, pp. 554–563. Springer, Cham (2017). https://doi.org/10.1007/978-3-319-62407-5_39

European Parliament Homepage. https://www.europarl.europa.eu/portal/en. Accessed 29 March 2021

Fernández de Losada, A.: The 2030 Agenda: A Policy Framework for a New Urban Future. ISPI, Milan (2020)

Casas, G.L., Scorza, F.: Sustainable planning: a methodological toolkit. In: Gervasi, O., et al. (eds.) ICCSA 2016. LNCS, vol. 9786, pp. 627–635. Springer, Cham (2016). https://doi.org/10.1007/978-3-319-42085-1_53

MiTE (Ministero della Transizione Ecologica) Homepage. https://www.minambiente.it/. Accessed 31 March 2021

NORAD (Norwegian Agency for Development Cooperation): The Logical Framework Approach (LFA): Handbook for Objectives-oriented Planning. 4th edn. NORAD, Oslo (1999)

OECD (Organisation for Economic Co-operation and Development) Homepage. https://www.oecd.org/. Accessed 31 March 2021

Project Everyone Homepage. https://www.globalgoals.org/. Accessed 05 April 2021

RAS (Regione Autonoma della Sardegna): Deliberazione N. 64/46 del, 18 December 2020

RAS (Regione Autonoma della Sardegna) Homepage. http://www.regione.sardegna.it/. Accessed 05 April 2021

UNGA (General Assembly of the United Nation): Transforming our world: the 2030 Agenda for Sustainable Development. United Nations (2015)

UNSD (United Nations Statistics Division) Homepage. https://unstats.un.org/sdgs/. Accessed 30 March 2021

UNSSC (United Nation System Staff College): The 2030 Agenda for Sustainable Development. UNSSC Knowledge Centre for Sustainable Development, Bonn (2017)

Wessa: Stepping up to the Sustainable Development Goals. Wessa (2016)

A Partnership for the Climate Adaptation: Urban Agenda for the EU

Anna Rossi[2], Luigi Santopietro[1]([⊠]) [iD], and Francesco Scorza[1] [iD]

[1] School of Engineering, Laboratory of Urban and Regional Systems Engineering (LISUT),
University of Basilicata, Viale dell'Ateneo Lucano 10, 85100 Potenza, Italy
{luigi.santopietro,francesco.scorza}@unibas.it
[2] Potenza Municipality, Potenza, Italy
anna.rossi@comune.potenza.it

Abstract. The EU Ministers Responsible for Urban Matters, meeting held in Amsterdam in 2016, established the Pact of Amsterdam: Urban Agenda for the EU. The Pact of Amsterdam defines Climate Adaptation as one of the priority themes to be addressed by the Urban Agenda. The Climate Adaptation Partnership was set up in 2017 and represents a multilevel and cross-sectoral cooperation instrument for the priority theme Climate Adaptation. The Action Plan developed by Urban Agenda for the EU Climate Adaptation Partnership is the result of a participatory process involving key stakeholders from the EU institutions, national governments, regional and local authorities. Climate Adaptation Partnership members are coming from all EU macro-regions, ensuring broad geographic representation including cities representative of different city size. Among them the Potenza Municipality, played a key role of Action Plan of the Climate Adaptation Partnership. This paper investigates the action promoted by the Potenza Municipality as a preliminary work to prepare the New Urban Agenda (2021–2027) for the development of the town according to a climate responsive perspective.

Keywords: New Urban Agenda · Decision making · Political Academy · Climate Adaptation

1 Introduction

The European Union is one of the most urbanized areas in the world and the development of urban areas will have a major impact on the future sustainable development (economic, environmental, and social) of the European Union (EU) and its citizens. Urban areas play a key role in pursuing the EU 2020 objectives and in solving many of its most pressing challenges. Urban Authorities (i.e. the public authorities such as local, regional, metropolitan and/or national authorities) are often the level of government closest to the citizens and play a crucial role in the daily life of all EU citizens. The success of European sustainable urban development is highly important for the economic, social and territorial cohesion of the EU and the quality of life of its citizens. In 2016, the EU Ministers Responsible for Urban Matters meeting held in Amsterdam, agreed on and

© Springer Nature Switzerland AG 2021
O. Gervasi et al. (Eds.): ICCSA 2021, LNCS 12957, pp. 605–614, 2021.
https://doi.org/10.1007/978-3-030-87013-3_46

established the Pact of Amsterdam: Urban Agenda for the EU [1]. The Pact of Amsterdam defines Climate Adaptation as one of the priority themes to be addressed by the Urban Agenda, fully in line with the EU 2020 strategy for smart, sustainable and inclusive growth. The Urban Agenda for the EU strives to involve Urban Authorities in achieving three pillars: Better Regulation, Better Funding and Better Knowledge (knowledge base and exchange).

The Action Plan prepared by Urban Agenda for the EU Climate Adaptation Partnership provides concrete proposals for the design of future and the revision of existing EU legislation, instruments and initiatives relating to the adaptation to climate change in urban areas in the EU. The development of the Action Plan was happened through a participatory process involving key stakeholders from the EU institutions, national governments, regional and local authorities that are represented in the Climate Adaptation Partnership and beyond.

In Sect. 2 the aims and the structure of the of the Climate Adaptation Partnership are commented and Action Plan, in Sect. 3 is given a specific focus one of the activities of the Action Plan engaged with the Potenza Municipality (member of the EU Climate Adaptation Partnership) while Sect. 4 is related to the discussion on main remarks and conclusions.

2   The Climate Adaptation Partnership and the Action Plan

The main focus of the Climate Adaptation Partnership according to the priority themes of Urban Agenda for the EU is *"to anticipate the adverse effects of climate change and take appropriate action to prevent or minimize the damage it can cause to Urban Areas. The focus will be on: vulnerability assessments, climate resilience and risk management (including the social dimension of climate adaptation strategies)."*

The Climate Adaptation Partnership members (altogether 22, see Table 1) originate from all EU macro-regions, ensuring broad geographic representation, are coordinated by the City of Genoa. The Climate Adaptation Partnership Members represent all governance levels – from the European to the local level - and key decision-makers and stakeholders engaged in urban adaptation to climate change in the EU.

Working groups (WGs) are made up by all members and are established in order to address 3 key areas of actions: Governance, Resources and Knowledge. The explanation of WG is the following:

- WG Governance is dealing with the political cycle, mandate, integrated strategic planning, decision-making, staff experience and similar topics;
- WG Resources is dealing with funding, human resources, cost-benefit analysis, climate adaptation monetizing topics and similar;
- WG Knowledge is dealing with data, expertise, methodologies, tools, risk assessments, monitoring indicator systems, capacity building, hazard/exposure, vulnerability analysis and other similar topics.

Each WG includes a mix of members representing the different governance and decision-making levels as well as diverse geographical locations and expertise. Every working group has a partner nominated as leader (see Table 2).

Table 1. Climate adaptation partnership members

Member states	Local/regional authorities	European commission	Other EU organizations/observers/stakeholders
France	Genova (IT) Coordinator	DG REGIO	EUROCITIES
Poland	Barcelona Diput. (ES)	DG CLIMA	CEMR
Hungary	Glasgow (UK)*	DG ENV	URBACT
Bulgaria*	Trondheim (NO)	DG RTD*	EEA
	Loulè (PT)	JRC	Covenant of Mayors
	Potenza (IT)		
	Sfantu Gheorghe (RO)		

*Partners that have not contributed or only to a limited extent to the Action Plan.

Table 2. Climate adaptation partnership members

	WG governance	WG knowledge	WG resources
Leader	Loulè (PT)	Potenza (IT)	Barcelona Diput. (ES)
Deputy		Trondheim (NO)	EIB
Partners	Genova (IT)	Genova (IT)	Potenza (IT)
	Glasgow (UK)	Loulè (PT)	DG REGIO
	Sfantu Gheorghe (RO)	Sfantu Gheorghe (RO)	EUROCITIES
	Potenza (IT)	EIB	Glasgow (UK)
	France	Glasgow (UK)	Genova (IT)
	Poland	DG RTD	France
	Hungary	France	CEMR
	DG CLIMA	CEMR	
	CEMR	EEA	
	URBACT	JRC	
	EEA		

The main objective of the Action Plan according to Urban Agenda is *"to operationalize suggested policy and governance solutions for the identified key bottlenecks hindering successful adaptation to climate change in the EU urban areas"*. The Action Plan fulfilling this objective, provides concrete action proposals for the design of future and the revision of existing EU legislation, instruments, and initiatives relating to the adaptation to climate change in EU urban areas tackling the three pillars of Better Regulation, Better Funding and Better Knowledge. It defines responsible institutions and organizations and implementation mechanisms for the proposed actions, proposing a timeline for the implementation of each of the actions. Furthermore, it provides the basis for the monitoring of the action Plan implementation by defining Completion Indicators for the proposed actions. The Action Plan is fully in the line with the current initiative of EU Global Covenant of Mayors for Climate and Energy (G-CoM), in term of coupling energy efficiency and climate adaptation/mitigation. On this track, G-CoM and ITI planning (Integrated Territorial Investments procedure promoted by EU Operative programs 2014–2020) have to be considered as operative tools for Municipalities, looking to energy efficiency and renovation of the building stock, improvement of infrastructure according to sustainable approaches [2–6], adopting solutions like nature-based solution to make cities climate-proof, reinforcing ecosystem services [7–10] and promoting sustainable urban mobility [11–14]. Previous research [15–19] explored this operative aspect at Municipal level, highlighting the opportunity for inland areas and small Municipalities to achieve ambitious targets in term of CO_2 reduction and climate adaptation/mitigation, supported by CoM structure.

3   Potenza Political Academy Geodesign Workshop

The NUA deals with growing urban areas as much as with declining rural context and it is evident that is a discontinuity related to the models provided by traditional planning. There is not enough availability of methodologies and approaches to tackle sustainable solution in order to manage urban decline of the small Municipalities competing with metropolitan areas [20, 21]. As discussed in previous works [22–24], we may put effort in such secondary challenges considering that in such declining context the following principles has to be adopted in order to change planning approach according to NUA common perspective and local needs:

1.   Planning "goes toward" Governance
2.   Planning Performance has to be assessed
3.   Inclusive, equitable, effective and sustainable strategies has to be designed

The process of developing a "vision" for a place and therefore to define a long-term strategy is far to be an easy matter. Generally, such approach, in a multi-agent's framework, delivers conflicts among groups, it takes time, it needs huge technical resources (especially constructing knowledge of the place).

GEODESIGN drives such processes in a framework reducing time for decisions and actions, comparing different interests and priorities, towards feasible decisions. Thus, in order to give specific training to local politicians (mayors, councilors, political local leaders...) [25] on the benefits of climate change adaptation, it has been simulated a process of urban design according to the rules of EU ITI planning. Through this simulation and the active participation of politicians and technicians of the Municipality of Potenza (Basilicata Region Capital city) the basic learning by doing approach had been developed. ITI promotes, within the complex procedures of Regional Operative

Program implementation, a way to give local authorities tools to self-define integrated investments programs. It becomes a critical stage of planning implementation where a Municipality can get the resources to realize its planning previsions. In current practice it becomes a political decision frame in which the results could be a list of investments, infrastructures, public aids, not balances, un-effective in a long-term strategy, oriented fix specific urban criticality without any systemic view of the whole urban structure.

In order to avoid this scenario in urban ITI delivering process, some methodological issues have to be talked: decision makers need methodologies in order to actively participate in the process, time has to be controlled in order to balance the intensity of discussion among the ITI, experience and competences to contribute in decision making process has to be owned by stake-holders.

Therefore, we decided to organize a training session for decision makers and technicians based on GEODESIGN workshop experience.

The workshop preparation had been delivered by the research team at LISUT lab, involving engineering master students. The selection of relevant systems, the territorial analysis and the land suitability evaluation maps was prepared at technical level and then proposed to the workshop participants.

The Workshop was organized by the Potenza Municipality in the frameworks of a broader transnational cooperation activities of the Climate Adaptation Partnership. One full day of activities had been performed in Potenza (17th January 2020) according to the main topic of the event: Political Academy.

The invited participants to the workshop were political representative of the town council of Potenza, including the Mayor, plus technical staff of the main municipal departments dealing with ITI planning and management. Researchers, PhD students and master students in engineering participated to the workshop as mentors, guiding actors through the methodological stages of the GEODESIGN and explaining technical analysis and the use of the online platform GeodesighHUB[1] (Fig. 1).

4   Final Remarks

The UN New Urban Agenda (NUA) [23, 26–28], adopted in 2016 at the HABITAT III Conference, set a shared strategic vision for sustainable urban development globally. It laid out standards and principles for planning, aiming at making cities a more livable place according to a shared vision of development.

We may agree with Las Casas et al. [27] that it refers to plan as a rational instrument in which approaches for sustainable, people-centered, inclusive and gender-based urban and regional development should be implemented by carrying out policies, strategies and at every level capacity building based on essential drivers including:

- urban policies development and accomplishment at an appropriate level;
- reinforcement of urban governance;
- actions to relaunch long term integrated planning and design at urban and regional directed to optimize urban model spatial dimension, guaranteeing all the benefits from the urbanization process;

---

[1] https://www.geodesignhub.com/ by Geodesign Hub Pvt. Ltd., Dublin, Ireland.

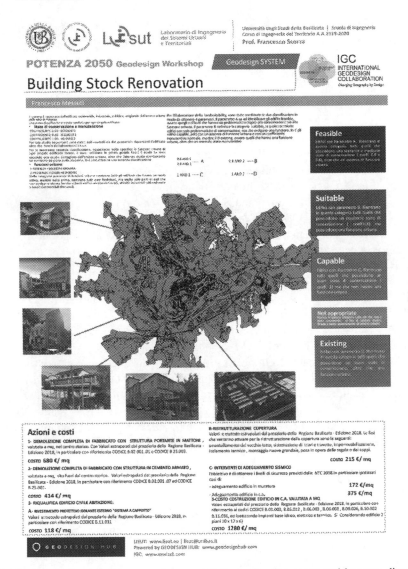

Fig. 1. Posters in the meeting room documented the evaluation maps and become discussion generator among technicians and politicians.

- support effective, innovative and sustainable funding frameworks and tools able to strengthen municipal financial resources and related fiscal system to create, support and share the added value produced by a sustainable urban development.

The Action Plan developed by the EU Urban Agenda, aligns with a number of its statements (in particular 13, 79, 80 and 101) and leads towards their implementation on the European scale. The Climate Adaptation Partnership and its Members strongly share the commitment towards promoting climate change adaptation and the Action Plan is designed with direct inputs from stakeholders who are the actual or future implementers of urban adaptation efforts in order to understand their needs and provide targeted and effective support. In the domain of the urban transformation great efforts are driven according to sustainable criteria (one of the key domain is represented by Smart City studies [29–32]).

In order to answer to the priority themes of Urban Agenda for the EU, GEODESIGN represents a suitable framework in order to develop "urban vision" in urban planning practices, as an effective way to organize and deploy participatory planning according to the negotiation approach and the experiences coming from scientific literature [33–39].

The challenge to anticipate the adverse effects of climate-change, is nowadays a relevant topic in the EU policies (i.e. European Green Deal [40]) or the EU initiatives such as The Covenant of Mayors for the Climate and Energy (G-CoM). The interest to them is highlighted by the widespread of G-CoM Signatories and their experiences among the EU countries.

Concerning the future developments of this research, they are related to:

- monitoring the results and the changes deriving from the practices of the Urban Agenda among the Partnership Members and the implementation of the planning processes at different levels;
- promoting different approaches [41, 42] and the methodological integration of collaborative planning approaches like GEODESIGN with Logical Framework Approach (among others [43]).

Potenza Municipality is committed to reinforce an integrated approach toward New Urban Agenda development benefitting from lessons learned of Climate Adaptation Partnership and promoting collaborative design practices following experience of the political academy.

References

1. European Commission: Urban agenda for the EU - Pact of Amsterdam, Amsterdam (2016)
2. Cerminara, I., et al.: Green chemistry, circular economy and sustainable development: an operational perspective to scale research results in SMEs practices. In: Gervasi, O., et al. (eds.) ICCSA 2020. LNCS, vol. 12255, pp. 206–213. Springer, Cham (2020). https://doi.org/10.1007/978-3-030-58820-5_16
3. Dvarioniene, J., Grecu, V., Lai, S., Scorza, F.: Four perspectives of applied sustainability: research implications and possible integrations. In: Gervasi, O., et al. (eds.) ICCSA 2017. LNCS, vol. 10409, pp. 554–563. Springer, Cham (2017). https://doi.org/10.1007/978-3-319-62407-5_39
4. Lai, S., Leone, F., Zoppi, C.: Implementing green infrastructures beyond protected areas. Sustainability 10, 3544 (2018). https://doi.org/10.3390/su10103544
5. Lai, S., Leone, F., Zoppi, C.: Assessment of municipal masterplans aimed at identifying and fostering green infrastructure: a study concerning three towns of the metropolitan area of Cagliari, Italy. Sustainability 11, 1470 (2019). https://doi.org/10.3390/su11051470
6. Scorza, F., Grecu, V.: Assessing sustainability: research directions and relevant issues. In: Gervasi, O., et al. (eds.) ICCSA 2016. LNCS, vol. 9786, pp. 642–647. Springer, Cham (2016). https://doi.org/10.1007/978-3-319-42085-1_55

7. Scorza, F., Pilogallo, A., Saganeiti, L., Murgante, B.: Natura 2000 areas and Sites of National Interest (SNI): measuring (un)integration between naturalness preservation and environmental remediation policies. Sustainability. **12**, 2928 (2020). https://doi.org/10.3390/su12072928

8. Pilogallo, A., Saganeiti, L., Scorza, F., Murgante, B.: Ecosystem services approach to evaluate renewable energy plants effects. In: Misra, S., et al. (eds.) ICCSA 2019. LNCS, vol. 11624, pp. 281–290. Springer, Cham (2019). https://doi.org/10.1007/978-3-030-24311-1_20

9. Mazzariello, A., Pilogallo, A., Scorza, F., Murgante, B., Las Casas, G.: Carbon stock as an indicator for the estimation of anthropic pressure on territorial components. In: Gervasi, O., et al. (eds.) ICCSA 2018. LNCS, vol. 10964, pp. 697–711. Springer, Cham (2018). https://doi.org/10.1007/978-3-319-95174-4_53

10. Scorza, F., Pilogallo, A., Las Casas, G.: Investigating tourism attractiveness in inland areas: ecosystem services, open data and smart specializations. In: Calabrò, F., Della Spina, L., Bevilacqua, C. (eds.) ISHT 2018. SIST, vol. 100, pp. 30–38. Springer, Cham (2019). https://doi.org/10.1007/978-3-319-92099-3_4

11. Scorza, F., Fortunato, G.: Cyclable cities: building feasible scenario through urban space-morphology assessment. J. Urban Plan. Dev. https://doi.org/10.1061/(ASCE)UP.1943-5444.0000713

12. Scorza, F., Fortunato, G., Carbone, R., Murgante, B., Pontrandolfi, P.: Increasing urban walk-ability through citizens' participation processes. Sustainability. **13**, 5835 (2021). https://doi.org/10.3390/su13115835

13. Fortunato, G., Scorza, F., Murgante, B.: Hybrid oriented sustainable urban development: a pattern of low-carbon access to schools in the city of Potenza. In: Gervasi, O., et al. (eds.) ICCSA 2020. LNCS, vol. 12255, pp. 193–205. Springer, Cham (2020). https://doi.org/10.1007/978-3-030-58820-5_15

14. Fortunato, G., Scorza, F., Murgante, B.: Cyclable city: a territorial assessment procedure for disruptive policy-making on urban mobility. In: Misra, S., et al. (eds.) ICCSA 2019. LNCS, vol. 11624, pp. 291–307. Springer, Cham (2019). https://doi.org/10.1007/978-3-030-24311-1_21

15. Scorza, F., Santopietro, L., Giuzio, B., Amato, F., Murgante, B., Casas, G.L.: Conflicts between environmental protection and energy regeneration of the historic heritage in the case of the city of Matera: tools for assessing and dimensioning of sustainable energy action plans (SEAP). In: Gervasi, O., et al. (eds.) ICCSA 2017. LNCS, vol. 10409, pp. 527–539. Springer, Cham (2017). https://doi.org/10.1007/978-3-319-62407-5_37

16. Santopietro, L., et al.: Geovisualization for energy planning. In: Gervasi, O., et al. (eds.) ICCSA 2020. LNCS, vol. 12252, pp. 479–487. Springer, Cham (2020). https://doi.org/10.1007/978-3-030-58811-3_35

17. Corrado, S., Giannini, B., Santopietro, L., Oliveto, G., Scorza, F.: Water management and municipal climate adaptation plans: a preliminary assessment for flood risks management at urban scale. In: Gervasi, O., et al. (eds.) ICCSA 2020. LNCS, vol. 12255, pp. 184–192. Springer, Cham (2020). https://doi.org/10.1007/978-3-030-58820-5_14

18. Santopietro, L., Scorza, F.: A place-based approach for the SECAP of Potenza municipality: the case of green spaces system. In: Gervasi, O., et al. (eds.) ICCSA 2020. LNCS, vol. 12255, pp. 226–234. Springer, Cham (2020). https://doi.org/10.1007/978-3-030-58820-5_18

19. Danese, M., Nolè, G., Murgante, B.: Visual impact assessment in urban planning. In: Murgante, B., Borruso, G., Lapucci, A. (eds.) Geocomputation and Urban Planning, pp. 133–146. Springer Berlin Heidelberg, Berlin, Heidelberg (2009). https://doi.org/10.1007/978-3-540-89930-3_8

20. Garau, C., Desogus, G., Coni, M.: Fostering and planning a smart governance strategy for evaluating the urban polarities of the Sardinian island (Italy). Sustainability **11**, 4962 (2019). https://doi.org/10.3390/su11184962

21. Torre, C.M., Morano, P., Taiani, F.: Social balance and economic effectiveness in historic centers rehabilitation. In: Gervasi, O., et al. (eds.) ICCSA 2015. LNCS, vol. 9157, pp. 317–329. Springer, Cham (2015). https://doi.org/10.1007/978-3-319-21470-2_22

22. Scorza, F., Saganeiti, L., Pilogallo, A., Murgante, B.: Ghost planning: the inefficiency of energy sector policies in a low population density region. Arch. DI Stud. Urbani e Reg. (2020)

23. Casas, G.L., Scorza, F.: From the UN new urban agenda to the local experiences of urban development: the case of Potenza. In: Gervasi, O., et al. (eds.) ICCSA 2018. LNCS, vol. 10964, pp. 734–743. Springer, Cham (2018). https://doi.org/10.1007/978-3-319-95174-4_56

24. Scorza, F., Pilogallo, A., Saganeiti, L., Murgante, B., Pontrandolfi, P.: Comparing the territorial performances of renewable energy sources' plants with an integrated ecosystem services loss assessment: a case study from the Basilicata region (Italy). Sustain. Cities Soc. 56, 102082 (2020). https://doi.org/10.1016/j.scs.2020.102082

25. Scorza, F.: Training decision-makers: GEODESIGN workshop paving the way for new urban agenda. In: Gervasi, O., et al. (eds.) ICCSA 2020. LNCS, vol. 12252, pp. 310–316. Springer, Cham (2020). https://doi.org/10.1007/978-3-030-58811-3_22

26. UN HABITAT: New Urban Agenda. United Nations (2017)

27. Las Casas, G., Scorza, F., Murgante, B.: New urban agenda and open challenges for urban and regional planning. In: Calabrò, F., Della Spina, L., Bevilacqua, C. (eds.) ISHT 2018. SIST, vol. 100, pp. 282–288. Springer, Cham (2019). https://doi.org/10.1007/978-3-319-92099-3_33

28. Las Casas, G., Scorza, F., Murgante, B.: Razionalità a-priori: una proposta verso una pianificazione antifragile. Ital. J. Reg. Sci. 18, 329–338 (2019). https://doi.org/10.14650/93656

29. Murgante, B., Borruso, G.: Cities and smartness: a critical analysis of opportunities and risks. In: Murgante, B., et al. (eds.) ICCSA 2013. LNCS, vol. 7973, pp. 630–642. Springer, Heidelberg (2013). https://doi.org/10.1007/978-3-642-39646-5_46

30. Batty, M., et al.: Smart cities of the future. Eur. Phys. J. Spec. Top. 214, 481–518 (2012). https://doi.org/10.1140/epjst/e2012-01703-3

31. Garau, C.: Smart paths for advanced management of cultural heritage. Reg. Stud. Reg. Sci. 1, 286–293 (2014). https://doi.org/10.1080/21681376.2014.973439

32. Garau, C., Pavan, V.M.: Evaluating urban quality: indicators and assessment tools for smart sustainable cities. Sustainability 10, 575 (2018). https://doi.org/10.3390/su10030575

33. Steinitz, C.: A Frame Work for Geodesign. Changing Geography by Design. Esri, Redlands (2012)

34. Fisher, T., Orland, B., Steinitz, C. (eds.): The International Geodesign Collaboration. Changing Geography by Design. ESRI Press, Redlands, California (2020)

35. Campagna, M.: Metaplanning: about designing the Geodesign process. Landsc. Urban Plan. 156, 118–128 (2016). https://doi.org/10.1016/J.LANDURBPLAN.2015.08.019

36. Nyerges, T., et al.: Geodesign dynamics for sustainable urban watershed development. Sustain. Cities Soc. 25, 13–24 (2016). https://doi.org/10.1016/j.scs.2016.04.016

37. Cocco, C., Rezende Freitas, C., Mourão Moura, A.C., Campagna, M.: Geodesign process analytics: focus on design as a process and its outcomes. Sustainability 12, 119 (2019). https://doi.org/10.3390/su12010119

38. Campagna, M., Di Cesare, E.A., Cocco, C.: Integrating green-infrastructures design in strategic spatial planning with geodesign. Sustainability 12, 1820 (2020). https://doi.org/10.3390/su12051820

39. Cocco, C., Jankowski, P., Campagna, M.: An analytic approach to understanding process dynamics in geodesign studies. Sustainability 11, 4999 (2019). https://doi.org/10.3390/su11184999

40. European Commission: The European Green Deal, Brussels (2020)

41. Scorza, F., Santopietro, L.: A systemic perspective for the Sustainable Energy and Climate Action Plan (SECAP). Eur. Plan. Stud. (2021)
42. Scorza, F., Casas, G.B.L., Murgante, B.: That's ReDO: ontologies and regional development planning. In: Murgante, B., et al. (eds.) ICCSA 2012. LNCS, vol. 7334, pp. 640–652. Springer, Heidelberg (2012). https://doi.org/10.1007/978-3-642-31075-1_48
43. Vagnby, B.H.: Logical framework approach 64 (2000)

Small Municipalities Engaged in Sustainable and Climate Responsive Planning: Evidences from UE-CoM

Luigi Santopietro[1]([⊠]) [iD], Francesco Scorza[1] [iD], and Anna Rossi[2]

[1] School of Engineering, Laboratory of Urban and Regional Systems Engineering (LISUT),
University of Basilicata, Viale dell'Ateneo Lucano 10, 85100 Potenza, Italy
{luigi.santopietro,francesco.scorza}@unibas.it
[2] Potenza Municipality, Potenza, Italy
anna.rossi@comune.potenza.it

Abstract. The Covenant of Mayors (CoM), a volunteer movement of local administrators established in 2008, has supported Municipalities to develop their Sustainable Energy and Climate Action Plans (SECAPs) and become energy and climate proof Municipalities. SECAP intended as an urban planning tool, allowed to EU Municipalities to develop adaptation/mitigation actions, facing the climate-change. Compared to this, the CoM started a new season of urban planning coupling the planning demand in terms of reduction of CO_2 emissions and the adaptation/mitigation to climate-change with the implementation of sustainable territorial development objectives. The European Signatories of CoM at May 2021 are 6789, and the 4312 of them (in percentage 63%) are small municipalities (i.e. under 10000 inhabitants). This high percentage of small Municipalities related to total has highlighted how SEAPs have been intended as instruments used to plan and provide funding for ordinary interventions in the urban areas instead of institutional instruments (i.e., urban planning regulations, operational plans and programs established by National policies). Therefore, the paper suggests an overview at European level to exploit the engagement of the small Municipalities, specifying the commitment and the SECAP's sectors chosen. It represents a useful framework interpreting the general results derived from the CoM official data and improving procedures related to the adaptation/mitigation climate-change in urban areas.

Keywords: SECAP · Covenant of mayors · Energy plans · Voluntary-based planning · European policies

1 Introduction

The Covenant of Mayors (CoM) since 2008 has supported the European Municipalities to become sustainable and climate responsive. In June 2016 the "Global Covenant of Mayors for Climate and Energy" (G-CoM) increased the targets in terms of greenhouse gases (GHG) reduction from 20% to 40% by 2030 and adopted an integrated approach:

© Springer Nature Switzerland AG 2021
O. Gervasi et al. (Eds.): ICCSA 2021, LNCS 12957, pp. 615–620, 2021.
https://doi.org/10.1007/978-3-030-87013-3_47

energy and climate change mitigation/adaptation. This initiative can be divided basically by two phases: the first (2008–2020) characterized by the Sustainable and Energy Action Plan (SEAP) and the second (2020 – ongoing) by the Sustainable Energy and Climate Action Plan (SECAP). The first phase focused on the energy efficiency, while the second on the coupling the energy efficiency with the mitigation/adaptation action facing climate-change. Fully in line with the UN Sustainable Development Goals [1], the G-CoM has started a new season of urban and territorial planning in Europe according to a volunteer approach in developing planning tools [2, 3] with the SEAPs and SECAPs. These planning tools are out of any normative obligation deriving from any planning law (national/regional) through effective practices such as useful technical contributions in selecting intervention priorities or design of feasible project frameworks for public and private investments. Recent works have analyzed the magnitude of the CoM experience in European and/or National contexts [4–8], highlighting a generalized success of the G-CoM policy both in terms of an effective contribution towards achieving the GHG reduction targets and in terms of commitment of local administrations and local communities towards EU policies objectives. An interesting feature of the CoM widespread is the high number of Municipalities signed up with resident population under 10000 inhabitants. In May 2021, these Municipalities are the 64% of the whole CoM Signatories, and it highlights that CoM is more supported by the "small" than the "big" Municipalities. We are focusing on inland areas [9, 10], where an insularity [11] effect can be a measure of spatial segregation [12]. The research aimed to explore better these "small" Municipalities in Sect. 2 presents some general statistics from the EU small Municipalities. Section 3 explores the SECAP sectors chosen by the CoM Signatories focusing on the most "favourite" sectors, while Sect. 4 is related to the main outcomes and the conclusions.

2   Statistics from Small CoM Municipalities

The CoM official website provides a database that supports advanced searches in terms of: region of origin, population, SECAP sectors, CO_2 emissions target reduction, target year set for the CO_2 reduction for every CoM Signatory. In May 2021, among 6792 CoM Municipalities, 4316 (corresponding to 63% of the whole Signatories) are small Municipalities. The small Municipalities (with resident population under 10000 inhabitants) have been classified by the CoM as XS Signatories. Thus, it has been counted the number of XS Signatories for each CoM country, and in Table 1 are proposed the top five countries with the highest number and percentage of XS Signatories.

It is interesting look at the number of the XS Signatories, only between Italy and Spain there are 3940 XS Municipalities, corresponding to the 91% of the whole XS Signatories. The remaining 376 XS Signatories have distributed 28 countries EU and not EU, with a mean percentage under the 1%.

Considering the CO_2 emissions target reduction set, (see Table 2) the 88% percent of XS Signatories have set a CO_2 target in the range 20–30%, close to the 20% 2020 target fix by the CoM. Only the 12% of the Signatories have set a more ambitious target over the 30% according to the G-CoM target (i.e. the reduction at least of 30% of CO_2 emissions).

Table 1. Top five countries with highest number of XS Signatories

Country	XS signatories	Percentage on the total XS CoM signatories
Italy	**2502**	**75%**
Spain	**1438**	**77%**
Belgium	**98**	**2,3%**
Portugal	**34**	**0,8%**
Malta	**23**	**0,5%**

Table 2. Number of XS signatories and percentage CO_2 emissions target reduction set

CO_2 emissions target reduction set	Number of XS signatories
20–30%	**3449**
30–40%	749
40–50%	575
>50%	174

3 XS Municipalities and SEAP/SECAP Sectors

The actions developed in the SEAPs and SECAPs are planned through a standard set of sectors concerning environmental, social and urban topics. The vision by sectors, has allowed to design actions with a detailed information concerning budget allocated, stakeholder involved or timeframe expected. A further distinctive aspect of this sectorial approach is the certainty of the action's timeframe for each Municipality, compared to the CoM procedures and self-defined actions. In Table 3 are proposed the occurrence of the SEAP/SECAP sectors of the XS Signatories and the percentage of the sector on the total XS Signatories.

Data from SEAP/SECAP sectors highlights that the XS Signatories have a preferential interest in developing actions related to sectors basically "public" like public lighting or municipal building equipment facilities. Considering the "private" sectors (involving not only public actors but also private company, stakeholders etc..), there is a widespread success of SEAP/SECAP policies of sectors related to the improvement of the energy production and the energy efficiency of the buildings. The remarkable number of SEAP/SECAP with transport sector that is considered as a main target in CO_2 emissions [13, 14], shows a changing of the idea of mobility oriented towards sustainable ways, fostering the emissions reduction.

Table 3. Count of occurrences of SEAP/SECAP sectors of XS CoM signatories

SEAP/SECAP sector	Occurrence of sector on total XS CoM signatories	Percentage of sector on total XS CoM signatories
Agriculture	**966**	**22**
Industry	**722**	**17**
Local electricity production	**3099**	**72**
Local heat cold production	**840**	**19**
Municipal buildings equipment facilities	**2940**	**68**
Others	**1389**	**32**
Public lighting	**3482**	**81**
Residential buildings	**3370**	**78**
Tertiary buildings equipment facilities	**2045**	**47**
Transport	**3260**	**76**

4 Discussions and Conclusions

Analyzing data coming from SEAP/SECAP occurrences among the XS Signatories, it highlights a widespread success of the CoM policies and SEAP/SECAP chosen by these small Municipalities as instruments used to plan and provide funding for ordinary interventions on the urban areas instead of institutional instruments (i.e. urban planning regulation, operational plans and programs established by National policies). A critical step for small Municipalities is represented by technical support that may affect the effectiveness of the entire process of CoM implementation at a local level. Thus, SEAPs first and SECAPs after, could be a boost for the small municipalities in the domain of the planning oriented towards result and performance in terms of energy/climate objectives. The sectorial approach seems to be (see also [15, 16]) the solution to the planning tools in urban areas where there are complex and fragmented planning laws. Furthermore, the considerable number of small Municipalities signed-up to CoM compared to whole number of signatories, highlights how these planning tools out of any normative law, are highly widespread in EU scenario. This new season of urban and territorial planning is representative of the high demand in implementation of sustainable territorial development objectives [17] and a generalized success of the current EU policies, achieving the EU 2020 emissions target. Previous researches [18–24] remark the fruitful aspect of the sectorial approach, facing the climate-change, however the cities should not be considered by sectors but by set of systems (such as green spaces, green infrastructures [25] waterproofed soils, energy system [26], active mobility [27–29] etc..). This represents the domain of further developments oriented toward an alternative approach for the foreword season of the SECAP: the cross-system assessment [30].

References

1. United Nations: Transforming our world: the 2030 Agenda for Sustainable Development. In: Sustainable Development Goals, pp. 333–374. Wiley (2019). https://doi.org/10.1002/978111 9541851.app1
2. Casas, G.L., Scorza, F.: Sustainable planning: a methodological toolkit. In: Gervasi, O., et al. (eds.) ICCSA 2016. LNCS, vol. 9786, pp. 627–635. Springer, Cham (2016). https://doi.org/ 10.1007/978-3-319-42085-1_53
3. Las Casas, G., Scorza, F.: A renewed rational approach from liquid society towards antifragile planning. In: Gervasi, O., et al. (eds.) ICCSA 2017. LNCS, vol. 10409, pp. 517–526. Springer, Cham (2017). https://doi.org/10.1007/978-3-319-62407-5_36
4. Santopietro, L., Scorza, F.: The Italian experience of the covenant of mayors: a territorial evaluation. Sustainability. **13**, 1289 (2021). https://doi.org/10.3390/su13031289
5. Abarca-Alvarez, N.-L.: Valenzuela-montes, campos-sánchez: European strategies for adaptation to climate change with the mayors adapt initiative by self-organizing maps. Appl. Sci. **9**, 3859 (2019). https://doi.org/10.3390/app9183859
6. Reckien, D., et al.: Climate change response in Europe: what's the reality? analysis of adaptation and mitigation plans from 200 urban areas in 11 countries. Clim. Change **122**(1–2), 331–340 (2013). https://doi.org/10.1007/s10584-013-0989-8
7. Reckien, D., et al.: How are cities planning to respond to climate change? assessment of local climate plans from 885 cities in the EU-28. J. Clean. Prod. **191**, 207–219 (2018). https://doi. org/10.1016/j.jclepro.2018.03.220
8. Coelho, S., Russo, M., Oliveira, R., Monteiro, A., Lopes, M., Borrego, C.: Sustainable energy action plans at city level: a Portuguese experience and perception. J. Clean. Prod. **176**, 1223–1230 (2018). https://doi.org/10.1016/j.jclepro.2017.11.247
9. Curatella, L., Scorza, F.: Polycentrism and insularity metrics for in-land areas. In: Gervasi, O., et al. (eds.) ICCSA 2020. LNCS, vol. 12255, pp. 253–261. Springer, Cham (2020). https:// doi.org/10.1007/978-3-030-58820-5_20
10. Curatella, L., Scorza, F.: Una valutazione della struttura policentrica dell'insediamento nella regione basilicata. LaborEst. 37–42 (2020). https://doi.org/10.19254/LaborEst.20.06
11. Garau, C., Desogus, G., Stratigea, A.: Territorial cohesion in insular contexts: assessing external attractiveness and internal strength of major mediterranean islands. Eur. Plan. Stud. (2020). https://doi.org/10.1080/09654313.2020.1840524
12. Torre, C.M., Morano, P., Taiani, F.: Social balance and economic effectiveness in historic centers rehabilitation. In: Gervasi, O., et al. (eds.) ICCSA 2015. LNCS, vol. 9157, pp. 317–329. Springer, Cham (2015). https://doi.org/10.1007/978-3-319-21470-2_22
13. Croci, E., Lucchitta, B., Janssens-Maenhout, G., Martelli, S., Molteni, T.: Urban CO2 mitigation strategies under the covenant of Mayors: an assessment of 124 European cities. J. Clean. Prod. **169**, 161–177 (2017). https://doi.org/10.1016/j.jclepro.2017.05.165
14. Kona, A., et al.: Covenant of mayors in figures: 8-year assessment. Publications office of the European Union, Luxembourg (2017). https://doi.org/10.2760/64731
15. Romano, B., Zullo, F., Marucci, A., Fiorini, L.: Vintage urban planning in italy: land management with the tools of the Mid-Twentieth century. Sustain. **10**, 4125 (2018). https://doi. org/10.3390/su10114125
16. Scorza, F., Saganeiti, L., Pilogallo, A., Murgante, B.: Ghost planning: the inefficiency of energy sector policies in a low population density region. Arch. DI Stud. Urbani E Reg. (2020)
17. Las Casas, G., Scorza, F., Murgante, B.: New urban agenda and open challenges for urban and regional planning. In: Calabrò, F., Della Spina, L., Bevilacqua, C. (eds.) ISHT 2018. SIST, vol. 100, pp. 282–288. Springer, Cham (2019). https://doi.org/10.1007/978-3-319-92099-3_33

18. Scorza, F., Santopietro, L., Giuzio, B., Amato, F., Murgante, B., Casas, G.L.: Conflicts between environmental protection and energy regeneration of the historic heritage in the case of the city of matera: tools for assessing and dimensioning of Sustainable Energy Action Plans (SEAP). In: Gervasi, O., et al. (eds.) ICCSA 2017. LNCS, vol. 10409, pp. 527–539. Springer, Cham (2017). https://doi.org/10.1007/978-3-319-62407-5_37

19. Santopietro, L., et al.: Geovisualization for energy planning. In: Gervasi, O., et al. (eds.) ICCSA 2020. LNCS, vol. 12252, pp. 479–487. Springer, Cham (2020). https://doi.org/10.1007/978-3-030-58811-3_35

20. Santopietro, L., Scorza, F.: A place-based approach for the SECAP of potenza municipality: the case of green spaces system. In: Gervasi, O., et al. (eds.) ICCSA 2020. LNCS, vol. 12255, pp. 226–234. Springer, Cham (2020). https://doi.org/10.1007/978-3-030-58820-5_18

21. Campagna, M., Di Cesare, E.A., Matta, A., Serra, M.: Bridging the gap between strategic environmental assessment and planning: a geodesign perspective. In: Environmental Information Systems: Concepts, Methodologies, Tools, and Applications, pp. 569–589. IGI Global (2018). https://doi.org/10.4018/978-1-5225-7033-2.ch024

22. Lai, S., Leone, F., Zoppi, C.: Assessment of municipal masterplans aimed at identifying and fostering green infrastructure: a study concerning three towns of the metropolitan area of Cagliari. Italy. Sustain. 11, 1470 (2019). https://doi.org/10.3390/su11051470

23. Danese, M., Nolè, G., Murgante, B.: Visual impact assessment in urban planning. In: Geocomputation and Urban Planning, pp. 133–146. Springer Berlin Heidelberg, Berlin, Heidelberg (2009). https://doi.org/10.1007/978-3-540-89930-3_8

24. Campagna, M., Deplano, G.: Evaluating geographic information provision within public administration websites. Environ. Plan. B Plan. Des. 31, 21–37 (2004). https://doi.org/10.1068/b12966

25. Lai, S., Leone, F., Zoppi, C.: Implementing green infrastructures beyond protected areas. Sustain. 10, 3544 (2018). https://doi.org/10.3390/su10103544

26. Scorza, F.: Towards self energy-management and sustainable citizens' engagement in local energy efficiency Agenda. Int. J. Agric. Environ. Inf. Syst. 7, 44–53 (2016). https://doi.org/10.4018/IJAEIS.2016010103

27. Scorza, F., Fortunato, G.: Cyclable cities: building feasible scenario through urban space-morphology assessment. J. Urban Plan. Dev. https://doi.org/10.1061/(ASCE)UP.1943-5444.0000713

28. Scorza, F., Fortunato, G., Carbone, R., Murgante, B., Pontrandolfi, P.: Increasing urban walkability through citizens' participation processes. Sustainability. 13, 5835 (2021). https://doi.org/10.3390/su13115835

29. Fortunato, G., Scorza, F., Murgante, B.: Hybrid oriented sustainable urban development: a pattern of low-carbon access to schools in the city of Potenza. In: Gervasi, O., et al. (eds.) ICCSA 2020. LNCS, vol. 12255, pp. 193–205. Springer, Cham (2020). https://doi.org/10.1007/978-3-030-58820-5_15

30. Scorza, F., Santopietro, L.: A systemic perspective for the Sustainable Energy and Climate Action Plan (SECAP). Eur. Plan. Stud. (2021)

Impact Evaluation: An Experiment on Development Policies in Agri Valley (Basilicata, Italy) Compared with New Urban Agenda Themes

Priscilla Sofia Dastoli[1]([✉]) ⓘ, Francesco Scorza[2] ⓘ, and Beniamino Murgante[2] ⓘ

[1] DiCEM, University of Basilicata, CdS Architecture, Via Lanera, 20, 75100 Matera, Italy
priscilla.dastoli@unibas.it
[2] School of Engineering, Laboratory of Urban and Regional Systems Engineering, University of Basilicata, 10, Viale Dell'Ateneo Lucano, 85100 Potenza, Italy
{francesco.scorza,beniamino.murgante}@unibas.it

Abstract. The Cohesion Policy of the European Union was established with the aim of redistributing wealth between regions and countries and to stimulate growth in lagging areas. It is the most important structural policy in terms of financial commitment, geographical dimension and timing. The management of the EU Structural Funds (SF) highlights problems related to monitoring and evaluation; the latter aims to measure the effectiveness, efficiency and impact of programs; however, in the regional evaluations of operational programs, the impact assessment is underestimated.

This paper is based on the results developed within the RI.PROVA.RE project and is aimed at defining an impact evaluation proposal based on the data emerging from the analysis of a specific case study.

By the collection of territorial data on public investments financed by EU Structural Funds and other regional funds in the Agri Valley area, several graphic representations on the distribution of funds were made. In addition, the investment priorities were compared with the themes of the New Urban Agenda: the analysis of coherence between the objectives of the previous programs and the future perspective of urban development policies made it possible to identify weaknesses in rebalancing structural territorial trends.

Keywords: European and local policies · Impact evaluation · New Urban Agenda

1 Introduction

The European Commission, for the Cohesion Policy of the 2021–2027 programming cycle, proposes a series of important changes with a view to simplicity, flexibility and efficiency. In particular, the 11 thematic objectives of the period 2014–2020 are replaced by five broader objectives: a smarter Europe, a greener and low-carbon Europe, a more connected Europe, a more social Europe, a Europe closer to citizens [1]. The theme of

© Springer Nature Switzerland AG 2021
O. Gervasi et al. (Eds.): ICCSA 2021, LNCS 12957, pp. 621–633, 2021.
https://doi.org/10.1007/978-3-030-87013-3_48

the impact evaluation is very current, especially if a paradigm change is foreseen based on the results, positive and negative, of the previous programming cycle [2].

This research was developed in the framework of the project "Re-inhabiting countries. Operational Strategies for the Enhancement and Resilience of inland areas" (RI. P.R.O.VA. RE); the research project was funded by the "Call to promote research projects to support the implementation of the National Strategy for Sustainable Development (SNAI)" in the theme "Resilience of communities and territories"; the call was encouraged in 2019 by the current Ministry of Ecological Transition (MiTE). The project is structured around three research objectives [3]: 1. Redesigning the geography of inland areas, 2. Understanding the Resilience of inland areas, 3. Defining strategies for sustainable and resilient development; the latter objective includes the activity aimed at carrying out an Analysis and Evaluation of ongoing policies. The RI.P.R.O.VA.RE project focuses on two regions in southern Italy: Campania and Basilicata. Following the results of the objective 1 activity, three areas of experimentation were identified in the two regions: Matese and Ufita in Campania Region and Agri Valley in Basilicata Region, for a total of 58 municipalities in the inland areas.

The departments involved in the RI.P.R.O.VA.RE project are the Department of Architecture and Industrial Design of the University of Campania Luigi Vanvitelli, the Department of Civil Engineering of the University of Salerno and the Department of European and Mediterranean Cultures, University of Basilicata (UniBas).

The UniBas research unit deals with the Agri Valley, which is located in the southwestern quadrant of Basilicata, between the Tyrrhenian and Ionian coasts. The research program covers territorial development investments, concerning EU instruments and a specific program active in the context of the Agri Valley called the Agri Valley Operational Program (POV). The POV is an impressive program of actions, inspired by regional economic planning lines and covering an enlarged territorial area, which activates the operation of all administrative levels, from regional to municipal. The Program is active in the regional territory affected by oil extraction, to invest the compensatory funds of royalties in a series of actions aimed at economic development, industrial growth and the development of renew energy sector [4–10]. Previous studies investigated the conflicts in current development strategies running in this area highlighting structural weaknesses of the planning process [11–16].

The analysis and impact assessment activities of territorial development policies [14, 17–20] are oriented to understand the Resilience of the inland areas, to deliver planning tools able to define strategies for sustainable and resilient development. The project's choice to focus on the inland areas is also functional to explore the usefulness of the concept of "Resilience", which is still the subject of different interpretations, in the triggering of processes of the revitalization of the inland areas [3]. The theoretical reference model to articulate the concept of Resilience in the RI.P.R.O.VA.RE project comes from the Gunderson and Holling studies [21] on the resilience of socio-ecological systems, of which territorial systems are clearly an expression. The authors point out that socio-ecological systems tend to develop according to evolutionary cycles structured in four phases: exploitation, conservation, release, and reorganization that leads to the triggering of a new evolutionary cycle, characterized by new configurations of the system.

The transition phase of the system - from decline to reorganization - requires high potential and high resilience [22].

A backward design approach has been adopted to identify critical development issues affecting local policies implementation the case study area: the Agri Valley in Basilicata region (Italy), as a precondition to stimulate a process of innovation and to develop a strategic perspective coherent with the principles of the New Urban Agenda (NUA) [23].

The New Urban Agenda was adopted in Quito (Ecuador), during the conference "Habitat III", held from 17 to 20 October 2016. The overall objective that is to be achieved is that of the 'right to the city', which means ensuring acceptable requirements in terms of equity, accessibility, security, healthiness, resilience and sustainability [24]. The 175 points are structured in three parts: sustainable urban development, tools for effective implementation, modalities for monitoring and revising the action plan.

The NUA identifies 12 priority themes that are mainly aimed at cities, where 65% of global energy is consumed and 70% of CO2 emissions are produced. However, in a country such as Italy, where 85% of municipalities have fewer than 10,000 inhabitants - mainly located in the inland areas - it is also necessary to pay attention to the policies and strategies of small municipalities and to the objectives that must be achieved by the "citizens" who live there [5, 25]. The study, therefore, proposes a consideration on the investment priorities of the Funds of a small inland area compared with themes of the NUA and on the coherence between former programs objectives and the future perspective of urban development policies.

2 European and Local Policies: Key Issues Related to Impact Evaluation

According to European Commission, in the evaluation process, you can identify three different types of evaluation related to distinct moments: ex ante, itinere and ex post. The impact assessment is part of the ex-post evaluation but focuses only on the impacts, i.e. the (non-immediate) changes caused by the interaction of cluster projects on the territorial system affected by the interventions. The impact evaluation should try to answer the question "What is the impact or effect of the interventions carried out on the condition of the target groups or territories?" [26].

The literature on public policy evaluation is very extensive [27–31]; the original meaning of the term evaluation has a very broad meaning, used in various contexts, which therefore needs to be framed within the limits of the analysis of the effects of public policies. A definition of evaluation encompasses the salient concepts of "effects of action" and "analytical activity" is as follows: "Evaluation is a multidisciplinary analytical activity that uses the methods of the social sciences to judge the effects produced by the implementation of public action" [32]. It is also necessary to understand what the meaning of the implementation of the evaluation activity is; the evaluation is useful in two areas: on the one hand, to produce information that can help improve the program, on the other, to measure the impact of the program on the target groups. Regulation No 1303/2013 [33] lays down general rules for the operation of Community funding and programs; the Regulation in article 54 specifies «evaluations shall be carried out to improve the quality of the design and execution of programs and to assess their effectiveness, efficiency and impact».

The information brochure prepared by the European Commission [34] for the period 2014–2020 states that «Managing authorities, together with project beneficiaries, must show the citizens of the region, as well as the media and politicians at all levels, the results of the investments made, while EU taxpayers have the right to know how their money is spent».

In Italy, the management of the Structural Funds improved for the 2014–2020 programming cycle with the introduction of information and communication rules to address the critical issues that had arisen in previous cycles [35]. The Agency for Territorial Cohesion has remedied some of these critical issues with the creation of the OpenCoesione web site (it is a portal of the Agency for Territorial Cohesion created in 2012 and dedicated to information on the implementation of cohesion policy interventions). Monitoring systems of this type are useful for constructing indicators that refer to the quantitative data of interventions, bringing out several problems.

In addition to the communication and information aspects, institutions are obliged to draw up evaluation documents during the implementation phases of Community programs to establish the effectiveness, efficiency and impact of the measures implemented. Evaluation documents are generally drawn up by regional offices because the regions and autonomous provinces represent the decentralized managing authorities of Community resources. It is a question of identifying a set of result and output indicators for each Axis of the Structural Funds, entering the data at the beginning of the implementation of the program and establishing intermediate and final targets that must be achieved based on the funding allocated to Axis. The evaluation takes place according to the degree of achievement of the objectives, comparing the deviation of the values from the initial data. Impact indicators are rarely included and calculated in evaluation documents, despite extensive literature on the subject of impact assessment by the European Community under the Structural Funds [34, 36–40].

A large set of result and output indicators is present in the database of territorial indicators for development policies, the construction of which represents one of the products provided for in the Convention concluded between the National Statistical Institute (ISTAT) and the PON Management Authority "Governance and Institutional Capacity 2014–2020", relating to the implementation of the Territorial and Sectorial Statistical Information Project for cohesion policies 2014–2020. The database contains 327 indicators (258 + 56 gender) available at a regional and provincial level, for macro-area and the target areas of the different development policy cycles, to have updated spatial data and indicators to observe the results gradually achieved by policies in the territories and support any reprogramming of resources [41–43]. Again, impact indicators are not included.

Currently the evaluation of Community policies is possible only based on the result and output indicators, without being able to monitor the effects of the same policies. In addition, this type of monitoring is normally aggregated to the scale of the entire region, so one cannot know the spending capacity or the margin for improvement of a part of the territory, such as inland areas or industrial areas. These are homogeneous data for the entire region that do not consider the inland dynamics of the same, even for sub-regional areas already prepared for other policies.

The impact evaluation has little application because - to understand the real effects on the territory - suitable and differentiated evaluation tools for sub-regional areas would have to be implemented, starting from the information of the municipal level. Suffice it to say that the Italian municipal administrations, with 4,060 projects, are the beneficiaries who, after private individuals, manage the most significant amount of resources of the ERDF 2014–2020 program, equal to 3.2 billion euros out of a total of over 20 billion [44].

So far, extensive studies have been produced focused on understanding the dynamics of innovation, growth and employment in the regions. Much less, the effort has been made by researchers to analyze the effects of policies. Only recently has an emerging international scientific literature on cohesion policy [45, 46] offered new evaluation evidence produced in a counterfactual perspective [47]. Theoretically, according to this approach, the effect is defined as the difference between what happened after the implementation of a policy (factual situation) and what would have happened if that same policy had not been implemented (counterfactual situation): this definition is based on all the evaluation of the effects with the counterfactual approach [48].

3   Methodology

3.1   A Case Study from the Basilicata Region

The data on the policies affecting the Agri Valley territory were acquired on the official website of OpenCoesione - concerning information on community and national policies at the municipal level - and on the website of the Agri Valley Operational Program (POV) for information on local policy. On the OpenCoesione website, it is possible to download projects (projects.csv / metadata.xls) grouped both for each municipality and for the entire region of interest. The information that has been acquired for each project of the municipalities of Agri Valley [6, 49–51] are as follows: Public cost, payments made, the progress of the project, Nature (Type of operation), Theme, Program, Axis. On the POV website, on the other hand, local policy data are available, organized within Annual Reports on the activities carried out by all implementing actors.

The first activity was to identify policies active in the areas of experimentation: the European Structural Funds, the national and local policies. Then there was the verification of the availability of data at the municipal level, which was followed by a phase of collection in a spreadsheet and georeferencing of the same in the GIS environment. All data were collected in a comma-separated values (.csv) table and join with the resident population data as of 1 January 2020 from ISTAT to be able to perform basic statistics identifying per capita impacts.

The collection phase is fundamental to build maps, which serve to understand the trend in the use of Community resources throughout the area, making a comparison between municipalities and between different types of funds. Maps are the basis for starting to reflect on the impact evaluation and spending capacity of small municipalities in an inland area.

In the next activity, each Axis of financing instruments has been compared with the 12 themes of the NUA, to understand in what aspects the economic resources of the policies concerned affect; the comparison made it possible to find a table of correspondence (see Table 1).

Table 1. Investment priorities at the EU and local levels compared with the themes of the New Urban Agenda.

	1 INTEGRATION OF MIGRANTS AND REFUGEES	2 AIR QUALITY	3 HOUSING	4 URBAN POVERTY	5 CIRCULAR ECONOMY	6 CLIMATE ADAPTATION	7 ENERGY TRANSITION	8 URBAN MOBILITY	9 DIGITAL TRANSITION	10 PUBLIC PROCUREMENT	11 JOBS & SKILLS IN LOCAL ECONOMY	12 SUSTAINABLE USE OF LAND AND NATURE-BASED SOLUTIONS
Plan FSC - Environment												✸
Plan FSC - Infrastructure										✸		
Plan FSC - Ultra-broadband									✸			
Plan FSC - Hydrogeological instability												✸
FSC - Tourism, Culture and Natural Resources Enhancement					✸						✸	
Axis 1 FSE. Create and maintain employment					✸						✸	
Axis 2 FSE. Strengthen and innovate active inclusion in society	✸		✸	✸								
Axis 3 FSE. Develop learning rights and quality and support smart innovation in key sectors					✸						✸	
Axis 1. ERDF: Research, technological development and innovation									✸			
Axis 2.ERDF: Digital agenda									✸			
Axis 3. ERDF: Competitiveness					✸						✸	
Axis 4. ERDF: Energy and urban mobility		✸				✸	✸	✸				
Axis 5. ERDF: Environmental protection and efficient use of resources												✸
Axis 6. ERDF: Transport systems and network infrastructures		✸				✸	✸	✸				
Axis 7. ERDF: Social inclusion	✸		✸	✸								
Axis 8. ERDF: Strengthening the education system											✸	
Measure A. POV: Safeguarding and improving the context of environmental liveability		✸				✸	✸	✸				
Measure B. POV: Strengthening of the supply of essential infrastructures									✸			
Measure C. POV: Improvement of the provision of services for the enhancement of the quality of life	✸		✸	✸								
Measure D. POV: Increase of the conditions and opportunities for lasting and sustainable employability					✸						✸	

It is important to stress that this step makes it possible to disregard policies affecting a specific area and to frame the analysis within the framework of the Sustainable Urban Development Goals.

In some cases, the themes have been grouped to constitute a single area of impact; this is the case of social inclusion in which they have merged: 1. Integration of migrants and refugees, 3. Housing, 4. Urban Poverty. Each area of impact, or thematic, corresponds to the share of economic resources of the relevant Axes.

After processing this initial information, the next step was to carry out an impact evaluation of Community and local policies on the whole territory of interest.

The experimentation with impact evaluation is based on the composition of indicators that can assess the effects on the community and the environment for each theme. For each impact area, one or more indicators have been composed, based on the possibility of acquiring statistical data on the subject. Here, too, there is a gap on the part of the institutions: Municipal statistics in the public domain on issues related to the implementation of development policies, both Community and local, are lacking; ISTAT produces a lot of statistical data, but they are mostly aggregated by region or province, sometimes by provincial capital.

Facilitation is given by the Statistical Atlas of Municipalities (ASC), a dynamic webtool which collects only ISTAT data at a municipal level. The indicators, therefore, were built on the available municipal statistical data, which must be acquired in two not close time moments, to see a change. One of the main reference years, if we consider above all ISTAT data, is 2011; the other reference year varies, but generally relies on the permanent population census 2018–2019. In the data acquisition phase, the ideal condition occurs when considering time moments coinciding with the extremes of programming cycles (i.e. 2014 and 2020), but since the absence of data represents a gap in the assessment of the impact on territories, a first experiment was put in place with the available data.

The approach used for impact evaluation [32] is based on the construction of indicators that can assess the effects on the community and the environment for each theme. The impact evaluation for the theme "11. Jobs & skills in the local economy" is reported as an example (see Table 2), which is connected to the topic of employment in the strict sense, and to the educational system for entry into the world of work. The main questions for assessing the impacts of EU and local policies are as follows: What impact have they had on employment and skills in the local economy? What impact have they had on strengthening the education system?

The indicators that could be constructed are: Change in the workforce (2011–2019), Change in the % of the workforce in the total number of residents (2011–2019), Change in the % of graduates residing > 9 years (2011–2019), Change in the % of graduates residing > 9 years (2011–2019) 2011–2019), Change in university en enrollees (2015–2017), Change in the % of university enrollees in the total number of residents (2015–2017).

The data have been acquired for each municipality and the indicators were calculated. In the Table 2, a symbol indicating the trend was included. The complete table is included as an annex to this paper (see Appendix A [1]), here only data from three Municipality and the whole Study Area are presented. The sum of the statistical data for the twenty municipalities made it possible to understand what the trend was also for the entire area of the Agri Valley, relative to that theme.

Table 2. The following table exemplifies the evaluation process that considers the amounts in euros of all separate policies for the issues of the NUA, the impact indicators and the trend for three municipalities, up to an overall trend for the entire area.

Impact theme	Indicators	Year of Analysis	Aliano	Armento	Corleto Perticara	...	All the municipalities of the Agri Valley
			€ 403.232	€ 9.529	€ 1.278.534	...	€ 20.728.270
	Workforce (employed and job seekers> 15 years) ISTAT	2011	420	278	1051	...	18064
		2019	337	238	1048	...	18547
	Change in the workforce (2011-2019)		⬇	⬇	⬇	...	⬆
	% workforce (out of total residents> 15 years) ISTAT	2011	43%	47%	45%	...	44%
		2019	41%	46%	47%	...	46%
	Change in % of the workforce on total residents (2011-2019)		⬇	⬇	⬆	...	⬆
11 Jobs & Skills In Local Economy	Degree of education of the resident population> 9 years (% secondary school graduates)ISTAT	2011	23%	29%	27%	...	27%
		2019	30%	36%	32%	...	34%
	Change in% of graduates resident> 9 years (2011-2019)		⬆	⬆	⬆	...	⬆
	The total number of residents enrolled in the university (ASC)	2015	34	12	99	...	1739
		2017	38	13	86	...	1598
	Change in university enrollments (2015-2017)		⬆	⬆	⬇	...	⬇
	% university enrolled on total residents (ASC)	2015	3,3%	1,8%	3,9%	...	3,6%
		2017	3,9%	2,2%	3,4%	...	3,5%
	Variation in the% of university students on the total number of residents		⬆	⬆	⬇	...	⬇

At the same time, the economic resources which have been invested by the policies taken into account have been indicated for each municipality and each theme. At this point, you can really answer the initial question: what is the impact or effect of the interventions carried out on the condition of the target groups or territories? For theme "11. Jobs & skills in the local economy", community and local policies, against an investment of more than 20.7 million euros, had a positive effect on the theme of work, with an increase of about 500 units corresponding to 2% of the workforce on the total number of residents. The results show that around EUR 42 000 has been spent on each new person employed, if we consider the entire investment only on employment; it is neither a little nor a lot but it clearly emerges that there is still a strong disparity between the municipalities of the examined area. The impact of policies on education, on the other hand, shows that the level of education of the resident population has been increased; however, the number of university en enrolees fell by 141, but this corresponds to only 1% of residents.

4 Conclusion

This contribution indicates the elements and main contents of a first experimentation on the theme of impact evaluation - at the municipal and local scale - which achieves preliminary results. It can be said that in Italy the debate on data, on the impacts and on how the results of development policies must be achieved - according to the specific territorial characteristics - is not at the top of the agenda of decision-makers and regional management authorities. Concern is expressed about the evidence emerging from the evaluations conducted in this research: the attention of operators (including beneficiaries) and institutions has focused only on the use of resources rather than working to network procedures, regulations and best practices, which could favour both a concrete assessment of the impacts on territories and institutional models of management of the same most useful resources.

Secondly, there is a lack of monitoring and production of data and indicators at the municipal scale, which represents the basic level from which to start an impact evaluation on territorial areas that do not coincide with the regional territory, as in the case of the Agri experimentation area. In the Community resource evaluation plans, a local level of monitoring should already be investigated, in which to evaluate the effects through statistical data and indicators built specifically for that territorial scale. At this level of disaggregation, there is a lack of municipal statistical data on the issues of agriculture (Utilized Agricultural Area), digital divide (Families with Internet access from home), energy transition (% of hybrid or electric total means of transport) and active mobility [53–55].

The experimentation in Agri Valley revealed that there is no strict coherence between investments and effects on the variables considered; probably, because the variables are few, or these variables are not able to describe the expected effects, but since there are no significant variations on these aspects, there is a weakness in the overall strategy in this territory, which as a whole fails to generate concrete results and actual changes [56]. The effective use of resources depends on numerous variables; already in an internal area such as the Agri Valley, there is a significant imbalance which is the expression of a weak territorial subsystem that is unable to participate in these development processes. For this reason, it is essential to arrange structural accompanying actions in the weakest territories that can be identified only after having evaluated the effects, based on integrated and effective management of municipal data collection, monitoring of results and evaluation of effects on the territory.

References

1. Reppel, K.: Future Cohesion Policy objective 1: A smarter Europe-innovative and smart economic transformation (2020)
2. Murgante, B., Borruso, G., Balletto, G., Castiglia, P., Dettori, M.: Why Italy first? health, geographical and planning aspects of the COVID-19 outbreak. Sustain. **12**, 5064 (2020). https://doi.org/10.3390/su12125064
3. Galderisi, A., Fiore, P., Pontrandolfi, P.: Strategie Operative per la valorizzazione e la resilienza delle Aree Interne: il progetto RI.P.R.O.VA.RE. BDC. Boll. Del Cent. Calza Bini. 20, 297–316 (2020). https://doi.org/10.6092/2284-4732/7557
4. Santopietro, L., Scorza, F.: A systemic perspective for the Sustainable Energy and Climate Action Plan (SECAP). Eur. Plan. Stud. (2021)
5. Santopietro, L., Scorza, F.: The Italian experience of the covenant of mayors: a territorial evaluation. Sustainability. **13**, 1289 (2021). https://doi.org/10.3390/su13031289
6. Izzi, F., La Scaleia, G., Dello Buono, D., Scorza, F., Las Casas, G.: Enhancing the spatial dimensions of open data: geocoding open PA Information using geo platform fusion to support planning process. In: Murgante, B., et al. (eds.) ICCSA 2013. LNCS, vol. 7973, pp. 622–629. Springer, Heidelberg (2013). https://doi.org/10.1007/978-3-642-39646-5_45
7. Scorza, F.: Towards self energy-management and sustainable citizens' engagement in local energy efficiency agenda. Int. J. Agric. Environ. Inf. Syst. **7**, 44–53 (2016). https://doi.org/10.4018/ijaeis.2016010103
8. Saganeiti, L., Pilogallo, A., Faruolo, G., Scorza, F., Murgante, B.: Territorial fragmentation and renewable energy source plants: which relationship? Sustain. **12**, 1828 (2020). https://doi.org/10.3390/SU12051828
9. Nolè, G., Lasaponara, R., Lanorte, A., Murgante, B.: Quantifying urban sprawl with spatial autocorrelation techniques using multi-temporal satellite data. Int. J. Agric. Environ. Inf. Syst. **5**, 20–38 (2014). https://doi.org/10.4018/IJAEIS.2014040102
10. Murgante, B., Las Casas, G., Sansone, A.: A spatial Rough Set for extracting the periurban fringe. Extraction et Gestion des Connaissances, EGC **2008**, 101–126 (2008)
11. Las Casas, G., Scorza, F., Murgante, B.: Conflicts and sustainable planning: peculiar instances coming from val d'agri structural inter-municipal plan. In: Papa, R., Fistola, R., Gargiulo, C. (eds.) Smart Planning: Sustainability and Mobility in the Age of Change. GET, pp. 163–177. Springer, Cham (2018). https://doi.org/10.1007/978-3-319-77682-8_10
12. Casas, G.L., Scorza, F.: Discrete spatial assessment of multi-parameter phenomena in low density region: the val d'agri case. In: Gervasi, O., et al. (eds.) ICCSA 2015. LNCS, vol. 9157, pp. 813–824. Springer, Cham (2015). https://doi.org/10.1007/978-3-319-21470-2_59
13. Las Casas, G., Murgante, B., Scorza, F.: Regional local development strategies benefiting from open data and open tools and an outlook on the renewable energy sources contribution. In: Papa, R., Fistola, R. (eds.) Smart Energy in the Smart City. GET, pp. 275–290. Springer, Cham (2016). https://doi.org/10.1007/978-3-319-31157-9_14
14. Casas, G.L., Scorza, F., Murgante, B.: Razionalità a-priori: Una proposta verso una pianificazione antifragile. Sci. Reg. **18**, 329–338 (2019). https://doi.org/10.14650/93656

15. Scorza, F., Saganeiti, L., Pilogallo, A., Murgante, B.: Ghost planning: the inefficiency of energy sector policies in a low population density region1. Arch. DI Stud. URBANI E Reg. 34–55 (2020)
16. Elfadaly, A., Attia, W., Qelichi, M.M., Murgante, B., Lasaponara, R.: Management of cultural heritage sites using remote sensing indices and spatial analysis techniques. Surv. Geophys. **39**(6), 1347–1377 (2018). https://doi.org/10.1007/s10712-018-9489-8
17. Casas, G.L., Scorza, F.: Sustainable planning: a methodological toolkit. In: Gervasi, O., et al. (eds.) ICCSA 2016. LNCS, vol. 9786, pp. 627–635. Springer, Cham (2016). https://doi.org/10.1007/978-3-319-42085-1_53
18. Las Casas, G., Scorza, F.: A renewed rational approach from liquid society towards anti-fragile planning. In: Gervasi, O., et al. (eds.) ICCSA 2017. LNCS, vol. 10409, pp. 517–526. Springer, Cham (2017). https://doi.org/10.1007/978-3-319-62407-5_36
19. Murgante, B., Borruso, G., Lapucci, A.: Geocomputation and urban planning (2009).https://doi.org/10.1007/978-3-540-89930-3_1
20. Danese, M., Nolè, G., Murgante, B.: Visual impact assessment in urban planning (2009).https://doi.org/10.1007/978-3-540-89930-3_8
21. Holling, C., Gunderson, L.H.: Resilience and adaptive cycles. Panarchy Underst. Transform. Hum. Nat. Syst. 25–62 (2002)
22. Galderisi, A.: Articolazione del progetto RI.P.R.O.VA.RE: resilienza (2021)
23. Commission, E.: Urban agenda for the EU. Pact of Amsterdam, Amsterdam (2016)
24. Caprotti, F., et al.: The new urban agenda: key opportunities and challenges for policy and practice. Urban Res. Pract. **10**, 367–378 (2017). https://doi.org/10.1080/17535069.2016.1275618
25. Casas, G.L., Scorza, F.: From the UN new urban agenda to the local experiences of urban development: the case of potenza. In: Gervasi, O., et al. (eds.) ICCSA 2018. LNCS, vol. 10964, pp. 734–743. Springer, Cham (2018). https://doi.org/10.1007/978-3-319-95174-4_56
26. Di Napoli, R., Ricci, C.: Vademecum. La valutazione di Leader a livello locale (2019)
27. Dziekan, K., Riedel, V., Müller, S., Abraham, M., Kettner, S., Daubitz, S.: Evaluation matters. a practitioners' guide to sound evaluation for urban mobility measures. Tesinska Tiskarna, A.S., Münster - New York - München - Berlin (2013)
28. Rossi, P.H., Lipsey, M.W., Henry, G.T.: Evaluation: A Systematic Approach. SAGE Publications (2018)
29. EVALSED: The Resource for the Evaluation of Socio-Economic Development (2008). https://doi.org/10.2776/8296
30. Weiss, C.H.: The interface between evaluation and public policy. Evaluation **5**, 468–486 (1999). https://doi.org/10.1177/135638909900500408
31. Weiss, C.H.: Theory-based evaluation: Past, present, and future. New Dir. Eval. **1997**, 41–55 (1997). https://doi.org/10.1002/ev.1086
32. Martini, A.: Cinque modi di interpretare la "valutazione." In: Valutare gli effetti delle politiche pubbliche. Metodi e applicazioni al caso italiano. pp. 19–32. Stampa Tipograf srl, Roma (2006)
33. Rete Rurale Nazionale 2014–2020 Homepage - Regolamento n. 1303/2013. https://www.reterurale.it/flex/cm/pages/ServeBLOB.php/L/IT/IDPagina/14733. Accessed 06 May 2021
34. European Commission: Ensuring the visibility of cohesion policy: information and communication rules 2014–2020 (2014). https://doi.org/10.2776/69343
35. Di Rienzo, M.: La trasparenza nell'uso dei fondi strutturali. Il ruolo delle pubbliche amministrazioni beneficiarie (2012)
36. European Commission: Guidance document on monitoring and evaluation. , Bruxelles (2014). https://doi.org/10.2776/969657.
37. European Commission: Selection and use of indicators for monitoring and evaluation - vol 2. In: MEANS COLLECTION. , Luxembourg (1999)

38. Scorza, F.: Improving EU cohesion policy: the spatial distribution analysis of regional development investments funded by EU structural funds 2007/2013 in Italy. In: Murgante, B., et al. (eds.) ICCSA 2013. LNCS, vol. 7973, pp. 582–593. Springer, Heidelberg (2013). https://doi.org/10.1007/978-3-642-39646-5_42

39. Scorza, F., Casas, G.B.L., Murgante, B.: That's ReDO: ontologies and regional development planning. In: Murgante, B., et al. (eds.) ICCSA 2012. LNCS, vol. 7334, pp. 640–652. Springer, Heidelberg (2012). https://doi.org/10.1007/978-3-642-31075-1_48

40. Las Casas, G., Scorza, F., Murgante, B.: New urban agenda and open challenges for urban and regional planning. In: Calabrò, F., Della Spina, L., Bevilacqua, C. (eds.) ISHT 2018. SIST, vol. 100, pp. 282–288. Springer, Cham (2019). https://doi.org/10.1007/978-3-319-92099-3_33

41. ISTAT Homepage, https://www.istat.it/it/archivio/16777. Accessed 07 May 2021

42. Saganeiti, L., Pilogallo, A., Scorza, F., Mussuto, G., Murgante, B.: Spatial indicators to evaluate urban fragmentation in basilicata region. In: Gervasi, O., et al. (eds.) ICCSA 2018. LNCS, vol. 10964, pp. 100–112. Springer, Cham (2018). https://doi.org/10.1007/978-3-319-95174-4_8

43. Martellozzo, F., Amato, F., Murgante, B., Clarke, K.C.: Modelling the impact of urban growth on agriculture and natural land in Italy to 2030. Appl. Geogr. **91**, 156–167 (2018). https://doi.org/10.1016/j.apgeog.2017.12.004

44. La Repubblica (2019). https://www.repubblica.it/dossier/esteri/fondi-strutturali-europei-progetti-italia/2019/12/31/news/l_europa_in_comune_quando_i_fondi_strutturali_aiutano_il_sindaco-244709880/

45. Becker, S.O., Egger, P.H., Von Ehrlich, M.: Absorptive capacity and the growth and investment effects of regional transfers: a regression discontinuity design with hetero_geneous treatment effects. Am. Econ. J. **5**(4), 29–77 (2013)

46. Bachtrögler, J., Fratesi, U., Perucca, G.: The influence of the local context on the implementation and impact of EU Cohesion Policy (2017)

47. Crescenzi, R., Guia, S.: Politica di coesione in Europa: a quali Paesi conviene? Un confronto di evidenze controfattuali per Germania, Italia, Regno Unito e Spagna. In: L'impatto della politica di coesione in Europa e in Italia. pp. 57–66. Senato della Repubblica Italiana, Roma (2018)

48. Strada, G., Martini, A.: L'approccio controfattuale alla valutazione degli effetti delle politiche pubbliche. Mater. UVAL. **22**, 28–45 (2011)

49. Scorza, F., Casas, G.B.L., Murgante, B.: Spatializing open data for the assessment and the improvement of territorial and social cohesion. In: ISPRS Annals of the Photogrammetry, Remote Sensing and Spatial Information Sciences, pp. 145–151. Copernicus GmbH (2016). https://doi.org/10.5194/isprs-annals-IV-4-W1-145-2016

50. Carbone, R., et al.: Using open data and open tools in defining strategies for the enhancement of basilicata region. In: Gervasi, O., et al. (eds.) ICCSA 2018. LNCS, vol. 10964, pp. 725–733. Springer, Cham (2018). https://doi.org/10.1007/978-3-319-95174-4_55

51. Scorza, F., Casas, G.L., Murgante, B.: Overcoming interoperability weaknesses in e-government processes: organizing and sharing knowledge in regional development programs using ontologies. In: Lytras, M.D., Ordonez de Pablos, P., Ziderman, A., Roulstone, A., Maurer, H., Imber, J.B. (eds.) WSKS 2010. CCIS, vol. 112, pp. 243–253. Springer, Heidelberg (2010). https://doi.org/10.1007/978-3-642-16324-1_26

52. Pontrandolfi, P., Dastoli, P.S.: Comparing impact evaluation evidence of EU and local development policies with New Urban Agenda themes: the Agri Valley case in Basilicata (Italy) (2021)

53. Scorza, F., Fortunato, G.: Cyclable cities: building feasible scenario through urban space-morphology assessment. J. Urban Plan. Dev. (2021). https://doi.org/10.1061/(ASCE)UP.1943-5444.0000713

54. Fortunato, G., Scorza, F., Murgante, B.: Hybrid oriented sustainable urban development: a pattern of low-carbon access to schools in the city of potenza. In: Gervasi, O., et al. (eds.) ICCSA 2020, LNCS, vol. 12255, pp. 193–205. Springer, Cham (2020). https://doi.org/10.1007/978-3-030-58820-5_15
55. Scorza, F., Fortunato, G., Carbone, R., Murgante, B., Pontrandolfi, P.: Increasing urban walkability through citizens' participation processes. Sustainability. **13**, 5835 (2021). https://doi.org/10.3390/su13115835
56. Scardaccione, G., Scorza, F., Casas, G.L., Murgante, B.: Spatial autocorrelation analysis for the evaluation of migration flows: the Italian case. In: Lecture Notes in Computer Science (including subseries Lecture Notes in Artificial Intelligence and Lecture Notes in Bioinformatics), pp. 62–76 (2010). https://doi.org/10.1007/978-3-642-12156-2-5

Author Index